To Gwen, Jodi, and Scott

THE ILLUSTRATED
HANDBOOK OF
DESKTOP
PUBLISHING
AND
TYPESETTING

THE ILLUSTRATED
HANDBOOK OF
DESKTOP
PUBLISHING
AND
TYPESETTING

by Michael L. Kleper

Professor
Division of Visual Communication Careers
Printing Production Department
National Technical Institute for the Deaf at the
Rochester Institute of Technology
Rochester, New York

TAB Professional and Reference Books

Division of TAB BOOKS Inc.
P.O. Box 40, Blue Ridge Summit, PA 17214

Other Publications by Michael L. Kleper

The following publications that are still in print are available
from Graphic Dimensions, 8 Frederick Road, Pittsford, NY 14534.

Understanding Phototypesetting (out of print)
Positive Film Make-up
Graphic Arts Pen Techniques
Practical Control of Phototypographic Quality (media package)
Elementary Phototypesetting Systems Concepts (media package)
How to Build a Basic Typesetting System
The Illustrated Dictionary of Typographic Communication
The Personal Composition Report (by subscription)

Cover photograph courtesy of Sunrise Computers, Norland Shopping Center, Chambersburg, PA.

FIRST EDITION
FIRST PRINTING

Library of Congress Cataloging in Publication Data

Kleper, Michael L.
    The illustrated handbook of desktop publishing and typesetting. .

    Includes index.
    1. Electronic publishing.   2. Computerized typesetting.
    3. Microcomputers—Programming.   4. Printing, Practical—Laser use in.
    5. Word processing.   I. Title.   II. Title: Desktop publishing and typesetting.

Z286.E43K54   1987   070.5'028'5   86-23149
ISBN 0-8306-2700-6
ISBN 0-8306-0700-5 (pbk.)

Edited by Suzanne L. Cheatle

Designed by Jaclyn Saunders

Contents

Preface

There is probably no one event nor single set of circumstances, no one invention nor method nor process that has had such a profound effect on the production of typographic images as has the microcomputer. Since its introduction in the latter half of the 1970s, it has grown steadily to become a significant tool, both as an input device for traditional phototypeset output, and as a self-contained publishing system utilizing its own on-line output devices.

The major reason for the popularity of microcomputers in conventional typesetting stems from the fact that they are exceptionally versatile input devices, and that the typesetting process is primarily one of generating keystrokes in order to drive a typesetting machine. The relative low cost, the multifunctionality, the variety of software, the availability of peripherals, and the ease of use have all added to the impetus surrounding the adoption of microcomputers over dedicated typesetting keyboards.

Just as the growth in the popularity of the automobile necessitated a sophisticated network of highways, the growing popularity of the microcomputer resulted in a demand for more sophisticated output options for micro-processed information. That demand has been addressed in a multitude of ways, some of which are only beginning to be developed.

Microcomputers are being used for typographic input and output in many diverse ways, and for many diverse purposes. An orthodontist produces a newsletter for his patients; a housewife working at home keyboards a manuscript for a local typesetter; a hardware wholesaler generates the input for his parts lists; a CPA's secretary creates invitations for an office party; a gasoline refiner produces its annual report; a pet store owner designs window signs and labels; a grammar school teacher creates handouts; a restaurant manager designs menu pages; a department store supervisor produces sales bulletins; a bank vice president generates transaction reports; an art supply store clerk creates weekly sale announcements; a stock market analyst produces a monthly newsletter; an electronics exporter produces custom shipping labels; a ten-year-old child generates a birthday card; a boating club membership chairman produces a membership list; a stamp dealer generates his weekly catalog.

The move from word processing to desktop publishing can be a single-step operation, utilizing enhanced dot matrix output from existing word processing files, or passing the files through a translation device to output them through a typesetting machine. It also can be a multiple-step operation where the user creates his own character designs and graphics and assembles them through coding or on-screen manipulation. The number of ways to move from word processing to desktop publishing are many, and the range of results spans the spectrum from marginally acceptable to unquestionably excellent.

Acknowledgments

Many people were exceptionally helpful in the preparation of this book. Among them are:

Abaton: Pat Casey
Activision: Melinda Mongelluzzo
Adobe Systems: John Warnock, Liz Bond, Linda Gass
Aldus Corp. Inc: Paul Brainerd, Ben Bauermeister, Jill Bamburg
Altsys: Jim Von Ehr
Artsci: Bill Smith
Apple Computer: Jean Louis Gassée, Elizabeth Yerxa, Martha Steffen
Bestinfo: Jim Bessen
Letraset: Russ McCann
Century Software: Michael Mace
Cauzin Systems: Brandon Nordin
CasadyWare: Robin Casady, Richard Ware
Compugraphic: Harry Zane
Data Transforms: Duke Houston, Bob Van Arsdale
EDO: Peter Kussell, Matthew Weiss
Hewlett-Packard: Bob Granger, Bill McGlynn
InfoSphere: Evan Solley
Itek: Dave DeBronkart
Knowledge Engineering: Bill Bates
Linotype: Bill Van Buskirk, Steve Byers
Manhattan Graphics: Martin Rosenberg, Ken Abbott
Microlytics: Mike Weiner
Microtek: S.C. Lee
Microsoft: Jonathan Prusky
Prometheus Products: Tom McShane
Rochester Institute of Technology: Don Beil, Bob Tompkins, David Pankow
Sensible Software: Roger Tuttleman
Silicone Beach Software: Charlie Jackson
Softcraft: Bob Finchell
Springboard Software: Judy Lund, Kathy Quinby
Studio Software: Peter Clarno
TAB BOOKS: Ron Powers, Jaclyn Saunders, Suzanne Cheatle, Ray Collins
Tangent Technologies: Steven Simpson
U.S. Lynx: Scott Kelly, Mike Krieger, Rene Clark
VariTyper: Jan Nowak
Videx: Bill Leinewebber
VS Software: Diane Crane, Benjamin McCorkle
Xerox: Ravi Sahay, Abhay Bhushan
Xyquest: John Hild

Introduction

Accounts differ as to the form and origin of the earliest type characters. It is known that entire pages of characters were carved in wooden blocks as early as 400 A.D. by the Chinese. The blocks were inked and pressed against paper in much the same way that linoleum block prints are made today.

The control, however crude, over the layout of an entire page of information has been the goal of practitioners of the art and craft of printing since the very beginning of graphic communication. The invention of movable type was at one and the same time one of the most significant inventions in the history of mankind and a move away from the single-piece, integrated page master, as exemplified by the incised wooden blocks of the Chinese. Today sophisticated phototypesetters, laser platemakers, and page printers are making the integration of page components a reality.

A major portion of the history of typesetting is composed of stories of the efforts of many large and small companies, independent inventors, and ingenious tinkerers who all worked toward the goal of automating the process of setting type. Although typesetting has outgrown the narrow perspective of being concerned solely with typographic characters, it is still perceived—and in most cases rightly so—as being a small part of the larger process of graphic communication.

There is weighty evidence to support the claim that typesetting always has been a rather removed, mechanical activity by which the words of an author are processed into a new, aesthetically pleasing form that is specified and controlled by one or more people usually unknown to the text originator.

The impact of the microcomputer on the typesetting process has been twofold. First, it has pushed back the keyboarding phase of typesetting directly to the author's hands. This development has, in most cases, reduced typesetting costs, increased accuracy (by eliminating retyping and the errors inherent in the process), and reduced the overall turnaround time involved in getting the text originator's thoughts into print. The microcomputer also has provided a number of software tools, such as spelling, grammar, and style checkers; on-line writing aids (synomym searches, readability ratings, etc.); and hyphenation routines.

Second, the microcomputer has developed its own identity as the nucleus of an on-line typesetting system. The system might use a dot matrix or page printer with the ability to set complete pages of text and graphics, or it might use an interface to connect directly to a phototypesetter. Sophisticated software packages are giving the microcomputer the capability to act like an integrated design station that not only originates text and graphics (and even photographs), but also combines them into a page format.

The application of microcomputer technology to the typesetting process has had a tremendous influence on both the hardware and software configurations of trade vendor offerings, as well as the definition of the multifunctional nature of such systems. Typesetting systems now routinely offer word processing and business applications, while off-the-shelf microcomputers can be used for serious typesetting input.

The results of this tumbling together of technology are that typesetting capabilities are now available to more people and the methods and tools of typesetting production have multiplied. Although the meaning of our words and the value of our thoughts might not be altered significantly by microcomputer technology, the graphic form in which they take life will become increasingly aesthetic, easier to read, and more compact.

This book provides an in-depth look at all of the ways that personal computers can be used to produce typesetting and composed pages. It begins with type, the building blocks of printed human communication, and takes you through a complete range of typesetting options, from low-cost dot-matrix output to do-it-yourself phototypesetting.

Numerous hardware and software products are presented from the viewpoint of the user. A major objective of this book is to show the products available for producing typographic output using a personal computer, what they do, and how they can be beneficial.

A few years ago, the prospect of persons not within the printing or affiliated industries setting their own type was as unlikely as it must have seemed for people to take their own pictures prior to Eastman's invention of the Kodak camera in 1888. The emergence of the desktop publishing phenomenon has made every desktop with a personal computer a launching pad for hurling words into higher quality forms.

The need to amplify printed communications by making them more eye-appealing is universal. There is almost no field of endeavor, from automotive design to zoology, that can not benefit from the use of this accessible new technology. The detail contained in this book will likely be more than sufficient for more practitioners of desktop publishing, and even for those providing professional typesetting services.

Most readers will have had some experience with word processing. This activity of entering words into a computer and rearranging them into final editorial form is the starting point for processing words into readable, compact, and attractive typeset output. Desktop publishing and typesetting methods and techniques can help to organize thoughts on a page, emphasize important information, and provide numerous design options that can lead to more effective printed communication.

This book presents a foundation of the typographic basics necessary to evaluate a desktop publishing or typesetting program and to use one effectively. Readers will find it beneficial for learning what they can do with their present computer equipment and what it will require to accomplish more ambitious objectives.

Chapter 1

TYPE!

The Building Blocks of Printed Communication

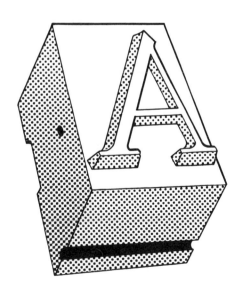

THE TYPEWRITTEN LEGACY

In most computer installations that provide some word processing capability, be they micro or mainframe, there are usually two forms of printed output available: dot matrix and letter-quality characters (FIG. 1). Both varieties of printer that generate such characters are engineered to produce output which conforms to requirements for standard office documents, such as work drafts, reports, tabular matter, and, depending upon the quality level of the character forms, correspondence.

Correspondence quality has become a default standard in evaluating the quality of line printer output. This "standard," which has never been formally defined, is nothing more than an objective measure of how well the line printer produces characters similar to those of a typical office typewriter. Thus, instead of computer technology providing a better-appearing output than has been available in the home and office since the introduction of the typewriter, the goal has been the imitation of standard typewriter output.

The idea for the typewriter was first stated in 1714 by Mr. Henry Mill, an Englishman who took out a patent for a machine which he described as "an artificial machine or method for impressing or transcribing of letters, singly or progressively, one after another as in writing, whereby all writings whatsoever may be engrossed in paper or parchment so neat and exact as not to be distinguished from print." Mill's machine failed; however, his idea obviously did not. In 1867, C. Sholes and Samuel W. Soulé, printers in Milwaukee, and their associate, Mr. Carlos Glidden, continued development of what was to become known as the *type-writer*. By 1873, they had completed a practical working model, which was manufactured shortly thereafter by E. Remington and Sons of Ilion, New York. The acceptance of the machine by business and industry stimulated other inventors to produce similar machines. By 1886 there were over 50,000 typewriters in use.

Ironically, the typewriter was invented to imitate printer's type, and the earliest typewriters actually used pieces of metal type mounted on the typebars. The typewriter, while providing only a coarse typographic image, did serve to automate the handwriting process, and by so doing, to change the way in which offices conducted business (FIG. 2).

The Typewriter as a Typesetter

Soon after the typewriter became popular it had an unexpected effect on the printing trade. It appeared that typewritten correspondence commanded a great deal of respect and, perhaps, curiosity. This interest was so overwhelming that in 1884 the Central Type Foundry of Boston introduced a typeface for printers called Type-Writer. This typeface reportedly had a larger sales volume than any other metal typeface ever issued. According to one account, the design was suggested by a stationer from Huntingdon, Pennsylvania, Mr. J.C. Blair, who was reputedly a typographic expert. The typeface was sold with the intention that "circulars could be made to resemble genuine correspondence, and thus secure for them the attention which it was previously so hard to get." By the turn of the century nearly every type foundry had a similar design in its specimen book. Quite ironically, the typewriter, which had been invented to simulate printing, was universally being simulated in print (FIG. 3). Today, most typesetting machine vendors still offer a typeface that resembles typewritten characters.

It was not until the 1930s, however, that the typewriter became a legitimate device for the setting of type. At that time there was a need for a compatible method for generating ''type'' for use on the mimeograph machine. The major typesetting alternatives at that time were the hot-metal linecasting machines, such as the Linotype and Intertype, and the more complicated character caster, the Monotype. These machines were too sophisticated and expensive to meet the needs of an office reproduction department, so the typewriter, having undergone considerable improvements in construction and capabilities since its introduction, became an office typesetter.

A number of machines were introduced that were much more than ordinary typewriters yet much less than typical typesetters. The IBM Executive Typewriter provided proportionally spaced characters, while the Friden Justowriter offered justified (equal margins) output and paper tape storage. The VariTyper was one of the first typewriter-like machines specifically made for typesetting applications (FIG. 4). It remained in a class by itself until 1967 when the IBM Selectric Composer was introduced.

FIG. 1. Enlargements of dot matrix characters and the printer that produced them, and letter-quality characters and their printer.

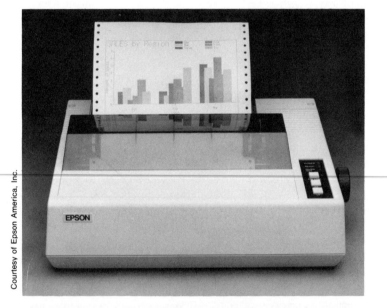

Courtesy of Epson America, Inc.

Courtesy of Dynax, Inc.

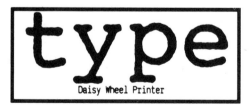

FIG. 2. The Sholes Typewriter, patented in 1871, was devised to bring printer's typesetting capability into the office environment. The keyboard arrangement has remained virtually unchanged for well over 100 years.

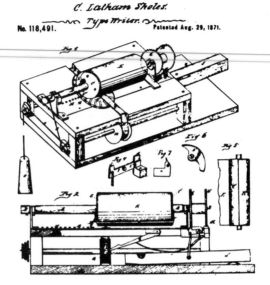

These specialized machines that provided limited typographic capabilities became known as *direct impression*, or *strike-on*, typesetters. Many people referred to their output as *cold type* (as contrasted with hot-metal typesetting), and the term has been used loosely, though erroneously, to describe any typesetting method that does not involve the casting of molten metal.

As the offset printing process (FIG. 5) replaced or augmented other forms of office reproduction, the strike-on method of typesetting grew in popularity. Unlike ordinary carbon-ribbon typewriters, strike-on machines produced sharp, dense (black), proportionally spaced characters suitable for reproduction.

A consequence of the reliance upon the typewriter to generate office documents has been the emergence of what is today termed *office-quality* reproduction. This level of quality can be defined as monospaced typewritten characters of a single style and size, appearing in single- or double-spaced line format, in either justified or unjustified mode, and usually occupying a standard 8.5-×-11-inch sheet. Many of these attributes are virtually unchanged from those achieved on the earliest typewriters, despite the computer processing power that is available today.

Why Typeset?

Typesetting provides many more advantages than simply a better appearance than typewritten output. Yet, appearance is, perhaps, the major factor in opting for typesetting. There are literally thousands of typeface choices suitable for a wide variety of specialized uses, to convey almost any feeling or mood. Consider the lightly flowing script typeface on an elegant menu, or the bold, commanding typeface in a truck advertisement (FIG. 6). The selection of an appropriate typeface is very important in communicating a message, and we'll examine how to make that choice later.

The use of appropriate typefaces not only helps to communicate, but also adds an element of prestige to printed material. The image that a company or an individual projects is enhanced by good typography, and this increased attractiveness helps to catch and hold the reader's eye. Getting and maintaining the reader's attention is critical for effective communication because the message that will be read is the one which has more visual appeal (FIG. 7).

FIG. 3. Examples of typewriter typefaces, as shown in the 1923 edition of the American Type Founders specimen book.

POPULAR TYPEWRITER FACES

12 Point New Model Remington Typewriter   20 A 100 a

The safety movement, to be effective, must be kept
continually before us, as is the case with advertising. You cannot place one advertisement and forever
keep the merits of the product before the public.
Neither will one "Safety Rule" forever keep us free
from accident. The need for intelligent cooperative
safety work is greater today than ever. Ten per cent

Characters in Complete Font—1/10 Inch Set

ABCDEFGHIJKLMNOPQRSTUVWXYZ&$1234567890abcdefg
hijklmnopqrstuvwxyz.,-'' '":;!?()¯*@¢/%#

Fractions are fonted $\frac{1}{4}\frac{1}{2}\frac{3}{4}\frac{1}{8}\frac{3}{8}\frac{5}{8}\frac{7}{8}$ and furnished separately

12 Point Silk Remington Typewriter   20 A 100 a

Every intelligent traveler who travels with a purpose
outlines his route, selects the places of interest
which he desires to visit, and carefully apportions
his time. If one is to traverse a certain area of
territory in a given period, his movements should be
guarded by forethought and method. Reading is mental
traveling through regions far more various and with

Characters in Complete Font —1/10 Inch Set

ABCDEFGHIJKLMNOPQRSTUVWXYZ&$1234567890abcdef
ghijklmnopqrstuvwxyz.,-'":;!?()¯*@¢/%#

Fractions are fonted $\frac{1}{4}\frac{1}{2}\frac{3}{4}\frac{1}{8}\frac{3}{8}\frac{5}{8}\frac{7}{8}$ and furnished separately

Special high period, comma, colon, semi-colon and apostrophe furnished to order

12 Point Silk Remington Underscored Typewriter (for use with Silk Remington)   10 A 32 a

In order to maintain color harmony, and still retain
beauty throughout, the advertisement must be planned.
The copy and illustrations are to be created--not
simply made to any size, but to fit a given space.
This working plan is bound to simplify and reduce to
a standard all work that may call for unusual and
quick execution. Consider the minor details at every

Characters in Complete Font—1/10 Inch Set

ABCDEFGHIJKLMNOPQRSTUVWXYZ&$1234567890abc
defghijklmnopqrstuvwxyz.,-'":;!?

Justifiers for all typewriter faces are put up in 1-pound and 5-pound fonts and furnished only when specially ordered

NOTE.—The matrices for the Typewriter Faces shown on this page were cut to match closely the characters used on the typewriting machines represented. In order to get satisfactory results in matching, these types should be printed through silk or ribbon with ink made for the purpose. (See examples on pages 525, 526, 527 and 528.)

While a difference in type style helps to attract the reader's eye, it is the difference in type size that helps to organize information in terms of its relative importance. Typewritten text is all the same size despite the fact that all of the information it represents is not necessarily of the same factual value. While the content display for typewritten text has very little flexibility other than utilizing all capitals, underlining, changing from double space to single space, or changing the margins, typeset output has much flexibility (the exact amount depending upon the typesetter used) in displaying pieces of information according to their relative importance. This capability makes it easier for the reader to locate the information that the message originator considers most important.

FIG. 4. The VariTyper machine, although resembling a typewriter, has many typographic capabilities, including changeable typefaces, a range of type sizes, and justified output.

FIG. 5. The offset printing process involves many steps. (*a*) The production cycle begins with the recognition of a need for the printed item. This need may take written form through the efforts of a copywriter or other person familiar with the message, or the need may have been previously established by either an author, in the form of a manuscript, or an advertiser, in the form of copy. (*b*) In any event, drawings, illustrations, and the overall design are handled by an artist. Pictures are taken by a photographer. Type is specified (spec'ed) and set by the typesetter. The elements are brought together and assembled in page format in a process called "art and copy preparation." The artwork, photos, and type are "pasted-up" in position to produce a mechanical, a completed page layout by the mechanical or paste-up artist. (*c*) The mechanical is placed on the copyboard of a darkroom camera and photographed by the reproduction cameraperson. The result is a photographic film negative. (*d*) The negative is "stripped" by the stripper into position on a sheet of opaque orange (goldenrod) paper or plastic, which is the exact size of the press plate. The negative, taped in position on the paper or plastic, is called a "flat." (*e*) The platemaker contacts the flat, under vacuum pressure, to a flexible plate which has a light sensitive coating on its surface. The plate is exposed, through the flat, to an intense light source. The exposed plate is then chemically processed. (*f*) The finished plate is then mounted by the pressperson on an offset press plate cylinder. Chemically treated water keeps the non-image areas free of ink, while the image area attracts and holds ink. The plate cylinder turns against a rubber blanket cylinder onto which the image is "offset" or transferred. Paper passes between the blanket cylinder and an impression cylinder, "offsetting" the image onto the paper.

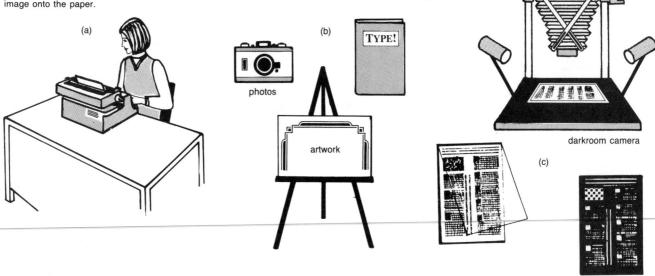

(a)

photos (b)

artwork

darkroom camera

process negative (c)

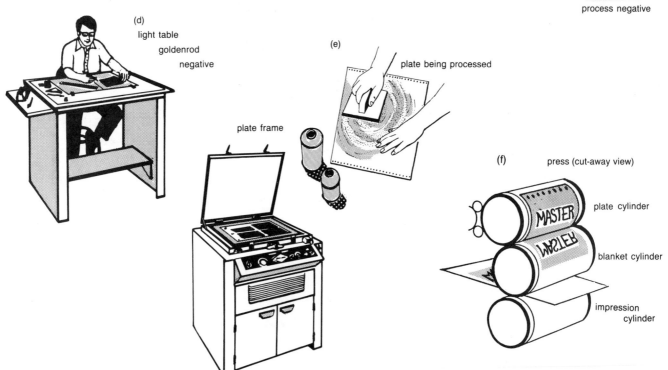

(d) light table

goldenrod

negative

plate frame

(e) plate being processed

(f) press (cut-away view)

plate cylinder

blanket cylinder

impression cylinder

Some of the most compelling reasons why many businesses choose typeset output are purely economical considerations. Typesetting provides increased *character density*. While typewritten characters usually are limited to ten characters per linear inch, typeset characters can be from 50 percent to over 200 percent denser in terms of their compactness on the line. Combine this increased density with the capability of minutely controlling the vertical spacing of lines, and typeset matter can easily transmit more information in a given space than can typewritten matter (FIG. 8). Estimates of this space-saving factor range from 40 percent to about 60 percent, depending upon the type sizes and styles involved.

Just as microfilm dramatically reduces the bulk of paper records, the process of converting information into typeset form has a similar positive effect on reducing paper bulk. It is this reduction in the space that information needs to occupy which provides economical benefits for typesetter users. Reduced space requirements mean less paper to buy, less paper to use, less paper to convert (cut, fold, insert, etc.), less paper to handle, less paper to distribute (mail), and less paper to store. Not only are significant dollar savings possible, but the reduction in handling time means that information can move faster and more efficiently.

Typesetting equipment does not need to be on-site or in-house in order to realize its major benefits. However, when the entire typesetting operation is captive within a company it provides significant additional benefits as compared to having typesetting performed by an outside service. The most immediate benefit is that of control. The typesetting personnel are now company personnel, and the typesetter now serves only one client. Information is typeset according to company needs and priorities, and sensitive, confidential, or valuable company data never leaves the premises. With fewer, and only company, people involved in the process, company data is more secure.

FIG. 6. The proper selection of a typeface reinforces a message by providing a visual structure to information content.

Entry PROHIBITED!
Authorized Personnel Only

You are cordially invited

to attend the world premiere

of the revolutionary

Lumiset
Laser Typesetter

Exceptional Resolution
Phenomenal Speed
Impressive Price

FIG. 7. This advertisement from AM VariTyper graphically compares typewritten with typeset output (Courtesy. AM VariTyper).

If you like word processing, you'll love phototypesetting.

With our powerful telecommunications link, you can go from word processing to high-quality typesetting in one easy step, without re-keyboarding copy.

The results will be better printed communications and lower costs.

Cut the fat out of your paperwork.

Ounce after ounce, bulky typewritten documents cost you thousands of dollars in paper, printing, postage and production time.

Typesetting can dramatically reduce these production costs. As you can see in the photo, typesetting can actually cut paper bulk in half.

Typeset documents communicate better.

Today, every business is flooded with information. Page after page of look-alike typewritten documents just won't command attention anymore.

Typesetting instantly transforms bland typewritten pages into dynamic, professional-looking presentations. And our Comp/Edit 6400 digital typesetter can set type in hundreds of sizes and styles, and to automatically create bold, italic, condensed or expanded type.

What jobs should be typeset?

Every single one that's important: financial reports, new business proposals, product releases, newsletters, manuals, announcements, price lists, technical bulletins... the list goes on and on.

To find out how Varityper can dramatically improve the look of your printed communications (and your bottom line) call toll-free 1-800-631-8134. In Alaska, Hawaii and New Jersey, 1-201-887-8000, ext. 999.

The type for this ad was entirely composed on the Comp/Edit system.
Comp/Edit and Varityper are registered trademarks of AM International, Inc.
© 1983 AM International, Inc.

Varityper

FIG. 8. Compare the typewritten specimen on the top with the typeset specimen on the bottom. Not only is the typeset information easier to read, but it also makes more efficient use of the space it occupies.

Most contemporary typesetting keyboards are highly reliable, with error rates not usually exceeding 1 in 30,000 keystrokes. People, however, are usually less reliable. It is human error which most directly affects the highest attainable level of quality in any typesetting system. Studies have shown that the average human error rate is, at best, in the range of 1 to 10 errors per 6000 keystrokes.

TYPEWRITTEN

Most contemporary typesetting keyboards are highly reliable, with error rates not usually exceeding 1 in 30,000 keystrokes. People, however, are usually less reliable. It is human error which most directly affects the highest attainable level of quality in any typesetting system. Studies have shown that the average human error rate is, at best, in the range of 1 to 10 errors per 6000 keystrokes.

TYPESET

FIG. 9. Gutenberg's invention of the handheld mold was responsible for helping to spread literacy by creating the mass production of books.

Having typesetting equipment located within a company also provides increased convenience. The problems of communicating information over telephone lines or sending or carrying media to an outside source are eliminated. Turnaround time is reduced because there is no need to wait for messengers to pick up and deliver work, nor to spend time seeking sources of supply or explaining over the telephone how the job should have looked. Last-minute changes and alterations are handled according to priorities set internally, without delay, and without financial penalty.

TYPOGRAPHY: THE ART OF TYPESETTING

Typography is the process of selecting typefaces, sizes, and spacing requirements for the layout of a printed job. It is a process that requires considerable care and attention because actual harm might be done to a printed piece by careless and inappropriate typographic decisions.

Typesetting has its roots in metal. The earliest metal type used in Western civilization was cast by Johann Gutenberg in the fifteenth century. Prior to that time entire book pages had been carved in wood, a very slow and exacting craft that left no margin for error. Gutenberg's invention of a hand-held mold to cast identical character images made the mass production of type a reality. Not only could pages of type be assembled faster, but the type could be used again and again (FIG. 9).

Much of the terminology used today in typesetting is derived from the use of metal type. Many of the terms used to describe each piece of metal are human descriptors (face, feet, shoulder, body), as is its overall label of "character" (FIG. 10). Type has been given many human qualities over the centuries, in prose and in poetry, to provide testimony to its contribution to mankind.

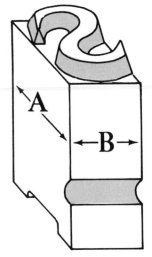

FIG. 10. A piece of metal type, the building block responsible for popular literacy, and the first form of mass communication.

The point size of the type is determined by measuring the height of the type body (FIG. 10A). Since the typeface design is limited to the physical dimensions of the type surface, the point size appearing in print (be it a metal impression, a phototypeset letter, or other) is found by measuring the distance from the uppermost limit of an upward-reaching letter (an *ascender*), such as b, d, f, h, l, or t, to the lowermost limit of a downward-projecting letter (a *descender*), such as g, j, p, q, or y.

Each typographic character is alloted a dimension proportional to its width (FIG. 10B). An m has a wider set width than an i, and an h is wider than an l.

The set width of an alphabet is based upon *em* measurement. Simply stated, the em is the square of the point size. In a 12-point em, each side of the face of the em is equal to 12 points (FIG. 11A). A 30-point em measures 30 points on each of the four sides of its face (FIG. 11B).

When all of the characters in use have identical widths, such as in typewriting, calculating the number of characters that will fill a line is easy. However, when characters of various widths, various designs, and various sizes will occupy a line, calculating characters per line is a much more difficult task. For this purpose, the em of each typeface design is divided into a number of vertical slices called *relative units* (RU). There are usually no fewer than 18 relative units to the em, and on more sophisticated typesetting machines, the number might surpass 100 units.

When a 48-point em and a 72-point em have been divided into 54 relative units (FIG. 12), we say that we are working with a 54-unit system. The widest characters, such as the W, the fractions, and the copyright and trademark symbols, each are assigned the full 54-unit value. The comma, the narrowest character, receives a unit assignment of 12. All other characters receive a unit assignment directly related to their relative width. The G is equal to 42, the v receives 27, and the f gets 18.

Notice that each particular character listed in FIG. 12 has the same unit value, regardless of its point size. In other words, a lowercase g has a unit value of 30 regardless of whether it is in reference to a 48-point em, a 72-point em, or any size em for that

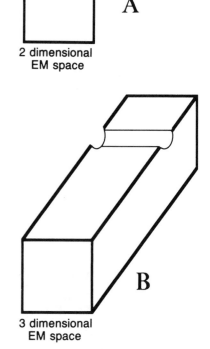

2 dimensional
EM space

3 dimensional
EM space

FIG. 11. The em is the square of the point size, regardless if the type is three-dimensional (metal) or two-dimensional (strike-on, phototypeset, laser printer, etc.).

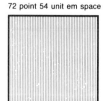

48 point 54 unit em space

72 point 54 unit em space

FIG. 12. To determine numerical values for each character of a type style, the em space is divided into vertical divisions called *relative units*, which are assigned to characters on the basis of their widths.

FIG. 13. Size is an effective method of indicating relative importance and organizing information for the reader.

matter. Yet, comparing the relative width of a 48-point g with that of a 72-point g, it is obvious that they are not the same size, which is where the *relative* part of the term *relative unit* assumes real meaning. In 48 point, the g's relative unit value of 30 is 30/54 of 48, or about 27 linear points. In 72 point, the g's relative unit value remains 30, or 30/54 of the 72-point em. In this case the g has a value of about 40 points.

Keep these ideas in mind while you look at the typographic measurement system. We'll then combine your knowledge of relative units and typographic measurements to show how a typesetter keeps count of the characters filling a line.

Typographic Measurement

Although most people recognize that type is measured in points, few actually know how large a point is. There are 72 points to the inch, each point being equal to 0.0138 inch. Type sizes in the 9- to 12-point range usually are used for reading matter, and are classified as *text sizes*. Type sizes of 14 points and larger usually are used for headlines (heads) and subheadlines (subheads), and are classified as *display sizes* (FIG. 13).

Page dimensions, column widths, and line lengths are measured in larger units called *picas*. There are six picas in 1 inch, and 12 points in 1 pica (resulting in 72 points in 1 inch). The length of a line of type is called the *measure*, and is sometimes indicated by an X, as in X24, meaning a line length of 24 picas.

The typeset line measure is comparable to the typewritten line width; the major difference is the difficulty of determining how many characters of a certain typeface will fill a typeset line. On a standard typewriter there are either 10 characters to the inch (*pica*) or 12 characters to the inch (*elite*). In a typesetter any one of thousands of different type designs might be in place, in any one of dozens or possibly hundreds of different sizes. To cope with this problem of estimating how many characters will fit on one line, called *copyfitting*, and how many lines (or possibly pages) will be needed, typesetters use a measurement called the *character count*.

The character count (c.c.) is an approximation of the number of characters of a specific typeface, in a specific size, that can be set in one linear pica. This value usually is provided by the vendor of the typesetting equipment, although it can be derived quite simply by measuring the width of the lowercase alphabet of the typeface in question and dividing this width into 342.

As an example, the typeface Granjon in 12 point has a character count of 2.45. In other words, approximately 2.45 characters of Granjon can be set in one linear pica. A line length of 18 picas would mean that 18 picas × 2.45 char/picas = 44 characters of 12-point Granjon can be set in one line. If there are 30 lines per page (30 lines × 44 char/line), then there is sufficient space for 1320 characters per page. If a typewritten manuscript containing approximately 165,000 characters was to be copyfit in this format, then 165,000 char ÷ 1320 char/page = 125 pages would be required to copyfit the manuscript.

Copyfitting calculations always take into account an allowance for word spaces. As a general rule, the typical word length is considered to be five characters. Because each word must be followed by a space, the copyfitting estimate for the average word length is then six characters. If the total number of characters in a document is known, an approximation of the number of words can be derived by dividing the total by six.

When type was set using metal characters, the sizes of the spaces were fixed fractional divisions of the em space. The em itself served as a spacing unit, usually for indentation at the beginning of paragraphs or to fill out short lines. The em was divided in half vertically to form two en spaces, also used for indenting and, since it had the same width as the figures, for setting (aligning) columns of numbers. In FIG. 14 a line of metal type illustrates the height relationship between the spaces and the characters.

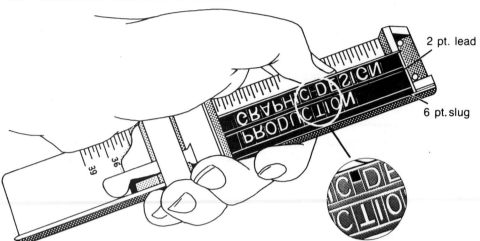

2 pt. lead

6 pt. slug

FIG. 15. The amount of space used to indent a paragraph should follow the prescribed recommendations in this table.

Indention	
0-18 picas	1 em
19-23 picas	1½ ems
24-30 picas	2 ems

Spaces, which do not print, are considerably shorter than characters. The amount of indentation is based upon tradition, and is directly related to the length of the line measure (FIG. 15).

The en space is too wide to serve as a normal space between words, and so the em space is further divided into three vertical divisions, the *3-to-em* or *3-em* spaces. The 3-em space is the normal space used between words. The em space is further divided into four (4-em space) and five (5-em space) increments to provide more spacing options (FIG. 16).

California job case

FIG. 16. The 3-em spaces, normally used as word spaces, are prominently positioned near the front of the type case. The California Job Case, although complicated-looking, was actually devised according to the frequency of use of characters appearing in the English language. Notice that the most commonly used characters, such as *e* and *a*, have proportionally larger compartments.

The Use of Space

It is the control of space that determines, in many instances, the quality of the typesetting. Take, for example, the problem of *justification*. Justification is the process of adjusting the space between words to force a line of type to completely fill its line measure. Accomplishing justification on an ordinary typewriter is quite simple. First the copy is typed, with attention given to the amount of space remaining at the end of each line. In the example shown in FIG. 17, x's have been used to indicate the amount of excess space remaining. When the copy is retyped, the excess space is distributed between words to space out the line and fill the measure.

Justifying metal type is also a two-step process. First the line is assembled using 3-em spaces between words. As the end of the line approaches, it becomes obvious to the compositor whether the last word will leave the line short, will need to be hyphenated, will need to be carried to the next line, or would fit if there was slightly more space. The decision then becomes whether to expand (space out) the line to fill the measure, in which case minute increments of space made of slivers of copper, brass, and paper are added to the 3-em spaces, or whether to contract (spaced in) the line to make room for the last word, in which case some or all of the 3-em spaces are replaced by smaller spaces or multiple spacing materials.

This decision-making process is carried on in an electronic form by sophisticated typesetting machines. Recall that each character has a unit assignment based on its width, and that the unit system is devised by the manufacturer of the typesetting equipment with *x* number of units to the em. Remember, too, that the unit assignments vary from one typeface design to another.

```
This is an example of howx
an ordinary office type-xx
writer can be used to com-
pose justified lines ofxxx
type.


This is an example of  how
an ordinary  office  type-
writer can be used to com-
pose  justified  lines  of
type.
```

FIG. 17. The justification process can be performed on a typewriter by distributing the excess space at the end of each line. Two typings are required: the first to determine the excess, the second to distribute it.

The typesetting machine stores within its memory a table of width values for each typeface it is using. When a line measure is specified, the typesetter converts that number into em units for internal calculation. For example, the line measure might be 18 picas and the type size might be 10 points. First, the machine determines how many 10-point ems will fit in an 18-pica line measure. Remember that an em is the square of the point size, so each 10-point em requires 10 linear points. To divide the line measure by 10 points, the line measure first must be converted from picas to points. There are 12 points in each pica; therefore, the 18-pica measure is equal to 216 points. Dividing the 216 points by the 10-point em yields 21.6 ems per line. Second, the machine multiplies the ems per line by its units-per-em value. For this example, a 36-unit system is being used; therefore, there are 36 units in one em and there are 777.6 units (21.6 ems × 36 units/em) in a single line that is 18 picas wide and is composed of 10-point characters.

As each 10-point character is processed, its unit value is subtracted from 777.6. The minimum and maximum word spaces are assigned fixed unit values as well, with the minimum unit value used for initial calculations. As the end of the line approaches (the justification or hot zone), the machine's logic determines if there is enough room for part or all of the next word. If the word or partial word fits, its unit value is subtracted; if it does not, it is carried to the next line. The excess units remaining at the end of the line are equally divided among the word spaces, which then expand to fill the line measure. After the calculation is complete, the line of characters is typeset (FIG. 18).

FIG. 18. The process of electronic machine justification involves (a) converting the line measure into points, (b) calculating the number of ems of the point size that will fit on the line, (c) calculating how many units of space the line measure represents, (d) subtracting the unit width of each character and space that will fit on the line, and (e) distributing the remaining units among the word spaces to expand the line to fill the measure.

a Line measure = 24 picas = 192 points

|← ———————————— 24 picas ———————————— →|

b Point size = 10 points
Em = 10 points square
192 points / 10 points = 19.2 ems per line

c Unit system = 18 units/em
19.2 ems X 18 units/em = 345.6 units/line

d
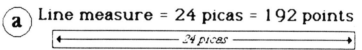
Placement tests have been conclusive in providing

P = 13 units
l = 5 units
a = 10 units   **Total unit count for this line = 264 units**
c = 8 units
e = 8 units

e Line length of 345.6 units minus
Character unit count of 264

345.6
-264
81.6 units

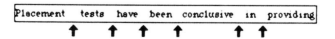
Placement   tests   have   been   conclusive   in   providing
↑   ↑   ↑   ↑   ↑   ↑

81.6 units of remaining space / 6 spaces =
an additional 13.6 units added to each word space

The process that takes place on a typewriter or on most word processing printers is considerably more gross in its execution of interword space allotment. In many cases the characters are monospaced, and the spaces used to justify lines are multiples of the fixed character width. Justifying spaces are therefore either as wide as any character, or are two or more times as wide. This process makes for loose-fitting lines.

Returning to our example, what if the total unit count of characters and spaces equals exactly 777.6? If it were to happen, the line would be set with minimum-width word spaces. This is perhaps the ideal situation, since tight (close-fitting) word spaces are preferable for increased ease of reading. However, what if the opposite were to happen, wherein there was either considerable space left at the end of the line, or so few spaces in the line that they quickly reached their maximum allowable expansion? What would become of the remaining space?

The usual solution is to add small increments of space between characters in a process called *letterspacing*. Letterspacing is not considered good typographic practice because it pulls words apart, making them less recognizable as patterns for the readers' eye (FIG. 19). Letterspacing has no place in the typewriter or word processing environment since the size of a space is usually no smaller than the width of the average character.

Although justification is a very common way of orienting lines of type, it is by no means the only way. Lines can be centered (*quad center*), wherein the remaining space at the end of the line is equally divided between the beginning and end of the line, or they can be either flush left (*quad left*), or flush right (*quad right*), wherein all of the remaining space is placed either at the end or the beginning of the line, respectively (FIG. 20).

The composition of justified lines of text has a long tradition in the graphic arts. Prior to the invention of printing, scribes laboriously copied manuscripts by hand. Because paper was very expensive, they paid special attention to filling each line with as many characters as possible. All of their lines were carefully written to be of consistent length, regardless of how words were broken (hyphenated). Early printers imitated this style in their effort to make the new craft of printing approach the quality of the established art of hand inscription.

FIG. 19. Compare the properly spaced lines in the paragraph on the left with the excessively letter-spaced and word-spaced lines in the paragraph on the right.

She had little idea what he actually meant by his casual remark, although she felt truly hurt. Did he really mean that he considered her insensitive and cold? His untimely departure put distance, as well as space between them. Only Reilly was aware of what was on Drew's mind when he confronted Lisa, and he was the least able to adequately explain any of it to her. Reilly, after all, had his own problems, and his devotion to his workers was of considerably less importance than his need to have his business survive.

She had little idea what he actually meant by his casual remark, although she felt truly hurt. Did he really mean that he considered her insensitive and cold? His untimely departure put distance, as well as space between them. Only Reilly was aware of what was on Drew's mind when he confronted Lisa, and he was the least able to adequately explain any of it to her. Reilly, after all, had his own problems, and his devotion to his workers was of considerably less importance than his need to have his business survive.

FIG. 20. Good typesetting is the control of white space.

The star around which the earth and other planets revolve, by which they are held in their orbits, from which they receive light, and which has a distance from earth of 93,000,000 miles, a linear diameter of 869,000 miles, a mass 332,000 times greater than earth, a mean density about one fourth that of earth, and a chemical constitution like that of earth, but so hot that it remains gaseous

A POLY-HEDRON WITH ONE BASE WHICH IS ANY POLYGON AND ADDITIONAL FACES CALLED LATERAL, WHICH HAVE TRIANGLES WITH A COMMON VERTEX... AN ANCIENT MASSIVE STRUCTURE OF HUGE STONE BLOCKS FOUND IN EGYPT HAVING TYPICALLY A SQUARE GROUND PLAN OUTSIDE WALLS IN THE FORM OF FOUR TRIANGLES THAT MEET IN A POINT.

WIND SAND & STARS—WIND SAND & STARS—WIND SAND & STARS—WIND SAND & STARS—WIND SAND & STARS—WIND SAND & STARS—WIND SAND & STARS—WIND SAND & STARS—WIND SAND & STARS—WIND SAND & STARS—WIND SAND & STARS—WIND SAND & STARS—WIND SAND & STARS—WIND SAND & STARS—WIND SAND & STARS—WIND

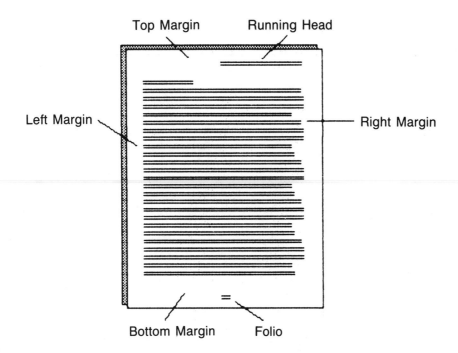

FIG. 21. The anatomy of a generic typewritten page.

Top Margin   Running Head

Left Margin

Right Margin

Bottom Margin   Folio

The Typographic Basics

There are four elements that are common to every typeset job. These elements are descriptors, which can be used to specify how typewritten text should be arranged on a page.

Consider the typical typewritten document (FIG. 21). If it became necessary to communicate a description of this page over the telephone so that the person you were talking to could duplicate the layout, what elements would you choose to describe? Assuming that a standard sheet of 8 1/2 × 11 inches will be used, it might be appropriate initially to specify the margins (their sizes and, in the case of the right and left margins, whether they are flush on one or both sides). Subtracting the values of the left and the right margins yields the length of the line of characters if justified, and an approximation of line length if not justified. The first descriptor then is the ''line length.''

Measuring the number of characters per inch will determine the pitch—pica or elite. This descriptor can be labeled ''character size.''

Many typewriters have changeable type elements, as well as many variations of the characters, which are immediately reorganizable as typewritten. It might be difficult, as it sometimes is in typesetting, to determine the exact identity of the type style that was used. Assuming that both you and the person on the other end of the telephone have a specimen sheet of common typewriter designs, you can then specify the ''style.''

The remaining physical attribute is quite easy to evaluate. It is the vertical spacing increment, generally called ''single or double spacing.''

If these four elements can be specified in advance of producing a typewritten page, the appearance of the product is very predictable. The same concept applies in typesetting, and similar descriptors, or *parameters*, must be specified.

Look now at the typeset job shown in FIG. 22. From your experience with the previous typewritten example (FIG. 21), you should have a good idea of what values you must derive before producing such a job. In the typeset example you must also have a *line length* or *line measure*. This parameter indicates how wide the lines that you typeset will be. It is specified in picas. If the line measure consists of any fractional part of a pica, as in 27 1/2 picas, the fraction is expressed in points, in this case 6

FIG. 22. A simple typeset job has four basic parameters.

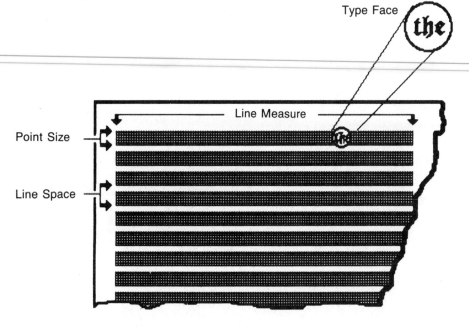

Type Face

Line Measure

Point Size

Line Space

points (6 points = 1/2 pica). Exactly how typographic parameters are specified depends upon the particular typesetting system you are using. The line measure of 27 1/2 picas, for example, might be expressed in many different ways, such as 2706 (27 picas 6 points), or 27.5 (27 1/2 picas).

The next parameter, although the order of specification is usually of no consequence when you are writing the codes for a typesetter, is "type size." Determining the size of previously typeset material is somewhat tricky because some typesetters can set in increments as small as 1/2 point (and even 1/10 point), and because the sample being measured might have passed through a reproduction system (photo offset, photocopier, etc.) that could have altered the size of the characters. There is no way to determine how much change in type size might have occurred without a careful comparison between the printed sample and the original output from the typesetter. For most work, a minute difference in type size is not significant; however, for some legal, business, and government jobs, type size specification can be critical.

Measuring type size usually is done with a clear type gauge or a magnifier with a special reticle. Purchase of a few measuring tools is a good investment for anyone involved in the specification of typographic information (FIG. 23).

A good approximation of the size of the type is the measurement between the top of the ascender and the bottom of the descender (FIG. 24). If you are familiar with the typesetter that is used to generate the type you are measuring, it is sometimes easier to approximate the size since it must fall within the incremental range the typesetter is capable of setting. If, for example, you measure the characters as 9.75 points and the closest sizes the typesetter can set are 8 point and 10 point, it is safe to assume that the characters measure 10 points.

The next parameter that must be determined is the "typeface," or type *font*. A font is the collection of all of the letters, figures, punctuation, and special characters of a particular typeface in a particular point size. Determining the type font that has been used is probably the most difficult task in this exercise. Before we go any further, however, remember that we are working backwards in this example, trying to reconstruct a previously typeset job. This is not the usual approach. In most cases, the choice of typeface is from a list, and the selection is based on criteria related to the purpose of the message or the function of the printed piece.

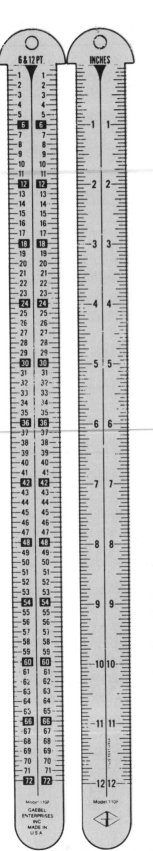

FIG. 23. A printer's metal line gauge, clear plastic overlay gauge, and magnifier are all useful in determining typographic measurements (Courtesy Gaebel Enterprises and Compugraphic Corporation).

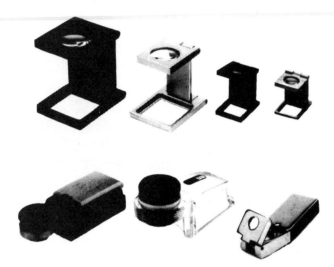

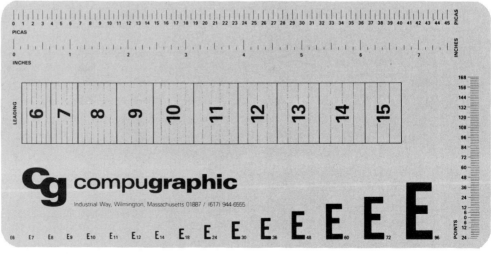

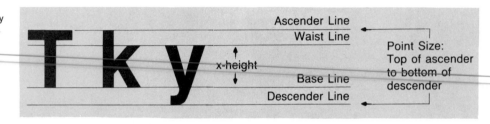

FIG. 24. To find the point size of previously typeset material, locate an ascender and a descender in proximity to one another and measure the distance between their outer limits. Familiarity with the point size range of a particular typesetter can make the determination of point size much easier.

FIG. 25. (Below) *Line spacing* is horizontal space added between lines of type to either improve readability or to vertically justify lines to fill a page depth.

Packing: In computer programming, grouping two or more units of information into one unit to save storage space and reduce transmission time. The unit can later be "unpacked" and the original units reconstructed.
8/8

Packing: In computer programming, grouping two or more units of information into one unit to save storage space and reduce transmission time. The unit can later be "unpacked" and the original units reconstructed.
8/9

Packing: In computer programming, grouping two or more units of information into one unit to save storage space and reduce transmission time. The unit can later be "unpacked" and the original units reconstructed.
8/10

Packing: In computer programming, grouping two or more units of information into one unit to save storage space and reduce transmission time. The unit can later be "unpacked" and the original units reconstructed.
8/11

Packing: In computer programming, grouping two or more units of information into one unit to save storage space and reduce transmission time. The unit can later be "unpacked" and the original units reconstructed.
8/12

Packing: In computer programming, grouping two or more units of information into one unit to save storage space and reduce transmission time. The unit can later be "unpacked" and the original units reconstructed.
8/13

If the particular typesetter on which the example was set is known, then the universe of type style choices is much reduced, and the problem becomes one of comparing the printed characters to a set of specimen sheets. However, if the typesetter is not known, you must depend upon your knowledge of typefaces and their subtle differences in design.

The last of the basic typographic parameters is the space between lines, the "line spacing." While the typewriter usually provides only single or double spacing, the typesetter can specify line spacing increments as small as 1/2 of a point and even, in some cases, as small as 1/10 of a point. As previously mentioned, the line spacing is measured from the baseline of one line to the baseline of the next (FIG. 25).

The similarities between the typewritten and typeset pages are many, as well they should be since the typewriter was invented as a typesetting machine for the office and the home. Not surprisingly then, each of the four basic typographic parameters has a parallel value in typewriting:

TYPEWRITING		TYPESETTING
line length	=	line measure
character size	=	type size
style	=	typeface
single/double spacing	=	line spacing

ALL ABOUT TYPE

The earliest metal type was cast by Johann Gutenberg in the fifteenth century (FIG. 26). Describing and defining *type* was fairly easy when type was physically formed from metal. Type was a piece of metal—composed of lead, tin, and antimony—0.918 inch high with a character or symbol in relief on one end. Since strike-on, phototypesetting, and laser printing methods have been introduced, the word *type* has become somewhat abstract, because it now refers only to the resulting typographic image, and not the image source itself. Some people called type derived from nonrelief masters *flat type*, to emphasize the difference. Yet all type that appears on paper (or other substrates) is flat, even if it was printed from metal type, so what is needed is a definition of type as it appears to the reader, and not the creator of the graphic images.

Does a typewriter create type? Some early designs of the typewriter actually used printers' type on the typebars. Yet even today, after over 100 years of typewriter development, in most cases it is easy to differentiate typewritten characters from typeset characters (FIG. 27). To answer the question, typewriters do not create type. For that matter, traditional typesetting machines, such as strike-on devices and phototypesetters, are only a segment of a growing population of devices with typesetting capability.

There are qualities associated with typeset characters that make them unique and immediately identifiable. A list of such attributes would include: sharp, clean character edges • proportional spacing • range of point sizes • variations in character strokes

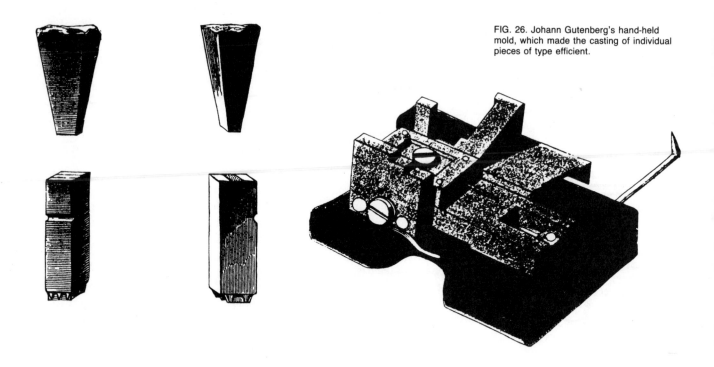

FIG. 26. Johann Gutenberg's hand-held mold, which made the casting of individual pieces of type efficient.

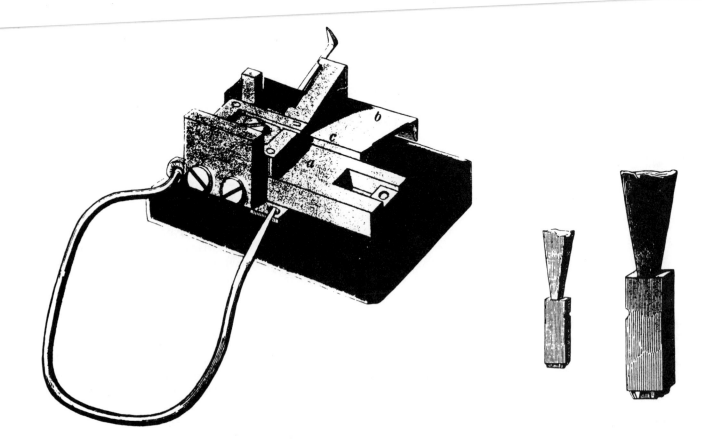

Dot Matrix Printer

Daisy Wheel Printer

Laser Printer

Phototypesetter

FIG. 27. Enlarged characters from a dot matrix printer, a daisy-wheel printer, a laser printer, and a phototypesetter.

(thick and thin) • variety of typeface designs • design variations of a single style (italic, bold, condensed, expanded, etc.). The first two attributes are the most useful (perhaps critical) in determining the quality level obtainable from a typesetting device. Evaluating them often is based solely on subjective judgments. At graphic arts trade shows, the typeset output from competing typesetters often is compared under a magnifying glass, by experts and tradesmen alike. Usually, the result is that there is little agreement over which is best or why.

There are, then, a range of acceptable standards for typeset output. The particular level chosen probably is based upon the purpose for which the type will be used (utilitarian, glamour, business), the environment using it (home, office, shop), the needs of the user (space factors, sizes, typefaces), the size and needs of the audience (short-lived information, archival storage, entertainment, and the methods of reproducing the message (copier, conventional printing).

Determining if a sample of characters can be classified as type is a fairly easy task using the five listed attributes. What is difficult is evaluating how good the characters are as specimens of the typographic form. The answer to this question must be determined by the user, who considers all of the factors that are significant in his situation.

uppercase or CAPITAL	ABCDEFGHIJKLMNOPQRSTUVWXYZ
lower case	abcdefghijklmnopqrstuvwxyz
SMALL CAPITALS	ABCDEFGHIJKLMNOPQRSTUVWXYZ
F LIGATURES	ff fi fl ffi ffl
FIGURES	1234567890
FRACTIONS	1/3 1/3 1/2 3/4 1/4
POINTS, OR THE MARKS OF PUNCTUATION	,."!;:-!)([]&?
MARKS OF REFERENCE	¶ §†‡
COMMERCIAL AND MONETARY SIGNS	$#%
SUPERIOR FIGURES	A1234567890
SPECIAL CHARACTERS (sorts—not a normal part of the font)	© ®•
Mathematical Signs	÷ = + × /

FIG. 28. Right: A complete font of type.

Typeface Geometry

Type can be found almost everywhere we look: on store windows, on the sides of buses, on candy wrappers and frozen foods, on billboards and tax forms, on money, and even on medicines. The proper use of type begins with some attention to the smallest parts of the letters, and some special terms used by typographers:

- The *arm* of a character is a horizontal projection or short, upward-sloping stroke.
- A *bar* is an enclosed horizontal stroke.
- The *stem* is the main part of the letter.
- A *cross stroke* is the part of the letter that cuts across the stem.
- The *tail* is a downward projection.
- The *apex* is the uppermost point or where the stems come together.
- The *vertex* is the lowermost joint where the stems join.
- The *ear* is the projection found on certain lowercase gs.
- The *spur* is the finishing stroke on certain uppercase Gs.

When describing any of the thousands of typeface designs in use, typographers frequently speak of the characteristics of specific styles using these terms. Notice that the physical elements of typewritten characters can be identified in a like manner by using these descriptions.

The collection of all of the various characters and symbols of a particular type design in a particular size is called the *font*. Fonts vary in size, from the basic alphabet to well over 100 characters (FIG. 28).

The relationship of characters in a font to one another is assessed most easily by viewing the characters in relation to the four typographic lines of reference. These lines are used by typeface designers to determine such things as the relative height of the lowercase characters to the uppercase characters (the *x-height*) and the amount of dip that rounded lowercase characters such as e and o will require. In FIG. 29 you will notice that all of the characters rest on the baseline. Directly above it is the upper limit of the main part of all lowercase characters, which is called the *mean line*. The distance between the baseline and the mean line is called the x-height, because it is the height of the lowercase x. Typefaces that have large x-heights usually are easier to read.

The two remaining lines are the extreme limits of the lowercase character shapes. Lowercase characters that descend below the baseline (g,j,p,q,y) are called *descenders*. The lowermost point of a descender is the *descender line*. Conversely, lowercase characters that ascend or project upward (b,d,f,h,k,l,t) are called *ascenders*. The uppermost point of an ascender is the *ascender line*, or as it is sometimes called, the *cap line*.

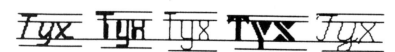

A selection of 24 point typefaces

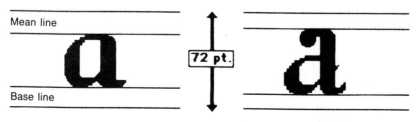

FIG. 29. The typographic lines of reference determine the relative sizes of uppercase and lowercase letters.

Arms

Bars

Stems

Cross strokes

Tails

Apex

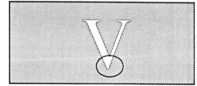

Vertex

Ear

Single Typeface Variations

When type is being set, it is common practice to deal with different elements of a page layout in different ways. Although the same statement could be made about typewriting, there is considerably more flexibility in typesetting, even when limited typographic resources are being used. Headlines or other composition that separate text should be set so they stand out. Words in text that are to be emphasized also require special attention. It is possible to meet these needs by using variations of a single type design.

Routine typesetting and typewriting involves the use of capital and lowercase letters. Two obvious variations are all-capital composition and all-lowercase composition. NOTICE THAT ALL-CAPITAL COMPOSITION CAN BE USED FOR EMPHASIS, AND ALSO THAT IT IS MORE DIFFICULT TO READ. We'll have more to say about the readability of type later. All-lowercase composition is easier to read, yet robs the reader of important information that capital letters provide. Like all-capital composition, it should be used with discretion.

Traditionally, printers have used the italic and boldface forms to emphasize text, and to organize information for easier reading. Most typesetting machines have *families* of type available, which are standard variations of a basic typographic design. The family usually includes an italic, boldface, lightface, condensed, and expanded version, although it also might include designs formed from a mix of these versions, such as condensed lightface, or an expanded boldface. Type family members all have physical attributes that make them design-compatible, and therefore, good choices for composing work involving multiple typefaces (FIG. 30).

A less common single face variation is the use of small capitals. Small capitals, or *small caps*, as they generally are known, are capital letters that have a lower cap line than the normal capital version of the same size. The small cap letters are, in fact, as high as the x-height of the lowercase characters. Because small caps have limited function, they are not usually part of the repertoire of characters available on a typesetting machine. To overcome this deficiency, typesetting keyboardists combine two sizes of capitals to produce a small cap variation that equals or approaches the size of the x-height (FIG. 31).

Spur

A Composite Picture of the complete GOUDY TYPE FAMILY is here shown for the first time
Goudy Catalogue
Goudy Catalogue Italic
Goudy Oldstyle
Goudy Italic
Goudy Cursive
GOUDY TITLE
Goudy Bold
Goudy Bold Italic
Goudy Handtooled
Goudy Handtooled Italic
AMERICAN TYPE FOUNDERS COMPANY

FIG. 30. The Goudy type family members all bear a close physical resemblance to one another.

FIG. 31. (*Top*) Examples of all-capital composition set in a range of point sizes. (*Bottom*) Combinations of various point sizes set in all capitals to produce small-capital composition.

HAVE A NICE DAY...SOMEWHERE ELSE
HAVE A NICE DAY...SOMEWHERE ELSE
HAVE A NICE DAY...SOMEWHERE ELSE
HAVE A NICE DAY...SOMEWHERE ELSE
HAVE A NICE DAY...SOMEWHERE ELSE

HAVE A NICE DAY...SOMEWHERE ELSE
HAVE A NICE DAY...SOMEWHERE ELSE
HAVE A NICE DAY...SOMEWHERE ELSE
HAVE A NICE DAY...SOMEWHERE ELSE
HAVE A NICE DAY...SOMEWHERE ELSE

Varying type size is probably the most common method of producing variety in the appearance of typeset matter. Typesetting machines are manufactured with a built-in range of sizes that they are capable of producing. The ranges can be in discrete steps, such as twelve sizes between 6 point and 72 point, or can be a continuous range, such as every half-point size between 5 point and 96 point. Regardless of the extent of the range, it usually embodies two categories of type-size range: text size and display size. The text range generally is considered to be sizes between 9 and 12 point. These sizes are used for the body matter of books, newspapers, magazines, and the like. The display range includes all sizes larger than 14 point. These sizes are used for headlines and subheads in combination with body matter. A portion of a size range is shown in FIG. 32.

Typeface Classification

One of the most perplexing problems confronting someone new to typesetting is the overwhelming variety of typeface designs from which to choose. There are literally thousands of styles available, many of which have families drawn as well. Printers have devised many methods of classifying typefaces, based upon either the physical attributes of the designs or their historical development. The complexities of organizing such a vast population of designs, coupled with the subtle design differences of similar typefaces, make identification of particular typefaces difficult, even, in some cases, for experienced typographers. For this reason, only a basic scheme of typeface classification will be offered here.

A typeface either has or does not have *serifs*. Serifs are ending strokes on the arms, stems, and tails of some typeface designs. If a typeface has serifs it is termed a *roman* typeface. If the typeface is without serifs, it is called a *sans serif* typeface. Typefaces that slant to the right, be they serif or sans serif, are called *italic* variations. Almost all type families include an italic member, and usually a boldface member as well (FIG. 33).

The designation of serifed typefaces as roman is complicated by the fact that any typeface which stands upright in comparison to an italic form is also called roman. This system of designation is somewhat confusing since both roman and sans serif typefaces have italic forms (FIG. 33).

The earliest typefaces—those from the Gutenberg workshop—were copies of the letterforms found in handwritten manuscripts. As a group they are called *Blackletter*, a version of which is referred to as *Old English*. These letters appear heavy and ornate, and have angular serifs (FIG. 34).

Printing from movable type spread from Germany south to Italy, and there the classical letterforms of Humanist manuscripts became the model for the roman typefaces. The earliest roman forms (as shown in FIG. 34) were called *old style*.

The roman forms underwent many changes during the period from approximately 1470 to 1775. In 1775 Giambattista Bodoni introduced a type design of mechanical structure, with heavy stems and light serifs. His design is classified as a *modern* typeface (FIG. 34).

Around the turn of the nineteenth century, a new commercial interest in type design began. One significant result of that attention was the formation of a group of type designs called the *square serifs*. Square serifs have squared off serifs at the extremities of each character (FIG. 34).

In 1816, William Caslon IV designed a typeface with no serifs. This design was in itself an innovation of major proportions. It was the first sans serif typeface, the first of many and the beginning of a major classification (FIG. 34).

FIG. 32. An example of a point size range for a single typeface. In general, the larger the point size, the more attention it gets from the reader. The selection of point sizes usually is based upon the relative importance of the information that is being displayed.

ABCDEabcde123
8 point

ABCDEabcde123
10 point

ABCDEabcde123
12 point

ABCDEabcde123
14 point

ABCDEabcde123
16 point

ABCDEabcde123
18 point

ABCDEabcde123
20 point

ABCDEabcde123
22 point

ABCDEabcde123
24 point

ABCDEabcde123
26 point

ABCDEabcde123
28 point

ABCDEabcde123
30 point

ABCDEabcde123
32 point

ABCDEabcde123
34 point

ABCDEabcde123
36 point

(a)

Scenic Greeting Cards
Scenic Greeting Cards
Scenic Greeting Cards

(b)

Scenic Greeting Cards
Scenic Greeting Cards
Scenic Greeting Cards

Typefaces imitating handwriting were first used in the sixteenth century. They appear to be drawn with pen and ink, and are classified as *scripts* and *cursives*. The letters of a script typeface are joined, while the letters of a cursive typeface are not (FIG. 34).

Typefaces that do not fit into any of the previous classifications can be grouped in a category called *decorative* and *display* (FIG. 34).

FIG. 33. (*a*) A serif typeface with italic and bold variations. (*b*) A sans serif typeface, also with italic and bold variations.

Making Type Easier to Read

There are two measures used to assess how easily a typeface can be comprehended by a reader. The first is the *legibility* of the typeface, how well each character design conveys its symbolic form to the reader. It is obvious that the various letter R's in FIG. 35 are not all equally identifiable as that character. The degree of legibility that a typeface possesses is controlled by the typeface designer. Although the legibility is designed into the typeface and its features cannot be changed by the user, the manner in which the typeface is used can very directly affect how easy the type is to read. The use of the type in its position in a layout, in its relation to other graphic elements, and in its specific form (type size, line length, line spacing) on the page are all aspects of *readability*, the second measure of typeface comprehension, and are all under the control of the user.

There has been, in typographic circles, the question of how, in a printed piece, it is possible to divorce the legibility of the typeface from the readability of the printed material. The consensus is that realistically it is not. The legibility of a typeface—roman or sans serif, italic or bold—is just as much a factor in readability as are line length, line spacing, and point size. In other words, too long a line length, little or no line spacing, and the wrong choice of point size can ruin the legibility of a typeface by altering the criteria under which it was designed. Conversely, an illegible, poorly designed, or extremely ornate or complex typeface cannot easily be improved by the variables of readability. Since legibility and readability are so intimately related in their influence on the effectiveness of graphic communication, the term *legibility of print* has been devised to refer to both.

Numerous studies have been conducted to determine the typographic factors that are most significant in increasing the legibility of print. Most of this research has used the measurement of work as the method of assessment. Since 1896 this measurement has been defined as the speed, in time, at which subjects are able to read and to locate answers to problems.

Reading has been defined by two experts as "the perception of graphic symbols. It is the process of relating graphic symbols to the reader's fund of experience." Reading has, therefore, two main variables: the graphic symbols and the reader.

To the mix of variables associated with the legibility of print we can add those that the reader touches, such as the tactile feel of the paper surface, and those that the printer has chosen and the reader sees, such as the color of the paper and ink, and the overall color or contrast of the page.

FIG. 34. These eight categories of type comprise a simple scheme of typeface classification.

FIG. 35. Six examples of the letter *R*. How would you rank them in terms of their legibility?

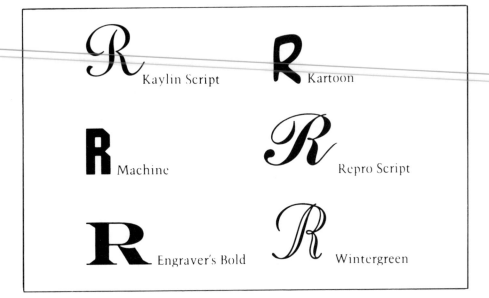

Kaylin Script   Kartoon

Machine   Repro Script

Engraver's Bold   Wintergreen

The reader presents his own mix of variables: his personality, age, sex, I.Q., maturity, willingness to learn, frustration tolerance, and reading skills, including eyesight. Other factors are the textual intent, whether pleasure-oriented or work-oriented, the length of text matter, the degree of interest, and the rate of speed and fatigue.

As early as 1907, Ruediger, a reading researcher, concluded that the eyes are easily able to cover ten times the number of words they actually do. The main impediments to speed, he found, were the comprehension and the quality of the text. He found that fluency of comprehension was directly related to smooth, rhythmical eye movements. The eye tends to divide a line of text into even units and fixates upon these delineations in even jumps. This phenomenon is called *point vision*. Dr. E.W. Dolch has concluded that ''the good reader is not fixating words or phrases of sentences. He is actually and literally fixating parts of the line.''

These facts have had a direct and quite meaningful impact on the use of type. Since the fewer fixations the eye must make causes greater speed of reading, it makes sense to use a minimum of space between words (word spaces) and to avoid wide or extended typefaces, which are now known to reduce reading speed and to cause eye fatigue.

Around the year 1910, Bertram Goodhue, the designer of the typeface Cheltenham, wrote that reading speed is dependent upon a reader's ability to make ''pictures'' out of words. Almost 25 years earlier, Cattell had showed by experimentation that the eye is capable of perceiving a whole word as quickly as a single letter. The block outlines of lowercase words provide a distinctive form, one not to be found in all-capital composition (FIG. 36).

FIG. 36. Words that appear in uppercase and lowercase form are easier for the eye to perceive as ''pictures.''

COMPOSITION   Composition

Cheltenham Bold

HOW IS ONE TO ASSESS AND EVALUATE

How is one to assess and evaluate a type face in term

The composition of all capitals has been proven to decrease the legibility of print. In extensive studies, G.W. Ovink found that differentiating characteristics of capitals must be clearly discernible. For example, the cross stoke at the bottom of the Q, which differentiates it from the ''O,'' must be obvious. He also found that the middle arm of the E and F should be shorter than the top arm and should not be too narrow, and that hairline stems and serifs and heavy or long serifs should be avoided.

Lowercase letters having more variation in shape have a greater legibility in print. Investigations by Ovink, Roethlein, Sanford, and Tinker all reached this same conclusion. Among their findings was that the relative width of the lowercase letter is a factor in legibility. Compare how easily an e or an i is read as opposed to an m or a w. They also found that the more simple the outline of the letter, the more legible the letter; that the serifs affect legibility; that shading, or variation of stress, affects legibility; and that the white space, or spaces within the outline of a letter, is a strong influence on that letter's legibility—the greater the space, the greater the legibility.

Much research has been conducted into the mechanical aspects of type design. Some of the earliest interest was expressed by Benjamin Franklin in a letter to Noah Webster concerning type contour, in which he wrote ''[it] makes the line more even, but renders it less immediately legible; as the paring of all men's noses might smooth and level their faces, but would render their physiognomies less distinguishable.'' In the early 1880s, Javal suggested the reconstruction of letter forms and the shortening of descenders. He based his recommendations on his observations from first covering the top half of a line of text, then the bottom. He concluded that it was much easier to read the top half with the bottom half covered than vice versa (FIG. 37). The eye does seem to define word forms in terms of their upper structural components.

The size of text type that is used does not seem to have a significant effect on the legibility of print. Studies by Paterson and Tinker, as well as Luckiesh and Moss have found that sizes between 9 and 12 points do not differ appreciably in this regard.

The weight of a typeface—that is, its degree of boldness—surprisingly does not have much affect on reading speed (FIG. 38). A study by Paterson and Tinker revealed, however, that 70 percent of those taking part in the investigation (320 subjects) had a definite preference for the normal weight of type as opposed to the bold.

Generally speaking, the typefaces in common use are equally legible, so even the inexperienced user runs little risk of selecting a text typeface that is terribly inappropriate. Readers seem to prefer a typeface that is neither light nor bold, but approaches boldness. Readers also prefer a serif to a sans serif typeface, although there is no difference in reading speed between the two. Italic typefaces tend to slow the reader, and should therefore, only be used for emphasis. As Ovink has stated, ''The typographer . . . who did not hit upon the specially appropriate type, will not have done actual harm to the transmission of the meaning of the text, but he has missed an opportunity to intensify the force of impression of the text in a considerable degree.''

There are a number of fairly simple guidelines that even the novice typesetter can follow that will improve the appearance of his typeset output. The first relates to line length. The manuscript writers and scribes of an age long past started the practice of consistently ending their handwritten lines at the same point. Early printers imitated this style. The uniformity of line length has influenced the printer so greatly that he sacrifices, in some instances, normal word spacing to achieve it. As the late Eric Gill wrote in his *Essay on Typography*, ''We have become accustomed to wide gaps between words, not so much because wide spacing makes for legibility as because the Procrustean Bed called the Composing Stick has made wide spacing the easiest way out of the difficulty caused by the tyrannical insistence upon equal length of lines.'' Generally speaking, readers dislike line lengths that are too short or too long (FIG. 39).

Paragraph Indentations. Even subtleties in text arrangement, such as paragraph indentation, can significantly affect legibility of print. An *indentation* is a space that sets the paragraph apart from other lines of type. It helps the reader's eye to identify and organize blocks of text. Only the first paragraph of a chapter or major subdivision does not require the indentation since the reader has no difficulty determining the beginning of a series of paragraphs. Studies conducted in the 1960s by Miles Tinker found that

FIG. 37. The upper half of a line of type provides more visual clues as to its identity than does the bottom half.

> The top of this line is covered from view.
>
> The bottom of this line is covered

FIG. 38. The effect of weight upon the Spartan typeface (light, book, medium, heavy, and black weights).

THE EFFECT OF WEIGHT UPON SPARTAN
light, book, medium, heavy, black

A B C D E F G H I J K L M N O P Q R S T U V W X Y Z
a b c d e f g h i j k l m n o p q r s t u v w x y z

A B C D E F G H I J K L M N O P Q R S T U V W X Y Z
a b c d e f g h i j k l m n o p q r s t u v w x y z

A B C D E F G H I J K L M N O P Q R S T U V W X Y Z
a b c d e f g h i j k l m n o p q r s t u v w x y z

A B C D E F G H I J K L M N O P Q R S T U V W X Y Z
a b c d e f g h i j k l m n o p q r s t u v w x y z

A B C D E F G H I J K L M N O P Q R S T U V W X Y Z
a b c d e f g h i j k l m n o p q r s t u v w x y z

FIG. 39. The optimum line lengths for various sizes of text type, based on research by Miles Tinker.

OPTIMUM LINE LENGTH
Single Column: 25-26 picas
Double Column: 17-18 picas

Type Size	Line Length
12 pt. s	17-37 picas
12 pt. l	17-33 picas
10 pt. s	17-27 picas
10 pt. l	14-31 picas
8 pt. s	13-25 picas
8 pt. l	14-28 picas
6 pt. s	9-25 picas
6 pt. l	14-28 picas

(set solid [s], with line space [l])

indentation can improve legibility significantly. As a general rule, paragraphs with line lengths up to 18 picas should be indented 1 em space; those with line lengths from 19 to 23 picas should be indented 1 1/2 em spaces; and those with line lengths between 24 and 30 picas should be indented 2 em spaces. Editorial style, however, might dictate otherwise.

Quadding. The last line of a paragraph usually does not fill the line measure. In hand composition, large metal spaces two or three times as large as an em were used to fill the space to the right of the final line. These spaces were called *quads*, and the process of using them was called *quadding*. In typeset output from a phototypesetting machine, for example, space is simply the absence of an exposure of light to photographic material. Quadding becomes a machine command controlling the positioning of less than a full line of type. The last line of a paragraph is pushed to the left, and therefore is called quad left (QL or sometimes flush left). A line pushed to the right is designated as quad right (QR or flush right). Centered lines are designated as quad center (QC or centered).

When lines are quadded, they gain the benefit of uniform word spacing. Because all excess space in a line is placed to the left, the right, or divided between the two, the fit of words in quadded lines is usually easier to read. Many publications have adopted the practice of setting all lines quad left, in a style known as *ragged right*, or flush left, ragged right. This style of line orientation has been shown to be easier to read. It also helps to avoid what George Bernard Shaw described as "rivers of white [which] trickle down between words like raindrops on the window pane."

Most readers are not aware if the text they are reading is ragged or justified. Do you know which style your daily newspaper uses? Check it out the next time you pick up a copy.

Letterspacing. The justification of lines of text sometimes is attempted under the worst of conditions. The line measure might be too short, or the words might be too long and unhyphenated, or the minimum word space might be too wide. The result is copy that is poorly spaced and difficult to read (FIG. 40).

Words can be spaced only so far apart before they lose their cohesiveness and become difficult to read. For this reason most typesetting systems have typographic spacing controls, which allow the user to set minimum and maximum expansion limits for word spaces. When the maximum word space value is surpassed, and if the user has specified the option, small increments of space are added between individual characters in the line. This letterspacing degrades the word shapes on which the readers' eye depends for quick recognition (FIG. 41). Letterspacing should be avoided if possible.

Kerning. The opposite of letterspacing is *kerning*. Instead of adding space between letters to fill a line, minute increments of space are subtracted from between certain character pairs in order to improve their fit and therefore make them more eye-appealing. Kerning is most common in display advertising, where differences in character fit are most obvious and aesthetically unacceptable (FIG. 42).

Some typesetting systems have an additional character-spacing option, usually referred to as *character compensation* or *tracking*. This option permits the user to specify a small increment of space that is to be uniformly removed from between all characters. The result of character compensation is tighter-fitting, although not necessarily more readable nor more eye-pleasing, typography. Character compensation can be used effectively to save space by squeezing characters closer together.

Hyphenation. The hyphenation process is linked intimately with the process of justification. The objective of line justification, as we have already discussed, is to pack as many characters on one line as will reasonably fit, while maintaining optimum word spacing and avoiding letterspacing. Hyphenation becomes necessary when a word falling at the end of a line causes the line to exceed the point where it should be ended (the *justification range*).

FIG. 40. Examples of poorly justified text.

The typographic implications of this capability are enormous. Not only can customer's input be received over the telephone (immediately, and from any distance), but, by using a dedicated computer which offers electronic mail, customers may leave files for pick-up at the convenience of the typesetter operator (usually at night when the telephone rates are lowest). Completed typesetting can then be mailed back to the customer. Even with the speed of the Postal Service, this method of doing business can be more efficient than current practices.

Information on manufacturer's products and prices is believed to be accurate as of the time of publication. Be advised that vendor's product descriptions and specifications are subject to change without notice. Where available, complete addresses and telephone numbers have been listed. The publisher maintains no liability or responsibility for the accuracy of claims, nor the performance of capabilities stated by manufacturers or their representatives.

FIG. 41. Excessively letterspaced lines slow the reading rate since the reader must determine where one word ends and the next begins.

She had little idea what he actually meant by his casual remark, although she felt truly hurt. Did he really mean that he considered her insensitive and cold? His untimely departure put distance, as well as space between them. Only Reilly was aware of what was on Drew's mind when he confronted Lisa, and he was the least able to adequately explain any of it to her. Reilly, after all, had his own problems, and his devotion to his workers was of considerably less importance than his need to have his business survive.

FIG. 42. Kerning helps to compensate for the placement of irregular character shapes in proximity to one another. (*Top*) Normal, (*Bottom*) Kerned.

The unTrivial Pursuit of Excellence

The unTrivial Pursuit of Excellence

Early phototypesetting machines required perforated tapes with all end-of-line information included; in other words, the lines had to be justified prior to typesetting. These justified tapes could be prepared on a counting keyboard, which calculated the unit width of each typed character and indicated to the operator when the justification zone was reached. Another method involved running an unjustified tape through a reader on a special computer so that a new justified tape could be prepared.

The first use of a digital computer in the typesetting area was in the early 1960s, when a general-purpose computer, used for accounting and payroll functions, was programmed for typesetting. Removing the end-of-line decision-making function from the perforator operator resulted in two major benefits. It increased the throughput speed and also allowed the operator to produce a tape from a less sophisticated and less expensive keyboard.

One of the first computers built to perform a specific (special-purpose) typesetting task was the Compugraphic Linasec. It was used to justify tape, but lacked the storage capacity necessary for hyphenation, thereby requiring a human monitor to respond to word breaks appearing on a CRT screen. The Linasec was followed by the Compugraphic Justape, which had the ability to accept an unjustified tape and output a justified tape, all without the aid of a human monitor.

Today most typesetting machines have the hyphenation and justification (popularly known as H & J) capabilities built in. We have seen that justification can be controlled by minimum and maximum word spacing and letterspacing ranges set by the user. Hyphenation can be user controlled as well.

When the last word in a line exceeds the line measure, one option is to carry the entire word to the next line and make up the space by using interword and intraword spacing. If all such hyphenation decisions are made in this manner, the result is *hyphenless justification*, which gives the appearance of very loose lines. Hyphenless justification is a poor typographic style that should be avoided.

The alternative is to hyphenate the word and carry only part of it to the next line. Most typesetting machines accomplish this process by using one or a combination of three different methods.

The first method of hyphenation relies totally on the judgment of the keyboard operator. The operator might anticipate that the typesetter's computer logic cannot differentiate between certain words, such as pre-sent and pres-ent, nor be able to handle the hyphenation of certain technical terms or unusual names. In such cases, the operator would insert a code called a *discretionary hyphen* at the proper points to make the correct break points obvious to the computer, should that particular word exceed the justification zone. If such words do not fall at the end of the line, the discretionary hyphenation codes are ignored during processing.

The second hyphenation method relies on the rules of English language logic. The typesetter computer is programmed with information based upon grammatical usage. Such instructions include not breaking a word a) after less than two letters, b) so that three or less letters are carried to the next line, c) after a consonant followed by a vowel and d) before a punctuation mark, as well as many others. Logic programs are not perfect because there are many exceptions to accepted rules of English usage. At best such programs are about 98 percent accurate.

The third and most precise method of hyphenation is by *dictionary look-up*. In this method, an entire dictionary is stored on hard disk and consulted as needed. Although this method is very effective, it is also very expensive and requires continuous updating for new words. A variation of this method is an *exception-word dictionary*, a special collection of words that a particular user or company frequently encounters. The exception word dictionary is used in conjunction with a logic program and with discretionary hyphenation, as well in cases of confusing word pairs.

Guidelines for Good Typographic Judgment

It is the responsibility of the type designer to make his design legible; that is, to make each character clearly depict the letterform it is meant to represent. Because of the great variety of typefaces that are available (conservation estimates place the number in excess of 5000 in popular use), the selection of appropriate typefaces is sometimes difficult, especially for an inexperienced person. The most popular typefaces, therefore those that are seen in print most often, tend to be very legible and, therefore, appropriate for most categories of work. Times Roman, a serif design, and Helvetica, a sans serif, are among the most popular in the world because of their clean designs and high legibility (FIG. 43).

Not only is the selection of the typeface important, but also how the typeface is arranged and used. How the typographer (or type consumer) executes the use of the typeface determines its readability. There are few strict rules that govern typographic arrangement, but there are some guidelines which are useful in planning an easy-to-read layout:

- Use a line spacing value that is approximately 20 percent of the type size. If the type measures 10 points, then an appropriate line spacing value would be 12 points (20% × 10 points = 2 + 10 point type = 12).
- The width of word spaces should be kept to a minimum.
- General reading matter should be typeset in a size between 10 and 12 points.
- Where appropriate, the typeface should match its intended use. An advertisement for a crystal goblet should be set in a light and free-flowing script typeface, while a letterhead for a trucking company should be set in a bold sans serif.
- Words in headlines should be arranged according to their content, as well as their length. Consider, for example, how these two headlines are broken and which is easier to read:

OUR ONCE IN A BLUE
MOON SALE STARTS AT 9
SHARP TOMORROW MORNING

OUR ONCE IN A BLUE MOON SALE
STARTS AT 9 SHARP TOMORROW MORNING

- Use italic and boldface to emphasize and to help organize logical units of text.
- Avoid using ornate typefaces for text matter.
- Don't use a line measure that is either too short or too long.
- Don't use all-capital composition in text material.
- Don't set blackletter (commonly referred to as Old English), script, or ornate typefaces in all capitals.
- Avoid excesses in both letter and word spacing, and eliminate letterspacing altogether if possible.
- Don't use condensed or expanded typefaces for reading matter.

Helvetica Thin

Helvetica Light

Helvetica

Helvetica Medium

Helvetica Medium Flair

Helvetica Bold

Helvetica Ultra Black

Helvetica Light Italic

Helvetica Italic

Helvetica Medium Italic

Helvetica Bold Italic

Helvetica Regular Condensed

Helvetica Bold Condensed

Helvetica Extrabold Condensed

Helvetica Ultra Compressed

Helvetica Extra Compressed

Helvetica Compressed

Helvetica Regular Extended

Helvetica Bold Extended

Helvetica Extra-bold Extended

Helvetica Medium Outline

Helvetica Bold Outline

Helvetica Italic Outline

Helvetica Bold Condensed Outline

Helvetica Extrabold Condensed Outline

FIG. 43. These two typefaces, Helvetica and Times Roman, are considered among the most legible. Legibility studies usually are conducted using sophisticated optical devices that display typographic characters for split-second intervals to test subjects. (Phototypositor specimens courtesy of M.J. Baumwell Typography, New York, N.Y.)

HOW IS ONE TO ASSESS AND EVALUATE A TYPE FACE IN TERMS O **ITS ESTHETIC DESIGN? WHY DO THE PACE-MAKERS IN THE ART O**

12
point

How is one to assess and evaluate a type face in terms of its esthetic design? Why do the pace-makers in the art of printing rave over a specific face of type? What do they see in it? Why is it so superlatively pleasant to their eyes? **Good design is always practical design.** And what they see in a good type design is, partly, its excellent practical fitness to perform its work. It has a "heft" and balance in all of its parts just right for its size, as any **How is one to assess and evaluate a type face in terms of its esthetic design? Why**

(with regular descenders on twelve point body)

How is one to assess and evaluate a type face in terms of its esthetic design? Why do the pace-makers in the art of printing rave over a specific face of type? What do they see in it? Why is it so superlatively pleasant to their eyes? **Good design is always practical design.** And what they see in a good type design is, partly, its excellent practical fitness to perform its work. It has a "heft" and ba   g j p q y **How is one to assess and evaluate a type face in terms of its esthetic design? Why**

(with long descenders on thirteen point body)

ABCDEFGHIJKLMNOPQRSTUVWXYZ&
ABCDEFGHIJKLMNOPQRSTUVWXYZ&

abcdefghijklmnopqrstuvwxyzfiflffffiffl   [($£,.:;'-'?!*†‡§¶)] 1234567890
abcdefghijklmnopqrstuvwxyzfiflffffiffl   [($£,.:;'-'?!*†‡§¶)] 1234567890

Matrix Information: 12△570. Lower case alphabet, 148 points. Figures, .0899; comma, period and thin space, .0449. Smallest slug on which this face will cast is 12 point; with long descenders on 13 point—*specify style of descenders desired.* Code word, ZOMIB.

Chapter 2

Word Processing as a Part of Typesetting

Similarities in the keyboarding skills between word processing and typesetting make them an obvious pair.

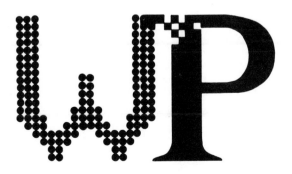

THE HISTORY OF WORD PROCESSING HAS BEEN DIRECTLY INFLUENCED BY MANY PEOple closely associated with printing and typesetting. Beginning with the inventors of the typewriter, which is generally perceived as the rudimentary basis for the word processor, people practicing the craft of printing have played a major role in nurturing the development and defining the usefulness of the word processor.

It was a goal of early typewriter inventors not only to automate the process of handwriting, but also to bring the printing process into the home and office environments. However, a number of mechanical problems necessitated design simplifications, which resulted in an image quality considerably lower than obtainable by the then standard practices of hand and machine typesetting.

THE AUTHOR: ORIGINATOR OF TYPESETTING INPUT

As early as the late nineteenth century, noncraftsmen began to operate mechanical typesetting machines to eliminate rekeyboarding. One of the first proponents of this was Tolbert Lanston, the inventor of the Monotype machine (FIG. 1), a composing device with a particularly complicated keyboard. His idea met with little or no interest.

Authors did take an immediate liking to the typewriter, however. It was easier to use, and not only gave their work a look of prestige, but also eliminated the ambiguity of handwritten copy. Compositors were pleased to receive typewritten copy because it was easier to read and easier to follow. The typewriter had a profound effect on the business community, and within a relatively short period of time it became a standard for the contemporary office. With great numbers of typewriters in use there were great numbers of proficient (or at least "trained") typists. The typewriter was hailed as the office printing machine, and unlike the craft of printing, presented numerous employment opportunities for women.

The obvious similarity between typewriting and typesetting processes did not go unnoticed, although the keyboard layouts were very much different. By the end of the nineteenth century, young, lady "typewriters" were being trained in St. Paul and Minneapolis publishing houses to run Linotype machines. Mergenthaler Linotype Company itself became actively involved in the training of typists into typesetters. The *Inland Printer* magazine of February 1899 reported: "Not one typewriter . . . became an acceptable operator when put to work in a composing room. Dexterity in manipulating keyboard, without technical knowledge of the printing business, is of no practical value in a printing office." The general tone of other articles published around the same time suggests that men were not very receptive to having women in the composing room, and were, therefore, not enthusiastic about seeing them succeed. Although the hopes of a few were never realized, neither were the fears of many—namely that these machines would completely eliminate requirements for skilled compositors. One verse from the poem "The Typesetting Machine," printed in the *Inland Printer* in July 1889, reads:

The editor will touch the keys, and deftly "set" his work;
The "special" man, his articles into the thing will jerk;
The "night man" and the "local" will quickly spread their notes;
The "funny" man will calmly smoke and click his anecdotes;
The "fashion" man and the "sporting sharp" their screeds will neatly do;
The machine will edit copy, yes, and punctuate it, too.

FIG. 1. The Monotype keyboard is among the most complicated in the typesetting industry, yet its inventor, Tolbert Lanston, advocated its use by authors and other text originators. (Brown Brothers, Sterling, PA 18463.)

The machine age of typesetting presented clear and present dangers to those whose livelihoods depended upon the typesetting process. To those who manually assembled type, the typesetting machine was a real economic threat—one that could eliminate, virtually overnight, most members of a composing room. Those who did use the machines, either as operators or owners, felt threatened by "amateurs," women workers, and the ever-present problem of machine sabotage.

TYPESETTING BY TYPEWRITER

One of the first typewriters to be produced as a typesetter was the Hammond machine. James Bartlett Hammond, its inventor, was a young Civil War correspondent who was dependent upon the telegraph to wire his handwritten stories to his newspaper. Telegraphers frequently misinterpreted his writing, leading to misprints and causing frequent embarrassment and anger. Hammond conceived of a typewriter that would print his story so clearly that even a careless telegrapher could easily follow it. His first model was produced in 1881, and featured a changeable typewheel for different faces and sizes.

The Hammond Company was acquired by Ralph C. Coxhead in the early 1930s. Coxhead renamed the Hammond machine the VariTyper, because of its typographic flexibility. The VariTyper (Chapter 1, FIG. 4) was more of a refined typewriter than a simplified typesetter, but nonetheless, typists were easily trained to set "type."

The VariTyper, which was one of the first typewriterlike devices to be manufactured for typesetting purposes, remained the default standard for direct-impression typesetting until the introduction of the IBM Selectric Composer (FIG. 2) in 1967.

Although direct-impression machines incorporate composition components such as typeface variety, point size range, line spacing, line length, letterspacing, word spacing control, justification, and proportional character fit, they are not cost-effective when compared to other typesetting alternatives. In the realm of commercial typesetting, the direct-impression machine never really had a place. Its significance today in the noncommercial market is definitely on the wane.

FIG. 2. The IBM Selectric Composer was instrumental in bringing typeset quality into the office and small shop environments. The justification of lines required two typings: one to generate a color/number code, and the second to actually produce the justified line. In early 1975, IBM introduced the Electronic Selectric Composer with a built-in memory of 8000 characters, permitting the operator to store, replay, and manipulate keyboarded copy. Additionally, only one typing was required since mistakes could be corrected by writing over the error, and justification in a number of formats was automatic.

TTS AND THE TYPEWRITER LAYOUT

In 1928, typists and typesetters again crossed paths. Walter Morey, himself a Monotype operator, invented the Teletypesetter (TTS) system. The Teletypesetter used a six-unit perforator to prepare a punched tape for input to a specially adapted linecaster. Three linecasters operated by tape could produce as much as seven linecasters run by operators.

TTS keyboards used standard typewriter layouts, which made the use of typists quite practical. It was so practical, in fact, that it was proposed that news reporters and editors use the perforators to directly keyboard their stories. Again, as had been the case with Lanston, the idea was not well received.

Although the TTS keyboard was similar to the standard typewriter layout, it was not identical. There were 19 additional keys, plus justification pointers, which required close attention. Despite these differences, the Teletypesetter Corporation advertised that beginning typists could produce 400 or more newspaper lines[1] of type per hour.

While TTS opened the door to typesetting input for typists, it closed the door to some linecaster operators. Those trained on a linecaster keyboard (FIG. 3) did not usually have typing skill, and so retraining was necessary. So great was the need for TTS operators that union schools were opened. The International Typographical Union (ITU) went so far as to develop the Brewer Keyboard, invented by Claire N. Brewer. This keyboard, resembling a linecaster layout, fit over the TTS keyboard, and let the linecaster operator keyboard as if sitting at a linecaster.

---

[1] A newspaper line of type is generally regarded as 8- to 9-point type on a 10- to 11-pica line measure.

In the 1930s, precisely the opposite had been done. Newspapers and printing companies had often found themselves in labor disputes or unable to find qualified operators. The solution was the "Type-O-Writer," a device manufactured by the Mergenthaler Linotype Company. The Type-O-Writer was a typewriter keyboard that fit over the linecaster keyboard, permitting operation by a typist.

THE TYPIST AND THE EARLY PHOTOTYPESETTER

The typist/typesetter issue was raised early in the marketing of commercially viable phototypesetting machines. William Garth Jr., who was the driving force behind Photon, the first commercially available second-generation phototypesetter, said in 1953 that "You can hire a typist today and she will be setting a book tomorrow even though she has never seen the machine before, and she will be doing it as fast as she can type." That statement was backed by Katherine Petmezakis, Garth's secretary, who publically demonstrated the Photon 200 (FIG. 4). Additionally, the first book produced by Photon, *The Wonderful World of Insects,* was set by "a girl typist with no previous experience in composition."

WORD PROCESSING TAKES ITS PLACE IN HISTORY

It is generally agreed that modern word processing began with the introduction of the IBM Magnetic Tape Selectric Typewriter (MT/ST) in Germany in 1964. The usefulness of the system was not recognized immediately, and it was not until 1965 that the term *textuarbeitung*, meaning "programmed paragraph assembly," was coined to describe the notion of automated word assembly, or *word processing*. The earliest version of this machine used one or more Magnetic Tape Selectric Typewriters to prepare tapes for output on a Selectric Composer, thereby providing "typeset" composition at the rate of about 14 characters per second. The first entrant into the realm of word processing, was, therefore, an automated version of the IBM direct-impression product, a quasi-typesetter.

FIG. 3. The standard keyboard on the Linotype machine was arranged from left to right according to the frequency of use of the characters.

The MT/ST provided features that were to characterize the early generation of word processors: the use of magnetic tape storage (in this case providing storage density of 20 cpi, almost twice that of paper tape at 11 cpi), reusable media, search and retrieval capability, and relative ease of operation.

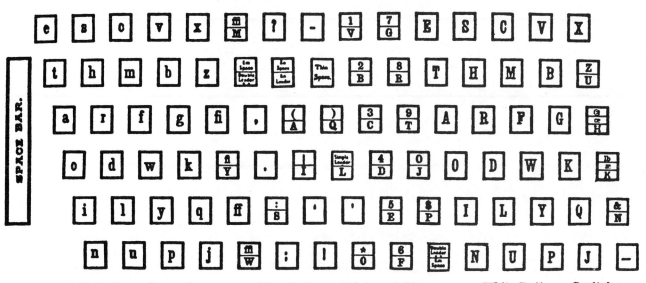

Black Buttons—Lower Case   Blue Buttons—Points and Figures   White Buttons—Capitals

In 1969, IBM introduced its Mag Card word processor, which incorporated the concept of one page of text to one magnetic card. Competition was slow to come, as was the market to develop, but in 1971 Redactron introduced a word processor and TyData followed suit. In 1972 the first video display systems were introduced by Lexitron and Linolex. In the following years, the market was literally to explode with new vendors, including such established office suppliers as Olivetti, Wang, Savin, Royal, Xerox, A.B. Dick, Lanier, Digital Equipment Corporation, Norelco, AM International, and Dennison.

As the market became established, so did the meaning of word processing. No longer was *word processing* interpreted as hardware only, but rather the collective activity through which information was transformed into typewritten form, not only by using the machines called word processors, but also by applying defined procedures, using trained operators, and providing supervision by a management committed to overall business efficiency.

HOW WORD PROCESSING AND PHOTOTYPESETTING ARE ALIKE

The parallel, sometimes intertwining, development of word processing and phototypesetting has resulted in two technologies with many similarities, both of form and purpose. The components that modern technology offers have been applied to each,

A Finger Flick—A Page of Type

FIG. 4. The skills required of an ordinary typist versus those of a trade craftsman have always been played against the similarities between a typewriter and a phototypesetter. This photograph is from the Christian Science Monitor, February 5, 1953. (Courtesy Mr. Louis Moyroud).

Gordon N. Converse, Staff Photographer

"It's easy," says Katherine Petmezakis as she shows how even an amateur can set up a page of type with Photon, the revolutionary new electronic typesetter. Standing by (left to right) are L. M. Moyroud and R. A. Higonnet, inventors of the machine, and S. H. Caldwell and W. W. Garth of the Graphic Arts Research Fondation, where Photon was developed. Mr. Higonnet is holding a copy of "The Wonderful World of Insects," the first book produced by Photon, while Mr. Caldwell examines one of photographic page plate films from which the engraver's page plates were made. These films were set by a girl typist with no previous experience in composition.

and so in physical form they closely resemble one another. Typically, a word processor, be it a dedicated system that only does word processing or a microcomputer-based system using word processing software, has the same basic parts as a typesetter input station: a CRT, a keyboard, a mass-storage device (diskette or hard-disk based), and a computer enclosure (which also can be a part of the disk drive enclosure or can be incorporated with the keyboard). The Compugraphic Personal Composition System (FIG. 5), actually used an Apple Macintosh XL personal computer to generate input for a variety of output devices.

Many phototypesetting systems, such as the Itek Quadritek 1600 (FIG. 6), use the same hardware components to accomplish both typesetting input and word processing tasks. A change of software converts the workstation from one to the other or to a general-purpose business computer. Many of the major typesetting vendors either sell the WordStar[2] word processing program for their systems or offer CP/M or MS-DOS capability to support the use of WordStar or other word processing packages.

FIG. 5. The Compugraphic Personal Composition System used an Apple Macintosh XL with custom typesetter driver software written by Compugraphic. The actual choice of typefaces and type sizes (from a limited selection) are manipulated easily on the XL screen.

FIG. 6. The Itek 1600 provides a CP/M environment in which WordStar word processing software can be run. Itek directly supports WordStar and offers software to facilitate the transfer of WordStar files into the typesetter operating environment for further processing.

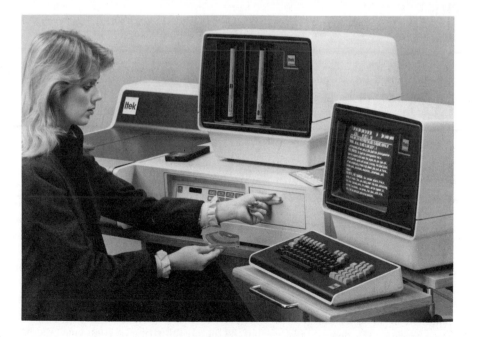

[2]WordStar by MicroPro International is one of the most popular word processing programs available for CP/M-compatible computers. (See Page 65.)

WHY WORD PROCESSING IS
A NATURAL PARTNER FOR TYPESETTING

Quite early in the commercial development of the word processing phenomenon it was realized that keystrokes captured on a word processor could be utilized by a phototypesetter. This possibility was not as obvious as it might seem today since early word processors and phototypesetters had little or no compatibility in media or in code structures.

Regardless of the number of obstacles, early proponents of interfacing based their beliefs on an analysis of the typesetting process, the outcome of which should make sense to anyone even remotely familiar with the basic functions performed in typesetting. The analysis, conducted by the National Composition Association (NCA, a division of Printing Industries of America), showed that the average phototypesetting costs for most categories of work were divided as follows:

Keyboarding	30%
Proofreading	22%
Corrections	14%
Make-up	10%
Typesetting	19%
Proofing/materials	5%
	100%

Of these major categories, keyboarding, proofreading, and corrections all can be done efficiently and effectively on a word processor prior to running the information through the phototypesetter output unit.

These statistics were convincing enough to start a movement affectionately termed the "marriage of word processing to phototypesetting." Not only has the marriage been successfully consummated, but the couple can reside compatibly in the same hardware or communicate effectively using a number of different methods.

THE ROLE
OF THE WORD PROCESSOR OPERATOR IN TYPESETTING

The input that eventually reaches the phototypesetter for processing is composed of two different sets of information. The first is the *information content,* the actual characters that will be typeset. These are the one and the same characters that are captured at the word processor. The second set is the commands that direct the form of the output—the typographic descriptors that indicate how the processed characters will physically appear on the output material.

It is clear that the word processing operator is responsible for providing clean input for typesetting, but the addition of the typesetting codes might or might not take place during the word processing phase of the operation. Philosophies and practices as to when the typesetting codes should be input differ, and are dependent primarily on the typographic understanding and skill level of the word processing operator, as well as the complexity of the jobs, the work relationships within a company, the pay scale or job skill level of the operator, the established procedures of a company or a typesetting service, the severity of the penalties for coding errors, and other considerations.

If the word processing operator is responsible for inputting the typesetting commands, then there are also various degrees of sophistication that might be employed in the process. The operator might input the literal, full string of commands required for each execution of a typographic change, or might instead input some shorthand codes that indicate a predefined format or methodology for handling a particular section of copy, such as headlines or footnotes.

Deciding who should do the typesetting coding and when it should be done are, to a high degree, dependent upon the specific set of circumstances in which an organization finds itself. In general, an organization should consider the implementation of typographic coding at the word processing input stage if a significant number of the following are true:

- The nature of the work is typographically noncomplex.
- The operators are completely trained, totally comfortable with the equipment in use, and relatively stable in terms of job permanence.
- A designated typesetting expert is resident in the immediate environment.
- Work destined for typesetting does not usually need to be output on letter-quality devices as well (eliminating the need to keep two versions of each job: one with embedded typesetting codes, the other without).

CREATING INPUT FOR A PHOTOTYPESETTER

The use of a word processor generally has as its objective the formation of typewritten words on paper. Pages usually conform to the 8 1/2-×-11-inch format, and margins, page headings, captions, footnotes, and other elements are handled in a fairly routine manner, with little or no flexibility in output format.

Even with all of the incredible editing and file management capabilities of word processors and of computers using word processing software, the output—either by daisy wheel, dot matrix, ink-jet, or laser printer—usually appears very much as though it were output from a standard nonautomated typewriter. Although this appearance is more by design than by accident, the fact remains that the path to phototypesetting output is more than half traveled when the word processing file is saved on disk.

There are a number of approaches to preparing word processing files for phototypesetting. All of them depend in whole or in part on the requirements and capabilities of the phototypesetter. Even in the simplest case, where the typographic default values of the phototypesetter will be used and the word processing file is composed of straight text and therefore requires literally no coding, there are certain conventions that must be followed. Typesetting is not exactly like typewriting, and this list of differences should be read with care:

- Successive spaces, such as between sentences, should not be used. The reader's eye does not require the additional space to separate sentences that is required in typewritten communication.
- The letter *l* (*el*) should not be used in place of the number one. Likewise the letter *O* should not be used in place of the number zero.
- A typesetter uses beginning and ending quotes rather than the single set of double quotes appearing on many word processing keyboards. (The IBM PC has both.)
- Typeset paragraphs are indented using fixed spaces (em and en spaces) rather than the variable space bar key. The width of each fixed space is relative to the size of the type in use, and the width of the indentation is related to the length of the line being composed.
- On a typesetter, a break in thought is indicated by an em dash (—), rather than by a series of hyphens (- -).
- Words that are underlined on a word processor for emphasis are set in either italics or boldface (depending upon user preference) on a typesetter.
- Fractions, usually indicated on a word processor as two numbers (or series of num-

bers) separated by a slash (i.e. 1/2 or 38/64) are set on a phototypesetter either as a superior/inferior character combination or as a special character.

- Words that are hyphenated in a word processing file will retain their hyphens when typeset. To avoid this situation, no words should be hyphenated, but instead wrapped around to the next line.

Capturing All That is Good

At some point before the actual typesetting of the file generated by the word processor, the file will undergo a translation operation. There are a number of ways by which this operation can take place, and we will cover them in detail later. For now, suffice it to say that unless the media produced by the word processor or microcomputer is 100 percent compatible with the phototypesetter, which it usually is not, some translation must take place.

The translation operation not only is necessary, but it can reduce or eliminate further editing of the file. By passing the word processor file through the translation table, each code takes on a value meaningful to the phototypesetter. An *A* remains an *A*, an underlined word is converted to italic, a centered headline remains centered. Likewise, multiple spaces between sentences automatically are reduced to single spaces; special lineprinter codes (such as reverse platen), which are meaningless to the phototypesetter, are stripped out; and special predefined mnemonic codes (such as for basic typesetting parameters) are converted to true typesetting commands.

Expanding the Capability of the Word Processor Keyboard

Accessing all of the typographic functions and special characters resident on a phototypesetter from a limited word processor or computer keyboard requires considerable planning. Many, many years ago this same problem arose in the typesetting industry when paper tape perforators were utilized. It was recognized then that just as the shift key essentially doubles the accessible character repertoire on a typewriter, the addition of a super shift (SS) key to the paper tape perforator opened access to all of the necessary typesetter commands and special characters. The super shift is called a *precedence code* because it changes the meaning of the character or characters that follow it.

The super shift was built into the paper tape perforator, but does not, of course, appear on a word processing or computer keyboard. Conceptually, however, the same kind of procedure can be used to accomplish the same end. The user of the word processor or computer, in agreement with the associated typesetting personnel, can define any rarely used keyboard character, such as [,], or ^, to serve as the precedence code. Likewise, other character strings preceded by unlikely characters such as a dollar sign or a slash can be used as the precedence code.

As an example, let's use the slash as such a code. The slash is not commonly used for other purposes, and we can retain the use of it as a character by assigning it its own definition. When the phototypesetter or the translation table encounters the slash, it will recognize that the following sequence of characters is not to be typeset, but rather is to be interpreted as commands or special characters.

The precedence code is like a flag, which signals that the string of characters coming is to undergo conversion. Specifying what those commands or characters are to be is accomplished by the use of *mnemonics*, two-letter abbreviations that refer to a longer string of characters. Mnemonics are a way of helping us remember what these shorthand codes mean. The mnemonic for line length, for example, might be LL, and the mnemonic for size, similarly, might be SZ.

Many typesetter commands require not only the specification of the mnemonic, but also a value to associate with it. In both the case of the LL and the SZ mnemonics, some value must be specified in order to complete the command. The full syntax, or order of entry, of these commands is:

1	2	3
PRECEDENCE CODE	MNEMONIC	VALUE (AS REQUIRED)

All typesetting jobs have a minimum of four typographic parameters, as described in Chapter 1. As a quick review they are:

Line Length. This parameter indicates how wide the lines to be typeset will be. Line length is measured in picas. The line length value is specified by four numbers. The first two digits indicate the pica measure of the line; the second two digits indicate the number of points. A line length of 45 picas would be written as *4500* (45 picas, 00 points). A line length of 26 1/2 picas would be written as *2406* (24 picas, and 6 points). All four digits must be specified. A line length of 7 picas, for example, would be written as *0700.*

Font. This parameter indicates the type style. Phototypesetting machines commonly have from 4 to 16 type styles available at one time, although some have as many as 100 or more. Fonts usually are accessed by number rather than by name, with the number referring to its physical location or storage area within the phototypesetter. The font in the first position is *1*; the font in the second position is *2*, and so on.

Size. This parameter indicates the size of the type. Depending upon the phototypesetter, the size value can be specified by either two or three digits, or a variation thereof. If the typesetter does not have half-point sizes, then two digits usually are used. If it does have half-point sizes, then either three digits are used, with either a 1 or a 5 as the third digit, or a period is used to precede the other two. A 10 1/2-point type might be indicated as either *101, 105,* or *.10*, depending on the specific phototypesetter. If three digits are required, then all three must be used, as in indicating 6 1/2-point type as *065*.

Line Space. This parameter indicates the vertical measurement of space between lines. Like size, it is measured in points and half points (and sometimes tenths of a point).

Putting It All Together

The code string for each parameter, command, or special character must be constructed using the proper syntax. To fail to do so will not only yield the improper results, but might completely ruin the format of the typeset job. This risk is sufficiently real to convince some users of typesetting services that they should leave all of the coding to trained typesetting personnel. Much of that decision depends upon careful consideration of job complexity, operator skill, time restraints (is there time to do the job over if necessary?), and economic factors (How much is saved by supplying the typesetter with fully coded files? How much more will it cost to have the typesetter insert the codes as compared to paying a more skilled operator to prepare the file beforehand? Is the potential monetary savings worth the risk of paying for correcting more errors?).

At the beginning of each job there must be a preliminary string of codes that defines the beginning job parameters (any of which may change at any time). These four main job attributes—line length, font, point size, and line spacing—are strung together, like so:

/LL1800/FT1/SZ080/LS090

Their order usually doesn't matter, although their syntax certainly does.

Once an attribute is ascribed, such as font number, it remains active until it is changed. Consider a paragraph having one italic word somewhere in the middle. To change to italic, the code */ft2* might be used (where the second font position is italic).

At the end of the word another code string must be used to return to the original typeface. If this small detail is overlooked, the remainder of the job would be set in italic. One small coding error results in much unusable typesetting! The cost of such a simple error is difficult to estimate; the entire job might have to be reset, or at the very least some portions of it. If the typesetting personnel do not notice the error or if they assume that a long italic passage is what was required, considerable time might be lost in bringing the text into published form.

Keep in mind, as well, that the text as it appears on the computer or word processor display, or even on the printer, does not provide an approximation of how the job will look when it is typeset. Systems such as the Apple Macintosh are exceptions.

Beyond the Basic Parameters

Straight text requires only the four basic parameters to describe its expected outcome adequately. Yet the flexibility of a phototypesetter extends considerably beyond these four delimiters, and through the use of mnemonic coding can be accessed by virtually any computer[3] (with word processing or text-editing capability) or dedicated word processor.

The total set of commands used by phototypesetting systems is fairly large, numbering 100 or more. To cover them in some logical order, I have arranged them according to common functions.

Group One: End-of-Line Commands. This set of commands determines the line orientation, either singly or successively. Generally, if the lines are to be justified—that is, fill the entire line length—then no command is necessary. Lines that are shorter than the measure, such as the last line of a paragraph, must be handled differently. Such lines must be pushed (quadded) to the left margin. If such a command was not issued, the last line of a paragraph, which is usually shorter than the lines that precede it, would be spread out across the entire line length, resulting in a very loose, unattractive line, as follows:

Improperly   quadded   paragraph

The use of successively flushed left lines is common, and the resulting style is called, as was mentioned earlier, ragged right.

There are two other common line orientations: flush right, wherein the line is pushed against the right margin, and centered. Phototypesetters usually provide some means for indicating that only one line will undergo the specified treatment, or that all lines will until the command is canceled. In display advertising, there are frequent examples of individual lines handled in these ways (FIG. 7).

SAVE!
An Exclusive Offer
Now Better Than Ever . . . Plus
The Best
Full Color . . . Graphics
Photography
Exhibition Design

#1
For excellence
innovative design
meticulous quality
whenever wherever
plus much more
write or call
today
★

FIG. 7. The advertisement on the left illustrates the combined use of flush right, flush left, and centered copy. The advertisement on the right uses all centered lines. The command to instruct the phototypesetter to set all successive lines either centered, flush left, or flush right need only be input at the start of the job.

[3]Depending upon system configuration, properly prepared text from mainframes, minis, micros, intelligent or dumb terminals (connected to an appropriate host) can be used to drive a phototypesetting system.

Group Two: Hyphenation Commands. Hyphenation is a function that accomplishes one of the basic goals of phototypesetting, namely, squeezing as many characters onto a line as possible. There are two states that the hyphenation command may take: one in which hyphenation is "on," and therefore executed when possible; and the other wherein it is "off." If hyphenation is on, then the keyboard operator can override the typesetting machine hyphenation program by inserting discretionary hyphens as appropriate (see Chapter 1).

Group Three: Indents. A typographic indent is like an inside-out tab. While a tab defines one or more portions of a line that is to be occupied by type, an indent is one or more defined parts of a line that is not to be set. An indent is usually indicated by picas and points, and can be a left indent, a right indent, or an indentation of both right and left. The indentation remains until it is canceled.

Group Four: Tabs.[4] On a typewriter a *tab* is a predetermined stop used to align characters for column formations, for standardized indentations, or merely for vertical organization. On a phototypesetter the same purposes are satisfied, but the capabilities are expanded by additional tabbing functions, not all of which might be available on all typesetting systems:

- Actual. The size of each tab is specified individually. The machine determines the overall line measure, as well as the starting point of each successive tab.
- Arithmetic. The machine automatically calculates the size of each tab by dividing the given line length by the number of tabs specified by the operator.
- Automatic. A tab may be set at any point in a line during actual composition. This function can be used to establish a beginning point for an indented block of text, for a word underline, or for copy that is to be centered below a word or group of words which are not on the center of the line measure.
- Floating. This is a stored tab width, which can be inserted at any time in addition to, or in place of, normal tab positions.
- Multiple Justification. A basic tablike function that repeats a small fixed line measure across a page to form tab columns of equal length.
- Proportional. If, for example, the copy to be set appears to the operator to require twice as much space in columns one, three, and five as in columns two, four, and six, then the phototypesetter can calculate proportional tab settings. By inputting a string of codes such as *TAB 2,1,2,1,2,1*, the machine would recognize that tabs 1, 3, and 5 are twice as wide as tabs 2, 4, and 6. The machine would add the parts, $(2+1+2+1+2+1=9)$, divide the line length by the resulting value, and multiply the result by the tab factor.
- Typewriter Tabs. Each tab is of variable length and is numbered in order of its serial location from the left-hand margin. Typewriter tabs are fairly easy to plan on a typewriter because each typewritten character occupies a predictable amount of space (monospacing). The opposite is true for typesetting because line-ending locations usually cannot be anticipated without machine intelligence and operator judgment.

The number of tabs that can be positioned across a line measure varies from machine to machine. If an individual or organization has specific tabular needs that comprise a significant portion of his typesetting workload, then special attention must be paid to the tabbing capability in terms of its ease of use, complement of alternative methods, tab coding and accessing procedures, keyboard tab position indicators, and use of tabs with reverse in line spacing.

Group Five: Line Packing Functions.[5] Most phototypesetters are capable of generating repetitive characters, symbols, or line segments across an entire line measure, or any segment thereof. The most common are the insert rule and insert leader

---

[4]This section is taken from *How To Build a Basic Typesetting System,* by Michael L. Kleper, pp. 30-31.

[5]This section is taken from *How to Build a Basic Typesetting System,* by Michael L. Kleper, p. 31.

functions. A *rule* is a printer's term for line, and is composed of short segments exposed in series to form a continuous span like this:

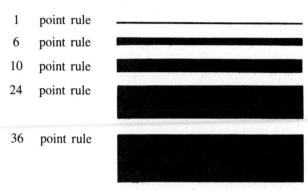

1	point rule
6	point rule
10	point rule
24	point rule
36	point rule

A *leader* is a baseline dot, usually a period, often centered on an en space. Its function is to "lead" the reader's eye across the page, like this:

Airbrushes 63
Airbrush Hoses 64
Air-Pressure Pump 119-121
Artist Pens 18
Artist Supplies 38-51

Although most phototypesetters can set horizontal lines, not all are capable of generating vertical rules. When the typesetting machine does not have this capability, the rules usually are added by hand after the type and horizontal rules have been set. In such a case, the paste-up artist or other skilled individual would use a technical drawing pen to rule directly on the typeset galley or on a clear plastic overlay. Another common method is to adhere graphic arts tape, available in a large variety of widths and designs, in their proper places on the paste-up.

Group Six: Line Spacing. Line spacing is, of course, one of the basic typesetting parameters. However, it also has some expanded capabilities, which enhance its usefulness.

Some typesetting systems allow for an auxiliary or secondary line space setting. This line spacing value would be used, for example, to separate paragraphs or other blocks of text. Another similar command allows for the insertion of a variable number of points (and sometimes fractional units of points) as specified by the keyboard operator. Small increments might be used to separate rules from text, whereas large increments might be used to leave blank space for the insertion of photographs or illustrations.

A commonly used member of the line spacing category is reverse line spacing. Whereas line spacing is the vertical movement down a page, *reverse line spacing* is movement in the opposite direction; that is, back up. This function is used for a number of common typographic effects, including the setting of multiple columns of type, and mathematical, statistical, and scientific formulae.

Group Seven: Character Fit. One of the main attributes that distinguishes typeset from typewritten material is the fit of the characters. Most typewriters are monospaced, distributing the same horizontal escapement to each character, regardless of its relative width. Typesetting machines use a proportional spacing scheme; yet despite their superiority over the output from the typewriter, they still sometimes lack some of the typographic niceties that are associated with fine typography. These niceties relate to the fit of various pairs of characters having shapes that combine to form unsightly spaces between them. Space reduction, or kerning, removes minute amounts of space between characters to improve their aesthetic appearance (FIG. 41, Chapter 1).

Many typesetting systems automatically compensate for predefined kerning pairs. Others are entirely under manual control, and compensation for kerning must be input during the keyboarding process.

As was stated previously, the opposite of kerning is letterspacing. Letterspacing is not usually a desirable objective, yet in rare cases it can be an effective tool. One example is to alter the appearance of the letter combination *rn*. In some cases (some typefaces, some typesetters, some heavily inked printed specimens), the *r* and *n* appear as an *m*, either confusing the reader momentarily or perhaps altering the meaning of the sentence, as in changing *modern* to *modem*.

Group Eight: Typographic Orientation. Like a typewriter, a typesetter has a two-sequence process of creating each character. First, the width of the character is escaped. Conceptually this sequence is quite similar to the way that a typewriter escapes to leave room for the next character to be struck. Second, the character is flashed onto the window that has been left for it.

Most typesetting machines allow for separate control over each of these two functions. There are occasions when the normal sequencing is not wanted. Take, for example, the problem of flashing a check mark into an election box symbol. In the normal space-and-flash sequence, the check mark would appear to the side of the box. By first setting the election box and then instructing the machine to flash the check mark without spacing, the width of the check mark would not be escaped, and therefore the check mark would be set in the same expanse as the election box.

An example of the use of the space-only command is the alignment of successive lines of type beneath an undetermined indent. In FIG. 8, the advantages of typesetting are enumerated, one exactly beneath the other. Determining the starting point of the advantage named in the first line was easy. It started one em space beyond the end of the title *Advantages of Typesetting*. Aligning the other lines with the same starting point is not difficult by first spacing over the width of the title, adding an em space, and then setting the copy normally. There are other ways (easier ways, in fact, such as using automatic tabbing) of accomplishing the same outcome, and it is true of typesetting in general that there is often more than one way of accomplishing the same end.

FIG. 8. The alignment of this list is achieved by spacing over the width of each of the characters in the title ''Advantages of Typesetting:''.

```
Advantages of Typesetting:  1. Time savings
                            2. Control of output
                            3. Convenience
                            4. Increased readability
                            5. Improved company image
                            6. Increased character density
                            7. Reduced printing & postal costs
```

Group Nine: Special Characters. The purchaser of a phototypesetting system usually has a choice in the selection of the keyboard layout that will appear on his input workstations (see FIG. 9). Although the alphanumerics and command keys are all basically alike for all models of the same typesetting system, the keyboard positions of special characters differ, depending upon the kind of work that will be produced. Special character sets have been devised to suit the particular needs of newspapers, book and magazine publishers, advertising agencies, scientific and technical printers, etc. The key identities that appear on the keyboard match the character set available on the phototypesetter, although additional typefaces on the phototypesetter might represent other layouts.

By dressing the typesetter with typefaces from more than one layout, the user gains an expanded repertoire of characters and can mix special characters of one design with another, provided that the styles' designs are compatible. In so doing, however, the operator must have enough presence of mind to keep track of which typeface is being accessed and which character is actually going to be flashed, regardless of the identity of the character printed on the keycap.

For users accessing a typesetting system from a remote computer or word processor, the problem is less apparent. The provider of the typesetting service gives each user a listing of all of the special characters, along with the instructions for accessing each. The mixing of various layouts is usually transparent to the user since a translation table usually will be used to move among typefaces in order to attain the necessary special characters.

USING A MICROCOMPUTER FOR WORD PROCESSING

A phototypesetter that receives input from a source other than its dedicated input keyboard(s) cannot readily differentiate how the codes were generated. The code values all conform to a standard: either TTS or the American Standard Code for Information Interchange (ASCII), a seven-level code structure that yields 128 distinct characters. The differentiating factors, then, are all considerations on the input side; that is, how easy it is to input the characters, to edit and correct what is input, to store and retrieve what is keyboarded, and to transmit or otherwise move what has been created into the typesetting realm.

One of the most popular uses of microcomputers is for word processing. As micro-based word processing programs have matured, their second-rate status, as compared to dedicated word processors, has all but vanished. In fact, the concept of dedicated word processors has vanished as well, and their reincarnation very much resembles the multifunctional micro-based systems that they had once surpassed in capability.

Whereas the operating software on a typesetting system is fairly immutable, the software on a microcomputer is very flexible, changeable, and available in great variety. What this situation means to the user who is contemplating typeset output is that there is a choice in the selection of a word or text processing package based upon an individual's or an organization's specific needs. Micro-based word processing packages have various levels of sophistication, various degrees of user-friendliness, various ranges of specialized capabilities, and various ratios of price/performance.

There are dozens of word processing packages available for the more popular microcomputers. Some are very basic, no-frills text editors that provide only the most basic editing capabilities. Others rival and surpass the functions that are built into dedicated word processors costing many thousands of dollars more. A word processing program that combines the low-cost advantages of micro-based systems with the functionality of dedicated word processing is the Word Juggler by Quark Incorporated.[6] The Word Juggler runs on the Apple *IIe, IIc*, IIGS or Apple III, and unlike most other systems, uses hardware modifications to transform the microcomputer into a professional word processing system.

The Word Juggler originally used a proprietary keyboard enhancer to extend the functionality of the limited Apple keyboard. Current versions are entirely software based. By using the escape, control, and open/solid Apple keys in combination with various alphanumerics, the program provides incredible capabilities. By replacing many of the keycaps on the Apple keyboard with a custom set supplied with the program, the Apple becomes something of a dedicated word processor.

After the Word Juggler has been booted (loaded into memory), the Main menu appears (FIG. 10). At the Main menu level, the Word Juggler bears some resemblance to other word processing programs in that it provides access to the disk catalog, to change the default disk drive (and directory), to edit the printer configuration, to initialize a blank disk, to enter the editor, to load a file from disk, to clear the editor, to purge a file from the disk, to store a file on the disk, and to quit the program.

[6]Quark Incorporated
2525 West Evans
Suite 220
Denver, CO 80219

FIG. 9. Keyboard layouts vary not only from one keyboard to the next, but also according to the final purpose of the composition.

CompuWriter II Keyboard Layout
(Book & Commercial Layout No. 1)

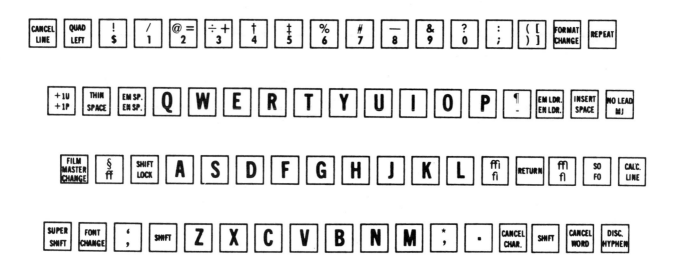

CompuWriter II Keyboard Layout
(Greek and Math Layout)

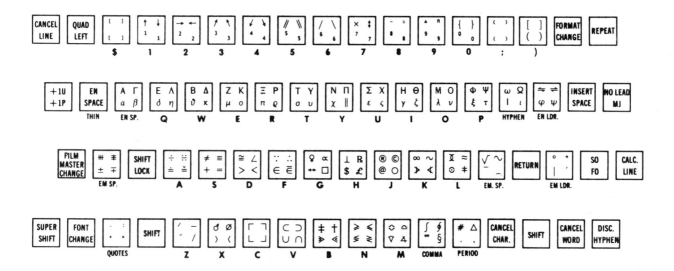

Symbols below boxes identify the keys which are used to access the characters show.

CompuWriter II Book & Commercial No. 3-SC

(Font 3—Bold Face)

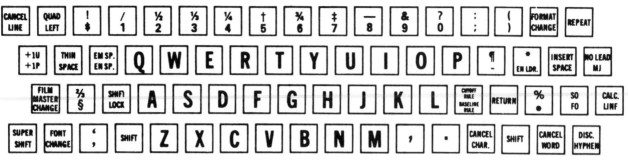

(Font 4—Caps, Small Caps, Superior & Inferior Figures)

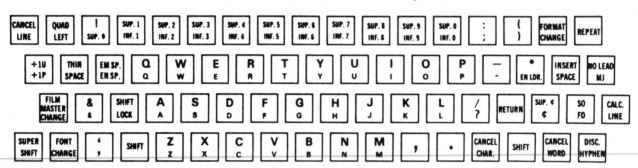

CompuWriter II Keyboard Layout

(Book & Commercial Layout No. 3)

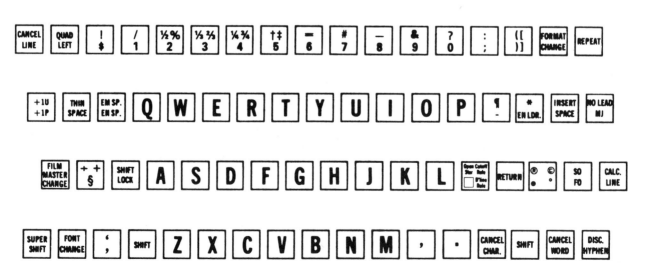

BOOK & COMMERCIAL LAYOUT #3 film strip is the standard layout for CompuWriter II. Keytops will show this arrangement. This layout must also appear in Font 1 (roman) and Font 2 (italic) of Book & Commercial Layout #3—SC (small caps).

CompuWriter II Keyboard Layout
(French-Canadian Piece Accents)

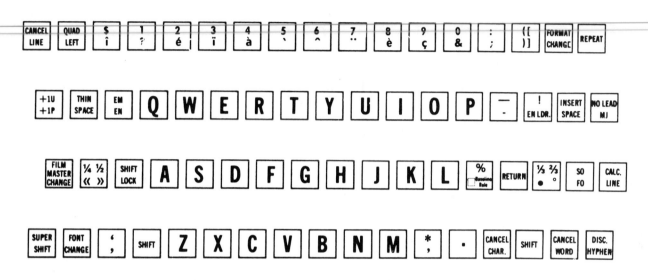

Piece accents are keyboarded before the vowel which is to be accented.

CompuWriter II Keyboard Layout
(Book & Commercial Layout No. 2)

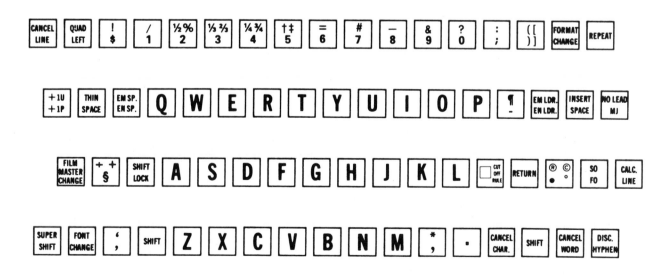

This keyboard arrangement is available with two fonts only and is accessed by Font 1 (LFM) and Font 3 (UFM). No composition can be obtained from Font 2 or Font 4.

CompuWriter II Keyboard Layout
(282F Arrangement)

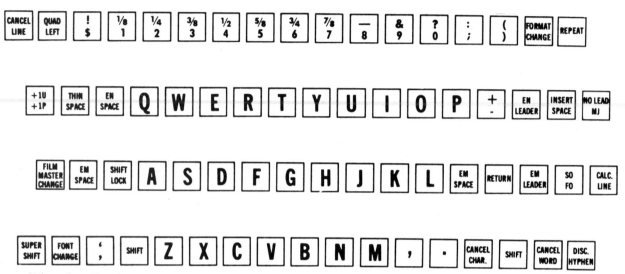

When the editor or text entry area is entered, the Word Juggler earns its name as a program that not only processes, but manipulates, or "juggles," words in almost any imaginable way. There are over a dozen cursor control functions, as well as over two dozen labeled editing keys for search and replace; block movement, copy, deletion, or store and delete; and deletion of individual characters (forward or previous), words, lines, or entire paragraphs. Additionally there are provisions for on-line help (which explains cursor movements), and for printing the present file in whole or in part, and with as many copies as required, without the necessity of first saving the document.

The Word Juggler does not provide a one-for-one correspondence of text being input with the printed output. Of course, this is of little or no significance when the input is destined for typesetting since input will not resemble typeset output in any circumstance. For text that is to be printed, the Word Juggler provides a display mode, whereby the document is displayed on the screen 23 lines at a time, exactly as it will be printed. Characters that are to be set in bold, or superscript, subscript, or underlined appear on the screen in inverse video.

While one obvious measure of assessing the quality of the Word Juggler is its range of editing functions, another is its special features, which are not commonly found in other word processing packages. The typing mode capability is of no special significance for typesetting input, although it does provide the useful ability to transmit individual lines of a document, for example, to address an envelope. The typing mode also can be used to place the Apple into a direct typewriter mode, whereby the user can fill in entries on a preprinted form, using the cursor keys to move in any direction. Ironically, a number of stand-alone programs are available that let a microcomputer mimic the typewriter, which it has all but replaced.

It is the implementation of variables that makes the Word Juggler especially suitable for specialized typesetting purposes. *Variables* are item identities that do not need to be declared until the job will be printed or transmitted. For example, a price list that is subject to frequent change could be updated easily just prior to typesetting by inputting current prices in place of variables previously input into the file. The same file, therefore, could be utilized again and again, with the variable information changed as required. The variable function also works in concert with Mountain Hardware's

Thunderclock, providing date and time stamping on documents that use predefined variable names for either date, year, month, day, or time.

The Word Juggler also accepts input in various forms. It will read standard Apple DOS 3.3 text files, as well as Apple Pascal text files. It also reads files from Apple's Quickfile database program and Software Publishing's PFS database program. The database programs can be used to generate such simple output as form letters and mailing labels, or such complicated output as telephone directories and parts catalogs.

Word Juggler output also can be controlled with the conditional operators IF, AND, OR, and NOT. Using these operators (which can be nested up to 127 deep), specific information can be extracted from documents according to specific criteria. Data that was input randomly can be organized according to any specific requirement. A document containing information on works of art, for example, can be output according to painters' names, or styles, or price ranges, or combinations of the three. This powerful capability is not commonly found in typesetting, although it is obviously very useful.

WHY WORD PROCESSORS DON'T ALWAYS MAKE GOOD TYPESETTER INPUT STATIONS

Although similarities abound between the functions of word processing and typesetting input, there is one fundamental difference, which can be decisive in determining the suitability of a standard word processing or micro-based input station for typesetting applications. This difference is the ability of the input station to count character widths.

Counting capability is what gives the operator an indication of line endings; it shows exactly how many characters will fit on a designated line measure. With this knowledge, the operator can fit an optimum number of characters on each line, hyphenating when necessary. This process, called hyphenation and justification, or *H & J* (see Chapter 1) is particularly important in the setting of fine books, tabular matter, and advertising typography, where line-ending information can be critical to the success of the typesetting.

```
              Word Juggler //e (version 2.5)

Options:

   1. NEW - Erases all text and goes to text entry mode.

   2. CATALOG - Lists all files in a directory.

   3. LOAD - Loads a document from disk and goes to text entry mode.

   4. STORE - Stores document on disk.

   5. PURGE - Removes a file from disk.

   6. FORMAT - Allows a diskette to be formatted.

   7. DEFINE PREFIX - Defines the prefix to be used for disk access.

   8. EDIT CONFIGURATION - Allows printer and default parameter selection.

   9. QUIT - Exits the Word Juggler program.

Which option (Press RETURN for text entry mode)?
```

FIG. 10. The Word Juggler Main menu selections provide access to the main word processing functions. Menus are considerably more commonplace on micro systems than on typesetters, and are quite helpful in providing a map of the various points of departure for accessing the main parts of a program.

Line-ending information is not, of course, of vital importance for all categories of work, and even in those cases where it could be a significant factor, it is still possible to take the input from a word processor and run H & J directly on the typesetting system prior to typesetting. So, while it would be beneficial to have interactive H & J at the word processing work station, it is not a necessity.

GETTING INFORMATION TO THE TYPESETTER

Dedicated and micro-based word processing systems provide quite effective ways of generating and storing text. For the captured information to be of any value for typesetting, some means must be employed to move the information into the typesetting system. Many methods are presently employed to perform this function; however, the choice of any given method will depend upon such considerations as:

- The average length of the text that must be sent
- The frequency at which text is sent
- The proximity of the typesetting system
- The urgency of the turnaround time requirements
- The computer and typesetting hardware presently in place
- The number of word processing or micro-based input stations to be supported by the typesetter
- The economic considerations associated with specialized hardware and software

Taking the Most Direct Route

The method by which typesetting can be accessed most directly is by an on-line connection to a phototypesetter. In this manner, files prepared at the word processor are sent out of the computer's serial or parallel port through a cable connected directly to the phototypesetter system. At the phototypesetter the file is either captured for further processing (editing or adding typesetting codes) or else typeset immediately. Most typesetting vendors offer some hardware to accomplish typesetting in this way.

A number of computer-to-typesetter interfaces are available that can mate word processors and computers with typesetters. Some of them are flexible enough to work with virtually any computer—micro, mini, or mainframe—and support text generation using almost any text or word processing program.

The MicroSetter interface[7] (FIG. 11) treats the phototypesetter as if it were the computer's printer. The ASCII codes that are sent through the connecting cable are translated by the interface into TTS codes which the typesetter can process. Typesetting functions and special character codes are accessed by enclosing codes within less than and greater than signs. Font one, for example would be indicated as < F1 >.

An inexpensive interface such as the MicroSetter, which works with both second- and third-generation phototypesetters and is obtainable for some typesetting machines for well under $1000, is among the most cost-effective ways of obtaining phototypeset output that is completely under the control of a single-site user.

Using a Computer-To-Typesetter Interface

Instructors at a large metropolitan technical institute use a computer-to-typesetter interface between an Apple *II*e microcomputer and a Compugraphic EditWriter 7500. They use this configuration to teach students in their graphic arts department about word processing, telecommunications, and typesetting.

Students begin at the Apple, learning to use the Magic Window IIe word processing program.[8] Many of the word processing skills acquired at the Apple are transferable, in concept if not in actual practice, to the EditWriter. Files can be created at the

[7]TeleTypesetting Company
224 Nickels Arcade
Ann Arbor, MI 48104
(313) 761-7664

[8]Artsci
5547 Satsuma Ave.
North Hollywood, CA 91601

Apple with typesetting and special codes in place, or the files can be created with no special attention to typographic requirements and the necessary typographic codes added later at the EditWriter.

After a file has been created (and saved on disk if required), it can be sent to the typesetter, the line printer, or both. Sending it to the line printer provides an inexpensive proof for examination, for mark-up, or for customer approval. The Magic Window IIe program provides an easy means of specifying which slot of the Apple will be used to output a file. For the line printer, slot 1, occupied by a parallel printer card is used. For the typesetter, slot 2, occupied by an RS-232 serial card, is used.

Before a file can be sent to the EditWriter, a few simple preparations must be made. First, the EditWriter must be turned on. When the file is sent from the Apple, it appears immediately on the EditWriter screen. If the automatic line-ending mode has been selected, the lines of type are justified (counted) as they are received on the EditWriter.

After the file has been sent, it can undergo further editing at the EditWriter console, be saved on disk, or typeset directly under remote control. The file can be held at the EditWriter for an additional input, if so desired, then saved on an EditWriter disk (this step is optional), and then typeset.

An Extension of the Classroom

Laboratory typesetting assignments at the same technical institute are completed using any computer terminal on campus that is connected to the institute's central computer system. Assignments are saved as electronic mail, addressed by the student to himself. In the graphic arts laboratory, the assignments are retrieved by using the Data Capture 4.0 software package[9] to turn the Apple into a terminal. Downloaded files then can be sent directly from the Apple using the same terminal software, or can be accessed using Magic Window II for further editing. Files are often put through the Sensible Speller IV spell checking program[10] prior to typesetting.

[9]Southeastern Software
7743 Briarwood Drive
New Orleans, LA 70128

[10]Sensible Software
6619 Perham Drive
West Bloomfield, MI 48033

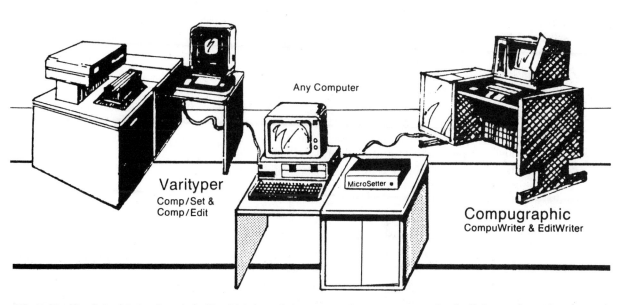

FIG. 11. The MicroSetter interface is part of a line of interfaces that marry a word processor or computer directly to one of a number of second- and third-generation phototypesetters (Courtesy of TeleTypesetting Company).

A number of Apple microcomputers are also available on campus for general use, and some students prepare their assignments using these remote computers. After the assignments are saved on disk, the students physically carry them to the laboratory for testing.

The computer-to-typesetter link also has provided access to typesetting for non-graphic arts students. Student resumés and type requirements for art, photography, AV, and media projects are typeset easily via electronic mail. The electronic mail system also has opened an extraordinary opportunity for the campus newspaper. The electronic mail system serves as a reporter network, with all stories eventually downloaded at the Apple in the graphic arts laboratory.

THE MEDIA COMPATIBILITY ISSUE

If the code structures and disk formats used in microcomputers and word processors were identical to those used in typesetting, the problems of interfacing the two would all but disappear. Unfortunately, the great variety of "proprietary" operating systems has fostered little cooperation among equipment vendors. The result is a marketplace full of machines with little direct media compatibility.

Notable exceptions to this state of affairs are two rather dated systems that were able to achieve this lofty goal of direct media compatibility. One is the AM Amtext 425 word processor and the AM VariTyper Comp/Edit. Since AM marketed both machines it was able to specify codes and formats for the word processor that would be compatible with the typesetter. The Amtext disk could be inserted directly into the typesetter disk drive, and with the insertion of typographic codes, could be used without modification. The other system, less notable than the first, was the Alphatype AlphaComp phototypesetter, which was mated with the Xerox 800 word processor.

MEDIA CONVERSION

If media compatibility is what is needed to use microcomputer and word processor input for a phototypesetter, then the use of a media-to-media interface is the answer. *Media-conversion interfaces* are microcomputer-controlled devices that are designed to read the information on a word processing or computer disk, translate its contents into a form readable by the typesetter, and then write it onto a new disk or transmit it to an editing terminal or directly to the typesetting system.

One such device that represents a flexible approach is the Cromwell Context Media Converter,[11] which is itself a complete Z-80 based microcomputer system. The system (FIG. 12) utilizes two dual disk drives: one for 5 1/4-inch and the other for 8-inch diskettes. Using its specialized hardware and software, the system is capable not only of exchanging data between dozens of different microcomputers, and word processors, but also of translating word and text processing instructions into usable typesetting codes.

Another feature of the system is a communications facility for capturing telecommunicated text. Although many typesetting systems support telecommunications directly, the process can, in some cases, interrupt the actual typesetting activity, thereby negatively affecting productivity. The Cromwell System can be left unattended, auto-answering client calls and saving the captured files on disk for processing at a later time. The system not only affects who the typesetter can communicate with, but also, in a very real sense, how he conducts his business. Virtually anyone possessing a personal computer can prepare usable input for typesetting. As a result, large typesetting jobs can be keyboarded by cottage labor, with complete machine independency. Peak-production situations can be handled without hiring more personnel or buying more equipment.

[11]Marketed by
The Electronics Language Center
Computer and Communications Service, Inc.
8115 Fenton St.
Silver Spring, MD 20910

FIG. 12. The Cromwell Context media conversion computer system. Cromwell states that "... setting type from personal computers will soon become a mainstay of the industry ... Disk-to-disk compatibility is the key to setting type from this growing market." (Courtesy Computer and Communications Services, Inc., 8115 Fenton St., Silver Spring, MD 20910, (301) 588-8706.)

The book or magazine publisher can utilize the Cromwell System to accept author's manuscripts. With an optional high-speed line printer, editors can print copies of manuscripts directly from the submitted disk. Disks also can be converted to match whatever system the editor uses so that copyediting can take place directly on disk. When the editing operation is complete, the disk can be converted again, this time for final typesetting.

While the Cromwell Context accepts input from virtually any source, it also can be configured to emulate the keyboard layout and character sets of many front-end systems. In such a mode it provides an extra, flexible workstation whenever needed. Additionally the machine is a full-featured microcomputer capable of running general-purpose, off-the-shelf software packages for word processing, accounting, estimating, proofreading, database management, and spreadsheet analysis.

MEDIA-CONVERSION DEVICE CONFIGURATIONS

The Cromwell Context is only one of many like devices that aid in establishing communication between dissimilar machines. The ways in which these devices are utilized are based upon the requirements of the client and the needs of the service provider, as well as the inherent capabilities of the hardware and software itself.

In a best-case situation there are a number of ways in which a word processor or personal computer user can use media conversion to deliver his data to the typesetter. They include:

- The physical delivery of the magnetic media to the typesetter. This may be in person, by messenger, U.S. Postal Service, or overnight package delivery. The sender always keeps a copy of his disk before releasing it for typesetting (or any other purpose). A hardcopy of the files also should accompany the disk. When the disk arrives at the typesetting site, it can be used in either of the following ways.

The disk can be rewritten in a form that is directly compatible with the typesetting system. Special word processing codes can be translated into their typesetting equivalents, or some or all of the peculiar word processing codes can be stripped out (deleted). The converted disk is then hand-carried to the typesetter.

In the second method, the disk can be read at the media-conversion device and the data sent on-line to the typesetting system. At the typesetting system, the data is stored on disk for further editing and final typesetting.

- The delivery of data to the typesetter can take place by means of telecommunications. The specifics of this process will be covered later. Simply stated, data is sent over telephone lines to the media-conversion device where it is either: converted into a typesetter-readable disk or read and translated by the conversion device and sent directly on to the typesetter, where it is retained on disk for further editing and final typesetting.

The major vendors involved in media conversion also convert word processing and computer disks into forms usable by other word processors and personal computers, as well as by typesetters as we have discussed here. Addresses of prominent vendors serving the typesetting (and to a lessor degree, the word processing/personal computer) marketplace are listed at the right.

Altertext
210 Lincoln Street
Boston, MA 02111

Antares Corporation
P.O. Box 159
Lake Elmo, MN 55042

Applied Data Communications
14272 Chambers Road
Tustin, CA 92680

Itek Graphics Systems
34 Cellu Drive
Nashua, NH 03060

Shaffstall Corporation
7901 E. 88th Street
Indianapolis, IN 46256

Chapter 3

Word and Text Processing Programs

Text destined for typographic output.

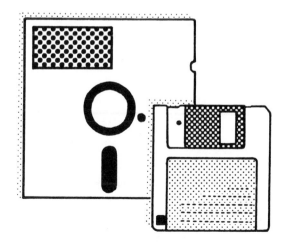

WORDSTAR:
Using the Default Standard in PC-Based Word Processing

The selection of the WordStar[1] word processing package by a number of vendors of phototypesetting equipment, as well as by manufacturers of personal computers for use as bundled or compatible software, has made the program something of a standard by which other word processing programs are judged. The popularity of this software offering is worthy of some attention.

WordStar is somewhat complex, but this is just another way of saying that it is unusually complete. It runs in either a CP/M or MS-DOS operating environment, and for efficiency, requires two disk drives. The first drive holds the WordStar program disk, while the second holds the text file disk, which stores documents and other text files. The text file disk is formatted using a program from WordStar called Format.Com. The program is run by typing an **R** followed by **Format**, and then depressing the Return key.

WordStar permits switching between it and *operating system commands*, commands that permit the use of utility programs and the actual running of application programs. When properly installed, the program begins by displaying its No-File menu (FIG. 1). "No-File" means that a file neither has been created, nor has been selected to be edited.

The No-File menu is the usual beginning place. If it is not displayed for any reason, it is usually obtainable by depressing the ESC (escape) key.

To begin a session with WordStar, it is necessary to access the text file disk, usually disk B. Since starting up the program requires the use of drive A, it is necessary to switch over to drive B. The drive that is in use is called the *logged disk drive*, and it is changed by using the L command. After the *L* key is pressed, WordStar explains what the logging function is, tells which disk is presently logged, and prompts the user for the name of the new disk to be logged. Responding to the prompt by typing **B:** changes the drive and returns the user to the No-File menu.

In WordStar terminology, creating a document requires *opening* a file. A file must be opened to either create or locate a previously created file. The "D" command is used from the No-File menu to create a file.

Next, a help message appears on the screen to remind the user what WordStar is expecting by way of file name. The message reads: "Use this command to create a new document file, or to initiate alteration of an existing document file." A file name is one to eight letters or digits, a period, and an optional one to three-character extension. The file name can be preceded by the disk drive letter—A, B, C, or D—and a colon; otherwise the current logged disk is used. The file to be created might be called

FIG. 1. The WordStar No-File menu is displayed before a file name has been assigned and after the editing of a file has been completed.

[1]MicroPro International
33 San Pablo Ave.
San Rafael, CA 94903
(703) 777-9110

```
           < < <  N O - F I L E   M E N U  > > >
 *  * * Preliminary Commands * *  * |*  File  Commands  *|* System Commands *
 L  Change logged disk drive    |  P  Print  a file  |R Run a  program
 F  File directory      off (ON) |  E  Rename a file  |X Exit to system
 H  Set help level              |  O  Copy  a file   |
 *  * Commands to Open a File *  *|  Y  Delete a file |* WordStar Options *
    D  Open a  document  file    |                    |M Run MailMerge
    N  Open a non-document file  |                    |S Run SpellStar ▪

 DIRECTORY of disk A:
 CHAPTR1.DOC  CHAPTR1.BAK  CHAPTR2.DOC  CHAPTR2.BAK  CHAPTR3.DOC  CHAPTR3.BAK
 CONTENTS.DOC CONTENTS.BAK FILE1.DOC    FILE1.BAK    FILE2.DOC    FILE2.BAK
 LETTER.DOC   LETTER.BAK   TEXT1.DOC    TEXT1.BAK    TEXT2.DOC    TEXT2.BAK
 MAILMRGE.OVR WS.COM       WSMSGS.OVR   WSOVLY1.OVR
```

TRIAL, and for ease of housekeeping the extension *.TXT* might be added to indicate that the file is text. The file name, then, is TRIAL.TXT. If an error is made while the file name is being input, WordStar provides editing commands on the screen to assist in making corrections.

Depressing the Return key takes the user into the Main menu (FIG. 2), which indicates the commands for moving the cursor, scrolling, deleting, inserting, finding/replacing, and other menus (help, block, print, etc.). WordStar is now ready for text entry. As text is input, the page, line, and column numbers appear at the top of the screen.

WordStar provides the standard cursor movements common to all word processing programs, and also an additional set of commands called Quick Cursor Movement Commands. These commands are accessible by depressing the Control key with the *Q*, providing entry into the Quick menu (FIG. 3). This menu displays the fast cursor commands and the find and replace sequences.

After paragraphs have been edited, WordStar can reform (rejustify) the paragraphs using the Control-*B* command. As the paragraphs are reformed, the cursor might stop if hyphenation is required—an unusual feature for a program of this variety. If the hy-

```
        A:TEST.DOC  PAGE 1 LINE 1  COL 1              INSERT ON
                  < < <      M A I N    M E N U      > > >
    * *  Cursor  Movement  *  *|* Delete *|  * Miscellaneous *  | * Other  Menus *
    ^S char left   ^D char right  |^G  char  |^I Tab    ^B Reform  | (from Main only)
    ^A word left   ^F word right  |DEL chr lf|^V Insert On or Off |^J Help   ^K Block
    ^E line  up    ^X line down   |^T word rt|^L Find/Replce again|^Q Quick  ^P Print
    * *    Scrolling    *    *|^Y line  |RETURN End paragraph|^O Onscreen
    ^Z line up    ^W line down  |            |^N  Insert a RETURN |
    ^C screen up  ^R screen down|            |^U  Stop a command  |
    L——!——!——!——!——!——!——!——!——!——!——!———R                     •
    ▪                                                            •
                                                                 •
                                                                 •
                                                                 •
                                                                 •
```

FIG. 2. The WordStar Main menu shows the basic commands for cursor movement, scrolling, deletion, and access to other menus. The degree of detail displayed in the menu is controlled by setting the help level (CTRL-J). As the user becomes more familiar with the program, less of the screen needs to be used for displaying often-used control sequences.

```
    ^Q      A:TEST.DOC  PAGE 1 LINE 1  COL 1              INSERT ON
                  < < <      Q U I C K    M E N U      > > >
    * *   Cursor Movement  *  *|* Delete *|  * Miscellaneous *  | * Other  Menus *
    S left side    D right side |Y line  rt|F Find text in file | (from Main only)
    E top of scrn  X bottom scrn|DEL lin lf|A Find and  Replace |^J Help   ^K Block
    R top of file  C end of file|* * *    *|L Find  misspelling |^Q Quick  ^P Print
    B top of block K end of block          |Q Repeat command or |   ^O Onscreen
    0-9 marker    Z up   W down            | key until  space |Space bar returns
    V last Find or block                   | bar  or other key |you to Main Menu.
    L——!——!——!——!——!——!——!——!——!——!——!———R
    ▪
```

FIG. 3. The WordStar Quick menu provides a display of control sequences which can be used to initiate fast cursor movements quickly, as well as perform other operations.

```
    ^K      A:TEST.DOC  PAGE 1 LINE 1  COL 1              INSERT ON
                  < < <      B L O C K    M E N U      > > >
    * Saving Files * |* Block Operations *|  * File Operations *| * Other  Menus *
    S Save and resume|B  Begin   K End  |R Read    P  Print  | (from Main only)
    D Save—done      |H  Hide / Display |O Copy    E  Rename |^J Help   ^K Block
    X Save and exit  |C  Copy    Y Delete|J Delete           |^Q Quick  ^P Print
    Q Abandon file   |V  Move    W Write |* Disk  Operations *|^O Onscreen
    * Place  Markers *|N  Column   off (ON)|L Change logged disk|Space bar returns
    0-9 Set/hide # 0-9|              |F Directory on (OFF)|you to Main Menu.
    L——!——!——!——!——!——!——!——!——!——!——!———R
    ▪
```

FIG. 4. The Block menu offers the means to save, move, copy, and hide/display files.

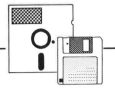

phenation point is acceptable, a hyphen is inserted manually. If it is not, the cursor can be moved right or left to a more acceptable position. If no hyphenation point is suitable, the Control-*B* command is used to cancel hyphenation for the line. As hyphens are added in this manner they are treated as soft hyphens; that is, they appear in the text only if the word actually breaks in that position. These hyphens differ from *hard hyphens*, which are input initially and remain in the text unless manually removed.

After editing has been completed, the file must be saved on the disk by holding the Control key with a **K**, followed by an *S*. WordStar saves the file according to the name given at the beginning of the work session, and then gives the user the opportunity to return to the end of the saved file and continue working. This feature is helpful in ensuring that valuable work is not lost (through carelessness, power failures, etc.). After resuming work on the same file, the user can use the Block menu (FIG. 4) to save the latest editing changes, save and resume editing, save and stop editing, save and exit, or abandon all of the latest editing changes since the file was last saved.

These are not all of WordStar's features, but they are enough to give an idea of the capabilities of the program.

XyWRITE II PLUS: Modeling a Word Processor After a Typesetting Front-End System

The availability of general-purpose software has had an enormous impact on creating the widespread acceptance of the personal computer for graphic arts applications. Graphic arts has been an especially receptive vertical market, both in using off-the-shelf software and hardware and in developing special-purpose programs for particular business and production needs. Few programs developed within the graphic arts, however, have found any degree of acceptance with the general public. A notable exception is XyWrite,[2] a word processing program created with the expert knowledge of two individuals who played a major role in developing the Atex front-end system for newspaper publishing.

Dave Erickson, who wrote parts of the Atex operating system, and John Hild, who engineered many of the Atex hardware interfaces to high-speed digital phototypesetters, began the development of XyWrite somewhat unwittingly in 1982. As the result of an Atex employee bonus, Erickson bought an IBM PC. His intentions were completely undefined, although as a systems programmer he quickly became dissatisfied with the DOS EDLIN line editor that had been provided with the system. Based upon his Atex experience, he set out to write an improved full-screen editor using IBM's Macro Assembler. When it was complete, he showed it to his friend John Hild, who recognized that as a word processor it was faster[3] and more responsive than any word processing program he had seen. After relatively little market analysis, but considerable favorable feedback from early users, the two left Atex to form XyQuest.

Since the initial program was developed while Erickson and Hild were Atex employees, it was agreed that Atex had some rights to the program. Therefore, the first version, XyWrite I, was licensed from Atex, although all successive versions have had no Atex claim.

Erickson's original goal of putting Atex functionality on a personal computer has been met. About one-quarter of XyWrite users have Atex system experience, and many newspapers use XyWrite on personal computers in place of more expensive Atex terminals. Atex supports the use of personal computer input through the use of PC-Interface software, which is licensed for a fee of approximately $10,000. On the *Providence Journal*, reporters and secretaries use over 150 copies of XyWrite, and the newspaper has developed a communications program called ComputerEase, which sends the PC input directly to the Atex system. Additionally, C-Text, a manufacturer of micro-based publishing systems, uses XyWrite as its text input system software.

[2]Xyquest
P.O. Box 372
Bedford, MA 01730
(617) 275-4439
Runs on the IBM PC and compatibles.

[3]This speed factor has distinguished all versions of XyWrite, which use custom keyboard routines rather than the standard IBM BIOS routines.

XyWrite uses the same basic input approach as Atex. The command field is at the top of the screen, followed by a prompt line and tab ruler line. Text input, in either full screen or text windows, fills the remainder. The user toggles between the two areas, initiating command sequences and inputting and editing text. Most of the commands are one or two characters, sometimes followed by a value or an alphanumeric identifier.

A number of the XyWrite commands, such as *ST*ore, *SE*arch, and *CH*ange, are identical to those used in the Atex system. There is certainly enough similarity to make XyWrite a reasonable complement to Atex input, and enough functionality to make it a fine word processor in its own right. Although at the editing and file level there are many common features, it is in the formatting and on-screen display where XyWrite more closely identifies with word processors than with typesetting front-ends.

The editor is rich in commands to move the cursor, move the editing window, and manipulate text. A number of commands, such as line positioning (*F*lush *R*ight, *F*lush *L*eft, *F*lush *C*enter), *D*iscretionary *H*yphen, *L*eadering, *L*ine *S*pace, and *W*idow and *O*rphan control, bear a close resemblance to their counterparts in typesetting.

According to Erickson, "A word processor should be able to put anything on paper you want to have there." XyWrite does. Hild adds that "It's as easy as you want it or as complex as you want it. It's as deep as you want to swim." Creating a simple file requires very few commands, and even at that, help screens are available at the touch of a couple of keys.

A number of features distinguish XyWrite as a valuable tool in formatting text for word processing, as well as for typesetting. Among them are:

- Changing Case: Text that has been defined, or *highlighted*, can be changed to the opposite of what it is, or to all uppercase or all lowercase.
- Automatic Upper Case: The program senses when the user has come to the end of a sentence, and automatically shifts the next character to uppercase.
- Save/Get: XyWrite programs frequently used phrases and character strings into a series of two-key sequences. These macros can be saved to disk and retrieved for future editing sessions. A set of current Save/Gets can be reviewed in directory fashion on the screen, as can a set stored on disk (without actually loading the set).
- Program: This feature allows the user to store any series of text or command keystrokes (alphanumerics, cursor moves, defines, deletes, searches, merges, etc.) in a file. Using the Run command these keystrokes can be played back. Because XyWrite supports direct access to DOS and the running of other programs from within it, interesting and useful effects can be achieved through programming.
- Command Field Arithmetic: Numbers can be added, subtracted, multiplied, or divided by inputting them into the command line. The result of the calculation can be lifted from the command line and inserted into the text by using the ALT-keys.
- Discretionary Hyphen: In order to maximize the number of characters that will fit on a line, and therefore avoid loose-fitting lines, a user can insert a tilde between syllables. If the word containing a tilde appears at the end of a line and is too long to fit, the program selects one of its discretionary hyphenation points at which to break the word and insert a hard hyphen. Any unused discretionary hyphens are ignored when the job is output.
- Index and Table of Contents: Items can be marked either for entry into the table of contents, or for subject or author indices. After a set is marked, it can be assembled in either alphabetical order, as for an index, or page number order, as for a table of contents.

- Forms-Handling Commands: A file can be created as a form, with fixed text field labels and open areas into which text can be keyboarded. The labels can be created in reverse display mode in order to easily differentiate them from information entered from the keyboard.
- Load Keyboard. The keyboard can be remapped and the new key identities can be saved in a file. This feature is useful for creating alternative keyboard layouts, such as the Dvorak, or for creating command keys for specialized functions.
- Mail Merge. Repetitive information can be saved in a file and be combined, at the time of printing, with a standard form letter.
- Extended Programming Language (XPL): Programs composed of keystroke information can be created using label statements, jump to labels, logical operations, conditional key sequences, and more.

XyWrite has developed a rather dedicated following, resulting in the formation of the XyWrite User's Group (XyWUG). The group newsletter is edited by Joe Russell, one of the earliest users of XyWrite. For information write to:

> XyWUG
> c/o Joe Russell, Editor
> 703 Market Street, Suite 1600
> San Francisco, CA 94103

SCENICWRITER:
Processing Large Publications into Pages

Untapping the typographic resources that are resident in laser printers, such as the Hewlett-Packard LaserJet and the Apple LaserWriter, is almost wholly dependent upon the software capabilities contained within the input workstation (i.e. personal computer). An evaluation of such software must be based on two fundamental questions: Can the program access all of the necessary printer capabilities? Can it do so in a manner conducive to productivity? One package that meets these criteria is ScenicWriter,[4] a professional publishing software package which incorporates the functions of a word processor, spell-checker, index and table of contents generator, and page formatter.

Commands

The ScenicWriter program (FIG. 5) is built around the Scenic Markup Language (SML), which provides the user with sets of macro commands for controlling the formatting and appearance of text. The macros are embedded within text files. They are interpreted and expanded by ScenicWriter just prior to printing, which means, of course, that the user does not see the result of the SML coding until the pages exit the printer.

FIG. 5. The ScenicWriter Main menu shows the major program divisions. The spell-checking program compares words in the user file to words contained in the system dictionary. User words that are not found in the dictionary are flagged as suspicious, although the program does not offer a correct spelling choice.

```
RAM: ScenicWriter Menu

<E> Editor
<F> File and Disk Management
<V> Set Working Volume
<S> Spelling Checker
<T> Formatted Printing
<B> Buffered Printing
<P> Plain Printing
<X> Execute a program


SYSTEM: Enter command <[]>
```

[4]Scenic Computer Systems Corporation
14852 N.E. 31st Circle
Redmond, WA 98052
(206) 885-5500
Runs on IBM PCs and compatible computers.

FIG. 6. A typical page from the ScenicWriter manual. The program also supports multiple-column formatting.

Formatting Documents

```
.RightPlayP 1.5i
.BoldP 'Page References' 91
ScenicWriter resolves both forward and backward cross references
automatically as the document is produced.  References are kept accurate
even when format changes cause page breaks to shift.

ScenicWriter automatically produces an alphabetized index (2 levels if
required) with correct page numbers in single or multi-column format.
Abbreviated words can be sorted and indexed as if spelled out in full
(Mt. indexed as Mountain).
.BoldP 'Graphics'
ScenicWriter allows unlimited mixing of the available fonts, symbols,
and graphics on every page in portrait or landscape orientation.
ScenicWriter is limited only by the capabilities of the printer.
.EndP
```

The above lines produce the following:

Page References   ScenicWriter resolves both forward and backward cross references automatically as the document is produced. References are kept accurate even when format changes cause page breaks to shift.

ScenicWriter automatically produces an alphabetized index (2 levels if required) with correct page numbers in single or multi-column format. Abbreviated words can be sorted and indexed as if spelled out in full (Mt. indexed as Mountain).

Graphics   ScenicWriter allows unlimited mixing of the available fonts, symbols, and graphics on every page in portrait or landscape orientation. ScenicWriter is limited only by the capabilities of the printer.

NOTE: You can boldface or italicize rightplay subheadings with the **.BoldP** **.ItalicP** commands described in the previous section. Notice that **.BoldP** was used in the example above.

5.5.6

Indented Paragraphs   The indented paragraph format is useful when your subheadings vary greatly in length or are especially long. Similar to **.LeftPlayP** paragraphs, the subheadings are left justified. The paragraph text, however, is indented and begins on the next line to allow maximum room for the subheading.

146

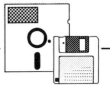

A number of commands have been devised to generically code a publication into its major parts, such as sections, chapters, subchapters, subsubchapters, appendices, subappendices, etc. A chapter format, for example, takes the form:

```
.Chapter '<heading>' <need>
```

The command is *Chapter*, and it, like other commands, always begins with a period in the first column of a line. The heading is the name of the chapter as it is to appear in the publication, both as a chapter headline and table of contents entry. It is enclosed within single quotation marks to delimit it from formatting information. The Need parameter is optional; it is the specification of the amount of space (i.e. the number of lines) that are required to keep the chapter heading and the first paragraph of text on the same page. If unspecified, this parameter defaults to five lines.

Each *dot command*, or generic code preceded by a period, is later translated into exact specifications, which indicate such details as the starting position on the page, the typographic treatments of the text elements, the text width and indentation, and the appearance and placement of rules and boxes (if any). The raw coding to accomplish all of these descriptors would be overwhelming for most users.

Although ScenicWriter is flexible enough to suit the page-layout needs of a variety of publications, as well as business correspondence and memoranda, it has a programmed bias toward the production of manuals. The ScenicWriter manual itself is a good example of how complex elements and details are attractively processed in a publication composed of 339 pages (FIG 6).

Keeping track of information, either as it is keyboarded or later during editing, is accomplished through the use of index entries. Items identified as index entries are automatically collected, sorted, and printed with their appropriate page numbers in a finished index. The index command takes the following form:

```
.Ix '<primary entry>:<secondary entry>'
```

The primary entry is the main entry, in the exact wording and case that are to appear in the index. The primary entry must be specified, although the secondary entry is optional. The colon is not used if the secondary entry is not included. The index command appears within the text as close to its reference as possible (to accurately reflect the correct page number). The following text shows two index items embedded within the paragraph.

```
The first working phototypesetter is generally credited to Eugen Prozsolt
.Ix 'Phototypesetting History: Eugen Prozsolt'
of Budapest. His machine, which appeared in 1894, had a typewriterlike
keyboard that elevated characters before a camera for photographing.
Some historians, however, consider a system patented by Michael Alisoff
.Ix 'Phototypesetting History: Michael Alisoff'
in 1876 as the first use of phototypesetting. Alisoff printed musical notes on
transparent sheets, cut them out, and pasted them in position on opaque
sheets ruled with staves. The paste-up was photographed and a plate made
from the negative.
```

These index entries would result in the following:

```
Phototypesetting History
  Eugen Prozsolt........................................78
  Michael Alisoff.......................................78
```

Among the more interesting indexing capabilities is the reference point, a command that prints the page number of a cross reference within a text passage. The command takes the form of .*RefPoint* <*term*>, and would be used to identify a point of reference by name, as in the following:

```
.RefPoint 'direct input phototypesetting'
The automation of some of the mechanics of the creative writing process
is the latest trend in direct input phototypesetting. Machines that allow
the writer to electronically keyboard his work, massage it into its
finished form, and then output it as finished galleys are changing the
task balance of the human/machine relationship in favor of the human.
```

The cross reference page number is linked automatically to another command: \ *$xr*__<*term*>, which prints the page number of the referent within the test, such as:

```
See page \ $xr__direct input phototypesetting for more information.
```

Which results in the printing of:

```
See page 89 for more information.
```

The ScenicWriter command structure is very sophisticated, and covers the following general areas:

- Macros related to headings, such as sections, chapters, etc.
- Macros related to titles
- Macros related to paragraphs
- Macros related to play (script) forms
- Macros related to tables
- Macros related to rules, frames, and screens
- Macros related to headers and footnotes
- Macros related to columns
- Macros related to folios and page breaks
- Macros related to data collection (indexing, etc.)
- Macros related to business correspondence

In addition to the large set of dot commands, there are other commands, which are used to enhance the typographic appearance of text, to adjust horizontal and vertical spacing, and to access special characters and symbols. These are the *backslash commands*, which, unlike dot commands, can be embedded directly within the text stream.

A common use for a backslash command, for example, would be to change type styles. The command to access boldface is \ *bf*, the command to return to the previously used typeface is \ *ro*. Within text, the operation would appear as follows:

```
The world's first \ bf available light phototypesetter \ ro was invented
by William Friese-Greene in 1898.
```

Backslash commands must end with a space, although the trailing space does not appear in the printed output. Font-related backslash commands can be used for italicizing, changing point size (within the range available on the printer), underlining, and framing (producing a fine-lined, round-cornered frame around a word or two).

Inputting to the System

The input of all commands and text may take place either inside or outside of the ScenicWriter environment. Unlike most IBM PC text processors, Scenic Writer uses its own operating system, which is based on the UCSD p-System. Although having its own operating system makes ScenicWriter text files incompatible with most other programs and vice versa, the program provides a conversion facility for using DOS ASCII and WordStar files.

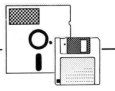

The ScenicWriter editor has three basic modes: command, insert, and delete. In the command mode, single keystrokes activate commands. Commands that have a need to repeat, such as Page Forward, accept a numerical precedence value, such as *3P* (advance three pages). This repeat-factor capability is also true for cursor movements. The Jump command moves the cursor on a gross basis. It can quickly move the cursor to the beginning or end of the page buffer (that part of the job in memory), to the first or last line of the file, or to preset tags or markers, which the user inserts to make the navigation of large files easier.

The Insert mode is entered by pressing **I**, in either uppercase or lowercase. In the Insert mode, each typed character appears on the screen as text. Each line must be ended manually by pressing the Return key (in the default state). In the Word Wrap mode (wherein each line does not need to be ended manually), the program can only leave one space between words, and therefore can justify lines. To return to the Command mode the End key is pressed.

The Delete mode has ten options, some of which support the use of repeat factors. Text that has been removed erroneously can be recovered, and the entire deletion session can be ignored by pressing the Escape key.

Although ScenicWriter does not support the creation or electronic paste-up of graphics, it does provide the means to leave expanses of blank space for the manual insertion of illustrations and photographs. The *.Figure Title '<title>' <space>* command causes the program to advance the space automatically (vertical distance specified), display the word *Figure* along with the proper sequential number, and input the title in the command line.

In the Paint mode, which is more a simple line-drawing mode, ScenicWriter does offer the ability to form boxes and other noncomplex shapes composed of horizontal and vertical line segments. Asterisks are used to indicate the path the lines are to take. Line macros also are available to produce horizontal lines with either set thicknesses of 1/64 inch or 1/32 inch, or in any specified increment. Increments for this parameter, as well as other commands that take a value, can be specified in an exceptionally wide variety of measurement systems, including:

Centimeter	c	3.5c
Inch	i	7i
Didot point (0.3759 millimeters)	d	52d
Horizontal motion unit (1/300 of an inch)	h	28h
Line space (default is 1.2 times the type height in use)	l	2 l
Pica	P	10P
Pica point (0.013837 inch, approximately 1/72 inch)	p	32p
Quad (square of the current font size)	q	2q
Type height (height of the vertical bar of the current font)	t	5t
Vertical motion unit (1/300 of an inch)	v	14v

The printing may be executed in either the Plain or Formatted mode. In Plain printing, the file is printed exactly as it appears on the screen, with all of the embedded commands in their natural state. The Formatted printing mode observes all of the commands that have been input, and responds to codes for setting margins, accessing typefaces, numbering pages, generating a table of contents and index, etc.

GUTENBERG:
Intergating Text and Graphics in a Typesetter-Like Environment

The Gutenberg[5] word processing program for the Apple II series is available in both a Junior and Senior version, and is unique among microcomputer-based word processors in that it shares much with the methods and procedures commonly used in

[5]Gutenberg Software Limited
47 Lewiston Road
Scarborough, Ontario, Canada MIP 1X8

typesetting. First, it employs an editor, which has capabilities found on typesetting front-end systems. Second, it separates the activity of inputting text from that of specifying its output appearance. Third, it approaches the task of pagination and page layout through the use of supermacros.

The program was written by Johann Wagner, who grew up near Mainz, Germany, the city of Gutenberg. It was in Mainz where he served his apprenticeship as a compositor. He emigrated to Toronto, Canada, in 1963 and has since worked as a software designer for three major typesetting companies in Toronto and Montreal.

Wagner's goal was to design a word processing package for the Apple II that would fulfill the text and graphics needs of the author while exploiting the full capabilities of specific dot matrix printers. In the Gutenberg package, he has met his objective, supplying the user with powerful text editing, flexible font and graphics creation, and full page make-up capability. Although it is more complex than most word processing programs, it does significantly more. Wagner spent over 10 years planning the program and worked over 20 months on the actual implementation on the Apple.

Wagner's concern for the aesthetics of typesetting has been carried over to the Gutenberg program. The lines are microjustified, with equal word spaces between each word, rather than uneven numbers of multiple full spaces between words. Those familiar with typesetting coding schemes will find some aspects of the program more like typesetting than word processing. The most obvious such aspect is the editor, where macros (brief indicators of lengthy format commands) are used extensively.

The editor permits text files of unrestricted length, up to the capacity of the disk. It also allows for split-screen operation, which lets the user view two parts of a single file at the same time, as well as transfer part of one file to another on disk.

Jobs prepared using the program are divided into a text file and a format file, both linked together by macros. This scheme is particularly well suited to typesetting input (after which it is fashioned), and is, in fact, used in some typesetting shops for that purpose.

The Gutenberg program uses its own disk-formatting scheme, which means that all disks must be formatted by using a utility program. Although this method of formatting makes Gutenberg files incompatible with other Apple programs, the user is compensated by the genuine ease by which files can be manipulated within their captive environment.

The Gutenberg Junior program is a subset of the Senior program, which was introduced first. The Senior program, being the full implementation of Wagner's original concept, is as complex as it is powerful. It attains its goal of producing fully composed pages of text and graphics by providing a means of designing and composing type fonts, painting and positioning illustrations, and defining and embedding complicated macro codes. The Junior software, which will be described here, provides the user with a fixed set of flexible macros that both simplify and restrict the range of attainable output appearances.

The editor permits movement in every conceivable direction and in every possible increment. Numbers may be input preceding a cursor command in order to prescribe the number of times it is to be repeated. Typing **5B**, for example, would move the cursor back five paragraphs. The deleting, inserting, overwriting, moving, and copying functions are similarly flexible in defining the text that is to be manipulated.

The Search function is another example of the flexibility available to the user. The Control-G command initiates the *GET>* after which the word or words to be found are typed in. The Escape key starts the search, which might have been further specified by the addition of a *mask*, which defines a particular set of occurrences that must be matched exactly.

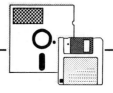

These are the masks and their effects:

- A ? permits any character including a space.
- A $ will permit any number, 0 to 9.
- A # will permit any character other than the one that immediately follows it in the specification.
- A % will permit the search to find any occurrence, regardless of whether it is capital or lowercase.

Searches may be conducted either forward or backward in the file. The masks make it possible to find such things as any occurrence of an *n* and a *t* not separated by a space (GET>n#t), which could result in finding such words as *can't* or *sun-time*, but not *in truth*.

The Search and Replace function is also quite flexible. The user may specify a number of words or phrases to be found and replaced in a single pass. On screen the procedure would look like this: *NEW>x∗y∗z OLD>a∗b∗c* (with the ∗ appearing in inverse). This sequence would change *a* to *x*, *b* to *y*, and *c* to *z*. There is no stated limit to the number of replacements that may be made at one time, and in addition, masks may be used to further specify items to be replaced.

A counting capability is built in, allowing the user to calculate the number of characters or words, or, by using masks, any occurrence of screen-displayed alphanumerics. A count may be made for the entire job or up to any prescribed place where the user has placed a stop indicator. This function is useful in typesetting for determining the total number of characters in a job, the number of characters of text, and the number of characters of control coding.

Nonprintable comments, a function not usually found in micro-based word processors, may be inserted at any point to indicate operator instructions, user comments, reminders, or any other information that is not meant to be printed on the final output. Comments appear on the screen enclosed within comment brackets, which are formed by using the Bracket key followed by control character sequences.

The keyboard can be modified to accommodate user-defined single- or double-key string storage. By typing Control-C from Command mode, the tag *CHG>* (Change) appears on the screen. The user then can define any key or combination of two keys, to result in the display of a string of up to 33 characters. A string definition is ended by typing **ESC**, at which time Gutenberg responds with the message -*GOOD*-, if the definition was acceptable. Thereafter, typing the key sequence will produce the programmed translation.

The Gutenberg program provides a font editor for the creation or alteration of characters specific to a particular use. The design matrix is 7 × 12 dots; however, characters that print together (joined as one) may be any reasonable number of matrices wide. The user may produce alphanumerics, special characters, mathematic and scientific symbols, ornaments, borders, and anything else that fits within the boundaries of one or more matrices.

The user can start with an established font and alter one or more characters as needed, or can design a new font from scratch. As characters are created, they are assigned to a specific keyboard location, or a *hex code identity*, so the editor can access them during the composition mode.

The creation of text and the specification of output appearance are separate functions, the latter being controlled by Gutenberg's repertoire of macros. In most cases the macros are just two characters delimited by the less than and greater than symbols (FIGS. 7 THROUGH 11). Failure to enclose the macro identifiers within these symbols will result in the macros being printed as ordinary text. Using the symbols without a predefined macro identifier will result in unpredictable output.

FIG. 7. Customizing formats.

CUSTOMIZING FORMATS

OPTIONAL START-UP FORMATS

[A1] – Automatic Accent Output Enable. 44 Alternate accented characters are automatically translated into regular printer characters plus floating accents. The floating accents are centered over the printer characters by the program. If [A1] is not issued at the beginning of a multi-lingual job, the accented screen characters are printed as graphics characters.

[A2] – Automatic Accent Output Disenable. Cancels the functions of [A1]. (Default)

[A3] – Print Roman Page Numbers.

[A4] – Print Arabic Page Numbers. (Default)

[A5] – Page Depth Reduction and Single Sheet Printing. [A5,3] shortens page depth by 3 lines and _halts_ print program between pages.

[A6] – Cancels [A5].

[A7] – As [A5] _without pause_ of print program between pages. [A7,2] shortens page depth by 2 lines.

[A8] – Cancels [A7].

[A9] – Print selected pages: e.g. [ZA,From,To,From,To][A9]. To extract pages 2 to 4, and page 6, issue the following command at the beginning of your input file: [ZA,2,4,6,6][A9]. A total of 8 arguments is allowed for a maximum of 4 groups of pages.

[B5] – Reduce Linewidth from 65C to 60C on wide-measure output, and from 31C to 29C on narrow-measure (double-column) output. The letter start-up formats [L1], [L2] and [L3] issue [B5] automatically. Each time another document is printed, the default column width is always reset to either 65C or 31C.

LINESPACING FORMATS

[S1] – Single line spacing (Default)

[S2] – 1-1/4 line spacing

[S3] – 1-1/2 line spacing

[S4] – 1-3/4 line spacing

[S5] – Double line spacing

[S1] through [S5] may be issued at the beginning of a document or _before_ any paragraph format to alter the linespacing. The linespacing will stay in effect during that print job until another [Sn] format is issued.

PRINT-STYLE FORMATS

[S9] – Change print style. E.g. [QO][S9] prints all following text in proportional print style #2.

FIG. 8. Standard paragraph formats.

STANDARD PARAGRAPH FORMATS
(All illustrated in DEMO520 and DEMO530)

STANDARD PARAGRAPHS

[P1] Indented paragraph

[P2] Unindented paragraph

[P3] Hanging paragraph

QUOTATION PARAGRAPHS

Left margin moved in:

[Q1]   Indented

[Q2]   Unindented

Left and right margins moved in:

[Q3]   Indented

[Q4]   Unindented

AUTOMATICALLY NUMBERED PARAGRAPHS

[E1] At level 1, using Arabic numbers

[E2]   Subordinated at level 2, using lowercase letters

[E3]   Subordinated at level 3, using lowercase Roman numerals

[E4] Indented unnumbered paragraph at the same left boundary as preceding paragraph

[E5] Unindented unnumbered paragraph at the same left boundary as preceding paragraph

MANUALLY NUMBERED PARAGRAPHS

[F1] At level 1

[F2]   Subordinated at level 2

[F3]   Subordinated at level 3

[F4] Indented unnumbered paragraph at the same left boundary as preceding paragraph

[F5] Unindented unnumbered paragraph at the same left boundary as preceding paragraph

[F1], [F2], and [F3] are two part formats. After the number, type a break (CTRL-B) to activate the second part which will input the text. Instead of numbers you may use letters, bullets, etc.

FIG. 9. Heading formats.

HEADING FORMATS

HEADINGS ABOVE TEXT

Nine basic styles of headings are provided. See also DEMO530. All except [H5] use downloaded printer fonts — FONTD.B and FONTD.I must be on the disk in Drive 1.

[G1] This is a G1 style heading

[G2] This is a G2 style heading

[G3] This is a G3 style heading

[G4] This is a G4 style heading

[H1] This is an H1 style heading

[H2] This is an H2 style heading

[H3] This is an H3 style heading

[H4] This is an H4 style heading

<u>This is an H5 style heading</u>

Any one can be centered by adding [QC]. If the heading includes an enumeration, a Break (CTRL-B) can be used after the enumeration to align the remaining text.

[H4][QC] This is a centered H4 style heading

- **[H4] This is an H4 style heading
  with enumeration**

HEADINGS BESIDE TEXT

These are illustrated in DEMO570.

      [J1] – Heading to left of [J2] or [J3] text

      [J2] – Normal text to right of [J1] heading

      [J3] – Enumerated text to right of [J1] heading. Type a Break (CTRL-B) after the
               enumeration to align the following text.

      [R1] – Optional rule to separate items.

FIG. 10. Typographic formats (*a*).

TYPOGRAPHIC COMMANDS

STANDARD PRINT PITCH COMMANDS

[PO] - PROPORTIONAL style #1

[QO] - PROPORTIONAL style #2

[CO] - CONDENSED 17 cpi

[DO] - CONDENSED 15 cpi

[EO] - ELITE 12 cpi

[MO] - MONO-SPACED 10 cpi

[UO] - WIDE-SPACED 9 cpi

EXPANDED PRINT PITCH COMMANDS

[PE] - PROPORTIONAL EXPANDED style #1

[QE] - PROPORTIONAL EXPANDED style #2

[CE] - CONDENSED EXPANDED 8.5 cpi

[DE] - CONDENSED EXPANDED 7.5 cpi

[EE] - ELITE EXPANDED 6 cpi

[ME] - MONO-SPACED EXPANDED 5 cpi

[UE] - WIDE-SPACED EXPANDED 4.5 cpi

DOUBLE STRIKE COMMANDS

[BO] - BOld (double-struck). Not the same as [B1]-bold format, which uses FONTD.B.

[KB] - Kill Bold (end double striking). End of paragraph has same effect.

UNDERLINING COMMANDS

[UL] - Start single UnderLine

[UU] - Start doUble Underline

[KU] - Kill Underline. End of paragraph has same effect.

LINE COMMANDS

LINE JUSTIFICATION COMMANDS

[QL] - Quad Left - flush left & ragged right

[QC] - Quad Center

[QR] - Quad Right - flush right & ragged left

[JU] - JUstify - both margins flush

FIG. 11. Typographic formats (*b*).

LEADER AND FILL LINE COMMANDS

[LD] - Print LeaDers . . . .

[FL] - Fill remainder of Line with blank space.

SPACING COMMANDS

HORIZONTAL

[FSn] - Forward Space. [FS3C] Forward space 3 character spaces. [FS2U] Forward space 2 unit spaces.

[BSn] - BackSpace. Arguments as FS.

[NBn] - Non-Break space. Arguments as FS.

VERTICAL

[UPn] - [UP6]xx[DN6] print xx superscript.

[DNn] - [DN4]xx[UP4] print xx subscript.

[SAn] - Space allowance. [SA4L] Insert white space of 4 lines.

PRINTING COMMANDS

OUTPUT CONTROL COMMANDS

[OF] - Turn OFf temporarily

[ON] - Turn ON printing (Default)

[OV] - OVer (terminate printing)

FILE LINKAGE COMMANDS

[NFn] - Next File. The current text file is terminated and "n"-file is processed. [NFMOUSE] The file MOUSE will be processed. It must be on the same disk.

PAGE NUMBER COMMAND

[PNn] - Set Page Number to n (default PN is 1) - See [A3] & [A4]

GHOST HYPHEN

$7F - Hex 7F is interpreted by the print program as a possible hyphenation point. It appears on the screen as a centered dot. On the Apple][+ type the following keys: (SLASH) (PERIOD) (7) (F). On the Apple //e type: (SLASH) (DELETE).

The Gutenberg Junior commands and macros can be divided into four general categories: • page layouts • paragraph forms • print style matters • various special matters. The Gutenberg Senior package provides for the respecification of existing macros, as well as the creation of totally new ones. This feature provides virtually unlimited flexibility for the handling of complex layouts involving such things as runarounds, shaped paragraphs, customized headers and footers, and logos (FIG. 12).

The Gutenberg Junior package comes with three format files. The main one provides predefined formats for creating reports, stories, term papers, resumes, newsletters, mailing labels, and more. The remaining two formats are used to generate envelopes (one with a return address, the other without).

FIG. 12. Miscellaneous formats.

MISCELLANEOUS

DOWNLOADED FONT SELECTION FORMATS

[B1] - **Start Bold.** FONTD.B must be on the disk in Drive 1.

[B2] - End Bold

[I1] - *Start Italic.* FONTD.I must be on the disk in Drive 1.

[I2] - End Italic

VERTICAL EXTRA SPACING FORMATS

[D1] - Down 1/2 extra linespace

[D2] - Down 1 extra linespace

[D3] - Down 1-1/2 extra linespace

[D4] - Down 2 extra linespaces

WIDOW CONTROL FORMAT

[W1,n] - [W1,4]: If 4 lines of print will not fit on the page at the time this format is issued, the page or column will be terminated. If issued in the middle of a line, the page or column may be ended at the next line break.

COLUMN SELECTION FORMATS FOR TEST PRINTING

To be used for testing individual paragraphs. May be modified by [B5].

[C1] - Selects one-column linewidth of 65C (6.5 inches).

[C2] - Selects two-column linewidths of 31C (3.1 inches).

PAGE-, COLUMN-, & DOCUMENT-ENDING FORMATS

[P7] - Force new column if 2-column printing, else like [P8].

[P8] - Force new page with footer and header on next page (if specified).

[P9] - Print footer (if specified) and end document or chapter.

SUPER MISCELLANEOUS

[R1] - Full-column rule to separate items

In actual use, the macros are input at appropriate locations to signal a change in the layout appearance of the document (FIGS. 13 AND 14). The manual provides a number of examples of the input coding versus the output appearance.

FIG. 13. The general macro input specification for a two-column newsletter.

SHORT TITLE

This is a basic [P1] paragraph. If you put this macro in delimiters at the beginning of your paragraph, it will print out like this sample. Every paragraph should begin with a macro. If you put this macro at the beginning of a paragraph, it will print out like this sample. If you put this macro in delimiters at the beginning of your paragraph, it will print out like this sample. Every paragraph should begin with a macro.

This is a basic [P1] paragraph. If you put this macro in delimiters at the beginning of your paragraph, it will print out like this sample. Every paragraph should begin with a macro. If you put this macro at the beginning of a paragraph, it will print out like this sample. If you put this macro in delimiters at the beginning of your paragraph, it will print out like this sample. Every paragraph should begin with a macro.

This is a basic [P1] paragraph. If you put this macro in delimiters at the beginning of your paragraph, it will print out like this sample. Every paragraph should begin with a macro. If you put this macro at the beginning of a paragraph, it will print out like this sample. If you put this macro in delimiters at the beginning of your paragraph, it will print out like this sample. Every paragraph should begin with a macro.

This is a basic [P1] paragraph. If you put this macro in delimiters at the beginning of your paragraph, it will print out like this sample. Every paragraph should begin with a macro. If you put this macro at the beginning of a paragraph, it will print out like this sample. If you put this macro in delimiters at the beginning of your paragraph, it will print out like this sample. Every paragraph should begin with a macro.

This is a basic [P1] paragraph. If you put this macro in delimiters at the beginning of your paragraph, it will print out like this sample. Every paragraph should begin with a macro. If you put this macro at the beginning of a paragraph, it will print out like this

sample. If you put this macro in delimiters
at the be
print out
should beg

This
put this
of your p
sample. E
macro. If
of a para
sample. I
at the be
print out
should beg

This
put this
of your p
sample. E
macro. If
of a para
sample. I
at the be
print out
should beg

This
put this
of your p
sample. E
macro. It
of a para
sample. I
at the be
print out
should be

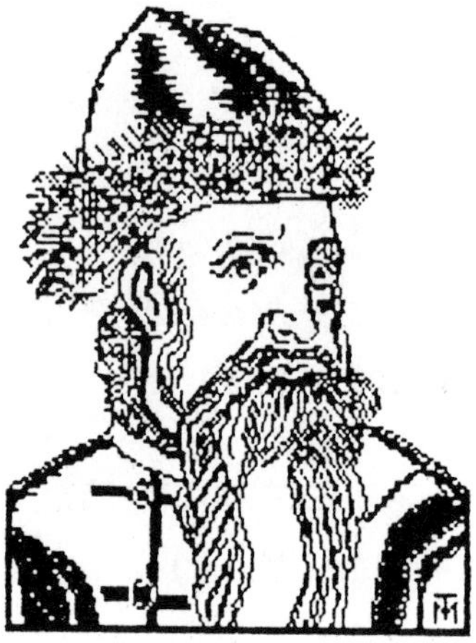

[M4]

INPUT APPEARANCE:

<C6>SHORT TITLE
<M4>

<-->YOUR TEXT. -- Use supplied formats.

<P9> At end of text.

This is a basic [P1] paragraph. If you put this macro in delimiters at the beginning of your paragraph, it will print out like this sample. Every paragraph should begin with a macro. If you put this macro at the beginning of a paragraph, it will print out like this sample. If you put this macro in delimiters at the beginning of your paragraph, it will print out like this sample. Every paragraph should begin with a macro.

THE Gutenberg Gazette

PUBLISHED NOW & THEN

FORMATTING, PLAIN AND FANCY

Your printer puts your text on a page of paper. Your word processor tells it how to arrange everything. You tell the word processor. Often the weak link in this chain is the middle one.

Some programs can only do single columns; some can do one or two. Gutenberg can do one, two, or three, or . . . in fact, any reasonable number. Gutenberg can start a page with one column, and switch to two or three — a single macro at the switch-over point does it all. You can even have a cut-in, as on this page.

Your page can have automatic headers and footers in infinite variety, with page numbering anywhere you choose in Arabic or Roman, or a, b, c, or A, B, C. Headers and footers can be different for odd and even pages, and the margins can be flipped.

That is, Gutenberg produces all the page layouts standard for word processing, but with a wider range of choice in each case. And it can produce others previously restricted to letter-press.

Indented, unindented, hanging indents, blocked quotations — any of the usual paragraph forms is created automatically to whatever specifications you choose.

The boxed paragraph on this page was produced automatically using a supplied format, as were the highlighted paragraphs on page 15. A selection of other simple, ready-to-use specialized paragraph formats is included in the package. Gutenberg Sr allows you to print a graphics masthead, as on this page. Or we could have had a picture inserted where we put the boxed paragraph. Or you can put diagrams in your text:

> Johannes Gutenberg died yesterday in Mainz a pfennigless and disillusioned man.
>
> His contribution of the casting of moveable type has revolutionized the bookmaking industry. Previously, all work was performed by monks in monasteries writing on small slips of paper. With Gutenberg's invention, the daily racing form became a staple of the man in the street.

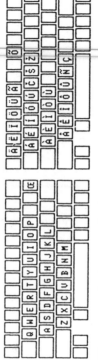

Indigo

Gutenberg's PAINT utility will enable you to create such artwork. But you don't have to draw everything. The structural diagram of Indigo, for example, was assembled from pieces selected from a stock of over 500 on a chemistry Applications Disk. Some lettering on page 11 was assembled from predrawn alphabets on still other Applications Disks.

You have another option: Headline Fonts that are larger than normal text letters (used in headings on pages 4-7) are available on an Applications Disk. Some artwork-like bits can be simply typed in: . These are just a matter of making special "characters" like .

Other things require not merely special characters, but also some fancy formatting:

$$\int_0^1 \sqrt{\log \frac{1}{x}} \, dx = \sqrt{\frac{\pi}{4}}$$

Here, one macro puts in the integral sign, then measures and places the indices; a macro produces each radical, and another the vinculum; and a fourth macro measures the numerator and denominator, then centers them properly with the division line. Any of the indices, numerators, or denominators could be longer. These formats (and many more) are on an Applications Disk.

All this formatting power results from Gutenberg's free use of short and flexible macros, instead of the long strings of print commands used in many programs. The definitions for the macros can be in format files, prepared in advance or as needed. The Gutenberg package contains ready-to-use formats in a wide variety. You can modify them easily. And you can write your own, but that will be necessary only for very special layouts.

GUTENBERG's DOUBLE KEYBOARD

The Apple has a single keyboard, but Gutenberg makes it, in effect, *two*, with the user free to choose the two from many possibilities. Perhaps the most generally useful combination is:

(To save confusion, we only show capital letters, there are lower case, punctuation, numerals, etc. — twice the usual allotment.)

When you are working on one keyboard, a simple command will get you a character from the other. You can type "Español" or "Française" using just one extra keystroke each. Or you can switch into the other keyboard and stay there for a while. Then you can write Greek or Cyrillic, one keystroke to a letter. A simple command will bring you back to the familiar keyboard and a different alphabet. Nothing can be simpler.

- 8 -

- 9 -

FIG. 14. The newsletter appearance based upon the macros shown in FIG. 13.

ULTIMATE ROM II:
Transcending Dependency on the Typesetting Input Place

The creative process of putting thoughts into words and words into coherent, organized blocks of text is the starting point of the personal publishing process. The removal of barriers separating the creator of the content from the designer, technician, and craftsman of the form has placed a new emphasis on the techniques and technical requirements for creating text. The author must anticipate the opportunities and limitations that are present when direct access to typographic characters and manipulable graphic images is at hand.

In most instances, the production of a desktop publication is place dependent. Although the equipment—personal computer, laser printer, scanner, proof printer, modem, and other accessories—is relatively compact compared to the traditional means of production, it will not usually be moved in the process of completing any one project. However, the process of developing the content is not necessarily tied to a physical location. The writing process might develop over a protracted period of time, with thoughts and ideas jotted on scraps of paper, processed repeatedly within an author's mind, and eventually keyboarded into a computer.

The sooner in the process that creative ideas and portions of textual content can be captured in silicon, the longer the germination process for developing well-constructed and organized information. The key to moving back the input phase to coincide with the author's random moments of creative genius is the *laptop computer*, a battery-operated, lightweight, compact computer, which frees the author of place-dependent information processing.

A laptop computer offers many benefits to the personal publisher. Among them are:

- Portable word processing. Articles, reports, and documents of all kinds can be created, edited, and revised with few limitations other than the constraints of available memory or media.
- Notetaking. Interviews and library research can be input directly into the computer rather than on paper.
- On-line communications. Most laptop computers have a built-in modem, providing the means to access a remote database for conducting research or to access a desktop computer for dumping text for output in publication form. Information that previously was input into a desktop computer can be downloaded to the laptop by direct cable connection, processed further independent of time and place, and uploaded back into the computer where it originated.
- Computer processing. The computer can be used to sort information quickly on the basis of given criteria. Lists of facts can be input randomly and organized according to need.
- Record keeping. Input sessions can be date-stamped; statistical information concerning files, such as the number of characters, words, and sentences, can be generated; time commitments and expenses in regard to particular projects can be logged.
- Work-in-process reporting. Hardcopy reports can be printed at any time with the use of a compatible printer, in order to involve others in the generation and reformation of information.
- Programming. A built-in language, usually BASIC, is generally available for writing custom programs to fulfill a wide range of individual needs.
- Time management. Appointments can be scheduled, publication deadlines can be tracked, job status can be logged, etc.

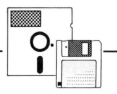
There are a number of laptop computers on the market; however, the Tandy (Radio Shack) Model 100 (FIG. 15), which was one of the first, is distinguished by the fact that it has gained the support of a number of third-party suppliers, who have endowed the device with capabilities far beyond those supplied by the original manufacturer. One such supplier is Traveling Software, Inc.,[6] a company supporting a number of different laptop computers and the manufacturer of The Ultimate ROM II.

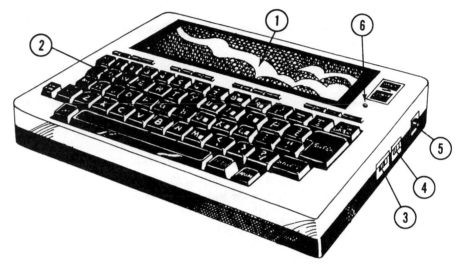

FIG. 15. The Tandy Model 102 consists of the following parts: (1) an 8-line-×-40-character Liquid Crystal Display (with the addition of the Ultimate ROM II, it can be expanded to up to 8 lines by 80 characters); (2) a standard typewriter-style keyboard with additional special-purpose keys, augmented by a row of function and cursor control buttons; (3) a power switch that is overridden if the computer is on but not used for more than 10 minutes; (4) a display adjustment dial to set the intensity of the LCD for optimum viewing; and (5) an external power adapter to extend the life of the internal batteries. (Courtesy of Tandy Corporation).

The Ultimate ROM II is a read-only memory chip that easily snaps into a socket located on the back panel of the Model 100 or 102. Installation and initialization take only a few minutes. The addition of the ROM adds a new menu item, UR-2, to the standard display. Selection of the "UR-2" option leads the user to a new menu accessing both the new features of the ROM, as well as the standard features of the Model 100.

The Ultimate ROM II provides three programs: a word processor, a database, and an outline processor, along with a display enhancer and a disk operating system. The disk operating system is a limited subset of TS-DOS, which is available as a separate product; however, the subset does permit the printing and previewing of files saved on Tandy's Portable Disk Drive. The display enhancer, called ROM-View 80, extends the Model 100's LCD display from its standard 8 lines by 40 characters, to 8 lines by up to 80 columns (up to 60 columns visible at one time, horizontally scrollable to 80).

T-Word: The Traveling Word Processor

The most important computer writing tool for the author is the word processor. Although the Model 100 has its own built-in text processor called TEXT, T-Word provides a number of additional features that aid in productivity and ease of use. These features are neither unique nor particularly exciting, but they are helpful improvements in what might be considered a fairly immutable product. Chief among them is the capability to switch between Insert mode and Type Over mode, and the capability to both search *and* replace. Of additional value to a personal publisher is the capability to ascertain, at any point in a document, exactly how many words and characters have been keyboarded.

The ROM-View 80 enhancement offers a visual change for the editing environment, permitting the user to specify a line length of 10 to 80 columns. (The same is true for the original TEXT, BASIC, and TELCOM applications, as well as for the Ultimate ROM II T-BASE, and IDEA! applications.) The potential for displaying a greater number of characters helps to overcome one of the serious limitations of such a small computer screen.

[6]Traveling Software, Inc.
11050 Fifth Avenue NE
Seattle, WA 98125-6151
(800) 343-8080
(206) 367-8090
The Ultimate ROM II is available for the Tandy M100, M200, 102; Olivetti M-10; NEC 8201 and 8300.

After T-Word is chosen, the File Selection screen appears. It looks like this:

```
                    Tandy 100 T-Word (vl. 11)
                 (c) 1986, Traveling Software, Inc.

    BOOK1     TEST      SETH      A&S1              PCR
    BOOK2     RIT                 TYPEX

    TS-DOS: Off              View80: On        Width: 80
    New Kill  Disk Edit          1388              UR-2
```

The screen displays all of the document files that are stored in the computer. The prompts along the bottom of the screen, corresponding to the function keys directly beneath them, offer access to creating a New file, Killing an existing file, printing or previewing files from the Disk, or Editing the file that is highlighted. The byte count for the highlighted, or currently selected, file also appears along the bottom of the screen. The user can return to the former menu screen by selecting the ''UR-2'' option.

One of the most significant features of the T-Word program is the text formatting capability, which is apparent in the Print menu. The Print menu, shown in the following illustrations, provides control over the way in which a document will be printed or saved to RAM. The options are fairly self-explanatory, providing the means to indicate margin settings, page length, justified or unjustified setting, single or multiple line spacing, a default font (specifically for the Epson FX-80 or compatible dot matrix printer, alterable to support other printers), the addition of a line feed with each return, the need to wait between pages (for noncontinuous feed paper), page-numbering options, the page that is to be printed first and last, and the number of copies to be printed.

```
              Model 100 T-Word (vl.11) (c) 1986, TSI

    [L]eft     10    [J]ustify   N    [N]um Start   1
    [R]ight    75    [S]pacing   1    [Q]uick       N
    [T]op       6    [F]ont      0    [1]st Print   1
    [B]ottom    6    [A]dd LF    N    [E]nd Print  99
    [P]g Len   66    [W]ait Pgs  N    [C]opies      1
       PCR
    TEXT Plot  PBrk   Disp Prnt  Par    Fil        UR-2
```

The prompts along the bottom of the screen are used to access the Text of the document, pixel Plot how the document will appear on the page (in preview form), scroll the job on the screen showing the page breaks (PBrk), display the job as it has been formatted (Disp), print the job according to the current print settings and any embedded print commands (Prnt), select the destination for the file (either a Parallel or serial printer, or to RAM), or return to either the File Selection screen (Fil) or to the Ultimate ROM II menu (UR-2).

Over 20 print commands can be embedded directly in text in order to format the appearance of a document. These commands affect such things as margins, the placement of headers and footers, page break decisions, and font selection. In order to center a headline, for example, a Control-C (^C) command would be embedded anywhere in the line.

A particularly useful feature of T-Word is the merging capability, whereby previously saved files and other information can be joined together to form a new file or a new document. The merging process consists of two file types: the Merge files, which will be inserted into other files at the time of printing (to paper or to RAM), and the Main files, into which the text will be inserted. The merging process can be used to print the current time or date, insert portions of stored files into a main file, insert

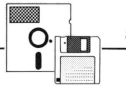

items from a database file into a main file, or insert entire files into a main file in order to chain-print them.

T-Base: The Traveling Database

T-base is a true relational database, which can be exceptionally useful in organizing a collection of information into a meaningful whole. Its relational functionality permits the user to borrow data from one file to another, and to perform automatic calculations based upon user-defined formulas. This cross-referencing capability can be exceptionally useful in research of all sorts. Of special significance is the fact that reports generated from T-base can be saved to RAM as well as printed to paper, thus ensuring that reports can be transferred to other computers, where they can be typographically formatted for publication, without the need to rekeyboard.

T-base uses three different kinds of files: Screen files, which define the items of information to be included in the database; Report files, which define what is to be printed, and in what order; and Data files, which actually store the data itself. The Screen and Report files are created by using the TEXT program. The Data files are created from within the T-base program.

The Screen file consists of two parts: first is a beginning line file definition, and second are the lines indicating field specifications. A typical file might look like this:

```
5,NAME,STREET,CITY,STATE,ZIP
Customer Name:,20,TM
Street:,15,T
City:,15,T
State:,2,T
Zip:,5,T
```

The file definition line shows the number of fields—five in this case—and the names of each field. The first field is always the key field, used for sorting and locating specific records. The field specifications show the name of each field followed by the field length and an indication as to the field type. The types may be composed of one or more descriptors, which indicate the kind of data stored in the field, as well as if the entry is borrowed from another source (another field of another database) or if it will store the result of a calculation. The field types are listed here:

FIELD TYPES

Primary Descriptors

T	Text
I	Integer
$	Dollar and decimal fraction
D	Date
U	User-defined

Secondary Descriptors

B	Borrowed
BS	Borrowed and stored
C	Calculated
CS	Calculated and stored
M	Mandatory entry

Although most of the descriptors do not require any explanation, the user-defined field is worthy of mention. It allows the user to define acceptable responses for an individual field. If a database was being constructed to collect information concerning page printers, for example, then the following item might be defined:

Downloadable Fonts (Y/N)?:,1,U,"YN"

The field name presents the prompt *"Downloadable Fonts (Y/N)?"* which will require a size of 1 character. The only acceptable responses are either a "Y" or "N."

After a screen file has been defined, information can be entered. The Data Entry screen shows the form with each empty field in reverse. The prompts at the bottom of the screen offer access to saving a record (Sav), deleting the current record (Del), finding a record according to its key field (Fin), displaying the previous record (Pre), displaying the next record (Nex), clearing the screen without saving (New), recalculating all calculated fields for which values have been changed (Cal), and exiting without saving data (End).

T-base reports are defined by using the TEXT program. Report definition commands are used to indicate such critical information as which database is to be used, if fields are to be sorted, what the page length of the report will be, how wide the report will be, where the report will be sent (to the screen, to the disk drive, to the cassette, to the printer, to the modem, or to memory), how the report heading will read, what the column labels will be, where the columns are to be positioned, which data fields will be used, where subtotals are to be tallied, if a grand total is to be included, and various other specifications.

Idea!: The Traveling Outline Processor

An *outline processor* is a powerful aid in helping to capture and organize an author's thoughts. Simply stated, an outline processor is a program that makes it possible to record the free flow of ideas, facts, observations, etc., in a structured way, organizing such information in a hierarchial fashion.

An outline processor can be useful for a great number of diverse activities, from planning an event or lecture to keeping a client list. It is an especially good way to begin writing about any subject, and is, therefore, very useful for personal publishing projects of all kinds.

Since the outline form is one familiar to virtually all writers, the Idea! program, no doubt, will seem elegantly simple. At the beginning of an Idea! file is a line displaying the file name, its status as of a given date, and the number of entries in the file (there is a limit of 250 per file). Below the line is a space for a numbered listing of the main topics, followed by a prompt line along the bottom of the screen. The easiest way to understand how the program works is to construct a simple example. The example file will be called "LASERS," and will deal with laser printers. To begin entering information, the user selects ADD. The number *1* automatically appears on the screen, and the entry **Background** is input, followed by the Enter key. The number *2* automatically appears on the next line, awaiting an entry. The word **Applications** is input, again followed by the Enter key. After a few minutes of contemplation, the screen looks like this:

```
LASERS IDEA! file as of 10/12/86 (5)
  1. Background
  2. Applications
  3. Major Vendors
  4. OEMs
  5. Major Advantages
Add  Edit  Del  Key2    Find  Top  Quit
```

Of course, there could be many more than five major topics input. In order to add a subtopic to any of the first-level topics, the cursor is moved to the target topic and the "Add" option is selected. The program automatically numbers a new indented subtopic entry. Successive levels of subtopics can be entered in the same way. Any subtopic can be expanded into a lengthy text entry by selecting the "Notes" option, which appears when the user is in a subtopic entry.

Major topics that contain subtopics are designated with a plus sign immediately following their numbers, as are subtopics that contain lower levels of entries. Subtopics containing notes are followed by an asterisk. An expanded portion of the example outline might look like this:

```
5.+   Major Advantages
      5.1   Speed
      5.2   Integration of text & graphics
      5.3   Plain paper output
      5.4+  High resolution options*
      5.5   Networking capabilities

   Exp  Add  Edit  Del  Key2    Find  Top    Quit
```

The "Exp" option on the prompt line expands a highlighted entry. Once chosen it toggles to its alternate state, "Cmpr," to compress the outline portion back to its next highest level. Expand/Compress will open or close each section, while pressing the Space Bar will fully expand or compress the whole outline.

The commands available on the initial prompt line are for adding new entries, editing existing entries, deleting entries, finding words, moving to the top of the outline, and quitting Idea! Selecting "Key 2" presents another prompt line offering the additional capabilities of moving and copying text, advancing subideas to the next highest level, sorting entries, and printing.

When an Idea! outline is complete, it can be read by the T-Word or TEXT programs and freely edited. Most of the preliminary work of structuring and researching an article, therefore, can be captured without rekeyboarding, thus impacting positively on both the creative and production processes.

Chapter 4

Text Creation, Generation, and Reformation Tools

*Helpful programs for improving
personal typesetting productivity.*

PROPORTIONALSTAR:
Producing Justified Output from a Word Processor

The realm of typesetting has some rather flexible boundaries, some of which have been stretched considerably in order to include character forms that are more akin to the typewritten than the typeset. Nonetheless, the distributors of such products and the publics that they serve give some credence to their wares, placing them in the quasi-typesetting category which some of the direct-impression typesetting devices (glorified typewriters used in the graphics arts) occupy.

An unknown, yet seemingly large, number of word processing users utilize un-adulterated word processing output as their final copy for reproduction. The copy is produced on either a dot matrix or letter-quality printer with no special consideration to typographic niceties. Such output is to be seen everywhere. Ironically, many of the manuals produced by typesetting vendors for their sophisticated typesetting machines are produced in this way.

While there are no laws to protect the public from bad character images, nor laws to compel users to take any special precautions in producing such images, one particular feature seems to surface in the issue of discriminating between "just plain word processing" output, and (marginally) acceptable "typeset" output. The feature is justification, and to many people without any typographic training nor any natural talent for spotting acceptable typographic spacing it is all-important.

Many word processing users go to extremes in order to justify their lines of output. These extremes tend to destroy their documents' word spacing, not only making it more difficult to read, but also considerably less appealing, and therefore less likely to be read.

A critical player within the world of word processing on microcomputers has been MicroPro's WordStar program. The reasons for its popularity are much less important than the fact that it has become the program of choice for an amazingly large number of users, a number of whom profess to use it for creating documents destined for direct reproduction. For example, the owner of an advertising/public relations/editing/writing service, who lives within the shadow of one of the largest typesetting shops in the country, regularly produces what he calls "typeset-quality" word processing on a Diablo 630 daisywheel printer with a portable computer and WordStar. Using this configuration, he produces newsletters, brochures, books, etc. to the complete satisfaction of his customers.

A curiosity of WordStar, which has a considerable impact on the quality of the printed output, is the fact that it does not directly support the output of proportional spacing on daisywheel printers. The result is that daisywheel output looks as though it were letterspaced, with lines appearing particularly loose and unattractive (FIG. 1)

FIG. 1. The normal appearance of a daisy-wheel type element in justified mode on WordStar.

This is how the typeface normally looks :

The information which follows will assist you in selecting a proportional spacing printwheel for your printer. However, you can take advantage of the some of benefits of PS even without a PS wheel. The PS tables may enhance the appearance of the 10 or 12 pitch wheel you are currently using.
(Set in Vintage 10 in 10 pitch, without PS logics)

A solution to this dilemma is the ProportionalStar program from Writing Consultants.[1] This program is based upon work included in the company's publication "Proportional Spacing on WordStar," which provided the user with a method of installing this feature directly in his copy of WordStar. The ProportionalStar program automates this installation process, making it simpler and less time-consuming to accomplish. According to the ProportionalStar publishers, "Proportionally spaced printing is very desirable because it gives a professional, typeset appearance similar to that used in books and magazines, and allows more text on a page without appearing cluttered. ProportionalStar allows WordStar's print command to send justified, proportionally spaced text directly to the printer without calling another program. ProportionalStar also improves WordStar's ability to print two or more justified columns on a page."

Whether or not the quality of image that proportionally spaced letter-quality printing can provide is acceptable for the typesetting needs of any particular user is a personal decision based upon taste, economics, and expediency (FIG. 2). Yet, it is another way in which the personal computer user can directly avail himself of control over the output of typographic images.

FIG. 2. A sample of text produced on a daisy-wheel printer using the WordStar and ProportionalStar programs.

You are reading text **printed by WordStar** on a daisywheel printer, using a Bold PS printwheel. Most professionally typeset books and magazines are set in proportional typefaces. Proportional spacing **provides a professional, typeset appearance,** it is **easier to read,** and **allows more words on a page.**

This new book provides complete details for printing in proportional spacing, **directly from WordStar.** The techniques will work on **all versions** of WordStar, including Xerox, Osborne, and IBM, driving **Diablo, Qume, NEC, C. Itoh,** and other daisywheel printers. Your printer does not require proportional spacing logics or firmware. Information is also included on how to set **two or more fully justified columns on a page,** underline spaces between words, and other techniques for first class output.

WORD FINDER:
Finding the Right Word for the Right Situation

The typesetting process deals with the conversion of words from their handwritten or typewritten form into something more aesthetic, more compact, and more communicative. In general, the activity of setting type has dealt almost exclusively with that transformation, leaving the realm of content to those whose talents are better suited to the task.

The microcomputer, and the avalanche of software which greatly enhances its value, to some extent has redefined the limits of the typesetting process, rolling it back closer to the text originator. For example, spell-checking, a common capability in the microcomputer word processing environment, is invaluable in typesetting because of its ability to find typographic errors. Almost all word processing programs have either a dedicated or a compatible word processing program available.

While some writing aids, such as spelling and grammar checkers, help to correct faulty writing, others actually work to improve it. One such program is the Word Finder[2] for CP/M, MS-DOS, and PC-DOS computers. Word Finder works with popular word processing programs such as WordStar and MultiMate. It installs as a pre-

[1]Writing Consultants
11 Creek Bend Drive
Fairport, NY 14450
(800) 828-6293
In NY (716) 377-0130
ProportionalStar modifies any version of WordStar, enabling it to perform proportional spacing on popular daisywheel and thimble printers (Diablo, NEC, Brother, Juki, C. Itoh, Silver Reed, Transtar, Dynax, and others), whether or not they contain proportional-spacing logics.

[2]Writing Consultants
A division of Microlytics
Techniplex
300 Main Street
East Rochester, NY 14445
(716) 377-0130

A demonstration version of WordFinder is provided in Softstrip form in the Cauzin section of Chapter 6.

boot, loading a small program that integrates within the host word processor (FIG. 3). To activate the thesaurus, the user places the cursor on a word and enters two keystrokes, such as CTRL-F6 on the IBM version. (The program allows users to respecify the keys that will be used to activate the thesaurus. (See FIG. 4.) The user is given a display of synonyms (FIG. 5). The left and right cursor keys are used to move among word selections. When the appropriate choice is located, a depression of the Return key deletes the old word and replaces it with the new one. The process is fast and does not require a user to remove his hands from the keyboard.

The program uses a proprietary database technique, which yields the equivalent of a 90,000-word dictionary. There are approximately 9,000 keywords, each with an average of ten synonyms, although some entries have as many as 50.

FIG. 3. The start-up screen for the Word Finder presents all of the instructions necessary for using the program. Note that the name has been changed from Synonym Finder.

```
                    SYNONYM FINDER  1.3
(C) Copyright 1984, 1985 Selfware, Inc.  All rights reserved, worldwide.

            Executive Editor:   Charles W. Woodford.
            Linguistic Editor:  Dr. Roger C. Schlobin.
            Programmer:         Jo Ann Reel.
            Adapted from previous works of Charles W. Woodford.


SYNONYM FINDER is now installed in memory for:  MultiMate
The synonym file (SF.SYN) is expected to be on the disk in drive:  A
The keystrokes to get synonyms are:  Ctrl-F6

When you are editing and you want a synonym, place the cursor on or
after the word.  Then use the keystrokes above.  Part of the screen
will be cleared and a list of synonyms will appear.  Press the arrow
keys to move the cursor to the desires synonym; press the return key
to have the word in your text automatically replaced with the desired
synonym; press the ESC key if you decide to use your original word.

SYNONYM FINDER remains installed until you reset the system by
simultaneously pressing the Ctrl, Alt and Del keys.
```

FIG. 4. The Word Finder provides the means to respecify the default drive and access keys according to the individual needs of the user.

```
                  SYNONYM FINDER by Selfware
                  ENHANCEMENT PROGRAM 1.0

  The SYNONYM FINDER ENHANCEMENT PROGRAM allows you to modify your
  SYNONYM FINDER program for your disk configuration and word processor.


      **   You can select the disk drive where you will locate
           the synonym file (SF.SYN).

      **   You can select a sequence of keys which you will use to
           invoke SYNONYM FINDER from your word processor.

      **   And you can input a message describing your key sequence to
           remind you of it each time you load SYNONYM FINDER.



  This program is sold for use on one computer.  Do not make copies
  for other computers or your friends.  Integrity benefits everyone.


  Press Esc to stop this program.  Press any other key to continue.
```

```
DOCUMENT: interfacing            |PAGE:   1|LINE:   7|COL:  25|
|1..»....»....».....................................................«
Communicating with an office typewriter is direct; a one-for-one
relationship of "key depressions" resulting in "character impressions."
The results are immediate, visual, and tangible. The placement of
characters, the limitations of line length and page depth, even the choice
of typefaces (on certain typewriters) are all under the physical control
of the typist. A phototypesetting machine, on the other hand, uses
image-forming techniques
```

```
┌───────────── The Synonyms displayed are for the closest word found. ─────────────┐
│ technique:  (n) code, codex, fashion, manner, method, mode, modus,               │
│ system, way.                                                                     │
│                                                                                  │
│                                                                                  │
│                                                                                  │
│                                                                                  │
│                                                                                  │
│                                                                                  │
└──────── ⁻ move left ───── ⁻ move right ───── Esc ⁻ exit ───── ↵ replace ────────┘
```

DocuMate/Plus:
Generating an Index Automatically

The usefulness of information is often a function of both the way in which it is arranged and presented, and the degree to which it is organized. Certain categories of printed work, such as text and reference books, and technical and professional journals, require that their contents be adequately indexed and listed in a table of contents. Furthermore, such works might require several indices, such as by subject, author, trade name, technical terminology, photograph credits, illustration listings, etc.

The generation of indices, cross-references, and tables of contents often are done manually—usually by the author, or by an editor who is fully versed in the intricacies of the manuscript content. Most indexing work is quite time-consuming and not terribly interesting. It is the kind of work that is particularly well suited to the sorting and organizing capabilities of a microcomputer.

Indexing programs for microcomputers usually work in concert with word processing programs. The identification and coding of words to be indexed can be accomplished either while the work is being created or after it has been completed. Regardless of when the codes are inserted, the microcomputer accomplishes the real work; that is, generating a map of words which assist the reader in quickly locating specific information.

An indexing program for use with MicroPro's WordStar is DocuMate/Plus[3]. In this program, a series of commands, which are inserted at appropriate places within the WordStar document, are used to generate separate files for a table of contents and index. These additional files can be printed or edited further using WordStar.

The coding structure used in DocuMate/Plus consists of four commands, each of which is preceded by three periods. The multiple periods are recognized by WordStar as comments, and are therefore not printed. To indicate the addition of a line for the table of contents, for example, the command **...T1** would be inserted in the extreme left of the line immediately above the line to be added. The *1* that follows the *T* indicates that the entry is a major section heading. Minor subject headings and subordinate topics are indicated by the addition of either a *2, 3,* or *4.* In a book about computerized type design, a section about designer Hermann Zapf might be indicated as follows:

...T2
Hermann Zapf: Designer of Modern Classics

FIG. 5. In this MultiMate screen, the user positioned the cursor on the words "technique" and pressed the CTRL-F6 keys. Nine synonyms were found.

[3]The Orthocode Corporation
P.O. Box 6191
Albany, CA 94706
(415) 753-3222
Distributed by
Digital Marketing Corporation
2363 Boulevard Circle
Walnut Creek, CA 94595
(415) 947-1000

When output, DocuMate/Plus uses user-defined settings to format the column width, page number width, prefix width (as in pages numbered A-1, A-2, A-3), number placement, margin width, and column indents (FIG. 6).

The index creation process works somewhat differently. Words that are to appear in the index must be listed on the page on which they appear using the command ...**X**. The word or words themselves must be typed immediately following the command, such as:

> . . . X Hermann Zapf

If the reference to Hermann Zapf appears on page 16, for example, then the index entry will be printed as:

> Hermann Zapf, 16

If references to Hermann Zapf appear on many pages, then DocuMate/Plus will collect them and list them all together like this:

> Hermann Zapf, 16, 22, 40, 104

Multiple levels of indexing also are supported, with the minor text entry or entries preceded by the major text entry, such as:

> . . . X Designers, Hermann Zapf

which would appear as:

> Designers, 16
> Hermann Zapf, 16, 22, 40, 104

Reference entries work in a similar way, and use either the . . . **R** command to indicate to "see" reference, or the . . . **A** command to indicate a "see also" reference. The syntax is similar to that used in the index entries. The following line:

> . . . R Hermann Zapf, Computer Aided Design, Software Tools

would be interpreted as:

> Hermann Zapf, 16, 22, 40, 104
> Computer Aided Design, see Software Tools

The authors of DocuMate/Plus anticipated the usefulness of the program for the preparation of typeset tables of contents and indices, and provide users with instructions and suggestions for such applications. One of their suggested procedures solves the obvious problem of the page references not agreeing on the WordStar and typeset versions of output. To overcome this difficulty, the document should be typeset nor-

FIG. 6. An index created with the program.

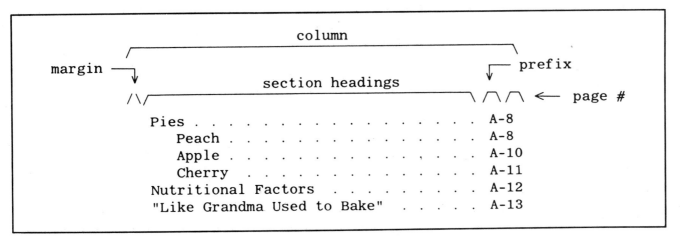

mally with no attention given to the DocuMate/Plus commands. After page breaks have been determined from the typeset page proofs or galleys, the WordStar version of the file is edited to match the typeset pagination. Commands are added to the WordStar document to prevent the word processor from making automatic page breaks, and then the DocuMate/Plus files are regenerated, with appropriate typesetting codes.

SMARTKEY II PLUS:
Packing More Meaning into Each Keystroke

A keystroke-intensive and character-extensive activity like typesetting relies upon methods of optimizing input to achieve efficiency. Long ago, manufacturers of typesetting keyboards realized that the standard typewriter keyboard was grossly deficient in providing access to the larger character repertoires of typesetting machines, and that adding more keys was not always the answer to greater operator productivity. Their simple solution was to add one key, which served as a flag to designate a supershift—a third order of shift after unshift and shift. The ''c'' key, for example, could produce the lowercase *c*, the capital *C*, or the copyright symbol, depending upon the shift condition that preceded it.

Some form of supershift is to be found on virtually all dedicated typesetting input keyboards. Some computer keyboards, such as that for the Apple Macintosh (with the use of the Option key), provide access to a third order of characters through the use of a similar precedence key.

The capability of adding a supershift case to a personal computer, as well as many other keyboarding enhancements, can be achieved through the use of the SmartKey II Plus program from Software Research Technologies.[4] This program, which was conceived as an experiment by microcomputer pioneer Nick Hammond in 1979, is generally regarded as the first of the ''pop-up'' utilities that operate in the background, in addition to the operating system and application software.

SmartKey is a small program which resides in the transparent memory area of the computer. Under PC-DOS, for example, it takes up just 2.25K of RAM. It is loaded prior to the applications software, and once installed remains until the computer is reset or shut off. Immediately after being loaded and anytime thereafter—whether in the operating system or within a program—SmartKey II Plus is available, waiting to define any keyboard key to another identity or string of characters or commands.

A key definition begins by pressing the Set-Up key. An audible beep provides feedback that SmartKey has been activated. When SmartKey is shipped from the publisher, it comes with the Set-Up key defined as the Escape key. The user may keep this as the designated Set-Up key or else choose another, by using the installation program. Next, the key to be defined is pressed—the asterisk, for example. The user sees the following prompt on the screen:

SMARTKEY: redefine < * > to <

The new identity for the asterisk key is typed. Then the Set-Up key is hit twice. Pressing the asterisk now results in the display of the programmed identity. The key can be redefined at any time to another identity or returned to its original identity by typing the Set-Up key, the key to be returned to its original identity, and the Set-Up key again.

Every key can be redefined as one or more characters or commands. The program includes a predefined SmartKey file, which redefines the entire keyboard to the Dvorak layout.

Key definitions that will be used repeatedly during more than one program session can be saved on disk and reloaded at any time. The definition programs optionally can be saved as text files and edited with a standard word processing program.

[4]Software Research Technologies
3757 Wilshire Blvd., Suite 211
Los Angeles, CA 90010
(213) 384-4120
Runs under a wide variety of personal computers using either PC-DOS, MS-DOS, CP/M, or CP/M-86.

Multiple-part definitions can be created for repetitive character strings that require operator input at one or more points within the string. For example, a parts list, which would have many repetitive and many variable aspects, would be a good application for a multiple-part SmartKey definition. The creation process is similar to the standard definition procedure, except that at each place where a pause (for operator input) is needed, the Set-Up key is pressed once. The procedure would be as follows:

```
SMARTKEY: redefine < * > to <first part of definition>
[set-up]
<second part of definition>
[set-up]
<third part of definition>
[set-up]
[set-up]
```

In use, the first part of the string would be displayed, and then pause until the operator input any variable information. The string would continue with the depression of the Set-Up key, and then pause again. The process would continue until the entire string was displayed.

The SmartKey program includes an Installation Option menu, which allows the user to customize the program according to individual preference or specific hardware/software requirements. This menu provides access to such options as defining the Set-Up key, setting the maximum size of the translation table, enabling/disabling input by hexidecimal notation, and setting the supershift character.

The supershift definition, in essence, enables twice as many characters (supershift and shift supershift) to be defined. The use of the supershift is critical since most users need to keep the keycap identities of common characters intact, so that pressing an alphanumeric results in that character. The supershift key, which is the slash key in the distributed version or another character designated during the installation procedure, is input immediately after striking the Set-Up key. To define the supershift of the "c" key as "Copyright 1987, New York, NY. All rights reserved." the following would be input:

```
[set-up] /c Copyright 1987, New York, NY.
All rights reserved. [set-up] [set-up]
```

SmartKey and similar programs are in use in many word processing and typesetting environments, extending the definition of individual keys into bursts of data (including lengthy boilerplate insertions) and command strings, while reducing the keyboarding time and complexity of repetitive keyboarding operations.

KEYWORKS:
Customizing the Operating System Environment

In the early days of microcomputing, before very many software companies had achieved name recognition and when the selection of available programs was limited, businesses and individuals in need of specific applications had little choice but to write their own programs or have them written by a contract programmer.

A result of much of the in-house development of software was, and still is, a growth in the availability of specialized software products reaching specific vertical markets, such as graphic arts and, in particular, typesetting. Many programs of a highly peculiar nature were developed for internal use and then marketed to meet a similarly specific need, and perhaps, to capitalize on a void in the software marketplace.

The expense of custom programming generally puts it out of the reach of most personal computer owners, and the variety and powerful capabilities of off-the-shelf packages are too enticing, and represent the investment of too many man-years, to try to duplicate in any form on a single installation basis.

Until recently no real compromises could be made in the area of software customization. Keyboard enhancers such as SmartKey, ProKey, and SuperKey are effective in extending the energy level of each key through the use of stored macros, but do not materially change the way in which software works. Although keyboard enhancers are of unquestioned utility in a typesetting environment, by making one key do the work of many, they essentially enhance the keyboard, not the software.

The first product in the category of software enhancement is Keyworks,[5] a program which was created to compete against keyboard enhancers, and in the course of its development took on a number of distinctive characteristics all its own.

As a keyboard enhancer, Keyworks is particularly easy to use. It is accessible in pop-down menu form at any time with the strike of a single user-selected key. The physical make-up of the menu (its size, style, color, etc.) and the attributes of the macros (their number and number of keystrokes) may be preset in a configuration file, which can be altered easily. The contents of a sample configuration file might look like this:

TYPE THIS:	COMMENT (PRECEDED BY A COLON)
F=2	:Set the foreground color to green
B=5	:Set the background color to magenta
M=100	:Set the max number of macros in memory to 100
K=5000	:Set the max number of keystrokes in memory to 5000
T=60	:Set the screen save delay in seconds; if no key is pressed, blank the screen to prevent image burn-in
S=2	:Set border style
C={F10}	:Set the menu key to the F10 function key

These and other parameters may be specified once and loaded automatically with the program, or changed on the fly, as conditions dictate.

Program Capabilities

The scope of the Keyworks program is sufficiently broad to necessitate listing its major capabilities before delving into specific features. These capabilities include:

Macro-Related Features.
- A description of up to 20 characters can be assigned to each macro.
- A list of all macros, with their descriptions, can be displayed at any time.
- Sets of macros can be saved and retrieved at any time, without leaving the application program in use.
- Macros can be freely edited from within the active application program using the Keyworks editor. Macros are saved as ASCII files and can also be edited using any word processor that can work with straight ASCII.
- Macros can be *nested*; that is, written to call other macros. Complex macro strings can be made from simple, short macros. Up to 20 levels of nesting are possible.
- Macros can call themselves; that is, *loop*. A looping macro will call itself endlessly until the Menu key is pressed. This capability is useful for filling a page with repetitive lines, such as a name and address, or other information which needs to be typeset many times.

[5]Alpha Software
30 B Street
Burlington, MA 01803
(800) 451-1018
(800) 462-2016 (in Massachusetts)
(617) 229-2924
Works with any IBM PC or compatible with a minimum of 128K and one disk drive.

• Macros can be created with fixed- or variable-length pauses. A macro that contains a pause will stop during playback in order to let the user input some information from the keyboard. A variable-length pause will let the user input keystrokes until the Return key is pressed. A fixed-length pause will wait only until the user has keyboarded a prespecified number of keys.

Menu-Related Features.

• Custom pop-down menus, with moving bar selection, can be created in order to control any single or multiple function or group of functions. This capability is what differentiates Keyworks from all previous classes of utility programs. It provides the means for a user to define how he would like to interact with a specific program.
• Text-only screens can be created to provide help, messages, instructions, etc.
• Menus and text screens can be created using menu *cosmetics*, which let the user specify such appearance-related items as the style of the border, the color of the foreground and background, the position on the screen (row and column coordinates), the display or suppression of the cursor, and the clearing of the entire screen before the displaying of the menu or text screen.

Additional Features.

• The user can access DOS commands, such as erasing and renaming files, from the main Keyworks menu, without leaving the active application program.
• Files can be encrypted for security reasons, and can only be unscrambled with the use of the proper password.
• When Keyworks prompts the user for the name of a file, the file name can be keyboarded or Keyworks' file-pointing capability can be activated. If the user presses the Up Arrow key when prompted for the file name, Keyworks will automatically display the current subdirectory, and a moving-bar pointer will appear so the user can select the required file.

A Simple Typesetting Application

While Keyworks is useful for optimizing the way in which an expert user interacts with software, it also is exceptionally helpful in simplifying the use of applications for the beginning user. When typesetting coding is a requirement for the computer novice, the problems are twofold: learning the intricacies of the word processor and learning the complexities of the typographic coding. Keyworks can be useful in such a case by supplanting any on-line help that the word processing program might provide, and by completely insulating the user from cryptic typesetting codes.

Take the example of a newsletter, which has three specific, repetitive elements: the headline, which introduces each news item; the text, which deals with the subject at hand; and the reference notation, which refers to the source of the story. The typographic coding for each element will always be the same, so these items are particularly good candidates for definition as macros.

To create a Keyworks macro, the Menu key is pressed. The Menu key is the Plus key by default, although it can be redefined to any other key. The Keyworks menu then appears on the screen (FIG. 7), with the first item highlighted. Items from the menu are selected by using the Up and Down Arrow keys to highlight the required choice, and pressing the Return key to make the selection. The "Record a macro" option is selected, and the user is prompted for the macro I.D. key; that is, the key that is to be programmed with a new identity. The choice must not be a key that performs a necessary function in the active application. Keyworks supports the use of any key, as well as key combinations, such as CTRL-F3. Additionally, the ALT key with the numbers from 1 to 255 can be programmed.

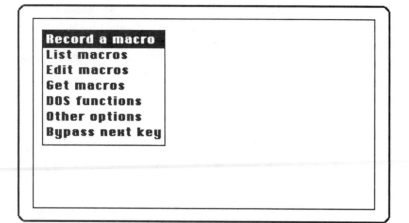

FIG. 7. The Main Keyworks menu is available by pressing the Menu key. The cosmetic appearance of the menu is alterable by choosing the "Other options" selection, or by editing the Configuration file.

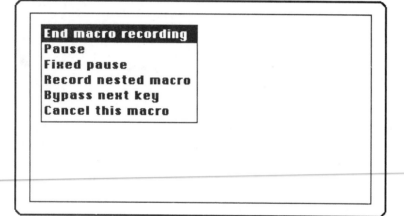

FIG. 8. The End Macro Recording menu presents options related to how the macro will be presented to the user in terms of actual keyboarding.

After the macro I.D. is selected, the user is prompted for an up to 20-character description of the macro. The description is helpful for reminding the user about the function of the macro, as well as serving as a possible menu listing. After the description has been keyboarded, the Return key is pressed. Next, the user keyboards the actual macro contents. Recording of the macro is concluded by pressing the Menu key, which results in the display of the End Macro menu (FIG. 8).

The newsletter macros might be input as follows:

Macro ID	Description	Macro
CTRL-F1	Headline	\<F1> \<SZ14> \<LS160> \<NL>
CTRL-F2	Body Copy	\<F4> \<SZ10> \<LS115> \<JU>
CTRL-F3	Reference	\<F2> \<SZ07> \<LS080> \<JU>

A macro is ready for use immediately after it has been defined. Pressing the CTRL-F1 key combination, for example, will result in the codes necessary for typesetting a headline.

A new user might have been told which macro keys to use, or might have been told how to list the available macros from the Keyworks menu. A far better way is to create a menu of the descriptions of the available typesetting code strings, and eliminate the need for the macro keys all together.

A menu is created by using the Keyworks editor. A key is selected that will activate the menu, perhaps CTRL-F4, and a title ("Newsletter Typesetting Elements")

and footer ("Enter your selection") for the menu are devised. The required form for this menu specification is:

{ {CTRL-F4}} <Typesetting Menu> {Menu} {Title}Newsletter Typesetting Elements\ {Footer}Enter your selection\ {CTRL-F1} {CTRL-F2} {CTRL-F3} {Menu}

The menu would be brought to the screen by pressing CTRL-F4, and would appear as:

Newsletter Typesetting Menu
Headline
Body copy
Reference
Enter your selection

The appearance of the actual macro I.D.s can be suppressed from the screen display since they no longer serve a function. A moving menu bar can be used to choose from the three menu selections, which will result in the explosion of the macro string on the screen.

This simple example is just one of the ways in which this powerful program can be utilized to customize off-the-shelf programs into highly specific typesetting applications.

LePRINT:
Post Processing Word Processing Files into Typesetlike Output

There are numerous routes that can be taken to move from the province of word processing to that of typesetting. Few, however, are as immediate as those that use the same word processing output device, namely the dot matrix printer, in order to accomplish the task. Not only is such a shared-output device among the least expensive typesetting alternatives, but the file-creation process in such instances almost assuredly can be handled by the same person.

It is the approach of the LePrint[6] program to provide an additional set of typographic formatting codes for MicroPro's WordStar word processing program in order to produce remarkably well-formed characters on a wide range of dot matrix printers. The LePrint program is actually a post processor, which takes the WordStar program as its input and produces typographically rendered pages based upon both the LePrint and WordStar dot command code sets.

The LePrint output greatly resembles that of a laser printer (FIG. 9). Although the quality is unusually high for a dot matrix printer, it is accomplished at a correspondingly slow speed, requiring as many as six passes to form normal-sized text characters, and many minutes to produce its maximum 10-inch-high characters.

Because the WordStar program ignores dot commands that it does not understand, LePrint-encoded jobs can be printed either as normal word processing files through the WordStar environment, or as typographically coded documents through LePrint. When LePrint processes a file, it takes into account the proportional attributes of the typefaces in use, and reforms paragraphs while respecting any implied parameters entered into the original WordStar document.

Justification is produced according to the attributes set in the WordStar file. If the original file used a ragged-right margin, for example, that is what LePrint will use. Hyphenation is based on both the hard and soft hyphens contained in the WordStar file. Soft hyphens, which only appear in print if they fall at the end of a line, can be added to or deleted from the original file to achieve more uniformly spaced LePrint lines.

[6]LeBaugh Software Corporation
2720 Greene Ave.
Omaha, NE 68147
(800) 532-2844
(402) 733-7600
Available for the IBM PC series of personal computers. Although the program was designed to work particularly with WordStar, it also can be used with any number of other popular word processing programs, including the Borland SideKick notepad.

About LePrint

LePrint may be used to print existing WordStar document files, without modification, producing print quality rivaling a daisy-wheel printer or laser printer.

You can switch from courier to pica just that easy.

Or if you prefer, Park Avenue.

Here is Times Roman.

Proportionally spaced.

A wide variety of sizes may be produced, like:

6 point

8 point

12 point

24 point

1"

2"

Type sizes up to a full page in height can be set.

FIG. 9. The LePrint program produces detailed typographic characters in a variety of sizes and styles.

LePrint dot commands (FIG. 10) are of two kinds. The normal dot commands appear alone on a line, preceded by a period and followed by a two-character mnemonic and additional parameter information. The dot command for a 24-point type size would be written as:

CH 24 PT

where *CH* equals character height.

The same instruction could be written within a line in the second kind of dot command: the embedded form. Embedded dot commands can be inserted at any point within a line, and are enclosed within braces. The same 24-point type size command would be written as:

Here is a sample of 24 point Helvetica: {.CH 24 PT} ABCDEFG . . .

FIG. 10. LePrint summary of dot commands.

DOT COMMAND	MEANING	ORIGIN
.AT	Auto-Tabbing	LP
.BP	Bidirectional Printing	WS
.CE	Center	LP
.CH	Character Height	LP
.CP	Conditional Page	WS
.CW	Character Width	WS
.DE	Define	LP
.FA	TypeFace	LP
.FI	File Insert	MM
.FM	Footing Margin	WS
.FO	Footing	WS
.HE	Heading	WS
.HM	Heading Margin	WS
.IG	Ignore	WS
.IW	Input Width	LP
.LH	Line Height	WS
.LM	Left Margin	MM
.LS	Line Spacing	MM
.MB	Margin at Bottom	WS
.MT	Margin at Top	WS
.OJ	Output Justification	MM
.OP	Omit Page Numbering	WS
.PA	New Page	WS
.PC	Page Number Column	WS
.PL	Page Length	WS
.PN	Page Number	WS
.PO	Page Offset	WS
.RM	Right Margin	MM
.SR	Subscript Roll	WS
.UJ	Microjustification	WS

WS = WordStar   MM = Mail Merge   LP = LePrint

There are many units of measurement that the Character Height command (and some other dot commands) will accept: points, inches, ems, ens, centimeters, didot points (European, approximately 1/68th inch), millimeters, and picas. Through the use of command sequences, two frequently used fonts can be specified as the normal and the alternate font. This process is accomplished by defining CTRL-N as one typeface and size, and CTRL-A as another, such as this:

```
^N
.FA TIMES
.CH 12 PT
^A
.FA TIMESITL
.CH 12 PT
```

The use of the CTRL-N or CTRL-A at any point within a line would issue a font call for the predefined font attributes.

After a file has been created, it is processed by typing **LP [file name]** at the A> prompt. The user has the option of previewing the job on the computer monitor. If a color/graphics adapter is installed, the display will show a representation of the document as it will be printed. If a monochrome adapter is used, the document will appear only in the normal screen text size.

TYPEFACES:
Enhancing Word Processing Output on a Dot Matrix Printer

Typefaces,[7] a program for the Apple II family of microcomputers, bills itself as a printing tool—a program that not only works in concert with word processors to enhance their output, but also stands alone to produce signs, letterheads, announcements, and other such work directly.

Typefaces (FIG. 11) is one of the only programs of its kind that comes with an audio tape as well as printed documentation. A tour of the program takes one of two distinct routes: either the Simple mode or the Comprehensive mode (FIG. 12). The Simple mode is just that. A line editor with limited capabilities is used to create simple, "typeset" output. Each session requires the assignment of a file name (FIG. 13) and the direct input of the text that it describes (FIG. 14). When the input is complete, pressing CTRL-C returns the user to the Main menu. From the Main menu (FIG. 11), option 3 "Print a saved file," is selected. The user is prompted for the kind of printer in use (FIG. 15) and which of the resident fonts will be used (FIG. 16). The result is the printing of the selected file in the chosen typeface (FIG. 17).

The program supports Apple DOS 3.3 files, as well as CP/M files. Option 2 from the Main menu provides the user with a number of file utilities, including those to list files names, list file text on the printer, delete a file from the disk, format a blank disk, back-up a disk, copy a DOS text file, copy a CP/M file, and more.

The program has a set of built-in print commands (FIG. 18) which control the appearance of the output. These commands are composed of a precedence character (a period) followed by a two-character mnemonic. These commands can be used in either the Simple or the Comprehensive mode, as well as from within word processing files.

The Comprehensive mode puts a more powerful editor directly into the hands of the user, without exiting the Typefaces program. The editor is line-oriented and provides for finding and replacing text, removing and adding text, and moving around within the file. Files of up to 325 lines long are supported. Longer files can be printed by using the ".so" Page Organization command to join files.

[7]Alpha Software Corp.
6 New England Executive Park
Burlington, MA 01803
(617) 229-2924
Written by Philip Baun
Printer support for IDS 460/Prism 80, IDS 560/Prism 80, Epson 80/100, Trendcom 200, and others.

FIG. 11. The Main Typefaces menu provides access to the direct input of text or the processing of an existing word processing file.

```
TYPE FACES MAIN MENU
====================

1 - Enter or edit text
2 - List or update files
3 - Print a saved file
4 - Exit program

Enter number (1 -> 4) : 1
```

FIG. 12. Two text-entry modes are provided: one for simple work, another for more complex composition.

```
TYPE FACES TEXT ENTRY MENU
==========================

1 - Simple mode
2 - Comprehensive mode

Enter number (1 -> 2) : 1
```

FIG. 13. The opening screen in the Simple mode offers instructions of the limited editing capabilities available. It is also at this point where the user must name the file to be created.

```
TEXT ENTRY INSTRUCTIONS
=======================

Use backarrow to backspace
RETURN to start new line
CTRL-w for upper case.
CTRL-u and RETURN to delete line
CTRL-c after last return

Enter file name: MUSIC
```

FIG. 14. Three lines of text have been input in the file "MUSIC." The input procedure is terminated by keyboarding CTRL-C.

```
TEXT ENTRY INSTRUCTIONS
=======================

Use backarrow to backspace
RETURN to start new line
CTRL-w for upper case.
CTRL-u and RETURN to delete line
CTRL-c after last return

Enter file name: MUSIC

    Now enter your text!

  1: Those Glorious MGM Musicals
  2: Singing in the Rain
  3: Easter Parade
  4:
```

```
TYPE FACES PRINTER MENU
========================

1 - IDS 460/Prism 80
2 - IDS 560/Prism 132
3 - Epson 80/100
4 - Trendcom 200
5 - Silentype

Enter number (1 -> 5) : 3
```

FIG. 15. The printer in use must be specified.

```
TYPE FACES FONT MENU
====================

   ri - Roman indexical
   ii - Italic indexical
   gi - Greek indexical
   rs - Roman simplex
   gs - Greek simplex
   ss - Script simplex
   rd - Roman duplex
   rc - Roman complex
   ic - Italic complex
   gc - Greek complex
   sc - Script complex
   rt - Roman triplex
   it - Italic triplex
   ig - Italian gothic
   eg - English gothic
specs - Special simplex

Use abbreviations above to select
primary font type : it
```

FIG. 16. A typeface must be selected for the output file. A different face can be used each time the file is processed.

Those Glorious MGM Musicals
Singing in the Rain
Easter Parade

FIG. 17. The processed output, suitable for a sign, label, or other use.

The main purpose of the print commands, however, is to embed them within word processing files. This process is generally easier since the user is familiar with the operation of the word processor and need not learn, nor be limited by, the editing procedures provided in the Typefaces program.

Unlike other programs that provide a font-creation capability, Typefaces only supports the 16 character sets which are supplied on the program disk (FIG. 19). No further character sets nor modification to the supplied fonts is possible.

FIG. 18. The set of print commands that are embedded with text to control the appearance of the printed output.

THE PRINT COMMANDS

This Appendix presents commands used in both the Simple mode and the Comprehensive mode. They appear in alphabetical order. For your convenience, the Print commands are also organized by function:

Print Commands

Page Organization

.pp New Paragraph
.pi Paragraph Indentation
.bp New Page
.he Header
.fo Footer
.ne Lines Needed
.pl Page Length
.so Join Files

Line Organization

.ce Center
.fi Fill Line
.in Indent
.ti Temporary Indent
.ju Right Justify
.nj No Right Justify
.rm Right Margin
.ex Spread Words Over Line
.np Non-paddable Blank
.nf Input Line=Output Line
.br Line Break

Spacing

.ln Underline Distance
.ls Space Between Lines
.lz Line Height
.sp Blank Line

Print Enhancements

.ul Underline
.cs Change Character Set
.ra Regular Print
.fa Fancy Print

This is Roman Indexical

This is Italic Indexical

Τηισ ισ Γρεεκ Ινδεξιχαλ

This is Roman Simplex

Τηισ ισ Γρεεκ Σιμπλεξ

This is Script Simplex

This is Roman Duplex

This is Roman Complex

This is Italic Complex

Τηισ ισ Γρεεκ Χομπλεξ

This is Script Complex

This is Roman Triplex

This is Italic Triplex

Ohis is Italian Gothic

This is English Gothic

⚘✝✗❀ ✗❀ ◇△✦✦✠ ◇✗❀△

FIG. 19. A complete showing of the character sets available in the Typefaces program.

ZYINDEX:
Processing Typesetting Information Via a Textual Database

The typesetting environment is one that is burdened with an enormous amount of textual information. The information usually takes one of two forms (sometimes both): it might be in a raw form which must be converted into typesetter input, or it might be in the converted (coded) form. Among the more critical aspects of dealing with this transformation are the organizing, filing, and retrieving of any portion of text quickly and easily.

Electronically stored files are identified by a job name, which is often limited by a computer's disk operating system to as few as eight characters. The name can be specified as an internal work order number, a job ticket number, a customer number, or a descriptive and usually abbreviated word. Despite the sophistication of the cataloging method, the file label usually does not contain sufficient detail to provide a clear picture of the exact file contents.

A further complication is the fact that a single computer disk might contain dozens of files. Even if the right disk has been located, the job of finding a specific file still might take considerable time and effort.

One answer to the problem of locating specific text files through computer searching is ZyIndex,[8] a text management program that can index, sort, and retrieve information stored in both ASCII and non-ASCII file formats. ZyIndex is compatible with text files produced using WordStar, WordStar 2000, Leading Edge, EasyWriter, MultiMate, pfs:Write, Office Writer, Palantir, Smart, Spellbinder, Wang, Word Plus, Microsoft Word, Word Perfect, Volkswriter Deluxe II, and XyWrite. It also can process files generated from the IBM PC line editor (EDLIN) and information utilities such as CompuServe, Dialog, and Dow Jones News/Retrieval.

ZyIndex is a full-text information retrieval program, which treats text files as if they were part of a textual database. It does so automatically, without the need for creating record fields or keywords.

The ZyIndex programs consist basically, although not exclusively, of two parts: The Index program and the Search program. The Index program, which must be used first, creates an Index List that includes the names of all files indexed and the location of each word relative to other words. The Search program is used to search for a particular word, number, or combination of words located in the Index List.

In order to achieve greater speed, ZyIndex does not process prepositions, conjunctions, articles, and certain common verbs. These words, such as *of, is, with*, and *the* are categorized as *noise* words, and usually do not impact on the search process. The user can add or remove words from the Noise Word List according to his preference and need.

The indexing process can be initiated either through the use of a menu procedure or by direct DOS prompt specification. The Indexing Menu screen looks like this:

F9:help   F10:exit

INDEX FILES

LOCATION OF FILES TO INDEX

To index files from a floppy disk:

Specify letter of drive containing files
  —Example: a:

To index files from a disk with sub-directories:

Specify drive and directory containing files
  —Example: c:\myfiles

ENTER LOCATION:

[8]ZyLab Corporation
233 East Erie Street
Chicago, IL 60611
(312) 642-2201
Runs under PC-DOS and MS-DOS on all versions of the IBM PC and workalikes.

If only the name of the drive or directory is given, then all of the files from that location will be displayed on the File Selection screen. The file specification can be narrowed by using a *global file name*—one containing either a *?* or *∗*, which are wild card designators—or by actually typing the name of a particular file.

The File Selection screen looks like this:

```
F1:Select all new files   F2:Begin Indexing   F3:Change WP   F9:Help
  F10:Exit
```

Select files to index: move cursor to filename and press ENTER

OMNI.TXT	WORDSTAR.IBM	SOFTEST.IBM	MAGNA.IBM
DECISION.IBM	SIGNMSTR.IBM	LASERST.MAC	PAGPLNR.IBM
TYPEBILL.IBM	TEX.IBM	FONTAST.MAC	GENCODE.TXT
FANFONT.APP	TYPEFACE.APP	LASERJT.TXT	PYXEL.IBM
XYWRITE.IBM	WORD.MAC	GRPHSOL.APP	WRDFNDR.IBM
MITE.KAY	PAGEMKR.MAC	KEYPORT.IBM	PCTS.IBM
SCENIC.IBM	KEYWORK.IBM	BLAST.IBM	DIAGRPH.IBM
HERCULES.IBM	CRAYON.TAN	GUTENBRG.APP	RSG.MAC
GRAPHDPT.APP	PIXIT.IBM	GRAPHSYS.APP	MACPUB.MAC
LASERSET.IBM	MACAD.MAC	DOCUMATE.IBM	SMRTKEY.KAY
REPLACE.IBM	JOSTEN.APP	STL.KAY	MACLINK.MAC
WORDSTAR.KAY	PRINTSHP.APP	NEWSROOM.APP	FONTRIX.IBM
STYLO.MAC	CLICKART.MAC	MACVSION.MAC	MAGIC.MAC
MACPIC.MAC	FLUENT.MAC	CASADAY.MAC	LETTALK.APP
PNTMTE.MAC	PROFONT.MAC	SOFTFORM.MAC	SPECEFF.MAC
BEAGLE.APP	WORDJUG.APP	POSTSCRT.MAC	MTK.MAC

None of these files have been indexed with this pathname & disk name.
CURRENT WORD PROCESSOR IS: WordStar 2000

Each screen displays up to 64 files, any or all of which may be indexed. After files from one screen have been selected and indexed, successive screens of files may be processed.

As ZyIndex scans each file, it displays a count of the number of characters read. After the file is copied into memory and the data is prepared for indexing, it is processed into the Index List. As this operation is taking place, a dynamic message is displayed, which indicates the percentage of words processed. The total number of words displayed includes both noise words and content words, and therefore accurately reflects the word count of a particular file. In a typesetting environment, this particular piece of information can be useful for billing or production statistics.

The Search program is used to locate all indexed files that match a search request. Files that contain a search request may be displayed or printed. When the file is displayed, each occurrence of the search request is highlighted, and the file can be scrolled forward or backward a screenful at a time, or the user can choose to jump directly to each highlighted word.

After a file has been viewed, the user can mark and save portions of text in a separate file. In a typesetting environment, this ability can be particularly helpful to locate and save specific portions of one or more long files that must be reset exclusive of the major body of the job. Information also can be saved with such files to show the name of the original file whose portion is being saved, the original file's DOS creation date, the search request that was entered to retrieve the file, and a memo of up to 60 characters.

The search request is composed of as many as four components. These include:

- The Content word. All searches must contain at least one content word upon which to base the search.
- Connectors. These are special operators, such as AND, OR, and NOT, that serve to relate one content word to another.
- Wild cards. These are symbols that represent one or more actual characters and allow for a more expansive search.
- Special Content Words. These are two particular words that allow searching on the basis of DOS creation date and/or the name of a specific file.

Suppose that a series of files was created for producing an agricultural report. The search possibilities would include:

CONTENT WORD & PHRASES	SEARCH RESULT (files containing . . .)
farm	*farm* and *farms*
family farm	*family* followed immediately by *farm*
farm AND family	*farm* and *family* in any proximity
farm OR family	either *farm* or *family*
farm*	*farm, farmer, farming, farmhand, farmhouse, farmland, farmstead, farmyard*
far?	*far, fare, farm, faro*
far??	*farad, farce, farms*
NOT farm	words other than *farm*
farm AND NOT family	*farm* without reference to *family farm*
family farm AND NOT farm	*family farm* without reference to *farm*
farm W/10 family	*family* within 10 words of *farm*
farm OR agri* AND family	*farm* or any words beginning with *agri*, and any occurrence of *family*
farm OR agri* W/20 family	*farm* or any words beginning with *agri*, within 20 words of *family*
file=farm*	*farm* as part of the file name
file=farm* AND date=8/??/86	*farm* as part of the file name and file-creation date in August of 1986

The Search menu presents seven options:

F9:Help F10:Exit

SEARCH MENU

F1 Input request
F2 Modify request
F3 Display results
F4 Print results
F5 View disk directory

PRESS APPROPRIATE FUNCTION KEY

- F1 is used to input a new search request. It results in the display of a new screen.
- F2 is used to modify a request in the case where the search did not yield any results or did not yield the expected results.
- F3 is used to display any of the retrieved files.
- F4 is used to print any of the retrieved files.
- F5 is used to view the names of any files on any disk.

The Search Request screen contains the following information:

Enter any of the following:

Words and phrases from your files
Connectors: AND, OR, NOT, W/n
Wild cards: *, ?
Parentheses ( ) to group items

Edit search request with:
<Back Space>   erase previous character
<Del>   delete character at cursor
<arrow keys>   move cursor

ENTER SEARCH REQUEST:

A search request may be as long as 144 characters, although a content word may be no longer than 16 characters. If a content word with more than 16 characters must be specified, it may be entered as the first 15 characters and the "*" multicharacter wild card.

When a search has been completed, ZyIndex displays a message to indicate the number of files that it has found containing the search request.

Chapter 5

Telecommunications Methods

The efficient movement of electronic impulses from text origin to typographic output device.

THE MOST LIKELY MANNER BY WHICH WORD PROCESSING AND PERSONAL COMPUTER users will access typesetting services is through some form of telecommunications.

It was not long ago in the history of phototypesetting that communication between noncompatible (different models or different manufacturers) input and output devices was either an impossibility or just plain impractical. TTS coding, although considered an industry standard, still did not provide sufficient flexibility to suit the variety of special characters and function codes in use. Compounding this problem was the independent attitude of industry equipment suppliers who consciously designed their input devices to support only their typesetters.

There has been no single event that has shaken the industry enough to result in code standardization, but there has been a significant movement, which has led to a number of alternatives. The movement, of course, is the growing use of word/information processors and personal computers, which represent great storehouses of captured keystrokes that can, under the right circumstances, be released for typesetting output.

SETTING THE STAGE

The telecommunications scenario might unfold in a variety of different ways, depending upon the equipment, software, and services available, as well as the physical distance and cost of the data communications.

In its simplest form, the user directly dials the typesetting service and establishes a working communications link. This link might be accomplished totally under computer control at each end, or it might involve an initial voice contact to be sure that all communications requirements are met. No matter which method is used, once the link is established the word processing file is transmitted directly to the typesetting system, to a dedicated microcomputer system, or to a media-conversion device (FIG. 1).

FIG. 1. A simple telecommunications link involves a direct telephone connection between the sender and one of three receiving options.

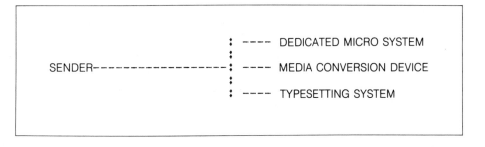

TERMINOLOGY

Even in its simplest form, however, the telecommunications process is quite involved and requires a whole new set of specifications for the new user. Therefore, quite a few new terms must be introduced before we can continue.[1]

[1]These terms are adapted from *Telecommunicating Typesetters,* by Michael L. Kleper, ©1982, Graphic Dimensions, Pittsford, NY.

access time—The time interval between the instant at which there is a request to obtain or store data, and the instant at which the operation is carried out.

acknowledgement—A character or group of characters generated by a receiving station to indicate if data has been correctly transmitted and when the receiver is ready to accept the next transmission.

acoustic coupler—A device that allows a conventional telephone handset to feed its signal into a modem, as opposed to a direct coupler, which feeds the signal directly into a telephone line.

alphanumeric—Shortened form of *alphabetic* and *numeric*. Pertaining to a character or group of characters that are either letters of the alphabet, numbers, or associated symbols. Special codes telling the typesetter or computer what to do are not usually alphanumeric.

alternate routing—A communications path that is used when the normal signal route is unavailable.

analog—1. Having to do with a computer that uses a signal which is of varying intensity, such as "more" or "less" rather than "on" or "off," and which is continuous rather than made up of individual codes. 2. Pertaining to the variable signal itself.

analog-to-digital conversion—The conversion of an analog signal into its digital equivalent. The converter measures the input voltage and outputs a digitally encoded number corresponding to that voltage.

answer back—An identifying code transmitted from a receiving station to indicate a signal has been received.

ASCII—Abbreviation for American Standard Code for Information Interchange, a code based on a seven-level or seven-bit structure, where each of the 128 permutations of the seven bits signifies a particular character. Sometimes an eighth level (bit) is used for a parity check. The ASCII (pronounced "as key") characters include the uppercase and lowercase alphabet, numbers, special symbols, and control codes. One ASCII character can be stored in one byte of memory.

asynchronous—Having a variable time interval between successive characters, bits, or events. Also called *async*.

asynchronous communication—Data transmission where the time interval between characters is allowed to vary. Each character is therefore arranged so as to have "start" and "stop" signals.

auto-answer—An equipment feature that allows a station to respond automatically to a call it receives over a network.

auto-dial—An equipment feature that allows the automatic dialing of a predesignated telephone number.

background processing—A computer operation mode in which two or more jobs or processes seem to be occurring simultaneously. In fact, some processes are assigned a lower, or *background*, priority, and the machine works on them only during those fractions of a second when it is not handling high-priority, or *foreground*, tasks. Electronic mail often is transceived in a background mode.

bandwidth—The difference (in hertz) between the upper and lower limits of wave frequencies transmitted over a communications channel. For example, *broadband* pertains to a communications channel having a bandwidth greater than a voice-grade channel, and therefore capable of higher-speed data transmission. *Narrow band* refers to communications facilities that handle up to 200 bits per second. *Wideband* pertains to a bandwidth capable of carrying large quantities of data.

batch—A group of records or programs that are dealt with as a unit during computer processing.

batch processing—A method of assembling work with similar characteristics for collective processing by a computer. Also referred to as *batching*.

baud—A unit of measurement of the speed at which data is transferred over wire, roughly equivalent to one bit per second. The transfer rate per second can be calculated by dividing the baud number by the number of bits required per character (including parity). Derived from its inventor, the French telegraphic engineer Emile Baudot.

baudot code—A code for the transmission of data in which five bits represent one character.

baud rate—The number of signals that travel over a transmission line in one second.

bell code—A TTS code first used to ring a bell to announce an incoming tape transmission; now used as a flag or precedence code.

binary number system—A number system written in base 2 notation (that is, using only the digits 1 and 0).

bit—1. A binary digit. 2. A data hole in paper or reinforced tape, or a recorded electrical charge on magnetic tape, that is used to signify character codes.

bisynchronous—Shortened form of binary synchronous, referring to a specific type of communications protocol wherein "header" signals are transmitted, followed by a series of synchronizing characters, then the text message, then the "end of text" message, then a checksum. The receiving device is then able to verify the accuracy of the transmitted message and request a repeat if necessary. Also called *bisync*.

black box—An electronic device with visible input and output components, or known input and output, but unknown or incomprehensible contents.

bps—Abbreviation for bits per second, a standard measuring unit of the rate at which digital data is transmitted.

buffer—The portion of a computer memory that stores input until the central processing unit is ready to process it.

byte—The number of consecutive binary digits a computer deals with as a unit. The term was coined by IBM.

check—An automatic or programmed means of testing the accuracy of information transmitted, manipulated, or stored by any unit or device of a computer.

compatibility—The ability of one device to interconnect with another as a result of having the same code, speed, and signal level.

conversational—Pertaining to an operating configuration between a terminal and computer in which each terminal entry is met with a computer response. During the computer response the terminal is locked out of operation.

cross talk—A form of electrical interference caused by the energy transfer from a "disturbing" circuit to a "disturbed" circuit.

dial-up—Pertaining to terminals and systems that have modems for accessing computers by dialing a special computer telephone number, as opposed to terminals that are directly wired to the computer.

download—Shortened form of downline-load, to transmit information from a central storage area to another device or a remote terminal.

driver—A program that controls (drives) the operation of a device or interface. The driver program interprets the computer data, providing the commands and signals required by the device or interface, or provides media output, which is then read by the device.

EBCDIC—Abbreviation for Extended Binary Coded Decimal Interchange Code, a code comprised of 256 eight-bit characters used primarily by IBM and IBM-compatible equipment which use bisync communications.

electronic mail—A message service using electronics and telecommunications to deliver hard or soft copies of information.

EOT—An ASCII code meaning End of Transmission.

error-checking—A method of verifying data transmission by sending redundant information with data so that the receiver can check the data's correctness.

exclusion key—A switch found on some modems that transfers the modem in and out of the telephone circuit in order to permit voice or data operation of the telephone.

explosion command—A keyboard symbol followed by one or two alphanumeric characters that indicate a stored, prespecified multiple-character or multiple-code chain to a machine's processing section.

file—A collection of information with a distinctive name that can be treated by a computer as a single unit.

fixed field—A field that always has a specific number of characters allocated, regardless of the number used or the amount of actual data in the field.

flag—A code used as a signal that the next code or codes will have a special meaning or require special treatment.

foreground—1. The space in the computer where processing tasks can be performed and/or monitored by the operator. 2. The space in the computer where processing tasks with higher priorities are performed.

frame—A screenful of information on a video screen.

frame-store—A technique for displaying information where each picture element of the frame is defined in the terminal's memory.

garbage collecting—In computer jargon, eliminating from a file the storage locations that are no longer needed.

garble—A disturbance or breakdown in the transmission or reception of information, causing a total or partial loss of the message.

general on-line distribution service—An organization that offers a number of databases across many subject and client interest areas, sometimes to a heterogeneous marketplace.

glitch—An unwanted voltage change of exceptionally short duration that a machine interprets as a legitimate signal.

half duplex—Pertaining to a transmission mode in which data can be sent in either of two directions, but in only one direction at a time.

handshaking—Pertaining to an interface wherein a transmitting device sends a signal, then the receiving device sends a "ready" signal before transmission continues.

hash—Electrical noise that disturbs information held in computer memory.

head-end—The electronic equipment located at the start of a transmission system, usually including antennas, preamplifiers, frequency converters, demodulators, modulators, and related equipment.

hexadecimal—Pertaining to a number system using a base of 16, wherein values from 0 to 15 each can be expressed using only one digit. (The values of 9 through 15 are assigned the digits A through F.) Hexadecimal is useful in a computer application since it can be reduced easily to binary figures and allows a fair amount of compacting of numerical data.

initialize—To set various counters, switches, and addresses to zero or another starting value.

integrated on-line database service—An organization that produces and provides access to one or more databases.

interlock—A protective feature, such as a log-on code, that prevents unauthorized access to stored data.

line protocol—The detailed procedure for the exchange of signals between a source and a sink for message transmission.

log—To sign onto (log on) or log off of (log off) a computer system or area. Log-on procedures might require operator passwords, or might be accomplished simply by designating the desired area.

massage—To process within a computer, especially in order to add line endings, page parameters, and positioning instructions. Text is said to be massaged between input and output.

menu—A listing of choices, elements, or references on a terminal display screen that requires an operator's selection in order to continue.

message switching—A technique in which a message is received, stored, and then retransmitted. No direct connection exists between the incoming and outgoing lines. Also called *packet switching*.

modem—Acronym for *mo*dulator/*dem*odulator, a device that converts a digital signal to an analog signal and vice-versa; often used to communicate signals from a telephone line to a computer.

multiplex—To transmit two or more messages simultaneously over the same communications channel to different receivers.

nak—Shortened form of negative acknowledgement, a communications transmission code indicating a message was not received. Also, an unacceptable transmission.

narrowband communications—A communications system capable of carrying only voice or relatively slow-speed computer signals.

noise—A disturbance that creates electrical interference which is interpreted by a system as meaningful pulses.

null-modem cable—A direct-connect cable between communicating devices for serial data transmission.

off-line—Pertaining to equipment or devices that are not in direct communication with the central processing unit of a computer system.

off-line interface—A data communications configuration wherein the two communicating devices are neither physically nor electronically connected. An example is a floppy disk (and the hardware and software needed to read from and write to the disk), which is readable by two like devices.

on-line—Pertaining to equipment or devices that are in direct communication with the central processing unit of a computer system.

paced transmission—A transmission mode in which the transmitter is turned off and on by a receiver to prevent data overflow.

packet—An addressed data unit of convenient size for transmission through a network.

parallel transmission—A transmission scheme that uses one data line for each bit.

parity check—A method of verifying the accuracy of a transmitted bit pattern by examining the code to determine whether its value is odd or even.

point-to-point—Pertaining to a protocol used to communicate between two devices that are identical.

poll—The activity of a central computer in monitoring each peripheral device in turn to see if the device requires processing time.

port—A communications channel between a computer and another device, such as a terminal or a tape reader.

protocol—The proper procedure for data transmission for a particular input device, with regard to code structure, identification of text stream, and code recognition. Common protocols follow.

2741—A protocol that transmits one line at a time, has no error checking, has a speed usually of 134.5 baud, and uses correspondence code.

BISYNC (2780)—A protocol that transmits one block of characters at a time, has error checking, has a speed usually of 2400 baud, and uses EBCDIC.

TTY—A protocol that transmits one character at a time, has no error checking, uses any speed, and uses ASCII.

CMC—A protocol that transmits one line at a time, has no error checking, has a speed usually of 134.5 baud, and uses a superset of correspondence code.

queue—A line of jobs in storage awaiting processing in the order the computer has specified. After jobs are stacked in queue, the operator is free to input other work. Queues can be FIFO (first in, first out) or LIFO (last in, first out).

RS-232—A technical specification for voltage levels and timing that describes the interface criteria for typesetters, word processors, computers, modems, and communications lines. Written by the Electronics Industries Association.

serial transmission—The transmission of characters on a bit-by-bit basis.

signal—The electrical quantity that conveys data from one point to another.

signal-to-noise ratio—The relative power of a data signal to the invalid noise in a message.

simplex—Pertaining to a circuit capable of transmission in one direction only. A television is a simplex device, since it cannot transmit data, only receive it.

simultaneous transmission—The transmission of data in two directions at once—both sending and receiving—by the same device.

sink—The receiving station or a data transmission or electrical connection.

spike—An irregular current surge that can disrupt a system and damage circuitry. Also called a *line hit*.

start bit—In asynchronous transmission, a marker preceding each character or character group.

stop bit—In asynchronous transmission, a marker following each character.

store and forward—An electronic mail technique in which many messages are collected and retained in a computer for eventual high-speed transmission in a single batch.

synchronous—Occurring concurrently and with a regular or predictable time relationship. In transmission, referring to the ability of the sending and receiving devices to run continuously at the same frequency. Also called *sync*.

telecommunications—The transmission of signals by telegraph, telephone, radio, satellite, or some other means that does not involve physical connection between the sending and receiving devices.

Teletypesetter (TTS)—A trademark for a six-level coding system first used by newspaper wire services for tape-driven hot metal typesetting machines.

transfer rate—The rate at which data is moved to and from a storage device.

transparent—Pertaining to a process that is not visible to the user or to other devices.

uplink—Transmission of a signal from an earth station to a satellite for retransmission to another earth station.

USASCII—Abbreviation for United States of America Standard Code for International Interchange.

voice-grade—Referring to the capability of a data transmission circuit to permit a transfer rate of up to 2400 bits per second.

XMT—Abbreviation for transmit.

MITE:
Establishing a Telecommunications Session

In a typesetting environment it is vitally important to be able to move information from one machine to another. This communication might be either the transmission or the reception of data. It might mean receiving information over the telephone line from a customer, or transferring data through a direct cable connection from a local microcomputer to an in-house typesetting machine.

Most microcomputers do not have an innate communications capability. In order to send and receive data, a microcomputer must have a serial port (RS-232), a modem[2] and communications software. There are many choices in terms of software and hardware combinations, features, and capabilities.

Hardware Considerations

In terms of the hardware, a number of considerations are important in selecting a modem. Among them are:

Speed. Modems are rated according to the number of bits of data they can send or receive in one second. The bits-per-second measurement, or *baud rate*, is generally ten times the actual number of alphanumeric characters that are communicated. A 1200-baud transmission rate, for example, would actually result in approximately 120 characters. The reason for the difference is that a character is composed of a string of eight ones and zeros. The string usually is preceded by a bit that indicates the beginning of the string and is followed by a bit that serves as an error check.

The optimum baud rate for any one communications situation can vary considerably. For long-distance telephone transmissions, a high baud rate is almost always preferable, although on untreated telephone lines higher baud rates tend to be more unreliable, and therefore require frequent retransmissions,[3] thus reducing the character throughput substantially. Higher baud rates also usually mean higher initial modem costs.

[2]A modem installed internally, on the microcomputer bus (i.e., in a slot), does not usually require a separate serial port connection.

[3]The retransmission of information is handled automatically by systems that utilize error checking.

Although the receiving or sending microcomputer might be able to attain very high baud rates, the communicating systems must match their baud rates, as well as a number of other items of communications protocol. (These items include duplex, file transfer protocol, parity, number of data bits, etc.) It is the highest baud rate common to both systems that is the highest common denominator for communication.

Auto-Answer/Auto-Dial. Computers usually use the same telephone lines that are used for voice communications, and are therefore prone not only to various forms of interference, but also to busy signals. An automatic dialing capability not only makes it possible to keep a directory of telephone numbers within the system (if supported by software), but also makes it possible to automatically redial a number until a carrier signal from a remote computer is detected (if supported by software).

An automatic answer capability, when activated, leaves the computer in a ready state, awaiting a call from a remote computer. When the call is received, the computer sends out a carrier signal, which electronically links the two systems in unison.

Call Monitoring. If every telephone call were successful, it would not be necessary to know why a call was not completed. Invariably, however, attempts to link two communications devices over telephone lines fail because of busy signals, poor connections, wrong numbers, line faults, and other equally annoying problems. Knowing that a call was not successful does not supply sufficient information to know how to proceed. A user needs to know why the call failed. Many modems have a speaker, which provides audible feedback of the dialing process, the line status (busy, ringing, or otherwise), and the response of the receiver.

Software Considerations

Gaining access to the capabilities within the modem is a function of the communications software. The software serves many general functions, such as providing control of:

- The physical communications settings, such as port location, baud rate, duplex, etc.
- The storage and retrieval of disk-based data.
- An on-line printer for simultaneous or delayed printing.
- The terminal display (number of characters per line, colors for background and foreground, terminal emulation, etc.).
- Disk access for file listing, removing, renaming, appending, and other maintenance operations.
- The specification of error-checking methodology.
- The specification, storage, and use of macro strings.
- The filtering of unwanted incoming characters.
- The addition of a carriage return (CR) and/or line feed (LF) at the end of each incoming line.
- The specification, storage, and use of auto log-on strings.
- The editing of incoming or outgoing text.
- The conversion of files from different operating systems.
- The transmission of ASCII or binary files.

Although not all communications software programs support these capabilities, others support these as well as additional features.

MITE

An example of a program that provides all of the software control just listed, as well as much more is MITE from Mycroft Labs, Inc.[4] MITE is a menu-driven program that supports data communications and file transfer over telephone lines, as well as through a hardwire connection.

The MITE screen provides a three-line system status, which remains throughout the communications session. It indicates the MITE version number; whether the remote device is directly connected, on-line, or off-line; the number of bytes that have been captured out of the total number of bytes the system can retain; whether the capture mode is on or off; and the identity of the remote communications site (FIG. 2).

At start-up, the program defaults to off-line mode status (see line #2 in the screen shown in FIG. 2). In order to set the system for telecommunications, the ''P'' option is invoked, resulting in the display of the Parameter menu (FIG. 3).

The Parameter menu provides the means of specifying the communications requirements for the session. Items are selected by typing a single letter, such as *B* for Baud Rate, and then a value. The telephone number must be added, as well as any other

FIG. 2. The MITE Main menu with its omnipresent three-line status display.

```
MITE v3.xx  - Copyright (c) 1983, Mycroft Labs, Inc.
OFFLINE. Bytes Captured =     0/#####. Capture = OFF.
Site ID =

MAIN MENU

     G - Go Start Communications
     H - Hang Up Phone
     I - Enter Site ID
     L - Load Parameters from Disk File
     S - Save Parameters on Disk File

            Sub-Menus:

     P - Parameter          O - Option
     U - Text File Upload    D - Text File Download
     B - Binary File Xfer    M - Macro Definition
     C - Command Processor   F - Character Filter
     T - Special Features    E - Emulation

     X - Exit to Operating System

Enter Option: _
```

FIG. 3. The Parameter menu.

```
MITE v3.xx  - Copyright (c) 1983, Mycroft Labs, Inc.
DIRECT.  Bytes Captured =     0/#####. Capture = OFF.
Site ID =

PARAMETER MENU

     B - Baud Rate              =   300
     D - Data Bits              = 7
     P - Parity                 = EVEN
     S - Stop Bits              = 1

     R - Role (ANS/ORG)         = ORG
     E - Entry Password         =
     M - Mode (Duplex)          = FULL

     A - Auto Redial Count      = 0
     N - Phone Number           =
     I - Modem Init String      =
     H - Dial Prefix            =

     X - Exit to Main Menu

Enter Option: _
```

[4]Mycroft Labs, Inc.
P.O. Box 6045
Tallahassee, FL 32314
(904) 385-1141

Available in versions for CP/M, CP/M-86, MS-DOS, PC-DOS, and Apple Macintosh.

parameter required for the session. For example, some modems have an internal command set that triggers certain functions, such as auto dial (AT or ATD), which would be inserted in selection ''I,'' Modem Init String. Typing ''X'' returns the user to the Main menu.

In the Main menu, the ''G'' selection initiates the communications process. The telephone number is dialed, the remote computer responds, and communication is established. Provided that all of the parameter specifications are met, MITE can be used to communicate with any computer, from a laptop to a mainframe.

A number of submenus, of which Parameter is one, offer increased functionality as well as individualization. Some of the capabilities include the following.

Option Menu Capabilities (FIG. 4).

- Defining an ''Escape Trigger'' character will permit the user to jump between being on-line with a remote system and accessing other parts of the MITE program, without breaking the remote communications link.
- Defining a ''Macro Trigger'' character, when followed by a digit between 0 and 9, will result in the display of a previously defined macro string.
- Defining a ''Break Trigger'' character will send a communications line-break function (a space condition for 150 milliseconds). This character generally is used to ''break out'' of a remote computer operation.
- Defining ''Local and Remote Command Trigger'' characters prompt the user for information concerning such things as reading and writing files, turning the screen on or off, initiating a character delay, checking the buffer statistics, and accessing the help files. These commands are a shorthand means of accessing capabilities that are available through normal menus, and normally are used only by more experienced users. The Remote Command Trigger allows the user of the remote computer to access capabilities in the MITE program, and therefore function as if sitting at the MITE-controlled machine.
- Selecting the ''Caps Lock'' option converts all incoming and outgoing characters to uppercase.
- Selecting the ''LF after CR'' causes a line feed to be sent to the local console any time a carriage return character is received. This is necessary because some computers only send a carriage return, this option would result in each line overprinting at the local computer, rather than advancing (scrolling) normally.
- Selecting the ''TWX Mode'' modifies MITE to allow the microcomputer to function as a Western Union TELEX terminal.

FIG. 4. The Option menu.

```
MITE v3.xx  -  Copyright (c) 1983, Mycroft Labs, Inc.
OFFLINE. Bytes Captured =     0/#####. Capture = OFF.
Site ID =

OPTION MENU

      E - Escape Trigger Char = 0AH = ^J
      M - Macro Trigger Char  = 1BH = ^C
      B - Break Trigger Char  = 02H = ^B
      K - Local Command Char   = 0BH = ^K
      R - Remote Command Char = 12H = ^R

      C - Caps Lock           = OFF
      L - Auto LF after CR    = OFF
      T - TWX Mode            = OFF
      D - Direct Connect Mode = OFF
      Q - Expand Tabs to CON  = ON

      X - Exit to Main Menu

Enter Option (? for help): _
```

- Selecting the "Direct Connect Mode" fools the computer into thinking that it has received the carrier signal and is connected to another computer. This mode is utilized for directly connecting two computers via direct cable (i.e., without a modem).
- Selecting the "Expand Tabs to CON" expands a tab character to the eighth space position on the receiving console line.

Text File Upload Menu Capabilities (FIG. 5).

- Selecting "Upload Text File" prompts the user for the name of the file that is to be uploaded from the local computer to the remote system. This option would be used, for example, to send a word processing file over telephone lines to a typesetting service.
- Selecting "Interchar. Delay" provides the user with the ability to slow down outgoing text from 0 to 255 milliseconds in order to meet the needs of a particularly slow remote system. In order to have any effect, the delay must be more than the normal delay associated with the baud rate. At 300 baud, for example, each character requires about 33 milliseconds to be transmitted; therefore, any delay value less than 33 will not have any effect. This option does not have any effect on baud rate, merely the rate at which characters are sent within the baud rate.
- Selecting "Await Char. Echo" gives the user the ability to require that the remote computer echo each character before another character is sent. This option ensures that data is not lost, although it usually results in halving the throughput speed.
- Selecting "CR/LR Handshaking" specifies that any time a carriage return is sent from the local computer, MITE will wait for the remote computer to send back a line feed command. This capability often is required on timesharing systems.
- Selecting "Turnaround Char." programs MITE to wait at the end of each line until it sees the specified turnaround character from the remote system. Some remote systems, for example, prompt with a question mark. MITE would recognize the "?" as indicating that the system is ready to accept another line. If MITE does not sense the turnaround character after 20 seconds, it automatically sends the next line.
- Selecting "Garbage Char. Count" refers to the number of characters that MITE will wait for after transmitting a line and before starting to send the next line. Each garbage character has a 1/2 second time-out.
- Selecting "Strip Controls" tells MITE to remove control characters from a file as it is being sent to a remote system. This option would be helpful, for example, for removing formatting and printing control sequences from WordStar files.

FIG. 5. The Text File Upload menu.

```
MITE v3.xx  -  Copyright (c) 1983, Mycroft Labs, Inc.
OFFLINE. Bytes Captured =      0/*****. Capture = OFF.
Site ID =

TEXT FILE UPLOAD MENU

    U - Upload Text File

    D - Interchar. Delay          = 000
    E - Await Char. Echo          = OFF
    H - CR/LF Handshaking         = ON
    T - Turnaround Char.          = 00H = ^@
    G - Garbage Char. Count       = 000

    S - Strip Controls            = OFF

    X - Exit to Main Menu

Enter Option (? for help): _
```

Text File Download Menu Capabilities (FIG. 6).

- Selecting "Capture Mode" instructs MITE to save all or part of a communications session on disk.
- Selecting "Capture Indicator" causes MITE to precede each incoming line with a colon to indicate that it is being captured. When the text buffer falls below 4K, the colon changes to an asterisk to warn the operator of a low buffer situation.
- Selecting "Append Captured Data" provides the user with the option of saving a portion of the buffer to a file and continuing. By so doing, multiple buffers-full can be appended to a single file.
- Selecting "Write Captured Data" causes any captured data to be written to the file that was originally specified when Capture mode was first enabled.
- Selecting "Reset Capture Buffer" clears the buffer.
- Selecting "Printer Echo" causes the printer to print whatever is being displayed on the console.
- Selecting "Type Capture Buffer" displays the contents of the buffer in blocks of 23 lines. The listing continues by typing a carriage return, or is aborted by typing **ESC**.
- Selecting "Flow Control" enables X-on/X-off handshaking, which is used to signal to the remote computer to send or stop sending data. MITE uses this handshaking when it needs to pause while data is being received in order to write to disk. The flow-control characters (normally CTRL-Q to start and CTRL-S to stop) are set using the "Q" and "S" options.

FIG. 6. The Text File Download menu.

```
MITE v3.xx  -  Copyright (c) 1983, Mycroft Labs, Inc.
OFFLINE, Bytes Captured =    0/*****, Capture = OFF,
Site ID =

TEXT FILE DOWNLOAD MENU

     C - Capture Mode          = OFF
     I - Capture Indicator     = ON
     A - Append Captured Data
     W - Write Captured Data
     R - Reset Capture Buffer
     P - Printer Echo          = OFF
     T - Type Capture Buffer

     F - Flow Control          = OFF
     Q - Flow Start Char.      = 11H = ^Q
     S - Flow Stop Char.       = 13H = ^S

     X - Exit to Main Menu

Enter Option (? for help): _
```

Binary File Transfer Menu Capabilities (FIG. 7).

- Selecting the "Protocol" option sets the protocol used to transfer binary files from one system to the other. The choices are MITE, XMODEM (typically used on RCPM systems), XMODEM/B (used to transfer a batch of files, such as: • all those ending in ".ASM") • CLINK (compatible with Crosstalk) • HAYES (Smartcom) • IBMPC (Asynchronous Support Package, no error checking or retransmission) • TEXT (ASCII text file protocol with error checking and recovery).

- Selecting "CRC Option (XMODEM)" activates the CRC error-checking routine for either XMODEM protocol.
- Selecting "Send File and Return to Link" causes MITE to prompt the user for the name of the file to be sent. As the file is sent, a period will appear on the console to indicate each block that is transmitted and acknowledged as correct. At the conclusion of the transmission, MITE will display the message: *File Sent.*
- Selecting "Receive File and Return to Link" causes MITE to prompt the user for the name of the file to be saved. As the file is received, a period will be displayed on the console to indicate each correctly received block. At the end of the transmission, MITE will display the message: *File Received.*

FIG. 7. The Binary File Transfer menu.

```
MITE v3.xx  -  Copyright (c) 1983, Mycroft Labs, Inc.
OFFLINE. Bytes Captured =     0/#####. Capture = OFF.
Site ID =

BINARY FILE TRANSFER MENU

     P - Protocol            = XMODEM
     C - CRC Option (XMODEM) = OFF

     S - Send File and Return to Link
     R - Receive File and Return to Link

     X - Exit to Main Menu

Enter option (? for help): _
```

FIG. 8. The Macro String Definition menu.

```
MITE v3.xx  -  Copyright (c) 1983, Mycroft Labs, Inc.
OFFLINE. Bytes Captured =     0/#####. Capture = OFF.
Site ID =

MACRO STRING DEFINITION MENU

     0: mailck^M
     1: mail read^M
     2: post scan cp/m^M
     3: off^M
     4:
     5:
     6:
     7:
     8:
     9: ^M@W^M@E@T=d1^M@T@c 30128^M@T>id tcm495 xxxxx^M

     X - Exit to Main Menu

Enter Option (? for help): _
```

Macro String Definition Menu Capabilities (FIG. 8). This menu provides the user with the capability to view and define up to 10 macro strings, each of which can be up to 62 characters in length. Printable as well as control characters can be entered.

Unwanted Character Filter Menu Capabilities (FIG. 9). This menu allows the user to specify up to 10 characters that should be ignored if sent from the remote computer. The ASCII character value can be specified in either decimal or hexadecimal form.

FIG. 9. The Unwanted Character Filter menu.

```
MITE v3.xx  -  Copyright (c) 1983, Mycroft Labs, Inc.
OFFLINE. Bytes Captured =      0/#####. Capture = OFF.
Site ID =

UNWANTED CHARACTER FILTER DEFINITION MENU

        0: 7FH =
        1: 1AH = ^Z
        2: 00H = ^@
        3: 00H = ^@
        4: 00H = ^@
        5: 00H = ^@
        6: 00H = ^@
        7: 00H = ^@
        8: 00H = ^@
        9: 00H = ^@

        X - Exit to Main Menu

Enter Option (? for help): _
```

Special Features Menu Capabilities (FIG. 10). This menu (not available on all versions) provides access to serial port selection and serial port address. Color monitor display attributes also can be set.

Most communications situations require only a handful of settings, although having access to the variety of settings available in a program such as MITE ensures that the greatest number of communication encounters will be satisfied.

FIG. 10. The Special Features menu.

```
MITE v3.xx  -  Copyright (c) 1983, Mycroft Labs, Inc.
OFFLINE. Bytes Captured =      0/#####. Capture = OFF.
Site ID =

SPECIAL FEATURES MENU

        C - Comm Port                  = 1
        B - Port Base Address          = 03F8H
        V - Interrupt Vector Address   = 0030H

        N - Normal Foreground Color    = E
        M - Normal Background Color    = 1
        H - Hi-Lite Foreground Color   = E
        I - Hi-Lite Background Color   = 4

        X - Exit to Main Menu

Enter option: -
```

BLAST: Ensuring Data Integrity

Two of the necessary requirements for telecommunications within a typesetting environment are the assurances that data is received accurately and that the communication link responds reliably. Without the absolute certainty that the data that is received is exactly the same as what was sent, a typesetting operation would be prone to typographic and content-related errors. The consequences of an erroneous transmission could be as simple as typographic errors of a textual nature, which might be discovered during proofreading, or as serious as numeric errors in financial information, which might not be detected at all.

Data Transmission

Data generally is communicated in one of two data formats: either eight-bit binary or seven-bit ASCII. In binary form, a file is coded in machine language, representing either an executable set of computer instructions or binary-coded text. A string of eight binary bits, such as 10011111, would be interpreted as the contents of a *register* (a single word of memory that is directly accessible by the microprocessor), and would not have a direct alphanumeric identity. In ASCII coding, which is used for the communication of text data, each character is composed of a string of seven binary bits, the leftmost bit (eighth bit) always being zero since it is not used. In ASCII coding, an *A* is represented as 01000001. Almost every communications situation provides the user with the option of selecting a byte size of either seven or eight bits. A seven-bit byte usually would mean that only text data is being transmitted, whereas an eight-bit byte specification would mean that either text or computer instructions could be received.

Textual information that is useful for typesetting generally comes only from a portion of the ASCII code table (FIG. 11). The codes in the range of 32 to 127 (decimal) are what are termed the *printable characters;* that is, the alphanumerics. The other codes, ranging from 0 to 31 (decimal) are the *ASCII control codes,* which handle such things as line feeds and end-of-transmission signals.

There is a need to distinguish between two different types of ASCII files. The standard ASCII text file is composed solely of printable ASCII characters plus four impor-

FIG. 11. The ASCII character set, along with decimal and hexadecimal equivalents (From the BLAST manual, courtesy of Communications Research Group).

ASCII Character Set

dec	hex	ascii	!	dec	hex	ascii	!	dec	hex	ascii	!	dec	hex	ascii
0	00	nul	!	32	20	space	!	64	40	@	!	96	60	'
1	01	soh	!	33	21	!!	!	65	41	A	!	97	61	a
2	02	stx	!	34	22	"	!	66	42	B	!	98	62	b
3	03	etx	!	35	23	#	!	67	43	C	!	99	63	c
4	04	eot	!	36	24	$	!	68	44	D	!	100	64	d
5	05	enq	!	37	25	%	!	69	45	E	!	101	65	e
6	06	ack	!	38	26	&	!	70	46	F	!	102	66	f
7	07	bel	!	39	27	'	!	71	47	G	!	103	67	g
8	08	bs	!	40	28	(	!	72	48	H	!	104	68	h
9	09	ht	!	41	29	)	!	73	49	I	!	105	69	i
10	0A	lf	!	42	2A	*	!	74	4A	J	!	106	6A	j
11	0B	vt	!	43	2B	+	!	75	4B	K	!	107	6B	k
12	0C	ff	!	44	2C	,	!	76	4C	L	!	108	6C	l
13	0D	cr	!	45	2D	-	!	77	4D	M	!	109	6D	m
14	0E	so	!	46	2E	.	!	78	4E	N	!	110	6E	n
15	0F	si	!	47	2F	/	!	79	4F	O	!	111	6F	o
16	10	dle	!	48	30	0	!	80	50	P	!	112	70	p
17	11	dc1	!	49	31	1	!	81	51	Q	!	113	71	q
18	12	dc2	!	50	32	2	!	82	52	R	!	114	72	r
19	13	dc3	!	51	33	3	!	83	53	S	!	115	73	s
20	14	dc4	!	52	34	4	!	84	54	T	!	116	74	t
21	15	nak	!	53	35	5	!	85	55	U	!	117	75	u
22	16	syn	!	54	36	6	!	86	56	V	!	118	76	v
23	17	etb	!	55	37	7	!	87	57	W	!	119	77	w
24	18	can	!	56	38	8	!	88	58	X	!	120	78	x
25	19	em	!	57	39	9	!	89	59	Y	!	121	79	y
26	1A	sub	!	58	3A	:	!	90	5A	Z	!	122	7A	z
27	1B	esc	!	59	3B	;	!	91	5B	[	!	123	7B	{
28	1C	fs	!	60	3C	<	!	92	5C	\	!	124	7C	|
29	1D	gs	!	61	3D	=	!	93	5D	]	!	125	7D	}
30	1E	rs	!	62	3E	>	!	94	5E	∧	!	126	7E	~
31	1F	us	!	63	3F	?	!	95	5F	_	!	127	7F	del

tant ASCII control characters: <return> (carriage return), LF (line feed), FF (form feed), and HT (horizontal tab). A word processing file, on the other hand, usually contains some eight-bit binary codes, many ASCII control codes, and of course the printable ASCII characters. The control codes activate such things as page (margins, headers, etc.) and character (bold, italic, etc.) formatting. Such a file must be treated as a binary file rather than a text file.

Many word processing programs have utilities that let the user save a file either as a normally encoded binary file or as a plain ASCII file. In general, plain ASCII files are what are sent to typesetting services, because of the lack of ambiguity as to each code's identity. In some cases, however, it is beneficial to capture some of the binary control codes in order to convert them into meaningful typesetting commands. A word processing code that activates a change to italic, for example, might be translated to the proper typesetting command for that result, and thus save considerable time in recoding.

The common error-detection methods that are generally used might or might not be effective. In the transmission of asynchronous data, for example, parity often is used as a means of ensuring that each byte is properly composed. A single byte would look like this:

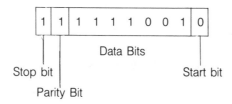

The function of the parity bit is to provide a consistent odd or even count of the number of 1's. If the parity is set to "even," then the parity bit will be set to either 1 or 0 in order to make the count of 1's an even value. Odd parity would work in a similar way. If an incorrect parity count is received, any of a number of possible actions might ensue. The receiving terminal might display an error message, it might activate an audible tone, or it might execute some corrective measures. Although parity can be set to "odd" or "even," in order to detect errors, it also can be set to "none" in order to deactivate it.

Error-Free Protocol

Two of the major causes of errors in data transfer are noisy telephone lines and circuits that are subject to *propagation delay* (a measure of the time required for a pulse to pass through from device to device). Two such circuits are satellite links and network virtual circuits. In these situations, the communications methods commonly used are often unreliable. A solution is the BLAST[5] asynchronous communications error-free protocol.

BLAST is a communications program that incorporates the BLAST error-free file-transfer protocol for use with binary or text files. It can be used with dial-up modems, hard-wire hook-ups, and network virtual circuits. It is a significant alternative communications standard, which has been implemented in software products for more than 100 different micro, mini, and mainframe computers. Many of its versions also support terminal emulation, text file upload and capture, and auto-dial modem capabilities.

A key to the BLAST error-free concept is the use of the BLAST software on both the sending and receiving computers. The BLAST protocol sends data in very small serial strings, called *blocks*. The smallness of the blocks makes them easier targets to

[5]Communications Research Group
8939 Jefferson Highway
Baton Rouge, LA 70809

Previous portions of this section are based upon information in the MS/DOS BLAST manual, Rev. 7.

capture at the receiving end, and makes them more likely to navigate a noisy telephone line without becoming altered.

The BLAST protocol works in *full duplex;* that is, it can simultaneously send and receive data. As data is being sent, BLAST monitors the remote computer in order to determine which blocks were properly received and which need to be sent again. This type of communications monitoring is termed *sliding-window* operation.

Because BLAST effectively can communicate in both send and receive modes at the same time, it can effectively halve long-distance telephone costs, and cut communications time in half when files need to be sent in both directions.

For the BLAST error-free protocol to be initiated, both systems must be properly configured with the BLAST software and placed in Log-On mode. In Log-On mode the program outputs an eight-bit log-on code once every second. This code can be displayed on the computer screen as the letter *P*. When the program has received two identical log-on codes in a row, it assumes that it is communicating with another BLAST system and that is has an eight-bit data path between the two devices. It then displays the *Communications Established* message on the screen. This message must appear at both sites before communications can commence.

There are four options that can be selected during an error-free data transfer session:

- Files can be sent to the remote system.
- The remote system can be requested to send a file to the local system.
- Messages can be sent to the remote system (for informational purposes only).
- Operating system file-management commands, such as ''DIR,'' or ''RENAME,'' can be sent to the remote system.

To confirm that a BLAST configuration is operating properly, Communications Research Group, the publisher of BLAST, maintains a 24-hour-per-day, 7-day-per-week dial-in line. Using log-on information supplied with the purchase of the program, a user is able to communicate with the CRG computer running BLAST and practice file-transfer procedures.

During a telecommunications session, BLAST monitors the quality of the outgoing and incoming telephone circuits, reporting it in terms of its throughput of ''good blocks'' (FIG. 12). It also displays the percent of the transfer that has been completed and saved to disk on the receiving computer. A display of the number of blocks to be sent (block count) is shown, and is decreased as each block is sent and acknowledged.

Commands input to control one or more communications functions can be entered interactively or input from a file. When they are input from a file, a series of functions can be specified, as they are in an autoexec file on an IBM PC. For example, if a typesetting service wanted to retrieve Chapter 4 from an author's computer, send a report concerning the status or completed work, delete a remote file of a previous report, and send a message concerning artwork, the file would look like this:

COMMAND	MEANING
get	get a file
chap4.txt	name of file to get
send	send a file
reprt03.txt	name of file to send
remote-functions	access Remote Functions menu
erase	erase remote file
reprt02.txt	name of file to erase
xit	return to Error-Free menu
message	send a message

Where are the illustrations for section 3.2?

```
        E R R O R - F R E E   C O M M U N I C A T I O N S   M O D E

   S-send file   ST-send text file    M-send message      R-remote functions
   G-get file    GT-get text file     L-local functions   C-continue display
                                                           X-exit to main menu
                          Enter desired option:


   ............................. LOCAL DISPLAY AREA .......................
   *** Waiting for logon with remote system
   *** Communications established with remote system




                          REMOTE DISPLAY AREA ......................



   ............ line quality ............ xfer pct completed ............ block count ............
        SND=    % / RCV=   %      SND=   % / RCV=   %      SND=    / RCV=
```

FIG. 12. The BLAST Error-Free Communications Mode menu (Courtesy of Communications Research Group).

```
        R E C E I V E   T R A N S L A T I O N   T A B L E

        | 0  1  2  3    4  5  6  7    8  9  A  B    C  D  E  F
   :::: |................................................................................
   00 | -- -- -- --    -- -- -- 07   08 09 0A 0B   -- -- -- --
   10 | -- -- -- --    -- -- -- --   -- -- -- 1B   -- -- -- --
   20 | 20 21 22 23    24 25 26 27   28 29 2A 2B   2C 2D 2E 2F
   30 | 30 31 32 33    34 35 36 37   38 39 3A 3B   3C 3D 3E 3F
      |
   40 | 40 41 42 43    44 45 46 47   48 49 4A 4B   4C 4D 4E 4F
   50 | 50 51 52 53    54 55 56 57   58 59 5A 5B   5C 5D 5E 5F
   60 | 60 61 62 63    64 65 66 67   68 69 6A 6B   6C 6D 6E 6F
   70 | 70 71 72 73    74 75 76 77   78 79 7A 7B   7C 7D 7E 7F
      |
   80 | -- -- -- --    -- -- -- 07   08 09 0A 0B   -- -- -- --
   90 | -- -- -- --    -- -- -- --   -- -- -- 1B   -- -- -- --
   A0 | 20 21 22 23    24 25 26 27   28 29 2A 2B   2C 2D 2E 2F
   B0 | 30 31 32 33    34 35 36 37   38 39 3A 3B   3C 3D 3E 3F
      |
   C0 | 40 41 42 43    44 45 46 47   48 49 4A 4B   4C 4D 4E 4F
   D0 | 50 51 52 53    54 55 56 57   58 59 5A 5B   5C 5D 5E 5F
   E0 | 60 61 62 63    64 65 66 67   68 69 6A 6B   6C 6D 6E 6F
   F0 | 70 71 72 73    74 75 76 77   78 79 7A 7B   7C 7D 7E 7F
```

Enter hexadecimal value of character to change (or <return> only to exit):

FIG. 13. The Receive Translation table is user-alterable in order to convert any incoming code into any other code. To read the table, first determine the hexadecimal value that the remote system is sending. For example, if it is C2, first locate the value C0 along the outer left column. Next locate the number 2 along the top row. The intersection of the two values is the number 42, which represents the ASCII character B (Courtesy of Communications Research Group).

In its terminal mode, some versions of BLAST support the use of translation tables during both the reception and transmission of data (FIGS. 13 AND 14). A translation table is used to alter the identity of an incoming or outgoing character, or to totally eliminate it from the communications process.

As a BLAST session is initiated, the user can create a log file, in order to keep an exact listing of all of the actions taking place in both the local and remote display areas.

A powerful capability of BLAST is the Batch Control command feature, which provides the user with the capability to: • branch to a label • conditionally branch to a label • set and test a loop counter • pause a specified period of time • wait until a specified time of day.

A batch control file contains batch control commands, labels (which can be used to branch from point to point), menu selections, and any normal response that would be entered during an interactive session. Such a file can be used to automatically log onto a remote system at some future time, retrieve information and leave information, and sign off. It also can be used to construct a "bulletin board," entering a slave mode in response to incoming calls.

The BLAST protocol method is one way to ensure that the send/receive environments of two physically separated, and possibly dissimilar, systems share sufficient common processing routines to guarantee 100 percent data integrity.

FIG. 14. The Transmit Translation table works in a similar way to the Receive Translation table. It is useful for stripping out codes that the receiving computer cannot process, and for communicating with a remote system that is not equipped with BLAST (Courtesy of Communications Research Group).

```
      T R A N S M I T    T R A N S L A T I O N    T A B L E

 :::  | :::::::::::::::::: ::::::::::::::::: ::::::::::::::::::: ::::::::::::::::
      | 0  1  2  3     4  5  6  7     8  9  A  B     C  D  E  F
 00   | 00 01 02 03    04 05 06 07    08 09 0A 0B    0C 0D 0E 0F
 10   | 10 11 12 13    14 15 16 17    18 19 1A 1B    1C 1D 1E 1F
 20   | 20 21 22 23    24 25 26 27    28 29 2A 2B    2C 2D 2E 2F
 30   | 30 31 32 33    34 35 36 37    38 39 3A 3B    3C 3D 3E 3F
      |
 40   | 40 41 42 43    44 45 46 47    48 49 4A 4B    4C 4D 4E 4F
 50   | 50 51 52 53    54 55 56 57    58 59 5A 5B    5C 5D 5E 5F
 60   | 60 61 62 63    64 65 66 67    68 69 6A 6B    6C 6D 6E 6F
 70   | 70 71 72 73    74 75 76 77    78 79 7A 7B    7C 7D 7E 7F
      |
 80   | 80 81 82 83    84 85 86 87    88 89 8A 8B    8C 8D 8E 8F
 90   | 90 91 92 93    94 95 96 97    98 99 9A 9B    9C 9D 9E 9F
 A0   | A0 A1 A2 A3    A4 A5 A6 A7    A8 A9 AA AB    AC AD AE AF
 B0   | B0 B1 B2 B3    B4 B5 B6 B7    B8 B9 BA BB    BC BD BE BF
      |
 C0   | C0 C1 C2 C3    C4 C5 C6 C7    C8 C9 CA CB    CC CD CE CF
 D0   | D0 D1 D2 D3    D4 D5 D6 D7    D8 D9 DA DB    DC DD DE DF
 E0   | E0 E1 E2 E3    E4 E5 E6 E7    E8 E9 EA EB    EC ED EE EF
 F0   | F0 F1 F2 F3    F4 F5 F6 F7    F8 F9 FA FB    FC FD FE FF


 Enter hexadecimal value of character to change (or <return>
 only to exit:
```

Let's Talk:
Recording and Storing Telecommunicated Text On-line

The telephone remains one of the most popular and powerful means of moving information from a text originator to a typesetting service. Telephone lines link virtually any two points together, with a minimum of hardware complexity and site preparation. Yet, for communication to take place, there must be a coordinated effort on both ends of the telephone line—with the originator of the communication and with the receiver.

Typesetting operations are, by their very nature, time-sensitive environments. The information that is processed into typeset form is often perishable, with strict deadline requirements. It is, therefore, usually unreasonable to interrupt the typesetting process in order to set up the typesetter for a telephone transmission.

There exist a number of dedicated media processing devices that monitor incoming telephone calls, filter transmitted data through a translation table (in order to render it in a compatible form), and record the converted data to disk. These devices not only tend to be expensive, but they also are limited in the functions they can perform and the machine formats they can support.

A more ideal situation would be a telephone monitoring system that would meet these criteria:

- Provide access to the receiving station only to legitimate users.
- Maintain complete file management of incoming data.
- Provide on-line assistance, i.e., help files, menus, and operator prompts.
- Provide security (password protection) for all client work.
- Provide an activity log of calls since the last system purge.
- Provide a means of displaying messages, updates, and other system instructions to remote users.
- Provide system statistics, showing the names of users, their log-on and log-off times, the size of their files, and the remaining file space in the system.

Such a system would operate on an unattended microcomputer connected to one or more dedicated, "clean" telephone lines. It would function in a manner similar to an on-line computer information service, offering the user a menu-driven shell that supports the means to access information as well as to upload files. This kind of capability is available for a number of microcomputers, including the Apple III, *IIe*, *IIc*, and IIGS, with the availability of the "Let's Talk" program from Russ Systems.[6]

```
01      00687        Edit                     Escape to QUIT
---------------------------------------------------------------------

ABOUT OUR PRICING

The P.O.R.T. pricing schedule is constructed in accordance with
customary charges assessed in the typesetting industry. In addi-
tion to a fixed cost per 1000 characters, we add a set-up charge
of $10.00 per job. Penalty charges are added in the following
situations:

        1. You failed to code your job with valid parameters. We
will call you collect, determine your requirements, and add the
necessary codes. The cost for this service is based on actual
time, and is billed at $25 per hour.

        2. You made an obvious coding error, such as failing to
leave the italic state. In such cases we will fix the error(s)
and charge you on a per foot basis for used materials.

---------------------------------------------------------------------
UP I)nsrt D)el F)ind C)opy S)et J)ump A)djust P)age X)change Z)ap
```

FIG. 15. The editor provides the means to create and edit files easily for use in Let's Talk. Markers can be set within the text so that the user can jump quickly from section to section. Deleted text is retained in a buffer so that it can be copied. Unwanted text stored in the buffer can be zapped.

[6]Russ Systems
1344 Pacific Ave.
Santa Cruz, CA 95060
(408) 425-INFO (Data)
(408) 458-5080 (Voice)

The Apple III requires 256K; the *IIe* requires the extended 80-column card and RS-232 port or equivalent; all systems require at least two floppy disk drives. Hard disk support is included with the program. A clock to record the connect log and time-out, and to time-stamp files, is optional.

Let's Talk is a set of programs operating under the Apple ProDos system that support the use of an appropriate Apple as a 24-hour-a-day unattended electronic mail, messaging, and information exchange system. The major hardware requirement consists of the addition of a modem supporting the Hayes SmartModem command set.

Let's Talk provides a structured environment consisting of only two elements: directories and text files. Directories are menu listings leading to either other menu listings or to text files. As the system structure is input, the program prompts the user to identify each element as being either a directory or a text file. The program then organizes the elements accordingly.

The program provides its own editor (FIG. 15) for creating text files and editing system files that are a part of the program. Examples of specific system files are those that appear upon log-on, when an error occurs, when the system times out, and at log-off. The user can use the built-in editor to customize these files to suit his particular requirements.

In the case of a hypothetical typesetting service, the connect message might appear as:

```
              You have landed in PORT
              P.   rofessional
              O.   n-line
              R.   eception of
              T.   ypographic input

Press  <SPACE-BAR>
```

To create this screen, the system file called "connect.message" would have been edited. The (*Press <SPACE-BAR>*) prompt is added automatically by the system in order to bring the caller to the first directory.

The Let's Talk structure defines two major divisions of the electronic messaging system: a public partition, referred to as *cruise*, and a private partition, referred to as *affiliates*. In the public partition the user is only permitted to view directory listings, read text files, and write to files when so prompted. In the private partition, which is protected by password access, the user can create and upload files, use the mail system, and view restricted information.

In the PORT system example, the first directory screen would reflect this structure, like so:

```
              You're at MAIN.MENU

              I)ntroduction
              P)ublic.menu
              A)ffiliates.only
              Q)uit

                        Choose__
```

Choosing "I)ntroduction," by pressing **I** will cause the following screen to open up for the caller to view:

Welcome to the Professional On-line Reception of Typographic input Service (P.O.R.T.). This system acts as an electronic telephone funnel, accepting your ASCII text file, with or without embedded typographic codes, for processing through our high-speed digital phototypesetting machines.
Your processed jobs are returned within two working days via first class mail, Express Mail, or your choice of other overnight letter services.
Please familiarize yourself with the guidelines and procedures listed in the information section of this electronic private access system.
Press (SPACE-BAR)

The menu structure, through which users flow from item to item, is formed by the use of path names. A *path name* is a succession of file names—each preceded by a slash—beginning with the volume name and leading to a particular file. Look at the following list of topics which could be included in the Public.menu:

General Information
Opening an account
   1) Customer information
   2) Password assignment
Billing
   1) Credit cards
   2) Prepayment
   3) Open accounts
   4) Report of job statistics
Errors and corrections
   1) Responsibilities
   2) Handling
   3) Penalties
Coding
   1) Describing what you want
   2) Mnemonic codes
   3) Shortcuts
       1) Formats
       2) Recursive codes
       3) Code definitions
       4) Translation strings
       5) Translation tables
       6) Stripping out codes
       7) Nonprinting comment lines
Extra services
       1) Proofreading
       2) Keyboarding from manuscript copy
       3) Grammar checking
       4) Indexing
       5) Sorting
       6) Code insertion
       7) Media conversion
Tips and suggestions
       1) Trade practices and customs
       2) Maintaining confidentiality
       3) Data security
       4) Online style manual
       5) Common user errors
       6) Getting HELP
       7) User suggestions

The path name specification is a listing of the order by which one file leads to another. If the volume (disk) name were "online.sys," the path name leading to "Customer information" would be as follows:

/online.sys/public.menu/general.information
/opening.an.account/customer.information

The program takes care of getting the user from the volume name to the "public.menu" and "affiliates.only" without entering "main.menu" as a path name. Path names may not exceed 64 characters, including slashes, and file names may not exceed 15 characters. This example is for illustration purposes only.

Creating an on-line system is facilitated by an Operator Main menu (FIG. 16), which leads the user to portions of the program for configuring the system (FIG. 17), editing files (FIG. 15), performing system maintenance and path name creation (FIG. 18), testing the system locally, placing the system on-line to await a call, interrogating the system for recent caller activities, receiving on-line help (FIG. 19), and printing selected files.

When defining the structure of an on-line system, the user must carefully plan how the caller will move from item to item. A simple chart needs to be drawn to indicate all file names (for both the public and private sections of the system) and whether a file will be a directory or a text file. These path names then are input by selecting "M)ake a directory/text file" from the Utilities menu (FIG. 18). The full path name is input for each item, and at the prompt, the user indicates if the file is a directory or a text file (FIG. 20).

After the path names have been input, they can be printed out using the "E)xtended list of files in all directory levels" in the Utilities menu (FIG. 18). This listing provides a clear picture of the structure of the system (FIG. 21).

Now that the structure of the system is completed, the text files must be created. The Editor is selected and the path name to the first text file is input. The system has a built-in prompt that offers the caller an expanded menu, providing more help in understanding what is available. Such a screen prompt might appear as:

You're at AFFILIATES.ONLY

1). BULLETINS

2). CONSULTANTS

3). PRICES

E)xpand this menu
H)elp
M)ain Menu
U)pload a text file

Choose [1,2,3,E,H,M,U]

If the user were to select **E**, the menu would reappear in the following form:

You're at AFFILIATES.ONLY

1). BULLETINS displays recent operational changes

2). CONSULTANTS is a menu listing certified members

3). PRICES reflects changes as of 1/1987

E)xpand this menu
H)elp
M)ain Menu
U)pload a text file

Choose [1,2,3,E,H,M,U]

```
LET'S TALK: v2.3            Main Menu
```
_____


```
        C)onfigure...the System.
        E)dit........edit or create text files.
        U)tilities...rename, remove, transfer, copy, or list files.
                     set system prefix or alter access atributes.
                     create directory and text files.
        T)est........see how online will appear to the caller.
        O)nline......wait for an incoming call.
        A)ctivity....printout of files added-to by callers.
        H)elp........just in case you need it.
        P)rint.......a text file.
        Q)uit........LET'S TALK


            Choose ?
```
_____

FIG. 16. The Main menu provides access to an on-line manual in a series of Help files.


```
LET'S TALK: v2.3            Configure            ESCAPE to Main Menu
```
_____


```
1) Pathname to PUBLIC SYS...: /ONLINE.SYS/PUBLIC.MENU
2) Pathname to PRIVATE SYS..: /ONLINE.SYS/AFFILIATES.ONLY
3) Pathname to online log...: /ONLINE.SYS/LOG
4) Pathname to program files: /PROGRAM

5) System wide password required.........  —NO——
6) Caller can Upload files...............  —YES—
7) Require passwords in uploaded files...  —YES—
8) Answer phone on ring [1..9]...........  1
9) Restrict minutes online to [1..55]....  55
0) Slot containing printer card [1..7]...  1

S)ave this Configuration
```
_____

```
Choose which option?
```

FIG. 17. The Configuration menu sets the highest level path names, as well as system specifications.

Utilities Menu   ESCAPE to MAIN MENU

L)ist the files in one directory level.
E)xtended list of files in all directory levels.
C)opy a file.
T)ransfer a file from one directory to another.
R)ename a file.
D)elete a file.
A)lter a file's access atributes (lock/unlock).
M)ake a directory/text file.
S)et System pathname prefix.
Q)uit the Utilities.

Choose:

FIG. 18. The Utilities menu offers access to file maintenance and system path name creation.

LET'S TALK: v2.3   System Help

You're at HELP.MENU

1) CONFIGURE is a Menu
2) EDITOR is a Menu
3) UTILITIES is a Menu
4) TEST: See how online will appear to the caller
5) ONLINE: Have computer ready and waiting for an incoming call
6) ACTIVITY: Printout of recently updated files
7) HELP: Operator Help (reference prog-disk/guide boot-disk)
8) PRINT: Print a text file to a printer
9) EXTRAS is a Menu

M)ain Menu

Choose [1,2,3,4,5,6,7,8,9,M] __

Press <CONTROL> S to Stop the display... <SPACE-BAR> to Continue

FIG. 19. The System Help menu presents detailed assistance on all aspects of the program operation.

```
                    Make a File          ESCAPE to Utilities Menu
```

```
System Prefix:/ONLINE.SYS

        Make what file?

        PUBLIC.MENU/GENERAL.INFO/FLASH
        D)irectory
        T)ext

        Type of file:    T
```

FIG. 20. The system structure is input by specifying the path name to each file, and then indicating if the file is of a directory or text variety.

```
                          List Files
```

| /ONLINE.SYS......Contains 280 Blocks | | | | | | |
FILENAME	LOCKED	TYPE	BLKS	MODIFIED	TIME	EOF
PUBLIC.MENU	V	Directory	001	05/03/85	12:25	00512
GENERAL.INFO	WV	ASCII text	001	04/30/85	07:40	00384
NEWS	WV	ASCII text	001	04/30/85	07:40	00376
BULLETINS	WV	ASCII text	001	04/30/85	07:40	00381
CALENDAR	V	Directory	001	04/30/85	12:01	00512
MAY	V	ASCII text	003	04/30/85	07:41	00574
JUNE	V	ASCII text	003	04/30/85	07:41	00574
JULY	V	ASCII text	003	04/30/85	07:41	00574
AUG	V	ASCII text	003	04/30/85	07:41	00574
DIRECTORY	V	Directory	001	04/30/85	07:43	00512
EDUCATION	V	Directory	001	04/30/85	07:42	00512
GROUPS	V	Directory	001	04/30/85	07:42	00512
PRODUCTS	V	Directory	001	04/30/85	07:42	00512

```
                      PRESS <SPACE-BAR>
```

FIG. 21. The file listing shows the organization of the path names, as well as the file attributes, file type, size, and date and time of creation.

The expanded information is input when the text file is created, and is, in fact, the very first line of the file. It may be no longer than 75 characters. If the file is to be password-protected, the password must be the first line, and must be in the form: "PASSWORD:THE PASSWORD." The title line becomes the second line of the file.

Let's Talk supports electronic mailboxes, which not only utilize the password protection scheme, but also provide callers with the ability to delete unwanted messages from their mailbox. In order to do so they must have a *trash code,* a five-character code that is input just before the password, like so:

PASSWORD:THE PASSWORD

In order to remove messages the caller must choose to "add to" their mailbox file, then press CTRL-K to "K)ill" the messages. They would then be prompted for the trash code, which would activate the removal process.

Text files can be customized so as to set the attributes that determine if the file may be read and written to, and if additions left by other callers may be viewed. If a file is locked for "read access," then it does not appear on the menu. This locking feature can be used to remove a file or a directory temporarily from the screen presentation without physically removing it from the disk.

If a file is unlocked to permit "write access," the caller will be prompted to add comments after reading the file. Write-locked files may be read only. The text prompt that invites the caller to leave a comment can be written by the user (and must be answerable with a yes or no), or can be omitted, in which case the system default prompt is used. The default prompt reads as follows:

"This file has been left open for your comments. Would you like to add comments at this time pertaining to the information in this file? Y)es/N)o. Press <CONTROL>-D when you're Done commenting. OK begin."

FIG. 22. The file attributes determine how each file will be used. The attributes can be edited at any time.

A file that is unlocked for "view access" permits the caller to see all additions to files left by previous callers. Files are locked and unlocked by selecting the "A)lter access atributes [sic]" from the Utilities menu (FIG. 22).

```
          Alter access atributes    ESCAPE to Utilities Menu


System Prefix:/ONLINE.SYS

     In what file?
     PUBLIC.MENU/GENERAL.INFO
     Currently you are allowed to:

               R)ead from the file.           -Yes-
               W)rite to the file.            -No-
               V)iew additions to the file.   -No-
               C)hange the filename.          -Yes-
               D)estroy the file.             -Yes-

               L)ock all atributes.
               U)nlock all atributes.
               I)nstall these new atributes.


Choose:
```

As previously mentioned, the system provides certain files to properly direct the caller through the log-on session. These files, listed as follows, can be customized in the editor:

- /PROGRAM/CONNECT.MESSAGE: This is the first file that the caller sees after completing log-on.
- /PROGRAM/INTRODUCTION: This is the first choice available from the on-line Main menu.
- /PROGRAM/TIMEOUT.MESSAGE: This is the message that the caller sees before being automatically logged off as a result of exceeding permitted on-line time. The activity log indicates this occurrence with the notation ''Kicked Off.''
- /PROGRAM/ERROR.MESSAGE: The program can detect if the caller is trying to crash the system, and will display this message before automatically logging the caller off. The activity log will indicate this occurrence with the notation ''Jerk Removed.''
- /PROGRAM/CALLER.HELP: A subdirectory of help files that detail system operation.
- /PROGRAM/SYS.PASSWORDS: A file that contains all of the acceptable system entry-level or private system passwords.
- /PROGRAM/ADD.TO.PROMPT: A file indicating to the caller that a response to a file may be input.
- /PROGRAM/LOGOFF.MESSAGE: A file displaying a good-bye message at log-off. This is the last message that a caller sees on his screen, and it remains there until he erases it.

MYHOST:
Controlling a Personal Computer Host Remotely

The telecommunication of text from a remote microcomputer to either a communicating typesetter or to another microcomputer is accomplished today on a fairly routine basis. What is less common, although certainly utilized with some frequency, is the unattended use of a microcomputer or typesetter to gather files for batch processing. The setup of a dedicated (or semi-dedicated) microcomputer on its own telephone line can provide an efficient method of gathering files from diverse sources over an extended period of time. Not only does this method not require a high labor overhead, but since it can function even at night (when the work environment is usually devoid of human activity), it can provide lower-cost telephone access from distant customers.

A microcomputer used in this fashion need not be particularly sophisticated, although it must provide sufficient storage capacity to satisfy the demands of peak customer service periods. For this reason, a hard disk system is routinely employed. It also must use an auto-answer modem, which can automatically connect a remote computer to the computer's operating system or interactive communications software. A number of software packages are available to turn the microcomputer into an electronic mail system or automated file-transfer device.

In regard to remote access to CP/M-based microcomputers, there is Myhost, a program from Mycroft Labs Inc.[7] that provides the following capabilities:

- Remote access through either a modem or a direct cable connection.
- System protection through password specification.
- File transfer from the remote computer to the host using a variety of popular communications protocols.
- Automatic baud-rate detection.
- Automatic execution of another program at the beginning of a remote user's session.

[7]Mycroft Labs Inc.
2615 North Monroe Street
Tallahassee, FL 32303
(904) 385-1141

This program supports most CP/M-80 microcomputers.

The Myhost program actually lets the remote user utilize the host microcomputer as if it were a mainframe and the remote microcomputer were a system terminal. Although the power of a mainframe is lacking, the functionality is not. This capability provides the remote user with the ability to run programs and execute disk operating commands remotely. In such a mode the typesetting service could provide programs for customer support, such as copyfitting, editing, or hyphenation and justification, as well as permit its stated objective of supporting the uploaded files destined for typeset output.

When a remote computer is on-line it effectively functions as the remote console of the host microcomputer. It can perform everything that can be performed from the host keyboard, although its screen display varies somewhat from that of the host. Only the physical movement of disks and the total resetting of the host computer are restricted from remote control.

The Myhost program actually is composed of two programs: the Bye program, which initializes the system as the host, and the Xfer program, which supports the transfer of files.

In order to run the Bye program, three pieces of information are required: 1). What kind of remote connection will be utilized (auto-answer modem, dedicated line, or direct connection)? 2). What password (if any) will be required for system access? 3). What program should be run automatically upon successful sign-on? The user is prompted for this information when the Bye program is first run.

If the specified mode of operation is auto-answer, then the host computer returns to its "awaiting incoming call" status when the remote user concludes his session. In this way successive remote callers can be served.

Files can be sent both to and from the host computer using the Xfer program. In order to attain compatibility with a wide range of remote computers, the Xfer program supports five communications protocols: XMODEM/BATCH, XMODEM, CLINK, HAYES, and MITE (Mycroft).

To initiate the uploading or downloading of a file, the remote user must invoke the Xfer program followed by specification of the file name, a code to indicate the protocol, an *S* or *R* (for Send or Receive), and an optional code to turn on error checking (if the protocol accepts it). The command structure appears like this:

XFER F=filename, P=protocol-code,dir,ed

MacLink:
Converting Data via Telecommunication or Cable Connection

The movement of data between systems, from the source of input to the destination of output, is accomplished most commonly by reducing the input to standard ASCII characters. In the process there is usually the loss of valuable information that relates directly to the format or display of the original data. This information might specify the page characteristics of a document, the vertical and horizontal cell positions within a spreadsheet, or the field identities of a database. In general, the more information that can be captured successfully from the original input, the less editing and alteration that will be necessary to reconstruct the data for typesetting or output imaging.

The great number of word processing, spreadsheet, database, and other programs that run on a wide variety of personal computers makes it an impossible task to be fully proficient in translating format codes in one program on one system into meaningful format codes in another program on another system. In most cases, the diversity of needs reduces the form of data-input transmission to straight ASCII, since it is easier to add formatting information at the receiving end than to try to translate original format information into a new and fully usable form during data transmission.

A small but growing number of programs have been written to facilitate the exchange of information between specific dissimilar program/system combinations. One, MacLink from DataViz,[8] is a bidirectional data bridge between the IBM PC and the Apple Macintosh. The use of MacLink is one way in which documents prepared on the IBM PC can be output, with a minimum of editing, on the Apple LaserWriter printer.

The MacLink package consists of two program disks: one for the IBM PC and one for the Macintosh. If the two computers are near each other, they can be cable-connected using the optional eight-foot interface cable sold by DataViz. The direct-cable configuration supports the transmission of data at 9600 baud. Otherwise, file transfers can be accomplished through telecommunications, with a compatible modem connected to each computer. In telecommunications, the limiting speed factor is the slower of the two modems. In other words, if a 300-baud modem is in place on one computer and a 1200-baud modem on the other, the communications could only be accomplished at 300 baud.

Because of the ease of use of the Macintosh, all transfers, in either direction, are initiated from it. The IBM PC is set up to function in an unattended mode, awaiting a call from the Macintosh (FIG. 23). The PC menu provides settings for specifying the communications, security, telephone, and disk requirements.

At the Macintosh, the menu choices are virtually identical (FIG. 24). After all settings have been made, the ''Connect/Dial'' option is selected. If the computers are cable-connected, the Macintosh introduces itself to the IBM PC and secures the connection. If the computers are arranged for telecommunications, the telephone number of the IBM PC is dialed automatically.

After the computers have made connection and successfully compared their passwords, files can be selected and transferred by using the ''Select Disk'' dialog box, which automatically appears on the Macintosh screen (FIG. 25). At the Macintosh, the direction of the transfer is set (to or from the IBM PC) and a directory of files available for transfer is displayed. If the transfer is to be from the IBM to the Apple, a directory of files resident on the IBM PC's logged drive is displayed on the Macintosh. The directory shows the file name, its size, and its contents (i.e., text, 1-2-3 worksheet, etc.). The user clicks on the required file to select it.

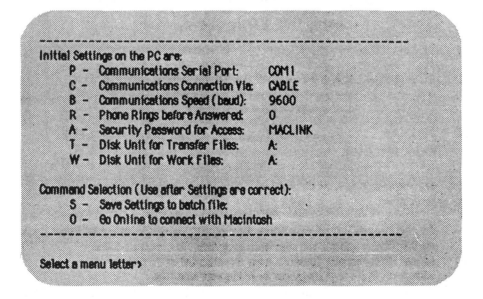

FIG. 23. The MacLink program consists of two program disks: one for the Macintosh and one for the IBM PC. This screen, from the IBM PC, shows the initial setup choices for communications.

[8]DataViz
16 Winfield Street
Norwalk, CT 06855
(203) 866-4944

MacLink reads the source file name and suggests a similar name for the target file. It also tries to sense what kind of data the source file contains, and presents a suggested translation table. The user can override the assumed translation table by clicking through the list of available tables.

The file transfer is initiated by clicking in the "Go" box of the "Move File" dialog box. As the transfer takes place, a status box keeps the user appraised of the operation's progress. For documents, the window displays a count of lines, blocks, or paragraphs. For spreadsheets, the window displays an indication of cell location.

When the transfer has been completed, MacLink reports on the number of translation warnings (indicating items that might require manual adjustment), translation errors (indicating items that were not completely translated), and transfer retrys (items that were sensed as erroneous and were retransmitted). MacLink saves a log of all errors for later examination.

FIG. 24. The initial Settings window of the Macintosh provides a display of current selections as well as access to changing the settings.

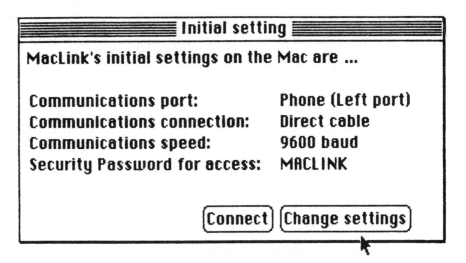

FIG. 25. The "Select Disk" dialog box allows the user to set the direction of communication as well as the logged disk drive.

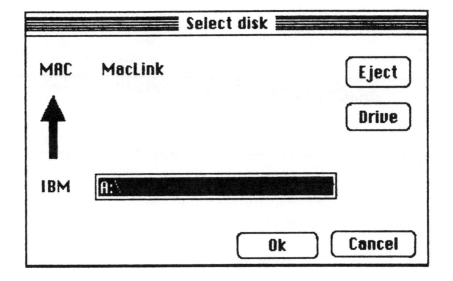

The transfer options available in MacLink include:

PC	To/From	MAC
Lotus	< - >	Multiplan
Lotus	< - >	DIF[1]
Multiplan	< - >	Multiplan
Multiplan	< - >	DIF[1]
DIF	< - >	Multiplan
DIF	< - >	DIF[1]
WordStar	< - >	MacWrite[2]
MultiMate	< - >	MacWrite[2]
Text	< - >	Text[3]
Binary	< - >	Binary
Binary-Mac	< - >	Binary-Mac[4]

[1]Data Interchange Format, a file format that is used to express the physical locations of text and numbers which are positioned in rows and columns, such as in spreadsheets.
[2]Files can also be used in Microsoft's Word.
[3]Used to move any ASCII data file.
[4]Transfers all data and Mac information "as is."

MacLink has been structured to accept new translation tables through program upgrades, so that future application programs can be handled in the same way.

TYPECOMM:
Communicating Using On-Line Data Translation

Any number of popular programs can be used to move text out of the microcomputer environment in which it has been created, over telephone lines, and into the typesetting environment where it will be processed into its final form.

Although the methods and procedures to initiate and perform on-line communications have become somewhat routine, passing codes accurately from the computer to the typesetter, so that they require no further human intervention, is far less than the typical case. The typesetting service that is the recipient of files which are not adequately prepared for typesetting must do some (or much) manual manipulation with the files in order to make them completely usable.

A program that combines text editing, data translation, and telecommunications is Typecomm from the 'Puter Group.[9] The program runs personal computers such as the Radio Shack Model III, IV, or IVP microcomputers and requires two disk drives, an RS-232 board and cable, and depending upon the purpose of the installation, one or both of the following: a null modem cable for local transmission and reception and an auto-answer telephone modem (300 or 300/1200 baud).

In a typical setup, the Typecomm program would be dedicated to a particular computer in the shop and would support a number of satellite systems. The satellite systems could be used for the input of text, and be attached to the main system through the RS-232 interface to download files for any text translation required by the typesetting system. Files received from outside the shop (i.e., from customers, reporters, or cottage laborers) could all be channeled directly through the dedicated computer, which is also responsible for communicating all files to the typesetter's front-end computer.

As incoming calls are processed, Typecomm automatically adjusts to match the protocol and baud rate being used by the remote computer. Any number of jobs can

[9]'Puter Group
1717 West Beltline Highway
Madison, WI 53713
(608) 273-1803

be handled, without a human operator, at any time of day, so long as the jobs do not exceed the storage capacity of the disk. Typecomm keeps an accurate account of each call, including the name of the caller, the time of the call, the size of the file, and the presence of any erroneous characters. The screen display of the caller log looks something like this:

<A>utomatic file reception

The disk in drive #1 contains the following files . . .

From	File	Date		Size
Ellis Wholesale	F1/TXT	3/16/85	09:05:11	2344
Beil Associates	F2/TXT	3/16/85	09:20:22	5629
Scottmark Corp.	F3/TXT	3/16/85	09:44:03	12305
Thornell Products	F4/TXT	3/16/85	10:01:36	1229

There are 137291 characters free on this disk.
Want to <U>se disk, <E>rase disk, or <A>bort {U} - - - >

Almost any word processing program will work with Typecomm, although the 'Puter Group recommends the use of Radio Shack's Model I Scriptsit™ since it is easy to use and copyable. The 'Puter Group also includes a number of useful patches for the program, including a directory display, a Dvorak keyboard, a type-ahead buffer, and routines for screen printing, user-definable keys, file-killing, zippy cursor movement, and page up and down movement.

A powerful part of the Typecomm package is the translation program, which can perform up to 500 code translations at one time. It also has the capability to: convert from EBCDIC to ASCII; convert from ASCII to TTS; convert from word processing codes to typesetting codes; uppercase to uppercase and lowercase; search by wildcards; replace by conditional operators; transmit any processed file to disk, printer, or out the RS-232 port for immediate processing; remove all multiple spaces (if so desired); and provide support for the embedding of up to 260 string formats.

The flexibility of this translation program permits the conversion of files that have been prepared for any typesetting system to be converted into a form readable by the typesetting system fed by Typecomm. Therefore, jobs that have been coded for a foreign system can be used on an in-house system without any recoding. This ability makes it easier for a typesetter using Typecomm to lure customers away from competitors, since it will not be necessary for the customers to learn a new coding system.

Typecomm is menu-driven (FIG. 26) and provides a ''help'' facility by typing **H** at any time. When the ''(A)utomatic text reception'' option is activated, the TRS-80 computer is placed in the Await Call mode. When a caller is on-line, the computer responds with a tone, sets itself according to the communication needs of the caller, and asks for a password (optional). The program then displays the company logo of the typesetting operation to the caller, who is prompted for his name. The Typecomm logs the call to a log file and sends the call (optionally) to a line printer in order to provide the user with a quick visual summary of all jobs awaiting further processing. Typecomm then provides the caller with an estimate of how much space is available for copy, and indicates that the caller should begin transmission. The program writes the text on disk, ends transmission, and resets itself to await the next caller. If the storage space on a disk falls below 20,000 characters, the program automatically switches to another drive. If the remaining disk space is dangerously low, the operator is alerted by an audible signal (as an option).

The other options on the Main menu perform the following functions:

- (M)anual text reception: This mode is used in those cases where the Typecomm program is unable to match the protocol used by the remote computer, or when the remote computer does not have communications software.
- (S)end text file: This mode is used to pass files that are ready for typesetting from the TRS-80 to the typesetter or front-end system using the local RS-232 line. Up to 128 files can be placed in a file queue and transmitted automatically. If any of the files reside on different disks, the Typecomm program will prompt the operator to insert the required disk when necessary.
- (C)ommunications program: This mode converts the TRS-80 into a terminal that can communicate with any other computer. The 'Puter Group provides a TRS-DOS 1.3 version of this program, which can be copied and provided to typesetting service customers free of charge.
- (R)eceive text locally: This option is used to receive files from in-house computers such as laptop computers, mainframes, and other microcomputers.
- (L)ist a file: This mode permits the quick reading of a file in order to check its contents. It also lists a file showing the code or ASCII value for each character in the file. These values are helpful in devising a translation file to convert commands and characters that fall outside the normal repertoire of the keyboard character set.
- (D)isk directory: This option provides a list of all files, their size, and when they were created.
- (T)ranslate text files: This option runs the translation program (called Replace), converting computer and word processing files into typesetter-ready format.
- (W)ord processor: This option brings the user into the word processing program, where new files can be created or existing files can be edited.
- (P)artition large files: This option allows the user to reduce the large files into smaller files that can be edited more easily by the word processor.
- (K)ill or rename files: This option displays the first ten lines of a file before the file is either eliminated or renamed.

- (E)xtract formats: The Typecomm program supports *formats,* which are defined sections of text that can be assigned to a simple code in the text file. This option copies the format definitions from a file and places them in a separate file. By calling this file, it frees the user from the necessity of redefining formats at the beginning of a new section of copy.
- (V)iew search & replace files: This option displays the information stored in translation files. Each search string is shown beside its corresponding replace string. The information can be either displayed on screen or printed on the line printer.
- (X)file fix: This option recovers files with bad sectors or parity errors. It also converts files with ''nulls'' (ASCII zero) into a readable form. Scripsit and other word processors interpret the null as an end-of-file marker and will not read it. This option converts each null into a space.
- (B)ackup and (F)ormat: These options are used to copy a disk and format a new disk, respectively.

The Typecomm program makes it possible to communicate with a wide variety of input sources (FIG. 27) and feed a number of different typesetting front-end systems or typesetters. Using the MCS-Transfer program (see Chapter 6), it is also possible to produce Compugraphic MCS-compatible disks directly on the TRS-80 or IBM PC.

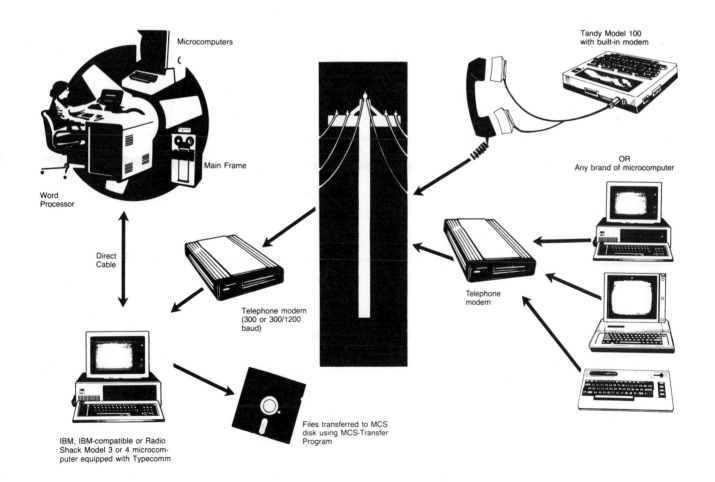

FIG. 27. The general scheme by which Typecomm benefits the typesetter. It not only provides a communications link, but performs the complete translation of incoming text into a usable form for typesetting (Courtesy of The 'Puter Group).

Chapter 6

Data Manipulation and Conversion

Changing existing data into more valuable forms.

COMPAT: Converting Media between CP/M and MS-DOS

The incompatibility of software products is a problem for almost every microcomputer user to some extent, ranging from mild inconvenience to utter frustration and despair. For the typesetter it is a special problem since he, more than a professional in almost any other line of work, must deal with customers utilizing a wide variety of media formats. The files that reside on disks of various formats must be converted to a common denominator in order to be typeset.

There are specialized media-conversion devices that accept magnetic media of one kind and convert it into magnetic media of a different kind. In general, these dedicated systems are exceptionally flexible, although they tend to be expensive, and in some cases, difficult to use. An alternative for most modest disk conversion needs is software utility programs, which convert magnetic media between systems that share certain features, most particularly the size of the diskettes or the version of the operating system.

A program composed of many such utilities is Compat from Mycroft Labs Inc.[1] It performs four fundamental operations:

- It can initialize blank 5 1/4-inch diskettes in a variety of CP/M and MS-DOS formats.
- It can convert one or both system drives into a specified CP/M format.
- It can copy (either to or from) files and display directories of a variety of MS-DOS formats.
- It can transfer information between disk files and/or devices.

After a disk has been created using the Compat utilities, it is virtually indistinguishable from one created on the original hardware system. If it contains eight-bit .COM files, which are native to the CP/M operating system under which Compat runs, then the files can be executed (although CRT screen codes that control character movement and display might be incompatible, as might be hardware-dependent programs and programs native to different operating systems).

The Format utility (version 3.2) initializes blank 5 1/4-inch diskettes in the following CP/M formats: • 48 tpi (tracks per inch) single sided • 48 tpi double sided • 96 tpi single sided • 96 tpi double sided. It also initializes 5 1/4-inch diskettes in MS-DOS formats: • Single sided, 8 sector/track • Double sided, 8 sector/track • Single sided, 9 sector/track • Double sided, 9 sector/track. These common disk specifications cover well over 90 different microcomputer disk formats.

The MS utility is used to access disk directories and move files to or from a variety of MS-DOS and CP/M formats. A set of commands are available to afford the user considerable flexibility in selecting and transferring files. Among these commands are DIR, which is used to display a disk directory; GET, which is used to get files from MS-DOS and move them to a CP/M disk; PUT, which is used to put files on an MS-DOS disk from a CP/M disk; TYPE, which is used to specify a file to display on the console (CRT); ERA, which is used to erase a file from an MS-DOS disk; and SPACE, which displays information about the MS-DOS disk in the following form:

MS-DOS Disk Type = Single/Double Sided, 8/9 Sector	
Total Directory Entries	= nnn
Used Directory Entries	= nnn
Available Directory Entries	= nnn
Total Space on Disk	= nnnK Bytes
Used Space on Disk	= nnnK Bytes
Available Space on Disk	= nnnK Bytes

[1]Mycroft Labs Inc.
2615 North Monroe Street
Tallahassee, FL 32303
(904) 385-1141

Available for several CP/M-80 based microcomputers, including Kaypro II/83, II/84, IV/83, IV/84; Sanyo MBC 1000, 1150, 1250; Zenith Z100, Z100HD; Zorba 7, QD; and Memotech MTX 512.

The Compat program also includes an extended File Copy utility, called Mycopy, to replace the standard CP/M utility, called PIP. Mycopy simplifies the process of copying an individual or group of files by using ambiguous or unambiguous file name expressions to indicate all files of a certain type that are to be copied or are to be selectively excluded.

TIMESAVER 10: Ridding Word Processing Files of Unwanted Data

Programmers, like cooks, add special ingredients to their creations in order to personalize them and make them more individualistic. This compulsion is easily seen in the diversity of word processing programs that are available. Although the files created with some word processors can be blended with those of others, thus enhancing the flavor of the combination, many cannot. The universal pot of electronic alphabet soup is unpalatable to many tastes.

Providing the right recipe to convert ingredients into generic forms is the Timesaver 10 program from Sunray Sales Incorporated.[2] This set of utilities provides the means for using files from a multitude of origins in typesetting and communications applications.

There are many elements within word processing files that are known to cause problems in typesetting. The Timesaver 10 programs address each one of these concerns, either individually or in a group, producing a standard ASCII file. The utilities perform these functions:

1. Remove the eighth bit and nonprinting characters except for carriage return, line feed, and tab.
2. Remove WordStar's soft spaces.
3. Remove WordStar's soft carriage returns.
4. Add line feeds to all carriage returns.
5. Add carriage returns to all line feeds.
6. Remove WordStar's dot commands.
7. Remove the eighth bit.
8. Double-space (add a carriage return and line feed to each carriage return and line feed).
9. Remove single carriage returns and line feeds and convert to spaces. (Does not remove double carriage returns and line feeds between paragraphs.)
10. Combine the functions of #1, #2, #3, and #6 for treating WordStar files.

While these utilities specifically address certain inherent problems with WordStar output, they also are usable with a wide variety of word processing files. Also included in the program package are specific utilities for converting OfficeWriter, WordStar 2000, and MultiMate files into plain ASCII.

The utilities all use a simple syntax to indicate the operations that need to be performed on each file, as well as the specific file to be converted and the name for the newly created ASCII file. The notation takes this form:

UTILITY NAME	FILE TO BE CONVERTED	OUTPUT SYMBOL	NEW FILE NAME OR DEVICE
cws2000	night.txt	>	day.txt

Note: This example uses the CWS2000 utility to convert a WordStar 2000 file called NIGHT into an ASCII file called DAY. As well as creating files, the user may specify that the converted information is sent to the computer screen or to the printer.

In addition to the list of generic utilities, a Search and Replace utility allows the user to find one or more characters and replace them with single or multiple characters. This function, while useful, is limited in that only one string may be specified at one time. The character strings may be specified in either ASCII or hex notation.

[2]Sunray Sales Incorporated
707 North Freeway, Suite 119
Fort Worth, TX 76102
(817) 338-1217

Available for the IBM PC and compatibles. Comes with a multiuser license agreement that allows up to ten users per disk.

The hex values of characters and codes can be derived by using the Display utility, which shows the hex value of each code directly beneath it.

Converted files do not remain captive in their newly achieved ASCII status. A utility called SHIPX.COM provides the means to send the file out the computer's serial port using the X-on, X-off protocol. This handshaking procedure controls the orderly flow of data out of the computer, synchronizing the transmission and the reception so that nothing is lost or misinterpreted. The data flows via telecommunication (modem) or a hardwire connection to a typesetting machine or a front-end input and editing system.

REPLACE: Searching and Replacing on a Large Scale

There are many idiosyncrasies in the ways computer programs perform that are likely to keep computers and word processors from achieving 100 percent compatibility with typesetting systems. Even if the disk format, the operating system, and the text format all are compatible, it is almost a certainty that the text preparation program (word processing, text editing, text processing, line editing program, etc.) will utilize codes for formatting its output that either will be meaningless or erroneous in the typesetting environment. What this means is that, although the alphanumeric characters will be captured through the media reading or telecommunications process, the meaningless word processing formatting codes will need to be stripped out, and the meaningful ones will need to be converted.

Fortunately, this tedious process need not be done manually. The Replace program from the 'Puter Group[3] performs up to 1,500 search/replace pair substitutions at the rate of 450 characters per second on a floppy disk system and almost 1,000 characters per second on a hard disk system.

In addition the program can do the following:

- Convert short mnemonic code sequences input by a customer into lengthy and/or complex typesetting commands.
- Locate and translate hidden or embedded word processing format codes into their typesetting counterparts. The word processing printer codes for designating a double-strike character, for example, could be translated into a bold typeface command.
- Convert files with nonstandard formats into standard formats such as ASCII or EBCDIC.
- Convert files that have been prepared for a specific target typesetter to the necessary coding for a different typesetter.
- Add typographic refinements, such as kerning, the addition of alternate line spacing (such as between paragraphs), or discretionary hyphenation, to a file.
- Convert ASCII coding to another coding system that a specific typesetting system requires.
- Convert typesetting files back into a form compatible with a specific word processing program.

The Replace program can be invoked either by itself, or from within the 'Puter Group's Typecomm or MCS-Transfer program's Translate option. It requires a standard text file as input. The translation file, which is also in the form of a text file, can include up to 50,000 characters of search and replace strings, each of which may be up to 120 characters long. Files of any size can be processed, provided there is sufficient disk (floppy or hard) storage to accommodate them. It is disk storage capacity, not memory, that is the limiting factor.

The translation file that specifies what is to be replaced is created using a standard word processing program. The file is composed of successive lines showing what is to be searched for, followed by what it is to be replaced with. A file containing the

[3]'Puter Group
1717 W. Beltline Highway
Madison, WI 53713
(608) 273-1803

Available for IBM/PC/XT/AT, and compatible computers. Specifications on other versions should be obtained from the 'Puter Group. Also see entries for the MCS-Transfer program in the next section and the Typecomm program in Chapter 5.

abbreviations of United Nations agencies could be expanded to the full agency names using a file such as this:

```
＼ UN agency translation file [comment line]
FAO
Food and Agricultural Organization
GATT
General Agreement on Tariffs and Trade
IMCO
Intergovernmental Maritime Consultative Organization
ICAO
International Civil Aviation Organization
*end*
*end*
```

The translation file may use comment lines, which are indicated by a backslash, as a means of explaining what a particular replacement string is to accomplish. Each file must end with two items (such as the words *end* *end*) that are sure not to be found in the source text file.

An additional capability of the Replace program is the support of *formats*, which are sequences of frequently used words or commands that are both defined and used in a text file. In use, the creator of the text file defines the format once, and then activates it with a simple three-letter command. The program supports up to 268 formats, but the number of formats reduce the total number of search and replace characters that are available.

When a file is specified for processing, the Replace program allows the addition of up to three parameters. The "S" parameter indicates that any multiple spaces in a file are to be removed. Since word processing files usually have multiple spaces at the beginning of paragraphs, between sentences, and in various other positions, this option is very useful. The "H" parameter is used to remove the "high bits" from the source text file. Certain word processing programs, such as WordStar, set the high bits (which increase the ASCII value of a character by 128) for certain internal characteristics of the program. The "V" parameter is used to force the program to display the source file on the video as it is being processed. Doing so, however, slows down the processing of the file.

If the Replace program was in disk drive A:, the source file and translation file were located in disk drive B:, and all three parameters were to be invoked, the command line would look like this:

```
A> REPLACE  B:SOURCE.TXT  B:DEST.TXT  B:SUBS.TNS  S  H  V
```

This command would read the source file, pass it through the substitution file, remove multiple spaces, strip the high bits, display the text, and write a converted file called DEST.TXT. If the word *replace* is typed without any parameters, the program prompts the user for the needed information.

The real flexibility of the Replace program is in its use of escape codes. Escape codes serve three purposes: they create characters that cannot be typed from the keyboard; they specify wild cards, and they indicate some special function. Escape codes are specified by using the "at" sign @ followed by a code identity. Creative use of escape codes can do such useful things as convert all uppercase characters to uppercase and lowercase, insert rules (lines) between items on a price list, interpret the tab code on a word processor to the tab code on a typesetter, specify that words of four letters or less are not to be hyphenated, and define formats.

The Replace program also includes a number of additional programs. The RSORT program sorts the translation data in order to maximize its efficiency. The CODELIST program lists a file to the screen showing the decimal value below each character. This capability makes it possible to identify any hidden word processing codes that need to be stripped out or converted. The VUE program allows the user to view the translation data on the computer screen or print it to a printer. The NUM program numbers the replacement strings consecutively, creating a new file with numbered strings. During the translation process the numbers are displayed, indicating which string was used. This program can be especially useful when constructing complex translations. The UTILITIES are a group of programs that permit the following: • stripping nulls • translating reserved characters • dividing large files into smaller ones • extracting formats • creating a correction file. A correction file is one created from a file in which those paragraphs and headlines that need to be retranslated have been marked by an open brace to begin and a closed brace to end. Corrections thus can be typeset without rerunning the entire file.

MCS-TRANSFER: Generating Typesetter Compatible Media

It is an established fact that microcomputers make acceptable-to-excellent input stations for phototypesetting output. However, where the microcomputer processing of text usually becomes somewhat troublesome is in the transfer of keyboarded information from the computer to the typesetter. Although the information can be transferred by such methods as telecommunication, direct channelling through a cable connection between computer and typesetter, or conversion through expensive hardware into an acceptable media form, the ideal solution is to have the microcomputer output media be 100 percent compatible with the typesetter.

A program that produces Compugraphic MCS typesetter compatible disks from a Radio Shack Model III or IV or an IBM PC is the MCS-Transfer program from the 'Puter Group.[4] The program in essence converts the microcomputer into a fully compatible typesetting workstation through a two-step software-conversion process (FIG. 1).

[4] Puter Group
1717 W. Beltline Highway
Madison, WI 53713
(608) 273-1803

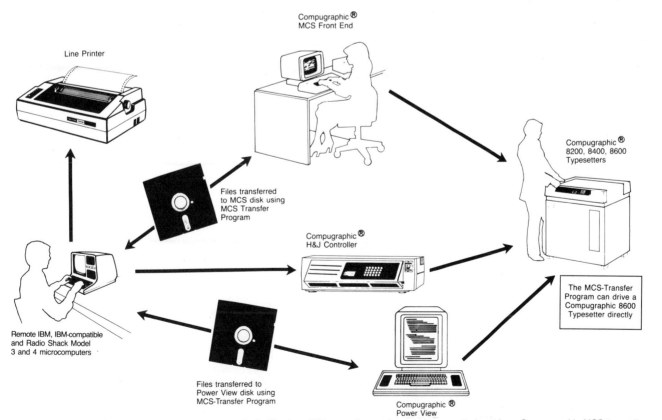

FIG. 1. A diagram showing the various ways in which a Radio Shack or IBM computer can be used to generate input for a Compugraphic MCS typesetter, or accept input from the MCS for editing or proofing on a line printer (Courtesy of The 'Puter Group).

The first step in this process is to run a file destined for typeset output through a program called Replaces on the TRS-80, or Replace on the IBM. The Replaces program translates a number of nonstandard characters generated by the microcomputer into new values that are recognizable by the typesetter. An example is the dollar sign, which is represented on most microcomputers as a decimal value of 36. The Compugraphic MCS represents the dollar sign as a decimal value of 20. The Replaces program converts this and many other characters into their MCS-readable forms.

The Replaces program also is used to solve the problem of generating special typesetting characters and functions for which there are no keys on the microcomputer. In order to produce an em space, for example, the user could define a mnemonic string, such as ''%m,'' which the Replaces program would convert to the proper MCS decimal value for an em space.

The second step in the conversion process is to run the Transfer program. This program simply asks for the current name of the file and the new name it will have in its MCS form. The file will be transferred and the disk then can be removed from the microcomputer and placed directly in the MCS disk drive. The IBM version of the program performs both step one and two automatically.

The MCS-Transfer program also performs a number of other useful functions. In the case of the Radio Shack version (for which all of the following comments apply), it will transfer a file from the Compugraphic MCS disk format into the Radio Shack TRS-80 disk format. In this form it can be edited using any Radio Shack word processor or editor (the 'Puter Group recommends Radio Shack's Scriptsit™ program) and proofed on a line printer. The program also supports the display of either a TRS-80 directory or an MCS directory, and the conversion of files from the TRS-DOS 1.3 format to the LDOS format. The MCS-Transfer program uses the LDOS operating system, and therefore expects all files it handles to be in this form.

The program also includes the LED text editing program, which is a general-purpose editor resembling Radio Shack's Scripsit. LED is used to create and alter translation files, as well as to create actual files that will be typeset. Any program that generates ASCII characters can be used for text entry.

DiskMaster: Converting Media on a Phototypesetter

The disk operating systems used on most phototypesetting systems are proprietary, and little or no information about their internal functioning is provided to the end-user. The initial popularity of the CP/M operating system in the microcomputer realm has had a positive effect on typesetting systems, many offering it as an option. The CP/M option makes it possible to run CP/M software on the typesetter, provided that the software is available on a compatible disk format.

Moving files from CP/M into the typesetting environment, or vice versa, is a conversion that not all typesetting systems which offer CP/M can provide. An answer to this problem is, sometimes, software offered by third-party vendors, such as Composition Software, Inc.[5] This company's DiskMaster program is a collection of software tools that run directly on the AM International Comp/Edit series of phototypesetting machines and convert from CP/M format to Comp/Edit. The program also supports the direct translation of MicroPro's Wordstar word processing files into Comp/Edit-compatible files ready for typesetting.

DiskMaster performs two distinct functions: character/code translation and media translation. The program will accept as input any ASCII file consisting of characters, and optionally, Comp/Edit $ (dollar sign) mnemonics. Mnemonics are input in a word processing file to specify codes upon which the typesetting machine can act. The specification of a line length of 37 picas and 9 points, for example, would be defined as ''$LL3709.'' DiskMaster is able to accept the $ mnemonics as input and to output on a compatible medium a properly coded file with the precise Comp/Edit equivalents in place.

[5]Composition Software, Inc.
213 West Institute Place, Suite 508
Chicago, IL 60610
(312) 248-4559

Media translation is a direct and simple operation that can be accomplished either one file at a time or in batch mode. The program automatically deletes files having the same name from the destination disk, and also generates an alphabetized directory file of the job names on either the CP/M or Comp/Edit disk.

When it is translating Wordstar files, DiskMaster will accept either a file with $ mnemonics or one completely unprepared for typesetting. In the latter case, it automatically translates WordStar commands for underlining and bold into data locations on the typesetter, which later can be defined as italic, bold, or normal typeface. Additionally, DiskMaster automatically performs the following operations to change the WordStar file into a Comp/Edit-compatible file:

- Quotes are automatically opened and closed. The single typewriter quote character is converted into typeset open or closed form.
- Multiple spaces are reduced to one. Any string of two or more spaces, as would normally separate sentences, is translated as a single space.
- Two hyphens are converted to an em dash.
- Soft returns are stripped out automatically.
- Soft spaces are stripped out automatically. Multiple spaces used to justify lines are reduced to single word spaces.
- Hard returns are translated into data. The hard returns at the end of paragraphs can be converted into quad left return, quad left return plus an indent for the beginning of the next paragraph, or whatever else is required.
- Soft hyphens are converted into discretionary hyphens.
- Multiple hard returns are translated into data. These multiple returns can be defined as additional line-spacing values.
- Any Comp/Edit $ mnemonic is translated into its typesetting equivalent.

TABLEMASTER: Creating Table-based Information for Typesetting

Among the most difficult categories of typesetting jobs are those that require the complex setting of *rules*—lines which must accurately delineate areas in a form or a table. Most phototypesetting machines do not easily support this application; others support it partially, with the setting of horizontal rules, but not vertical; and others do not support it at all. The TableMaster program from Composition Software, Inc.[6] simplifies the setting of complex ruled forms by acting as a preprocessor for phototypesetting on the AM International Comp/Edit series of machines.

TableMaster is a table-formatting program that is based on the TBL utility in the UNIX operating system. It requires four basic operations:

- Prepare an input file using a CP/M-based word processor.
- Process the file through TableMaster to produce an output file containing the typesetting codes for the Comp/Edit.
- Transfer the TableMaster file to the Comp/Edit.
- Typeset the file.

The user enters information in a conceptual form, specifying the appearance of the table rather than the codes it requires. The specification of column width, copy entering (horizontal and vertical), rule insertion, column alignment, and typesetter code generation are all left to the program.

For purposes of explanation, a simple table will be constructed composed of the following information:

[6]Composition Software, Inc.
213 West Institute Place, Suite 508
Chicago, IL 60610
(312) 248-4559

Requires the CP/M environment and at least 60K of RAM.

Jane	President	1st floor royal office	$10.75
Wang	Vice-President	3rd floor suite	$0.99
Hank	Treasurer	basement vault	$4.50
X	Secretary	an anteroom	$6.00
Smithy	Gofer	very mobile	$22.12

The body of a table must always reside between two table specifications: one for start (.TS) and one for end (.TE). The Table Start command occupies a single line and is followed immediately by a format section, which describes the layout of the table. An example of a format section for this table information would be:

r l c n.

which indicates "right, left, center, numerically aligned." What this format is saying to TableMaster is that there are four vertical columns, and the information in each is to be positioned according to the specified format.

The format section is followed by the data section, which contains the data to be typeset. Each column entry is separated from the next by a colon. The table shown in FIG. 2 is the result of input that appears as follows:

```
.TS
r    l    c    n.
Jane:President:1st floor royal office:$10.75
Wang:Vice-President:3rd floor suite:$0.99
Hank:Treasurer:basement vault:$4.50
X:Secretary:anteroom:$6.00
Smithy:Gofer:very mobile:$22.12
.TE
```

Jane	President	1st floor royal office	$10.75
Wang	Vice-President	3rd floor suite	$0.99
Hank	Treasurer	basement vault	$4.50
X	Secretary	anteroom	$6.00
Smithy	Gofer	very mobile	$25.12

FIG. 2. The typeset table resulting from simple descriptive codes.

Multiple format lines may be used, with the final format line indicated by a period at its end. Adding a line of headlines to the table using an italic typeface would make the first few lines of the table input look like this:

```
.TS
r fi l fi c fi r fi
r    l    c    n.
Name:Office:Mail Stop:Pay Rate
Jane:President:1st floor royal office:$10.75
```

The correspondence of format lines with data lines is an important consideration in TableMaster. The first format line commands stay in effect until a succeeding format line is called into play.

The generation of more complex tables can be accomplished by adding more codes. TableMaster is endowed with codes to accomplish most table requirements. Among the more useful are the horizontal rule, which is indicated by an underscore character, and a thicker rule, which is indicated by an equal sign.

The table shown in FIG. 3 was constructed from the input at the top of the next page. Note the doublebox command, which put a box around the entire table; the vertical rule commands, which placed vertical rules between each column; and the "s" command, which centered the headline over all columns.

Employees of XYZ Corporation			
Name	*Office*	*Mail Stop*	*Pay Rate*
Jane	President	1st floor royal office	$10.75
Wang	Vice-President	3rd floor suite	$0.99
Hank	Treasurer	basement vault	$4.50
X	Secretary	anteroom	$6.00
Smithy	Gofer	very mobile	$25.12

FIG. 3. A fairly complex ruled table produced with relatively few TableMaster codes.

```
.TS
doublebox;
c   fb    S     S              S.
r   fi   !  |   fi   !  c    fi  !   r   fi
r        !  |        !  c        !   n   .
Employees of XYZ Corporation
=
Name:Office:Mail Stop:Pay Rate
=
Jane:President:1st floor royal office:$10.75
_
Wang:Vice-President:3rd floor suite:$0.99
_
Hank:Treasurer:basement vault:$4.50
_
X:Secretary:anteroom:$6.00
_
Smithy:Gofer:very mobile:$22.12
_
.TE
```
Note: ! used in place of vertical rule symbol.

Although the syntax of TableMaster might take some practice to learn, it can greatly reduce the trial-and-error procedures that typify the composition of most categories of complex tabular work.

TEXTMASTER: Preprocesing Word Processing Files with Hyphenation and Justification

The link between word processing files and phototypesetting machines very often is accomplished by bringing the word processing data into the typesetting environment by first passing it through some sort of translation process. The translation process converts incoming characters and commands into a form that the typesetter can utilize, stripping out those which are meaningless and substituting typesetting commands where appropriate. The converted word processing file, however, still must depend upon the hyphenation and justification logic of the typesetting machine in order to reach its ultimate output form.

A program that bridges the gap between micro-based word processing in the CP/M environment and phototypesetting is the TextMaster program from Composition Software, Inc.[7] Supporting the creation of text input for the VariTyper Comp/Edit series of phototypesetting machines, TextMaster in essence places user-alterable translation capabilities in a preprocessor on the microcomputer. It accepts as input a word processing file and hyphenates it, justifies it, paginates it, translates it, and converts it into a form that can be used by the phototypesetting machine.

The translation capabilities of TextMaster operate at three levels. First, there is the direct translation of word processing descriptors into their typesetting counterparts. Word processing commands such as bold, italic, paragraph indent, secondary lead between paragraphs, and tabs are directly converted into like typesetting codes. Second, there is the translation of Comp/Edit commands that have been input mnemonically in the word processing file into command sequences which the Comp/Edit can process directly. Third, there are up to 100 user-defined search and replace operations for handling special characters and simple mnemonics.

As a preprocessor, TextMaster provides capabilities that the typesetting machine either cannot do or cannot do easily. It can do pagination, multiple columns, and footnotes. It can also support the definition of numerous formats, which can be saved on disk and utilized repeatedly for similar types of work, such as newsletters and books.

[7] Puter Group
1717 W. Beltline Highway
Madison, WI 53713
(608) 273-1803
Requires CP/M (version 2 or 3) with at least 60K of usable memory.

The operation of the program is best described by its author, Martin Schechtman: "TextMaster works by reading an *input file* containing the text to be set, interspersed with commands that control its style and positioning. This file is known as the *primary input stream.* TextMaster also reads *font files,* which specify the widths of the characters being used, and *format definition files,* which define the general format being used.

"The output of TextMaster is written into an *output file,* known as the *primary output stream.* This output file contains a complete Comp/Edit job file, which may be transferred to the typesetting machine, and set in the usual manner. No operation intervention is required at the typesetting machine while the job is being set."

For TextMaster to properly determine the necessary line endings for its input text, it must reference an on-disk file that stores the width values for the font disk(s) the Comp/Edit will be using. This character-width information is copied from Comp/Edit disks onto the microcomputer disk, where it must reside with the main TextMaster programs.

TextMaster is invoked by typing the program designation, **TXT**, followed by the name of the input file, the name of the output file, and any necessary options. Options would include things like running the program in batch mode, wherein processing does not stop when errors are encountered. In this mode a separate file is specified to store error listings. The specification of an alternate drive can be used to access font files, TextMaster program files, and temporary work files, which TextMaster uses during normal processing.

When TextMaster encounters errors, it displays an error message on the display screen, along with a listing of the line number in which the error occurred. If the error is *fatal,* meaning that TextMaster cannot recover and continue, the user is returned to the CP/M operating system. If the error is less serious, the user is given the opportunity to continue, and TextMaster will cope as best it can with the erroneous information it has encountered.

As an incoming stream of text is processed, TextMaster uses its fill mode to fit as many characters on the specified line measure as possible, just as the Comp/Edit normally does when operating in its automatic mode. In this mode, the line endings that were created in the word processing file are ignored. In TextMaster's no fill mode, however, the line endings from the original input file are maintained, as they are in a similar way on the Comp/Edit itself when it is in the manual mode.

Commands to specify typographic descriptors are included in the input file in one of two ways. A line that begins with a period (which may be respecified by the user), the *command character,* is considered a command line. The command character is followed by two lowercase characters and then by any necessary parameters. To space 12 points down a page, for example, the code string *.sp 12p* would be input.

Commands also may be input by using escape sequences, which need not be specified at the beginning of the line, but rather at any convenient or necessary place. Escape sequences are preceded by a backslash and followed by two characters (and sometimes a parameter) that indicate some sort of action to be taken. The escape sequence \ *fb,* for example, indicates a change to a boldface type.

Whenever a numerical parameter is required, it usually is followed by a *units indicator,* which specifies the kind of units that the parameter must utilize. The available units indicators are:

UNITS INDICATOR	MEANING
p (lower)	points
P (upper)	picas
m	ems
n	ens
i	inches
c	centimeters
v	primary vertical spacing (a multiple) of the primary line spacing. If, for example the primary line spacing is 10 points, then the command **12v** would be equal to 120 points.
u	basic units (1/10 points) used by TextMaster for internal calculations.

TextMaster also supports *arithmetic operators* $(+,-,*,/,\%)$ and *logical operators* $(<, >, <=, >=, =, \&, :)$, making possible command strings such as *.sp 2u*(30p−1v)+1c*, meaning "space a distance equal to the quantity (30 points minus the current baseline spacing), times 2, plus an additional centimeter."

Because of the coding flexibility inherent in the program, some strings of commands might be somewhat confusing to persons other than the one who wrote them. To solve this problem, as well as aid in eliminating others, TextMaster supports a *comments capability,* which permits the inclusion of explanatory remarks that are readable by the operator but are not typeset. Commands are indicated by either starting a line with ". \ '" or using the escape sequence " \ " anywhere in a line. An example of a line using a comment is:

.sp 2i   \ '' leave 2 inches of space for photo

TextMaster uses its own hyphenation algorithms to produce what its author terms "acceptable hyphenation." Hyphenation points also may be specified manually, using discretionary hyphenation, or may be determined by using an exception word dictionary, which would be invoked prior to processing through the TextMaster program. Furthermore, the user may specify other hyphenation parameters that will affect the overall appearance of the job, some examples of which are:

.hu 4   \ '' at least 4 chars left on the end of line
.hd 3   \ '' at least 3 chars carried down to next line
.hl 3   \ '' don't hyphenate more than 3 in a row

Copy processing is made more efficient by a flexible implementation of strings and macros. Strings and macros are codes that permit the user to define blocks of text and commands which are used frequently as a much shorter series of characters. Defining the string "Whereas the party of the first part" as *fp* would, for example, be written as:

.ds fp Whereas the party of the first part

The command ".ds" means "define string."

One of the most significant features of TextMaster is the implementation of a command called a *trap.* A trap is a flag, which signals that some action (automatically invoking a macro) is to take place when the text reaches a certain vertical position on the page. A trap might be set to spring, for example, when the lowest point on a page is reached; at which point a footnote is inserted or a page number is set.

Pagination controls also can be specified by the use of a set of commands that determine page format. These commands can control:

• the length of the page
• the start of a new page
• the insertion of a page number
• the page offset (margin)
• the reservation of space of photo insertion
• the marking of a vertical position for a return to position

The specification of typographic commands, page formatting, textual controls, and operators extend far beyond this summary. Suffice it to say that the TextMaster program provides a very strong bridge from word processing files to the Comp/Edit typesetting environment.

TYPEFACE: Utilizing Word Processing Codes for Typesetting

There are certain document descriptors that both word processors and typesetters might have in common. Changes of typeface, centered lines, and paragraph endings, among others, might be similar in definition in both typewritten and typeset form. Of help in this regard is that many typesetting systems utilize translation tables when communicating with the computers that provide them with input. These translation tables usually accomplish two important functions. First, they convert predefined strings of characters into commands that the typesetting machine can process internally. Second, they stripout unrecognizable codes, such as those used to drive a line printer, and unusable codes, such as multiple word or line spaces or graphic characters.

Few word processors have the native intelligence to deal directly with both line printers and typesetters. One notable exception is TypeFace, a companion program to Quark Incorporated's[8] Word Juggler word processing program.

TypeFace is a utility program that provides the facility to send documents directly, via either on-line connection or modem transmission, between an Apple III and any typesetter which can both accept ASCII information through an RS-232 port and uses translation tables. It is also useful in those cases in which the typesetting installation is able to directly read Apple disks (Pascal ASCII file format).

Quark recognizes the limitations of the program, and cautions new users that the translation capabilities will not eliminate cut and paste and do not provide hyphenation and justification prior to typesetting. Despite these shortcomings, the program does provide the unique capability of allowing the user to produce one version of a file that can be output in two very different forms.

The operation of the TypeFace conversion could be characterized as paragraph oriented in nature. At the beginning of each paragraph, a string of codes, called a *Sequence,* is inserted to indicate typesetting information such as the line spacing (single, double, or triple), the line formatting (ragged right, ragged left, centered, or justified), and the font description. Each of these items are only specified if they have changed since the previous paragraph.

The Sequence is followed by the paragraph text. If at any point within the paragraph a descriptor needs to be changed, a new Sequence is inserted, composed only of that descriptor.

Certain word spaces also receive special attention during the translation process. Spaces at the beginning of a paragraph are converted into an indent Sequence. This step is necessary because individual typeset spaces are of variable width, dependent upon the mix of character widths that share the line with them. Of course, variable width is not a concern on a line printer that uses an equal horizontal escapement for each character and space. Another concern is the convention in typewriting which dictates that there are to be two spaces between each sentence. When the TypeFace program encounters either a period, an exclamation point, a question mark, or a single or double quote followed by two spaces it replaces the spaces with an EOS (End Of Sentence) Sequence. Paragraphs are ended with an EOP (End Of Paragraph) Sequence (FIG. 4).

The program also provides for the specification of true typesetting line-spacing values, line widths, and point sizes. In addition, superscripts, subscripts, and tabs are supported.

The TypeFace program is installed directly on the Word Juggler program disk and is easily accessed. After the file has been created, a special menu is provided in order to expedite the delivery of the file contents to the typesetting machine. The first menu option is ''CHECK,'' which examines the file in memory for erroneous TypeFace commands. If it should encounter one, the user can reenter Text Entry mode by pressing ESC, which will put the cursor on the line containing the error. The second option

[8]Quark Incorporated
2525 West Evans, Suite 220
Denver, CO 80219
(303) 934-2211

is "SEND," which puts the Apple into Terminal mode so that it can communicate directly with the typesetter. The final option is "WRITE," which creates a text file version on disk (FIG. 5).

FIG. 4. Sequence names for TypeFace.

SEQUENCE NAMES

PREAMBLE	Sent preceding document transmission.
POSTAMBLE	Sent following document transmission.
PINDENT	Indicates a paragraph indent. (Active only in TEXT mode)
EOS	Replaces the two spaces at the end of a sentence. (Active only in TEXT mode)
EOP	Marks the end of a paragraph.
BLANK	Sent to indicate a blank line.
SPACES(count)	Replaces a run of spaces with length greater than "count". (Active only in TABLE mode)
RAGGEDRIGHT	Turns on ragged right.
RAGGEDLEFT	Turns on ragged left.
JUSTIFY	Turns on justification.
CENTER	Turns on centering.
SINGLE	Turns on single spacing.
DOUBLE	Turns on double spacing.
TRIPLE	Turns on triple spacing.
NORMAL	Turns off bold and underlining (normal font).
UNDER	Turns on underlining. Turns off bold.
BOLD	Turns on bold. Turns off underlining.
BOTH	Turns on both bold and underlining.
STARTSUPER	Starts superscripting.
ENDSUPER	Ends superscripting.
STARTSUB	Starts subscripting.
ENDSUB	Ends subscripting.

FIG. 5. Sending special commands to the typesetter using the TypeFace program.

TypeFace™

SENDING SPECIAL COMMANDS TO THE TYPESETTER

COMMENT
TS:*sequence*

To send special characters, use "$" followed by a two-digit hexadecimal code for the character (e.g. "$0D" sends a carriage return). Note that to send just a "$", you must use "$$".

SPECIAL COMMANDS TO TYPEFACE

COMMENT
WJ:*command*

The valid commands are:

RESTORE	Resets all special sequences to their default values.
TEXT	Indicates that paragraphed text is being transmitted.
TABLE	Indicates that tables of values are being transmitted.

ASSIGNING NEW VALUES TO SPECIAL SEQUENCES

COMMENT
WJ:*sequence name=sequence*

Each sequence may contain up to 32 characters. For special characters, use "$" followed by a two-digit hexadecimal code for the character (e.g. "$0D" is a carriage return). Note that for just a "$", you must use "$$"

NUMERIC KEYPAD LAYOUT DURING "SEND"

Baud Rate Select	Handshake Toggle	BREAK
Parity Select		
Send LF Toggle		
Echo Toggle		Send Document
Delete Prev. Character	Return to TypeFace Menu	

To change character used for Delete Previous Character Key, press CONTROL – on the keypad.

READYSETGO-MP:
Converting Low-Resolution Personal Computer Text
and Graphics into High-Resolution Phototypeset Output

Achieving phototypeset or high-quality output of images generated on a microcomputer is an area of increasing growth. Such output may or may not increase the resolution of the image, but will, nonetheless, increase its definition by producing sharper, more well-formed, and more uniformly dense images than are presently produced by the typical output device, such as a dot matrix printer.

A number of programs have been written to convert microcomputer-generated graphics and text directly into an analogous typeset output form. One software product that provides direct typeset output of Apple Macintosh MacPaint drawings is the ReadySetGo-MP program from Manhattan Graphics[9] (FIG. 6). This dual software pack-

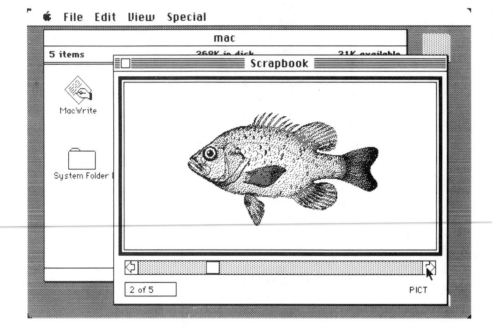

FIG. 6. Visual results of using the ReadySetGo-MP and producing the picture on the Imagewriter printer.

ReadySetGo-MP

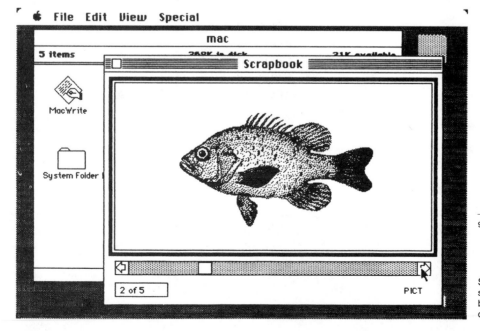

Imagewriter

[9]Manhattan Graphics
163 Varick Street
New York, NY 10013
(212) 924-3110

Site license information available. (The considerable memory utilization of the Macintosh bit-mapped graphics make the use of the hard disk a requirement.)

age, which connects the Macintosh (via direct cable connection) to the Compugraphic MCS-8400 system, consists of two translation programs: one at the Macintosh and one at the MCS editing workstation. Illustrations are drawn normally using MacPaint and saved locally at the Macintosh. Using the ReadySetGo-MP program, the file or files are selected and transmitted to the MCS, which is equipped with Compugraphic's Advanced Communication Interface and a hard disk.

The MacPaint file that is received at the MCS workstation appears on the screen as computer gibberish and cannot be altered, although it can be integrated with other MCS files for page layout. Prior to typesetting, the actual MacPaint image can be displayed on the MCS passive display device, the Preview, which provides a good approximation of how the image will appear when it is typeset.

A second member of the Manhattan Graphics family is the ReadySetGo-MW program, which facilitates the typesetting of Macintosh MacWrite documents (FIG. 7). The conversion to typesetting provides not only more typeface choices, but also better spaced, easier to read, and automatically hyphenated output.

The ReadySetGo capability can be utilized through a service-bureau arrangement offered by Manhattan Graphics for those Macintosh users who do not have direct access to their own MCS-8400 typesetter. For a prescribed amount, Manhattan Graphics or its licensees accepts Macintosh disks and converts any number of files into typeset output.

The MacPaint and MacWrite conversion programs are the precursors to sophisticated desktop publishing programs, developed by Manhattan Graphics and marketed by Letraset U.S.A.

FIG. 7a. The version as seen on the Macintosh screen.

ReadySetGo-MW Now Available !

New York

ReadySetGo-MW, the second member of Manhattan Graphics ReadySetGo product line, connects Apple's Macintosh with Compugraphic's MCS-8400 typesetting system and provides the ability to typeset **MacWrite** documents.

The Macintosh fonts are converted into **real type fonts** and the user can specify the exact conversion required. All MacWrite typographical functions are supported such as font change, point size change, line spacing, line length, justification etc. Since ReadySetGo-MW composes the text with real fonts, it can make better line ending decisions and provides full hyphenation capabilities.

ReadySetGo-MW is available to MCS-8400 owners immediately for a one-time license fee of $2,500. Owners of ReadySetGo-MP will receive a 30% discount on the MW product. For Macintosh owners without the MCS typesetting system, Manhattan Graphics will provide an output service. MacWrite documents will be typeset for $10 per (Imagewriter) page plus a set-up fee of $50 per job. The set-up fee covers the Mac to MCS font conversion.

ReadySetGo-MW Now Available !

FIG. 7b. Typeset from MacWrite.

New York

ReadySetGo-MW, the second member of Manhattan Graphics ReadySetGo product line, connects Apple's Macintosh with Compugraphic's MCS-8400 typesetting system and provides the ability to typeset **MacWrite** documents.

The Macintosh fonts are converted into **real type fonts** and the user can specify the exact conversion required. All MacWrite typographical functions are supported such as font change, point size change, line spacing, line length, justification etc. Since ReadySetGo-MW composes the text with real fonts, it can make better line ending decisions and provides full hyphenation capabilities.

ReadySetGo-MW is available to MCS-8400 owners immediately for a one-time license fee of $2,500. Owners of ReadySetGo-MP will receive a 30% discount on the MW product. For Macintosh owners without the MCS typesetting system, Manhattan Graphics will provide an output service. MacWrite documents will be typeset for $10 per (Imagewriter) page plus a set-up fee of $50 per job. The set-up fee covers the Mac to MCS font conversion.

CAUZIN SOFT STRIPS: Creating Publishable Media

Many desktop publishing projects involve gathering information from a number of sources and then assembling it into a publication. One of the main objectives in moving and manipulating information is to avoid rekeyboarding. Rekeyboarding is time-consuming, and can result in the introduction of new errors.

If existing information is only available on paper, then the options, until now, have been limited to OCR scanning or manual input. A third method, the Cauzin Strip System,[10] is a low-cost alternative for inputting information from dissimilar computer systems, as well as outputting information on plain paper for distribution or storage.

What the System Can Do for a Desktop Publisher

A desktop publisher's goal is to communicate thoughts and ideas effectively and efficiently, with a minimal expenditure of time and money. In order to do so, he must be able to make use of information that has already been stored in both electronic and hardcopy forms. The Cauzin System supports both the reading and writing of multiple narrow data strips on ordinary paper. Each strip is composed of a precise pattern of minute black and white rectangles. The arrangement of the rectangles is interpreted by the Cauzin Reader (FIG. 8) into binary data that can be processed by the host computer.

Computers that are supported by Cauzin, such as the Apple II series, the Apple Macintosh, and the IBM PC, both can interpret and create Softstrips. The capability to both read and print Softstrips makes it possible for all supported computers to exchange certain types of information freely, most notably ASCII text files.

10 Cauzin Systems, Inc.
   835 South Main Street
   Waterbury, CT 06706
   (800) 533-7323
   (203) 573-0150

Connecting the System to a Computer

The Cauzin Softstrip System Reader is purchased with the appropriate computer accessory kit. The kit consists of a software disk, sample Softstrips, an instruction manual, a subscription offer for the Cauzin Softstrip newsletter, and the cables necessary to connect the reader.

Installation takes no more than a few minutes. The accessory cable connects the reader to the serial port of the computer, and the power cord connects the reader to an AC outlet.

FIG. 8. The Cauzin Reader is an optical/electronic scanner with a moving "truck" that scans the length of a data strip in about 30 seconds. It uses an LSI chip and microprocessor to transfer the SoftStrip ASCII-encoded date to the internal memory of the personal computer. The reader can connect to any personal computer that has either an RS-232C or cassette input port (Courtesy of Cauzin Systems).

FIG. 9. A SoftStrip data strip is composed of the header (a), the start line (b), the checkerboard (c), the rack (d), the data area (e), and the alignment marks (f).

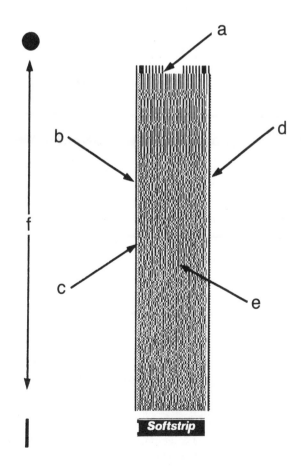

The Softstrip Data Specification

A Softstrip is composed of six different parts (FIG. 9). At the top of the strip is the *header* (FIG. 9a), which holds information concerning the number of bytes in a line, the height of each line, and the paper-to-ink contrast level. Each horizontal line is bounded by the *startline* (FIG. 9b), the *checkerboard* (FIG. 9c), and the *rack* (FIG. 9d). These elements help the reader identify the track that it is to follow and also help maintain alignment. The actual *data area* (FIG. 9e) is contained between the checkerboard and the rack. The user positions the reader by setting it on the *alignment dot* and *black line* (FIG. 9f).

The Scanning Process

In order to begin a scan, the host computer must be running the Cauzin Communications program (FIG. 10), and the Reader must be properly attached and powered. The following series of events comprise a complete scanning session using the Macintosh as an example:

- The Reader is aligned over the first data strip. Programs that consist of more than one data strip have numbers beside each of the short black alignment lines indicating the scanning order.
- The scan is activated by positioning the cursor arrow in the Read Strip box, located near the bottom of the screen, and clicking the mouse. A message appears at the top of the screen, indicating that the read is in progress. A small arrow located to the right of the screen data strip image moves down the strip, indicating the actual reading speed.
- After a strip has been read, information concerning its name, file, type, and size, are displayed on the screen (FIG. 11). If additional strips are part of the program, the user is prompted to align the next data strip in sequence, and click in the Read Strip box.
- When all of the associated data strips have been read, the communication program automatically initiates any necessary file conversion. The user then is prompted to accept the displayed file name for saving to disk. The saved file is now ready to use.

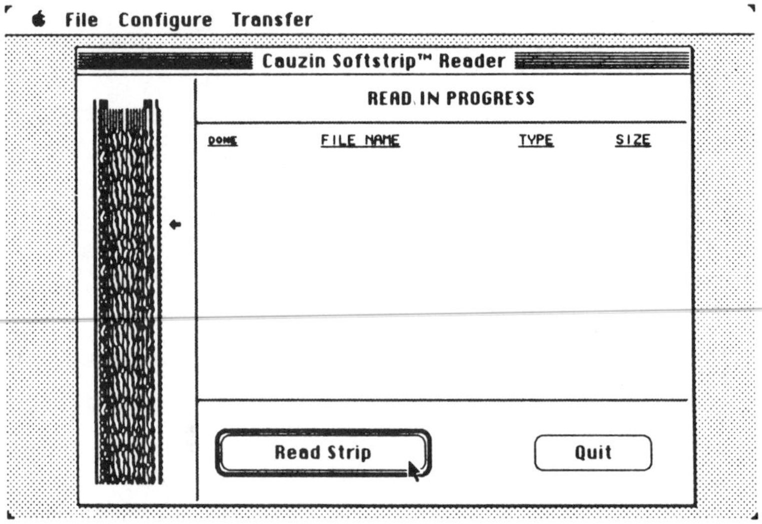

FIG. 10. The Cauzin Communications program shows an animated display of the scanning operation.

The Strip Creation Process

Part of the excitement, and much of the potential utility, of the Cauzin System is in its publishing capability. Significant amounts of data can be published compactly and inexpensively using conventional printing and duplicating methods. Although a user must commit to the one-time expense of a Reader, Softstrips can be reproduced in mass quantities at a per unit cost unrivaled by any competitive method.

Softstrip System users can buy a program to produce their own data strips, using either a dot matrix printer (StripWare Stripper) or a laser printer (StripWare Laser Pro). The quality of the printed output determines the data density that is obtainable, ranging from a low of 1075 bytes per eight-inch strip using a dot matrix printer, to a high of 3675 bytes using a laser printer.

The Macintosh version of the StripWare Stripper is simple to use. The user selects up to 10 files to convert into SoftStrip form. As the files are selected, their names and sizes appear on the screen, along with an indication of the number of data strips and number of pages that will result (FIG. 12).

The laser printer version of the program, which is considerably more expensive, provides more publishing design options. These options include rotating the strips, changing their lengths, and adding descriptive text.

FIG. 11. The input file's name, type, and size are shown following a successful scan.

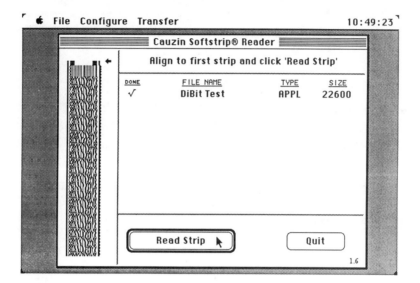

FIG. 12. A desktop publisher can produce SoftStrips quickly and easily using a dot matrix or laser printer. The three selected files in the window shown will result in 46 data strips on 6 pages of dot matrix output.

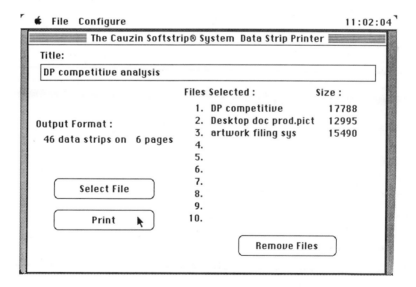

Checking for Accuracy

Softstrip data strips use double parity and a checksum for error checking, providing higher accuracy than magnetic media. Although they are printed on ordinary paper, they are durable and can be read through creases, ink, coffee stains, and other desktop calamities.

The Cauzin Reader is engineered to read an accurate data strip 999 times out of 1000. Under normal circumstances, the 1 out of 1000 exception will only require a second reading in order to be input properly.

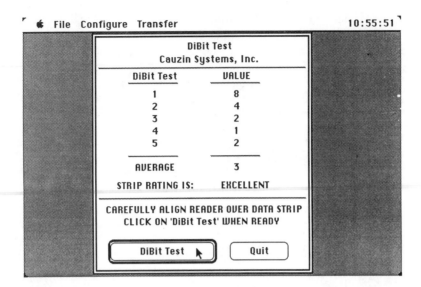

FIG. 13. The DiBit Test program, which is included with the Stripper program, makes repetitive scans of user-produced data strips, to ensure that they are readable.

An evaluation program, called the DiBit text (FIG. 13), is used to evaluate the accuracy of strips and also the printer that produced them. The program is used to certify the reading of a strip, not the data it contains.

After the DiBit program is run, the reader is aligned over a data strip. When the reader is activated, it makes five abbreviated read cycles. Several scans of the same line are made, and the results are displayed on the computer screen. The possible values are as follows:

Average 0-6	Excellent
Average 7-12	Good
Average 13-20	Marginal
Average 20+	Make a new one
Average***	Unable to read

The DiBit program is essential for verifying that a data strip is usable prior to reproducing it in quantity. A visual inspection of a strip can be made by using a magnifying glass, and selecting a strip that has equally sized black and white areas.

Reproducing Data Strips

Multiple sheets of data strips can be made directly on a dot matrix or laser printer; however, that process is usually rather slow. Faster, more efficient reproduction can be done using a photocopier or offset press.

Although the dot matrix output is the original and the photocopier output is a first-generation copy, the reproduction capability of a properly maintained office copier might be better than that produced by a dot matrix printer. However, a copy of a copy, or a *second-generation copy*, is more prone to toner specks, which can create noise and introduce errors. Copiers also are affected by mechanical motion and optical distortion, which can result in changes in the dimensions of the copied images. Although a data strip can vary as much as 6 percent in any dimension, copies should not be made beyond two generations.

High volumes of data strips are best reproduced using offset printing. Offset printed sheets have images formed from a thin layer of ink, which is usually absorbed into the paper. Images produced by this process are more resistant to scratching and flaking, and less likely to be affected by creasing or folding.

Softstrip Program 1. *Computer:* IBM PC
Program: Word Finder Demo, *Publisher:* Microlytics, Inc.
Capability: Find synonyms to a limited number of words.

IMPROVE YOUR WRITING
...IN FIVE SECONDS OR LESS!

Find the right word for your thought without taking your hands off the keyboard or your eyes off the screen. With Word Finder, you just place your cursor on the word you want a substitute for, and up pops a window with a list of alternate words with similar meaning. Put the cursor on the word you want, and press the return key. The new word instantly replaces the old word right in the document, even retaining the exact punctuation and capitalization.

"I recommend Word Finder from Abandon to Zeal."   Peter McWilliams

"Word Finder is an affordable adjunct for whipping (flogging, thrashing) your prose into shape quickly and efficiently, without leaving the document file you're working in."
                    David Obregón, PC Magazine

". . . Give serious consideration to making Word Finder a permanent resident in your electronic reference library."
                    Barbara Lewis, PC World

". . . A joy to use." "Compared to Borland's Turbo Lightning Word Finder requires less memory, has four times as many synonyms in a file that is only twice as big . . ."
                    Bill Todd, Chicago Computer Society

OPERATING INSTRUCTIONS

Read the five data strips on the right into your data disk. Return to the A: prompt and type the word **DEMO**.

The demo is as easy to use as the Word Finder program. There are complete on-screen instructions and the demo is self-running. Quit anytime by pressing F10.

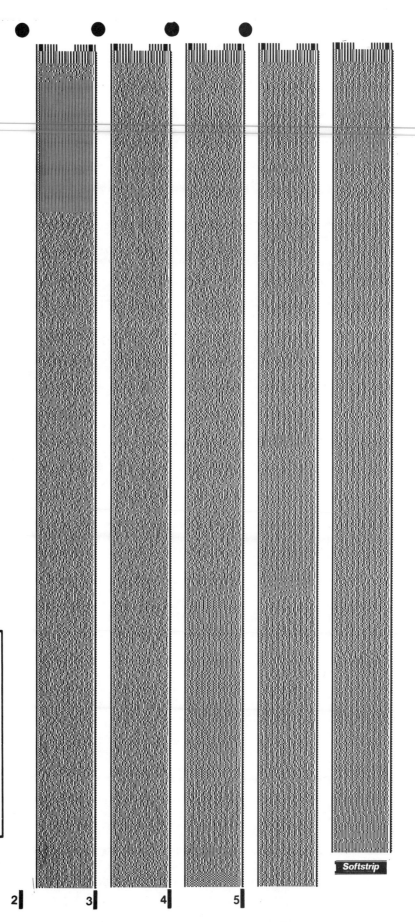

Softstrip

1   2   3   4   5

Softstrip Program 2. *Computer:* Apple Macintosh
Program: Stripware Laser Pro Preview, *Publisher:* Cauzin Systems
Capability: Design bitmap typographic characters.

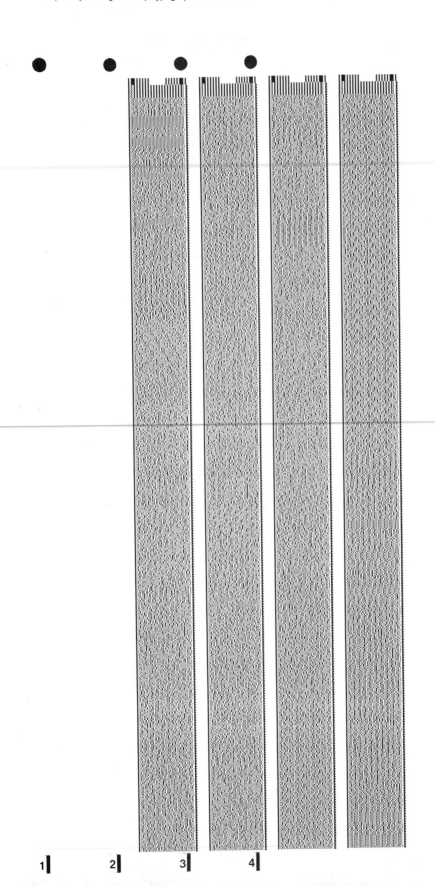

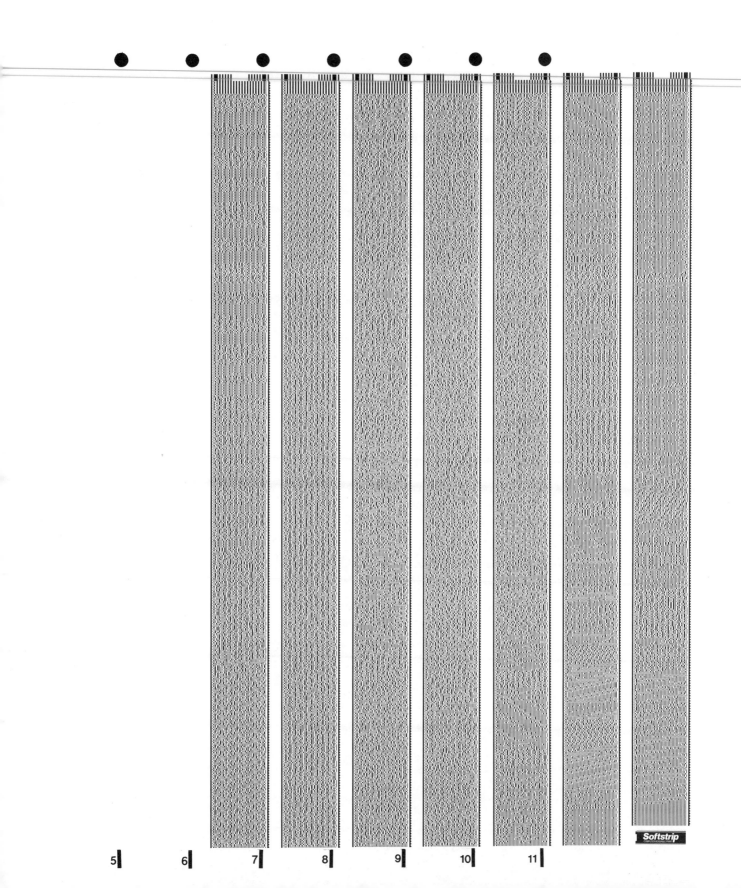

Softstrip Program 3. *Computer:* Apple Macintosh
Program: FONTastic Font Editor Demo, *Publisher:* Altsys Inc.
Capability: Produce Softstrips using the Apple Macintosh and Apple LaserWriter.

FONTASTIC

Softstrip

13 | 14 | 15 | 16 | 17 | 18 | 19 |

Chapter 7

Typesetting Hardware Tools

Accessories and programs which enhance productivity, efficiency, and, in some cases, enhance the appearance of the output.

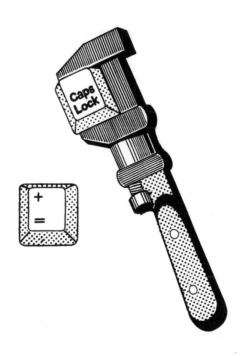

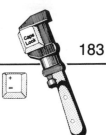

THE CHAMELEON-LIKE QUALITY OF THE MICROCOMPUTER IS ATTRIBUTABLE TO THE MAjor changes in screen appearance and keyboard operation that are brought about by the use of different software programs. This element of versatility is at the very center of most microcomputers' engineering and marketing specifications. Not only can a microcomputer change in overall functioning—from a database manipulator to a word processor, from a word processor to an intelligent terminal, from an intelligent terminal to an arcade machine, etc.—but it can change significantly in functioning on the basis of the power and sophistication of the particular software package in use. All the while, however, the hardware in use remains the same.

The process of typesetting is a keyboard-intensive activity. Although software can work in many ways to reduce the time necessary to accomplish certain functions and to enhance the efficiency of others, it is the keyboard that remains the ultimate barrier to communicating information from the outside world to the micro environment. There are, fortunately, a number of ways to increase *keyboard productivity* for certain microcomputer models; that is, either making all or some keys do the work of many or making all or some of the keys more accessible.

A BRIEF HISTORY OF THE KEYBOARD

The keyboard, as a human/machine interface device, was invented as means of controlling what is believed to have been the first automated typesetting machine. According to an account published in the report "Direct Entry Phototypesetting":[1]

In 1822 in Birmingham, England, visitors to William Church's workshop could witness a most strange contraption (FIG. 1). It was a large hardwood frame, rectangular in shape, and supported upright by two oversize feet. It had across its upright pillars various metal mechanisms, all quite alien to any observer. A foot petal was used to supply power to a complex network of clockworks and weights. Eighty keys, arranged in four rows of twenty, dominated the front of the machine. Upon inquiry, Church, a medical doctor, who abandoned his profession in favor of tinkering with machines, would have explained that this device was a type of composing machine. And indeed it was, by most accounts the first successful attempt at mechanizing the typesetting process.

The most significant feature of the Church machine is its keyboard, and it has obviously had a profound effect on human/machine interfacing ever since. There is, interestingly enough, a close alliance between the mechanics of early typesetters and the construction of musical instruments. Part of the keyboard mechanism on Church's machine, for example, was fashioned after similar parts on a harpsichord. The 1839 Kiegl Composer, and the 1840 Clay and Rosenberg Typesetter and Distributor, both closely resembled upright pianos. The Clay and Rosenberg machine could be run by crank or steam power, and it was suggested by another contemporary inventor that it be run by perforated tape. James Young and Adrian Delacambre invented the Pianotype (FIG. 2), based in part on Church's principles, and again very much resembling a piano.

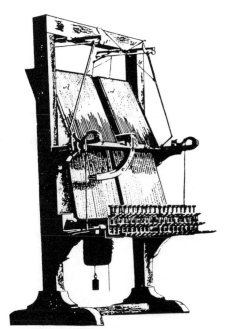

FIG. 1. The Church machine is generally regarded as the first mechanical typesetter. (Courtesy of Richard E. Huss.)

[1]Michael L. Kleper
Graphic Dimensions
(Pittsford, NY)
1978, pp 3-4

The development of the typesetting keyboard and the typewriter have evolved along parallel lines, crossing many times and eventually intertwining. The keyboard layout on most of today's microcomputers, word processors, typesetters, and other related devices is descended from early work in typesetting and typewriting development.

The first commercially successful typewriter was invented by Christopher Latham Sholes, who was actually the 52nd man to invent the typewriter, but the first to overcome all of the mechanical and economic problems surrounding the machine. His role in the history of typesetting devices is significant since his keyboard layout has endured to the present day.

Sholes' QWERTY keyboard layout, common to most keyboards today, is believed to have been the result of mechanical limitations inherent in the design of the typewriter itself. It seems that originally the typebars were arranged in such a way that the machine could not be operated at any speed without resulting in a jam. Sholes set out to determine the most inefficient layout of the alphabet possible, so that users would be forced to move their fingers greater distances, and therefore reduce the possibility of keybar jams.

Sholes gave the assignment of devising a suitable keyboard to his brother-in-law, who was a mathematician. The result was the QWERTY arrangement and fewer jammed typebars.

Sholes' influence on typesetting was to occur almost immediately. It seems that one of Sholes' close friends was a financial backer of Ottmar Mergenthaler, who invented the Linotype machine (FIG. 3), the machine that was to become the first commercially successful typesetter. To maintain good relations with his backer, Mergenthaler is believed to have altered his keyboard mechanism to incorporate some of the design characteristics of the aforementioned typewriter.

Although some early experimental typesetting machines used the QWERTY keyboard layout, most did not. In fact, it can be concluded that, in many cases, the keyboard layout was a result of the mechanical limitations of the machine design, rather than a conscious plan based on keyboarding efficiency. Mergenthaler's Linotype is a good example of an enduring (though dying) typesetting machine whose keyboard layout resulted from a mechanical requirement; that is, the need to have the most frequently used characters in the closest proximity to the assembling elevator. The layout of the keys on the Linotype relates one-to-one to the horizontal arrangement of matrices in the magazine channels. Although the frequency of use of characters is provided for, the Linotype keyboard puts seven of the most often used characters under the control of the operator's left hand, resulting in an unbalanced work distribution.

One of the first typewriters to be produced as a typesetter was the Ham-

FIG. 2. The Pianotype (1840), invented by Young and Delacambre, gave early meaning to the phrase "to be composing type." (Courtesy of Richard E. Huss.)

FIG. 3. The Linotype machine circa 1950. It was given its name in 1886 when one of the first machines was installed at the New York Tribune. Editor Whitelaw Reid called the metal slug exiting the machine a "line-o-type," and the apt description stuck. (Courtesy of Eastman Kodak Company.)

mond machine. James Bartlett Hammond, its inventor, was a young Civil War correspondent who was dependent upon the telegraph to wire his handwritten stories to his newspaper. Telegraphers frequently misinterpreted his writing, leading to misprints and causing frequent embarrassment and anger. Hammond conceived a typewriter that would print his story so clearly that even a careless telegrapher could follow it easily. His first model was produced in 1881, and featured a changeable typewheel for different faces and sizes.

The Hammond Company was acquired by Ralph C. Coxhead in the early 1930s. Coxhead renamed the Hammond machine the VariTyper, because of its typographic flexibility. The VariTyper was more of a refined typewriter than a simplified typesetter, but nonetheless, typists easily could be trained to set "type." The machine is still in use today for very limited applications.

Although typesetting keyboards today usually incorporate dedicated keys to access typographic functions, special characters, or other machine capabilities, the main keyboard uses the same QWERTY character arrangement that is found on virtually all other keyboards, regardless of their application.

KEYBOARD ENHANCEMENT

Many studies have been conducted to prove what has been known from the start: that the QWERTY keyboard arrangement is inefficient. Lillian Malt, a British pioneer in keyboard training and keyboard layout design, found that the QWERTY keyboard layout generates fewer than one-third of the average English-language words from the home-row keys. A study comparing her Malton II layout to the QWERTY showed that QWERTY produced 44 percent of the 100 most used English words from the home row as compared to Maltron's 90 percent. (FIG. 4a).

The total Malt Method of improved keyboarding combines a multimediated training program along with the Malt keyboard and Malt keyboard layout. The Malt keyboard, which is like no other, provides two dish-shaped concave key assemblies, one for each hand. The slope of the keys compensates for the differences in the lengths of the user's fingers. Although scientifically proven to be more efficient, the Malt keyboard has not found much acceptance in the United States.

The answer to improved keyboard layout seems to be the rediscovery of the work of August Dvorak, which was conducted in the early 1930s. Dvorak, working under a Carnegie Corporation grant, was named the director of the Carnegie Foundation for the Advancement of Teaching Study of Typewriting. Using time-and-motion studies of typists filmed by Frank and Lillian Gilbreth, Dvorak was able to formulate a set of nine principles that he believed applied to the physical activity of typewriting. These principles, combined with a study of the frequency and order of letters appearing in the English language, prompted Dvorak to conclude in December of 1943 that "it is possible to make at random dozens of typewriter keyboards which are as good or better than the Sholes Universal Keyboard. If the letters and characters in the lower three rows of keys are drawn from a hat and placed by pure chance, keyboard arrangements frequently are secured on which the total hand and finger loads are more equitably divided, on which there are fewer one-hand words, and on which there are fewer awkwardly stroked letter-sequences than on the mentioned Sholes Universal Keyboard."[2]

Dvorak's work resulted in an improved layout (FIG. 4b), which he patented in 1936. In studies conducted on the use of the keyboard, it was shown to improve productivity and reduce fatigue, yet the firmly entrenched population of QWERTY-trained operators seemed to ignore its apparent benefits. It was not until November 19, 1982, that the Dvorak layout achieved an adequate measure of recognition. On that date, The American National Standards Institute, Inc. approved it as an alternate standard to the QWERTY keyboard arrangement for alphanumeric office machines.

FIG. 4a. A variety of Maltron keyboard layouts. The Maltron provides increased operator comfort by relieving postural stress and the resultant fatigue. By dividing the keys into two separated groups, the operator's wrists can remain straight. This change frees the space in the center of the keyboard so that keys can be allocated to the thumbs, which are strong and versatile. (Photo courtesy of P.C.D. Maltron Ltd., 15 Orchard Lane, East Molesey, Surrey KT8 OBN, England, 01-398-3265).

[2]Michael L. Kleper
"DVORAK: The New Keyboard Layout Standard" Graphic Dimensions, 1983

What has followed is an incredible amount of support from keyboard manufacturers, software houses, and third-party manufacturers to provide Dvorak layouts on a wide, and ever growing, variety of keyboard-based equipment.

Many of the micro-environment typesetting software packages mentioned in this book that provide the user with the ability to design characters and map them to the keyboard can easily support the generation of the Dvorak layout (or any other for that matter). Many systems are also available directly from their manufacturers (and had been for many years before the adoption of the standard) with the Dvorak layout. Some keyboards, such as that on the Apple *II*c and IIGS, are switchable between the Dvorak and the QWERTY.

Hardware conversions are available for a number of microcomputers. Those handy with the modification of electronic circuitry sometimes can convert their keyboards by themselves, while others might want to purchase a conversion kit such as that sold by Southern California Research Group[3] for the Apple II. The company's hardware device, called The Magic Keyboard, converts the Apple's keyboard into any two (switch-selectable) of many alternate keyboard layouts. The external set of switches allows the user to select between two of these several available keyboard configurations and to return to the standard QWERTY instantly.

The installation of The Magic Keyboard takes under 15 minutes and is accomplished easily. Three sheets of decals are supplied for relabeling the keycaps according to the most frequently used layout. Among the standard keyboard alternatives provided are the Dvorak, the American Simplified Keyboard, Alphabetical Order, The Montgomery, One-Handed Left, One-Handed Right, four variations of ten-key numeric keypads, and four variations of hexadecimal keypads. A user also can design his own keyboard layout and order a custom PROM for a slight charge.

ACCESSORY KEYBOARDS

The use of microcomputers as typesetting input stations has become commonplace. Their use by trade and commercial craftspeople, office and clerical personnel, word processing and secretarial service employees, authors and technical writers has cut across all traditional methods of generating keystrokes for phototypesetting output.

There are a number of alternate keyboards available for many microcomputers, from the membrane keyboard Timex-Sinclair and Atari 400, to the more sophisticated old Apple Macintosh and IBM AT.

[3]Southern California Research Group
P.O. Box 2231
Goleta, CA 93118
(805) 685-1931

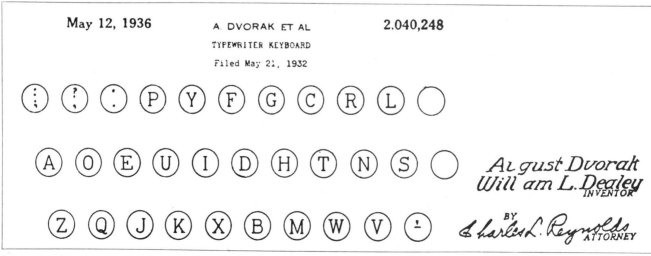

FIG. 4b. The Dvorak keyboard arrangement. A typist's fingers working at 100 words per minute would travel 10 to 20 miles over a standard keyboard in one day, while the same work would result in just over 1 ;mile of travel on the Dvorak, a reduction of over 90 percent.

KEY TRONIC PLUS: A Detached and Enhanced Keyboard

When used exclusively in a typesetting environment, the microcomputer keyboard in most cases is lacking many of the features that are considered standard on traditional dedicated input devices. Such things as a working shift key, displayable uppercase and lowercase characters, cursor controls, programmable function keys, and editing keys might not be present. A family of alternate keyboards incorporating many of these features is manufactured by Key tronic Corporation,[4] and distributed by SSE Products Inc.[5] Key tronic offers the KB 200 for the Apple II, II+, and IIe (FIG. 5), and the KB 5150 for the IBM PC. Both keyboards are completely compatible with their respective microcomputers, have expanded layouts and detachable units, and feature an ergonomic design.

Getting On-Line

For purposes of evaluation, the Key tronic KB 200 for the Apple II+ was used. It took about one-half hour to install the keyboard, the major part of which was devoted to the partial disassembly and reassembly of the Apple housing. The unit renders the Apple keyboard inoperable, but a soft-switch is available that will permit the use of either keyboard (if such is considered necessary).

After the unit is installed, the Apple itself need not be placed on the work surface, or even within sight. Provided that all necessary cabling will support the placement of the Apple on a shelf or under a desk, the work surface need only accommodate the keyboard, monitor, and disk drives. This capability not only results in a neater work surface, but allows for complete modularity in placing each element in an ergonomically efficient manner.

[4]Key tronic Corporation
Spokane, WA 99216
(509) 928-8000

[5]SSE Products Inc.
791 Meacham Ave.
Elmont, NY 11003
(516) 872-9001

Eleven Function Keys Streamline Multiple Key Operations

Full Shifting Capability

Keys in Familiar Typewriter Locations

Numeric Pad

10 Foot Cable For Portability

FIG. 5. The KB 200 from Key tronic is an Apple plug-compatible replacement keyboard that includes a function keypad, numeric keypad, and status LED for power and shift lock. The company also makes a variety of alternate keyboards and keypads for a wide range of computers.

Keys Dedicated To Their Jobs

As a direct replacement for the Apple II+ keyboard, the Key tronic KB 200 offers many advantages, mainly in increasing the efficiency of the user in utilizing native Apple commands related to the disk operating system. There are dedicated keys, for example, to catalog or boot a disk, and to list, load, save, delete, or stop a program. Each one of these keys reduces a multiple-key sequence to a single-key entry. The numeric keypad on the right provides one-hand entry of numeric information—useful not only in programming an item entry in applications software, but also for typesetting applications involving numeric tabular work and mathematics.

Although the keyboard itself does not provide any programmable keys nor any keys specifically dedicated to typesetting input, it should be obvious that the efficiencies derived from the increased ease of use of the Apple disk operating system will have a direct impact on the effectiveness of the keyboard as a typesetting input device. Files created on the Apple are, after all, resident in the Apple disk operating system, and as such, their manipulation by single-key commands will positively affect the speed and ease of keyboarding for typesetting output.

A Design That Wins Hands Down

Of the many alternate keyboards available, the Key tronic KB 200 has one of the lowest profiles, both in terms of its cabinet and its key cap slope. The low profile in itself can have a significant effect on operator comfort and reduced fatigue level, since studies suggest that typing is most efficient when the arms are at a 90-degree angle to the body. In Europe, work-station design is subject to governmental regulation. The Germans specify a maximum height for the keyboard of just over 1 inch.

European standards also specify a detached design for a keyboard, which is a major feature of the Key tronic KB 200. With its coiled cord, the unit can be placed in any comfortable position, and two small hidden legs on the underside of the keyboard can be lowered to slightly increase the angle of the keybank.

The feel of the keys on the KB 200 is different than that of the Apple, as would be true when comparing the feel of almost any two dissimilar keyboard devices. It seems to be somewhat spongy, although not disagreeable nor uncomfortable. The auto-repeat feature is a timesaver, and it can be enabled or disabled by pressing the power indicator key.

EPS KB A3

One of the fantastic capabilities of a microcomputer is its ability to take on a number of different characteristics based upon the software that resides within its memory. This versatility gives users the choice of a variety of different text and word processors for creating input for phototypesetting output. This choice of configuring an input system now is extending to hardware as well. Another keyboard peripheral is the EPS KB A3 from Executive Peripheral Systems, Inc.[6] This device for the Apple II, II+ (FIG. 6), and optionally *II*e, has some unique features that make it adaptable to a number of software-specific applications.

Developing a Fond Attachment

The installation of the KB A3 is probably as easy as any installation of this type could be. It can be accomplished in about 15 minutes, and depending upon the installer's dexterity and the size of his hands, requires no tools. Very simply, the top of the Apple II+ is removed, the keyboard cable is unplugged, and the KB A3 interface board is plugged in its place. The interface board has a short cable attached with a telephone-type jack attached. This jack hangs out of the back of the Apple, and the KB A3's 6-foot coiled cord plugs into it to complete the installation. In a normal installation

[6]Executive Peripheral Systems, Inc.
800 San Antonio Road, Suite 1
Palo Alto, CA 94304

FIG. 6. The EPS KB A3 replacement keyboard provides plug-in PROMware modules which reconfigure the keyboard to match popular software packages, thereby reducing or eliminating complex command sequences.

the Apple keyboard would be rendered useless, but EPS provides an optional soft-switch in order to keep the Apple keyboard activated.

Let's Go To the PROM

Perhaps the major strength of the KB A3 is its use of the programmable read-only memory (PROM) for specialized applications. The PROM stores a program that defines the meaning of 12 format keys, which provide up to 48 command strings, and special key sequences, which greatly enhance the use of the Apple disk operating system, CP/M, and a number of popular software packages such as WordStar, AppleWriter II, and VersaForm. A recent development is the availability of the Dvorak keyboard layout for most software packages.

Each PROM-ware module is housed in a small plastic cartridge, which plugs into a concealed compartment located along the top of the keyboard. The compartment provides storage space for nine such cartridges and the overlay masks that indicate the new key definitions. Each cartridge provides mapping for two specific applications, the choice of which is accessed by properly setting the program key in the upper right row of keys.

In addition to providing reserved format keys, the KB A3 has a full-size numeric keypad, editing keys, and full cursor controls. The auto repeat function is available on the cursor control, numeric keypad, alphanumeric, and some editing keys. The keyboard also utilizes a 60-character type-ahead buffer which, in certain circumstances, will store characters in advance of the Apple's ability to process them. A small but innovative feature is the use of deep-dish keycaps on the *f* and *j* keys, making home-row finger placement easier.

For each application, all possible input requirements are not only available, but are accessible with fewer keystrokes—a significant feature not only for reduced operator fatigue, but also as a productivity enhancer, making the keyboard a cost-effective accessory for typesetting input, or any other use for that matter.

Making WordStar Shine

WordStar is one of the most popular word processing programs available for use on microcomputers. Both Itek and Compugraphic have marketed WordStar for their phototypesetting systems. Their versions are almost identical to those sold for dozens of other computer systems, with the major exception that they have been modified to make use of the specialized keys resident on typesetting keyboards. For this enhancement, the user pays a premium, but also benefits from the resulting increase in efficiency that this key mapping provides.

The KB A3 provides similar key mapping. However, instead of modifying the software to match the hardware, EPS provides a PROM, which redefines the keyboard. The new key functions match the input that WordStar expects to receive in order to execute any of its dozens of commands. In essence, the KB A3 becomes a WordStar keyboard, not only making it easier to create textual matter in the work sense by eliminating much of the overhead time necessary for both recalling (and often looking up) commands and inputting their multiple key identities, but also in the creative sense by having the functions operate more by tactile than cerebral input.

The use of the KB A3 with WordStar is at first feel a luxury, relieving the user of the heavy task of remembering numerous codes that do not, in all cases, make perfect mnemonic sense nor suggest logical assignment. Within a short time the user probably will develop a close attachment for the keyboard, recognizing that it has relieved a major burden of the use of WordStar; making input easier, faster, and perhaps more creative.

The use of WordStar for typesetting input is an excellent choice. It has many features not commonly found in the typesetting environment, and is supported by MicroPro, its publisher, with companion programs. Additionally, there are numerous complementary programs, from a number of vendors, that assist in sorting, footnoting, telecommunicating, annotating, and cataloging WordStar files. The use of a compatible keyboard greatly enhances the usefulness of WordStar for typesetting input, not only by increasing its friendliness to the operator, but by equalizing the disparity between the quality of microcomputer and typesetting keyboard hardware.

Having it Your Own Way

While EPS offers PROM-ware modules for many popular software packages, it also makes available a low-cost device for users to program their own modules. This device enables the keyboard interface to the computer to take on any attributes that the user wants, be it for other applications software packages, a custom-designed program, or a special typesetting job requiring numerous formats or repetitious names and phrases. This flexibility is heretofore unknown, and places a powerful facility in the hands of users.

For typesetting users this customizing ability is particularly advantageous. It can be used to map a keyboard to drive any specific phototypesetter, using that typesetter's peculiar set of commands and/or mnemonics. With a quick change of a module, the KB A3 could be reconfigured as a totally different input keyboard, supporting either a different typesetter or a different category of typesetting.

The implications for typesetting services that support microcomputer users are far-reaching. A micro user having a KB A3 could buy a specially prepared PROM from a typesetting service which would map his keyboard with prepared formats meeting his own individual needs and matching the output capabilities of the service's phototypesetter. Typesetting services also could provide such keyboards at no cost or low cost to micro users who maintain a monthly minimum of typesetting purchases.

Since many Apples are used for typesetting input, it is worthwhile to investigate the use of devices such as these, especially if the Apple keyboard currently being used is beginning to show signs of wear. The cost of alternate keyboards is modest, and becomes increasingly so when compared to the repair or replacement costs of the Apple keyboard itself.

POLYTEL: A Large-Format Membrane Keyboard

There have been two primary philosophies of keyboarding efficiency: one states that there should be one key for each character, special symbol, and function. This arrangement of *dedicated keys* leaves no ambiguity as to the manner by which each aspect of the typesetting process is executed. Each key is labeled with its one and only identity. The opposing philosophy states that the use of mnemonic character strings—that is, a succession of characters which signify a particular function, such as Control-S for "Save", or a particular special character, such as Escape-De for "degree sign"—results in higher productivity. The use of mnemonics requires fewer physical keys, although more actual keystrokes, and is a means of enhancing typesetting input since it keeps the keyboardist's fingers on the main keyboard.

Although it was not specifically designed for typesetting input, an accessory keyboard for the Apple II family of microcomputers provides an extraordinary 717 dedicated keyboard positions, surpassing the character and command function repertoires of most typesetting systems. This keyboard is the Keyport 717,[7] an advanced-technology flat-membrane keyboard that measures 12 × 25 × 2 inches (FIG. 7). It plugs into the game controller socket of the Apple and can be configured with the appropriate program disk and flexible plastic overlay, as one of a number of available packaged applications or as a completely user-defined keyboard.

The active area of the Keyport measures 9 inches × 22 inches, and a typical application uses between 150 and 300 keys. Unused keys do not appear on the overlay, which can be designed to indicate key positions with any combination of words, symbols, colors, graphics, or pictures. A single key can be programmed to execute a series of commands or a string of characters. Additionally, the programmer can reserve a bank of key locations as end-user format keys (user-defined keys), which can be programmed to the particular job in progress.

The Keyport does not affect the use of the main Apple keyboard, which remains the primary input device, since touch-typing is not easily accomplished on the Keyport. Neither a separate power supply nor discrete integrated circuits are needed for the Keyport, which as a result of its simplicity, can be located up to 200 feet from the computer. It can be mounted on the wall, on a desk, or on a machine, and without its case it measures just 1/10th inch thick.

The actual functioning of the device is described this way: "Pressing a key changes two electrical resistances in the Keyport between the Input line and X and Y Output lines. The computer then polls the Keyport by sending it a ONE or a ZERO on the Input line and monitoring the X and Y lines for the return signal. The Keyport circuit delays the signal by an amount proportional to the X and Y coordinate of the key. By timing the return of the signal, the computer identifies the key.

"The decoding circuits containing the resistors are printed on pieces of polyester film which are then laminated together. This membrane "sandwich" uses thick-film technology to create a giant integrated circuit containing the individual circuit elements. The key-reading routine, stored in the computer's memory, features a table with data about each key, the Key Data Table or KDT. The KDT includes the functions, commands, words, or single characters assigned to each key. It tells the program what to do when a key is pressed. The KDT allows the computer to perform the desired functions with a single keystroke, without using menus or language analysis. A new KDT is loaded with each program, so different keys can have different meanings in different programs. Changing the Keyport overlay changes the visual key pattern so that it corresponds to the functions in the KDT."

[7]Polytel Corporation
1250 Oakmead Parkway, Suite 310
Sunnyvale, CA 94086
(408) 730-1347

The Keyport comes with the software tools necessary to make any number of Key Data Tables for defining the identities of any of the Keyport key locations. Utility programs also are included to link the key assignments to a user-written BASIC program. A blank, clear key layout sheet is included with each Keyport for devising and testing, and Polytel assists in the design and reproduction of professional full-color overlays for both high- and low-volume applications.

A derivative of the Keyport 717 technology is the Keyport 300 for the IBM PC/XT, a considerably smaller, yet, in some ways, more functional device. The model 300 is fully user programmable and is designed to simplify and expand the use of all computer applications software. The model 300 functions like an on-line keystroke recorder, allowing the user to program into each of its keys a number of keystrokes representing an application procedure or a string of characters. These key assignments are saved in Key Definition Tables, just as on the model 717, although in this case the key assignment activity takes place while the application is being executed. Any number of KDTs may be created and saved for later use.

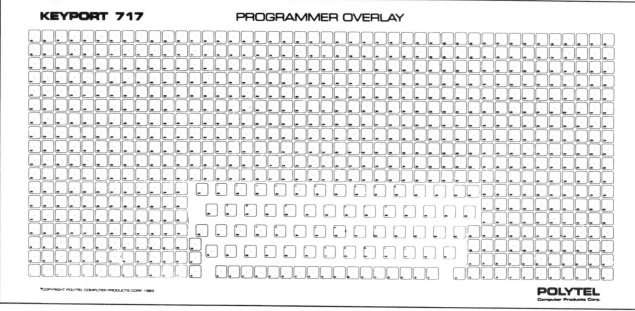

FIG. 7. The Polytel Keyport 717 keyboard is built into a hard shell case, which opens to store additional keyboard overlays, program disks, and documentation. The programmer overlay shows all of the 717 key locations that may be programmed by the user (Courtesy of Polytel).

This hardware solution has been implemented in software by a number of software houses. Software Research Technologies' Smartkey II Plus, for CP/M and IBM personal computers and their compatibles, and RoseSoft's ProKey 3.0, for IBM Personal Computers and their compatibles, are totally RAM-resident programs that permit the user to define keys on the computer keyboard. The keys retain their normal alphanumeric identities, as well as assume new identities, which are accessed by using multiple-key sequences.

POLYTEL KEYPORT 300: An Accessory Flat Membrane Keypad

The path that leads from the origination of information to the output of typeset galleys and pages almost always travels through the keyboard interface. There is, at present, no substitute that is as flexible, reliable, and universally understood as is the standard QWERTY keyboard.

The achievement of higher input productivity has come mainly from technology which enhances the use of the keyboard, rather than from that which has tried to replace it. In the typesetting environment, keyboard productivity increases have been realized by either adding more keys (dedicating specific functions and characters to additional keys); using multiple-key command, bell, or supershift code sequences; or using mnemonic code sequences for commands and special characters. The high overhead in command and special character keys utilized in typesetting requires a particularly skilled keyboard operator.

The acceptance of the personal computer as an input device for typesetting is a good example of creative adaptation. Although the typical computer keyboard has none

FIG. 8. The Keyport 300 system software supports the attachment of up to two Keyport keypads on a single personal computer. Changeable keypad overlays and stored key definition tables make it easy to change between applications (Courtesy of Polytel).

of the special function, command, or character keys required for typesetting, methods and techniques have been devised to allow the personal computer user to access readily all of the alphanumeric, special character, and appearance-related commands required in the typesetting environment. To do so, however, has meant that multiple keystrokes have been required for virtually all nonstandard alphanumeric characters, and virtually all system commands and functions.

A means of argumenting the character complement of the standard keyboard and eliminating the multiple, and sometimes illogical sequencing of unrelated keys is possible with the use of the Keyport 300, a touch pad interface from Polytel[8] (FIG. 8). The Keyport 300 is a flat-membrane pad with 300 programmable keys positioned on a 15 $\times$ 20 array over an 8 1/2-$\times$-11-inch area. The pad, which is compatible with the IBM PC, XT, AT, and word-alikes, attaches to the computer's game port adapter card. Up to two Keyports may be attached to a single computer using a single game port card.

The heart of the touch pad consists of a single mylar membrane that is screen-printed with a silver conductive grid and two resistive strips. When a key is pressed (actually the location on the pad representing a key), two electrical resistances are sensed. The system software has been written so as to constantly poll the touch pad and measure any resistances through the game port. The resistances are interpreted as individual touch pad key identities.

After a key has been identified, the system software searches through a key definition table (KDT) to determine if the key has been defined previously. If it has, the contents of the key are displayed on the screen, just as if they had been keyboarded in real-time. The contents of the key may be any string of keyboard keys and/or commands, with the exception of those that halt the operation of the currently running application. More specifically these exceptions include the following keystroke sequences: [CTRL]-[Break] and [CTRL]-[ALT]-[DEL]. The Keyport Development System can be used, however, to define a key as [CTRL]-[BREAK]. A diagnostic program is provided to test and verify the operation of each key.

The process of programming an individual key consists of first loading the Keyport 300 system software. The Keyport program occupies an unused portion of memory and does not interfere with any applications program. After it has been loaded, individual touch pad key locations are programmed by simultaneously pressing the [ALT] key and the required Keyport key. A beep provides immediate feedback that the Keyport unit is responding properly. Next, the user types in any sequence of commands and characters on the main keyboard or the Keyport. There is no set limit to the size of a key definition, although the maximum key definition table size is 22K. The recording process is terminated by pressing the [ALT] key and Keyport key again.

Each one of the 300 keys can be programmed in the same way. In addition, the user can program the shift position of each key by pressing the shift key along with the [ALT] key when initiating the recording process. Any key can be redefined at any time, replacing its previous key identity. With two Keyports attached to a computer, there is the capacity to program 1200 keys.

The defined Keyport identities can be saved to disk by accessing the Keyport menu by pressing the [CTRL] key and any Keyport key. The Keyport menu appears on the bottom three lines of the screen and offers the user the options of turning the Keyport off or on, loading a previously saved key definition table, saving the present Keyport definitions, or canceling the menu display. The optional Keyport Development System program can be used to define a Keyport key to ''Load/Save'' a key definition table. This capability makes switching KDTs quite simple.

The Keyport 300 Development System is one of a number of software products produced specifically for the Keyport. Polytel calls such programs *keyware*,[9] since

[8]Polytel
1250 Oakmead Parkway, Suite 310
Sunnyvale, CA 94086
(408) 730-1347
(800) 245-6655

[9]The Word Processing keyware, which supports WordStar and MultiMate, is of special interest for a typesetting environment since many of the editing commands are similar. Keyware consists of a plastic overlay and predefined KDTs.

they functionally change the personality and operation of the Keyport. The Development System keyware extends the capabilities of the Keyport well beyond the elementary storage of character strings, and provides the means for defining an entire KDT, for up to two Keyports, all at one time.

The process for using the Development System keyware is basically composed of three stages: designing the Keyport overlay (the key assignments for each function, character, or operation), writing the key definition statements, and producing the key definition tables. The Development System contains a number of transparent and opaque overlays, as well as die-cut labels, which can be used to determine the layout for an application. Key groupings can be made by type, by function, by sequence, or by whatever operational organization makes sense to the user.

The actual key definitions, called the *Key Definition Source* (KDS), are composed using a standard text editor. Each key definition follows the same form, containing four fields:

- Identification of the key type. Is it repeating (R) or nonrepeating (K). Is it shifted (S) or unshifted (N)?
- The number of the Keyport key (1 through 300) to be defined.
- The number of the function that the key is to perform.
- Details concerning how the function is to be performed, what information the function is to be processed, or what text is to be displayed.

A sample assignment statement might be written as follows:

KN, 73, 8 ~ ^032You are ready to begin~

The fields, which are separated by commas, have the following meaning: make the key nonrepeating, unshifted; assign this function to Keyport key identity number 73; use function 8; display the following text at the bottom of the computer screen using color 032.

The function capability supports the processing of string constants, string variables, numeric constants, numeric variables, and special variables (DATE, TIME, FLAG, and ERROR). The available functions are:

1: Assign a string of characters to the key.
2: Assign a sequence of Keyport keys to the key.
3: Assign to the key a pause for user input.
8: Assign to the key a message to be displayed.
13: Produce a CTRL-BREAK.
20: See if the variable meets certain conditions.
21: Assign a value to a variable.
22: Send the value of a variable as characters.
23: Clear all variables to zero or nothing.
25: Perform one of the Keyport menu options.
26: Wait for a certain number of seconds.

The Key Definition Source file, which is essentially a text file, is converted (or compiled) into an executable object file by using the MAKEKDT.EXE program. It translates the KDS into a KDT.

These more powerful programming capabilities, coupled with some ingenuity, can be used to streamline typesetting input. Tab start information, for example, could be passed from one tab to the next, eliminating repetitive input. Ordered lists could be numbered automatically, publications could be generically coded, predefined form areas could be assigned, etc.

The ease of use and immediacy of response make the Keyport 300 a particularly productive tool in the typesetting environment. Not only can complex command and character sequences by assigned to a single key, but the Keyport can be set up to provide easy access to the operating system environment, offering custom menus, on-line help, and system and program documentation. In addition, the visual nature of the keypad is always presenting a clear picture of all system's options to the operator. The keypad overlays are changeable, and Polytel provides preprinted overlays for specific applications, as well as die-cut stickers for the design of custom applications.

KEYWIZ VIP: An Accessory Full-Stroke Keypad

There are two fundamental typesetting tenets. One is to reduce to a minimum the number of command keys struck, and the other is to increase the degree of keyboarding accuracy as much as possible. The attainment of both objectives has been met with a typesetting aid that is available for users of the Apple II, II+, *II*e, and their workalikes (with others to be announced). It is the Keywiz VIP[10] (FIG. 9), a 31-key auxiliary keyboard that is completely programmable and reprogrammable, with up to eight command codes or characters per key. Each key can be programmed in both its shift and unshift position, yielding 62 such assignments. Four distinct keyboards are accessible by pressing the Keyboard Select key, resulting in 248 unique key locations. A seven-segment light-emitting diode (LED) displays which of the four keyboards is in use, and user-designed templates fit over the keyboard to identify each key assignment.

It is somewhat ironic that a device made for the general-purpose use of the microcomputing community should be named VIP, a name long associated with the typesetting industry by virtue of Mergenthaler's name selection for its line of second-generation phototypesetters (Variable Input Phototypesetters). VIP, in this case, stands for *V*ery *I*ntelligent *P*eripheral, an apt name for what its marketing company calls "the first user programmable keyboard." In the realm of typesetting, the assignment of code

[10]Creative Computer Peripherals Inc.
Aztec Environmental Center
1044 Lacey Road
Forked River, NJ 08731
(609) 693-0002

FIG. 9. The KeyWiz VIP is one of a number of add-on keypads made by Creative Computer Peripherals. A selection of preprinted template overlays are included, as well as blanks for programming user-defined selections (Courtesy Creative Computer Peripherals).

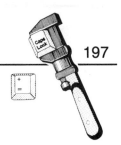

and character strings to format user-definable keys is fairly routine. Frequently used names or function codes are assigned to format keys so that repetitive keyboarding can be reduced to a minimum. This same objective is met by the Keywiz, only on a much grander scale. Unlike many typesetting system keyboards, the Keywiz uses nonvolatile memory, meaning that the key assignments remain even when the power is turned off. The assignments and the operation of the unit are completely software independent.

The power of the Keywiz rests in its ability to take on the characteristics of any one of a number of specific user-selected keyboarding functions. This ability makes it ideal for typesetting applications, since any sequence of up to eight keystrokes can be stored under a recognized typesetting identity. Such typesetting functions as typeface change, line length, and centering usually are input via the microcomputer keyboard as a precedence code followed by mnemonics and sometimes numbers. While mnemonic systems are usually fairly easy to learn and to remember (such as ql = quad left, sz = size), they are sometimes lengthy and sometimes awkward to use. Assigning such strings to the Keywiz, the user has the choice of renaming these strings with names identical to those used on the host typesetter or those most familiar in-house, or those most comfortable for the operator or the working environment. An end-of-paragraph sequence can, for example, be composed of a quad left command, a return, and a beginning-of-paragraph indention. This whole sequence can be reduced to a single key on the Keywiz, labeled with any name that makes it comprehensible to the operator. It, therefore, makes keyboarding input easier for those who are unfamiliar with typesetting requirements and technical terminology.

The variety of word processing and text editing programs available for microcomputers and their suitability for the preparation of typesetting input differ considerably. The variability extends not only to distinct capabilities of software packages, but also to the means by which specific commands are accessed. The Keywiz becomes the common denominator for dissimilar command sets, reducing awkward commands to the same key with the same label on any of the eight Keywiz keyboards. In this way, typesetting input can be accomplished by using a number of different text inputting programs, the selection of a particular one being based on the requirements of a specific typesetting job. The operator virtually is freed of remembering the unique command sets for individual software packages, and can concentrate instead on the accuracy of input.

There are two distinct parts to a typesetting job: the alphanumeric characters that compose the graphic content, and the codes or commands that control its ultimate appearance. Errors of the first kind have a direct and undesirable effect on output, yet can be overcome with the use of a spell-checking program or by manual paste-up techniques. Errors of the second kind are more potentially damaging. Incorrectly specified command sequences can cause a job to take an unexpected form, or at worst, to be aborted. The Keywiz certifies that each and every code sequence is exactly as specified, eliminating the major cause of typesetting errors.

The Keywiz installs in less than 30 minutes, and requires no special technical skills. On the Apple *II*e, the user removes the case, reassigns the keyboard ROM to the Keywiz board, and modifies one other chip with a jumper. A fairly long cord is supplied so that the Keywiz can be positioned comfortably for easy access.

There are four dedicated keys on the Keywiz. The *S* key is used to select the keyboard identity. There are eight keyboard layouts, four keyboards in both shift and unshift positions. The *P* key is used for the actual programming of individual keys. A shift and a shift-lock key provide access to the alternate positions of the four main keyboards. The LED indicates which of the four boards is in use, and a small dot beside the displayed number indicates if the shift position is activated.

Programming the Keywiz is an easy procedure (FIG. 10). First the keyboard identity is selected, and then the **P** key is depressed. A **P** then appears in the LED window to verify that the unit is in the programming mode. Next the key to be programmed is depressed. The keys to be stored then are struck on the computer keyboard. When the string is complete, the **P** key is depressed again to indicate the end of the procedure. The key is now programmed and will retain its stored identity until it is reprogrammed. This procedure can be repeated again and again for the same key as the user's needs change. However, with 248 distinct key assignments available, it should not be necessary to make frequent changes.

The Keywiz not only provides for mapping key assignments used repetitively for specific word processing programs (FIG. 11), but provides for scratchpad assignments

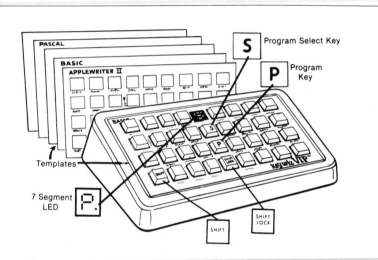

FIG. 10. The programming procedure for the KeyWiz VIP is very simple, and quick to execute.

PROGRAMING A FUNCTION KEY

NOTE: We will program the key in the Lower Right hand corner with **H E L L O** for this example.

STEPS

1. Touch Program Key (to start programing).

2. Touch key you wish to program.
   (We will use key in lower right hand corner for our example)

3. Type the characters **H E L L O** on your computer keyboard

4. Touch program key again (to stop programing).

THAT'S IT!!!!

Now when you depress the function key in the lower right hand corner it will provide the 5 characters **H E L L O** in a single keystroke on your computer monitor.

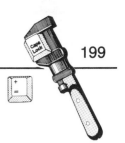

for specific typesetting jobs. A book, for example, will require a change of typeface, point size, and line spacing for chapter titles, major heads and subheads, body copy, footnotes, etc. The Keywiz can be programmed easily and quickly to identify a dedicated key for each, simply labeled for identification. Long string series requiring more than eight keystrokes can be stored in adjacent Keywiz keys and accessed by striking the keys in sequence.

The Keywiz is among the most practical peripherals yet produced for the microcomputer typesetting market. Although it is expensive relative to other devices that attach to micro systems, its cost can be justified in the typesetting environment on the basis of the time it saves and the level of accuracy it ensures.

FIG. 11. A suggested template organization for MicroPro's WordStar word processing program. The KeyWiz simplifies the use of command-intensive programs such as this by converting control sequences into user-specified English.

COMMAND DESIRED	ACTUAL KEYSTROKES TO BE PROGRAMMED INTO DESIGNATED KEY	"ENGLISH" DESIGNATION TO BE WRITTEN ON TEMPLATE
Return Key	RETURN	RETURN
Go to beginning of file	CTRL QR	HOME
Go to end of file	CTRL QC	END
Left one word	CTRL A	←W
Right one word	CTRL F	W→
Tab right	CTRL I	TAB→
Delete character right	CTRL G	D CHR→
Center text	CTRL OC	CTR
Insert mode on/off	CTRL V	INS ON/OFF
Reform text on screen	CTRL B	REFORM
Insert blank line	CTRL N	INS LN
Top of screen	CTRL QE	TOP
Bottom of screen	CTRL QX	BTTM
Block beginning	CTRL QB	BLK BGN
BLOCK end	CTRL QK	BLK END
Tab set	CTRL OI	T SET
Tab clear	CTRL ON	T CLR
Delete to end of line	CTRL QY	D LN→
Delete to beginning of line	CTRL QDEL	←D LN
Delete line	CTRL Y	D LN
Left one character	CTRL S	←
Right one character	CTRL D	→
Up one line	CTRL E	↑↓
Down one line	CTRL X	
Set left margin	CTRL OL	S LEFT MAR
Set right margin	CTRL OR	S RIGHT M.
Release margins	CTRL OX	REL MAR
Variable tabbing on/off	CTRL OV	V TAB
Start of last find/rplace	CTRL QV	FD/RPL
Up screen full	CTRL C	▲ SCRLL
Down screenfull	CTRL R	▼ SCRLL

PRODUCTIVITY TOOLS

The mouse is one answer to finding a better way of helping to move information from the originator (or his agent) into a computer. The first mouse was invented by Douglas Engelbart at the Stanford Research Institute (SRI) in 1964. Using government funding, SRI developed a number of alternate man/machine interfaces between 1964 and 1965. From the start, the mouse seemed to show the greatest promise, and it was tested successfully against the light pen, the joystick, the Grafacon (a curve tracer no longer made), and the knee controller.[11]

The purpose of the mouse, and other devices of a similar nature, is to move the cursor quickly and efficiently around the screen in order to carry out various operations. In its simplest application it merely replaces or augments the cursor (arrow) keys, which indicate compass direction.

Although the mouse is not available on all computer systems, nor is it supported by most software products, it has become generally known as a result of the popularity of the Apple Macintosh. The Macintosh is essentially mouse-bound, relying on the mouse for the selection of menu items, the specification of applications parameters, the creation and movement of graphics, as well as the rapid placement of the venerable cursor.

In the typesetting environment, the mouse can be useful in making gross editorial changes. These changes generally follow the keyboarding operation and, therefore, do not interrupt it. The quick specification of text, its movement, deletion, and duplication, are all important and necessary operations in editing text bound for typesetting output.

JANE: Mousetrapping and Manipulating Text

The Arktronics' mouse (made by Apple), which is used in the company's Jane software[12] (FIG. 12), is a mechanical, one-button design that utilizes a rolling rubber composition ball. The mouse controls five tools, which are used in each of the integrated programs Janewrite, Janecalc, and Janelist. The *hand* is used to move around the screen and indicate position or point to other tools. The *scissors* is used to cut out unwanted text or numbers. The *paste jar* is used to glue in text or numbers that either have been cut with the scissors or copied by the camera. The *arrow* is used to insert new text

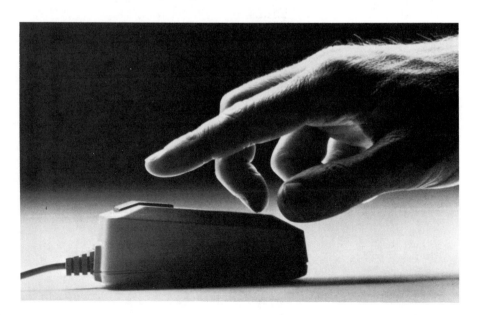

FIG. 12. The Arktronic's mouse (the standard Apple mouse) uses a single button. Other mouse varieties use up to three buttons to select and manipulate their prey.

[11]Schnatmeier, Vanessa
"A Modern Mouse Story"
A+, Vol. 2, No. 7
July, 1984, pp. 32-33

[12]Arktronics Corporation
P.O. Box 4190
Ann Arbor, MI 48106
(313) 769-7253
Jane runs on the Apple II, II+, *IIe*, and other compatible computers.

or numbers. Finally, the *camera* is used to copy text or numbers so that they can be moved using the paste jar.

In FIG. 13 the order of two paragraphs is reversed. The text of the second paragraph was highlighted (with a sweep of the mouse), cut out (by clicking the mouse button), and then placed in its new position by changing the mouse tool (clicking on the picture of the paste jar), moving the picture of the paste jar to the new location, and again clicking the mouse. Although somewhat long by way of explanation, it is still a faster way to perform this operation than most other methods.

FIG. 13. The Arktronic Jane program uses mouse-selectable icons to choose applications and functions.

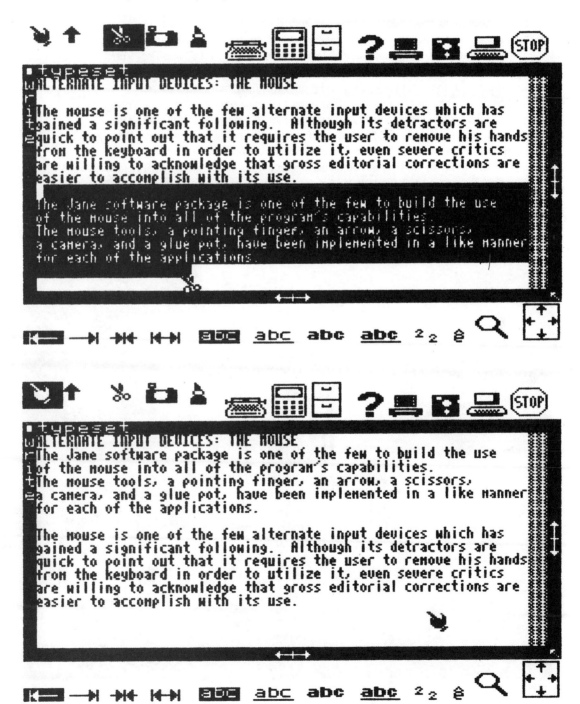

DIGITAL PAINTBRUSH:
Creating and Integrating Text and Graphics

The typesetting community has long been plagued by the problem of typeface design misappropriation. Because there is no solid legal protection for typographic forms, every typesetting vendor produces its own versions of popular typefaces and assigns them its own names. This practice has resulted in considerable confusion in typeface identification, as well as reducing an artist's incentive to produce original typeface designs.

To encourage the continued creation of quality typographic forms, protect the interests of the designer, and provide the typesetting industry with consistent master letterforms, two companies—The International Typeface Corporation (ITC) and The World Typeface Center (WTC)—have been formed. These companies stimulate new designs and disseminate uniform drawings for use by an expanding market of users.

In the microtypesetting realm, a similar event has taken place. The Data Transforms' font library has been licensed to The Computer Colorworks,[13] for their Digital Paintbrush System for the IBM PC and Apple II series of microcomputers. What this means, is that fonts, either sold for Data Transforms' Fontrix program, or created with it, can be used with the Digital Paintbrush system. This cooperative effort results in a significant enhancement for both products.

What the Digital Paintbrush System Does

The Digital Paintbrush system (FIG. 14) combines a hardware input device and a

[13]The Computer Colorworks
A Division of Jandel Corporation
3030 Bridgeway
Sausalito, CA 94965
(415) 331-3022

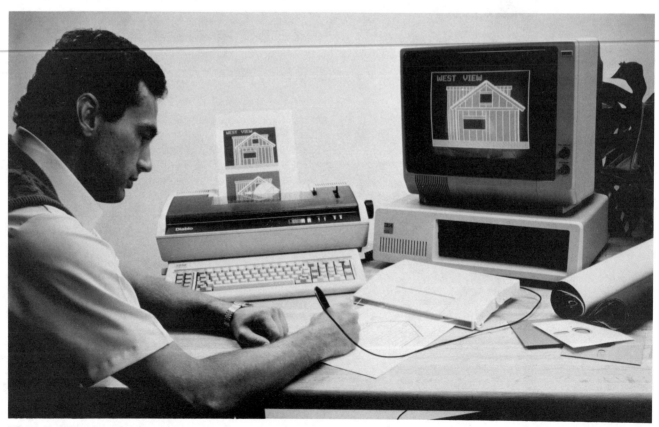

FIG. 14. The Digital Paintbrush System shown in use on the IBM PC. Unlike many other input devices, the Digital Paintbrush provides a means of natural freehand drawing (Courtesy of The Computer Colorworks).

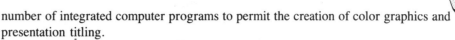

number of integrated computer programs to permit the creation of color graphics and presentation titling.

The Digital Paintbrush hardware input device consists of a hand-held pen that is tied to two thin dacron lines connected to two wheels inside the unit housing. As the pen is moved, the wheels turn potentiometers, which send their relative positions to the computer. The pen is used not only to indicate locations on the computer's high-resolution screen, but also to initiate various actions by depressing the pen tip. A button on the side of the pen is used to toggle the Main menu display on or off, and to cancel the presently selected drawing option. The software also supports the use of a joystick (or paddles, touch tablet, etc.), in which case button 0 is equivalent to the pen tip and button 1 is equivalent to the pen button.

The Graphic Design Program screen is fashioned after higher priced professional systems. A menu bar running along the right side of the screen presents the major options (FIG. 15), some of which lead to additional menu choices. (Although both the Apple and IBM versions are similar, the descriptions that follow apply most particularly to the Apple version.) These selections include:

Brush. This option presents a palette of colors as well as a choice of drawing instruments (FIG. 16). Each drawing tool (brush) is available in a variety of sizes—a total of 38. The cursor assumes the shape of the currently selected brush. Colored patterns also can be created using combinations from the color charts.

Shapes. This menu offers selections for the construction of lines, boxes, circles, curves, and freehand drawing. Each shape appears in the color selected, as well as assumes the shape or outline corresponding to the chosen drawing instrument.

Fill. Selection of this item fills the chosen area with the currently selected color or pattern.

Micro. Rather than providing a zoom feature for the close-up editing of graphics, The Digital Paintbrush provides a Micro frame. This frame defines a small editing area (approximately 2 inches square on a 12-inch monitor), in which gross pen movements result in micro movement on the screen. Any of the shape options can be executed while in the micro mode.

Edit. This option permits the selection of an area of the screen to be cut. The cut area then can be moved, resized, or duplicated. Colors can be removed selectively or copied by selecting either ''All Colors,'' ''Only Current Color'' (separates only the currently selected color from the editing area), or ''No Current Color'' (separates all colors except the current selection).

The ''Library'' option from the Edit menu permits access to a graphic library collection, which includes such categories as communication, audio/video, home, cooking, medicine, industry, symbols, and office. Each graphic category has a number of images. The ''Travel'' category, for example, has images of boats, cars, gas pumps, stoplights, trains, planes, and motorcycles. Each graphic image can be incorporated in a user-designed graphic and edited as required (FIG. 17). In addition, the user can design library images and categories as needed.

Grids. This option draws a grid of a user-selected ruling as a guide for the accurate division of screen space. The grid can be toggled on or off.

Alpha. This selection is the means by which typographic images are composed on the graphic screen. It is the way by which fonts, either supplied with The Digital Paintbrush or compatible with Fontrix, are typeset. Fonts are loaded by selecting the ''Disk'' option (FIG. 18) from the Main menu, followed by the ''Get Font'' selection. The disk holding the required font is inserted in the drive, the disk is cataloged (if so requested), and the name of the font is typed. After it is loaded, it is immediately available for composition.

Selection of the ''Alpha'' command results in the display of four flashing dots,

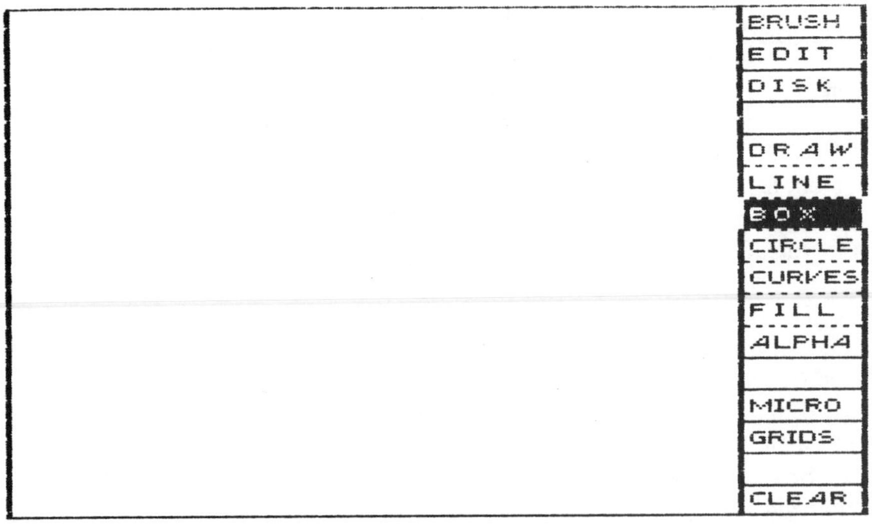

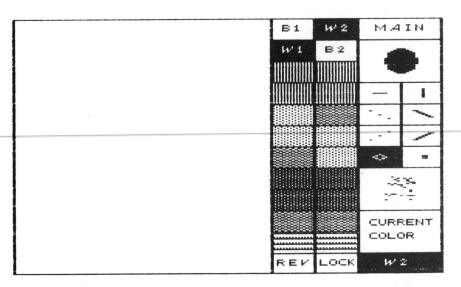

FIG. 15. The Digital Paintbrush Graphic Design Program's Main menu. The menu bar can be toggled on or off by pressing the button on the pen.

FIG. 16. The color palette and Drawing Tool menu provide access to 38 drawing tool shapes. Colors also can be blended by the user.

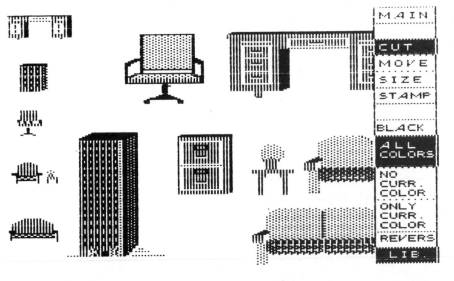

FIG. 17. This screen shows the "Office" category from the Graphic Library. Any image can be cut and moved to the main Graphic screen.

which indicate the appearing size of the characters. The position of the characters can be specified either by pen movement or pixel-by-pixel manipulation via control sequences from the keyboard. Characters appear initially in white, although their color can be changed by making a new selection from the color palette.

Graphic Applications

The general usefulness of graphics in the fields of communication, industry, medicine, sales, education, design, business, marketing, engineering, and science are well known. The Digital Paintbrush provides a means of easily creating color graphics that can be used in a wide variety of ways.

- Outputting to paper using a dot matrix printer (black and white or color). The Printout program supplied with the package supports 37 different printers without the need for a graphics dump interface card. The program provides the capability of choosing the number of copies to be printed, the magnification (from 1X to 5X), the image orientation (normal or inverse), the vertical position (from 1 to 9 lines of blank space), the horizontal position (flush left, flush right, or centered), the page width (either 8 1/2 inches or 14 inches), and the type of paper (continuous form or single sheet).
- Outputting to the screen as a graphic slide show. The Presentation program allows the user to create an automatic or manually advanced slide show (FIG. 19).

FIG. 19. The Slide Projector menu allows the user to arrange images into "Slide Trays," and to present them for variable lengths of time.

```
         SLIDE PROJECTOR        VER 2.0

M MANUAL / AUTO          T TIME= 10 SEC.

B BLEND ON / BLEND OFF

P START PROJECTOR

C CATALOG

L LOAD NEW SLIDE TRAY

S SELECT SLIDES

         ENTER SELECTION
```

In automatic mode the slides can be programmed to appear from 3 to 99 seconds, and can be specified as advancing full frame only, or blending from the current image to the following one.

- Photographing the screen as a 35mm color slide. The images can be photographed using a 35mm camera with conventional procedures for directly capturing the screen, or a special-purpose camera can be used.
- Using graphic screens as a part of a program. The Digital Paintbrush provides programming suggestions for including graphic screens in custom-written programs.
- Integrating graphic screens in video presentations to title or to insert line illustrations and textual explanations.

Tele"graphic" Communication

A unique feature of The Digital Paintbrush system is the capability to telecommunicate color graphics interactively between Apple systems, whether they are in the same room or across the country. Using similarly equipped systems, with the recommended modems and modular y-connectors so that a telephone can be plugged into the same jack as the modem, two people can communicate graphically, by voice, or by typing. This capability is a significant tool for designers of page layouts, magazine covers, logos, and other graphic images that require visual conferencing.

The Telephone-Graphics program has its own menu of design choices (FIG. 20), as well as its own color palette. Icons provide access for freehand drawing; making straight lines, circles, squares, and rectangles; filling in areas; adding text; capturing areas of the screen to move or copy; and also moving to the Transport menu. The Transport menu provides for toggling between interactive drawing and voice communications, dialing the telephone, displaying the telephone book, answering or hanging up the telephone, initializing a disk, sending a disk file to a remote disk, saving the screen to disk, starting or ending a session file, deleting a file from disk, showing a catalog of the disk, getting a picture from the disk, retrieving a session file, selecting a disk drive, and transferring back to the Graphics menu.

In some cases the quality of the graphic output produced by the Digital Paintbrush will be satisfactory for a specific application, in which case a design studio could create graphic images and telecommunicate them to a client who uses a similar model of Apple computer. The client would not necessarily need the Digital Paintbrush System because there are software packages that support the reception and processing of standard Apple graphics over telephone lines. In other cases, the graphics produced with the system could be used as (same-sized) guides for redrawing, using conventional graphic arts drawing tools and typesetting machines.

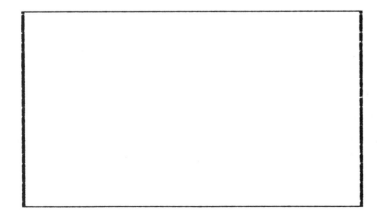 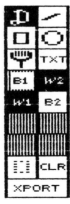

FIG. 20. The Telephone Graphics Program provides many of the same drawing options found in the main Graphic Design Program. With similarly equipped Apple systems, two users many miles apart can work interactively on the same graphic screen.

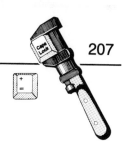

PRINT-IT! Transferring Screen Images to Paper

The typographic and graphic images created on a computer screen are not always easily moved to another form of visual presentation. Some software packages have built-in routines to dump the contents of the computer screen to the printer, but most, unfortunately, do not. Captive images are of limited usefulness since they only can be displayed with the use of the computer and its accompanying software, or be photographed directly off the screen using either specialized equipment or a conventional 35mm camera. These latter methods are usually time-consuming or expensive.

Transforming screen images into immediate printed copies can be accomplished in a number of ways, generally using a special-purpose printer interface card, or sometimes, as in the case of the Apple Macintosh, using capabilities built into the computer itself.

Many of the Apple II screen displays in this book were made using a push-button screen dump card called Print-It.[14] This printer interface card, which supports a wide range of both serial and parallel printers, allows the user to interrupt the operation of the Apple at any time, dump the contents of the screen to the printer, and then continue with the application in use.

Print-It! is one of a number of printer interface cards that provide capabilities in hardware which the applications software does not support. In addition to its main function of printing any screen display, Print-It! offers the user the option of specifying how the information will be printed. Among these options are printing the two Apple graphic screens side by side, printing the screen in double size, rotating the image 90 degrees, inverting the black-on-white image into white-on-black, printing the image at the left margin rather than in the center, and emphasizing the image by printing two closely spaced dots in place of one.

The Print-It! card generally is inserted in slot 1, where most software packages expect the printer card to be. The red Print-It! button is mounted at any convenient location, either on the Apple itself or on the work surface. At any time while information of any kind is displayed on the screen, the button may be pressed and the screen printed. When the button is pressed, a beep is sounded and the program stops executing. At this point the user types any combination of output format commands (or none at all), and then presses the Return key. The screen is printed according to the input commands, then control is returned to the computer, which continues executing the program as if nothing had happened. At any time during the printing process, output can be halted by pressing the Space Bar.

The ability to easily output work created on a computer is of considerable benefit, since a great deal of such work is usually destined for reproduction in paper form.

THE FONT MACHINE: Creating Fonts for Dot-Formed Typesetters

The Font Machine[15] is a hardware/software font-development system for the creation of character sets, symbols, logos, and artwork for output on dot matrix printers. Any type of printer using a dot matrix pattern—including ion deposition, laser, magnetic, thermal, or impact technologies—with a resolution of up to 600 dpi can be supported.

The system is aimed primarily at printer manufacturers, who need to develop libraries of typefaces and special characters to burn into PROMs or to provide to end-users on a disk (i.e., in a downloadable form). The Font Machine automates the process of converting line art graphic images into a generalized dot-map storage format in which individual characters (graphic or typographic) can be easily edited and combined into font sets.

[14]Texprint Inc.
8 Blanchard Road
Burlington, MA 01803
(617) 273-3384

[15]Maracom Corporation
648 Beacon Street
Boston, MA 02215
(617) 266-3630

The hardware (FIG. 21) consists of an IBM PC/AT 5170 Model 99 with an 80287 math coprocessor, second serial/parallel adapter, 128K memory expansion option, 5175 Professional Graphics Display, Professional Graphics Controller (640-×-480-pixel resolution), and a Mouse Systems PC Mouse. The video input system consists of the Chorus Data Systems PC-1000 four-bit Video Digitizer, AZI black-and-white television camera with a macro zoom lens, and an AZI Copy Stand. Other components include a Hewlett-Packard 7470 Graphics Plotter, and an Alloy Computer Products PC-QICTAPE Subsystem.

The video system is used to capture two-dimensional drawings of typographic designs or other images. The Font Machine software converts the digitized image into a dot-map representation of the matrix utilized by the target printer. In the case of an impact dot matrix printer, for example, the dot-map would correspond to the printhead pinfires required to image the character (FIG. 22).

The initial dot-map is totally within the control of the operator. Lines and curves can be smoothed, and characters can be drawn from scratch by placing dots upon a black character map. After characters have been edited adequately and proofed, the

FIG. 21. The Font Machine provides a specialized environment for the conversion of graphic and typographic images into imageable bitmaps suitable for a wide variety of printers.

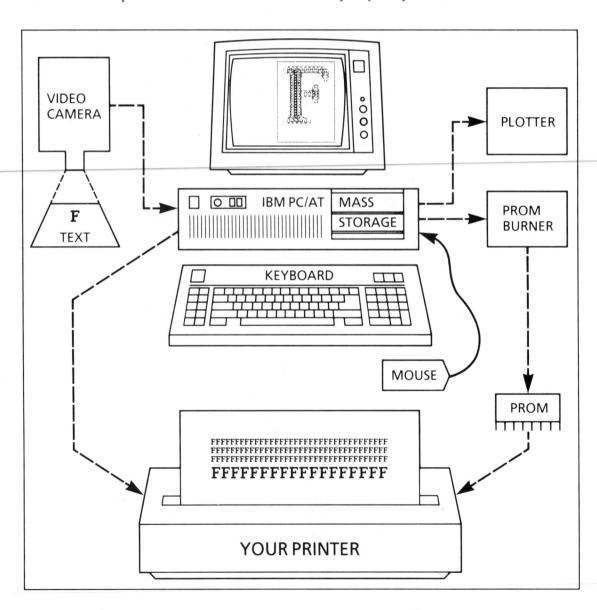

Chapter 8

Professional Typesetting Software for Personal and Professional Applications

Software packages which rival or surpass the results obtainable through traditional methods.

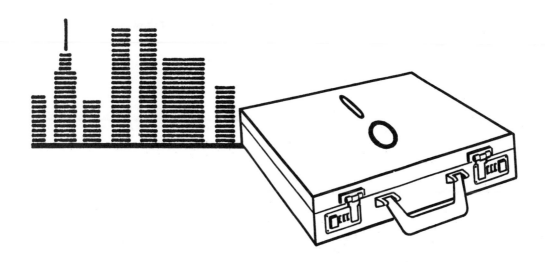

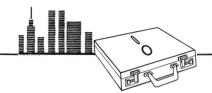

The application of microcomputers to the typesetting process has been occurring from the very earliest days of their introduction. Professionals in the typesetting trade were quick to recognize that microcomputers provide many advantages that dedicated typesetting keyboards either do not provide, or do not provide on a cost-effective basis.

One of the major advantages of using a microcomputer for typesetting input is that its usual configuration represents a complete stand-alone system. This situation is in contrast to most typesetting input keyboards, which are dedicated to a single task and usually rival or surpass the cost of a fully configured microcomputer system.

The dedicated typesetting keyboard might have a limited character display or no display at all, making the correction of errors difficult. Also, no matter how sophisticated typesetting input keyboards supplied by industry vendors are, they are usually locked into only one mode of operation—whether through hardwiring, ROMs, or the availability of only one version of software. Therefore, not only can the devices usually only be used for one purpose, but the manner in which they are used is limited, by design, from the very outset.

The microcomputer, on the other hand, is totally flexible, able to take on whatever characteristics are required by the job environment. This flexibility, of course, is accomplished by software—both the large and growing selection that can be purchased, and the user-defined programs that can be generated by the computer.

Without software, the microcomputer is just an empty box. Its usefulness and attractiveness is directly related to the availability of quality software. It is software that ''sells'' microcomputers, and the more microcomputers sold, the more software that is published, and therefore the greater the value of the microcomputer. Not only does the population of microcomputers spur the production of more software, but each microcomputer can be used to generate software. Therefore, unlike the typesetting industry, which is dependent upon particular vendors for programs for specific devices, the microcomputer environment actively generates low- to medium-priced software packages with regularity.

Until about 1984, the microcomputer market did not respond to the need for specialized typesetting input software, and for understandable reasons. Regardless, there has been no lack of usable text-creation software for typesetting applications. Depending upon system (microcomputer and typesetter) requirements, many different word processing and text-creation programs are not only adequate for, but in some cases have features not usually found in (although potentially helpful to), the traditional typesetting input process. Likewise, with a degree of irony, micro-based word processing software such as MicroPro's WordStar is offered as an option on a number of typesetting vendor systems, including Itek's Quadritek series and Compugraphic's MCS.

The editing and file management features found in word processing programs are similar to those used in typesetting. What the terminal and the software lack in typographic specifications can be overcome through the use of a variety of coding schemes.

Software written specifically for the creation of typesetting input plays upon the strengths of the two worlds, combining sophisticated typesetting input programs with powerful, user-configurable microcomputer hardware.

Exploring the microcomputer world first reveals numerous advantages over most dedicated typesetting input devices and workstations. Keep in mind that as microcomputers have grown in popularity, the offerings of typesetting vendors in the area of

FIG. 1. The Compugraphic MCS 4 is a noncounting off-line workstation that supports the Modular Composition System (MCS). After keyboarding raw text (text that has not been hyphenated or justified), the operator transfers the disk to a larger MCS system for processing. Notice that the system components closely resemble those of a microcomputer.

input devices have, in some cases, changed considerably. Many such systems look very much like microcomputers, being composed of a keyboard, disk drives, and CRT (FIG. 1). Nonetheless, there is a long list of reasons why microcomputers are a good alternative to dedicated input devices.

First, there is the matter of choice in the area of text-creation software. Package prices start at well under $100 for word processing software. Specialized typesetting software packages can cost over $2000, yet even so, there remains the element of choice since a number of programs run on the same microcomputer systems. This ability to choose from a variety of software makes it possible for users to build a library of programs, which can be used according to the characteristics of a particular job or upon individual user preference.

Second, most word processors and dedicated typesetting programs are supported with two companion programs (not necessarily provided by the same software source). One is a spell checker, an invaluable aid in the typesetting environment (although slow to be recognized as such), where output is usually reproduced in quantity and errors are expensive. The second is a mail list program, which permits the merging of lists of variable information into files generated by the word processing program.

Third, in some instances text files produced using one text-creation program can be used with another, or with another, unrelated program such as a spelling or grammar checker, or a communications program. Most specialized typesetting software packages support the processing of text files produced by other programs that have been created using the same operating system.

Fourth, when the microcomputer is not used for typesetting input it can be used for a multiplicity of other functions, such as accounting, payroll, database management, financial forecasting, modeling, production control, scheduling, estimating, costing, inventory, and many more (including programming, education, and games).

Fifth, the microcomputer system can grow to meet future needs. There is a large universe of peripheral suppliers who manufacture hardware accessories to extend the capabilities of microcomputers.

Sixth, microcomputer systems and software tend to be user-friendly. The manuals usually are written in a low-key, casual manner, and the software is usually menu-driven, often providing on-line help screens.

Seventh, service for most microcomputer systems is available on a local carry-in (or sometimes, on-site) basis. Some models even have diagnostic software available, which the user can run to pinpoint memory and hardware malfunctions. The relatively low cost of the system components makes the purchase of back-up systems a reasonable consideration.

Eighth, microcomputer systems routinely have a line printer, which can be used for hardcopy proofs. Such proofs are generally unavailable in low-cost typesetting systems. They provide another check on input text and commands, as well as provide a last-resort back-up for the storage medium.

Ninth, the popularity of the microcomputer has made it a consumer item. System components, peripherals, and supplies, therefore, are all available in the open market at competitive prices.

Tenth, with appropriate hardware, microcomputers can be networked to provide communications among users, with output designated to the typesetter, line printer, disk, or remote system.

Eleventh, because of the ubiquitous presence of the microcomputer, cottage labor becomes a cost-effective resource for publishers, printers, and typesetters. Input operators can be employed with a minimum of overhead expense, and all of their work can be telecommunicated rather than physically transported.

Twelfth, compact, portable, and battery-operated microcomputers can be used for input from almost any location. They can telecommunicate using ordinary telephone lines directly to an awaiting receiver (typesetter, another micro, etc.) or to a mainframe or other computer having electronic mail, which will hold the transmission until the other party (receiver) is ready to accept it.[1]

THE WORLD OF PROFESSIONAL TYPESETTING SOFTWARE

The do-it-yourself movement has had a major impact on the typesetting industry, as it has on many trades. As a result, there is the strong likelihood that both trade and lay people will use many of the same hardware and software tools to produce their work. Although the programs presented in this section by and large were developed for professional use, they are already being used effectively by those outside of traditional typesetting environments.

Professional software packages for typesetting applications generally share a number of common characteristics that significantly enhance their usefulness for generating input for typesetting.

Typographic Specification. These programs are all devised using accepted trade terminology, measurements, and syntax.

Screen Display. Many programs use screen displays that have been designed to approximate those of existing typesetting input stations. Some packages provide for the display of specialized character sets, which aid in the composition of typographically code-intensive work as well as work composed of fractions, special symbols, and other characters not normally generated by the host microcomputer.

Justification. All specialized typesetting software packages provide some means of justifying text—in other words, some way of counting the widths of individual characters in order to determine line endings.

Hyphenation. The accurate determination of necessary end-of-line word breaks in order to achieve proper intraline spacing is supported by some software packages to varying degrees. Most commonly, an algorithm is used, supported by an exception-word dictionary.

Typesetter Independence. Most specialized typesetter software will support a number of different typesetters. In most cases, the same software can be utilized for a variety of output devices: in a few, however, machine-specific versions of the program are required.

Operator Interface. Many programs have used existing typesetter front-end systems as models for their software design. As a result, an operator who has worked

[1]Adapted from *Microcomputers and Typesetting*
Michael L. Kleper
Graphic Dimensions
1982, pp. 2-3

on a specific typesetter can make the transition to such a micro-based system with little or no retraining.

Keyboard Limitations. The considerably smaller set of keys on a microcomputer has required the authors of typesetting software to make fewer keys accomplish more work. They do so by requiring the operator to strike a series of keys in order to access typesetting commands and special characters. In some cases the unique keyboard configuration of the microcomputer, such as the function keys on the IBM PC or the keypad on the Kaypro 2, have been mapped with dedicated typesetting functions.

CPU Support. Many typesetting programs are available in versions for the most popular models of microcomputers. Among the most popular microcomputers for typesetting applications are the IBM PC, Apple IIe, Apple Macintosh, Kaypro 2, and Tandy TRS-80 Models 3 and 4.

Typesetter Interface. The product of typesetter software is one or more files that are ready to be processed by the typesetter. Moving the files from the microcomputer to the typesetter, however, requires either some specialized hardware (which might or might not be built into the typesetter) or some means of converting the files into a form compatible with the typesetter's native media requirements. Some software vendors supply the necessary interface and cabling to access the typesetter; others provide a way of generating compatible media; while others require that the user solve this problem.

EASY-K:
Integrating Writing Functions with Typesetting Requirements

The Easy-K program from US Lynx[2] is unique in the world of microcomputer software for typesetting. First, it is part of an editorial system that does not provide any H&J capabilities, but nonetheless is rich in text-preparation features. Second, it is an integrator of applications rather than an actual application itself, and by so being it unifies and complements its parts to present an easy user interface. Third, it optimizes the effectiveness of a group of powerful companion programs to enhance their overall usefulness and increase productivity, yet its program shell generally remains transparent to the user.

The *K* in the Easy-K name stands for Kaypro, the microcomputer system that provides the CP/M environment for the program shell and applications. Any of the Kaypro model 2, 4, or 10 microcomputers can be used, the specific selection being dependent upon particular user requirements.

After the copy-protected Easy-K program is loaded, the screen looks like this:

EASY-K MENU

TEXT PROCESSING
B   Begin Typing a New File
E   Edit a File
L   List Files
D   Delete a File
S   Spelling Checker

ELECTRONIC TYPEWRITER
Q   Quick Type

COMPUTER UTILITIES
C   Copy Files to Floppy
I   Initialize Floppies
O   Online Communications
R   Rename a File
T   Telecommunications
M   Multiple Disk Conversion

PRINTING
P   Print a File

The Easy-K program was designed for writers, authors, editors, and others in a publishing environment. Its objective is to unify proven software and hardware tools into an integrated package that will have a learning curve of minutes rather than hours.

[2]US Lynx
853 Broadway
New York, NY 10003
(212) 673-3210

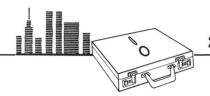

It accomplishes this goal by presenting clear menus rather than cryptic CP/M notation, and by reprogramming the Kaypro keyboard for single-key access to commonly used applications functions.

For the creation and manipulation of text, Easy-K uses Micropro's WordStar (or optionally Perfect Writer). For the checking of spelling, it uses The Word Plus from Oasis Systems (or optionally Perfect Speller). For the telecommunication of information, it uses Suprterm from Kaypro. Each of these programs in and of themselves usually require extensive documentation and training, especially WordStar, which is as complex as it is powerful. Yet the Easy-K manual, a document of less than 20 pages, states that "You should be able to begin writing and editing without knowing Wordstar or reading its manual." The Easy-K implementation is an impressive feat of simplification, to the end that authors' ideas do not need to transcend artificial software and hardware barriers in order to enter the publishing process.

On those Kaypro systems with sufficient disk capacity (those other than the Model 2), the Easy-K software, along with its associated applications, resides on a single disk. The software is provided completely installed and ready to use.

The Initial Act of Creation

A file is created by selecting **B** ("Begin Typing a New File") from the Main menu. This is the typical starting point for the creation of a new document or the continuation of a series of associated files, such as chapters in a book. The user is immediately passed into WordStar, where he is prompted for a file name of up to eight characters.

FIG. 2. The Easy-K keyboard template.

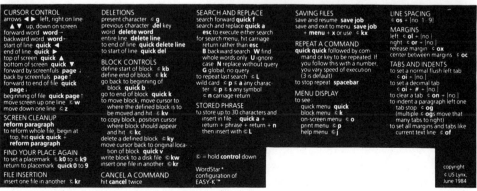

WordStar's popularity is based upon its power. The power of WordStar is at one time its greatest strength and its most limiting weakness. Although it has the flexibility to perform at a level equal to or better than dedicated word processors, it does present a level of complexity far beyond that found in most word processing packages sold for implementation on personal/business computers. The significant number of books, training guides, and tutorials available to support the program are adequate testimony to both its popularity and complexity.

The Easy-K package includes a keyboard template, which fits over the Kaypro numeric keypad and indicates the WordStar function that each key represents (FIG. 2). These dedicated keys provide immediate access to cursor control, word/line deletion, paragraph reformation, file printing, file saving, WordStar screens with instructions and help for accomplishing additional tasks, and a single key to access the main Easy-K menu.

As an editing tool, WordStar provides all of the capabilities that a writer reasonably would expect to have available. Complete cursor control: side-to-side, top-to-bottom, word-to-word, and character-to-character (in either direction) are all supported, along with automatic key repeat. The Search and Replace feature allows searching for a specified number of occurrences of a whole word, partial word, or particular occurrences of case (or without regard to case), in either forward or backward directions. Blocks of copy can be moved, copied, written to disk, inserted from disk, or deleted. Files can be combined, renamed, and deleted, and are automatically retained in backup form by WordStar.

The Easy-K program insulates the user from both the CP/M syntax with which WordStar was originally allied so closely and the special terminology that WordStar uses to refer to its files and their status.

On-Line Typo-Checking

The lost time and money that can result from the presence of typographical errors in printed text is sufficient reason to make spell-checking a required step in the editorial process. Easy-K facilitates this activity by making it simple to exit WordStar and enter The Word Plus spell-checking program. From the Easy-K menu, the user selects **S** ("Spelling Checker") and types the name of the file. An alternate method is to select **L** ("List Files"), use the arrow keys to locate the required file, mark the file to be selected by typing **E**, and then select **S**.

When it is normally invoked, The Word Plus first analyzes the document contents and makes a list of the unique words. It then displays this number on the screen and proceeds to check each unique word against the contents of its 45,000-word dictionary. Any words that do not appear in the dictionary are displayed on the screen.

Although this routine is Easy-K's default implementation of the spell-checking procedure, it is but one of the tools provided in The Word Plus program. Additional features include the capability of using special dictionaries of user-selected words, specifying the conditions under which the checking process will proceed (ignoring lines starting with certain characters, ignoring uppercase words, selecting the character to be used to mark typos, etc.), and indicating how suspect words are to be handled (marked, discarded, corrected, viewed in context, etc.).

A particularly useful function of The Word Plus is its Hyphen program, for the automatic hyphenation of words. This program can be used in either of two ways. First, and most beneficially in a typesetting environment, it can insert soft hyphens in words of a minimum specified character length. Second, it can be used on-line to display the proper hyphenation points for words that are typed into the computer.

The Hyphen program is a reasonable means of compensating for the lack of hyphenation capability in certain second-generation phototypesetters. The program provides a facility for redefining the soft hyphen character as a new value; in this case, as the discretionary hyphen character used by the phototypesetter. The hyphenation algorithm, which is based on a method devised by Donald Knuth of Stanford and described in his book *TeX and Metafont, New Directions in Typesetting,*[3] also relies upon a disk file of hyphenation exceptions, which the user can add to as necessary.

The Word Plus also provides on-line capabilities to: look up the correct spelling of words that are misspelled, but "close;" find all words of a certain length beginning with a given letter, as in **FIND R????**, which would result in a list of all five-letter words which begin with *R*; unscramble anagrams (word puzzles) and list all words of a certain length containing given characters, such as **??EE**, which would result in a list of all four-letter words ending in *EE*. In addition to the feature of allowing the user to create custom dictionaries of selected words and alphabetically sort them for convenience, there are two additional programs that are particularly useful to writers. First is the Word Frequency program, which provides a list, in order of the most frequently appearing word, showing how many times each word was used. The program also lists the total number of words, the number of unique words, and the number of words that appear only once. Second is the Word Count program, which provides an indication of the total number of words residing in a particular file.

Electronic Word Delivery

Rounding out the Easy-K package is the Suprterm program, which supports the telecommunication of the documents that have been created in WordStar and proofed in The Word Plus. Suprterm, along with a modem (built into the Kaypro 4) and a connection to a standard telephone jack, turns the computer into a terminal capable of communication with other computers.

Electronic delivery is the most direct route for remotely created text destined for publication. The Suprterm program can automatically dial the telephone number of another computer that is either similarly equipped or with dial-in access of some sort, sense a carrier signal, and display a log-in message. Information typed at the Kaypro is converted into serial codes, which are passed through the RS-232 port to the modem, where they are changed into audible tones that can be carried over regular voice-grade telephone lines. At the receiving computer, the modem reverses the process, changing the tones into serial signals that the computer can use.

Once the communications link is established and the user has accessed the area of the remote computer where he will deposit his document (perhaps as electronic mail), Suprterm's "Send" option is chosen. A short series of questions is presented concerning the mode by which the file will be sent. The file name is then typed, the send flag is toggled, and with the final ESC sequence the file is transmitted.

Through other menu selections, remotely transmitted files can be received, saved on disk, and printed.

CTEXTSETTER I & II: Creating Text for Batch Processing of Hyphenation and Justification

CTextSetter I[4] is a combination hardware and software package that mates the IBM PC with the Compugraphic CompuWriter. The CText software turns the IBM into a front-end system for the typesetter, satisfying the need for text editing, justification, and external manipulation of nearly all of the typesetter's capabilities.

[3]Digital Press
Bedford, MA
1979

[4]CText
1286 Eisenhower Place
Ann Arbor, MI 48104
(313) 971-1011

The CTextSetter hardware interface provides a means of processing files prepared on the IBM. The CompuWriter is manually set to a maximum line measure and a minimum line spacing increment. The typesetting software is then able to generate whatever values are necessary for any given typographic format.

The IBM is able to count the character widths of each font, and therefore justify each line, by utilizing binary-coded files of each font's width values. These files are created by the user by filling in a Font Width Table, requiring the input of the relative width of the character as well as the Compugraphic output code. Files may be copied or edited in order to use part of an existing file for the creation of a width table for a similar font.

The software provides for the generation of user-defined defaults, to be used when a required typographic value is not specified. If, for example, a typeface is not input, the default value, say typeface 2, is selected automatically.

The defaults are specified using a Setup Information Form, which presents the user with screen prompts for the input of a font, point size, line spacing, and line measure value. The information is editable should the need arise to change the default conditions.

When the Setup file is completed, the user returns to the system-level screen prompt. The editorial and typesetting programs are accessed by typing **EDIT**, and then pressing the Return key. Typesetting functions and special characters are entered in files as mnemonic codes, enclosed within a set of brackets. A line measure would be written as [**SM** *p*], where the mnemonics *SM* stand for "Set Measure," and the *p* stands for a pica and point value. In order to override the default values, mnemonic codes for the line length, point size, line spacing, and font must be specified in the very first line of the job. Such lines, which contain no printable text, are not counted in any page-depth calculations, and do not trigger the activation of line spacing advance.

After a job has been completely keyboarded, it must be justified prior to sending it to the on-line CompuWriter. That process is well described in The CText documentation:

"When the CJust function is called by an operator, the system first retrieves and examines the default file and the font width files that correspond to the fonts selected for the file or job. The tables within the files are then copied, or 'loaded' into a memory area that the system can access easily.

"Based on the values recorded in the tables, CJust begins accumulating the widths of each character in the first line, beginning with the first character in the file. As the accumulated sum approaches the line length specified by the Set Measure markup command, the CJust programs 'reads ahead' on the line to determine whether or not the line has been quadded by an operator. Quadded lines, or text entered in a quadded mode, are never justified by CJust. If the line is a typical, justifiable line, CJust calls forward the line-break algorithm.

"The algorithm is a formula that enables CJust to determine the best logical breaking point for a line. In much the same way that a human operator might, the CJust program examines the line for wordspaces, punctuation marks or discretionary hyphens that indicate an acceptable place at which to end a line and keep it at or below the set measure.

"Once CJust decides on a good breaking point for the line, it inserts or subtracts word or letter spaces required to make the line meet the set measure exactly. These hidden spaces, not visible on the terminal screen, are recognized by the CompuWriter and inserted into the justified copy as it is being set.

"Any copy that no longer fits in the justified line is automatically sent down to the beginning of the next line, and the justify routines then begin on that line; the routine is continued until every justifiable line on the job or file is complete."

The justification process performs an error-checking routine, searching for command errors (erroneous mnemonics) as well as for invalid command parameters, such as a line measure value beyond the typesetting machine's capability.

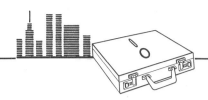
When the justification process is complete, the job depth in lines, picas, and points is displayed near the top of the screen. The justified job is displayed, with flashing returns indicating the line-ending decisions made by the justification program. Although the job has been justified, it remains editable. However, major revisions are best handled by invoking the "Unjust" command, which removes all of the flashing end-of-line indicators and returns the file to its prejustified condition.

After a job has been justified, it displays the actual length of each line as it will appear when typeset. As a further aid to assisting the user in visualizing the processed text, CTextSetter I supports a variety of display screen modes. These modes, composed of varying intensities of display as well as underlined characters, can be mapped to specific typefaces so that bold, for example, always appears on the screen as brighter than other typefaces. Completed files can be processed in Background mode by typing "**do ts** [*output filename*] Return" from the command line. The job is sent through a typesetting preparation program that uses calculation procedures similar to those performed by the justification program. When the job has been preprocessed, it is placed at the end of a "queue" of jobs that are awaiting typesetting. The foreground operation of the editor remains active for the generation of new jobs or the editing of old ones.

CTextSetter II is an upgraded program that runs on more sophisticated typesetters such as the Compugraphic 8600, Mergenthaler 202, and Autologic APS micro 5. It also uses the IBM PC as its host computer, yet greatly extends the system capabilities to include a number of specialized features (for publishing, commercial, and in-plant environments) such as news-wire collection, "aged story" purging and archiving, ad-taking forms (FIG. 3), scheduling, pricing, and others.

FIG. 3. The Adtaker screen on the CText-Setter II program provides customer information for production and billing, as well as a display of the justified ad text.

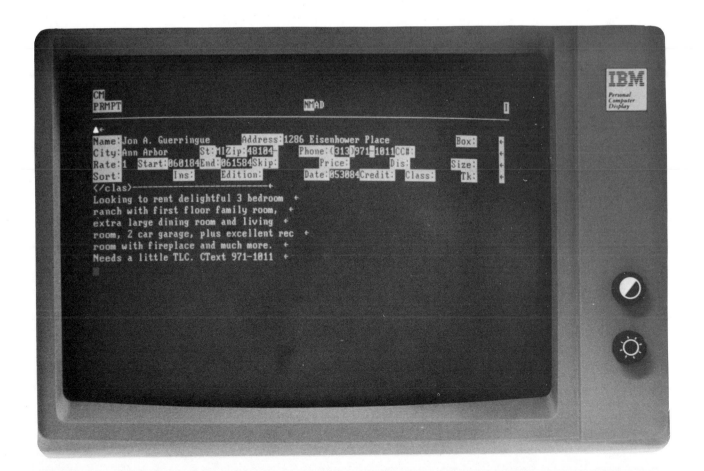

PAGEPLANNER: Integrating Text Entry, Hyphenation and Justification, and Page Make-up

The PagePlanner[5] program is an integrated package which combines text entry, hyphenation and justification, and page make-up. It is compatible with many microcomputers, most notably the IBM PC, as well as many typesetters.

The operation of the program requires the insertion of a hardware security device, called a *dongle*, which is plugged into the Centronics port of the microcomputer. Failure to use the dongle results in the erasure of the program disk. The user is permitted, however, to make multiple backups of the program disk using normal copying procedures.

At the start-up of the system, the program disk is inserted in the primary disk drive and a formatted data disk is inserted in the secondary drive. After the program is read into memory, the Primary menu appears on the screen (FIG. 4). The Primary menu is capable of supporting up to 14 entries, and is completely user-definable in terms of both the sequence of line items and the wording of selection choices. Security locks, in the form of passwords, also can be assigned to important or sensitive programs or maintenance procedures.

Text input begins by selecting the Text Entry and Editing menu (option 1). At this point, a new file can be specified and identified with a name of up to eight characters, or an existing file can be recalled. After the file name is specified, the Text Entry form (FIG. 5) is displayed on the screen. Among the items included are:

- File—The file name, identified either by the name of the operator or the name of the job.
- Id—The identification of the type of file being processed, either ''TXT'' (text), ''HAJ'' (hyphenated and justified), or ''PMU'' (processed through the Page Make-up process).
- Date—Automatically imprinted when the system is started up. The date information stays with each file as a part of its history.
- Char/Count—The number of characters set or in a file.
- Page—Up to three alphanumerics used to identify pages.
- Edition—Up to six alphanumerics used to identify the publication edition.
- Ver—The version of the program that is being edited. Each time that the file passes through one of the parts of the program, the version number is incremented by one. The user always has the current version, plus a backup should something go wrong.
- Depth in pts—A measurement of the depth of the job in points, displayed after the file has undergone H & J.
- Depth in cms (inches in the USA)—Shows an inch conversion of the value displayed in the point depth field. In editorial environments, this value is used to fill columns to reassigned depths. If the depth displayed is too short or too long, it can be edited and hyphenated and rejustified.
- Face—Displays the typeface currently in use.
- Size—Displays the point size currently in use.
- Width—Displays the point size width of the currently selected size. If the output typesetter is digitally based, the width value usually can be changed to expand or condense the appearance of the typeface.
- L/s—The line space value currently in use.
- Measure—The line length, in picas and points, currently in use.
- Indent—The value of the indent as specified in the text area.
- Ragged—Specifies if the margins are to be aligned on either the left, right, or both sides.

[5]New American Page Planner
One Maple Street
E. Rutherford, NJ 07073
(800) 526-5368

PAGEPLANNER PRIMARY MENU

Job Description
1. Text Entry/Editing
2.
3. Hyph/Justification
4.
5. Page Make-up
6.
7. Typesetter
8.
9. Lineprinter
10.
11. Housekeeping
12. Utilities
13.
14. End processing

Enter the no. of job required and press ESC

FIG. 4. Access to all of the PagePlanner capabilities are available from the Primary menu.

FIG. 5. (upper right) The PagePlanner Text Entry screen is similar in many respects to those found on dedicated typesetting input terminals.

FIG. 6. The Hyphenation and Justification menu provides users with control over how they would like their files to be processed.

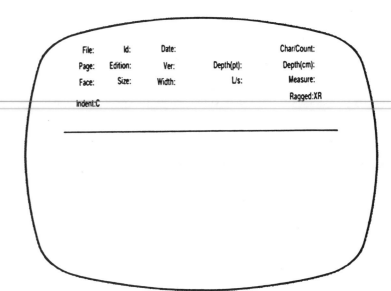

File:	Id:	Date:		Char/Count:
Page:	Edition:	Ver:	Depth(pt):	Depth(cm):
Face:	Size:	Width:	L/s:	Measure:
				Ragged:XR

Indent:C

HYPHENATION AND JUSTIFICATION

1. Check for available space

2. Change data disk (Drive B)

3. View data disk directory

4. H&J an existing text file

5. Hyphenation by prefix? - Currently 'Yes'

6. Hyphenation by suffix? - Currently 'Yes'

7. Hyphenation by logic? - Currently 'Yes'

X Exit from this program

Select the required option and enter appropriate code:

As each field is filled in, the ESC key passes the user to the next. A number of command options are available from the text entry area by pressing the ESC key. These options let the user do such things as end the job (up to 50,000 characters may inhabit the memory at one time), abandon a job in memory, recall a format library (of predefined code strings), save the file intermittently as it is being created, create temporary format keys, search and replace, read in text from another file, send the current file out for H & J and then return it, and many more.

The editing features are comprehensive and include a number of commands that can be used to delete or insert characters, words, lines, sentences, or blocks, as well as move or copy defined text blocks, or write them directly to disk.

After a job has been entered, it is processed through the Hyphenation and Justification program (FIG. 6). The user has the option of determining how the hyphenation process will be performed; that is, by prefix, suffix, or logic. If an error is detected during the hyphenation and justification attempt, processing will stop and the user will need to return to the text entry area in order to make corrections. The site of the error will be marked with a question mark, usually indicating that information is missing or an illegal parameter has been input.

Following hyphenation and justification, the file can be returned to the text entry area for final checking. At this point, word breaks and line ending can be altered manually by using discretionary hyphens (which indicate a preferred hyphenation point) and hard line endings (carriage returns that H & J processing does not alter).

Properly processed text files can be combined for processing through the Page Make-up program (FIG. 7), where they are assembled in graphic form on the microcomputer screen. The displayed page represents the actual page proportions of the printed page.

The page-creation process begins with the assignment of a name for the page file. It is followed by the input of page descriptors for width and depth. Next, the names of all of the text files that will be used to create the page are input. There can be separate files for each distinct part of the job, such as headlines, subheads, captions, and body copy. After this information has been processed, the user returns to the Page Make-up menu and selects option 3, "Process the page file."

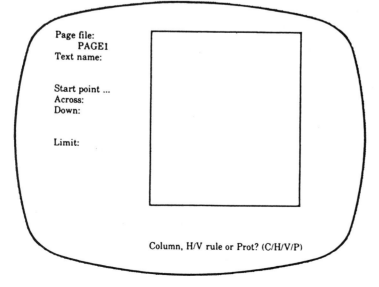

PAGE MAKE-UP MENU

1. Create a new page file

2. Extend an existing page file

3. Process the page file

4. Change data disk (Drive B)

5. View data disk directory

X. Exit from this program

Select required option and enter the appropriate code:

FIG. 7. The Page Make-Up menu provides access to the page-creation, page-processing, and page-editing functions.

Page file:
PAGE1
Text name:

Start point ...
Across:
Down:

Limit:

Column, H/V rule or Prot? (C/H/V/P)

FIG. 8. The Page Creation screen gives the user considerable flexibility in defining the location of all page elements.

The user is presented with a screen representation of a page (FIG. 8) in its proper proportion to the width and depth previously specified. The screen prompts the user for information related to the text file being processed, the column divisions, the placement of horizontal and vertical rules, and the boundaries of protected areas that must be reserved for photographs and artwork. Small markers appear on the screen to indicate column positions. The placement of horizontal rules, for example, is specified by inputting their starting position from the left-hand margin, their depth from the top of the page, their width across the page, and their weight (any of ten different line thicknesses). After all of these items have been specified for each rule, the user is presented with a repeat prompt, providing the opportunity to specify the automatic insertion of similar rules at defined intervals. Protected areas are specified in a similar fashion; that is, their relative locations on the page are indicated.

The assignment of the positions that text will occupy is initiated by pressing ESC, which presents a new prompt: *P/T/R/E/Q*. Each of these letters provides access to a different page-layout function. The *P* (Page layout) lets the user return to the page-layout stage to redefine areas and remove text that has been entered. The *T* (Text fill) lets the user "paint" text into the defined areas. The *R* (Refresh) lets the user repaint the whole screen at once. The *E* (End normally) lets the user write the completed page file to disk. Finally, the *Q* (Quit) lets the user end the session without saving any of the work, and return to the primary menu.

At this point, the page is properly prepared to accept text. Pressing **T** prompts the user for the name of the text file to be utilized. A series of prompts follow. These prompts specify the exact page location that the text will occupy. The text is painted on the screen, at which point the user has the options of accepting it and continuing, viewing the column ending to check for widow or orphan lines (and changing the column ending if necessary), redefining the lower column limit for better fit, or refitting the text block in another position (FIG. 9).

The PagePlanner program provides a number of utilities for handling file management (copying, deleting, recovering, and renaming files) as well as typesetter-specific information (pi fonts, kerning pairs, width tables, and format libraries).

FIG. 9. A completed page as it appears on the computer screen. Column endings may be displayed in character-readable form for end-of-line decision-making.

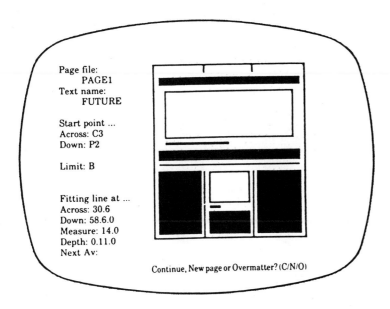

STL: Creating Typesetter Input
In-House for Service Bureau Processing

STL[6] is the Simplified Typesetting Language, a software package which is marketed differently than most others. There are two distinct parts to STL: one that an end-user buys, and another that a typesetting service (type site) buys.

The end-user of the STL program does not typically have a typesetting machine within his environment, although there is nothing to preclude him from implementing the entire STL program. In the usual circumstances, however, the end-user uses STL to create files for typesetting and telecommunicates them to a type site, where they are translated through another STL program for processing on a particular typesetting system.

The STL program basically converts a number of different microcomputers[7] into counting keyboards. What this means is that the user can input typographic coding and have instant feedback on the fit (justification) of each line. By using a configuration facility provided in the program, the user can set up the microcomputer to drive a number of different typesetters.

The end-user is dependent upon the type site for the critical information that will make the program perform satisfactorily. Of primary importance is the character width information, which the program needs in order to determine accurately how many characters will fit on each line. Font files, representing width tables of user-selected typeface designs, are supplied to end-users by the type site either via telecommunications or on disk.

The font widths are only one of many details that must be defined prior to configuring the STL program to operate properly with a specific typesetting machine. Among the other considerations, which are in many instances also of use to non-STL users who need to access typesetting services, are the following.

Maximum Line Length. This information relates to the maximum paper width that the typesetting machine can accommodate: 45 picas for machines using 8-inch paper, and 70 picas for machines using 12-inch paper.

The Sensitized Material. Whether the typesetting machine uses resin-coated (RC) or stabilization paper.

Size Range. The minimum and maximum point size attainable on the typesetter, as well as the point sizes in between. The STL program supports the input of sizes from 2 point to 99 point, in whole- and half-point increments.

Font Order. STL supports up to eight fonts in any one job; however, some typesetters can access only four typefaces during normal processing. In addition to the restriction on the number of typefaces, there is the restriction of working only with those typefaces that are available to the typesetting machine at one time. If, for example, the typesetter uses a spinning disc type master with four typefaces on it, then the STL user would not only be limited to using four typefaces, but would have to use the four faces on that particular disc, and in the order in which they appear on the disc. Failure to adhere to the order in which the type site has arranged its typefaces will result in incorrect output.

Line Advance/Reverse. All typesetting machines have a line spacing function, but not all have provision for a secondary line spacing function or a reverse-feed and multiple-column positioning function.

Leader Characters. STL supports the input of up to nine leader characters in the STL Leader Table. A *leader*, which is a single character repeated in a line to ''lead'' a reader's eye across the page, can be defined as any character. Type Source suggests

[6]Type Source
2022 Traval #609
San Francisco, CA 94116
(415) 564-9104

[7]Microcomputers presently supported include the following CP/M systems: Kaypro, Osborne, Televideo, Northstar, Actrix, Eagle II, Apple (with CP/M card and two drives), Franklin, Cromwell Disk Reader; and the following IBM compatibles: Columbia, Compaq, Corona, Hyperion, Eagle PC, Televideo PC (1605 series) MS-DOS, Tava PC, Sanyo MBC 555, Chameleon, Panasonic Senior Partner, Zenith Z-100, Leading Edge, Microcraft Dimension w/IBM option, Otrona Attache 8088, Handwell, IBS, NCR, Sperry, Fujitso, ITT XTRA, Burroughs, ATT (Olivetti), Tandy 2000 MS/DOS, and DEC Rainbow MS/DOS. Other systems are under development.

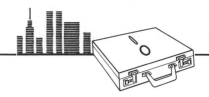

that the most commonly used leaders will be the dot rule, medium rule, bold rule, and dash rule.

Pi Characters. The complement of characters available in any one font, other than alphanumerics, varies considerably. Typesetting machine vendors offer a wide range of font layouts designed for specialized applications such as books, newspapers, mathematical and scientific typesetting, advertising, and foreign languages. The identification of these characters, along with their unit values and any additional instructions, must be communicated by the type site.

Fixed Space. Fixed spaces must be properly defined. *Fixed spaces* are those that maintain their horizontal dimension, unlike *variable spaces* (space bar), which expand or contract in order to justify a line. Each fixed space that an end-user chooses to use will need to be communicated to the type site. Fixed spaces are created by using a user-defined code (UDC) in front of the Fixed Space command.

Word/Letter Space Defaults. The end-user must utilize the same word-spacing range (3 units minimum, 12 units maximum) as the type site. Any alteration to this default must be arranged in advance with the type site.

Insert Space. When input in a line, this function expands the line outward in both directions from the point of insertion. If used more than once in a line, it equally divides whatever remaining space is available at the end of the line between the points of insertion. Not all typesetting machines support this command, although with proper planning it can sometimes be generated by the type site through the conversion process.

Quotations. STL supports the use of the less than and greater than keys to generate open and close quotes. The Inch key is used to generate the inch character, although some users might use the Inch key as the open and close quote. If it is necessary to use the less than and greater than characters in the job, it will be necessary to define two pi characters for the quotes.

Tabs. There is wide variation on the way in which tabs are stored and accessed in different typesetting machines. Precise tab coding information will need to be specified by the type site.

User-Defined Codes. Gaining control of the vast differences between typesetting machines from the STL program is possible by using user-defined codes. These codes have no inherent meaning to the STL program, and only take on an identity when they are converted at the type site into a code string that the typesetting machine can process. Complete specification of user-defined codes must take place prior to the communication of any STL-generated files to the type site.

Starting Up the System

- Two copy-protected STL program disks: the original and the backup.
- A template with typographic functions labeled to correspond with a 10-key numeric keypad.
- A set of two transparent type measurement tools used for calculating type size, line length, line spacing, and indentations.
- The STL Users Manual, which contains the instructions, a description of all typographic functions, operator aids, reference charts, and lessons.
- A quick reference card listing the major STL functions and codes.
- The Type Site Directory, listing all of the typesetting services that accept STL files.

The numeric keypad is programmed according to the conventions required of the specific microcomputer in use. The ten keys take on these dedicated attributes:

KEY		FUNCTION	MEANING
Number 0	=	<ESC>EM	Em Space
Number 1	=	<ESC>QL	Quad Left
Number 2	=	<ESC>QC	Quad Center
Number 3	=	<ESC>QR	Quad Right
Number 4	=	<ESC>SZ	Size
Number 5	=	<ESC>PL	Primary Line Spacing
Number 6	=	<ESC>FT	Font
Number 7	=	<ESC>LL	Line Length
Number 8	=	<ESC>TS	Tab Start
Number 9	=	<ESC>TE	Tab End

The STL program must be properly configured for the operating system in use. Specific instructions for accomplishing this procedure are supplied with each version of the program.

When STL is first run, a Configuration menu is presented to the user. This menu lets the user specify his choice of many typographic variables, as previously discussed. When these items are completed, they are copied onto another disk that holds the font-width information. This disk is placed in the secondary drive while the STL program disk is placed in the primary drive.

After STL has been loaded and the title screen has been exited, the following menu appears:

STL CONFIGURATION MENU

(0) TYPESETTING PARAMETERS
(1) FONTS
(2) PI CHARACTERS
(3) LEADER TABLE
(4) DEFAULT DISK DRIVE
(5) USE CURRENT VALUES AND START STL
(6) EXIT TO OPERATING SYSTEM

Please enter your choice:

Selection of option 0 presents the following screen:

THE CURRENT DEFAULT SETTINGS ARE AS FOLLOWS:

1. Maximum Line Length	70	(picas)
2. Paper Type	S	(stabilization paper)
3. Letterspacing	0	
4. Word Space Lower	03	(minimum word space)
5. Word Space Upper	12	(maximum word space)

Enter # to change or [ESC] to menu:

All of these settings have been previously discussed.

Selection of option 1 presents a series of eight font identifiers, prompting the user for the name of each typeface that will be used. The typeface width information must be resident on a user disk (either the logged disk or another), and must be entered in the order in which the typefaces are accessed on the typesetting machine.

The fonts that are supplied by the type site contain only the lowercase and upper-case alphabet, numerals, and punctuation. Any additional, or *pi*, characters must be entered manually by the end-user. The ''Pi Characters'' table, option 2, allows the end-user to specify the mnemonic identity of each character, enter a description, and indicate its unit value. Any two letters may be used to name a pi character, except

those reserved by STL for normal processing. Because certain pi characters are only available in certain fonts, it might be necessary to initiate a font change prior to accessing particular characters. These details need to be clearly specified when defining the Pi Characters Table. This is the way that the Pi Character table appears on the screen:

Character	Description	Units
BU	Bullet	10
ST	Star	12
CR	Copyright	12
BX	Box	14

Enter Character or [ESC] to return to menu:

Up to 20 entries may be made in the Pi Characters table. If additional pi characters need to be accessed, they must be input in the table in place of existing characters.

Certain characters that are present on most microcomputer keyboards—such as @ (at sign), = (equal), and + (plus)—must also be entered into the Pi Characters table if they are to be used in the typesetting job.

The "Leader Table," option 3 from the Configuration menu, provides the end-user with the opportunity to specify repetitive characters. The unit value for all leader characters must be the same. If a special character with an unlike unit value is specified, the character will be the only leader that will be operative for any given job.

The selection of the "Default Disk Drive" is option 4. Since most microcomputers have two disk drives and the default is set to the secondary drive, this setting usually does not need to be changed.

When menu option 5, "Use Current Values and Start STL," is selected, the active fonts and pi characters are loaded into computer memory. Upon successful loading, the user is prompted to remove the font file/configuration file disk and insert a job disk. Previously prepared files from compatible word processors may be entered into the STL program environment for further processing.

Using STL

Reflecting the needs of virtually all typesetting machines, STL requires that the four basic typesetting parameters—point size, line length, font, and leading (line spacing)—be entered before any work can be processed. These typesetting instructions must be at the top of every file sent to the type site. If any one is not included, the typesetting machine will use its last recorded value (or a default value) for that parameter, which most likely will result in incorrect output.

The STL screen (following) closely resembles that of a direct-input phototypesetter. The top four lines are reserved for the specification of typesetting information, operator prompts, and messages. The remaining screen lines are the text input area, which can be scrolled up and down within the limits of the text buffer. The maximum text buffer size varies among computers.

```
Units Remaining= 756.0  Buffer= 2,377  Depth= 669.0  Mode= JU
Size= 12.0  Line Length= 24.00  Leading= 120.0  Font= UNIVERS.LT
Count Mode= AUTO  Insrt= ON  Tab Count= 0  Indt= 0.00
Multiple Spaces are not allowed in Typesetting
```

Because STL was written to drive a wide variety of typesetting machines, it embodies certain generic features that are common to most typesetting systems. Among them are the following.

Unit Count. The number of units of space available in a line is a function of the unit system used by the typesetting machine (units to the em space), as well as the length of the line being set, and active point size. Because the width information for each font is available in memory, the unit value of each character is subtracted from the unit count as each character key is struck. When the remaining units in a line reach a value small enough to achieve satisfactory justification, the line is ended automatically.

Buffer. The buffer counter keeps track of the number of characters that have been keyboarded. This count is important not only as a gauge of the size of the job, but also as an indication of the remaining space available for input.

Depth. The depth indicator reflects the measurement, in points, of the accumulated line spacing at the cursor location. Line spacing is measured from the baseline of one line to the baseline of the next. This value will reflect reverse line spacing if the type site system supports it.

Mode. The mode refers to the arrangement of lines, either justified, ragged left, ragged right, or ragged center. The system defaults to justified upon start-up. The ragged commands stay in effect until they are canceled by reentering the justification mode.

Parameters. Values for size, line length, leading, and font are input according to the job requirements. An error check is made to verify that the leading value is not smaller than the point size, an error that would result in overlapping lines of copy. If it is smaller, the message *YOUR LEADING IS SMALLER THAN YOUR SIZE* is displayed.

Count Mode. The operator has the option of having the STL program automatically end each line when the justification range is entered, or of ending it manually. Manual end-of-line decisions sometimes are preferred because they allow the operator to specify word breaks (STL does not directly support automatic hyphenation), and therefore achieve more tightly spaced lines. Job requirements also might suggest that manual count mode is advantageous.

Insert. The creation of text is accomplished under one of two modes—either insert or overstrike—similar to the functioning of many word processors. When the Insert mode is "off," the program is in the Overstrike mode.

Tab. The tab field shows which of the up to 20 tabs is active.

Operator Messages. The incorrect specification of typesetting functions and/or values will generate a screen message, accompanied by an alarm if the microcomputer hardware supports its use. The keyboard will lock out until the problem is fixed.

The files created with STL are simple ASCII files, which can be read by most word processing programs and printed on most line printers (those having the capability of adding line feeds). Likewise, ASCII files prepared on word processors or captured via telecommunications can be read into STL and formatted for typesetting. When the files are read into STL, all extraneous coding related to word processing is stripped out.

The operator has access to on-line help at any time by typing **CTRL-Q.** A series of screens are presented listing the control characters, keypad characters, command characters, individual keyboard characters, and their resultant actions. The Typesetting Parameters menu, Fonts Table, Leader Table, and Pi Characters Table are also available for on-line review.

The maximum file size that can be processed by STL is limited by the available buffer. In the CP/M version, for example, the job must be written to disk before the 10K limit is reached. The job disk must have sufficient space to accommodate the file, or else the program will crash and will return the user to the CP/M system. After the

file has been written successfully to disk, it is returned to the STL buffer. If it is no longer needed, STL must be restarted by striking **CTRL-C**, which clears the buffer and the function field and prompts the user for the input of the four primary parameters.

The buffer count value is helpful as an indicator of the potential cost of typesetting the file, since many type sites calculate their billing on the basis of the number of characters that they process.

Depending upon whether the user has the complete STL software and dedicated typesetting equipment or utilizes only the end-user portion of STL and a type site, completed files are either sent on-line to the typesetter, telecommunicated to the type site, or mailed on media to the type site for processing.

At one time, end-users of STL had the option of buying a complete typesetting system, of which STL was a major component. The STL package was bundled with a remanufactured AM VariTyper Comp/Set 500, a Kaypro 2 microcomputer, and a Data Frontier's El Cid interface by B & G Micro Systems, Inc.[8] This system was a low-cost turnkey package that combined microcomputer-based front-end processing with affordable phototypeset output.

PC-TS: Emulating a Vendor Typesetting Front-End System

The technological "trickle-down effect," resulting in sophisticated processing being available on modestly priced microcomputer equipment, is evident in many areas of the graphic arts. The emulation of an expensive dedicated computerized workstation, for example, on an inexpensive microcomputer has changed the marketing emphasis and product mix of industry vendors, as well as the equipment selections and production routines of end users.

The manner by which a microcomputer not specifically designed for a certain typesetting task is transformed, through software, into an emulator of a system built for a dedicated purpose is a testament to human ingenuity. Such a program is PC-TS from Hampstead Computer Graphics.[9] The PC-TS program converts an IBM PC or compatible into an interactive emulator of the Compugraphic MCS text-input station.

In use, the PC-TS disk is loaded in drive A, and the width disk is loaded in drive B. After start-up, the following menu is displayed:

```
            1. UTILITIES
            2. TYPESETTING
            3. TYPESET OUTPUT
            4. EXIT

            SELECT FUNCTION : -
```

The first task the user encounters is to load in the width values for the typefaces that will be used in the jobs to be created during the work session. Up to 60 width tables, representing 60 typefaces, may be in memory at one time.

Item 1 is selected, and the following menu is displayed:

```
            1. LOAD WIDTHS
            2. INITIALIZE DISK
            3. COPY DISK
            4. DEFINE KEYS
            5. LOAD UDKS
            6. LIST UDK FILES

            SELECT UTILITY :-
```

[8]Similar systems are available from:
Baseline
3800 Monroe Ave.
Pittsford, NY 14534
(716) 385-3149

[9]Hampstead Computer Graphics
P.O. Box 469
Hampstead, NH 03826
(603) 329-5076

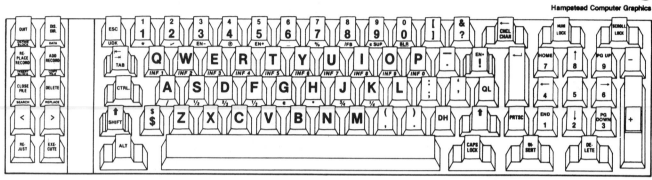

PCTS   **MCS-500**   **hcg**
                                                                              Hampstead Computer Graphics

Control "C" = Quad Center   Control "F" = Tab Return   Control "K" = Carriage Reset   Control "R" = Quad Right   Control "T" = Thin Space
Control "E" = Em Space   Control "I" = Tab End   Control "N" = En Space   Control "S" = Insert Space Control "Z" = End Line

FIG. 10. The mapping of the IBM keyboard provides access to all of the capabilities of the Compugraphic MCS-500 keyboard layout.

```
Fn:TECH     D:A Rn:01                                                      B

PS=012.0 SW=012.0 LS=0012.0 FT=0030 TB=00   LLR=24.00 DC=028.00=004.66    IM 1265

and useful, its character surface must be inked¬
and impressed against paper. The type itself¬
serves to impress the image it carries on its sur-¬
face directly to the printing substrate. This print-¬
ing process is called ''letterpress,'' and it was the¬
dominant printing process from Gutenberg up to¬
the 1960's. Although letterpress printing and¬
metal typesetting systems are not extinct, they¬
have given way to the offset lithographic print-¬
ing process. ''Offset'' (sometimes called ''litho,''¬
''lithography,'' or ''photo offset'') requires type¬
characters composed on a flat surface, usually¬
photographic paper or film. For this reason, and¬
for a very long list of others, phototypesetting¬
has become the dominant method of setting¬
type today.(1)

(1)See Michael L. Kleper: HOW TO BUILD A BASIC¬
TYPESETTING SYSTEM, Graphic Dimensions,¬
Rochester, NY (1979), p.19.
```

FIG. 11. A representation of the PS-TS screen. The top line indicates that this file name is "Tech" and it is on disk drive "A," and that this is record 01. Other information apparent from the display is that the point size is 12, the set width is 12, the line space is 12, the font is number 30, the tab is 0, the line length remaining is 24 (the cursor is at the beginning of a line and the line measure is full; it is decremented as characters are keyboarded), the depth of copy is 28 picas or 4.66 inches, Insert mode is active, and there are 1265 characters in the job.

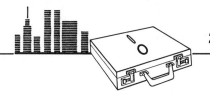

The IBM keyboard is mapped (FIG. 10) to provide access to all typographic commands, functions, and characters. It becomes, in essence, a Compugraphic MCS keyboard, accomplishing the same objective with fewer keys. It does so by combining sequences of control characters, user-defined keys, and dedicated function keys (in both normal and shift modes).

When all necessary width tables have been loaded, the "Typesetting" option is selected from the Main menu. The user is prompted for a file name—either a new one for a new job, or an existing one for a previously keyboarded job that must be edited, revised, or completed. Individual pages of a job can be accessed individually by specifying the file name and the appropriate record number. Files created by word or text processing programs or received through telecommunications can be converted from PC-DOS or MS-DOS into a form usable by PC-TS.

After the job name is processed, the editor work screen is displayed. It is arranged in a fashion similar to interactive screens found on direct-input phototypesetters (FIG. 11). At the beginning of the job, the user inputs the initial job parameters for point size, line space, typeface, and line measure. These values are displayed in the parameter field at the top of the screen. Also displayed are a depth counter, indicating the vertical depth of the composition in both picas/points and inches. At the extreme right of the field there is a keystroke counter, as well as an editing mode indicator (IM = insert mode). Other parameter and job-related information that is displayed relates to command and error messages, indents, and tabs.

The job text is displayed in 21 copy lines of up to 80 characters each. As additional lines are keyboarded, the previous text is scrolled upward into the text buffer. Typographic codes appear on the screen in half intensity to make it easier to differentiate them from the text.

The parameter field is updated instantly as changes to typographic values are made. As each text character is keyboarded, its width value is subtracted from the overall line measure. When the line contains sufficient character widths to provide acceptable fit (justification), the line is automatically ended with a return code. The way the line appears on the screen is the way it will appear when typeset. When changes to text or commands are made, it is necessary to recount (rejustify) the job in order to reestablish the fit of each line. PC-TS has a very fast rejustification capability.

The program provides hyphenation capability by automatic logic, manual insertion, and the selection of appropriate user-suggested discretionary hyphenation points.

In the editing mode, the PC-TS program has all of the text-manipulation capabilities that have become standard for text-input programs. Blocks of text can be defined and moved, deleted, copied, or saved. Word strings of up to 20 characters can be searched for and replaced, or deleted.

All of the text keys can be programmed by the user, and a one- or two-key sequence can represent a long string of codes and characters. The total memory allocated for this feature is 2048 characters, which can be divided among the 62 available text keys in any ratio. A number of series of these assignments of user-defined keys (UDKs) can be saved on disk and loaded as deemed necessary by the user. The UDK define, store, and load capabilities are part of the Utilities menu.

While the PC-TS program provides access to virtually all typographic needs, a number of Hampstead accessory programs provide easier means to accomplish certain complex typographic effects, such as runarounds and complex indentations.

Completed jobs can be output on MCS-compatible disks or directly on a number of different phototypesetters.

PCTYPE: Incorporating Typesetting as an Office Function

As typesetting becomes more of an everyday office activity, it is more likely that it will become one of the many functions performed by a so-called *knowledge worker*. A knowledge worker is someone who originates, synthesizes, and processes information. In the course of his daily work, he directs and coordinates the flow of information to and from a variety of audiences, serving them with both electronic- and paper-based versions of his cerebral output.

Few typesetting programs take into consideration anything other than the process of creating input for a typesetting machine. They typically ignore the fact that those people responsible for the creation of text, the coding of preexistent text, or both, are also usually members of a team of similar workers; and, if they happen to be classified as creative people, they probably perform a number of other functions related to their more general office responsibilities.

A program that differs in this respect of multifunctionality is PCtype.[10] Although the program can be used by a single user, it has been devised to support a multiple-user environment, providing detailed logs of file information as well as password protection. Each user is provided with a personal appointment calendar, an alarm clock, a name and address database, an electronic mail facility, a notebook database, and a personal file library. Each of these supportive functions is available after a user has logged on, and all information is maintained as private.

The Main menu presents the following options:

```
1) Create a New Document
2) Edit an Old Document
3) Print Options
4) Communications
5) Typesetting
6) File Management
7) Other
```

When a new file is created (option 1), a document summary is generated. The summary lists a computer-supplied access name, a user-supplied description (up to 50 characters), the name of the author, the name of the operator, a short list of keywords, and both the date of creation and date of last modification. A typical summary might look like this:

```
                 Document Summary
     Access Name:  DOC036
     Description:  Telemarketing Research Report
          Author:  GS
        Keywords:  tri-state, phone poll, product futures
    Date Created:  01/06/86
Date Last Updated:  01/19/86
```

The system screen is very much like that of a word processor, displaying the input mode (insert or overstrike), page number, line number, logged disk drive, and document name across the top of the screen. All of the typical word processor editing, searching and replacing, and text-formatting capabilities are supported. After a document has been input, it can be printed on a line printer for proofing purposes.

An unusual feature (for a typesetting input-generation program) of PCtype is its math and calculator functions. Addition, subtraction, multiplication, and division are fully supported, as are 17 other math registers, or memories. The Math mode is entered by pressing Function-N. The words *Calculator Mode* appear on the second line of the screen. At that point, the following functions are available:

[10]Modtek, Incorporated
12 South Walker Street
Lowell, MA 01851
(617) 454-1620

Available for the IBM PC family of personal computers.

+	addition
−	subtraction
×	multiplication
/	division
=	result
c	clear last entry
cc	clear calculator accumulator
m*x*	memory access key (*x* is any letter)
sm*x*	store memory
cm*x*	clear memory
@	copy to calculator from text
d	copy to text from calculator
Return	Addition
Execute	Leave Calculator Mode

One of the objectives of the PCtype program is to insulate inexperienced users from the peculiarities of typesetting. It does so by providing easy commands to accomplish what seem to be word processing functions. Common functions that are used to specify italic, indicate centered text, and signify tab locations, for example, have their counterparts in typesetting. Although the text immediately takes on a screen appearance indicative of a typewritten page appearance, it is, in reality holding the associated codes in reserve. To see the actual embedded codes, the user types **Function-V**.

Another useful function of the program is its ability to sort information contained in lists. It handles either alphanumeric or numeric information, in either ascending or descending order. Although it is dependent upon a number of factors, the sort operation proceeds at the rate of about 50 entries every 3 seconds.

After a file has been completed, it is checked against the built-in spelling verification program. Words that do not appear in the dictionary (of over 130,000 words) are highlighted, and the operator has the option of correcting the spelling, skipping the word, or adding the corrected word to the dictionary.

A communications capability is built into the program, providing the means to receive, as well as to send, information. Incoming or outgoing files can be passed through a conversion file to translate certain codes into more meaningful forms. The code used on a word processor to indicate the start of underlining, for example, might be translated into the code required to indicate an italic typeface.

A user may write as many conversion tables as is needed. Entries are written in the form of two parts separated by an equals sign. If every occurrence of the word *oz.*, for example, was to be translated into *ounce*, the entry would appear in the conversion file as:

$$[oz.] = [ounce]$$

Text, hexadecimal, embedded commands, and PCtype-reserved names can be indicated freely in the conversion equation.

The final exit point of the program is the typesetting operation. This procedure supports the use of a *style file,* which is a translation file that converts certain document codes into particular codes supported by the typesetter. Each job may have its own style file, or many jobs may share the same file. Style files can be written by the user and modified at any time using the program's normal editor.

A further capability of the program is the Glossary feature. The Glossary is powerful in that it can be used to reduce the number of keystrokes required for repetitive input, alter or redesign the layout of the keyboard, and customize documents in application-specific ways.

Like other PCtype support files, there may be many Glossary files on one disk. However, only one Glossary file may be used at any one time.

A Glossary entry consists of an *access code* and a list of actions that the code is to perform. An access code consists of a single character, either uppercase or lowercase, which is the mechanism that triggers the event specified in the entry. A typical instruction might be: "go to the beginning of the document, find the previous space, and see if the number in column 4 is less than $75.00."

Using the Glossary capability, a PCtype user was able to modify a three-year financial data summary sheet, which was contained within a document. A year after its creation, a Glossary was written to automatically delete the entries in the oldest year's column, accept the latest year's data, and compute the percentage difference between the data of each of the remaining years. These changes were made by crafting the Glossary, with the use of built-in programming tools, rather than manually editing the document.

TYPE PROCESSOR ONE:
Seeing What You are Going to Get Before You Get It

There is quite a difference between the activities of setting type and composing type. In the former, typographic characters are assembled according to the most basic criteria (type size, typeface, line spacing, and line measure), and the result is usually a long strip of photographic paper that must be assembled manually into page form. In the latter, the exact specifications for all aspects of page layout must be dealt with, and the result is usually fully made-up pages. There are certainly many more machines and methods that deal with setting type than with composing it.

A program for the IBM PC, XT, and AT that performs the typographic composition of text and rules is The Type Processor One.[11] Among its features are the capabilities of drawing column outlines with indents and runarounds, automatically filling in text, cutting and pasting blocks of text, changing sizes and fonts and having them appear on the screen instantly, automatically kerning ill-fitting characters, drawing rules (lines) using the keyboard arrow keys, and vertically justifying pages.

There are two ways in which type can be composed using the program. In the first method, the user defines a form area into which previously created word processing files are flowed. In the second method, the text and rules are input in real time. What appears on the IBM screen is essentially what will appear on the typesetter (FIGS. 12 AND 13).

The Main menu presents five choices: Create/Edit form, Fill form, Compose, Output to typesetter, and Exit. During the course of input, most keys on the IBM keyboard will be interpreted normally, although some acquire a special meaning. The keypad on the right of the keyboard retains its special keypad meanings, rather than its numeric identities. The following keys take on new meanings:

- The Double Quote key becomes a single left-hand quote
- The Apostrophe becomes a single right-hand quote
- The Backslash becomes an em dash
- The Shift-Backslash key becomes a vertical rule
- The Minus key becomes a hyphen
- The Caret key (Shift-6) becomes a cent sign
- The Underline key becomes a baseline rule

[11]Bestinfo
The First Pennsylvania Building
130 South State Road
Springfield, PA 19064
(215) 328-2900

FIG. 12. A reproduction of the Type Processor One screen showing its representative typefaces. The background grid is calibrated in 1-inch squares with 1-pica increments.

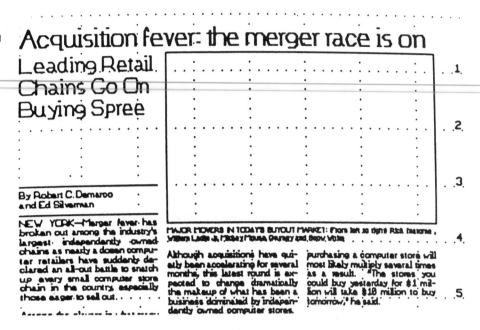

FIG. 13. The typeset result of the screen shown in FIG. 12.

Acquisition fever: the merger race is on

Leading Retail Chains Go On Buying Spree

MAJOR MOVERS IN TODAY'S BUYOUT MARKET: (From left to right) Rick Inatome , William Ladin Jr, Mickey Mouse, Grumpy and Snow White

By Robert C. Demarco
and Ed Silverman

NEW YORK—Merger fever has broken out among the industry's largest independently owned chains as nearly a dozen computer retailers have suddenly declared an all-out battle to snatch up every small computer store chain in the country, especially those eager to sell out.

Among the players in what many are calling the "computer store wars of '84" are some of the biggest names in computer retailing, including Inacomp Computer Centers Inc., Compushop Inc. and ComputerCraft Inc.

Although acquisitions have quietly been accelerating for several months, this latest round is expected to change dramatically the makeup of what has been a business dominated by independently owned computer stores.

Now, most retailers are saying, the long-predicted consolidation will happen very quickly.

But as one computer retail executive pointed out, the cost of purchasing a computer store will most likely multiply several times as a result. "The stores you could buy yesterday for $1 million will take $10 million to buy tomorrow," he said.

Another executive, William E. Ladin Jr., president of the 30-store ComputerCraft chain said last week, "After Comdex, I came away with the feeling that there (continued on page 138)

As type is composed, it appears on the IBM display in a set of simulated fonts representing a roman and italic typeface. The position, type size, width, weight (light, medium, bold, and ultrabold), and character orientation (condensed and expanded) are all correct, although the character positions might vary by a point or two. A reference grid appears in the screen background marked in increments of picas and inches. The grid area measures 8 inches wide by approximately 5 inches deep, and can be scrolled to a depth of over 18 inches. As the page is constructed, the zoom feature provides a way of viewing the entire job at from 1 to 100 percent of actual size.

An explanation of how a few of the more frequently used functions work provides an insight into the effective way in which the user interface has been blended into the IBM hardware. For example, changing the size of type is particularly easy (FIG. 14). The cursor is moved to the character that is to be changed, and then the F1 function key is pressed. The message *Size* appears on the bottom of the screen. By pressing the up arrow, the character increases in size over a range of predefined steps. Pressing the down arrow decreases the point size. The size of type also can be changed to any size from 6 to 99 point, or the maximum size available on the typesetter, by typing CTRL-A followed by the point size.

The exact positioning of characters can be accomplished by moving them horizontally or vertically within the screen window (FIG. 15). This movement is accomplished by pressing the F2 function key after the character to be moved has been typed. The message *space* appears at the bottom of the screen, and the character can be moved in two-point increments by using the arrow keys. When the character is in the correct position, the Enter key is pressed.

Special typesetting characters, such as a copyright symbol or ballot box, are accessed and displayed by using the IBM's ALT key and a single character or number simultaneously. The copyright symbol would be set by typing ALT-L, and the ballot box by typing ALT-T.

The fit of typographic characters is one parameter that distinguishes good typesetting from average or poor typesetting. The Type Processor One program has the capability of either uniformly varying the space between all characters (FIG. 16), positively (adding space) or negatively (subtracting space), or only varying the space between specific character pairs (FIG. 17). Although the control of space between two characters is the kind of flexible intervention a typographer requires, the program is somewhat restricted in that the screen display typeface is only a representation of the true typeface appearance, and the spacing which appears on the screen is only an approximation. However, an operator's experience with typesetting, character fit, and the use of the program will compensate for these hardware limitations.

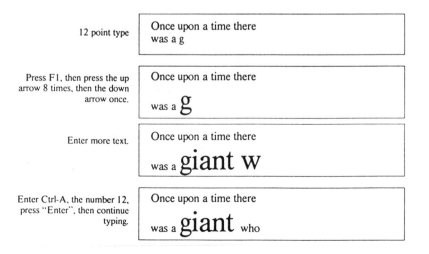

12 point type	Once upon a time there was a g
Press F1, then press the up arrow 8 times, then the down arrow once.	Once upon a time there was a g
Enter more text.	Once upon a time there was a giant w
Enter Ctrl-A, the number 12, press "Enter", then continue typing.	Once upon a time there was a giant who

FIG. 14. The keyboarding procedure (on the left) and resulting screen display result (on the right) for the process of changing type size.

FIG. 15. Characters are moved horizontally and vertically within the area of the screen through the use of the arrow keys.

Sweaters $

18 point type

Sweaters $1

Press F2 and use the right arrow and up arrow to move the dollar sign into position. Then enter "1" and ctrl-A, 36, then "Enter".

Sweaters $134

Press F2 then use the down arrow to move the number 1 down. Enter 3 and 4.

Sweaters $13⁴⁹

Enter Ctrl-A 18 to size down the 4. Then press F2 and the up arrow to move it up. Enter number 9, then flush left with F3 "Enter."

Sweaters $13⁴⁹each

Enter letter e, size it down then press F2 . Use the arrow keys to move it into position (it may partly erase some characters). Then continue.

FIG. 16. The intraword spacing between all characters may be specified as a number from − 100 to 100.

Normal spacing

Letters can be spaced out_

Press Ctrl-C, enter "10", press "Enter."

Letters can be spaced out_

Press Ctrl-C, enter "-3", press "Enter."

Letters can be spaced out_

FIG. 17. The kerning or letterspacing of characters may be achieved by using the left and right arrow keys, and making a visual determination.

AV_

Press Ctrl-K, then press the left arrow key several times, then press "Enter".

AV_

FIG. 18. Margins are set by specifying the placement of the cursor in its required right and left marker locations.

Using justified columns with automatic line ending.

Once upon a time in a far, far distant land
—

Press Ctrl-S, then move the block cursor with the arrow keys. Press "l" to set the left margin.

Once upon a time in a far, far distant land

Move the cursor further right and press "r".

Once upon a time in a far, far distant land

Press "Esc" and continue typing.

Once upon a time in a far, far distant land there lived an old man and_

Margins can be executed at any time by initiating a CTRL-**S** key sequence. The change in margin values is used primarily to produce indents and runarounds, which are used to flow text around photographs or illustrations that appear within the boundaries of a column of type. When this command is used, the current margin settings are displayed at the bottom of the screen, appearing as short vertical lines with a block cursor at the left. The right and left arrow keys are used to move the left edge of the cursor to the required location. For more exact positioning the block cursor can be changed into a cross-hair cursor by entering CTRL-**H** (and back into the block cursor by entering CTRL-**H** again). Typing **L** sets the left margin; typing **R** sets the right (FIG. 18).

Being a professional typesetting package, The Type Processor One has a number of built-in aesthetic determinants that prevent the program from supporting the creation of ill-fitting words or lines. The default line-ending mode, for example, is column justification. As text exceeding the end of a line measure is input, it is automatically carried to the next line. The algorithm used to determine when the end of the line is reached allows for a maximum word space and letterspace expansion. If the line cannot be ended within the preset range of acceptable values, the computer beeps, displays *Cannot Break*, and automatically positions the cursor over the first character that exceeds the line measure. The operator then must make a decision as to where the line can be properly ended. The operator also can override the default column justification mode and specify flush left, flush right, or centered.

Although the direct input of text might be most efficient for some jobs, the use of word processing or telecommunicated files in the Formfill composition mode probably will be the predominant method of composing pages since it permits the use of the software and hardware in its most valuable capacity. In Formfill the user draws the outline of a page layout on the screen (using a cursor directed by the arrow keys) indicating indents, runarounds, and even wordwraps, and then pours text into the forms, passing it through a hyphenation and justification process. Standard forms can be used again and again, or existing forms can be edited for specific applications.

The files used in Formfill may be created by any text editing or word processing program that produces ASCII files. Formatting codes that are native to the text-creation program, such as tabs and justification commands, should be avoided. Typographic commands in the form of mnemonic codes should be entered within the text. These codes must be delimited both before and after by a Backslash character. The command ＼**ft2**＼, for example, indicates a change to font 2.

The Type Processor One is appropriate for ad make-up and short jobs of a limited number of pages. It has been joined by a second program, SuperPage, which incorporates all of The Type Processor One features in a more sophisticated version that is capable of doing full pagination.

MICROGRAPHIX:
Producing Text, Page Layouts, and a User Database

There are many applications that seem to be particularly well suited to computerization. Jostens, the world's largest producer of school yearbooks, has taken the three major tasks associated with yearbook production—the generation of copy, the design of page layout, and the compilation of student body information—and devised software to assist yearbook staffs in streamlining production.

[12]Jostens
5501 Norman Center Drive
Minneapolis, MN 55437
(612) 830-3300

The Jostens' Micrographix software[12] is composed of three programs, all of which run on the Apple II series of microcomputers. The Layout Program provides a graphic means of assembling page elements in position according to design principles built into the program. The Word Processing Program offers an easy way to input text destined for phototypesetting output. Finally, The Indexing Program gives users the means to establish a student database for typeset listings, as well as for administrative record-keeping. We will take a look at the first two applications.

Beginning a Layout

Jostens' approach to yearbook production is to provide its customers with all of the necessary tools in order to effectively plan and design their yearbook content. This objective is clearly followed in The Layout Program, which contains a lengthy educational section meant to orient the user to planning techniques and the general rules of good layout and visual appeal. An interactive tutorial gives the user information about the five most popular layout styles: column, mosaic, mondrian, modular, and isolated element. Descriptions of each kind of layout are provided, as well as animated graphic presentations that show how each is composed.

Each of Jostens' programs serves to simplify the job of both the client school and the production department within Jostens itself. The Layout Program, for example not only instructs the yearbook staff in the basics of good layout and design, but also provides the software tools to specify exact positioning of each graphic element. After the pages have been committed to disk, Jostens' manufacturing operations use the computer images as a guide to assembling the pages.

The Layout Program's Main menu (FIG. 19) provides access to the layout tutorial, layout quiz, layout specification, and database editing. Each layout (FIG. 20) is composed of a double-page spread divided into four quadrants. The elements within each quadrant conform to a number of simple layout rules, such as maintaining equal white space between all elements and forcing all white space to the outside of the grouped elements (which, incidentally, leaves space for autographs).

FIG. 19. The Layout menu provides general information and a tutorial, as well as the means to lay out, modify, and efficiently store page designs.

```
LAYOUT TOOL MAIN MENU


1. INSTRUCTIONS FOR THIS PROGRAM.

2. INSTRUCTIONS FOR GOOD LAYOUT.

3. LAYOUT TUTORIAL AND QUIZ.

4. GRAPHICS AND LAYOUT DESIGN.

5. EDIT LAYOUTS IN DATABASE.

6. REPORT ON LAYOUT DATABASE.

7. END THIS PROGRAM.


PRESS <SPACE> TO MOVE YOUR CHOICE.
PRESS <RETURN> TO PROCEED TO CHOICE.
```

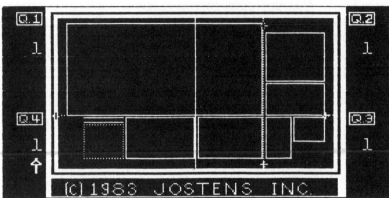

A number of layout styles are explained and shown:

- Column—This layout uses 2, 3, or more vertical columns per page. Photographs and text are placed within one or more adjacent columns (FIG. 21).
- Mosaic—This layout places a dominant photograph toward the middle of the double-page spread, with smaller elements and text clustered around it (FIG. 22).
- Mondrian—This layout uses an intersecting horizontal and vertical line, both off-center, serving as guidelines for the placement of page elements (FIG. 23).
- Modular—This layout depends upon the initial placement of a large horizontal or vertical square or rectangular element, to which all remaining elements are carefully fit (FIG. 24).
- Isolated Element—This layout draws attention to a single photograph or piece of artwork by segregating it from clustered elements on the double-page spread (FIG. 25).

For the program to actually lay out pages, information about each page must be entered into a page-specification form, which contains the date, whether the page contains process color, the section identification name, the page numbers (for double-page spreads), whether the page is mondrian or column layout, and an optional special category ID. After the information has been input and saved on a data disk, the screen clears and the user is presented with the graphic layout screen and on on-screen menu of positioning choices (FIG. 26). These choices include features to both lay out and edit page elements across the double-page spread.

Among the menu choices are selections that: present the page data screen, clear the present layout, retrieve a previously saved layout, change the layout to reflect any of the ten professionally designed layout schemes available within each quadrant, move among quadrants, save the layout to disk, save up to ten screens for printout using an accessory program (Zoom Graphix from Phoenix Software), draw reference indicators in each element for identification (FIG. 27), and exit from the program.

As each double-page spread is input, it becomes part of a database. The database is composed of specific information about each element on each page; specifically, the layout style used, the identification and size of each element, the presence of color, the name of the section, and of course, the page numbers. The information in the database is a valuable aid in gauging the progress of the planning and in determining the actual layout specification at the factory.

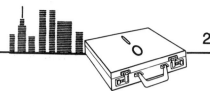

FIG. 21. A simple six-column layout.

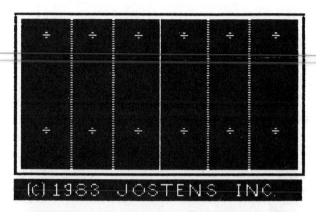

FIG. 22. The mosaic style of layout fits elements together like pieces of tile.

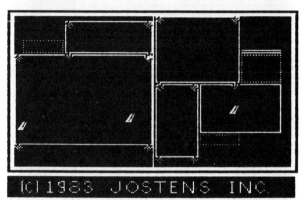

FIG. 23. The modrian style layout positions elements from off-center horizontal and vertical guidelines.

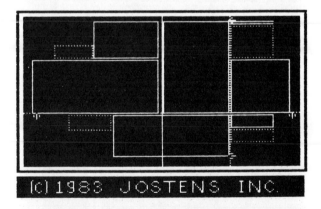

FIG. 24. The horizontal modular style of layout groups large horizontal blocks of photographs.

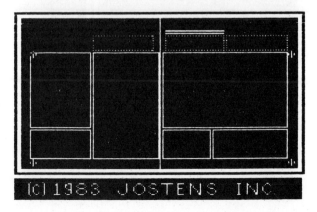

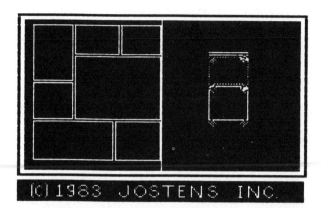

FIG. 25. The isolated element style of layout sets a small element to the side, completely surrounded by white space.

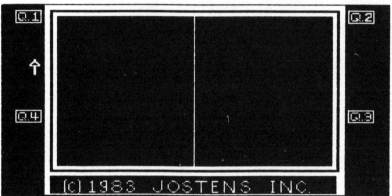

FIG. 26. The Layout menu provides access to page specifications, quadrant positioning, and disk access.

```
( P )PAGE DATA       (C,R)CLEAR/RETRIEVE
(I,M)CHANGE LAYOUT  (J,K)CHANGE QUADRANT
( S )SAVE DBL-PAGE   ( D )DRAW COPY REFS.
( Z )SAVE FOR ZOOM   ( X )EXIT          ?
```

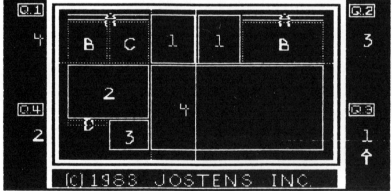

FIG. 27. Copy references can be added to each element in order to specify further the exact positioning of text, photographs, and artwork.

```
( P )PAGE DATA       (C,R)CLEAR/RETRIEVE
(I,M)CHANGE LAYOUT  (J,K)CHANGE QUADRANT
( S )SAVE DBL-PAGE   ( D )DRAW COPY REFS.
( Z )SAVE FOR ZOOM   ( X )EXIT
```

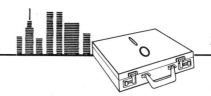

Composing the Text

Jostens' text-input program is fashioned after the popular Bank Street Writer, written by staff members of the Bank Street College. Upon initial start-up, it provides access to a setup screen (FIG. 28), wherein certain system capabilities are detailed and user preferences are chosen. Furthermore, additional screens are presented that offer the user the opportunity to select typefaces, paragraph styles, and justification schema for captions/body copy (FIG. 29) and headlines (FIG. 30).

The word processor screen toggles between the Page menu (FIG. 31) and the Edit/Write menu by using the Escape key. Toggling between executing a command and inputting text in the word processor is accomplished by hitting CTRL-**A**.

In the Edit/Write menu, copy is input by first specifying its position (FIG. 32). The position attribute has three values: one for its position on the page (a value from A to ZZ), a second for its type of copy (Caption, Headline, Body Copy, Subheadline, or Division Page Headline), and a third for its line width in picas.

After copy has been input, it can be edited (deleted, moved, searched, replaced) by selecting the appropriate commands in the menu. Portions of the text can be designated for special typographical treatment; that is, as either italic, bold, or bold italic variations. In order to specify which word or words are to be set in a variant style, the user simply positions the cursor at the beginning and end of the text section, which in the process becomes highlighted (FIG. 33). If the highlighted section is acceptable, pressing **Y** (Yes) automatically inserts the necessary typesetting codes that will ultimately cause the Jostens typesetting machine to change to the proper type style and back again (FIG. 34).

Although the word processor does not count the character widths of the text in real time, it does provide a background count. Selecting command #6, "Fit Copy," causes the program to count the number of characters, display the number of characters that will fit on one line, and show the column depth in picas and points (FIG. 35).

FIG. 28. The Set-Up menu for the Jostens' word processing program allows control of printer requirements, disk drive specifications, and screen display.

```
SET-UP ITEMS AND CURRENT VALUES


A.LINE FEED ON CARRIAGE RETURN?..N
B.PRINTER SLOT #.................1
C.DATA DISK SLOT #...............6
D.DATA DISK DRIVE #.............1
E.PAUSE BETWEEN PAGES?..........N
F.FORM FEED CHARACTER ACTIVE?....Y
G.FORM FEED CHARACTER...........140
H.PAGE EJECT?...................Y
I.KEYCLICK ON?..................N
J.CURSOR TYPE...................U
K.SEND PRINTER CONTROL CODES?....N


ENTER THE LETTER OF VALUE TO CHANGE:
        (A THRU K; X TO QUIT)
```

```
           CAPTION/BODY TYPE SPECIFICATIONS

      PICTURE CAPTION
           1.  TYPE FACE NUMBER: ?019
           2.  TYPE SIZE:   08


      BODY COPY
           1.  TYPE FACE NUMBER:   019
           2.  TYPE SIZE:   08
           3.  PARAGRAPH STYLE:   2
               1 = INDENT
               2 = NO INDENT - BLANK LINE


      JUSTIFICATION:   3
           1 = JUSTIFIED
           2 = UNJUSTIFIED LEFT
           3 = UNJUSTIFIED RIGHT


      CORRECT WHERE NECESSARY. ELSE RETURN
```

FIG. 29. The Caption and Body Copy Specifications menu sets the default typographic values for the entire yearbook. Typeface numbers correspond to Jostens' list of available styles.

```
            HEADLINE TYPE SPECIFICATIONS

      SUB HEADLINES
           1.  TYPE FACE NUMBER:   ?019
           2.  TYPE SIZE (14,18):    14

      MAIN HEADLINES
           1.  TYPE FACE NUMBER:    019
           2.  TYPE SIZE (24,30,36):    24

      DIVISION PAGE
           1.  TYPE FACE NUMBER:   019
           2.  TYPE SIZE (24,30,36,42,48,60):   30

      NOTE: COPY STYLE - LOWER AND UPPER CASE
            WILL BE USED JUST AS YOU USE IT
            WHILE ENTERING TEXT.


      CORRECT WERE NECESSARY. ELSE RETURN
```

FIG. 30. The Headline Type Specifications menu sets the style and size of each sub-head, main headline, and division headline.

```
                  PAGE MENU            CMD
      1 OPEN PAGE  4 RENUM PAGE   7 PRINT
      2 ENTER POS  5 CHG POS LBL  8 INIT DISK
      3 SAVE PAGE  6 DELETE       9 QUIT

      +--------------------------------------+
      |                                      |
      |                                      |
      |                                      |
      |                                      |
      |                                      |
      |                                      |
      |                                      |
      |                                      |
      |                                      |
      |                                      |
      +--------------------------------------+
```

FIG. 31. The Page menu provides the means to store or retrieve a file, specify a page position, renumber a page, change a position label, delete a file, print a file, initialize a disk, or quit.

FIG. 32. The Copy Position prompt requires information to describe the page location, variety of type usage, and line measure.

```
COPY POSITION
     ENTER POSITION(A-ZZ): A
     ENTER TYPE(C,H,B,S,D):H
     ENTER WIDTH IN PICAS(1-99): 36
```

FIG. 33. In order to change words to the italic form, it is first necessary to highlight them by marking their beginning and end.

```
ITALIC
     ARE YOU SURE YOU WANT
     THE HIGHLIGHTED AREA
     SET IN ITALIC(Y/N)?      _

{POS   A   HDL   36W   00-01D CHRS 0000}

Debate Team Wins Fifth National
```

FIG. 34. The Edit/Write screen is the actual word processing creative environment.

```
PAGE 1              EDIT/WRITE           CMD
  1 ERASE      4 REPLACE      7 BOLD
  2 MOVE       5 ADD MARK-UP  8 ITALIC
  3 LOCATE     6 FIT COPY     9 BOLD ITALIC

{POS   A   HDL   36W   00-01D CHRS 0000}

Debate Team Wins {obFifth{ub National
```

```
COPY FIT           HDL
    PICA WIDTH 36     TOTAL CHARS 0031
    CHRS/LINE 046     DEPTH       02-04
    PRESS RETURN TO CONTINUE     _

┌─────────────────────────────────────────┐
│ {POS  A  HDL  36W  02-04D CHRS 0031}     │
│ Debate Team Wins {obFifth{ub National    │
│                                          │
│                                          │
│                                          │
│                                          │
│                                          │
└─────────────────────────────────────────┘
```

FIG. 35. After copy has been input, it can be copyfit to yield its page depth and number of characters. (See the first line within the editing box showing POSition, HeaDLine notation, Width, Depth, and number of CHaRacterS.)

```
PAGE RENUMBER

      ENTER NEW PAGE NUMBER(1-999): 89_
      RETURN ONLY LISTS PAGES

┌─────────────────────────────────────────┐
│ {POS  A  HDL  36W  04-06D CHRS 0089}     │
│ ***                                      │
│ Surprint head over team photo           │
│ ***                                      │
│ Debate Team Takes {obFifth{ub National   │
│ Title Under the Sponsorship of the       │
│ /afEli Whitney Foundation/nf             │
│                                          │
│                                          │
└─────────────────────────────────────────┘
```

FIG. 36. An item that must be moved to another page can be respecified using the Page Renumber command.

On occasion it is necessary to attach some special instructions along with a text element in order to provide information to the typesetter. The program provides an "Add Mark-up" feature, which lets the user insert any number of nonprinting comment lines. These instructions appear within two rows of three asterisks (FIG. 36).

A final command, "Page Renumber," lets the user reassign a section of text to another page should the layout requirements change.

The proofreading function is conducted using the Sensible Speller.[13] This program utilizes an on-disk version of the Random House Dictionary, which contains over 80,000 words with provision for a user-constructed dictionary of 10,000 words.

GALLEY PREPARATION SOFTWARE
NEWSSET

The Concept Publishing System[14] is composed of 14 programs encompassing integrated typesetting, spell-checking, ad setting, wire service editing, and telecommunications. Marketed for the small newspaper, the system is built around an Apple *II*e microcomputer, which uses a custom-designed 80-column card that supports the display of special typesetting symbols and pi characters. The Apples can be networked on a Corvus central data system, which is capable of supporting up to 63 workstations. Hyphenation and justification is handled by the output typesetter, which can be either the Compugraphic VideoSetter, EditWriter, or 8600. Input into the Apple network can be accepted from Radio Shack TRS-80 Model 100 lap computers through the use of additional software and hardware. Additionally, the Apple workstation can be used to generate raw ad copy for manipulation on the Compugraphic Advantage ad make-up terminal.

[13]Sensible Software, Inc.
210 S. Woodward, Suite 229
Birmingham, MI 48011
(313) 258-5566

[14]Concept Publishing
805 Park Avenue
P.O. Box 558
Beaver Dam, WI 53916
(414) 887-0321

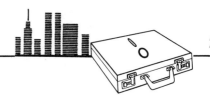

THE DEFT PHOTOCOMPOSITION PACKAGE

The Deft Photocomposition Package[15] is a combination of programs that run on the Wicat microcomputer and allow the user to input, edit, and make up text into pages. Output is to a variety of modern phototypesetting equipment. All h&j takes place as text is input. Tabular matter is displayed with indents and offset numbering strings correctly aligned. A number of single-key commands also simplify the setting of complex and repetitive tabular work. The page make-up program supports vertical justification and horizontal and vertical ruling. The hyphenation dictionary is editable for particular applications, such as medical texts, and for particular languages, such as French. A facility also is provided for controlling the character sets in use at the keyboard, on the user screen, and on the typesetter font layout. An additional software package called TDS-80 provides a set of programs for database typesetting, allowing the user to create, update, delete, sort, and extract text records in an intelligent fashion.

ETC

The ETC software package[16] consists of four programs that are used with the Radio Shack Model III and SuperSCRIPSIT. It is specifically for users of a CCI typesetting computer with TypeLink software.

According to the supplier, it works in the following way: "A manuscript is sent out to a typist who then enters it into a Mod III using SuperSCRIPSIT. The typist then uses PRT/CTL to convert the file to ASCII and perform a character count. The disk is then sent into the plant where it is placed in a Mod III that is connected to the CCI system. A typist then enters the names of the files that are to be sent to the CCI system. If ten files are to be sent then ten file names would be entered. The typist then tells the Mod III to send the files. The typist is now free to perform some other task. The Mod III will send each file in turn until all files have been sent. This process can be reversed so that files can be taken off the CCI and put onto Mod II disks so that they can be sent to a typist or a customer to be edited. Note that the Mod III can be connected to the CCI with hard wire or over the phone with a modem."

FIRST MAIN COMPUTER SYSTEMS

First Main Computer Systems[17] offers a number of typesetting and data entry systems utilizing popular microcomputers. Their systems are modular, and unlike other vendor's systems, can be tailored to specific applications. Furthermore, systems can be upgraded at a later time to perform additional tasks without disrupting current operations. Most upgrades require only plug-in circuit cards and additional software.

The AP100. This system is based on a specially configured Apple II computer. A special video character set is supplied which features lowercase characters with true descenders and displayable TTS characters. Also supplied with the system is an enhanced text editor, a standard disk operating system, a self-test and diagnostic utility, and a proof print utility (which requires an optional printer and interface). Special memory cards are available that will support programs for typesetter drivers, communications, OCR, etc.

The Mainwriter. This is the AP100 system with an expansion ROM, letter-quality printer, and interface (printer interface is $295). It allows the Apple to be used as a sophisticated word processing system. The flexibility of the AP100 Text Editing system is combined with a powerful print formatter to give complete control of a printed document.

[15]Deft Computer Systems Ltd.
51 South Street
Dorking, Surrey RH4 2JX
ENGLAND
(0306) 886627

[16]Elizabeth Typesetting Company
26 North 26 Street
Kenilworth, NJ 07033
(201) 241-6161

[17]First Main Computer Systems, Inc.
P.O. Box 795
Bedford, TX 76021
(817) 540-2491

In addition to having business letters and forms stored on disk, the Mainwriter option will allow the freelance writer to create manuscripts rapidly and effectively on the AP100 and to print a complete manuscript suitable for submission to a publisher.

The Mainwriter ROM plugs into the master PROM board of the AP100.

AP100 Direct Typesetting. Many typesetters currently in use can be driven directly by the AP100 terminal through the use of the DTS typesetter interface option. This system consists of special typesetting software in ROM, a typesetter interface card for a specific typesetter, and an interface cable to connect the typesetter to the AP100.

Copy to be typeset is entered and edited in the normal manner. All typesetter control codes are entered along with the text, allowing all control codes to be manipulated like plain text for editing purposes. The file is saved to disk for storage. When the Typesetting option is activated, the disk is read, and one or more files are converted into TTS codes and transmitted to the typesetter.

Although the DTS is compatible with the majority of typesetters on the market, there are some exceptions. DTS will not generate justified output, nor will it support head fit or copy fit because the AP100 is a noncounting keyboard. Therefore, it will not interface to typesetters that accept only justified copy.

Pricing will vary for different typesetters because of differences in interfacing, typesetter capabilities, etc. Multiple typesetters of the same type may be connected to a single DTS via a switch box, but only one may be active at a time.

AP100 Communications. Two communications options are available on this system. The first is the MCOM, which provides bidirectional communications at 300 to 19,200 baud between two AP100 terminals. MCOM is ideal for transfer of AP100-compatible text files from remote sites to the main plant. With the Auto Answer option there is no need for operator intervention; it will automatically answer, save the data to disk, and hang up.

The second communication option is the UCOM. This configuration lets the AP100 terminal communicate with a system other than another AP100. The UCOM will take the AP100 text file, convert it to codes compatible with the host system, and transmit this data to the host system, where it is saved on its own database. UCOM is a custom package, tailored specifically for the user's application and host system.

Typset 80. This front-end system is based on the TRS-80 Model III. Text is entered using the First Main text editor, and the completed copy is stored in a floppy disk file. For users of ATEX and CSI, special software can be used to transmit text from the terminal to the host system via telephone, OCR port, or RS-232C port.

EDITERM 90

The Editerm 90 System[18] uses the Radio Shack TRS-80 (unmodified) with special interfaces to drive the Compugraphic 8600 and Edit Writer 75/7700, Mergenthaler VIP, Linoscreen 7000, Mycrotek, Omnitek, CRTronic, and Linotron 202. The Editerm 90 features full editing capabilities, large video screen, disk storage, optional hard copy printer, telephone communication, and paper tape to disk conversion.

Keyboarding is simplified by use of the Universal Translation Program (UTP), which is a code-substitution table that allows the user to avoid learning cumbersome typesetting codes. Any operator can simplify input coding by not having to key typeset codes into the data file. Anywhere a machine command or repetitive blocks of copy are required, an operator simply types target strings (a mnemonic designator such as **, +a, /bd/, etc.) of up to four characters in length. The standard program will accept up to 99 translation strings, which are stored on disk. Before the data files created by the operator are output to the typesetter, the formats are called from disk and loaded into the terminal's memory. As the data file is sent to the typesetter, the UTP automatically and instantly substitutes the entire format (up to 254 characters) for the four-letter callout.

[18]Marcus Computer Services Inc.
243 Riverside Drive, Suite 1002
New York, NY 10025
(212) 678-0406

The TypeMate 2000

The TypeMate 2000[19] is a publications precomposition system specifically for the Mergenthaler VIP phototypesetter. Each workstation consists of a terminal, a dual disk drive, 500 user-definable formats, multitasking capability, and full feature editing. All h&j, advanced typographic programs, exception word dictionaries, and formatting are performed using the intelligence resident in the VIP.

PAGE MAKE-UP SOFTWARE

TYXSET 1000

The TYXSET 1000 system software[20] runs under UNIX on a sophisticated 16-bit supermicrocomputer capable of supporting up to 24 terminals. The system software includes a word processor with all of the universal editing commands, and a menu-driven document descriptor generator to define the output format of such instructions as indentations, headers/footers, and multiple columns. The system is capable of producing graphics (logos, charts, etc.), as well as textual information.

The procedure for using the system is fairly easy, despite its relative complexity. Use begins with a log-in procedure using a user name previously assigned. Successful log-in results in a three-item menu providing three choices: document formatter, document processor, and forms processor.

''Document processor'' is used to create and alter completed files. It has its own eight-selection menu that provides options for such choices as composing a new document, editing a previously composed document, proofing, deleting, and cataloging.

Output is through either a Canon Laser Printer or a Mergenthaler Omnitech 2100.

SCRIBE

The Scribe document preparation software[21] runs on a number of time-sharing computers, such as the DEC VAX/VMS, IBM 370, and PRIME PRIMOS. A text editor, native to the computer system, is used to generate a manuscript file. This file is then processed through Scribe to produce a document file that can be output to a variety of devices, ranging from line printers and laser printers to phototypesetters. It is document-oriented rather than page-oriented, in that it is concerned with the many elements which make up an entire document, such as a table of contents, chapters, sections, subsections, indices, etc.

Scribe contains a database of document format definitions that describe the exact rules for formatting an extensive collection of styles. For most applications the user need not be concerned with such formatting decisions since Scribe contains complete instructions for their execution, making a best attempt at proper formatting regardless of the capabilities of the output device.

BUSINESS APPLICATION SOFTWARE

PUBLISH-ER7

Publish-ER7[22] is a series of three programs specifically designed for the weekly newspaper market. Advertise-ER is a computerized accounting system that generates invoices and management reports. Mail-ER is a circulation management system that supports up to 3,000 addresses per disk. Edit-ER is an editing system that provides word processing capabilities along with single-key commands for often-used typesetting functions. Each program runs on Commodore computer equipment, which is sold as part of the publishing package.

[19]Wave Mate, Inc.
14009 S. Crenshaw Blvd.
Hawthorne, CA 90250
(213) 978-8600

[20]TYX Corp.
1250 Roger Bacon Drive, Suite 16
Reston, VA 22090
(703) 471-0233

[21]Unilogic, Ltd.
160 North Craig Street
Pittsburgh, PA 15213
(412) 621-2277

[22]Interlink, Inc.
Box 134
Berrien Springs, MI 49103
(616) 473-3103

LTCAP INC.

LtCap. (pronounced LiTe CAP) software[23] is presently available in three versions.

The MICRO-system. This package contains all of the necessary software for creating and maintaining a customer database, invoicing procedure, and accounts receivable system.

The MINI-system. This package provides all of the software for cost accounting and billing, including customer and employee databases, time sheet entry, daily production report, job cost summaries, detailed invoices, and miscellaneous utility programs.

The TYPOGRAPHER. This is the full-featured cost and billing system with all of the features of the MINI-system plus work-in-progress and dual-format invoice programs, transfer file capability, and profitability and revise.

MICROCLASSIFIEDS

The microCLASSIFIEDS software package[24] runs on the LNW80, TRS-80 Model III, CP/M S-100 compatibles, and CP/M-enhanced TRS-80 Model II's, Model 16's, Apples, and Franklin microcomputers for typesetting using any CompuWriter, EditWriter, or UniSetter.

Advertisements originate with an ad taker working at the computer console. The program prompts for complete customer information, including name, address, telephone, ad category, ad format, start date, and kill date. The ad text is keyboarded into the computer, which then automatically inserts the typesetting format codes necessary to set the ad in any of four user-definable ad formats.

Ads are stored on floppy disk and can be recalled at any time. The program calculates ad charges based on user-specified input, and generates an invoice, if required. The program provides documentation for the utilization of captive ad information for later transfer to an accounts receivable program. Such a transfer probably would require the services of a professional programmer.

The ads are input randomly, sorted by the computer according to categories, and alphabetized within categories. The sorted file then is sent to the typesetting machine. Ad files also can be flushed at any time according to kill dates stored as part of the ad information. The result from the typesetter is galley copy ready for paste-up.

UTILITY SOFTWARE

CPMINTF

CPMINTF[25] is a software interface that is designed to provide the AM VariTyper Comp/Edit phototypesetter with the capability to use the CP/M-80 version 2.2 operating system. Installation of this program makes possible the running of many word processing, data processing, business, and computer language applications such as are common to microcomputers. It does not require any additional hardware; however, it is recommended that users have a line printer installed in order to derive the greatest benefit from the CP/M environment. The COMINTF program does not include the CP/M operating system itself, and is not compatible with the Comp/Set systems, since they utilize a different microprocessor.

[23]LTCAP Inc.
102 Oak Bluff Drive
Palm Harbor, FL 33563
(813) 937-8209

[24]Cybertext Corporation
702 Jefferson Ave.
Ashland, OR 97520
(503) 482-0290

[25]Helena Business
P.O. Box 4360
Mountain View, CA 94040
(415) 969-1642

3Rs

The following computer programs[26] are all written in BASIC and are modifiable to run on any personal computer. They are supplied in printout form and must be manually input by the user into his system. According to the supplier, "If you know BASIC programming, it is possible for you to add your own changes and enhancements to these programs. They all use the same variable names throughout and each program comes with an alphabetical listing of these variable names and their particular uses. Each program listing is accompanied by full documentation of the formats necessary for all the input variables."

Copy Fitting. This program determines the maximum type size and line spacing that may be used for a piece of textual matter, given the typeface and the number and size of printed units (i.e., book pages, columns, etc). Two different line measures and type sizes can be utilized at the same time, allowing for indentations of either size.

Column Inch Rate. This program enables the user to produce a printed table of column inch rates for straight text copy based on hourly charges. It produces rates for every full and half size from 6 to 12 point with a two-point range of extra line spacing in full-point increments.

Bidding and Estimating. This program computes the number of pages or panels a text job will require based on typeface, type size, line spacing, and line measure. It uses this information to produce a price bid based on the hourly typesetting rate, with options for surcharges for excessive font changes, tabbing, foreign language setting, statistical input, and rush work.

Job Pricing. This program calculates the column inch rate that should be charged for a specific job based on type size, line spacing, and line measure. It is computed using a predetermined hourly rate and consideration for penalty copy and fast turnaround.

Figuring Your Rate. This program computes the hourly rate that you should be using based on your gross expenses, fixed overhead, and the skill level of your operators. It provides the option of using various mark-up percentages depending on the market in which you are bidding.

Mumford Micro Systems

Mumford System,[27] which runs on the Radio Shack Model 3 or 4 computer, IBM PC, and Macintosh provides the user with the ability to produce magnetic media that is directly compatible with the Compugraphic MCS system. This capability affords the MCS user the opportunity to produce input on a relatively inexpensive computer using a text or word processing program costing from $20 to $200. The software consists of three programs: one to create and manipulate MCS-compatible disks, one to telecommunicate between the computer and the MCS system, and one to catalog multiple MCS disks as a means of locating needed files quickly.

MICRO/TELECOMMUNICATIONS SERVICES

Dream Electronics Typesetting Service

The Dream Electronics Typesetting Service[28] permits computer users to enter text at their own location, embedding appropriate typesetting commands, and then send the completed file on disk or transmit the file over telephone lines. Upon receipt of the data, Dream computes the typesetting charges, and upon approval from the customer, typesets the job, returning it (with the disk if previously sent) by return mail. Costs are applied to the customer's credit card (CitiBank or Visa).

[26]3Rs
  P.O. Box 592
  Winter Park, FL 32790

[27]Mumford Micro Systems
  Box 400
  Summerland, CA 93067
  (805) 969-4557

[28]Dream Electronics
  131 N.W. Second Street
  Corvallis, OR 97330
  (503) 752-4833

Advantages of the system include no additional investment in typesetting equipment and its associated costs for labor, maintenance, overhead, and inventory. The user also retains the ability to use his present word processing software, keeping a backup copy for editing and archival purposes.

Typesetting formatting commands are enclosed in backslashes and must be in capitals. All typesetting functions are accessible in this manner. Dream provides users with a detailed manual showing all of the commands and examples for the most common commands.

Costs include a one-time handling fee, a per-foot photographic material charge, and return postage. If the data is transmitted, the customer also bears the cost of the telephone call. At 300 baud (300 characters per second), a large file can be relatively expensive.

Chapter 9

Specialized Typesetting Languages

*Sophisticated solutions
for specific categories of typesetting problems.*

TEX: Preparing Text for Output Device Independence

TeX[1] is a sophisticated program that facilitates the setting of complex typographic matter, most notably of a mathematical nature. It was written by Donald Knuth of Stanford University. Although the program is most often used in a nonmicrocomputer environment, it is worthy of mention because of its grand implementation of typographic descriptors and its availability under the name of MicroTeX for IBM personal computers with very specific hardware configurations.[2]

TeX uses what Knuth refers to as "control sequences" to communicate the form in which a specified portion of text is to be processed. In most cases, this sequence begins with a backslash character followed by a coded command, which may be either a letter, a control word, or a single nonletter. There are about 900 control sequences that TeX is capable of processing, and the user retains the option of respecifying commands so he can remember them more easily.

FIG. 1. A sample MicroTeX file output, on an Epson FX-100.

MicroTEX™

MicroTEX is a full microcomputer implementation of Donald Knuth's technical text processing system, TEX, developed for the IBM PC/XT, AT, and PC with a hard disk by David Fuchs.

The following mathematical expressions exemplify TEX's state-of-the-art computerized typesetting capabilities:

$$\mathbf{S}^{-1}\mathbf{TS} = \mathbf{dg}(\omega_1,\ldots,\omega_n) = \mathbf{A}$$

$$\sum_{i=1}^{\infty} \frac{1}{2^i} = 1, \quad \{\overbrace{a,\ldots,a,}^{k\ a's}\overbrace{b,\ldots,b}^{l\ b's}\}, \quad \sqrt{1+\sqrt{1+\sqrt{1+x}}},$$
$$\underbrace{\phantom{\{a,\ldots,a,b,\ldots,b\}}}_{k+l\ \text{elements}}$$

$$A = \begin{pmatrix} a_{11} & \cdots & a_{1n} \\ \vdots & \ddots & \vdots \\ a_{m1} & \cdots & a_{mn} \end{pmatrix}, \quad \left(\int_{-\infty}^{\infty} e^{-x^2}\,dx\right)^2 = \pi,$$

$$2 \mid\mid k \stackrel{\text{def}}{=} 2^{2^{2^2}} \Big\} k, \quad \frac{f(x+\Delta x) - f(x)}{\Delta x} \to f'(x) \text{ as } \Delta x \to 0.$$

MicroTEX contains the power of TEX implementations on larger machines, and is fully compatible with all TEX82 implementations. MicroTEX offers writers and publishers the opportunity to produce professional looking text, including mathematics, both quickly and inexpensively. The most complex documents can now be processed on a personal computer and printed out locally on a dot matrix printer, or elsewhere on a laser printer or phototypesetter.

[1]See TeX and METAFONT
Donald E. Knuth
Digital Press, 1979
and The TeXbook
Donald E. Knuth
Addison-Wesley, 1984

[2]MicroTeX, developed by David Fuchs in conjunction with Addison-Wesley Publishing Company, Inc. System requirements are in IBM PC/XT, AT, or PC with hard disk, at least 512K RAM, PC or MS DOS version 2.1 or 3.1, an IBM Matrix or Graphics printer (or an Epson MX, RX, or FX, or an Okidata 92 or 93 with Plug'n Play EPROM), and at least 1.5 MB of hard disk space for a minimum configuration, or 4.0 MB for the complete program and all fonts.

TeX fonts are composed of 256 characters each, and are displayable as either roman ($\backslash$rm), slanted ($\backslash$sl), italic ($\backslash$it), typewriter ($\backslash$tt), or bold ($\backslash$bf). Type size specifications may be combined with typeface commands in a single command, such as $\backslash$**tenrm**, indicating a 10-point roman typeface.

The creation of a MicroTeX file can be accomplished by using any text editor that does not add formatting commands of its own. The editor must produce a plain ASCII file, such as that produced by WordStar in the nondocument mode.

After the file has been created, with all TeX commands in place, it is processed by the TeX program to create a device-independent file that contains the necessary formatting and typesetting commands for an "ideal" printer. This file is processed using another program, which translates the ideal set of output instructions into specific instructions for a particular output device (FIGS. 1 AND 2).

Along with the TeX program, Knuth has authored METAFONT, a program for the generation of typefaces. The user of METAFONT writes a program that defines the characteristics of individual letter or symbol shapes in declarative algebraic language. The language specifies where the shape is to be drawn and how, using "pens" and "erasers." The user-constructed program does not draw the characters; it simply provides the instructions for how to draw them.

MicroTEX™

MicroTEX is a full microcomputer implementation of Donald Knuth's technical text processing system, TEX, developed for the IBM PC/XT, AT, and PC with a hard disk by David Fuchs.

FIG. 2. The same MicroTeX file as FIG. 1 output on an APS-5 phototypesetter.

The following mathematical expressions exemplify TEX's state-of-the-art computerized typesetting capabilities:

$$\mathbf{S^{-1}TS} = \mathbf{dg}(\omega_1, \ldots, \omega_n) = \mathbf{\Lambda}$$

$$\sum_{i=1}^{\infty} \frac{1}{2^i} = 1, \quad \{\overbrace{a, \ldots, a}^{k\ a\text{'s}}, \overbrace{b, \ldots, b}^{l\ b\text{'s}}\}, \quad \sqrt{1 + \sqrt{1 + \sqrt{1 + x}}},$$
$$\underbrace{}_{k+l\ \text{elements}}$$

$$A = \begin{pmatrix} a_{11} & \cdots & a_{1n} \\ \vdots & \ddots & \vdots \\ a_{m1} & \cdots & a_{mn} \end{pmatrix}, \quad \left(\int_{-\infty}^{\infty} e^{-x^2}\, dx \right)^2 = \pi,$$

$$2 \uparrow\uparrow k \stackrel{\text{def}}{=} \left. 2^{2^{2^{\cdot^{\cdot^{\cdot^2}}}}} \right\}k, \quad \frac{f(x + \Delta x) - f(x)}{\Delta x} \to f'(x) \text{ as } \Delta x \to 0.$$

MicroTEX contains the power of TEX implementations on larger machines, and is fully compatible with all TEX82 implementations. MicroTEX offers writers and publishers the opportunity to produce professional looking text, including mathematics, both quickly and inexpensively. The most complex documents can now be processed on a personal computer and printed out locally on a dot matrix printer, or elsewhere on a laser printer or phototypesetter.

GENCODE: Coding Manuscripts Generically

The concept for a generic coding language, which addresses a document's editorial content as opposed to its typographic format, was first presented by William W. Tunnicliffe of the Courier Corporation in 1967. As a founder of the Graphic Communications Association,[3] he served as a director and as chairman of their Character Generation Committee. It was not until the late 1970s, however, that a formalized generic coding process was introduced. It was named the Standard Generalized Markup Language (SGML), or GenCode.

Generic coding deals with elements in a document according to their content, rather than their form. A caption, for example, might take the typographic form of an 8-point, Times Roman typeface, with 9 points of line spacing and a line measure of 18 picas, while generically it might be coded simply as <C> or <CAP>. When a generically coded job is output, either on a typesetter, line printer, or other such device, it is passed through a preprocessor, which translates the generic codes into machine-specific codes necessary for output.

Generic codes free the text originator from having to learn complex typographic coding. They also result in a document that can be output by any number of different devices without any alteration to the original coding. Additionally, generically coded documents can form a textually formulated database, which can be manipulated to output the entire document as well as selected portions for magazine formats, paperback books, bibliographic references, and even videotext.

The generic coding model is based upon an understanding of the structure of a document. A book, for example, is composed structurally of three zones: the *front matter*, the *body matter*, and the *back matter*. Similarly, each zone is composed of smaller parts, called *segments*. The front matter usually has three segments: the title, the preface, and the table of contents. The body matter is composed of segments called *chapters*. Finally, the back matter is composed of segments consisting of appendices, notes, and an index.

In use, each document element is tagged by using four special characters (FIG. 3). The ESMO (Element Start, Markup Open) is the delimiter that indicates the start of an element. It is indicated by the less than character, although the delimiter characters can be specified by the user. The ESMC (Element Start, Markup Close) ends what is called the *start-tag*. Within the start-tag is the generic identifier (GI) and all of its attributes. The end-tag is similarly constructed using an EEMO (Element End, Markup Open) and an EEMC (Element End, Markup Close).

[3]Graphic Communications Association
An affiliate of Printing Industries of America, Inc.
1730 North Lynn Street, Suite 604
Arlington, VA 22209
(703) 841-8160

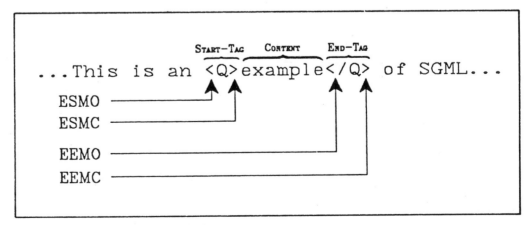

FIG. 3. The syntax required for identifying individual text elements.

Each zone and each segment of a book, as well as each smaller element of text, has a generic identifier associated with it (FIG. 4). A listing of suggested GIs follows:

FIG. 4. An example of GenCode generic codes (on the right) and the resulting manuscript output (on the left). (Copyright 1981, Graphic Communications Association, Arlington, VA)

Manuscript Format	*GenCode™ Application*
The following is an outline of terms:	**⟨P1⟩** The following . . .
	⟨LIST⟩ [first level list]
I. Capitalism is an economic doctrine based upon private ownership of the means by which goods and services are produced.	**⟨L1⟩** Capitalism is . . .
	⟨L1⟩ A democracy exists . . .
	⟨P1⟩ Modern democracies . . .
	⟨LIST⟩ [second level list]
II. A democracy exists where the power to govern is held by the people themselves, where government is conducted by, and with the consent of the people.	**⟨LI⟩** The fundamental . . .
	⟨L1⟩ The equality . . .
	⟨L1⟩ Majority rule . . .
	⟨L1⟩ Individual freedom . . .
	⟨/LIST⟩ [end second level list]
Modern democracies are indirect—that is, representative democracies—rather than direct (or pure) in form. Democratic thought insists upon belief in	**⟨L1⟩** Socialism . . .
	⟨P1⟩ Evolutionary . . .
	⟨/LIST⟩ [End first level list]
	⟨P1⟩ Studying . . .

A. The fundamental worth of every individual
B. The equality of all men
C. Majority rule and minority rights
D. Individual freedom

III. Socialism is a philosophy of economic collectivism, advocating public ownership of the major instruments of production, distribution, and exchange.

Evolutionary socialists are to be distinguished from revolutionary socialists; most of the latter are communists.

Studying those concepts will help the student gain a better idea of world governments.

Zone	GI
Front Matter	FM
Body Matter	BM
Rear Matter	RM
Segment	**GI**
Title	TITL
Copyright	COPY
Part	PART
Chapter	CHAP
Tabular Material	TABL
Table Box	TBOX
Index	INDX
Element	**GI**
Paragraph	P1, P2, etc.
List	L1, L2, etc.
Tabular entry	T1, T2, etc.

Although generic coding has been devised as a "simple" method of providing authors with format-coding capabilities, there are no restrictions as to where or when the generic codes must be added. In fact, the author may avoid coding altogether, and leave it to later editorial insertion, or may input a general level of coding, which would be further specified by editorial insertion later.

The aforementioned coding example is but a small sample of the full language implementation. The user is not required to follow the specific codes listed in the SGML guide. Look-up tables can be used to convert any "house style" coding scheme into a compatible form just prior to output processing.

INTERPRESS: Generating Pages in Binary Form

Interpress[4] is a device-independent page- and document-description language that was developed at Xerox Corporation's Palo Alto Research Center (PARC) for the purpose of printing complete documents within a network environment. Interpress is the model after which PostScript[5] was fashioned, and the two page-description languages share many similarities in their capabilities and basic imaging operation. Like PostScript, Interpress is based on the concept of passing an ink, or a color, through a mask or a stencil.

Interpress coding consists of binary data, as compared to PostScript's ASCII encoding, and is approximately twice as compact. This compactness results in faster processing through the target output device. A number of other differences exist between the two languages; however, they will not be dealt with here.

Principal Language Capabilities[6]

Xerox's work with device-independent printing formats dates back to 1974, when a number of raster printers were developed at PARC. In 1981, Xerox began shipping commercial products that incorporated Interpress. Since then, the list of supported devices has grown considerably, as has the list of third-party hardware manufacturers that either have expressed an interest in supporting Interpress or have begun development of Interpress-compatible printers and typesetters. Some of the reasons for the popularity of Interpress follow.

Device Independence. An encoded Interpress master is independent of a printer's specific characteristics, including its resolution, the coordinate system used to position

[4]Xerox Office Systems Division
2100 Geng Road
Palo Alto, CA 94303
(415) 496-6088

[5]See description in Apple Macintosh entry, p 378.

[6]Adapted from *Xerox Interpress Printing Architecture*, date and author unknown.

information on the printed page, paper size, the availability (or lack) of specific fonts, and the presence or absence of special characteristics, such as the ability to print two-sided pages, color, and scanned images. This device independence allows Interpress to be used for generating output on a broad range of electronic printers, fascimile devices, phototypesetters, plotters, and other output devices.

This device independence is an advantage for a software developer in that he need only include a single standard printer interface in his programs. The elimination of device drivers for different printers saves a significant amount of programming and testing time.

Functionality. It was a design goal of the Interpress development project to take full advantage of the capabilities of current raster printing technologies. To ensure that high-quality imaging can be achieved, Interpress provides:

- Commands for describing text fonts in either bitmapped or outline form.
- Commands for creating graphic images, and rotating and scaling them.
- Support for almost any color printer, regardless of its color capabilities. This includes simple highlight colors as well as full-process color.

Printing Control. The Interpress Printing Instruction set provides capabilities that:

- Enable the user to control the actions of the printer, i.e., two-sided printing, binding offset, or special finishing procedures such as stapling.
- Provide information necessary for the effective and efficient use of a printer within a multiuser environment. This information includes the name of the person who printed the document, the name of the client, and provision for the use of passwords to control the authorization of printing.
- Permit the declaration of resources required by a document. Such resources include the files, fonts, and font sizes needed to execute the printing process.
- Allow an up-front determination as to the ability of a given printer to print a document correctly, and enable the printer to access all of the resources it needs to do so.

Page Isolation. An Interpress document has a well-defined structure. A significant feature of this structure is page isolation. Within an Interpress master, the image description of each page is totally isolated from that of any other page. Page isolation allows documents to be printed in an arbitrary page order, such as last page first or the unusual printing sequences often required in two-page printing jobs. Page isolation also permits the creation of software routines to perform such tasks as creating a new Interpress master from pieces of existing masters, or creating two-up, head-to-toe, or signature masters commonly used in publishing environments.

Performance-Oriented Standard. Interpress supports high-performance printing of even very complex images, and works economically with both low- and high-speed printers. For example, the Xerox 9700 electronic printing system can print a complex Interpress master at up to 120 pages per minute.

Much of Interpress's efficiency stems from the fact that it is a printing architecture which clearly distinguishes the process belonging to the printing domain (those operating on the printer) from those belonging to the document-creation domain (those operating on the computer). For example, Interpress relegates decisions about kerning text, justifying lines, and hyphenating words to the computer's software, not the printer's software. By placing such decisions on the computer's side, Interpress increases printer efficiency.

Compact Encoding. Interpress uses special encoding techniques to create a compact representation of each page within a document. An Interpress master is a set of encoded instructions for building an image; it is not the image itself. This distinction is important. The information required to build the bitmap image of a single page can total 1,000,000 bits of data or more, but the encoded Interpress master for the same page might require only 100,000 bits. As a result, the page can be transmitted to the printer ten times faster than a full bit-map, and requires only 1/10 the amount of electronic file storage.

Software routines are available for the translation from the compact Interpress format to full English-language ASCII character representation, a useful feature for programmers analyzing Interpress output.

Network Environment Compatibility. Interpress can be incorporated readily into a far-reaching network environment. It therefore supports a uniform distributed printing environment in which computers in a local area network can send Interpress masters via telecommunications links to printers in distant networks.

Flexibility. Interpress is available in three functional sets. A Commercial Set supports office and data center applications; A Publications Set is for office, business, and technical/engineering documents; and a Professional Graphics Set provides specialized graphics facilities for complex publications.

The Commercial Set is for applications that include text, forms, and scanned images. It permits text to be printed in vertical, or *portrait*, and horizontal, or *landscape*, orientations. It also provides for vertical and horizontal lines; filled rectangles, for shaded and blacked-out areas on forms; and pixel arrays, for graphic elements, such as symbols and logos, and for scanned images. The Commercial Set addresses typical office applications and those in the computer data center environment.

The Publications Set is for office and business publications, and for technical/engineering documents. It incorporates all the facilities of the Commercial Set, and adds graphics capabilities such as straight and curved line trajectories, dashed lines, filled outlines, and solid gray-scale color for highlighting.

The Professional Graphics Set addresses specialized graphics artwork requirements typical of advanced publishing applications. It includes the facilities of the other two sets, and adds gray-scale pixels for process color, rotation of text and graphics at any angle, and clipping in any shape for graphics applications.

A Brief Look at the Language

Interpress is a language and, as such, has both a syntax and semantics. The syntax is in machine-readable binary form for enhanced processing speed and compactness, although it can be translated into a form readable by people for debugging.

When an Interpress master is sent to a printer, the software within the printer interprets it and builds a document one page at a time. As each page is printed, an interpreter processes the code that forms the page description.

Page images essentially are composed of three kinds of graphic representations: *characters, vector graphics,* and *pixel arrays.* Character-coded images are text strings in one or more selected fonts. Vector graphics are images composed of line segments, described in terms of trajectory coordinates. Pixel arrays are graphic images represented by bitmaps.

The content of an Interpress document is developed at a computer, referred to as the *creator.* The creator uses software that can format the document content into its ultimate page form, with fonts, sizes, graphics, and other page components selected and arranged. The creator uses software to translate the page description into a compressed, binary, Interpress form. The Interpress document then is transmitted to the printer, where it is decoded and used to direct the printer to create the intended result.

Interpress and its related standards are available without the need for licensing fees or royalty payments. Although Interpress can be used with a variety of character code and font standards, Linotype, Bitstream, Compugraphic, URW, Imagen, and Xerox have collaborated on a set of standard Interpress fonts conforming to the Xerox Font Interchange and Character Code standards. Such industry-wide agreement on implementation standards makes it possible for a user to confidently assemble a system composed of elements (computer, fonts, and printer) from different vendors.

DDL: Separating Document Content and Form

One of the most successful laser printers in the marketplace has been the Hewlett-Packard LaserJet. Official estimates of its sales volume credit it with over 80 percent of the market share as of the end of 1986. Despite its success, the machine has succeeded more for its speed, print quality, and quiet operation than for its typographic versatility and graphic imaging capabilities. Numerous software products have attempted to compensate for imaging deficiencies in the printer's control software; however, none have been completely successful.

It was apparent that one of the prime differences between H-P's original Canon CX-based LaserJet and Apple's Canon CX-based LaserWriter was Apple's implementation of Adobe's PostScript page-description language. PostScript is what Adobe President John Warnock calls the "glue" that holds together the graphic imaging system. Hewlett-Packard's "glue" is a *document description language* called DDL.

DDL was developed by Imagen Corporation,[7] a developer, manufacturer, and vendor of image processors and printing systems. It is the company's second description language, the first being imPRESS. DDL was released to the public domain in 1986.

Imagen manufactures product-specific language interpreters, such as the one for the H-P LaserJet, and makes them available to other vendors on a license basis.

What Is DDL?

DDL is a language for describing documents that are to be printed on raster devices. It is similar in some respects to both PostScript and Interpress (FIG. 5). Unlike other languages, DDL separates a document into two parts: the content of the pages, and the data describing how the pages are to be composed. In simple terms, DDL translates the way in which a software application sees a page into the way that the printer sees it. It is *output-device independent*, meaning that it can control raster devices of differing resolutions and printing processes. However, it is also *output-resolution targetable*. A target resolution may be set under the unit of measurement control of the application software. Specifying a target resolution can increase screen-to-printer WYSIWYG correspondence. If the output device can produce the target resolution, DDL "guarantees the integrity of specified dot locations." If the target resolution is not obtainable, DDL will transform the image to produce as consistent an appearance as possible.

DDL's base language is a general-purpose programming language that uses a stack-oriented, Postfix notation. It offers arithmetic, logical, and bitwise operations; named and indexed variables; and assignment operations. In addition, it has control operators to perform selection and iteration, and allows the definition of procedures. Unlike other description languages, DDL can accept input formats in both binary and ASCII forms, and can accept them simultaneously.

[7]Imagen Corporation
2650 San Tomas Expressway
POB 58101
Santa Clara, CA 95052-8101
(408) 986-9400

DDL's Imaging Model

DDL processes pages by converting the elements of an image, such as lines, curves, and characters, into components called *graphic objects*, which it then applies to the image (FIG. 6). As each image is interpreted, it begins as a blank rectangle. The rectangle is altered by the successive applications of sets of three types of objects:

- Print Objects place marks on the image.
- Clip Objects restrict the portion of the image to be modified.
- Transform Objects describe how the print objects are to be scaled, rotated, skewed, or otherwise modified.

FIG. 5. A comparison of three powerful, highly functional page or document description languages.

A Comparison of DDL, PostScript, and Interpress*

	DDL	PostScript	Interpress
Language Aspects			
Programmability	Full	Full	Limited
Representation	ASCII & Binary	ASCII	Binary
Storage Management	Automatic	Manual	N/A
File Access	Yes	Yes	Limited
Printing Instructions	Yes	No	Yes
Device Independent	Yes	Yes	Yes
Graphical Aspects			
Arbitrary Transformation	Yes	Yes	Yes
Line & Area	Yes	Yes	Yes
Texturing Mode	Transparent, Opaque & Compliment	Opaque	Transparent & Opaque
Priority Important	Always On	Always On	On or Off
Sampled Objects	Yes	Yes	Yes
Arbitrary Clipping	Yes	Yes	Yes
Color	Yes	Yes	Yes
Intelligent Scaling of bitmaps	Yes	No	No
Composite Objects	Yes	No	No
Document Layout	Yes	No	Limited
Performance			
Binary Representation (Compactness, Speed)	Yes	No	Yes
Object Cacheing	Full	Fonts Only	Fonts Only
Section Independence (Possible Parallel Interpretations)	Yes	No	Yes (Page basis only)

*Courtesy of Imagen Corporation, *An Introduction to DDL*, August, 1986.

Print objects are composed of two elements: a *mark* and a *material*. A mask describes which points are inside and which are outside of the boundaries of an object. These points can be stroked outlines of curves, bitmaps, typographic characters, or other graphic components. A material is defined by the way in which it alters the current image, such as changing all of the points to a particular color. Materials can be *solid*, whereby each point in the mask is altered in the same way, or *texturized*.

Collections of print objects can be combined into new print objects called *composite objects*. Furthermore, composite objects themselves can be combined to form other composite objects. Such objects can be processed as simple print objects, producing the successive application of each of their elements.

Input Stream Path for DDL

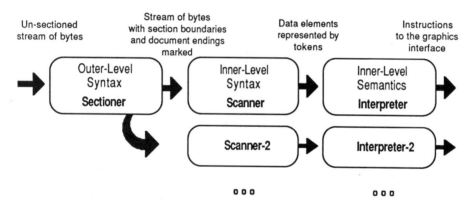

FIG. 6. A DDL document description is represented in a sequence of byte values called the *input stream*. The input stream first passes through the *sectioner*, which separates the document into one *preamble* and one or more *sections*. The preamble and sections then are checked for *tokens*, which are the semantic atoms, or smallest interpretable units of DDL. The tokens are interpreted to produce a document image.

Chapter 10

Desktop Typesetting

The creation, manipulation, composition and printing of original letter forms.

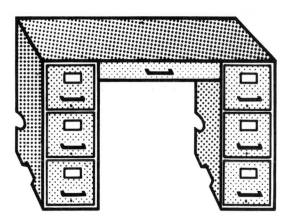

TYPOGRAPHIC CREATION AND DESIGN

All microcomputers have at least one native character set, which is used to present characters on the display screen. These characters are usually relatively coarse in terms of the amount of data that is allocated to describe and differentiate each character image. Many early microcomputer models displayed only capital letters, and were designed more for functionality than for aesthetics.

Yet, even as character sets were enlarged to include lowercase letters and a more complete complement of characters, punctuation, and symbols, the overall design of the display images remained relatively unsophisticated. The root of the problem stems from the small amount of information that is allocated to specify the shape of each alphanumeric character. Microcomputers generally utilize a small matrix to define the structure of each display image. The matrix size might be 5×7 or 7×9, but is, in any event, too limited to show anything other than the coarsest representation of identifiable images. This limitation precludes the generation and use of typographic images without the use of specialized software.

Many software packages provide typographic design and composition capabilities to microcomputer users. They differ in many respects, among them:

- The number of fonts provided with the program
- The character repertoire provided with each font
- The size of the character matrix used to define the font sets
- The kinds of input devices (keyboard, paddles, joystick, light pen, bit pad, etc.) supported for the actual design of characters in matrix form
- The degree of spacing control between characters, words, and lines
- The specification of color, texture, or pattern
- The ability to preview an entire font at one time
- The ability to measure in typographic units
- The ability to distort or otherwise manipulate the image orientation of the characters (slant, flip, overlap, invert, mirror, reduce, enlarge, etc.)
- The ability to combine typographic images with graphics
- The ability to alter and add to existing fonts
- The ability to overlay extant font images in order to design new ones (such as using an existing O to design a new Q)
- The ability to move composed typographic images on the display screen
- The ability to output composed typographic images in a variety of sizes
- The ability to combine display and text sizes in proper position for reproduction
- The ability to output composed typographic images to a variety of output devices (either different manufacturers of one kind of output device, such as line printers, or manufacturers of completely different kinds of output devices, such as plotters and laser printers)
- The ability to combine preexistent graphics and word processor text files into a composed form
- The ability to integrate composed typographic images into user-designed programs, computer slide shows, 35mm color slide productions, video productions, or printed reproductions

The selection of a software package for generating typographic images on a microcomputer is more likely to be made on the basis of finding a partially adequate or a generally suitable program than on the basis of finding a program with all required attributes. This is simply because there are no programs that meet all of the aforementioned criteria, and because the wide range of microcomputer models are not all equally supported by software vendors.

FONTASTIC:
Creating Fonts for Dot Matrix Output

The great majority of word processors that are available for microcomputer use do not have special character sets, nor do they have typographic design features built in. The additional complexity involved in the use of more capable programs is often too great for new users. However, once comfortable with a word processing program, users often find themselves ready for more challenging kinds of output. To meet this need, there are a number of programs available that work in combination with existing word processors, using their text files as input for further processing of output form.

One program that fulfills this need for IBM PC users is Fontastic,[1] a software package consisting of three programs. The first is IHSFONT, a font editor that allows the user to create or edit characters using either a scale 1 (12 × 8 matrix) or a scale 2 (24 × 16 matrix) proportion. The second is IHSPRINT, a program that enables a standard ASCII text file to be printed with Fontastic fonts, using any Fontastic text formatting commands which have been embedded in the file. The third is IHSUTIL, a utility program that gives the user the ability to perform major editing changes on font definition files.

Somewhat unique to the IHSFONT program is the facility to define proportional characters. By using a function key the user can indicate the boundary of each character as it is created. In this way, each character will occupy a linear width commensurate with its design intent when it is printed.

The user begins the font-creation process by choosing either an exiting font to edit or allocating disk space for the creation of an entirely new font. After the user indicates whether the font is, or will be, a scale 1 or scale 2, the Character Definition Matrix screen is displayed (FIG. 1). Characters are stored in a font file according to the order in which they are created, and are displayed on the matrix screen in that order. The IHSUTIL program can be used to place the characters in ascending order; however, there is no safeguard to prevent the user from mistakenly replacing a new character for an existing character and having both associated with the same ASCII character code.

As each character is completed, it is saved and then ''keyed'' to its associated ASCII value. A unique feature of the character definition matrix is the ability to completely reverse a character into a negative form (a white character on a black background). By using Function Key 2, all nonblank matrix positions are blanked, and all blank positions are changed to plus signs. This feature is useful for creating reverse fonts, as well as for designing certain complex characters.

At any point in the design process, the character under development can be sent to the dot matrix printer for proofing. If the characters are scale 1, they will appear horizontally in one line. If they are scale 2, they will appear individually at the far left margin of each line.

Additional function keys are used for setting the rightmost boundary of proportional characters, deleting a character from the font, randomly selecting a character for editing, selecting either the previous or the next character in sequence, and using a previous character as a ''mask'' or guide for the creation of a similar-appearing character, such as an *O* used as the mask for the creation of a *Q*.

Following the definition of one or more fonts or the selection of one or more fonts provided on the Fontastic font disk (FIG. 2), the user next can embed control words and characters in the text file by using whatever word processor was used initially to

[1]IHS Systems
4718 Meridian Ave., Suite 211
San Jose, CA 95118
(408) 265-5503

Supported dot matrix printers include Epson printers with Graftrax, the C.Itoh model 8510A, and others.

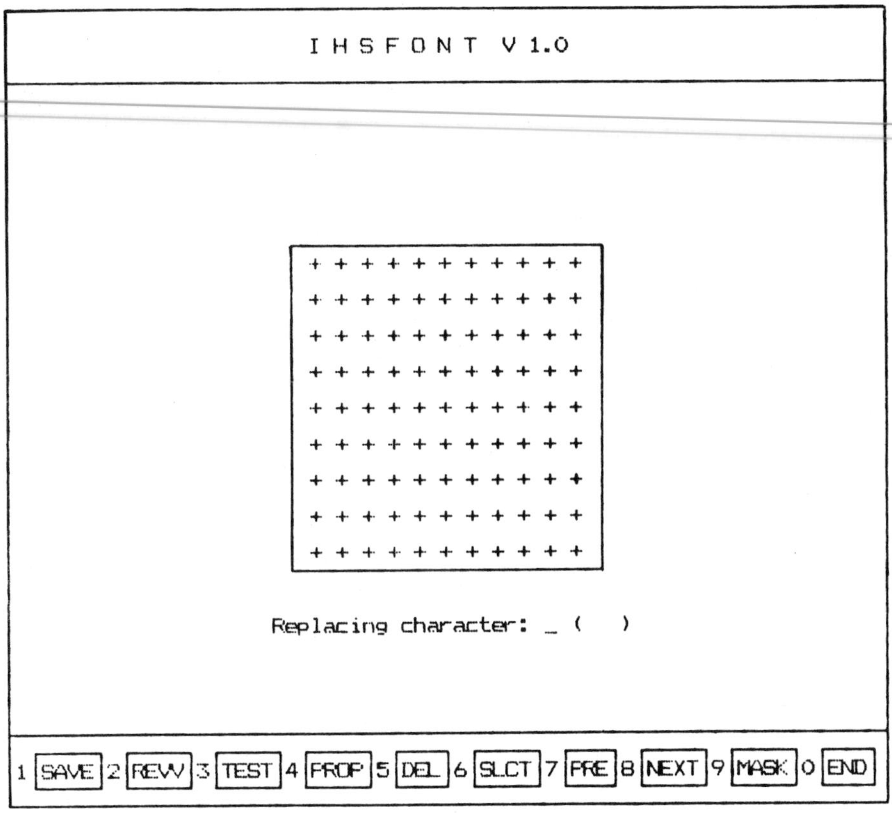

FIG. 1. The Fontastic Character Definition screen provides on-screen labels of the IBM PC function keys.

```
┌─────────────────────────────────────────────┐
│              I H S F O N T   V 1.0            │
├─────────────────────────────────────────────┤
│                                               │
│          ┌───────────────────────┐            │
│          │ + + + + + + + + + +   │            │
│          │ + + + + + + + + + +   │            │
│          │ + + + + + + + + + +   │            │
│          │ + + + + + + + + + +   │            │
│          │ + + + + + + + + + +   │            │
│          │ + + + + + + + + + +   │            │
│          │ + + + + + + + + + +   │            │
│          │ + + + + + + + + + +   │            │
│          │ + + + + + + + + + +   │            │
│          │ + + + + + + + + + +   │            │
│          └───────────────────────┘            │
│                                               │
│        Replacing character: _ (   )           │
│                                               │
├─────────────────────────────────────────────┤
│ 1 SAVE 2 REVV 3 TEST 4 PROP 5 DEL 6 SLCT      │
│ 7 PRE 8 NEXT 9 MASK 0 END                     │
└─────────────────────────────────────────────┘
```

FIG. 2. A selection of fonts provided in the Fontastic package. Additional fonts are available from the IHS Systems.

Calligraphy Font

DARKBOLD FONT

LItebold Font

Special Font

Gothic Font

Cursive Font

CONTROL WORD SUMMARY TABLE

FIG. 3. The Control Word Summary table contains an alphabetical listing of codes that are embedded in word processing files to control the output appearance.

Control Word	What does it do ?
♦:BDIR	Activates Bi-directional printing
:CCON	Activates Control Characters
:CCOFF	Deactivates Control Characters
♥ :CON	Turns ON the Compressed Mode
♥ :COFF	Turns OFF the Compressed Mode
♦:COMP	Activates Compressed print font
:CWI	Sets a new IHSPRINT Control Word Indicator
♥ :DSON	Turns ON the double strike mode
♥ :DSOFF	Turns OFF the double strike mode
♥ :DWON	Turns ON the Double Width mode
♥ :DWOFF	Turns OFF the Double Width mode
:EJECT	Ejects the paper to top of next page
♦:ELITE	Activates ELITE print font
♥ :EON	Turns ON the emphasized mode
♥ :EOFF	Turns OFF the emphasized mode
♥♦ :FONT	Selects an alternate font for printing.
♥♦ :ION	Turns ON the Italics character set
♥♦ :IOFF	Turns OFF the Italics character set
:JON	Maintain justification
:JOFF	Ignore justification
♦ :LOAD	Dynamically loads an alternate font set from the diskette.
:LPI	Sets the Lines Per Inch
♦:PICA	Activates PICA print font
♦:PRO	Turns ON proportional print font
♥♦ :SBON	Turns ON Subscript mode
♥♦ :SBOFF	Turns OFF Subscript mode
♦ :SCALE	When alternate fonts are selected, sets the printing scale (1-10).
:SPACE	Spaces n lines before printing
♥♦ :SPON	Turns ON Superscript mode
♥♦ :SPOFF	Turns OFF Superscript mode
♦:UDIR	Activates uni-directional printing
♥♦ :UON	Turns ON underscore mode
♥♦ :UOFF	Turns OFF underscore mode

NOTE: Control words marked with an (♥) will only work with the EPSON Graftrax™ feature. Graftrax is a registered trademark of EPSON AMERICA, Inc.

The function invoked by control words marked with a (♥) may also be invoked by using control characters (see below).

Words marked with (♦) will only work on the CITOH Model 8510A printer.

create it. All control words (FIG. 3) are preceded by a colon (default state), but can be changed to any ASCII character by using the :CWI control word. The control word indicator symbol and the control word must occupy a single line and be placed in the first position of the line.

Changing the appearance of individual words within a line is accomplished by the use of *control characters,* which are individual codes that control the various printer modes such as emphasized, italic, and underline (FIG. 4). Any of the control words and control characters may be used in combination, or *nested* as IHS documentation calls it.

When the IHSPRINT program is invoked, a full-screen series of prompts is presented (FIG. 5). First, the file to be printed must be specified. The additional processing information, such as single or double space, number of copies, lines per page, all have default values. The user can enter up to ten lines of preprocessing commands at the bottom of the screen. These commands, usually composed of individual IHSPRINT control words or optionally of normal text, are processed first. This facility makes it possible to use existing noncomplicated text files that do not require control words to be embedded at any place other than the beginning.

FIG. 4. Single character codes are used within lines to control the Print mode appearance of individual words and characters.

FIG. 5. The IHSPRINT screen provides further control over the output specifications of the file being processed. Preprocessing commands allow the user to output files that do not have any embedded control words within the text.

CONTROL CHARACTER SUMMARY

Code	What does it do ?
*	Turns emphasized on and off
!	Turns italics on and off
...	Turns underline on and off
%	Turns compressed on and off
=	Turns double strike on and off
#	Turns double width on and off
^	Turns Superscript on and off
~	Turns Subscript on and off
@n	Selects Alternate font n(0,1,2)

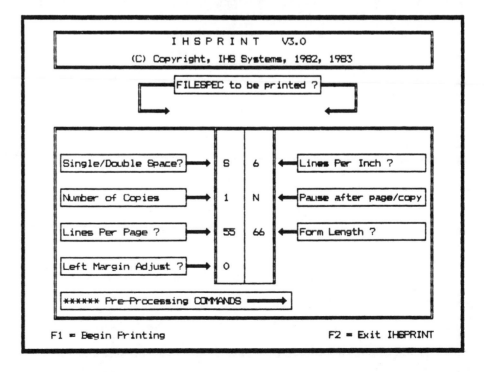

IHSPRINT V3.0
(C) Copyright, IHS Systems, 1982, 1983

FILESPEC to be printed ?

Single/Double Space?	S	6	Lines Per Inch ?
Number of Copies	1	N	Pause after page/copy
Lines Per Page ?	55	66	Form Length ?
Left Margin Adjust ?	0		

****** Pre-Processing COMMANDS ⟶

F1 = Begin Printing   F2 = Exit IHSPRINT

Printing of the file is initiated by pressing the F1 key. Printing may be halted temporarily by using the F9 key, or it can be stopped entirely by using the F10 key. When printing is stopped, the user is returned to the Print Prompt screen where all values have been returned to their default values. The file to be processed then must be respecified.

The IHSUTIL program (FIG. 6) provides a number of useful utilities. In particular, it gives the user the ability to merge any number of characters from one font into another. This feature can be very useful if a series of symbols or graphics must be common to more than one font. In order to accomplish this merge, the fonts must be loaded, and the user must indicate the direction of the merge, for example, from file 1 to file 2. The range of characters to be merged must be identified, as well as the starting location in the receiving file where the transferred characters are to be placed.

Another useful utility is the ability to proportionalize fonts that were originally designed as fixed character width sets. Fonts that undergo this conversion must be reviewed using the IHSFONT program to be sure that each character maintains its design integrity.

FIG. 6. The IHSUTIL interactive screen provides the user with a number of helpful utilities, including merging and reproportionalizing.

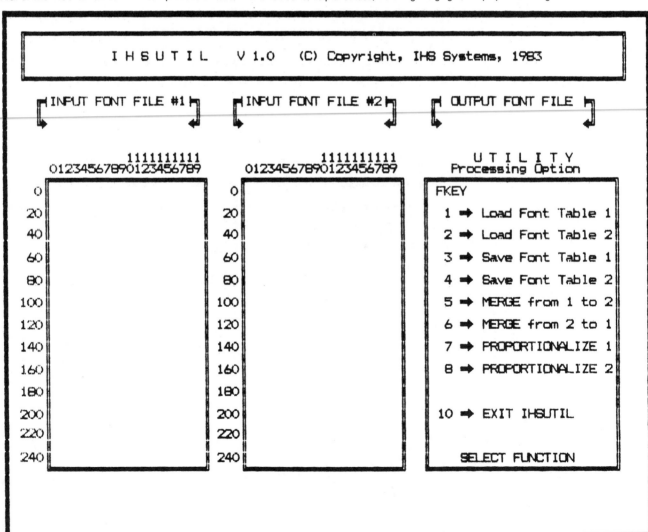

MICRO TYPOGRAPHER:
Manipulating Screen Fonts On a Pixel Basis

It is the capacity to precisely place characters on the display screen that determines the degree of control a microcomputer user has in aesthetically fitting characters together. To be effective, this control should be on a pixel-by-pixel basis, controlled either by cursor or other keyboard input, or by an alternative input device such as a joystick or graphics tablet.

A program that provides this control is The Micro/Typographer,[2] by Robert Scott, the author of GraphicMaster (discussed later in this chapter). This program for the Apple II series of microcomputers lets the user select one of three active fonts, type directly on the high-resolution screen, and then float the image around the screen by using a graphic input device (GID) such as a joystick or Koala Pad, in order to establish approximate positioning. A "Fine Tune" mode, which moves the typographic image in any compass direction, provides for precise positioning.

Other capabilities that expand the flexibility of the program are the abilities to run the active typographic element in any screen direction, erase all or part of it (including the whole screen), expand or contract the intercharacter spacing, change display colors, justify or quad, mix typefaces, add type to extant graphic images, and save to disk (FIG. 7).

As is true of similar software packages, The Micro/Typographer consists of two distinct parts: one to compose characters and another to create them. The font-creation portion of the program is called Vectorplot, and provides the options of creating an entirely new font (FIG. 8) or editing an existing one (FIG. 9).

Vectorplot displays a 14-×-16 dot grid in which to design each character. Dot positioning is under keyboard control, using the *I*, *J*, *K*, and *M* keys to locate dots, and the *1* and *2* keys to plot or remove dots, respectively. As the character is formed, a real-size representation of its display appearance is shown directly below the grid.

FIG. 7. The Micro/Typographer provides considerable flexibility in character design, placement, and orientation. In the Composition mode, the program options appear along the bottom of the screen. They are accessed by using the arrow keys, resulting in the active choice being highlighted.

[2]Tid Bit Software
P.O. Box 5579
Santa Barbara, CA 93108
(805) 969-5834

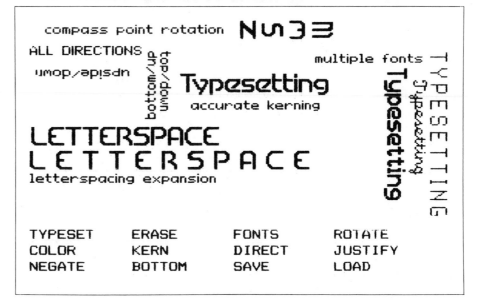

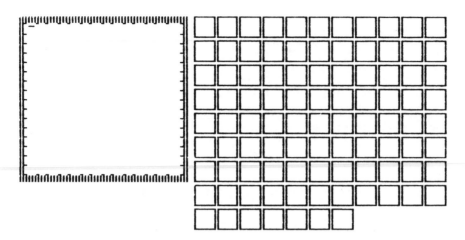

FIG. 8. The Vectorplot program provides a blank 14-x-16 grid for the design of an entirely new character set.

```
1-2,I,J,K,M,W,A,S,Z,E,T,Q,RTN
UPPER CASE !          CHAR # 2
```

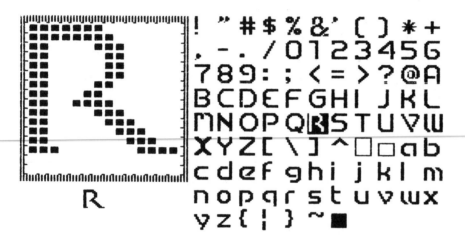

FIG. 9. The *R* has been selected for editing. Notice how the original highlighted *R* has been modified.

```
SELECT CHAR TO EDIT     (I,J,K,M)
UPPER CASE R          CHAR # 51
```

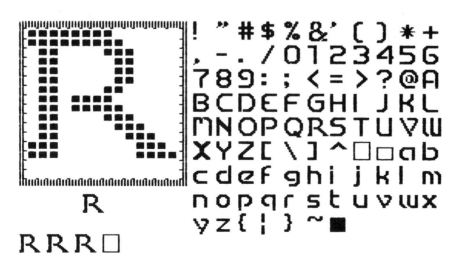

FIG. 10. The *R* has undergone further modification, and a character shift to the right. The "T"ype mode has been activated and three *R*'s have been typed to test the character's appearance.

After all or part of the character has been designed, it can be moved, as a whole, inside the grid in order to provide placement of dots outside of the original character boundaries. As dots pass beyond the limits of the grid, however, they are destroyed and must be manually replaced. This movement, accomplished by using the *W*, *A*, *S*, and *Z* keys, can serve as a means for quickly erasing unwanted parts of a character, as well as for providing an overall character shift.

At any point in the design process, the newly created character can be tested by typing it (as well as other characters in the font) along the bottom of the screen (FIG. 10). This testing gives the user the ability to see the new character in combination with other characters and symbols. When the character is finished, it can be replaced in its original keyboard position, or in any other. In this way, the font can be used to remap the keyboard for another language, a graphic symbol set, or an alternative keyboard layout, such as the Dvorak.

CRAYON DELUXE 2.0:
Processing Text and Graphics with Bit-Image Printing

It has been a goal in word processing and typesetting to build systems that provide, directly on the screen, an exact portrayal of the appearance of the output. This ''What You See Is What You Get'' objective has been quite elusive, and until the introduction of the Apple Macintosh, was not generally available in affordable systems.

A number of attempts have been made to provide users of certain microcomputers with complete control of the individual dot-printing abilities of their dot matrix printers. By so doing, the user is provided with the flexibility to produce both typographic characters and other graphic images in the same document.

The process of bit-image printing is clearly explained by Jerry Goodwin, the author of Crayon Deluxe 2.0,[3] a word processor/graphics editor/font creator/typesetter system for the TRS-80 Models 1, 3, and 4. According to Goodwin, ''Bit-Image printing is accomplished by addressing the individual pins in the print head of the printer. There are eight or nine pins in most of today's print heads. The following diagram indicates their arrangement on the Epson MX-80 printer:

Decimal #	Pin #
128	Pin 7
64	Pin 6
32	Pin 5
16	Pin 4
08	Pin 3
04	Pin 2
02	Pin 1
01	Pin 0

''Each time that the needles of the printer fire, any or all of them can be selected by setting the corresponding bit, in the number sent to the printer, to a one. Therefore, to send out a complete character in a 12 × 12 dot font matrix, it would require sending out 12 such numbers two times: once for the first row of eight needles, and once for the second pass consisting of 4 needles. This means that we would need a minimum of 24 numbers to store a character. We would need 960 numbers to print a full line in each pass, and we would have to keep track of where to find all of these numbers and other print functions. While Bit-Image printers are not new, actually all dot matrix printers are bit image printers, you can see that without programming, no one would try to accomplish more than a few small letters without the aid of a sophisticated program to keep track of things.''

[3]Pioneer Software
  1746 N.W. 55th Ave., No. 204,
  Lauderhill, FL 33313
  (305) 739-2071

Crayon Deluxe 2.0 requires 48K, at least 1 disk drive, and supports the following printers: MX-80, MX-100, FX-80, FX-100, Prowriter, C.Itoh 8510A, Gemini 10/15, and NEC-8023.

Crayon Deluxe 2.0 is a software package that claims it can print anything. By using six different modes, it provides the user with a high degree of control over the screen display, which corresponds directly to what will be printed. The two major modes, the Graphics mode and the Letter mode, essentially provide two different keyboards: one for the creation of graphic construction and drawing, and one for the entry and editing of text. The remaining modes are used for such things as disk access, display of user-defined characters, wide printing, and line-oriented editing.

Actual operation of the program requires that the user load in a font. Two 300-character fonts are provided on the program disk, and others are available at additional cost. The user, of course, has unlimited font-creation capability built into the program.

After a font is loaded, the following information appears on the screen:

M=08,N=16,S=00,R=00,L=00,C=00,F=00   Etc.

15 = Height
12 = Dot Width
80 = Characters / Line Maximum
52 = Lines / Page Maximum
12 = Dots Remaining
16 = Available Screens etc.

The top line of the display lists the page-display variables, which are ''carried'' with the font and define various characteristics of the printer output. These variables include such things as margin settings, the number of lines per screen, and the number of additional dots required for line spacing. The other information provides a description of the physical attributes of the characters themselves.

When a job is being composed, characters are displayed on the screen as images of the font stored in memory. Considerable flexibility is provided for editing content and form, as well as for justifying text. The Graphic mode provides almost 30 commands for the placement and editing of individual and group arrangements of pixel formations. The user can switch between composing characters and drawing graphics at any time. The cursor changes shape to visually confirm the mode status of the program currently available.

A reproduction of a page from the program manual is shown in FIG. 11. This page was produced entirely in position, with no cut and paste, using the Crayon Deluxe 2.0 program. Notice that text and graphic images are freely combined.

The FontMaker utility allows the user to create characters as high as 39 dots (.55 inch) and as wide as 127 dots (1.00 inch) using TRS-80 block graphics. Character sets may be comprised of as few as one character or as many as 256. The full character complement enables the user to access up to two complete character sets, a set of reversed block capitals, the full set of graphic image components, and 19 user-defined characters.

FIG. 11. A page created entirely in position using the Crayon Deluxe 2.0 program.

Section **D** **CRAYON DELUXE** 2.0 Page **D**-21

Entering Graphics

OVERVIEW ➡ The 64 different graphics pixel combinations can be set directly from the keyboard in the **GM**
by pressing the keys listed below. **T**he most elementary of
these commands sets the individual pixels. **T**he shape of a
graphic BYTE is shown below. **N**otice how the pixels are
numbered:

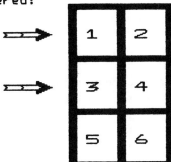

When you press the keys
numbered 1-6 on the keyboard
then you will see the corresponding pixel light up at the
center of the cursor. **T**he
shapes may be added together.
Therefore pressing the [1+3]
keys would light both pixels
pointed to by the arrows.

Additionally there are a number of other commands that can
be used to *set more than one pixel* at a time. **T**hese are
logically linked to the *letter keys* so that you can remember
them more easily. **T**hey are listed below along with the numbered pixels that will light up when you press each key.
You are encouraged to *try each one as you read it.*

KEY	MNEMONIC	PIXELS LIT
A	ALL	1,2,3,4,5,6
B	BOTTOM	5,6
C	CENTER	3,4
D	DOWN	3,4,5,6
E	ERASE	NONE
L	LEFT	1,3,5
R	RIGHT	2,4,6
T	TOP	1,2
U	UPPER	1,2,3,4
Q	ERASE	NONE

When the cursor is over a text character and want to make it
into a *graphic* ⊞ then you must ERASE the text first.

PROCEDURES

THE GRAPHICS DEPARTMENT:
Plotting, Charting, Lettering, and Graphics Editing

The value of information often is enhanced by its presentation. The typewritten-to-typeset transformation is an obvious example of that fact, and one which holds for most categories of information. When the information is numeric in nature, however, it is usually best presented in graphic form—as a chart or graph, or other form of illustration.

The production of a graph using conventional methods requires that the numerical data be manually plotted, in order to produce a guide for the paste-up artist. Type is set and combined with the graph, which can be produced using a technical pen and graphic arts tape and pressure-sensitive shading material.

The microcomputer analogy to the automated production of charts is The Graphics Department,[4] a program for the Apple II family of microcomputers. This software integrates many of the functions of a real graphic arts department: plotting, charting, lettering, editing graphics, and producing slides.

From the Main menu (FIG. 12) option 1, Charting Kit, is selected. This is the pivotal portion of the program (FIG. 13), providing the means to enter, edit, plot, recall, save, sort, and print data that will be the basis for producing bar, line, pie, or scatter charts.

Information for a new chart is entered by selecting option 2, Edit Data. The user is prompted for a title, and the identification of the x and y axes. Any two rows or columns of existing data that is produced from programs using Software Arts' DIF (Data Interchange Format)[5] can be utilized through The Graphic Department's software interface.

After the data has been identified by name and the axes labeled, the user is presented with blank columns to fill in:

```
x-axis name here I     y-axis name here
   1:             I   1:
```

Suppose that the information consisted of the actual measured size of typefaces at a 6-point lens setting. The columns then would look like this:

```
FONTS          I OUTPUT SIZE (PTS)
1: FT1         I 1: 6.5
2: FT2         I 2: 7.0
3: FT3         I 3: 5.5
4: FT4         I 4: 6.5
5: FT5         I 5: 4.75
6: FT6         I 6: 5.5
```

Upon completion of the input of data, the user would return to the main Charting Kit menu and either save the data for future use or go immediately to the "Plot Chart" option (FIG. 14). The "Plot Chart" portion of the program is both functional and fascinating. It is here that the user decides what type of chart will be displayed (FIG. 15). Any chart can be saved on disk as a standard Apple Graphics file and edited further either within The Graphics Department or else with other compatible software.

Facilities exist within the program to display data in many different ways, in order to best represent it graphically. Some of these facilities include the addition of an overlay grid, the specification of colors, the inclusion of statistical information, the use of manual axis scaling, and the production of side-by-side and stacked bar charts.

The speed and ease by which charts are produced require a temporary sacrifice in design and layout choices. The standard font used to label the chart components is a 7-×-9 dot matrix. The number of plots also limits the length of the words that can be used to identify the axes.

[4]Sensible Software, Inc.
210 S. Woodward
Birmingham, MI 48011
(313) 258-5566

[5]For an excellent tutorial see
The DIF File
Donald H. Beil
Reston Publishers, 1983

Considerable flexibility is provided in The Lettering Kit (option 2, see FIG. 12) to add other type styles, sizes, colors, and lettering directions (FIG. 16). These capabilities also can be used on graphic images generated by other Apple software packages.

The completed chart can be printed on a dot matrix printer. Accessory software packages provide printer utilities that extend the output variation to include such things as size change, image rotation, and image reversal (black on white, and white on black). Images also can be chained together to present a series of images directly on the Apple using the Slide Projector mode. An interesting use of this program, as well as others, is the output of the images in 35mm color slide form. The Graphics Department program includes a sample of a slide produced from a disk imaged by The Graphics Department and processed by the Computer Slide Express.

FIG. 12. The Graphics Department program consists of three diskettes. Access to any portion of the program is through the Main menu shown here.

```
GRAPHICS DEPARTMENT          VERSION 1.00

COPYRIGHT 1983 BY MINT SOFTWARE, INC.
DISTRIBUTED BY SENSIBLE SOFTWARE, INC.
=========================================

1. CHARTING KIT

2. LETTERING KIT

3. GRAPHICS TOOLS

4. SLIDE PROJECTOR      (ON THIS DISK)

5. PRINTER INTERFACE

6. FILE UTILITIES       (ON THIS DISK)

0. BOOT ANOTHER PROGRAM

ENTER OPTION (0 TO 6): ?
```

FIG. 13. Data is input, manipulated, displayed, and saved using the Charting Kit.

```
              CHARTING KIT
=========================================
FILE: NO FILE NOW IN MEMORY

1. RECALL DATA
2. EDIT   DATA
3. PLOT   CHART
4. SAVE   DATA
5. SAVE   CHART
6. PRINT  DATA
7. SORT   DATA

8. PRINT  CHART
9. DIF FILE CONVERSION
0. QUIT (CHARTING KIT)

ENTER OPTION (0 TO 9):
```

```
                    PLOT MENU

=============================================

CHART TYPES:

      BAR

      LINE

      PIE

      SCATTER

OTHER OPTIONS:

      GRID OVERLAY      (NO)

      MULTIPLE CHARTS (NO)

      RETURN - VIEW CHART

      ESC - RETURN TO CHARTING KIT MENU

ENTER OPTION :
```

FIG. 14. The physical attributes of the chart are determined by taking selections from the Plot menu.

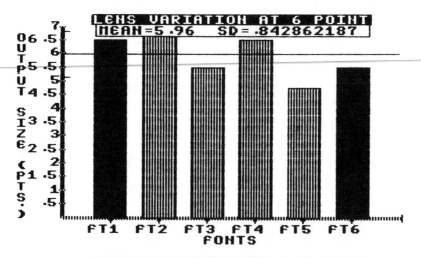

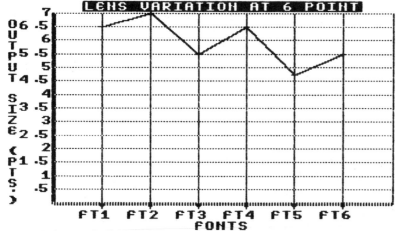

FIG. 15. Two charts made from the same data within moments of one another. The production of the charts was totally automatic, on the basis of simple menu choices.

FIG. 16. A showing of some of the 30 type styles supplied with the program. Eight different colors, five different sizes, and five different composition directions can be specified. Space can be added between characters, but cannot be reduced. The specimens shown here do not include any additional letterspacing.

BEAGLE TYPEFACES:
Creating, Editing, and Composing Typographic Fonts

Legendary to Apple computer users is the Beagle Brothers' line of software products.[6] They are original, clever, elegantly simple in design, and ingeniously sophisticated in execution. The Beagle entries into the typographic environment are parts of a program called Apple Mechanic, as well as a complete accessory disk of additional type designs called Typefaces.

The typographic programs consist of a Font Editor to create or modify type designs, a Type program to compose such fonts on the Apple high-resolution screen, and a third program which can be used as part of user-designed programs for font display.

The Apple Mechanic program is easy to use and is enhanced by the addition of a narrow chart, which folds and fits directly above the top row of keyboard keys. This chart indicates the following functions for the first six keys:

1 =	2 =	3 =	4 =	5 =	6 =
EDIT	SAVE	LOAD	CATALOG	DRIVE	DISPLAY
Shape	Shapes	Shapes	Disk	Change	Shapes

By using these functions, up to 95 high-resolution characters can be designed and saved on disk.

The Font Editor screen (FIG. 17) displays a grid on the left, and whatever character set is presently in memory on the right. Since no character set has been loaded yet, 95 single dots are shown instead, to indicate the maximum complement of characters. The Apple Mechanic disk is supplied with six fonts (FIG. 18).

The grid is ten times the size of the actual character appearance, and is one of two sizes: large or small. The large grid is 14-×-16 dots, while the small one is 7 × 8. The dots and the lines on the grid serve no purpose other than to act as a guide for consistent character design, maintaining the relationships between uppercase and lowercase, ascenders and descenders, etc.

[6]Beagle Bros Inc.
4315 Sierra Vista
San Diego, CA 92103
(619) 296-6400

Apple Mechanic was written by Bert Kersey for users of the Apple II, II+, IIc, IIe, and IIGS microcomputers.

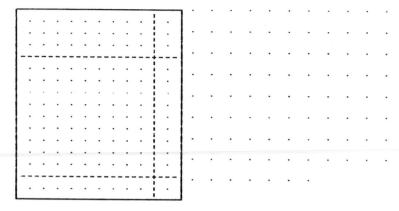

FIG. 17. The Shape-Font Editor screen in its large-font orientation provides a 14- x -16 dot grid.

SHAPE-FONT EDITOR   (C) 1982 BEAGLE BROS

SELECT FUNCTION FROM KEYBOARD CHART:?

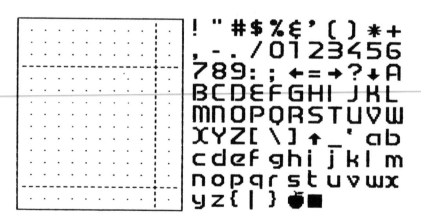

FIG. 18. Only fonts supplied with the Apple Mechanic program or its accessory disk, Typefaces, are compatible with the Font Editor. The guidelines on the grid are helpful in maintaining the integrity of the font design from character to character.

LOAD FONT NAMED:JAPPLE

BLOAD JAPPLE,A24832

The editing function is engaged by pressing the **1** key. A flashing cursor appears over the first character in the type set. The cursor is moved left and right by using the arrow keys, and up and down by using the *A* and *Z* keys. In the series of screens shown in FIG. 19, the *E* is selected (19a); it is drawn on the grid (19b); it is altered (19c); it is scanned (19d); it is replaced in its original ASCII position (19e); and it is displayed in its new form. Notice that changes made on the magnified character are reflected on its real-size counterpart.

When a character is selected for editing, there are three options as to how it will be displayed on the grid. First, as in the example just cited, it can be imprinted on the grid as a 10× enlargement. This option is convenient for making minor alterations, since the major part of the character is already drawn. Second, it can be entirely erased so that it can be redesigned. This option is useful if the new character will be

FIG. 19. The sequence of procedures followed to select and edit a character. (a) The cursor is placed over the E; (b) an enlarged image of the E is displayed; (c) the E is edited by adding some dots and removing others; (d) the edited character is scanned and its plotting information is read into memory; (e) the new character is tested on a one-line display.

FIG. 19(a).

A,Z,<-,->: SELECT CHARACTER TO BE EDITED
AND <RETURN>.

FIG. 19(b).

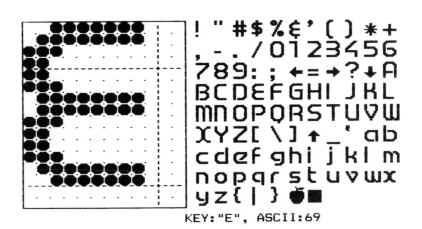

A,Z,<-,->: PLOT CHARACTER AND <RETURN>.
<SPACE BAR> = PLOT/NO-PLOT

FIG. 19(c).

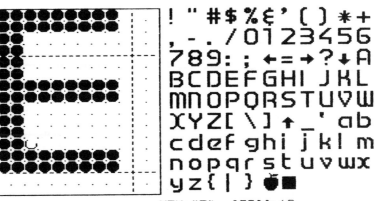

A,Z,<-,->: PLOT CHARACTER AND <RETURN>.
<SPACE BAR> = PLOT/NO-PLOT

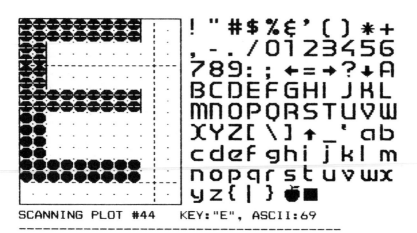

SCANNING PLOT #44   KEY:"E", ASCII:69

FIG. 19(d).

AaBbCcDdEe☐

FIG. 19(e).

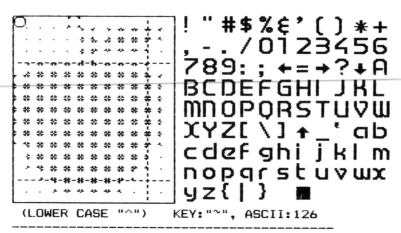

(LOWER CASE "^")   KEY:"~", ASCII:126

A,Z,<-,->: PLOT CHARACTER AND <RETURN>.
<SPACE BAR> = PLOT/NO-PLOT

FIG. 20. The shadow imprint of the apple character can be traced to produce a similar-looking shape.

radically different from the original. Third, it can be displayed as a shadow imprint (FIG. 20), merely indicating the location of the dots that originally formed the initial character shape.

After the characters have been created or edited, they are saved on disk so that they can be used in the type composition program, Xtyper. Any user-designed or Beagle-generated typeface can be used with this program, although typefaces not designed with the Beagle Font Editor will not be compatible. This font incompatibility is true for most programs of this kind.

Bert Kersey, the author of the software and himself a graphic artist, took great care to be faithful to the traditions of the typographic arts. Specimens of his six Apple Mechanic and 26 Typefaces fonts are adequate testimony. It is interesting to compare Kersey's dot matrix character sets with a traditional metal type specimen (FIG. 21).

FIG. 21. Typographic specimens, modern and traditional. (*a*) Samples of the typefaces provided with the Apple Mechanic program; (*b*) the 26 character sets found on the Type-faces disk; (*c*) a selection of metal typefaces from the Kelsey Catalog (P.O. Box 941, Meriden, CT 06450, (203) 235-1695). The numbers beside the *a*'s indicate the actual number of individual capital and/or lower-case *a*'s in the font.

]APPLE: Pack my box with five dozen liquor jugs. ABCDEFGHIJ

]BLOCK: Pack my box with five dozen liquor jugs. ABCDEFGHI

]STENCIL: Pack my box with five dozen liquor jugs. ABCD

]WESTERN: Pack my box with five dozen liquor jugs. ABCD

]SMALL SQUARE: Pack my box with five dozen

]SMALL STANDARD: Pack my box with five dozen

FIG. 21(*a*).

FIG. 21(*b*).

]ACES ABCD

]ASCII: ABCDEFGHIJK

]BROADWAY

]BRDWY..#2

]CHOMP: ABC

]COMPUTE

]COMPUTE/SMALL: ABC

]EMBOSSED

]English/Small: ABCDE

]FATSO: ABC

]FATSO/SMALL: ABCD

]ITALIC/UGLY: ABC

]JAGGED/SMALL: ABC

]L.E.D.: ABCD

]L.SHADOW

]MINI: ABCDEFGHIJKLMNOPQRSTUV

]MOD: abcdef

]OUTLINE: ABC

]OUTLINE/SMALL: ABC

]PARALLEL: AB

]Penman: ABCD

]SERIF/SMALL: ABCDEFGH

]SKINNY: ABCD

]SQUAREBALL

]TRICK/SMALL: ABCDEFGH

(]Widgets)

]ZOOLOO: ABC

FIG. 21(*c*).

PACK MY BOX 4

No. 9BC18	Large Font 8A	CAP Font 8A	Medium Font 4A

RED FOX JUM

No. 10BC18	Large Font 6A	CAP Font 6A	Medium Font 3A

RED FOX JU

No. 14-18	Large Font 7A 15a	CAP Font 7A	Medium Font 3A 7a

RED Fox jump

14-18CF		CAP & Figs. 7A

PACK MY B 3

No. 19-18	Large Font 9A 20a	CAP Font 9A	Medium Font 4A 10a

RED FOX jumps

19-18CF		CAP & Figs. 9A

PACK MY BOX 1

88-18CF		CAP & Figs. 12A

PACK MY BOX WIT 42

No. 91-18	Large Font 8A 28a	CAP Font 8A	Medium Font 4A 14a

Red Fox Jumps ov 70

No. 93-18	Large Font 9A 22a	CAP Font 9A	Medium Font 4A 11a

Red Fox Jumps ove 53

No. 96-18	Large Font 13A 30a	CAP Font 13A	Regular Font 4A 10a

RED FOX jumps over the .74

96-18CF		CAP & Figs. 13A

PACK MY BOX WITH FIVE $5

No. 97-18	Large Font 9A 20a	CAP Font 9A	Medium Font 4A 10a

Red Fox Jumps Ov 26

RED Fox Jump

19-24CF		CAP & Figs. 7A

PACK MY $9

No. 32-24	Large Font 7A 18a	CAP Font 7A	Medium Font 3A 9a

Red Fox Jumps 4

No. 82-24	Large Font 7A 15a	CAP Font 7A	Medium Font 3A 7a

RED Fox jumps 8¢

82-24CF		CAP & Figs 7A

PACK MY B 25

No. 88-24	Large Font 10A 15a	CAP Font 10A	Regular Font 3A 5a

RED Fox Jumps o

The objectives of the Xtyper program are not only to compose typographic characters on the Apple screen, but also to enhance high-resolution pictures that have been saved on disk previously. For this purpose, up to three fonts can be loaded at one time (FIG. 22), and others can be swapped as needed. Pressing the Return key presents the blank high-resolution screen. (If it's not blank, typing **CTRL-X** will clear it.) The fonts that are available are displayed at any time along the bottom of the screen by typing **CTRL-F**, after which they are selected by number (FIG. 23).

Movement on the screen can be done in either whole cursor increments or by single pixels. This fine degree of control provides precise control over character positioning. It can prove to be especially useful when adding type to irregular areas or shapes on a picture, or when putting different fonts or shapes together (FIG. 24).

The major frustration with the Xtyper and similar programs is that, after typographic images have been created, their boundaries cannot be protected. They can be mistakenly overwritten, presenting the challenge of reconstructing the original images in their exact locations. Additionally, errors and typos only can be eliminated character by character, or by whole line or whole screen deletions, thus limiting the real editing that can be executed during composition. Although the Xtyper and other programs lack the screen-manipulation capabilities that would make composition easier and more creative, there are graphics programs which will take screens such as the one in FIG. 24 and permit the selective addition and subtraction of individual pixels, the rotation of specified areas, the addition of frames and borders, the introduction of colors (Xtyper does support this feature) and patterns, and the movement of selected areas of the screen.

```
XTYPER LETS YOU TYPE CHARACTERS ONTO THE
HI-RES SCREEN USING SHAPE-FONTS. YOU MAY
SAVE THE COMPLETED PICTURE TO DISK AFTER
TYPING <CTRL-R> TO RETURN TO THIS MENU.

  TYPE A NUMBER TO LOAD A FONT:
------------------------------------------
<1> FONT:]BLOCK
<2> FONT:]SMALL SQUARE
<3> FONT:]COBBLER

  OR SELECT:
------------------------------------------
<X> CLEAR HI-RES SCREEN
<L> LOAD HI-RES PICTURE
<S> SAVE EXISTING PICTURE
<C> CATALOG DISK (LOCK/UNLOCK)
<D> DRIVE NUMBER (NOW 1)
<Q> QUIT PROGRAM

<RETURN> BEGIN TYPING
<CTRL-R> RETURN TO THIS MENU

SELECT: <  >
```

FIG. 22. The Xtyper menu supports the assignment of up to three fonts at a time.

```
SELECT FONT (1-3):    (CURRENTLY FONT 3)
    FONT 1:]BLOCK
    FONT 2:]SMALL SQUARE
    FONT 3:]COBBLER
```

FIG. 23. The blank Xtyper screen provides quick access to font information, as well as easy selection of an active character set.

FIG. 24. Composition of short examples set using Beagle Bros. fonts.

PENGUIN TYPE SETS: Enhancing an Existing Graphics Environment

In many programs that utilize typefaces, the creation and composition of the character forms is not the major emphasis of the software, rather it is a functional feature which enhances the overall graphics environment in which the user works. Such is the case with The Complete Graphics System and its companion disk, Additional Type Sets,[7] produced for the Apple II family of microcomputers.

The Complete Graphics System is a flexible set of graphics utilities that allow the user to draw, paint, create, and manipulate shapes, as well as add type to newly created high-resolution pictures. The Main menu (FIG. 25) lists the main categories of options. Notice that the ''(T) TEXT'' selection is just one of many. It is an additional feature, and not the main focus of the program.

Selection of the ''Text'' option results in a new menu (FIG. 26), which is displayed across the bottom of the screen. An examination of the menu shows that this part of the program gives the user two major capabilities. First is the ability to load a previously created picture onto the high-resolution screen, add type, and save it again. Second is the ability to edit a type set and save it under a new identity.

Selection of the ''(T)YPE'' option results in an entirely new screen display (FIG. 27). A box-shaped cursor in the upper left indicates the size of the character, which is restricted to one of two sizes: small (approximately 10 point) or large (approximately 18 point). The cursor is moved around the screen by two sets of cursor control keys. The CTRL-I, CTRL-M, and CTRL-K key combinations move the cursor one full step in any of the compass directions. Similarly, the CTRL-T, CTRL-V, CTRL-F, and CTRL-G key combinations move the cursor one dot at a time, greatly increasing the user's control of character fit. As the cursor is moved, its X and Y coordinate position is displayed, as well as its color number (77 is white) and default horizontal and vertical spacing values (HI and VI). Also shown is one of three typing mode states: destructive, nondestructive, and reverse type.

The proper selection of the ''TYPE'' mode state is important both when adding type over pictures and when creating custom typographic designs. In the destructive state, the characters are created with their own individual background, a black rectangular box. In the nondestructive state, the characters are created exclusively of the dots

[7]Penguin Software
830 4th Ave.
P.O. Box 311
Geneva, IL 60134
(312) 232-1984

Written by Mark Pelczarski with assistance from David Lubar, David Shapiro, and Dave Holle.

THE COMPLETE GRAPHICS SYSTEM
BY MARK PELCZARSKI, DAVID LUBAR,
AND DAVID SHAPIRO
COPYRIGHT 1984, PENGUIN SOFTWARE, INC.

TWO-DIMENSIONAL GRAPHICS

DRAWING
(1)JOYSTICK (2)TABLET (3)MOUSE (4)HIPAD

(T) TEXT   (R) TRICKS   (S) SHAPES

THREE-DIMENSIONAL GRAPHICS

(P) 3-D PANEL CREATOR
(V) VIEW 3-D FIGURES
(E) 3-D POINT EDITOR
(L) PLOTTER

(C) COLOR BARS   (M) MODIFY DISK ACCESS
(Q) QUIT

MASTER DISK:D1 DATA DISK:D1?

FIG. 25. The Main menu of the Complete Graphics System provides access to a broad range of graphic utilities.

(T)YPE (L)OAD PICTURE (S)AVE PICTURE
(G)ET TYPESET (K)EEP TYPESET ON DISK
(E)DIT TYPESET (^C)LEAR SCREEN (M)ENU
(C)ATALOG (F)ORMAT: PACKED

FIG. 26. The "(T)ext" option provides the means to add type to an existing picture, as well as to create or alter character sets.

[]

FIG. 27. The Composition screen provides information as to the location and status of the type set in use.

'CONTROL-H' FOR HELP
SIZE : SMALL   COLOR : 77
REVERSE   HI:7 VI:8
X:0 Y:0   ?

that comprise their shape, allowing overlapping, kerning, and other typographic creativity. In the reverse mode, characters appear in the color opposite from that of their background.

All of the information necessary for using all aspects of this part of the Complete Graphics System program is available immediately on a Help screen accessible by typing CTRL-H (FIG. 28).

Type sets can be mixed freely and placed anywhere on the screen. When the "TEXT" program option is entered, a small and a large type set are loaded automatically (FIG. 29). User-created character sets or additional designs available on the optional Type Set disk (FIG. 30) also can be loaded when needed.

FIG. 28. A Help screen is available at any time without exiting the portion of the program in use.

```
TYPING CONTROL COMMANDS

TO USE THE FOLLOWING, HOLD DOWN THE
'CONTROL' KEY.

CURSOR MOVEMENT:
CHARACTER   SINGLE DOT
    I              T
  J K            F G
    M              V

S - SMALL TYPE    L - LARGE TYPE
D - DESTRUCTIVE   N - NONDESTRUCTIVE
R - REVERSE       C - COLOR
X,Y - CHANGE X,Y SPACING
O - TEXT PROGRAM OPTIONS
E - SHIFT KEY FOR //E
ESC - SHIFT AND FULL SCREEN
?
```

FIG. 29. Character sets are of two sizes: small and large.

```
This is a test of the default font
in the small size.
```

```
This is the large
font.□
```

```
        'CONTROL-H' FOR HELP
SIZE : LARGE         COLOR : 77
DESTRUCTIVE          HI:14 VI:16
X:84 Y:72
```

FIG. 30. A sample of some of the 50 additional type sets available on an accessory disk to the Complete Graphics System. These character sets are usable only with the Complete Graphics System.

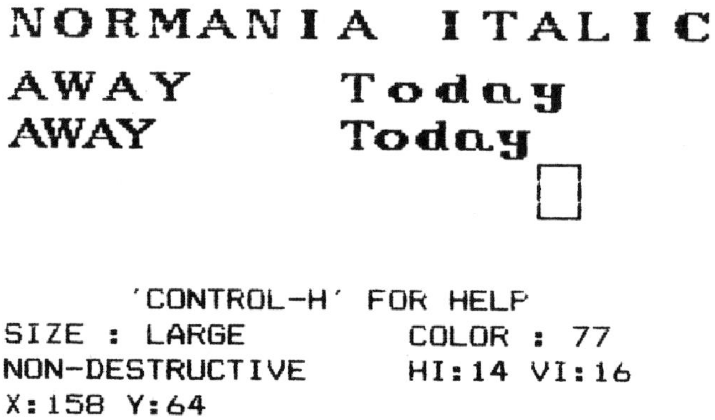

FIG. 31. This screen shows the setting of the words *AWAY* and *Today* as normally composed, and as kerned using the Non-destructive mode.

Any one of the available typefaces can be used as a point of departure for creating an entirely new or semimodified character set. For example, the Normandia Italic typeface, which is loaded from the Type Sets disk, not only can be composed flexibly on the high-resolution screen (FIG. 31), but can be flexibly altered, from a single dot to all of the dots composing the entire character set.

The process of altering or creating a new character set is initiated by selecting the "(E)DIT TYPESET" option. Character sets are basically of two kinds: small (7-×-8 dots) and large (14-×-16 dots). The user's first choice is to select one of these two major classifications. Next, a particular design is selected, either because it is to be modified or because it bears a resemblance to a new set that is contemplated. The initial editing screen with the Normandia Italic character set loaded is shown in FIG. 32.

FIG. 32. The character sets Normandia Italic loaded in the editor. The options at this initial point are to create new characters or to edit existing shapes.

```
! " # $ % &  '  ( )
* + , - . / 0 1 2 3
4 5 6 7 8 9 : ; < =
> ? @ A B C D E F G
H I J K L M N O P Q
R S T U V W X Y Z [
\ ] ↑ _ ' a b c d e
f g h i j k l m n o
p q r s t u v w x y
z { ¦ } ~ ▒
```

```
(C)REATE  (E)DIT  (RETURN)
?
```

FIG. 33(a). The capital B has been selected for editing. Note the minor changes made in the lower screen (b).

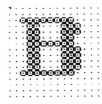

```
! " # $ % &  '  ( )
* + , - . / 0 1 2 3
4 5 6 7 8 9 : ; < =
> ? @ A B C D E F G
H I J K L M N O P Q
R S T U V W X Y Z [
\ ] ↑ _ ' a b c d e
f g h i j k l m n o
p q r s t u v w x y
z { ¦ } ~ ▒
```

B

```
IJKM Z-PLOT X-ERASE S-SAVE Q-QUIT
?
```

FIG. 33(b).

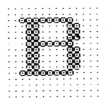

```
! " # $ % &  '  ( )
* + , - . / 0 1 2 3
4 5 6 7 8 9 : ; < =
> ? @ A B C D E F G
H I J K L M N O P Q
R S T U V W X Y Z [
\ ] ↑ _ ' a b c d e
f g h i j k l m n o
p q r s t u v w x y
z { ¦ } ~ ▒
```

B

```
IJKM Z-PLOT X-ERASE S-SAVE Q-QUIT
```

After a character set is loaded, the user has the choice of either editing an existing character or creating an entirely new one. If the character is to be edited, then it is selected (again by use of the compass-shaped control keys), and then modified by turning dots on or off. As changes are made, they are immediately reflected in an altered real-size image appearing directly below the character grid. Notice the minor changes made to the *B* shown in FIG. 33. If the character is to be totally replaced, either as a new design or as a new character (to remap the keyboard for example to produce a Dvorak layout), the character grid is erased (FIG. 34), and can be totally redesigned.

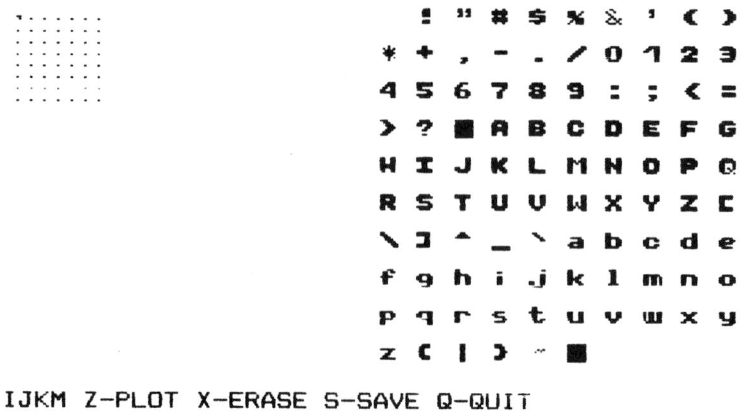

IJKM Z-PLOT X-ERASE S-SAVE Q-QUIT

FIG. 34. When the "Create" option is selected, a blank grid is displayed beside the character set. All or part of the character set displayed on the right can be altered or replaced.

GRAPHICMASTER:
Working Within a Graphics Presentation System

Graphicmaster is a visual presentation software system produced for the Apple II family of microcomputers.[8] Like other graphic production software packages, it provides typographic font-creation capabilities as a part of its design framework. Taken as a whole, the type design feature, called the Fontcaster, is one of five major system capabilities that can accomplish "professional" graphic presentations incorporating animation and color (FIG. 35).

Graphicmaster
The Visual Presentation System

```
(1) Fontcaster
(2) Bitmap Wizard
(3) Patternmaster
(4) Window King
(5) GR&MPS
(6) Picview/Save
(7) Demo
(8) Exit

Select by number
```

(C) 1983 TID BIT SOFTWARE V2.081

FIG. 35. The Main Graphicmaster menu provides access to font design, as well as graphic generation and manipulation.

[8]Tid Bit Software
P.O. Box 5579
Santa Barbara, CA 93108
(805) 969-5834

The Fontcaster program module is menu driven (FIG. 36), and supports the creation of fonts as large as 24 × 24 pixels, composed of either characters or shapes. The first menu selection, "Edit Existing Fonts," provides access to a sampling of fonts provided on the program disk itself. This option also would be used to load into memory a user-designed font that was previously saved on disk.

FIG. 36. The Fontcaster submenu provides easy access to all of the font-creation and font-editing capabilities.

F O N T C A S T E R

1) EDIT EXISTING FONTS

2) CREATE NEW FONT SET

3) SAVE FONT SET TO DISC

4) EXIT MAIN MENU

SELECT BY NUMBER

After an existing font has been selected and loaded into memory, a blank matrix is displayed along with a single-line screen menu (FIG. 37). The first four letters—"I," "J," "K," and "M"—are cursor keys, which direct the movement of the cursor within the grid. Four other characters—"U," "O," "N," and comma—which are not displayed, move the cursor diagonally on the grid. The numbers "1" and "2" are used to turn the plot and no-plot function on or off. When it is "on," a pixel is placed in the current cursor position.

FIG. 37. The blank Character Creation and Editing screen provides a display of the magnified character bitmap (matrix) on the left, and the character as it will be displayed on the right.

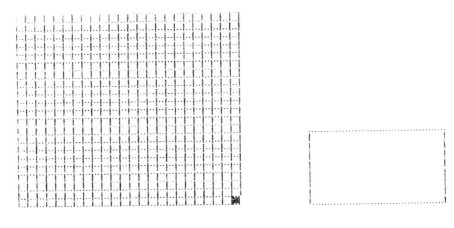

I,J,K,M,1-2,E,C,T,V,Q   CHAR> O

The "V" selection displays a view of the entire character set (FIG. 38). The use of the "E" selection places the display in the Edit mode. The right and left arrows are used to sequence through the character set. The designation *CHAR>* shows the character number currently selected, and the full-size image of the character appears in the display window on the lower right (FIG. 39). When the required character is located, hitting the Return key draws the character map on the grid (FIG. 40).

! " #$%& ' [ ]
*+ . - . /0123
456789 : ; <=
>?@ABCDEFG
HIJKLMNOPQ
RSTUVWXYZ

PRESS ANY KEY

FIG. 38. A display of an entire font accessed by selecting the "V" option.

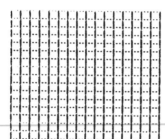

FIG. 39. Character number 33, which corresponds to the letter A, presented in the display window.

SELECT CHAR TO EDIT <,>,RTN   CHAR> 33

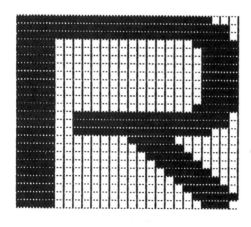

FIG. 40. The character R painted in the matrix and in the display window. As the R is altered, the smaller R on the left immediately reflects the changes. The smaller R on the right is not alterable.

I,J,K,M,1-2,E,C,T,V,Q   CHAR> 50

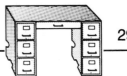
The "C" command clears the editing grid in order to start over again. The "T" provides the capability of transferring a character from one matrix to another in order to eliminate the need to redraw common character parts such as the stem for the *T* and the *I*. The "Q" command quits the editor and returns the user to the main Fontcaster menu.

The second choice on the Fontcaster menu (FIG. 36), is the "Create New Font Set." This selection provides for three design choices: a small, 8-×-8 matrix; a medium, 16-×-16 matrix; or a large, 24-×-24 matrix (FIG. 41). Depending upon the specification of "S," "M," or "L," a similar screen as appeared in menu choice 1 is displayed (FIG. 42).

After the new or edited font has been completed and the user has returned to the Fontcaster menu, the third menu selection, "Save Font Set to Disc," is chosen. At this point, the user gives his font a name. The program automatically appends the suffix *.FNT* at the end of the name for easy identification.

Once saved on disk, the font sets are utilized with other modules in the Graphicmaster program to produce graphic presentations for a wide variety of uses. The other program capabilities provide facilities for such things as changing the color of the characters, displaying them in inverse, and altering the character spacing.

FIG. 41. The Character Design Matrix Choice menu.

```
SELECT MAX CHAR SIZE

S 8X8   M 16X16   L 24X24



     S,M,L,RTN   ?
```

FIG. 42. The small 8-×-8 matrix ready for drawing.

```
I,J,K,M,1-2,E,C,T,V,Q          CHAR> 50
```

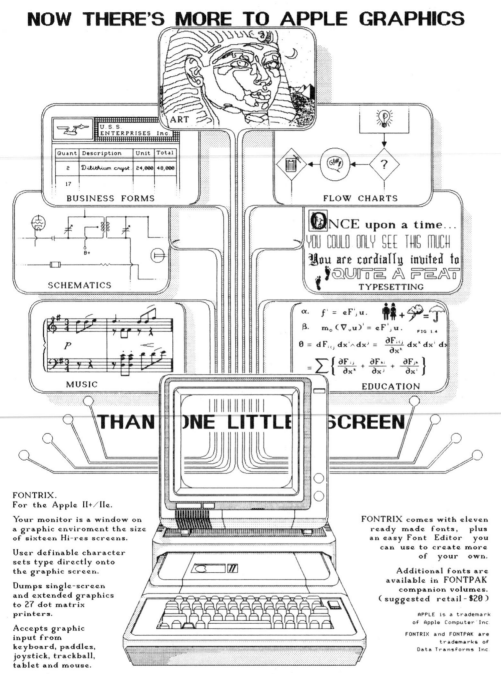

FIG. 43. An entire full-page advertisement composed using Fontrix. The program supports the multiple high-resolution screen composition of complex typographic and graphic information, as well as the creation of user-designed fonts and graphic image sets.

FONTRIX:
Integrating Font and Graphics Creation with Full-Page Make-up

The complete integration of text and graphics in page form has been the major elusive objective of builders of typesetting machines for many years. The complexities involved essentially have fragmented the production process, requiring the assembly of separate elements (text type, display type, photographs, illustrations, rules, borders, etc.) through an operation known as *paste-up*. The elimination of cut-and-paste operations has been reserved, until fairly recently, for only the most expensive typesetting systems.

A software package for the IBM PC and the Apple II series of microcomputers that provides considerable flexibility in the design of original fonts, the composition of complex typography, and the setting of complete pages is Fontrix from Data Transforms.[9] It achieves its power from a relatively simple idea, though certainly complex in its execution, that a page can be composed of a number of high-resolution screens, rather than a single one (like most other programs). The extended screen graphic capability is embodied in the notion of the *graffile,* a word coined by Data Transforms to refer to a graphic file that is composed of multiple screens. Fontrix provides an enlarged window upon which almost any kind of textual or graphic information can be composed.

The graphics window can be scrolled horizontally or vertically, providing access to a page-sized area and beyond. In the Apple version, the scrollable area is 16 times (4 × 4) the normal high-resolution screen. In the IBM version, the monitor provides a graphic worksheet 23 times the area and resolution of a single screen—up to 115 screens when using a hard disk system. A full page ad produced entirely on an Apple II+ without any postprocessing cut and paste is shown in FIG. 43.

In terms of capabilities, both versions of the program are similar and retain a like mode of operation. The IBM version, however, also incorporates pop-down menus, the direct input to a graffile from a standard ASCII text file, elastic drawing routines, the ability to keep up to nine fonts in memory at the same time, automatic italicizing and boldfacing, and 90-degree rotation on printout.

The start-up screen on the Apple (FIG. 44) provides access to all of the system capabilities. The IBM screen is virtually identical, and no further comparisons of the two versions will be mentioned.

FIG. 44. The Main menu of the Apple version of Fontrix provides information on the hardware configuration, as well as access to each of the major program subsystems.

```
FONTRIX 1.0          SYSTEMS MENU

....CONFIGURATION......................

     CARD: WESPER WIZARD BPO
     SLOT: 1
  PRINTER: EPSON FX-80
 GR INPUT: APPLE JOYSTICK

......................................

  <I>   INTRODUCTION & DEMONSTRATION
  <N>   NEW CONFIGURATION
  <D>   DISK ACCESS
  <F>   FONT EDITOR
  <G>   GRAPHIC WRITER
  <P>   PRINT GRAPHICS
  <Q>   QUIT FONTRIX SYSTEM


ENTER CHOICE: ?
```

[9]Data Transforms, Inc.
 616 Washington Street
 Denver, CO 80203
 (303) 832-1501

Versions run on the Apple II, II+, *IIe, IIc,* III, IIGS, Franklin Ace 1000, IBM PC, IBM XT, and 100% IBM compatibles.

The program is easily configurable to support many different interface cards, keyboard configurations, graphic input devices, and dot matrix printers. The Systems menu shows the current configuration choices, as well as provides access to changing the choices, by selecting a new configuration (menu selection "<N>").

The selection of fonts is virtually unlimited since the font-creation capability is built into the program. A small number of fonts are included with the program disk, and additional fontpaks (FIG. 45) are available at nominal cost. Many fonts, such as Folio Bold and Huxley Vertical, are Fontrix versions of "real" typefaces.

The creation of a font, special character, logo, border, or any graphic element or part thereof can start from scratch or can use existing characters in available fonts. The default font is a standard ASCII character set that is devoid of any significant design attributes.

From the Font Editor menu (FIG. 46), character sets may be loaded, saved, created, edited, or otherwise altered. As an example, the Folio Bold font may be loaded by selecting the appropriate computer slot, drive, volume number, and font name. Wildcards also may be used to locate a font quickly.

After the font is loaded, the user is returned to the Font Editor menu, which confirms that the current font in memory is, indeed, Folio Bold. At this point "<E>

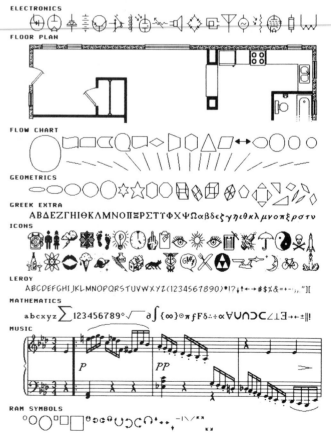

FIG. 45. Sample pages from the Fontrix specimen book of additional character sets. A number of the fonts that are available have been purchased by Data Transforms from users who have created them for their own use.

Edit Set'' is selected, which results in a listing of all of the displayable characters, the font attributes, the cursor control keys, and the editing options (FIG. 47).

Because of the size of the characters, not all of them can be viewed on the screen at one time, so they are divided among up to three screens. The Folio Bold font has no lowercase characters, and so it only occupies two screens (FIG. 48).

The character to be edited is either placed under the cursor from the ''Edit Set'' screen, or highlighted with a box cursor from the viewing screen. When Return is pressed, the selected character is displayed in side-by-side matrix construction form, and actual appearing form (FIG. 49). A new cursor appears inside the matrix, providing access to each image element. The Space Bar is used to turn existing character construction elements off or nonexisting elements on. The user also is provided with the capability of moving the entire character image within the grid, as well as superimposing one character over another, such as to form an *R* out of a *P*.

FIG. 46. The Font Editor menu defaults to the standard ASCII character set. The ASCII set very much resembles, in size and shape, the characters that appear on this screen.

```
FONT EDITOR

CURRENT FONT IN MEMORY: ASCII

MENU

L)   LOAD SET
S)   SAVE SET
D)   DISK ACCESS
N)   NEW SET
E)   EDIT SET
C)   CHANGE SET PARAMETERS
Q)   QUIT TO SYSTEMS MENU


ENTER CHOICE: L
```

FIG. 47. The Edit Set screen shows information concerning the first character position, the length (size) of the character set (LEN), the horizontal cell size (H), the vertical cell size (V), and whether the set is proportional or not (P).

```
EDIT SET              I.J.K.M: MOVE CURSOR
                      RETURN:  SELECT CHAR
FOLIO BOLD            V: VIEW      Q: QUIT
1ST=! LEN=63          C: COPY   O: OVERLAY
H=32 V=32 P=YES


   < SCREEN 1 >< SCREEN 2 >< SCREEN 3 >

       (  O  8  @  H  P  X  '  h  p  x

    ?  )  1  9  A  I  Q  Y  a  i  q  y

    "  *  2  :  B  J  R  Z  b  j  r  z

    #  +  3  ;  C  K  S  [  c  k  s  {

    $  ,  4  <  D  L  T  \  d  l  t  ¦

    %  -  5  =  E  M  U  ]  e  m  u  }

    &  .  6  >  F  N  V  ··  f  n  v  ~

    '  /  7  ?  G  O  W  _  g  o  w
```

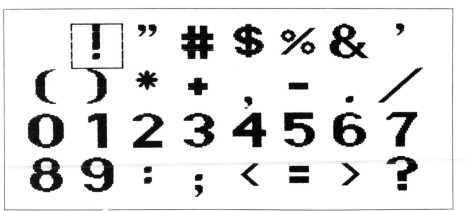

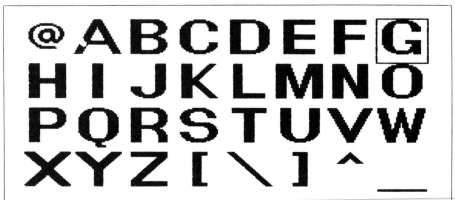

FIG. 48. The Folio Bold character set is so large in physical size that it must be viewed as two screens. The square cursor indicates the character that will be chosen for editing.

FIG. 49. The character G as it appears normally in the distribution font (left), and in the edited version (right).

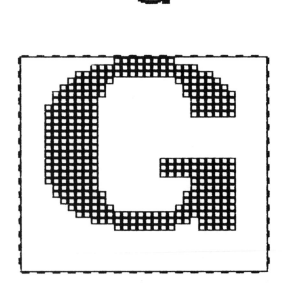

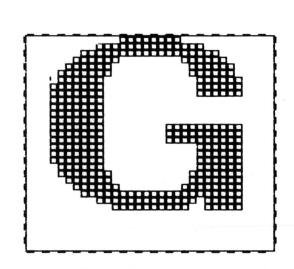

Any number of characters in a font may be changed, from a single character to the entire font. It then may be saved under the same name or a new one (FIG. 50).

To use newly created fonts (or any fonts or graphics), the user must return to the Main menu. The creation of graffiles takes place into the <G> GRAPHIC WRITER portion of the program. Selecting this option results in the display of a screen (FIG. 51) that presents options to load in a font, or load or save a graphic or graffile. A graffile must be opened and defined in terms of its size; that is, the number of high-resolution screens that it will cover. The smallest Apple graffile is 30 disk sectors—5 horizontal and 6 vertical—which is equivalent to a single screen. The largest graffile is 480 disk sectors, composed of any two horizontal and vertical values not exceeding 480.

FIG. 50. The Parameter menu, which is displayed when a font is saved.

```
SAVE SET


SET PARAMETERS

  1)    NAME OF THIS SET:    FOLIO BOLD
  2)    TOTAL CHARACTERS:    63
  3)     FIRST CHARACTER:    !
  4)     HORIZONTAL SIZE:    32
  5)       VERTICAL SIZE:    32
  6)        PROPORTIONAL?:   YES


    Q)    RETURN TO MENU
    C)    CHANGE SET PARAMETERS
    S)    SAVE SET

       ENTER CHOICE: S?
```

FIG. 51. The Graphic Writer menu provides a display of the font, graphic, and graffile in use, as well as the means to change them.

```
GRAPHIC WRITER

     FONT:ASCII
  GRAPHIC:VACANT
 GRAFFILE:VACANT


MENU

  D)    DISK ACCESS
  F)    CHOOSE FONT
  L)    LOAD GRAPHIC
  S)    SAVE GRAPHIC
  O)    OPEN GRAFFILE
  C)    CLOSE GRAFFILE
  W)    WRITE ON GRAPHIC
  Q)    QUIT TO SYSTEMS MENU

ENTER CHOICE: W?
```

The default font is the ASCII set, which would be changed at this point to another set, Folio Bold, for example. The "Write on Graphic" option provides entry to the high-resolution screen, first displaying a Help screen (FIG. 52) as a preview/review of available commands.

The high-resolution screen appears after any key is pressed from the Help screen display. A cursor, representing the size of the font matrix, appears in the upper left-hand corner. The user now has complete control over how the characters will be composed. The placement of any character on the screen can be manipulated pixel by pixel (FIG. 53). Background or character colors can be changed; line spacing can be altered; lines (rules) can be added; fonts can be changed; characters can be overlapped, replaced, reversed, or deleted.

With the use of a graphic input device such as a joystick or mouse, an active character can be "floated" around the screen to occupy any chosen position. In this mode, the character also can be composed in a step-and-repeat fashion, placing the same image repeatedly at any location.

Fontrix supports the use of a definable window, which can be placed anywhere on the screen. It is useful for filling in large areas of color or texture, erasing within given boundaries, or restricting cursor movement within a small area for easier construction of images.

```
GRAPHIC WRITER      COMMAND KEYS

CTRL A ASK FOR HELP CTRL N NORMAL MODE
CTRL B BKGRND COLOR CTRL O OVERLAY MODE
CTRL C CAPS LOCK    CTRL P POINT MODE
CTRL D DEFAULT WNDW CTRL Q QUIT TO MENU
CTRL E ERASE SCREEN CTRL R REPLACE MODE
CTRL F FRGRND COLOR CTRL S SPACE BTW CHR
CTRL G GRAPHIC INPT CTRL T TRNSPRNT MODE
CTRL H BACKSPACE    CTRL U FORWARD SPACE
CTRL I INVERSE      CTRL V VIEWPORT
CTRL J LINEFEED     CTRL W WINDOW
CTRL K RVRSE LNFEED CTRL X BACKSLASH
CTRL L LINE SPACING CTRL Y YANK SCREEN
CTRL M CARR RETURN  CTRL Z ZERO CURSOR

ESC I J K M MOVE CURSOR(ALSO USE ARROWS)

    >PRESS ANY KEY TO CONTINUE<
```

FIG. 52. The Graphic Writer command summary is displayed just before the high-resolution screen area is entered. It is available for reference at any time by keyboarding CTRL-**A** (ask for help).

GRAPHIC ART
TYPESETTING
PHOTOCOMP
COMPUTERS
COMMUNICATE

FIG. 53. A single screen composed using the modified Folio Bold font. (Notice the G's.) Characters have been kerned. (Notice the spacing between the a and t in the word *communicate*.) The line spacing between the bottom two words also has been reduced.

At any point, the user can leave the high-resolution screen area and return to the Help screen, or take another step back to the Graphic Writer screen. At this point, another font or graphic can be loaded, and work then can resume on the job in progress. In this way some very large and complex images can be constructed.

When the image is complete or when it needs to be proofed, it is saved on disk and then printed using either the screen dump or graffile dump from the <P> PRINT GRAPHICS menu.

Fontrix is compatible with other Apple graphics programs that store their output in the standard format. These graphics can be brought into the Fontrix environment from the Graphic Writer menu. Similarly, single screen graphics created with Fontrix may be utilized with other Apple graphics programs. Small graphic images also may be defined as characters in a font. The dragon in FIG. 54 was created using a dragon font composed of repetitive dragon parts.

FIG. 54. A dragon produced by Duke Houston on the IBM version of Fontrix. Various repetitious elements of the graphic were predefined as characters in a ''dragon'' font.

Ver Hague T Y P E:
Experimenting with Typographic Forms

The earliest printing was art imitating art. The work of the scribe was Gutenberg's model for his type design and page layout. The story goes that one scribe, upon a close examination of an early press sheet exclaimed, "it's nice, but it's not calligraphy." He was correct in a very real sense, since early printing merely approached extant methods, but did not rival nor surpass them. Gutenberg is known to have employed scribes, called *rubicators,* to create and embellish the ornate colored initials appearing on many Bible pages. Typesetting began, then, as a hybrid system joining the mass production of black text pages with the art of hand-lettered initials and decoration.

Throughout typesetting history hybrid systems have been employed to generate various elements of a page. Linecasters produced text while Ludlow machines produced headlines; direct-impression machines produced text while photolettering machines produced headlines; typewriters produced text while transfer type produced headlines. Numerous machine and process combinations are still in use which legitimize the historically proven concept of hybrid typesetting system usage.

In large part, the mix of machines and methods used to compose pages of type has been totally transparent to the reader. Today, even a trained eye would have difficulty determining by what means various elements of a page were generated. The problem of type origination is complicated further by the fact that microcomputers and word processors can be used to generate input for typesetters, making the path from mental thought to printed word virtually untraceable.

As a typesetting tool, the microcomputer is very versatile. It can be used to generate input for traditional typesetting output devices, such as phototypesetters and laser printers, as well as generate type on its own peripherals, such as plotters and dot matrix printers. In addition, it is an excellent partner in a hybrid typesetting system.

The essence of a hybrid typesetting system is the recognition that each part of the system has distinct attributes that benefit and enhance the whole. Although the use of a microcomputer for typesetting input is of unquestionable benefit, the microcomputer has additional features that make it well suited (to a greater or lesser degree) to the production of graphic elements which traditionally have been produced by other methods.

The Graphic Elements

A typical page is composed of many parts: text, headlines, photographs, captions, artwork, borders, etc. Relatively few composition systems are able to deal with all of these elements in their totality, and to compose them without using cut-and-paste methods. While a single-system solution to page assembly always has been a perceived goal, the multidevice approach has the benefit of extreme flexibility, allowing the user to choose the manner by which each page component will be produced.

Typesetting machines are, in the main, character-oriented. The creation of artwork and other graphic elements usually is accomplished separately, and then added to the page layout through a manual paste-up step.

Many microcomputers have graphics capabilities. While the resolution of the graphics might preclude their use in professional presentations and commercial applications, where there is a compromise in quality standards (or the helping hand of a professional artist) and perhaps the imposition of time constraints, they can be used effectively.

Artists have had considerable success in using microcomputer graphics software to design a wide range of artwork, from logotypes and custom characters to business graphics and full-page illustrations. Some have used the graphics exactly as they have been generated by the computer, while others have used the computer as a creative tool to give form to their ideas, and have then either hand-rendered the artwork or else altered the computer output to smooth ragged lines and edges.

FIG. 59. These designs were produced through experimentation by the author after a brief introduction to the program.

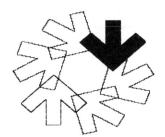
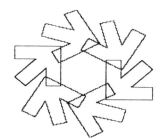
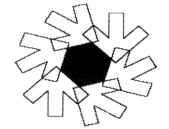

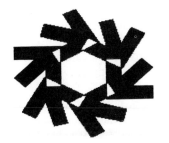
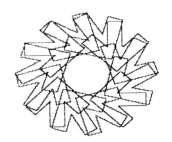

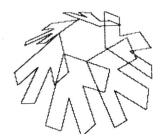

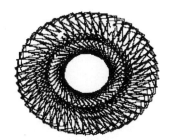
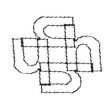
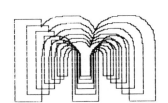

FANCY FONT: Editing Fonts for Use with a Word Processor

The continuing automation of words has outgrown the generally accepted definition of word processing. Today, word processing machines perform work, thought, and graphics processing, greatly surpassing the typewriter's mere automatic placement of words upon the page. This creative factor is what word processing on microcomputers is all about: the personal transformation of thoughts into graphic expression using powerful authoring tools.

Not only is the vehicle of creativity within reach of the originator's hands, but so, too, is the production of the finished product. A limited number of off-the-shelf word processing software packages offer more pagination, graphics, and character-design options than are generally available in most commonly used phototypesetting systems. However, they usually provide these capabilities with coarse character definition and slow output speeds—a compromise in quality to be sure, but a reasonable alternative to traditional graphic arts production for a number of applications.

Fancy Font[11] is a software package that is marketed as "A Personal Typesetter." With a character resolution of 216 dots to the inch (25,920 dots/square inch) from an inexpensive dot matrix printer, it is at a level of output quality that approaches the 300-dots-per-inch threshold which has become acceptable for office use.

The Fancy Font program is composed of three parts: a printing program (Pfont), a font editing program (Efont), and a font-creation program (Cfont). Although it is not intended as a word processing program, it does provide many features that normally are found in a standard word processor. Its main area of usefulness is as a sophisticated printing system that can be used in combination with many available word processors.

Eleven fonts are provided in the package, and they, along with many format commands, can be accessed either by embedding the commands within the word processing text file or by specifying them interactively, just prior to printing.

For example, a text file created with WordStar and named **text.ff** would be printed by typing that name preceded by **Pfont** at the system prompt (assuming that the system has been properly configured and that all necessary programs are loaded):

```
A>Pfont   text.ff
```

The Pfont program processes the file on the basis of whatever commands are embedded in the text or are provided just prior to printing. If, for example, it were necessary to specify an increase of 1/2 inch to the space between each line of text, first the user would invoke Pfont alone, which would result in a Pfont prompt (> >):

```
A>Pfont
> >text.ff +sp .5
> >
```

Any number of printing commands can be specified in this form; however, it is more common to embed the commands within the text using precedence characters and mnemonics.

All of the various printing parameters can be embedded within the text by preceding them with a backslash followed by one or more letters, followed sometimes by a value. The "Underline" command, for example, would be invoked by typing . . . \uFancy Font \u . . ., which would result in the name *Fancy Font* being underlined.

Fancy Font provides absolute printer control by allowing the user to specify the print head movement, either horizontally or vertically, to within one dot. For example, there are 120 dot positions per inch horizontally, resulting in a maximum horizontal value of 960 dots for an 8-inch printer. A column could be specified to start at exactly 3 inches from the left by using the code . . . \a0360 . . ., which states that the absolute horizontal motion of the print head should be 360 dots from the left.

[11]Softcraft
222 State St. #400
Madison, WI 53703
(800) 351-0500

Fancy Font runs on any CP/M computer, as well as the IBM PC under PC-DOS. A current list of supported printers, which includes most Epson models with graphics capability, is available directly from Softcraft.

Fancy Font provides for an extensive on-screen help facility in the Interactive mode. Typing **?** at the > > prompt causes a list of all available parameters to be displayed. Any single parameter followed by a **?** will result in a description of that parameter alone. For example, the rough draft parameter, indicated by **RD**, would be shown as:

```
> > +Rd ?
Expecting value for RD Rough Draft feature - an Integer
Between 0 and 2
Current Value: <Off>
RD Rough Draft>
```

Other information and assistance is available, such as a display of all current settings (typing **&**), a means of overriding existing embedded commands with interactive specifications (typing <), a way of displaying on the terminal a description of the special characters (CTRL-**V**), and editing controls for more efficient specification of interactive commands.

Unlike most font-creation programs, the font sets in Fancy Font can be edited using any standard text editor. Characters and logos also can be created in a text editor as a matrix of asterisks, each one representing a pixel, or printable dot. The Epson printer, for example, typically supports the printing of 216 dots per vertical inch and 120 dots per horizontal inch.

The Fancy Font Efont program is able to convert patterns of asterisks into dot patterns usable for printing. Font files also carry information concerning the left- and right-hand margins, or *character boundaries*, as well as a measure of the relative height of the top dot in the character. When an Epson printer is used, the largest character attainable is approximately 1 inch square.

The Cfont program provides the user with the ability to select up to 128 characters to comprise each font. Included in Fancy Font is the Hershey character database, comprised of over 1500 characters. The database was designed and implemented by Alan V. Hershey for the National Bureau of Standards (Wolcott, NBS Special Publication No. 424). By using the Cfont program, the user is able to select characters from the Hershey database and map them to ASCII character codes so that they can be used with the Fancy Font Pfont and Efont programs.

An example of this mapping technique is the creation of a font composed of a single character, a bell. The bell shape is present in the Hershey database as character number 380 (FIG. 60, LINE 7, CHARACTER 21). When Cfont is run, the interactive mapping capability is accessed by typing **M**. The user is prompted for the ASCII code to which the character (bell) is to be mapped. It seems appropriate to map a bell to the letter *B*, so the number **66** (the ASCII value for the letter *B*) is typed. Next the user is asked for the "Start of matching Hershey sequence," which is the identifier **380**. Since only one character is being specified, the answer to the next prompt, "End of sequence (Hershey number)," is also **380.** If 381 was typed, then Hershey character 381 would be mapped to C, etc. The user then invokes the "g" (generate) command which constructs the bell character and maps it to the *B*. The user then must specify the name of the output file in which this character will be stored.

For the bell to be used within text, it would need to be specified in the Pfont command line, and therefore loaded with the file being processed. It would be accessed by delimiting the character with backslashes, calling the font number, and typing the *B*, like so:

```
The Liberty \f1B\f0 rang
```

In addition to mapping characters to ASCII values, the Cfont program allows the user to scale Hershey characters up or down in order to reduce or enlarge them. Two increments can be specified in each direction: x1 and x2, and y1 and y2. Characters can be previewed from the Cfont program by specifying a range of characters to be sent to the printer for proofing.

FIG. 60. The Hershey Character Database of over 1500 characters provides the Fancy Font user with a full range of characters and symbols from which to build custom fonts. Additionally, over 30 ready-to-use fonts are included.

Selected Characters from the Hershey Database

There are over 1500 characters supplied with the *Fancy Font* system in addition to the regular fonts. The following are just a few of the available characters:

Φ Χ Ψ Ω A B C D E F G H I J ω a b c d e f g h

U B C D E F G H I K L M N O P Q R a b c d e

а б в г д е ж з А Б В Г Д Е Ж З И Й К Л Э Ю Я

δ ε ζ η ϑ ι κ λ μ ν ξ ο π ρ σ τ υ φ χ ψ ◯ ◯ ○

± ∓ × · ÷ = ≠ ≡ < > ≦ ≧ ∝ ~ ⌢ [ ] { } ♠ ♡ ◇ ♣

' ˙ √ ∪ ⊃ ∩ ∈ → ↑ ← ↓ ∂ ∇ √ ∫ ∮ ∞ % & ⟁ ∥ ⊥

@ $ # § † ‡ ⅂ ☉ ☿ ♀ ⊕ ♂ ♃ ♄ ☊ ♆ ♇ ☽ ⚹ ✳ ⚘ ✶ ⚶

♏ ♉ ♈ ♊ ♋ ♌ ♍ ♎ ♏ ♐ ♑ ♒ ☇ ✳ · ‿ ⌣ ○ ○ ● ♯ ♮ ♭

Font Style and Size Samples

8 pt. Roman	A good character is for remembrance.
10 pt. Roman	A good character is for remembrance.
11 pt. Roman	A good character is for remembrance.
12 pt. Roman	A good character is for remembrance.
18 pt. Roman	A good character is for remembrance.
18 pt. Roman Bold	**Boldness has genius, power and magic in it.**
18 pt. Italic	*Print it as it stands — beautifully*
18 pt. Sans Serif	Simplicity of character is no hindrance to sublety of intellect.
20 pt. Script	*Fancy may kill or cure.*
20 pt. Old English	This is the sort of English up with which I will not put.
40 pt. Roman	Big Bird for President
Gray Background	SoftCraft 8726 S. Sepulveda Bl. Ste. 1641, Los Angeles, CA 90045

Printed by the *Fancy Font*™ System (actual size)   **SoftCraft**

The Fancy Font program provides the user with considerable flexibility in defining the output appearance of files created with an ordinary (compatible) word processing program. A sample of the versatility which the package provides is shown in FIG. 60.

GRAPHIC ENVIRONMENTS WITH TYPOGRAPHIC CAPABILITIES

SIGN-MASTER:
Producing Signage with a Dot Matrix Printer or Color Plotter

The realm of applications for which typesetting is useful in offices, schools, and plants is deeply entrenched in all facets of their daily operations. However, a multitude of text pages, headlines, tables, charts, and signs often are produced with less than professional results using typewriters, markers, and common art supply items. The use of a microcomputer with a color plotter and the Sign-Master[12] software fulfills a need not easily met even by traditional graphic arts procedures and products.

Sign-Master is somewhat unique in that it supports both plotters and dot matrix printers. A plotter affords a number of advantages over a printer in that it can utilize a variety of colors (few printers can); it can produce its output in horizontal or vertical orientation; it can produce smooth line edges; it can produce fairly large character sizes; and it can sometimes produce an image area significantly larger than that obtainable on a printer.

A look at the master menu provides a glimpse of the overall capabilities of the program:

```
1  CREATE A SIGN
2  EDIT SIGN
3  HELP & INSTRUCTIONS
4  PLOT SIGN
5  CHANGE PLOTTING OPTIONS
6  STORE/RETRIEVE/DELETE SIGN
7  CHANGE/DISPLAY CONFIGURATION
8  QUIT
```

These major categories are fairly self-explanatory. ''Create A Sign'' is the text-input portion of the program; ''Edit Sign'' provides a means of making changes in the text; ''Help & Instructions'' gives the user assistance at any point in the program; ''Plot Sign'' offers a menu of various output media; ''Change Plotting Options'' determines the design format of the sign; ''Store/ Retrieve/ Delete Sign'' provides disk access for saving, loading, and removing files; and ''Display or Change Configuration'' offers the user the option of redefining the system configuration.

Assuming that the software is properly installed, the creation of a sign begins with the selection of option 1, ''Create a Sign.'' The Entry/Editing screen (FIG. 61) is composed of an Entry window and an Options Selection window directly below it. At the top of the screen is a number followed by a colon and another number. These numbers indicate the line number that is currently active and the total number of lines that comprise the sign.

The bottom of the screen consists of options that change the physical appearance of individual characters, words, or lines. These options control the size, type style, and color, and whether the text is justified, italicized, or underlined. The options for a change in text appearance must be specified before the text is keyboarded.

There are six type styles from which to choose. They are described as producing ''professional, typeset-quality'' output. They consist of a standard, a bold, a roman, a roman bold, a script, and a gothic. The default setting is the standard typeface.

The range of sizes spans 16 settings, designated as 1 through 9 and A through G, with 1 being the smallest and G the largest. These sizes bear no direct relationship to known typesetting point sizes. The default setting is size 7.

[12]Decision Resources
25 Sylvan Road
Westport, CT 06880
(203) 222-1974

Requires an IBM PC, XT, or compatible; 1 or 2 disk drives (320K); DOS 1.1 or DOS 2.0; 192K (256K for printer or Polaroid Palette output).

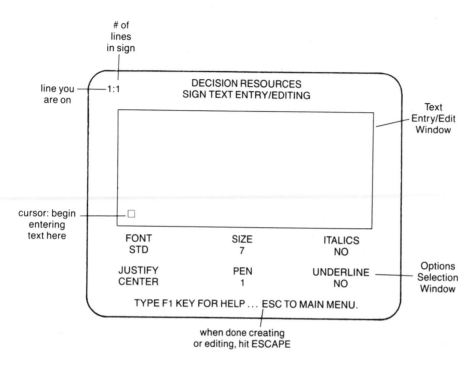

of
lines
in sign

line you
are on ——— 1:1

DECISION RESOURCES
SIGN TEXT ENTRY/EDITING

Text
Entry/Edit
Window

cursor: begin
entering
text here

FONT	SIZE	ITALICS
STD	7	NO

JUSTIFY	PEN	UNDERLINE
CENTER	1	NO

Options
Selection
Window

TYPE F1 KEY FOR HELP ... ESC TO MAIN MENU.

when done creating
or editing, hit ESCAPE

FIG. 61. The Sign-Master Text Entry/Editing screen.

The Italics command slants characters approximately 15 degrees. It is activated by changing the default "No Italics" setting to "Yes." The Underline mode, which also defaults to the off position, is activated in the same way.

The Justification setting is actually a determination of quadding, or line orientation. Lines can be set either centered, flush left, or flush right. The default setting is centered.

The color of the text is designated by pen color. Up to eight colors or pens can be used, depending upon the capabilities of the plotter in use. The choice of the pen number must correspond to a specific color on the plotter. If a two-pen plotter is used and three colors are necessary, pen 3 can be specified during the text-creation phase and the program later will prompt the user for the manual pen change when the sign is produced. Additional colors can be used with other plotters that have less than eight colors by utilizing the same manual pen change procedures.

A particularly strong capability of Sign-Master is its table-creation mode. The function keys on the left-hand side of the PC keyboard have been programmed to define delimiters for the tables. These functions indicate column delimiters, upper and lower right-hand and left-hand corner locations, and vertical lines (FIG. 62).

After text has been input, it can be edited by selecting option 2 from the Main menu. The Sign-Master editor permits the user to insert characters and lines; delete characters, lines, and portions of lines; and move around the screen. Typographic attributes for newly created lines also can be changed.

With the proper hardware, the sign can be previewed on the screen prior to being committed to paper. In Monochrome mode, the display is capable of a resolution of 640 pixels by 200 pixels. In Color mode, the resolution is coarser: 320 pixels by 200 pixels. If the preview results in unsatisfactory results, the user can return to the Editor to make corrections. If everything appears correct, the Plotting option is selected.

The Plotting menu is the most complex menu, and is composed of three screens of choices. The selections indicate the plot area for transparencies, for 35mm slide enlargement, for standard 8 1/2-×-11-inch paper, or for a specified size of paper; the sign orientation, either horizontal or vertical; the sign location, anywhere within the plotting area; the pen speed, which must be specified to correspond to the kind of output substrate being used (fast for normal bond paper, slow for transparencies); the pres-

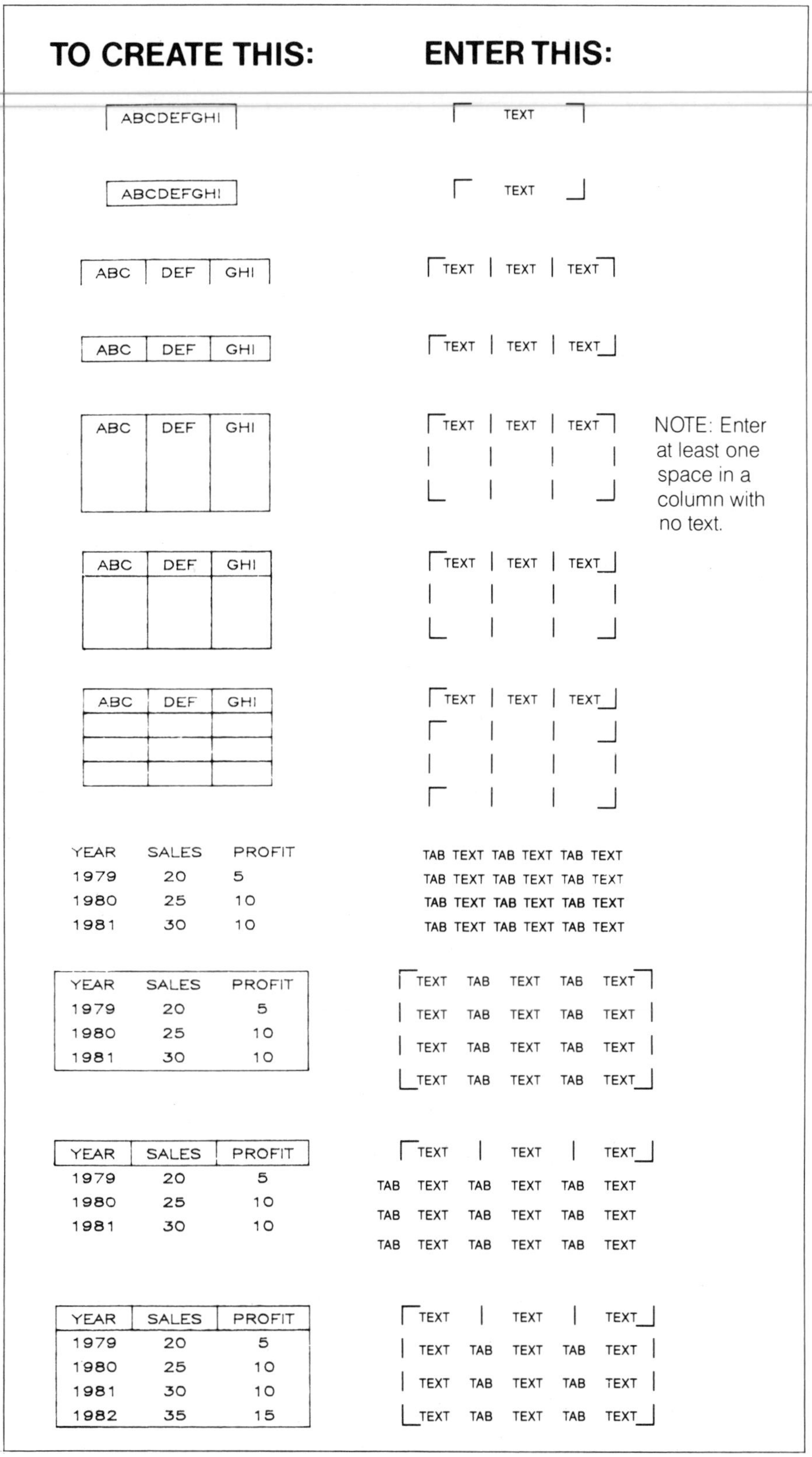

FIG. 62. The "Table Creation" capability provides a simple means of indicating column and row boundaries.

TO CREATE THIS: **ENTER THIS:**

| ABCDEFGHI | | ⌐ TEXT ¬ |

| ABCDEFGHI | | ⌐ TEXT ⌐ |

| ABC | DEF | GHI | ⌐TEXT | TEXT | TEXT¬

| ABC | DEF | GHI | ⌐TEXT | TEXT | TEXT⌐

| ABC | DEF | GHI | ⌐TEXT | TEXT | TEXT¬
(tall cells below) | | | |
                        L | | ⌐

NOTE: Enter at least one space in a column with no text.

| ABC | DEF | GHI | ⌐TEXT | TEXT | TEXT⌐
(tall cells) | | | |
                        L | | ⌐

| ABC | DEF | GHI | ⌐TEXT | TEXT | TEXT⌐
(gridded rows)   ⌐ | | ⌐
                        | | | |
                        ⌐ | | ⌐

YEAR	SALES	PROFIT
1979	20	5
1980	25	10
1981	30	10

TAB TEXT TAB TEXT TAB TEXT
TAB TEXT TAB TEXT TAB TEXT
TAB TEXT TAB TEXT TAB TEXT
TAB TEXT TAB TEXT TAB TEXT

YEAR	SALES	PROFIT
1979	20	5
1980	25	10
1981	30	10

⌐TEXT TAB TEXT TAB TEXT¬
| TEXT TAB TEXT TAB TEXT |
| TEXT TAB TEXT TAB TEXT |
L TEXT TAB TEXT TAB TEXT⌐

YEAR	SALES	PROFIT
1979	20	5
1980	25	10
1981	30	10

⌐TEXT | TEXT | TEXT⌐
TAB TEXT TAB TEXT TAB TEXT
TAB TEXT TAB TEXT TAB TEXT
TAB TEXT TAB TEXT TAB TEXT

YEAR	SALES	PROFIT
1979	20	5
1980	25	10
1981	30	10
1982	35	15

⌐TEXT | TEXT | TEXT⌐
| TEXT TAB TEXT TAB TEXT |
| TEXT TAB TEXT TAB TEXT |
L TEXT TAB TEXT TAB TEXT⌐

ence or absence of a frame surrounding the sign; the page formatting of the plot, either top, middle, or bottom placement, or vertical justification; and the specification in inches of the top, bottom, right, and left margins (FIG. 63).

The Plotting menu includes the direct creation of 35mm color slides or 3 1/4-×-4 1/4-inch color prints using the Polaroid Palette computer image recorder, which is a tabletop device. The Palette has its own set of software and hardware requirements. A list of these items is available directly from Decision Resources.

FIG. 63. A sample produced on a plotter. The frame was created simply by indicating on the menu selection that one was required.

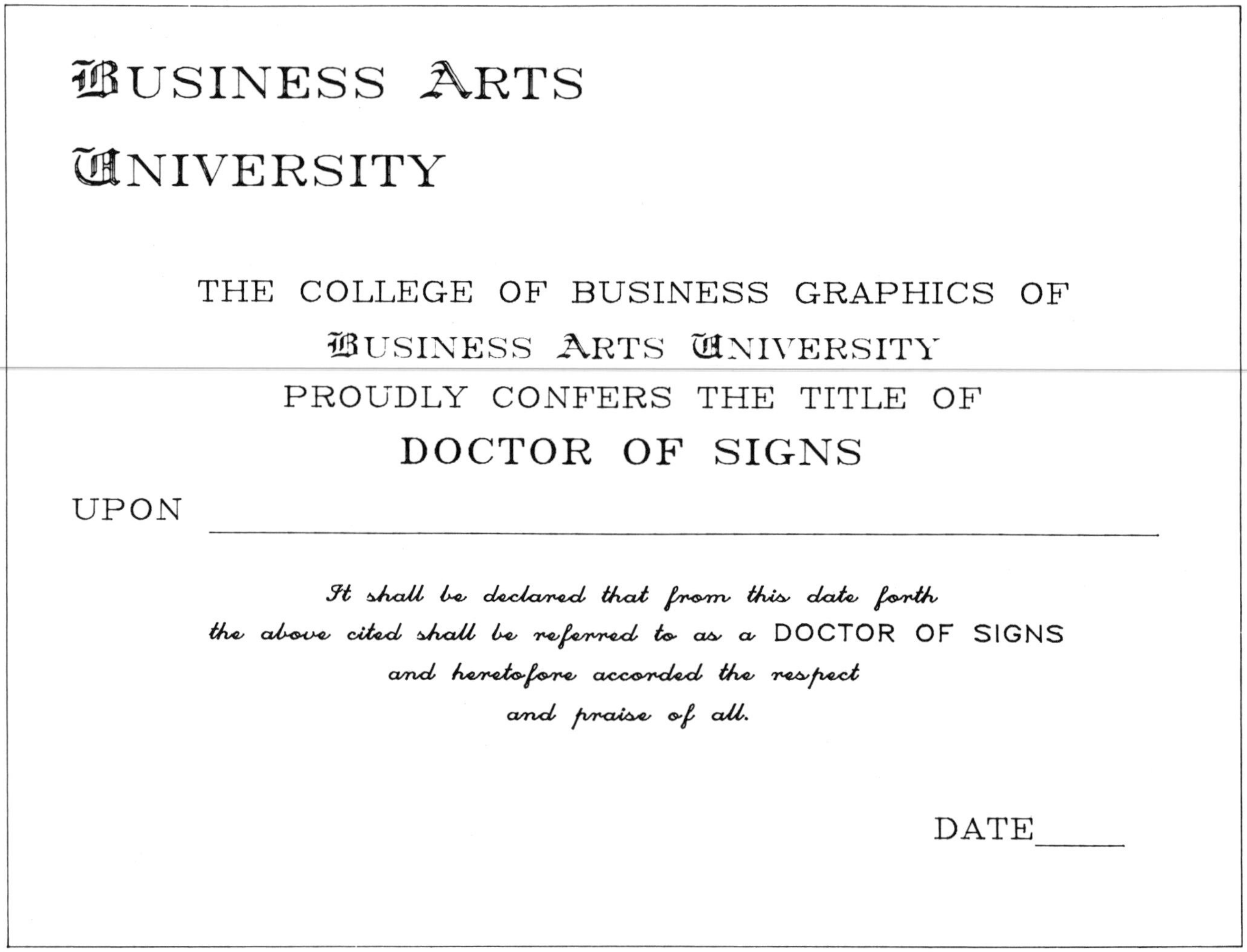

𝔅USINESS 𝔄RTS 𝔘NIVERSITY

THE COLLEGE OF BUSINESS GRAPHICS OF

𝔅USINESS 𝔄RTS 𝔘NIVERSITY

PROUDLY CONFERS THE TITLE OF

DOCTOR OF SIGNS

UPON _____

*It shall be declared that from this date forth
the above cited shall be referred to as a* DOCTOR OF SIGNS
*and heretofore accorded the respect
and praise of all.*

DATE_____

DIAGRAPH:
Composing Text and Graphics for Slide Production

Few graphic generation software packages have the flexibility of supporting dot matrix printers, plotters, and film recorders. One that does is Diagraph,[13] for the IBM PC and its compatibles. Diagraph is a menu-driven program that permits the user to select from a library of over 1600 symbols, categorized in such files as graphic aids, signs and icons, pictorials, and applications.

When composing a design for the creation of a slide, overhead, or sign, the user is prompted for the pattern of symbols that will be manipulated on the screen. The pattern divides the screen into a matrix of X items across and Y items down. Each window within the matrix becomes an active work area in which the image may be moved, resized, stretched, rotated, flipped, and copied. The window also may be specified as being 1×1, so that a single graphic element fills the entire screen (FIG. 64).

A library of 13 typefaces is provided (FIG. 65), and type may be added freely to any area of the screen. The typographic parameters include proportionality (P), size (S), justification (J), font number (F), bold (B), and italic (I) (FIG. 66). Text is input on the Text Menu screen (FIG. 67), where it is typed and its specifications are assigned.

Aside from its flexible graphic-manipulation capabilities, one of Diagraph's greatest strengths is the size and scope of its graphic libraries (FIG. 68). In addition to the graphics that are provided with the program, accessory libraries covering a variety of subjects are available at extra cost.

FIG. 64. A stock graphic to which a single line of type is added can be produced in a matter of minutes with Diagraph.

[13]Computer Support Corporation
2215 Midway Road
Carrollton, TX 75006
(214) 661-8960

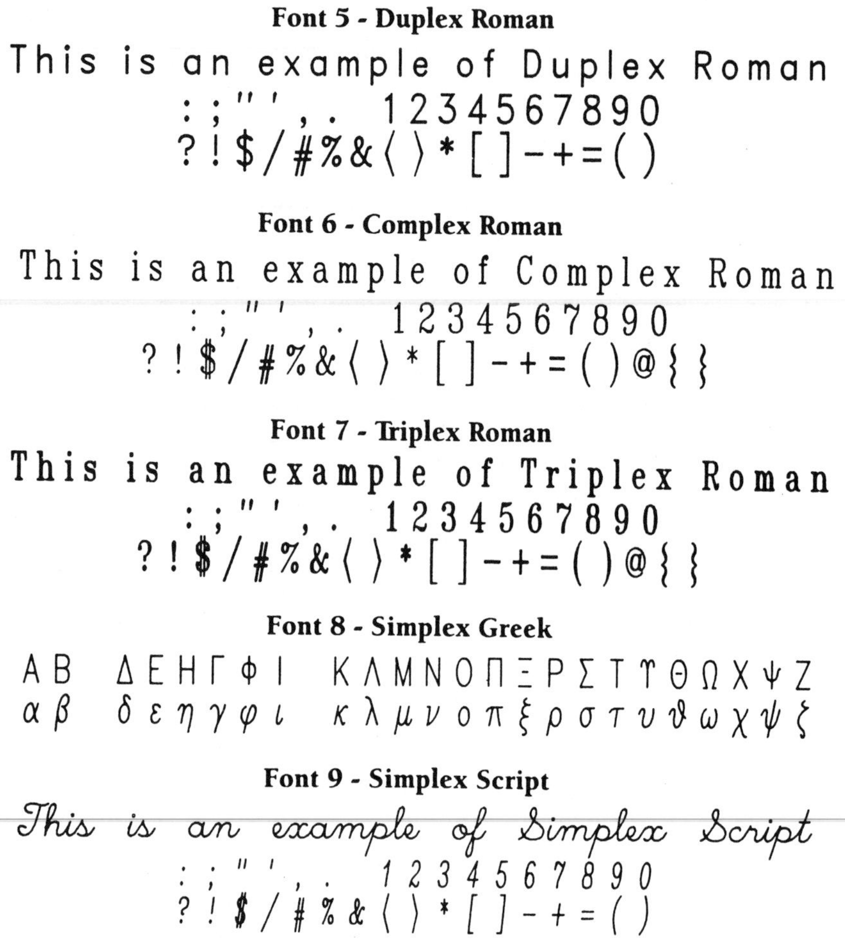

Font 5 - Duplex Roman

This is an example of Duplex Roman
: ; " ' , .   1234567890
? ! $ / # % & ⟨ ⟩ * [ ] - + = ( )

Font 6 - Complex Roman

This is an example of Complex Roman
: ; " ' , .   1234567890
? ! $ / # % & ⟨ ⟩ * [ ] - + = ( ) @ { }

Font 7 - Triplex Roman

This is an example of Triplex Roman
: ; " ' , .   1234567890
? ! $ / # % & ⟨ ⟩ * [ ] - + = ( ) @ { }

Font 8 - Simplex Greek

Α Β Δ Ε Η Γ Φ Ι Κ Λ Μ Ν Ο Π Ξ Ρ Σ Τ Υ Θ Ω Χ Ψ Ζ
α β δ ε η γ φ ι κ λ μ ν ο π ξ ρ σ τ υ ϑ ω χ ψ ς

Font 9 - Simplex Script

This is an example of Simplex Script
: ; " ' , .   1234567890
? ! $ / # % & ⟨ ⟩ * [ ] - + = ( )

FIG. 65. A selection of 5 of the 13 type fonts available for labeling Diagraph graphics.

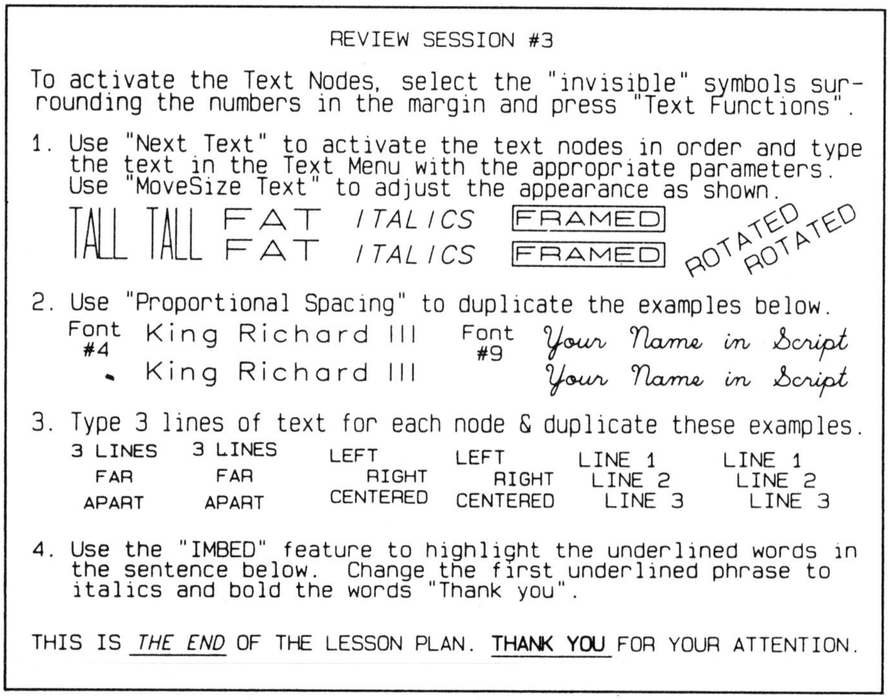

REVIEW SESSION #3

To activate the Text Nodes, select the "invisible" symbols surrounding the numbers in the margin and press "Text Functions".

1. Use "Next Text" to activate the text nodes in order and type the text in the Text Menu with the appropriate parameters. Use "MoveSize Text" to adjust the appearance as shown.

TALL TALL FAT FAT *ITALICS ITALICS* FRAMED FRAMED ROTATED ROTATED

2. Use "Proportional Spacing" to duplicate the examples below.

Font #4 King Richard III   Font #9 Your Name in Script
         King Richard III   Your Name in Script

3. Type 3 lines of text for each node & duplicate these examples.

3 LINES	3 LINES	LEFT	LEFT	LINE 1	LINE 1
FAR	FAR		RIGHT	LINE 2	LINE 2
APART	APART	CENTERED	CENTERED	LINE 3	LINE 3

4. Use the "IMBED" feature to highlight the underlined words in the sentence below. Change the first underlined phrase to italics and bold the words "Thank you".

THIS IS *THE END* OF THE LESSON PLAN. **THANK YOU** FOR YOUR ATTENTION.

FIG. 66. A variety of typographic effects is achieved easily under keyboard control.

319

FIG. 67. The Text Input screen provides the slate upon which lines of type are entered and their descriptors are specified.

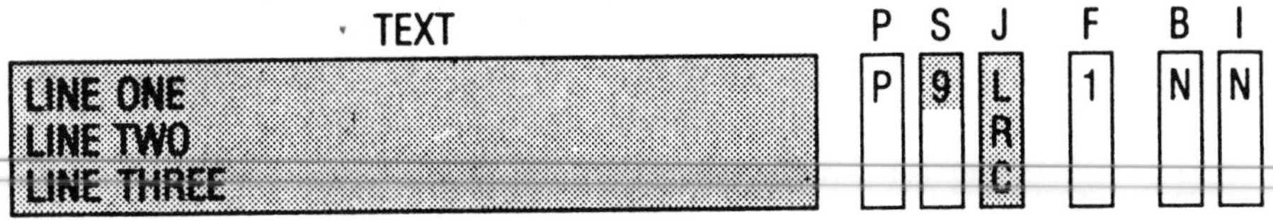

TEXT   P S J F B I

LINE ONE
LINE TWO
LINE THREE

P 9 LRC 1 N N

FIG. 68. A selection of symbols from the Diagraph Data Processing equipment library.

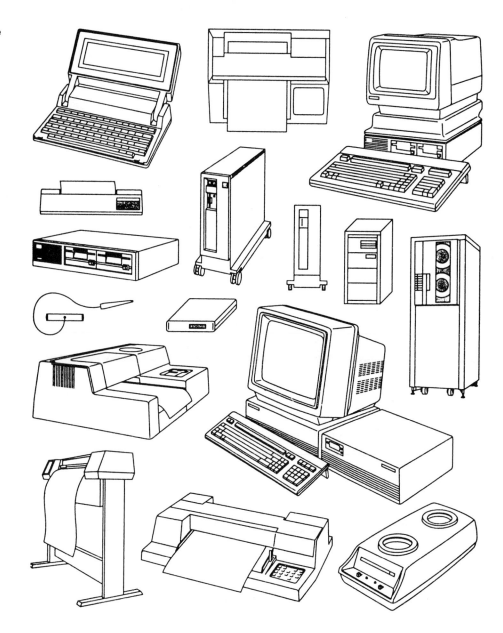

THE PRINT SHOP:
Reducing Typo/graphic Composition to a Cookbook Approach

A number of people in the community of typesetting users have, from time to time, expressed the opinion that the complexity of the typesetting process could be reduced greatly by implementing a "cookbook approach" to typesetting production. This new methodology, it has been reasoned, would increase the ease of use of typesetting systems by restricting the number of typographic design choices, thereby standardizing coding and eliminating most, if not all, of the errors associated with typographic formatting. Such a system was produced by Itek for its Quadritek series of phototypesetters. The story announcing this historic event was recorded in *The Direct Input Phototypesetting Newsletter* in September of 1980.[14] An excerpt follows:

ITEK ADVANCES DO-IT-YOURSELF PHOTOTYPESETTING

This is clever. Off-the-shelf programs for composing a wide variety of work on the Quadritek. Just a few years ago the concept sounded futuristic—a menu of typographic choices; find a preset specimen that fulfills your expectations, and go to work. Now with the Quad Quick package, a keyboard operator can do even fairly complex typesetting with almost no training. It is not even necessary to have completed the Operator Learning Program to use these special purpose programs.

The objective of the Quad Quick package is to make the operator and the machine productive immediately. This means that the capabilities of the phototypesetter do not go unused while an operator-in-training discovers what the machine can do. Even experienced operators do not always approach similar jobs in a systematic way, and so they really extend the time required to produce work since they need to replan and rekeyboard similar formats again and again.

The procedure with Quad Quick is simple. The customer or client is shown pages of jobs from the appropriate job category. The selection of jobs is fairly representative. The customer makes a selection, and his/her copy is so marked. The job then goes to the Quadritek operator. The operator has all of the Quad Quick formats on a floppy disk, or on magnetic cassettes. In the case of the disk system, such as we used, he/she calls the disk directory, and all categories of work appear on the screen. The operator then calls the chosen file (category), and enters it in memory. The customer's copy indicates the style which will be used, and the operator finds the corresponding page in the Quad Quick booklet. The sample in the booklet indicates the required format name (usually a single character) to produce each variation in form. The operator keyboards the format name, followed by the appropriate section of the customer's copy. The operator need not know or understand any of the formats. As each format is keyboarded, an operator prompt message appears below the parameter field, guiding the operator through the process. A typical business card job, for example, would take less than five minutes to keyboard, and the Quadritek Quad Quick program can automatically typeset them two across, four down, with trim marks in position.

While the Quad Quick package can accomplish quite alot, it should not be thought of as a surrogate for a well-trained operator, nor a substitute for the limitless versatility of the Quadritek's 99 stored formats.

Cost of the Quad Quick package of nine job categories is $1250. Individual parts of the package, which is comprised of Letterheads and Envelopes, Resumes, Invitations and Announcements, Brochures, Text, Newsletters, Post Cards and Tickets, and Business Cards are $250 each. The ninth part, a forms package is now being written.

[14]Michael L. Kleper, "Itek Advances Do-It-Yourself Phototypesetting," *Direct Input Phototypesetting Newsletter*, Vol. 2, No. 8, pp. 1, 5.

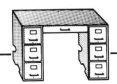

The concept of "canned" typographic formats, though proven valid by Itek, has not captured the imagination of other typesetting equipment vendors. It is somewhat ironic, therefore, that a program offering some similar, though considerably more limited, capabilities should be available for the Apple II and Macintosh families of microcomputers. It is called The Print Shop.[15]

The Print Shop is a menu-driven program that turns the Apple and one of a number of supported dot matrix printers into a self-contained printing system for the production of such items as greeting cards, letterheads, logos, advertising flyers, announcements, note cards, banners, stationery, report covers, bulletins, bookplates, certificates, signs, and more. The program offers a limited set of output alternatives for the production of each of the aforementioned classifications.

The easiest way to understand the operation of the program is to work through a simple example: the creation of a greeting card. From the Main menu (FIG. 69), the "Greeting Card" option is selected. Options are chosen by either keyboard input, joystick, or Koala Pad. The next screen (FIG. 70) prompts the user for a choice between a custom-designed card and a ready-made one. If the "Ready-Made" option is selected, the user is presented with another menu listing canned designs that only

FIG. 69. The Main menu of The Print Shop lists all of its major capabilities.

FIG. 70. The production of a greeting card can be speeded up considerably by using a ready-made design.

[15]Designed by David Balsam
Programmed by Martin Kahn
Broderbund Software
17 Paul Drive
San Rafael, CA 94903

Supports the Apple DMP, Imagewriter, and Scribe; the Okidata 92/93; the C.Itoh 8510 (Prowriter); the Star Micronics 10X/15X; the NEC 8023A; and the Epson RX-80/MX-80 and 100 and FX-80 and 100. No graphics card required.

accommodate the addition of personalization. These designs include birthday and holiday greetings, as well as invitations and notepaper. Selections are made by striking the Return key, or by pressing a joystick or Koala Pad button. The user has the option of returning to the prior screen by striking the ESC key.

The first design choice is a border for the front of the card. As the name of the border is highlighted, a sample of the border appears on the screen (FIGS. 71 and 72). Next there is the choice of which of the 60 supplied graphics will be used on the front of the card (FIG. 73). The user can select the graphic by typing its number (a reference card shows a display of all 60 images) or by displaying its picture on the screen (FIG. 74). After the graphic is chosen, its printed size must be selected. There is a choice of three sizes: small, medium, and large (FIGS. 75 and 76).

The layout of the graphic is the next design decision. It can be staggered, which will place 13 small or 5 medium images according to a predetermined arrangement, or can be tiled, which will place small graphics in a side-by-side arrangement. If the custom layout is selected, the user then decides which of the display positions will be occupied by the graphic (FIG. 77).

The type composition section is next. Eight all-capital fonts are available (FIG. 78). As each typeface is highlighted, a sample appears in the display window (FIG. 79). The user next enters the editor where he keyboards the copy (FIG. 80), as well as selects the line positioning (flush left, flush right, or centered), the form of the characters (solid, outline, or three dimensional), and their size (small or large) (FIG. 81).

The inside of the card is produced using a similar series of screen presentations. Just prior to printing, the user is given more choices, including adding a credit line to the back of the card and setting the number of copies that will be printed (FIG. 82).

The completed card (FIG. 83), a four-panel French fold, reflects all of the design decisions completed through the series of menus. The software package includes colorful tractor-feed paper and matching envelopes for a more creative touch. In addition, the publishers provide a source for colored printer ribbons and additional paper and envelopes.

The Print Shop provides other capabilities as well, including the ability to superimpose text over any design or picture, a facility to print graphics created with other software packages, and a kaleidoscopic animation system for creating background patterns. Furthermore, any of the 60 graphic images can be edited, and completely new ones created, by using the built-in graphic editor (FIG. 84).

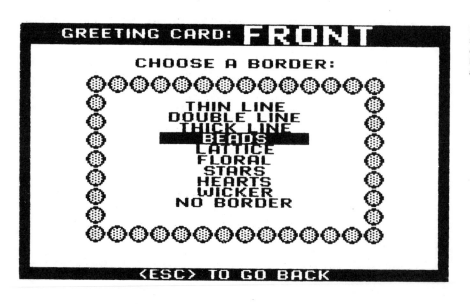

FIG. 71. A border for the front cover is selected by moving through the list of choices. As the name of each border is highlighted, an actual sample of the border appears on the screen.

FIG. 72. The nine border selections are built into the program.

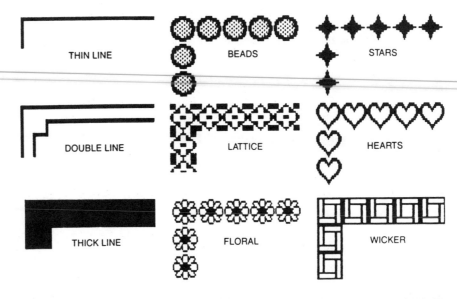

THIN LINE · BEADS · STARS

DOUBLE LINE · LATTICE · HEARTS

THICK LINE · FLORAL · WICKER

FIG. 73. The selection of a graphic is made either by number (from a reference card) or by picture display.

FIG. 74. Graphics may be examined prior to inclusion by opting for the "By Picture" selection.

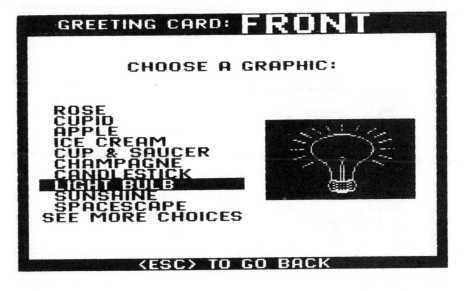

SELECT GRAPHIC SIZE:

SMALL
MEDIUM
LARGE

<ESC> TO GO BACK

FIG. 75. The graphic size is shown relative to the front cover of the card.

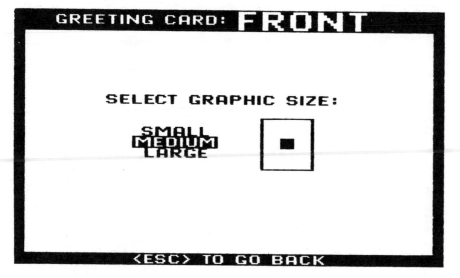

SMALL

MEDIUM

LARGE

FIG. 76. A sample of the three graphic sizes available. The larger the size, obviously, the more jagged the outline.

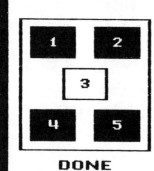

GREETING CARD: FRONT

1	2
3	
4	5

DONE

USE ← → , AND PRESS <RETURN> TO PLACE OR REMOVE GRAPHICS AT ANY POSITION ON THE PAGE YOU WISH.

<ESC> TO GO BACK

FIG. 77. The number of graphics that will fit on the front of the card is determined by the selection of the graphic size. Which of the graphic positions will be occupied is determined by the user.

FIG. 78. A showing of the eight typefaces available in The Print Shop. No lowercase alphabet is supplied.

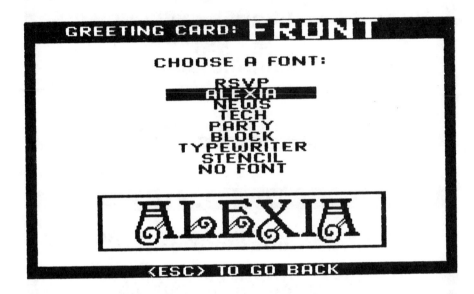

FIG. 79. As a typeface is highlighted, its name appears in the actual design in the display box.

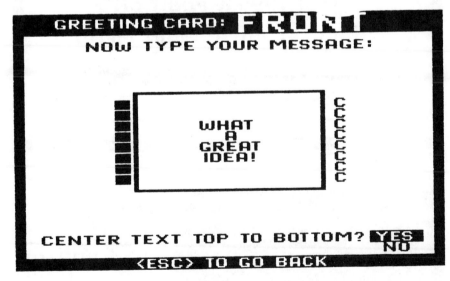

FIG. 80. The message for the front of the card is centered automatically as it is typed. The solid boxes to the left of each line indicate that the type will be filled in solid. The C's indicate that each line is centered.

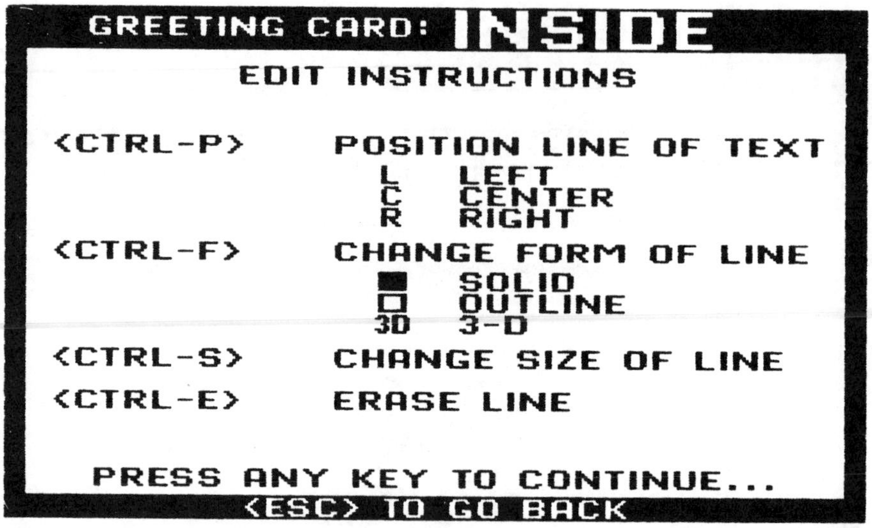

GREETING CARD: **INSIDE**

EDIT INSTRUCTIONS

\<CTRL-P\>   POSITION LINE OF TEXT
            L   LEFT
            C   CENTER
            R   RIGHT

\<CTRL-F\>   CHANGE FORM OF LINE
            ■   SOLID
            □   OUTLINE
            3D   3-D

\<CTRL-S\>   CHANGE SIZE OF LINE

\<CTRL-E\>   ERASE LINE

PRESS ANY KEY TO CONTINUE...
\<ESC\> TO GO BACK

FIG. 81. The editing instructions are available by typing CTRL-I from the editor.

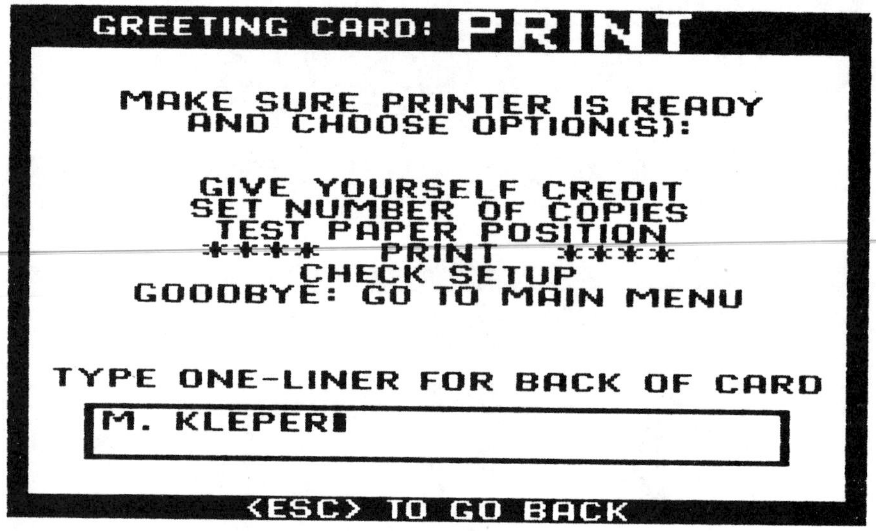

GREETING CARD: **PRINT**

MAKE SURE PRINTER IS READY
AND CHOOSE OPTION(S):

GIVE YOURSELF CREDIT
SET NUMBER OF COPIES
TEST PAPER POSITION
****   PRINT   ****
CHECK SETUP
GOODBYE: GO TO MAIN MENU

TYPE ONE-LINER FOR BACK OF CARD

M. KLEPER▮

\<ESC\> TO GO BACK

FIG. 82. The final menu prior to printing provides the user with the option of adding a credit line and selecting the number of copies to print.

FIG. 83 (facing page). The completed card, properly imposed for folding, is the result of all of the many individual design decisions.

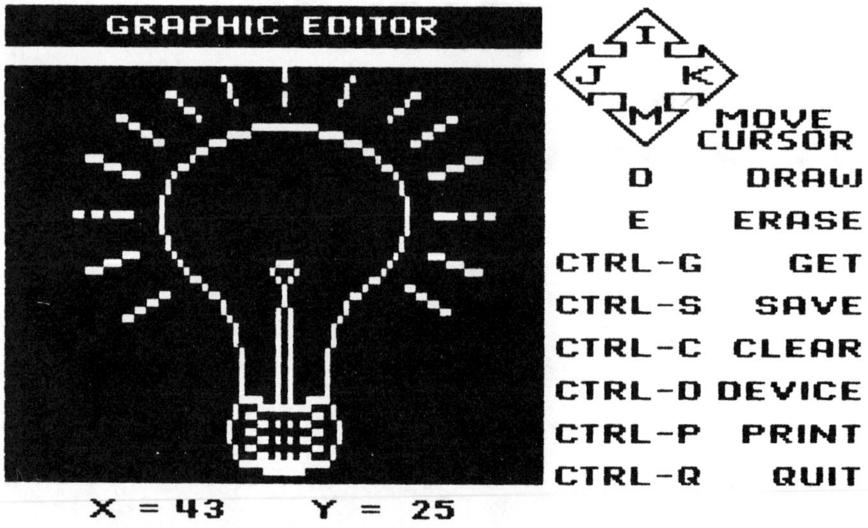

GRAPHIC EDITOR

I
J   K
M   MOVE
    CURSOR
D   DRAW
E   ERASE
CTRL-G   GET
CTRL-S   SAVE
CTRL-C   CLEAR
CTRL-D DEVICE
CTRL-P   PRINT
CTRL-Q   QUIT

X = 43   Y = 25

FIG. 84. The Graphic Editor permits the redesign of any of the library of graphic images, as well as the creation of original designs. The Editor matrix is 87 dots across and 51 dots down.

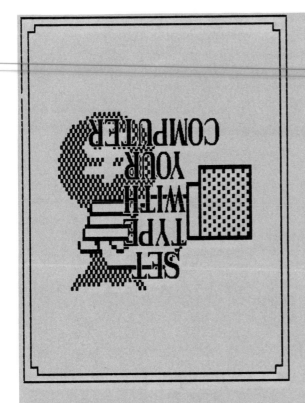

M. KLEPER

THE NEWSROOM:
Creating a Newspaper Micro-environment

Many computer programs are devised as microenvironments of real-world activities. Spreadsheets emulate accounting, word processors emulate writing, databases emulate filing, and on and on. Usually, the more complex the program, the more complete the emulation. A sophisticated word processor, for example, would do more than edit words; it would proof the document for spelling and grammatical errors, merge variable and fixed information, telecommunicate text, perform mathematical functions, and much more. As such, it combines the functions of writer, proofreader, filer, courier, and mathematician.

Few programs, however, have the breadth of scope to encompass all of the activities in a particular process. One that offers a good emulation of the various activities performed in the publishing environment is Springboard's The Newsroom,[16] aimed particularly at younger users, although suitable for the preparation of newspapers and similar publications for families, clubs, classes, schools, and businesses.

The Newsroom works on the premise that all pages are composed of two basic types of elements. There is the *banner,* the newspaper's means of identifying itself; and the *panel,* the rectangularly shaped blocks that in single or multiple units form columns of stories. A page can be composed of a banner and either six or eight panels, or simply all panels (FIG. 85).

The Newsroom is made up of six distinct tasks, which are required functions in the production of a newspaper (FIG. 86). They include the Photo Lab, where pictures

Banner		Panel	Panel	Banner		Panel	Panel
Panel	Panel	Panel	Panel	Panel	Panel	Panel	Panel
Panel	Panel	Panel	Panel	Panel	Panel	Panel	Panel
Panel	Panel	Panel	Panel	Panel	Panel	Panel	Panel

8½″ × 11″ letter size page with banner   8½″ × 11″ letter size page without banner   8½″ × 14″ legal size page with banner   8½″ × 14″ legal size page without banner

FIG. 85. A Newsroom page is composed of blocks that fit together as if composed as columns. These are the four layout possibilities.

FIG. 86. The Newsroom Start-Up menu is accessible from any of the various Newsroom departments.

[16]Springboard Software, Inc.
  7807 Creekridge Circle
  Minneapolis, MN 55435
  (612) 944-3912
  (800) 328-1223

Available on disk for the Apple II+, *IIe, IIc,* IIGS, and IBM PC, PC*jr.*

are taken and developed; the Banner production department, where the banner is designed; the Wire Service room, where text is sent to and received from remote reporters and newspapers; the Copy Desk, where text is composed and combined with photographs into panels; the Layout table, where the banner and panels are assembled; and the Press room, where the pages are printed.

One of the unique features of The Newsroom is that each of its different computer versions—Apple and IBM—can work together without restriction. Through the use of the wire service capability, previously incompatible computers can share text and graphics, outputting virtually identical pages from input generated in another part of the room or in another part of the world.

Just as in the real world, work in The Newsroom need not follow a fixed sequence. It is highly likely that the demands of creating a newspaper will necessitate frequent shuffling between various departments. Through its pictorial menu, The Newsroom provides access to any department at any time.

In the Photo Lab (FIG. 87), the photographer has a file of prepared photographs (clip art graphics) covering a variety of subjects. Access to the photo archives and to other studio tools and functions is made possible by a cursor, which moves vertically beside the lab icons. The cursor is moved either by keyboard keys or with an optional joystick, Koala pad, or mouse.

The photo archives are accessed by positioning the cursor beside the Face icon and activating the selection. A listing of file names is displayed (FIG. 88), which provides a choice of hundreds of graphic images located on both sides of The Newsroom

FIG. 87. The Photo Lab offers a number of tools to create artwork, as well as modify archive images.

FIG. 88. Each file of clip art contains a number of related images, with the exception of the Miscellaneous (MISC 1 through 7) series, which has collections of random drawings.

clip art disk. Additional images are available on accessory clip art disks, which are available at extra cost.

A selection of Miscellaneous images (FIG. 89) provides the photographer with a choice of many unrelated, individual items. A Hand icon appears over the clip art page for positioning over the particular piece of artwork needed. When it is activated, the screen returns to the Photo Lab, where the artwork appears floating on the copy board. Using the keyboard or another device, the artwork is positioned. Additional pieces of art can be brought before the camera in the same way.

The active image can be flipped—that is, its orientation can be reversed—by using the Double Arrow icon.

The Crayon icon opens a new palette of menu selections (FIG. 90) offering artist's tools for drawing lines (connected or nonconnected), circles, boxes; freehand drawing; erasing. It also offers a variety of ten pen points, ten textures, and a hand to reposition artwork. The typeface library of three large fonts and two small fonts also is located there.

The Magnifying Glass icon enlarges a selected portion of the copyboard so that an image can be edited pixel by pixel. The magnified screen shows a small window with an image section displayed in actual size (FIG. 91).

FIG. 89. A page of clip art showing the hand positioned over the image of a book. Any reasonable number of images can be copied from the clip art archives onto the Photo Copy Board.

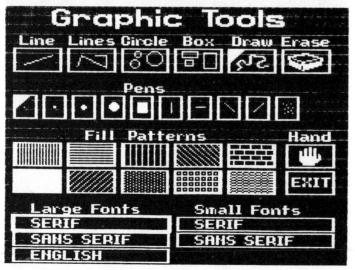

FIG. 90. The Graphic Tools menu, accessed by selecting the Crayon icon, offers considerable flexibility in creating and modifying images on the Photo Copy Board.

If an error is made, the last operation can be canceled by selecting the "OOPS" option. The "OOPS" option also can be used on itself to reinstate an operation mistakenly erased. The entire work area can be cleared by activating the Garbage Can icon.

Type can be added to a piece of artwork or to a design as an integral part, or as a cutline or caption. No editing capabilities are provided, although a mistakenly typed character can be replaced by overtyping.

The photograph is taken by selecting the Camera icon, which causes it to blink. The cursor is positioned in one corner of the artwork, and it expands under keyboard or joystick control into a box, which frames, or *crops,* the artwork. To take the photograph, the selection key or button is activated. The picture is saved by selecting the Disk icon, which provides entry to disk storage.

The Banner department has many of the same tools found in the Photo Lab, although it does not have the double-sided arrow, "OOPS," or camera options.

At the Copy Desk, photographs are combined with type to form panels, which are the modules that make up columns on a page. The Disk icon is activated in order to access photographs taken in the Photo Lab. When a photograph is brought onto the copy desk, it is positioned using the cursor keys or the joystick controller. The photograph's crop area becomes a protected block; that is, copy may be entered only in the remaining nonphotograph area (FIG. 92).

Five type fonts are accessible by selecting the Font icon (FIG. 93). Limited word processing capabilities, such as inserting and deleting text, are available. All text can be removed from the panel by selecting the Eraser icon, and the entire panel can be erased by selecting the Garbage Can icon. Panels are saved by choosing the Disk icon.

FIG. 91. The result of selecting the Magnifying Glass icon is a full-screen window view of a portion of the Photo Copy Board. Individual pixels can be turned on and off. A true-size window appears in the middle of the lower portion of the screen.

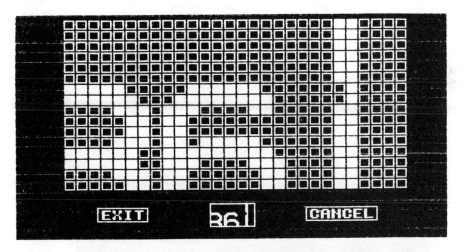

FIG. 92. The cropped boundaries of a photograph, positioned on a Copy Board panel, form the default area available for the input of text.

After all parts of the newspaper have been created, the elements must be assembled in the Layout department. During this operation, the layout artist chooses one of the four stock layouts: either 8 1/2 × 11 inches or 8 1/2 × 14 inches, with or without banner. As the layout artist moves from panel to panel, a listing of the possible placements for that panel appear in the panel's window. When the appropriate choice is highlighted, it is selected, and the panel is labeled thusly (FIG. 94). The layout then represents the page contents, and is saved under its own name as a page. For ease of use and organization, Springboard suggests that photographs, panels, and pages all be saved on separate disks. One data disk will suffice and reduce disk swapping.

A completely composed page, as well as any single page element, can be sent over a modem to another computer using The Newsroom's Wire Service department (FIG. 95). Using this capability, incompatible computers can be used to generate or receive input, as well as to produce facsimile pages at remote locations.

The Pressroom provides prompts for the selection of banner, panel, photograph, or page printing. The press can be used to proof individual elements to see how they will appear when printed, or to print the entire page (FIG. 96).

In addition to providing documentation for the operation of its software, Springboard includes an annotated treatment of how to create a newspaper and how to effectively design a newspaper, as well as a glossary of newspaper terms.

FIG. 93. Fonts can be mixed within the Copy Desk panel.

FIG. 94. In the Layout department, panels and the banner are assigned page positions.

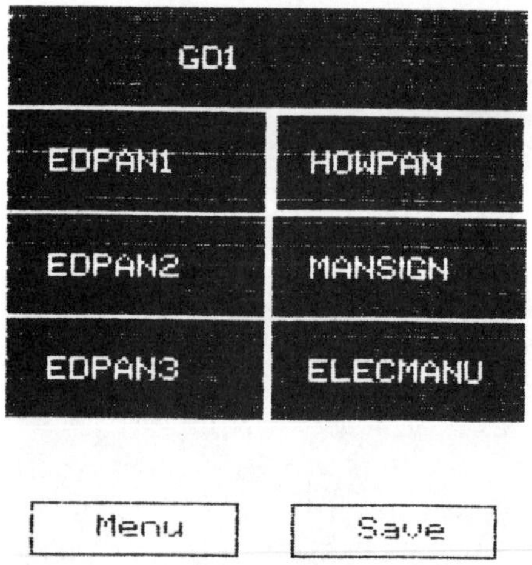

FIG. 95. The Wire Service office supports the transmission and reception of panels, photographs, and entire pages.

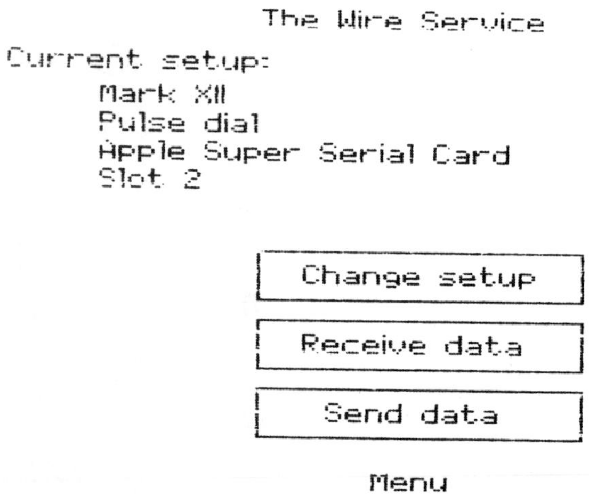

FIG. 96. A complete page made after just 1 hour of experience with the program. Notice in Column One that there are two blank lines, which should be removed. These were caused by mistakenly leaving a blank line at the bottom of the panel.

Graphic Dimensions

19 86

NEW PUBLICATIONS

Volume 1   Number 1   January, 1986

From the Editor's Desk

PC Typesetting Center

Graphic Dimensions has one of the most complete selections of books, reports, and print information covering the fields of typesetting, word/information processing, and microcomputing.

THE PERSONAL COMPOSITION REPORT (formerly

The Digest of Information on Phototypesetting) is edited by Prof. Michael Kleper of RIT, and issued ten times per year. This newsletter tracks the developments in typesetting, and the many converging technologies which are redefining its role and function in business, industry, government, and the home. Subscriptions are $40/yr. in the U.S. and $50/yr. foreign.

THE ILLUSTRATED DICTIONARY OF TYPOGRAPHIC COMMUNICATION, also by Prof. Kleper, is a 200 page book comprising almost 1000 definitions, and over 300 illustrations, covering the fields of typesetting, word/information processing, typography, computer science, photographic

processing, graphic design, and much more. The book is $19.

TYPESETTING BY MICROCOMPUTER are a set of reports on the usefulness of microcomputers in the typesetting environment, and specialized hardware and software available for implementation. The set of reports are $15.

Orders and requests for further information should be directed to:

GRAPHIC DIMENSIONS
8 Frederick Road
Pittsford, NY 14534

No phone orders please.

How to Build a BASIC TYPESETTING SYSTEM

"...an interactive tool that can reduce your alternatives, narrow your choices, and pretty much pinpoint your selection."
                    -Frank Romano
Here is the book that tells everything you need to know about every important aspect of contemporary typesetting, from system configurations to site preparation. A complete, easy to understand explanation of what a phototypesetter does and how it works with other machines to perform better and faster.

100 pp., 2 colors, 6" x 9"..................$10.00

We've added more words and pictures to our illustrated DICTIONARY!

Buy one before they are all gone.

Our Illustrated Dictionary has entered it's second printing!

Still $19.00

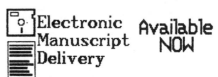
Electronic Manuscript Delivery   Available NOW

Graphic Dimensions is now soliciting manuscripts from authors who have their work on a personal computer. We have the typesetting equipment and skill to convert keyboarded files into virtually any typographic form.

We are especially interested in receiving manuscripts related to personal computing and graphic imaging.

Overhead Express:
Producing Overhead Transparencies

The traditional typesetting process has been typified by its extreme degree of flexibility. Although one typesetting process or one typesetting machine might be more efficient at producing ruled forms, tabular matter, or reverse images, in general, trade typesetting procedures are adaptable to a wide range of applications. However, the microcomputer, with its open programming environment and larger user base, has produced the opportunity for rather specialized typesetting and image-generation applications. A good example is the Overhead Express,[17] a program written for the IBM PC/XT to assist specifically in automating the production of overhead transparencies for presentation to business and professional audiences.

By defining a functional specification of such a narrow application, the program fulfills most, if not all, of the overhead projection text needs of the user. The program provides two editors: The Express, for accessing one of the 12 stored templates and a limited set of layout and design commands, and The Custom, for making custom templates and accessing the full range of Overhead Express commands.

The production of a program specifically for overhead presentations reflects a considerable effort, not only in designing a software means by which users can create their overheads, but also in analyzing the whole overhead projection scheme. This study of the types of overhead transparencies commonly used in group presentations resulted in the identification of these 12 groups:

- Budget: a listing of items with their associated costs. Dollar items are totalled.
- Bullet: a listing of items, each indicated by a small round bullet.
- Compare: two lists of text.
- Grid: a blank grid with printed annotations for hand-drawn graphs.
- List: a single list of text.
- Notes: a staggered arrangement of text.
- Outline: a progressively indented list of text.
- Prose: multiple lines of text.
- Table: a ruled form with x and y labels and their associated values.
- Title: full-width text lines.
- Window: a blank box with printed annotations used for the manual addition of a graphic or other illustration.
- 3 column: a listing of three columns of items.

Since most overhead transparencies conform to one of these groups, the user basically is prompted for the insertion of the variable text. All of the details for formatting and designing have been programmed, allowing the user to follow a simple cookbook approach to overhead production.

The Express Editor (FIG. 97) already has the appropriate commands listed in the Section Name portion of the screen. These section names indicate how the corresponding text will be handled. If multiple lines of text are to be grouped with a single section name, a plus sign is typed. After some of the text has been input, the overhead can be previewed on the screen in block form by pressing F2. The preview capability provides a rough view of how the text will appear when it is printed, and during the input process is helpful to obtain an idea of how the overhead is progressing. Pressing Return brings the user back to the editor for additional inputting. After the file has been saved, it can be reviewed on the screen in reduced, yet readable form. Any changes that need to be made can be executed by returning to the editor. If the overhead is acceptable, it is printed by selecting the "Printer" option from the Main menu. A range of dot matrix printers are supported.

---

[17]Business and Professional Software, Inc.
143 Binney Street
Cambridge, MA 02142
(617) 491-3377

Epson MX-80, FX-80, MX-100, and FX-100; IBM Graphics Printer; C.Itoh 8510, 1550, Prowriter, or Prowriter II; NEC PC-8023A-C (narrow or wide); Okidata Microline 84 Step 2; and the Apple Matrix Printer.

Both the Express and Custom Editors can make use of backslash commands. This group of 13 commands, which are input beside the text they will affect, do such things as change the font within a line, move the text right or left a number of pixels, and add shading to characters. A second set of commands, called *dot commands,* are implemented only in the Custom Editor. Dot commands are input only at the beginning of a line, are not followed by text, and stay in effect for more than a single line. Dot commands do such things as center blocks of text, draw a box of a stated size and line thickness, evenly distribute white space between lines, and allow for the input of comment (nonprinting) lines.

The typeface library (FIG. 98) consists of four designs, referred to as Classic, Popular, Script, and Modern. Each is available in three sizes, with the exception of Modern, which is provided in five sizes. The fonts are measured in dots, rather than points, with sizes ranging from 24 dots (18 dots for screen-only displayable fonts) to 75 dots. Each font consists of numerals, 26 uppercase and lowercase characters, and an assortment of punctuation. The Classic, Popular, and Modern typefaces also contain a collection of international characters. A special 21-symbol font consisting of such things as arrows, playing card symbols, boxes, circles, brackets, and stars is available in two sizes: 24 and 40 dots.

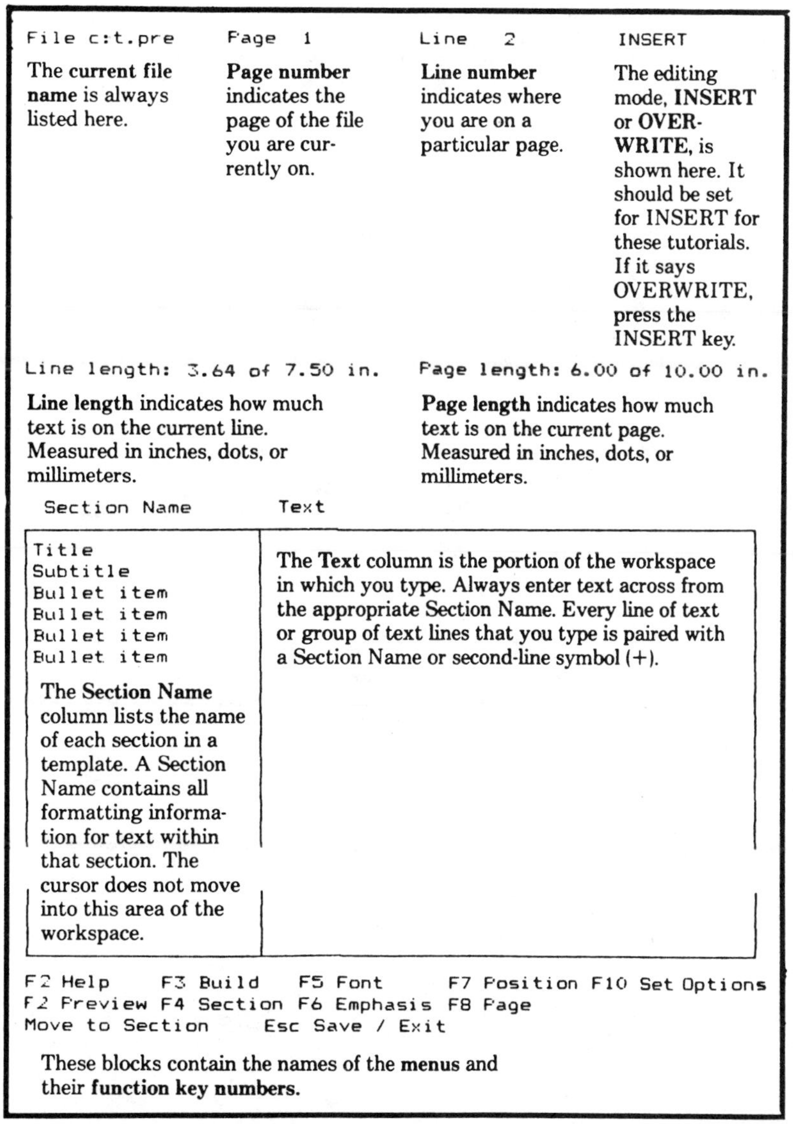

FIG. 97. A reproduction of The Overhead Express's Express Editor screen (with annotations provided by the publisher), as presented in the manual.

```
File c:t.pre      Page   1        Line    2        INSERT
```

The current file name is always listed here.

Page number indicates the page of the file you are currently on.

Line number indicates where you are on a particular page.

The editing mode, **INSERT** or **OVERWRITE**, is shown here. It should be set for INSERT for these tutorials. If it says OVERWRITE, press the INSERT key.

```
Line length: 3.64 of 7.50 in.      Page length: 6.00 of 10.00 in.
```

Line length indicates how much text is on the current line. Measured in inches, dots, or millimeters.

Page length indicates how much text is on the current page. Measured in inches, dots, or millimeters.

```
   Section Name        Text
```

```
Title
Subtitle
Bullet item
Bullet item
Bullet item
Bullet item
```

The **Text** column is the portion of the workspace in which you type. Always enter text across from the appropriate Section Name. Every line of text or group of text lines that you type is paired with a Section Name or second-line symbol (+).

The Section Name column lists the name of each section in a template. A Section Name contains all formatting information for text within that section. The cursor does not move into this area of the workspace.

```
F2 Help     F3 Build    F5 Font       F7 Position F10 Set Options
F2 Preview F4 Section F6 Emphasis F8 Page
Move to Section      Esc Save / Exit
```

These blocks contain the names of the **menus** and their **function key numbers.**

A B C D E F G H I J K L
M N O P Q R S T U V W
X Y Z
a b c d e f g h i j k l m n
o p q r s t u v w x y z
1 2 3 4 5 6 7 8 9 0
? . , ; : ! " " ' ' & • *
- + = / \ # $ % ( ) [ ]

FIG. 98. A showing of the Classic typeface with its full character complement and range of sizes.

AaBbCcDd
.font C60

AaBbCcDd
.font C60I

AaBbCcDdEeFf
.font C40

AaBbCcDdEe
.font C40I

AaBbCcDdEeFfGgHhIi
.font C24

AaBbCcDdEeFfGgHhIi
.font C24I

In addition to its main objective of producing overhead transparencies, The Overhead Express can be used to prepare presentations for display on the computer screen (FIG. 99). Many of the same commands used for controlling the printer can be used for a screen presentation. There are also a small set of commands reserved specifically for screen shows. These commands result in such actions as automatically ending the screen show, reversing the current screen lighting, and causing a delay, or pause, in the screen show.

The command structure of The Overhead Express provides additional flexibility, which is suggested by a number of advanced examples provided on the program disk (FIG. 100). These examples show how to produce complex borders, shadowed boxes, nested boxes, filled-in election boxes, bar charts and graphs, *x* and *y* matrices, organizational charts, a screen display with a moving hand-shaped pointer, and such typographic effects as hollow type, shadow type, white-over-black type, white-over-gray type, and black-over-gray type. It is suggested that the user study the coding used in these examples in order to create similar special effects for himself.

FIG. 99. An example of the coding (along the left) and the resultant screen display (on the right) produced with The Overhead Express's "Screen Show" option.

```
.page screen
.font C40 C40I
.scroll c s 40
.down 80
Comfortable Chair
International
.down 40
.wait 2
WELCOMES \ U YOU!
.wait 3
.page screen
.font C40
.elastic
Open House
.wait 1
.reverse
.wait 3
.elastic
.page screen
.font C24
.down 30
.box
.left
.block
Date: April 12
Time: 2:00 p.m. to
  5:00 p.m.
Place: Our Downtown
  Store
.block end
.box end
.wait 5
.page screen
.font C40
.elastic
See you there!
.elastic
.wait 3
```

Comfortable Chair International

WELCOMES YOU!

Open House

Date: April 12
Time 2:00 p.m. to 5:00 p.m.
Place: Our Downtown Store

See you there!

FIG. 100. Samples of the more complex designs produced by following the advanced coding examples provided on the program disk. Notice how reducing the size of these samples sharpens the edges of the characters that are shown in full size in FIG. 98.

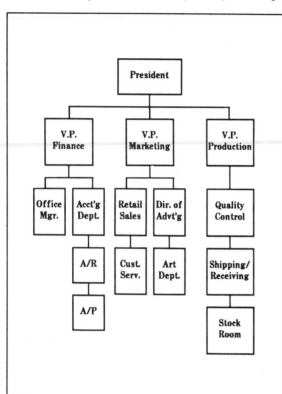

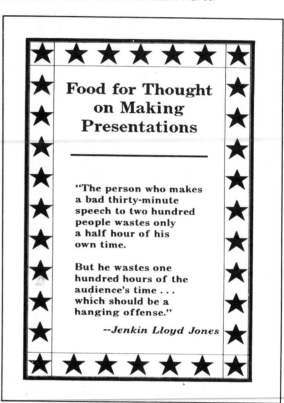

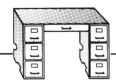

THE GRAPHIC SOLUTION:
Animating the Typographic Form

Using the microcomputer screen as a presentation palette, as opposed to the direct output of text via a printer or the postprocessing of text via a typesetter, makes possible a number of typographic capabilities that static images cannot produce. Animation, texture, color, three-dimensional drawings, sound, and the free interaction of text and graphics all combine to form an exciting alternative to paper-based output.

Capturing the images from a microcomputer screen requires a certain amount of technical expertise. In many cases, programs that have the capability of generating *slides*, or animation sequences, promote the use of the computer as the final medium of presentation. The microcomputer can serve as an automatic slide projector, sequencing a number of screen images in a prescribed order and for prescribed intervals of time. A number of slide projector programs are available that allow the user to generate screen images using other compatible graphics programs, save them on disk, and then combine them for presentation.

Using a microcomputer as a dedicated presentation system is not always economically feasible, nor universally convenient. Two more common means of rendering the screen images transportable are either by recording them using still photographic techniques, such as a tripod-mounted 35mm camera or a specialized on-line computer camera, or by recording them using video tape equipment. Trade services are also available to convert the images that have been recorded on computer-generated magnetic media into other presentation formats.

The graphics capabilities of the Apple II series of microcomputers have made them a popular choice for software designers. Many programs are available to create, manipulate, combine, and display graphics and text in a vast variety of ways. One program that provides the user with the ability to both draw shapes and make them move is TGS: The Graphic Solution.[18]

The purpose of TGS is best expressed by the first two sentences in the manual: "TGS is a sophisticated graphics editor and animation system for combining graphics and text in a manner similar to making a moving film. The 'actors' are state-of-the-art bit-map shapes that you build with simple keyboard commands."

The ability to animate ideas rather than be limited to static images makes the package particularly useful for generating training aids, educational materials, sales presentations, product demonstrations, animated title screens, film story boards, process flow diagrams, and more.

The main TGS menu (FIG. 101) presents the major options available to the user. From this point it is possible to load in a previously saved graphic sequence; create a new graphic sequence, or continue working on one that has been loaded; save a graphic sequence that the TGS projector can show; load in a background, which can be any standard Apple DOS 3.3 graphic file; save the current high-resolution screen as a background; draw a circle of any size anywhere on the hi-res screen; save the projector module on a user disk in order to show recorded sequences independent of the program; catalog the active disk; and delete files from the user disk. The user also can quit or enter page 2 of the menu, which provides access to: printing the hi-res screen; appending sequences (splicing); running the TGS expansion module, which supports the use of a specific hardware device, such as a light pen, or the performance of a specific additional task; or returning to the Main menu or quitting.

The creation of an animation sequence is similar to that required in conventional animation. Each minor change in the position of a shape must be drawn meticulously in order to produce smooth movement. Each stage of an animated shape can be devised by plotting, erasing, moving, expanding, contracting, and scrolling individual pixels.

[18]Accent Software
3750 Wright Place
Palo Alto, CA 94306
(415) 856-6505

When the individual shape is complete, it is "shot" like a frame in a film. The shape is altered slightly to suggest the next movement, then shot again. This process continues until the entire sequence is complete. This repetitive operation is simplified by a built-in macro capability, which lets the user define a series of common steps into a single key. By carefully planning the execution of movement, even complicated motion like walking can be achieved (FIG. 102).

The keyboard mapped-text capabilities of TGS are limited to a single character set, in normal and inverse video versions, although new character shapes created with TGS or other compatible programs can be used. Like other shapes, text can be animated, and like other graphic shapes can be used within Applesoft programs for a wide variety of purposes.

An additional, larger character set is provided for use with TGS as a set of shapes (FIG. 103). These shapes are manipulated in the same way as other TGS shapes. The precise placement of these letter shapes makes exact character fit, for proportional spacing and other typographic considerations, quite easy to achieve.

In addition to its prime function as an animation system, TGS is an effective graphics editor, which can process graphic screens produced by most other standard Apple graphics programs. Text, color, texture, and other graphic enhancements can be added to graphic screens created in other program environments (FIG. 104).

```
            TGS MAIN MENU

        1. LOAD SEQUENCE
        2. CREATE SEQUENCE
        3. SAVE SEQUENCE
        4. LOAD BACKGROUND
        5. SAVE BACKGROUND
        6. DRAW CIRCLES
        7. SAVE PROJECTOR
        8. CATALOG
        9. DELETE FILE
        Q. QUIT/MENU PAGE 2
        SELECT OPTION # >
```

FIG. 101. The Main TGS menu provides a brief overview of the program's capabilities. The manual provides short Applesoft programs, which can be integrated within users' programs in order to utilize animation sequences produced with the TGS.

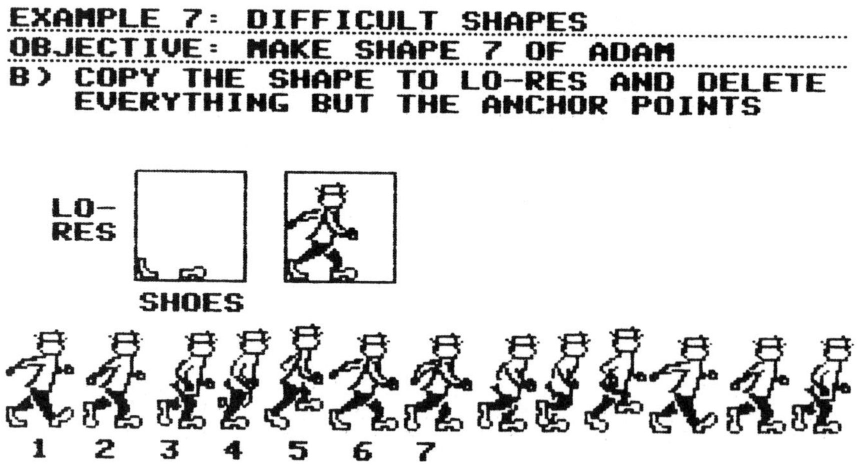

EXAMPLE 7: DIFFICULT SHAPES
OBJECTIVE: MAKE SHAPE 7 OF ADAM
B) COPY THE SHAPE TO LO-RES AND DELETE EVERYTHING BUT THE ANCHOR POINTS

FIG. 102. Animation sequences are conceived and produced in a fashion similar to animated cartoons. A series of repetitious movements can be saved as a macro.

FIG. 103. The larger, special character set is composed of a set of character shapes that can be animated.

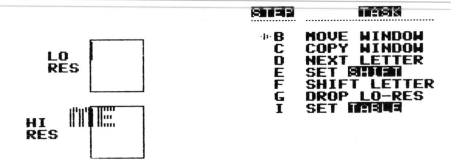

EXAMPLE 1: SPECIAL CHARACTER SETS
TASK: WRITE "MEMO"
(J): REPEAT ALL STEPS UNTIL DONE:

STEP	TASK
B	MOVE WINDOW
C	COPY WINDOW
D	NEXT LETTER
E	SET SHIFT
F	SHIFT LETTER
G	DROP LO-RES
I	SET TABLE

FIG. 104. A two-dimensional bar chart that has been converted to three dimensions using the graphic facilities of the TGS. Static graphic images such as this can be printed out on paper, a facility that is built into the program.

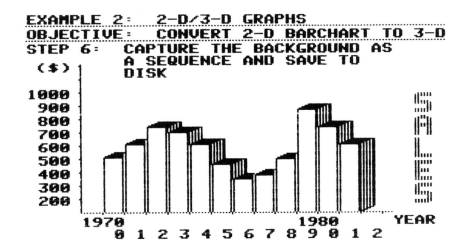

EXAMPLE 2: 2-D/3-D GRAPHS
OBJECTIVE: CONVERT 2-D BARCHART TO 3-D
STEP 6: CAPTURE THE BACKGROUND AS A SEQUENCE AND SAVE TO DISK

PYXEL VISUALS:
Creating Screen Displays for Presentations

In business, in science, in education, in government, in industry—in almost all areas of human endeavor, the graphic presentation of information is one of the most effective ways of communicating ideas, facts, and concepts. Within this realm, paper-based communications promises to remain as the dominant delivery system because it is easily afforded, easily transported, easily stored, easily imaged, easily altered, easily duplicated, and easily destroyed.

The microcomputer can be used as an electronic slate that can be edited, altered, and otherwise manipulated until all typographic and line graphic elements are satisfactorily selected and positioned. A software package that provides such capabilities is Pyxel Visuals,[19] for the IBM PC. This program gives the user the capability of creating screen displays for output on paper or as part of a screen presentation show.

The Visuals program makes use of the function keys available on the computer (FIG. 105). These dedicated keys provide the user with on-line help, disk access (to load or save an image), editing capabilities, the specification of simple typographic parameters, and the creation of lines.

[19]Pyxel Applications
2917 Mohawk Drive
Richmond, VA 23235
(804) 320-5573

Hardware and software requirements include an IBM PC, XT, or compatible; 128K RAM; PC-DOS 1.0, 1.1, OR 2.0; IBM Color/Graphics Adapter or compatible board; Graphics Monitor (color or monochrome); 1 disk drive (2 recommended); IBM Graphics Printer or Epson printer with Graftrax.

The first step in the creation of any visual should be a rough sketch that includes the text content (or specific references to it), gross indications of the placement of each graphic element, and clear indications of the relative size of each graphic element (FIG. 106).

FIG. 105. The Main Pyxel Visuals menu displays the values assigned to the ten function keys.

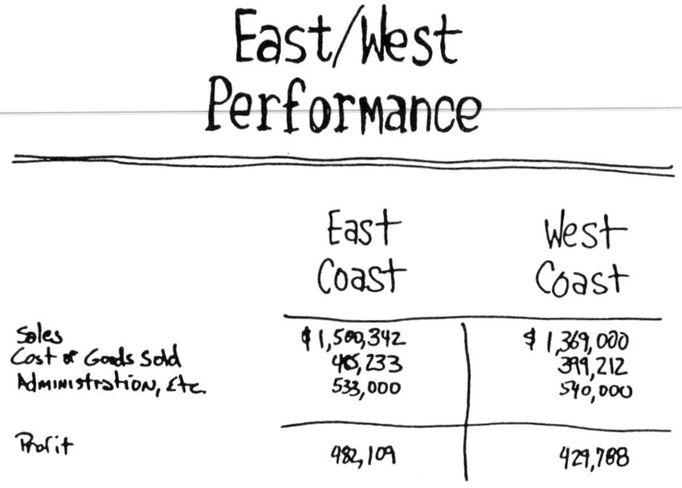

```
        Function Key Definitions
   F 1   NEW  -  Start developing new screen
   F 2   DISP -  Display Current Screen
   F 3   MOVE -  Move text lines to new positions
   F 4   LINE -  Draw lines using the cursor keys
   F 5   EDIT -  Edit or Add Text, Change Text Size
   F 6   SAVE -  Save present screen to disk
   F 7   LOAD -  Load previously saved screen
   F 8   PRINT-  Print Graphic screen on printer
   F 9   HELP -  Help in understanding an operation
   F 10  END  -  Stop execution of this program

       Select Option Via Function Keys
1 NEW  2 DISP  3 MOVE  4 LINE  5 EDIT  6 SAVE  7 LOAD  8 PRINT  9 HELP  10 END
```

FIG. 106. A rough sketch of a simple job, which could be produced as a screen display, report table, overhead visual, or presentation exhibit. Its overall shape conforms to the proportions of the computer screen.

To initiate a new screen, the F1, "NEW," key is pressed, resulting in the display of three lines on the monitor:

Line 1:

Character size:

/\

(Press "Esc" to EXIT)   24 Lines available for Text

The cursor appears beside the character size, awaiting the input of a number between 1 and 4. Each successive number larger than 1 is twice as big as its predecessor (FIG. 107). For this example, size 3 is appropriate for the first line. After the size has been selected, the prompt *Text:* is displayed on the next line. It is followed by a highlighted area, which shows the number of characters of the chosen size that will fit on the line. Below the highlighted area is a "ruler," marked with a caret at every fifth position, and a number at every tenth. The ruler assists in the alignment of vertical rows of information such as are found in FIG. 106.

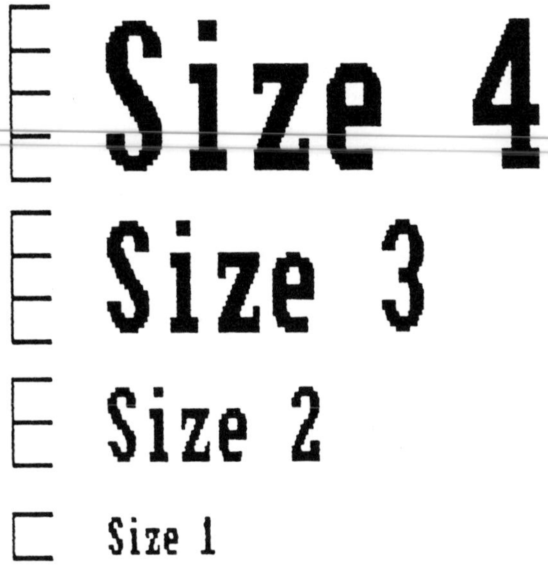

FIG. 107. The four sizes of type available. The size of the type also relates directly to the number of screen lines that it occupies.

Size 4

Size 3

Size 2

Size 1

After the first line of text has been input, the top of the screen will look like the following:

Line 1:

Character size: 3
Text: East/West
- - - - ^ - - - - 1 - - - - ^ - - - - 2 - - - - ^ -

Line 2:

Character size:

The same procedure is used to input all of the textual material. As each line is input, an indicator at the bottom of the screen displays the remaining number of lines available.

After the text input process has been completed, the user has the option of editing any of the information, saving the text to disk, or erasing it from memory and starting over. Assuming that all is correct, pressing the F2 key will display the information in its specified form (FIG. 108). In the Display mode, the uses of the function keys are altered: F1 provides access to the previously highlighted line, F2 moves to the next line, and F3 moves blocks of copy.

The cursor keys act on the highlighted line, moving it in any compass direction in increments of approximately 1/4 inch. Finer increments, composed of single pixels, are obtainable by holding down the Shift key while using any of the cursor movement keys. Using these procedures, the example can be manipulated to take the form shown in FIG. 109.

The example calls for the inclusion of lines, which can be added by entering the Line mode (F4). The Line mode redefines F1 as the line start indicator, F2 as the line end indicator, and F3 as the delete line function. Again, the cursor keys are used for positioning, in this case, moving a cross-hair around the screen.

Lines are formed by first positioning the cross-hair at the start of the line, pressing F1 to mark it, moving the cursor to form the line, and pressing F2 to end it. In this way, horizontal, vertical, and diagonal lines can be formed. Simple illustrations can be constructed of line segments and moved to any location on the screen. If an error is made, it is easily erased by pressing F3.

When the F3 key is pressed, it reassigns the functions of the F1 and F2 keys. F1 provides the user with access to the previously drawn line, while F2 highlights the line next in sequence to the current line selected. F3 deletes any line that is currently highlighted.

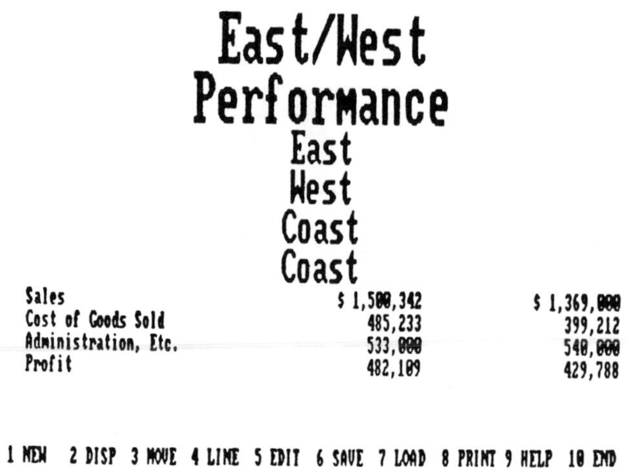

East/West
Performance
East
West
Coast
Coast

Sales	$ 1,500,342	$ 1,369,000
Cost of Goods Sold	485,233	399,212
Administration, Etc.	533,000	540,000
Profit	402,109	429,788

1 NEW 2 DISP 3 MOVE 4 LINE 5 EDIT 6 SAVE 7 LOAD 8 PRINT 9 HELP 10 END

FIG. 108. The unedited screen presentation of the textual input.

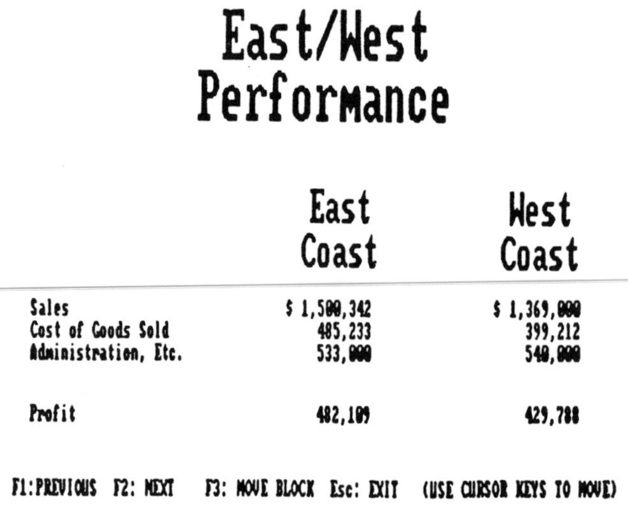

East/West
Performance

	East Coast	West Coast
Sales	$ 1,500,342	$ 1,369,000
Cost of Goods Sold	485,233	399,212
Administration, Etc.	533,000	540,000
Profit	402,109	429,788

F1:PREVIOUS F2: NEXT   F3: MOVE BLOCK Esc: EXIT   (USE CURSOR KEYS TO MOVE)

FIG. 109. The cursor keys are used to move highlighted items to their proper positions.

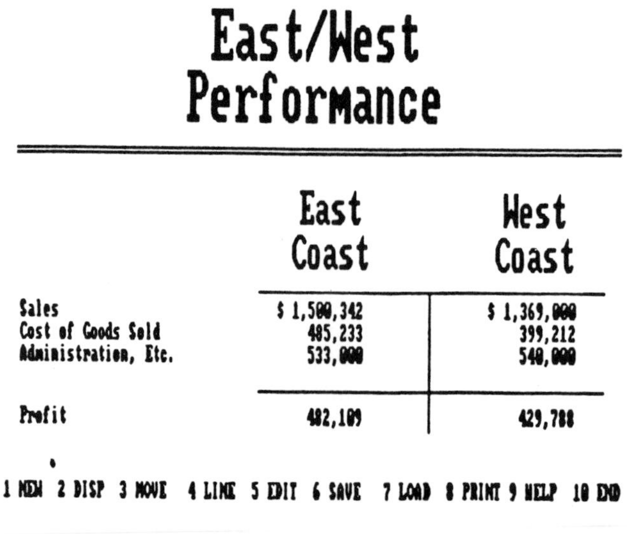

East/West
Performance

	East Coast	West Coast
Sales	$ 1,500,342	$ 1,369,000
Cost of Goods Sold	485,233	399,212
Administration, Etc.	533,000	540,000
Profit	402,109	429,788

1 NEW 2 DISP 3 MOVE 4 LINE 5 EDIT 6 SAVE 7 LOAD 8 PRINT 9 HELP 10 END

FIG. 110. The beginning and ending positions of lines are indicated by pressing appropriate function keys. The lines themselves are generated by using the cursor keys.

Any portion of the text or line construction area can be moved. Single or multiple text lines can be specified using function keys active in the Move mode. Areas composed of lines or lines and text areas must be moved using the "Move Block" function. In the "Move Block" mode, a cross-hair is moved around the required area to indicate corners of the area to be moved. An outlined area is created, which can be moved by pressing the appropriate cursor keys.

The completed job (FIG. 110) can be saved on disk and printed. The printing options include a Vertical format (for report covers and overhead transparencies) and a Horizontal format (for signs and displays). The Horizontal format produces a larger image and also has the option of printing a *dense horizontal,* which results in a considerably darker character image and a significantly slower printer output rate.

The printed appearance of the visuals can be enhanced through the use of a companion program called Batchprint, also published by Pyxel Applications. This program provides for the printing of visuals in high resolution and with proportional spacing. Up to 42 screens can be printed as a batch, either in Vertical or Horizontal mode. Four print modes are available: Low Resolution Medium, composed of 72 dots per inch vertically and 120 dots per inch horizontally; Low Resolution bold, composed of 72 dots per inch vertically and 120 dots per inch horizontally; High Resolution Medium, composed of 216 dots per inch vertically and 120 dots per inch horizontally; and High Resolution Bold, composed of 216 dots per inch vertically and 120 dots per inch horizontally (FIG. 111).

FIG. 111. Four print-resolution levels are available. The higher the resolution is and the bolder the characters are, the slower the printer output rate is.

Low Res Med
Low Res Bold
High Res Med
High Res Bold

DATABASE TYPESETTING

The objective of the typesetting process traditionally has been the conversion of hand and typewritten copy into typeset output. This function has dealt only with the form of the output, and not at all with its content. The value that typesetting adds is almost totally appearance-related: more aesthetic, less space-consuming, and easier to read. One of the most powerful applications in which microcomputers can serve as an adjunct to the typesetting operation is in the area of *database* manipulation. A database is a set or body of numeric or textual information that is manipulated by a storage, retrieval, and processing system, such as that provided by a microcomputer. Familiar database applications are such things as telephone directories, parts catalogs, and real estate listings.

When database processing is combined with typesetting output, the whole becomes greater than the sum of its parts. Not only will the report generated by the computer not have to be retyped, as is still common in many situations, but the completed typeset product accrues value in both form and content. Take for example a database composed of members of a large public service organization. The individual records might be composed of items or fields indicating such descriptors as name, title, address, city, state, zip code, telephone number, chapter, region, office held, committee memberships, and original membership date.

Implicit in a database computer program are the abilities to sort and select information on the basis of a specific set of requirements. A membership roster might be composed of member names, mailing addresses, and telephone numbers. A national directory might have five major sections: one listing members alphabetically, another listing them geographically, a third listing only officers, a fourth listing committees, and a fifth listing members of long standing, such as 5-, 10-, and 15-year anniversaries. For a convention, a listing of attendees might be generated as well as typeset name badges.

Database programs also usually provide for some kind of calculations, and so this fictitious directory might also provide for membership subtotals by chapter, by state, and by region, as well as a grand total for the membership as a whole.

DEVISING THE DATABASE

There are numerous database programs available for microcomputers. However, their usefulness for typesetting applications is not only dependent upon their suitability for accomplishing specific tasks, but also upon their compatibility with the related software and hardware necessary for passing the data from the computer environment to that of the typesetter.

One package that has been found useful for the typesetting of noncomplex database reports is the Incredible Jack program published by Pecan Software Systems, Inc.[20] The program, available in versions for the Apple II, II+, and IIe, and the IBM PC, is a combined word processor and database manager. For the following application, the Apple version was used.

As a test application, a list of keywords used in the 1983 edition of *The Digest of Information on Phototypesetting* was generated (FIG. 112). Each record contained fields for the keyword, the page on which it appeared, and the volume and issue numbers. The objective was to produce two listings: one sorted alphabetically by keyword, the other sorted numerically by volume and issue number.

The creation of the Incredible Jack form for entering keyword information was a simple procedure. The title of each field was typed, followed by a colon. The colon is used to indicate the end of a field, and the program automatically generates its own end-of-field indicator—a caret. If the caret which the program generates does not provide sufficient space for the typical entry, the user can override it and extend the field size to suit specific requirements.

[20]Pecan Software Systems, Inc.
1410 39th Street
Brooklyn, NY 11218
(718) 851-3100
(800) 45-PECAN

FIG. 112. These two typeset reports (A and B) were generated from the same database. In each case, the Report Formatting capability of the database program sorted the information according to the form needed by the user.

THE DIGEST OF INFORMATION ON PHOTOTYPESETTING
1983 Key Word Index

THE DIGEST OF INFORMATION ON PHOTOTYPESETTING
KEYWORD INDEX BY ISSUE 1983

After the form is defined, it is saved on disk. It can then be used to enter records. In this exercise, each keyword occupied one record. As the information for a record was completed, the record was saved on disk. The keyword database thus was composed of 625 entries or records.

Specifying the manner in which the output was to appear was accomplished using Jack Report, a companion program to The Incredible Jack. The report component provides for the selection of fields, the order in which they will appear, and field calculations such as column totals, averages, or item counts.

For the first report the keyword was input as the first column, the volume/issue as the second, and the page number as the third. No calculations were specified.

Up to this point the procedures used to create the database are identical to the manner and methods used to produce a database report destined for output on a line printer. In many instances such a report would be sent to a typesetter for complete rekeyboarding.

The critical difference occurs in the print subsystem where the final report will be sorted based on the selection criteria previously completed. Reports are output directly to the printer and are not written to disk; therefore the report must be transmitted directly to the typesetter in order to capture the keystrokes. Database programs that can write reports to disk are more flexible in bridging their output to a typesetting machine.

The Jack Report program is written in the Pascal programming language and expects to find the printer card located in slot 1 of the Apple. Because that destination could not be changed, a serial communications card was placed in that location. An RS-232 connection between the serial card and a computer-to-typesetter interface was made connecting it to a Compugraphic EditWriter 7500.[21] To both the Jack Report and the Apple, the EditWriter would look exactly like a printer.

In order to activate the interface, a short code was inserted preceding the alphanumeric data. The Jack Report conveniently allows for the addition of a title to be input just prior to the generation of the report. All of the commands required by the interface can be input in the title area.

The interface allows for character and code conversions, so the soft returns used by The Jack Report for its line printer output can be translated into "Flush Left, Return" commands on the typesetter. The design of the interface command language provides for considerable flexibility in the typographic formatting possibilities.

When the "Print" command of the Jack Report is executed, it starts the sort procedure based upon the column criteria that were selected. When the sort is complete, the program halts and displays a message indicating that the report is ready for printing.

The EditWriter is prepared by simply entering a set of parameters; that is, type size, line space, font, and line measure.

The report is output from Apple by touching the Return key. The data exits through the serial card. Since the title is the first string of characters that exit from the Apple, the command to activate the interface is sensed and the report begins to appear on the EditWriter screen.

After the report is completely transmitted, it is saved on the EditWriter disk and typeset. Additional editing also could be accomplished directly at the EditWriter keyboard.

Although this example is fairly simple and can be accomplished with reasonably priced hardware and software, it is significant to note that database applications typically are not performed by native typesetting systems. The software that is sold with such systems is specifically for the generation of traditional typesetting work, and not for the manipulation of information into forms previously unspecified by the copy originator. The ability to alter the form of a set of data and typeset it to meet specific requirements provides the typesetter with a salable service, not only in terms of the actual typeset product, but also in terms of fulfilling the role of a database manager: maintaining databases to meet clients' needs.

---

[21]Compugraphic Corp.
80 Industrial Way
Wilmington, MA 01887
(313) 536-1300

DOT MATRIX TYPESETTING: PRINTER UTILITIES

Dot matrix printers are manufactured with a limited number of sets of characters provided in ROM. By using control codes embedded in output files or in initialization sequences, these character sets can be accessed and combined with one another to provide some small degree of visual variety. The extent of the range of character set choices usually is limited to a roman face, a bold, an italic, and an underline version, and possibly a mix of these, such as a bold italic or an underlined bold (FIG. 113). These character sets almost always are monospaced, although many provide proportionally spaced character sets.

Because these character sets are not user-redefinable, the only way in which dot matrix printers can be utilized to output higher quality typographic images is through the use of bit-mapping, wherein a part of the computer's memory is converted by the printer's graphic interpreter as a series of printable dots, rather than as a series of predefined printable characters.

FIG. 113. A representative sample of the resident character sets on the Epson FX-80.

```
NORMAL type                    SUPERSCRIPT type

DOUBLE width                   SUBSCRIPT type

COMPRESSED width               SUPERSCRIPT compressed

DOUBLE width compressed        SUBSCRIPT compressed

DOUBLE strike                  UNDERLINED characters

EMPHASIZED type                ITALICS type

DOUBLE strike emphasized       DOUBLE width

                               COMPRESSED type
```

FONT DOWNLOADER AND EDITOR:
Downloading Character Sets to a Printer's Memory

A feature of some dot matrix printers is the provision for the installation of a user-designed character set. These character sets are designed and edited at the microcomputer, usually saved on disk, and then downloaded to the printer where they reside until the printer is turned off. An example of such a printer utility is the Font Downloader and Editor,[22] which provides this capability to many printers, such as the Apple Matrix Printer, the Prowriter, the OKI Microline 92, 93, 84 Step II, and the Epson FX printer, when driven by any member of the Apple II family of microcomputers.

The Font Downloader and Editor is a menu-driven system for designing an unlimited number of character sets, special symbols, patterns, or design pieces that will reside in the printer and be output as needed, most often when outputting a word processing file. After booting the disk a six-item menu is displayed (FIG. 114). The "Demo," number 3, would be the first selection made by a new user. Another menu of choices, in this case the four fonts that are supplied with the program, is presented (FIG. 115). One of the Demo fonts is loaded (FIG. 116), and its entire character set is printed by selecting menu item **5**. The Main menu is accessed by selecting item **0**.

The entire set of instructions is supplied on disk and is displayed on the screen

[22]Micro Ware
P.O. Box 113
Pompton Plains, NJ 07444
(201) 838-9027

```
FONT DOWNLOADER & EDITOR
   FOR EPSON FX80 & FX100

COPYRIGHT 1983  RAK-WARE


0 . . . EXIT

1 . . . DOWNLOAD FONT

2 . . . EDIT FONT

3 . . . RUN DEMO

4 . . . INSTRUCTIONS

5 . . . CONFIGURE I/F
        (WIZARD)

        SELECT:
```

FIG. 114. As the second line indicates, the Main menu shows the particular printers that the program has been customized to drive.

```
    FONT DOWNLOADER DEMO

0 . . . EXIT

1 . . . DOWNLOAD FONT.1

2 . . . DOWNLOAD FONT.2

3 . . . DOWNLOAD FONT.3

4 . . . DOWNLOAD FONT.4

5 . . . PRINT CHARACTERS

6 . . . PRINT TEXT

        SELECT:
```

FIG. 115. Four fonts are provided on the program disk. Micro Ware provides monetary incentives to users for user-designed fonts that it deems suitable for publication.

```
      FONT DOWNLOADER



ENTER FONT FILE NAME

    OR 0 TO EXIT


FONT.4?_____
```

FIG. 116. The font to be downloaded to the printer is specified on this screen.

or printed out by selecting option **4.** The main business part of the program is the editor, which is entered by selecting option **2.** Font 1 is loaded automatically and displayed in the largest part of the Editor window. Each character can be redesigned and replaced on the disk to form an entirely new character set. The Font Editor screen (FIG. 117) consists of the font set display, a square-box selection cursor, a character matrix display (upper right), and a message area on the bottom. An explanation of the avail-

FIG. 117. The Font Editor screen displays an entire font, as well as an interactive editing matrix.

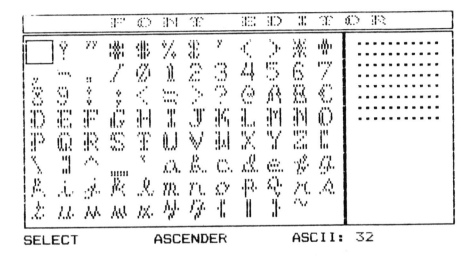

FIG. 118. Commands available in the Select mode.

VALID COMMANDS IN SELECT MODE

\<ESC\>	ENTERS EDIT MODE
I J K M	CHARACTER SELECT
\<RTN\>	MOVES CURSOR TO NEXT CHAR
R	REPLACE CHAR – ENTER EDIT
L	LOAD FONT FROM DISK
S	SAVE FONT TO DISK
D	DOWNLOAD FONT TO PRINTER
T	TOGGLE SOUND ON/OFF
Q	QUIT EDITOR

ANY KEY CONTINUES

able commands is provided by typing a **?** (FIG. 118). As each character is selected, it is displayed in the matrix window and another cursor becomes active, permitting the addition or subtraction of individual pixels. Help is again provided by typing a **?** (FIG. 119). This process allows the user to redesign characters or map entirely new character images to given ASCII identities (FIG. 120). By so doing, a special application character set—such as a foreign language, scientific, mathematical, or hobby set—could be devised. Furthermore, an entirely new keyboard arrangement, such as the Dvorak, could be produced easily.

The Font Downloader and Editor also provides two other useful capabilities in the Editor mode. The first allows the user to copy the outline of one character to use as a frame upon which to build a second character (FIG. 121). The second capability permits the user to shift the position of the entire character one dot in any direction (FIG. 122).

In practical use, the Font Downloader and Editor would be used prior to the loading of the word processing program. After the custom character set is loaded, it, as well as other built-in character sets, can be accessed through the use of control characters embedded in the word processing text file. A comparison of a normal set of characters and a custom set is shown in FIG. 123.

```
          VALID COMMANDS IN EDIT MODE
    <ESC>       ENTERS SELECT MODE

         I
    J    K       DOT SELECT
         M

    <RTN>       MOVES CURSOR TO NEXT DOT

      R         REPLACE CHAR - ENTER SELECT

      C         CLEAR EDIT AREA

      X         CLEAR WITH TRACE

      S         SHIFT CHAR 1 DOT

      T         TOGGLE DESCENDER/ASCENDER

    <SPC>       TOGGLE DOT ON/OFF

                ANY KEY CONTINUES
```

FIG. 119. Commands available in the Edit mode.

FIG. 120. The top screen shows the letter *J* as it appears in FONT . 1 supplied on the program disk. The bottom screen shows a modified *J*.

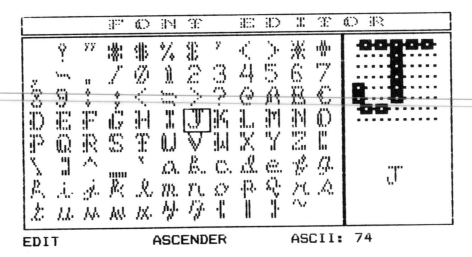

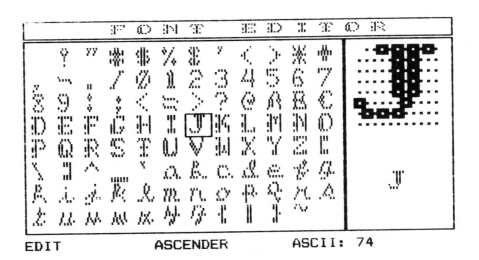

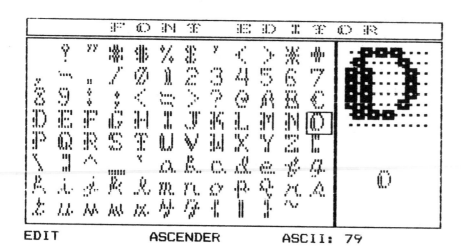

EDIT   ASCENDER   ASCII: 79

TYPE ? FOR HELP

FIG. 121. These three screens show how the shape of the letter *O* is used to form the outline of the letter *Q*. In the top screen, the letter *O* has been selected. In the middle screen, it has been placed in the Trace mode. In the bottom screen, the letter *Q* has been constructed partially.

EDIT   DESCENDER   ASCII: 79

TYPE ? FOR HELP

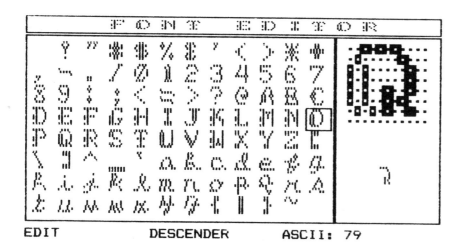

EDIT   DESCENDER   ASCII: 79

TYPE ? FOR HELP

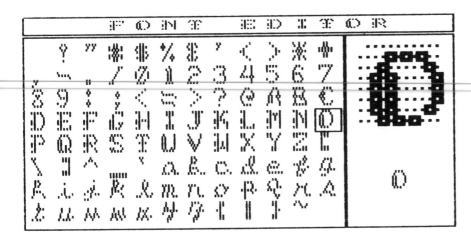

USE I,J,K,M KEYS FOR SHIFT DIRECTION

FIG. 122. The letter *O* shifted two dots to the right (top) and then one dot downward (bottom).

USE I,J,K,M KEYS FOR SHIFT DIRECTION

FIG. 123 (below). A comparison of normal printer output (left) and customized (right). Notice that the customized characters also take advantage of the display variations (underlined, bold, proportional, etc.) inherent in the host printer.

	BUILT-IN	CUSTOM
10CPI:	AaBbCcDdEeFfGgHhIiJjKk	AaBbCcDdEeFfGgHhIiJjKk
12CPI:	AaBbCcDdEeFfGgHhIiJjKk	AaBbCcDdEeFfGgHhIiJjKk
17CPI:	AaBbCcDdEeFfGgHhIiJjKk	AaBbCcDdEeFfGgHhIiJjKk
5CPI:	AaBbCcDdEeFf	AaBbCcDdEeFf
6CPI:	AaBbCcDdEeFf	AaBbCcDdEeFf
8CPI:	AaBbCcDdEeFf	AaBbCcDdEeFf

And let's not forget Enhanced and Underlined printing as well...

AaBbCcDdEeFfGgHhIiJjKk
AaBbCcDdEeFfGgHhIiJjKk

AaBbCcDdEeFfGgHhIiJjKk
AaBbCcDdEeFfGgHhIiJjKk

PRINTWORKS:
Controlling a Printer for a Variety of Application Needs

For many personal computer users, the only "typeset" output they will ever generate is that which is obtainable from a dot matrix printer. Although the typographic versatility of such devices continues to increase, the ease of accessing print appearance capabilities often is difficult or awkward. Printworks[23] is a program that provides complete control of over 30 dot matrix printers used by IBM PC and compatibles users.

Printworks is composed of a series of programs and files, which can be installed on a wide variety of applications program disks to provide printer control for word processing, spreadsheets, databases, and other programs that typically have printed output. Printwork's menu-driven design makes it easy to set up and alter.

The main Printworks menu (FIG. 124), accessible by typing **pw.exe** or more conveniently by creating an autoexec file that would automatically present the menu to the user each time the disk is booted, provides a simple interface to the printer. A multiple-line message area running along the bottom of the screen presents information on how to initiate various functions or what the result of a selection would be.

The standard menu presents access to both the standard printer modes, such as italic, emphasized, condensed, doublestrike, and wide, as well as to advanced capabilities, such as loading a graphic font—either one supplied with the program, or one created with the program's font editor. The routine printer control options include:

- Condensed: prints a typeface approximately 3/5 as wide as normal characters, comprising about 17 characters per inch.
- Doublestrike: prints a darker character by striking each character twice.
- Emphasized or Enhanced: prints a bold character by striking each character a second time slightly offset to the right.
- Overstrike: prints a better defined character by striking each character a second time, slightly offset and slightly lower.
- Wide or Enlarged: prints characters approximately twice the current character width.

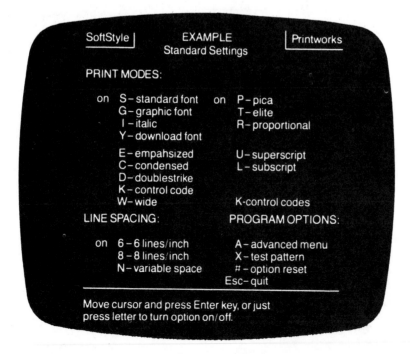

FIG. 124. The standard Printworks menu provides a simple user interface for controlling dot matrix printer features.

[23]SoftStyle, Inc.
7192 Kalanianaole Highway, Suite 205
Honolulu, HI 966825
(808) 396-6368

Supported printer manufacturers include IBM, Epson, Okidata, C.Itoh, and Star Micronics.

At any point during the set-up procedure, the settings may be proofed on the printer by selecting "X-test pattern." This option results in the printing of two lines of a specimen in the typeface that is specified.

When a graphic font is specified, the user is prompted next for the name of the text file that is to be printed. The name may be typed or the directory may be displayed, file by file, until the necessary file is located. If no file is specified, the graphic font remains the default font for printing. In most instances, the Printworks menu would be quit after making printer set-up selections, and the choices would remain active until the computer was rebooted or turned off. Therefore, whatever successive applications programs were used would benefit from the Printworks settings.

An advanced menu of capabilities is accessed from the standard menu by typing **A**. The advanced menu (FIG. 125) contains control settings for forms control (margin settings, number of lines per page, etc.), foreign language character sets, typewriter mode, and *pivot printing,* which uses special character sets to print information vertically rather than horizontally.

In terms of typesetting, the most interesting features of the program are the Font Editor and the graphic fonts that are supplied on the second of the two program disks (FIG. 126). Fonts can be devised from scratch, formed by editing existing fonts, or formed from the merger of two or more existing fonts.

Characters in a font are identified by their character positions within the ASCII code set. In ASCII, there are 256 codes, which can be used to represent printable characters. Although the ASCII code set is recognized as standard, only the character codes in the range of 32 to 127 generally are regarded as industry standards. The other ASCII code values are not necessarily applied uniformly.

The manufacturer of a dot matrix printer uses various sizes of dot matrices to form the printer's character set. The size of the dot matrix might vary from 11 × 7 to 37 × 24 dots (FIG. 127). At the time of manufacture, a dot pattern is assigned to each ASCII code. The font editor provides the means to change that dot pattern assignment.

FIG. 125. The advanced Printworks menu offers quick access to forms control, foreign language character sets, and the additional print modes of pivot (vertical) printing and real-time typewriting.

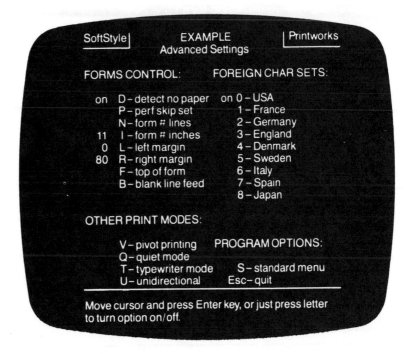

SoftStyle | EXAMPLE | Printworks
Advanced Settings

FORMS CONTROL: FOREIGN CHAR SETS:

on	D – detect no paper	on 0 – USA
	P – perf skip set	1 – France
	N – form # lines	2 – Germany
11	I – form # inches	3 – England
0	L – left margin	4 – Denmark
80	R – right margin	5 – Sweden
	F – top of form	6 – Italy
	B – blank line feed	7 – Spain
		8 – Japan

OTHER PRINT MODES:

V – pivot printing   PROGRAM OPTIONS:
Q – quiet mode
T – typewriter mode   S – standard menu
U – unidirectional   Esc – quit

Move cursor and press Enter key, or just press letter to turn option on/off.

The size of the dot matrix grid that appears on the Font Editor screen (FIG. 128) conforms to the matrix available on the printer for which the program is configured. The Configuration menu is presented to the user automatically when the Printworks program is first loaded.

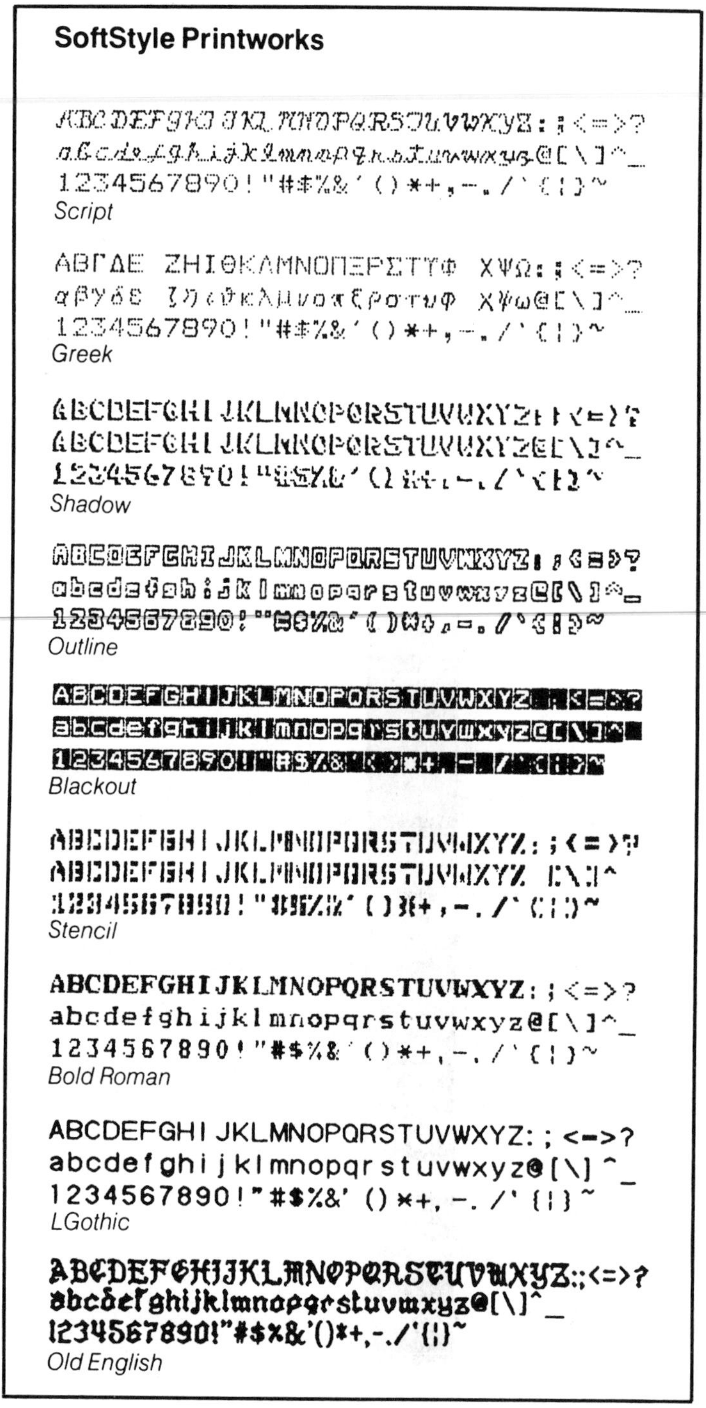

FIG. 126. A selection of the special graphic fonts provided with the Printworks package.

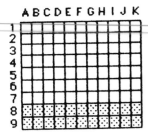
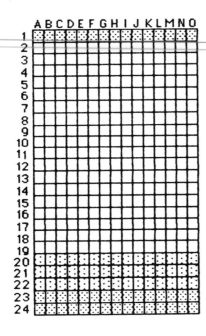
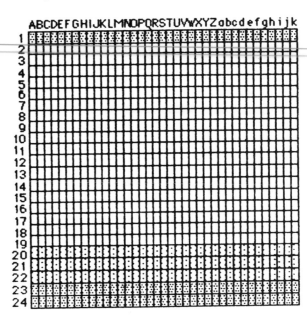

FIG. 127. Three common dot matrix patterns used on Printworks-compatible printers. The blank grids can be reproduced in quantity for designing characters.

FIG. 128. The Font Editor screen provides a display of all available options, as well as an on-line help facility.

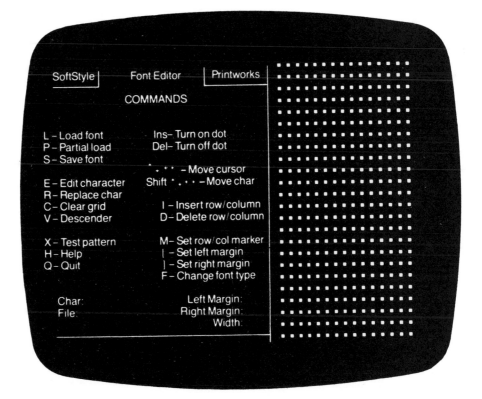

To begin an editing session, a font is loaded by selecting **L**. Individual characters are brought to the screen for editing by selecting **E**. In order to load a character, it must be specified by its ASCII code identity. When loaded, the character appears on the dot matrix grid. The character is altered by turning dots on or off, shifting the entire character within the grid boundaries, and adding or subtracting entire rows or columns of dots (FIGS. 129a and b). The character can be proofed as part of its complete font by selecting **X** (FIG. 129c).

When the font editing session has been completed, the font is saved to disk. It is loaded using the standard Typeworks menu and selecting the **G** (graphic font) option.

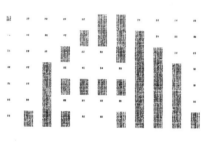

FIG. 129(a). The letter A as provided on the Roman Bold font. (b) The same character having undergone minor editing. (c) The Printworks test pattern. The ASCII code value of each character can be derived by adding the horizontal numeric value to the vertical numeric value. The letter A, for example, is ASCII 65 (60 plus 5). This A has been shifted down one row, making it misalign with other characters.

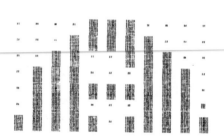

FIG. 129(b).

FIG. 129(c).

```
Printworks Test Pattern--BOLDROMN.PW2 font.
                 1         2
       12345678901234567890123456
       000000000000000000000000000
  0        (2<FPZdnx
  1        )3=GQ[eoy
  2        *4>HR\fpz
  3        !+5?IS]gq{
  4        ",6@JT^hr|
  5        #-7AKU_is}
  6        $.8BLV`jt~
  7        %/9CMWaku0
  8        &0:DNXblv
  9        `1;EOYcmw
```

DMP UTILITIES:
Creating and Using Downloadable Character Sets

DMP Utilities[24] are a set of integrated menu-driven programs that provide the Apple II user with easy access to the programmable printing features of the Apple Dot Matrix or Imagewriter printer, or the Epson FX-80 printer. According to the authors, there are four major uses for these programs:

"First, DMP Utilities will help those wanting their DMP [Dot Matrix Printer] to control printing parameters. Program listings, letters, and other printed output can always have nicely formatted pages. Margins, type sizes and styles may be saved, permitting you to produce consistent output without the trouble of looking up control codes.

"Second, the DMP Utilities includes character sets and the software to download them to the printer. These attention-getting character sets let you express yourself in italics, bold, script, or modern type styles effortlessly. They can highlight important words, or can be used throughout entire documents, depending on the effect you wish to convey.

"Third, DMP Utilities lets you replace individual characters with custom-designed characters. The days of wishing that your printer could print special characters are over. You can edit characters or character sets and save them to disk, permitting you to precisely match your character set to the task at hand.

"Finally, DMP Utilities lets your printer utilize a wide variety of character sets, beyond the two dozen provided. You can convert character sets produced by the [Apple] DOS Toolkit, [Synnergistic Software's] Higher Text II, or a host of other hi-res character generators to formats compatible with your printer. This permits immediate access to over 30 additional character fonts (not provided here)."

When the DMP Utilities disk is booted, it polls the system to try to determine the printer interface card and printer in use. If it is successful in doing so, it displays the Main menu (FIG. 130). If it is not, it presents a menu in order to properly configure the program to support the hardware in use.

FIG. 130. The Main menu provides access to the printer setup, font editing, and conversion of high-resolution fonts from the Apple Toolkit or Synergistic Software's Higher Text II.

[24]Vilberg Brothers
P.O. Box 4576
Madison, WI 53711
(608) 274-6433

```
DMP UTILITIES DISK                    V 4.6


          SELECTIONS:

          -> SETUP PRINTER

             EDIT CHARACTER FONTS

             CONVERT HIGH RES FONTS

             (END)


     PRESS ARROWS TO SELECT PROGRAM
```

The "Set-up Printer" selection is commonly the first one that is accessed (FIG. 131). It permits the specification of such things as the number of characters per inch, the left margin setting, the page length, and a number of other items. One of its most significant specifications is the indication of the character set(s) that will be downloaded to the printer (FIG. 132). After these items have been input, they can be saved on disk for repeated use.

If the selected character set is not more than 8 characters wide, the user may specify a portion of a second set to download. Only the characters from ASCII 32 to 111 of the second set may be loaded, meaning that the user cannot access lowercase *p* through *z*, the vertical bar, the tilde, and both curly brackets (ASCII 112 to 126).

After the setup is complete, it is sent to the printer for initializing with the user selections. The DMP Utilities disk is removed, and the user can proceed to use another application program, such as a word processor, and retain the printer settings (so long as the system is not reset or turned off).

Although the DMP Utilities provides two dozen new fonts for downloading, the user has the option of creating new fonts or altering versions of existing fonts. This process is accomplished with the DMP Font Editor, which is accessible from the Main menu (FIG. 133). The user chooses between fixed width and proportional width and also selects the width of the characters in dots, normally 8 or 16. (Any value between 1 and 16 is acceptable.) An 8-dot-wide character is equivalent to the 9-$\times$-8 dot matrix of the normal DMP character set.

```
DMP SETUP                                    V 4.6
```

FIG. 131. THE DMP Setup menu permits specification of the character, spacing, and location parameters.

```
HORIZ SPACING        10 CPI (PICA)
LEFT MARGIN          0 CHARACTERS
VERT SPACING         6 LPI (STANDARD)
LENGTH OF PAGE       66 LINES
PAGE SKIP            0 LINES
ENHANCED             OFF
EXPANDED             OFF
PRINT LINES          BIDIRECTIONAL
FOREIGN              USA
FONT SELECTED        CUSTOM 1
CUSTOM FONT 1        AVANTE GARDE.8
CUSTOM FONT 2        -NONE-


    SELECTIONS:

        CHANGE SETTINGS
     -> SEND SETTINGS TO PRINTER
        SAVE SETTINGS TO DISK
        GET SETTINGS FROM DISK
        END SETUP PROGRAM
```

The purpose of the mouse, and other devices of a similar nature, is to move the cursor quickly and efficiently around the screen, in order to carry out various operations. In its simplist application it merely replaces or augments the cursor (arrow) keys, which indicate compass (NSEW) direct on.

In the typesetting environment, the mouse can be useful in making gross editorial changes. These changes generally follow the keyboarding operation and do not, therefore, interrupt it. The quick specification of text, its movement, deletion, and duplication, are all important and necessary operations in editing text bound for typesetting output.

FIG. 132. (above right) A sample of text produced on the Apple Imagewriter using its default character set. (right) A sample of text produced using one of the 24 fonts provided on the DMP Utilities disk.

The purpose of the mouse, and other devices of a similar nature, is to move the cursor quickly and efficiently around the screen, in order to carry out various operations. In its simplist application it merely replaces or augments the cursor (arrow) keys, which indicate compass (NSEW) direction.

In the typesetting environment, the mouse can be useful in making gross editorial changes. These changes generally follow the keyboarding operation and do not, therefore, interrupt it. The quick specification of text, its movement, deletion, and duplication, are all important and necessary operations in editing text bound for typesetting output.

FIG. 133. The Character Editor menu provides access to stored fonts, to the editing matrix, to the printer for proofing a character set, to the disk for saving a new or edited set, and to the option for exiting from the editing session.

DMP CHARACTER EDITOR   V 4.6

SELECTIONS:

-> LOAD CHARACTER SET FROM DISK

   EDIT CHARACTERS

   PRINT SAMPLE OF CHARACTER SET

   SAVE CHARACTER SET ON DISK

   END EDITOR PROGRAM

COPYRIGHT 1983   BILL & TOM VILBERG

In normal operation, a character set is loaded from disk, the character to be edited is chosen, it is displayed in the character matrix (FIG. 134), and it is modified by turning dots on or off. As the characters are completed, they are accepted by pressing Return, and successive characters are chosen. When the editing session is completed, the set is saved to disk. The Font Editor menu also provides a selection to test a character set by printing a sample directly onto the printer.

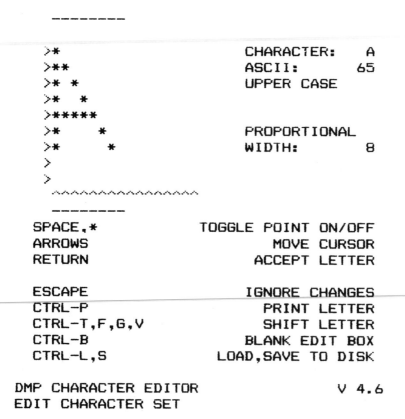

FIG. 134. The editing matrix displays the selected character and permits interactive modification.

```
--------

>*                        CHARACTER:    A
>**                       ASCII:        65
>* *                      UPPER CASE
>*   *
>*****
>*      *                 PROPORTIONAL
>*        *               WIDTH:        8
>
>
    ∧∧∧∧∧∧∧∧∧∧∧∧∧∧∧∧∧∧

--------
SPACE,*              TOGGLE POINT ON/OFF
ARROWS                      MOVE CURSOR
RETURN                    ACCEPT LETTER

ESCAPE                   IGNORE CHANGES
CTRL-P                     PRINT LETTER
CTRL-T,F,G,V               SHIFT LETTER
CTRL-B                   BLANK EDIT BOX
CTRL-L,S             LOAD,SAVE TO DISK

DMP CHARACTER EDITOR              V 4.6
EDIT CHARACTER SET
```

Chapter 11

Desktop Publishing

The Apple Macintosh Environment.
The IBM Desktop Publishing Alternatives.

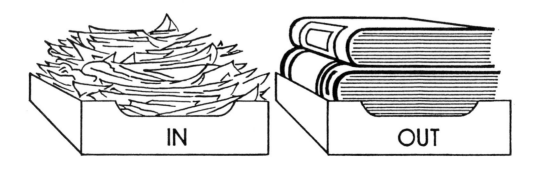

DESKTOP PUBLISHING

THE DERIVATION OF THE NAME *DESKTOP PUBLISHING* IS GENERALLY ATTRIBUTED TO Paul Brainerd, president of Aldus Corporation of Seattle, Washington. Brainerd conceived the PageMaker program, which was the first credible software link between the Apple Macintosh and the Apple LaserWriter. At the time of its introduction in 1984, PageMaker was the first program to easily integrate text and graphics, thereby eliminating paste-up and incorporating the composition process in a what-you-see-is-what-you-get (WYSIWYG) environment.

Desktop publishing provides the user, usually the text originator or author, with the capability to produce reader-ready or camera-ready originals without the need (necessarily) for successive prepress operations. The tools of production are sufficiently compact to fit on a desktop and provide the user with total control over the content and form of the output. In general, prerequisite skills include a working knowledge of word processing, the ability to create and position graphics, and a sense for what constitutes acceptable layout and design.

The significance of desktop publishing is threefold. First, it provides the author with the tools to express thoughts and ideas in word, graphic, and sometimes photographic (halftone) form. These elements are pieces of the publication production process that have traditionally required the services of trade professionals to assemble into final form. Second, the author has immediate feedback on the appearance of the final publication form. The page relationships of the elements, their sizes, and their physical characteristics are immediately visible and infinitely editable. Third, the paper output from the system is in finished form, ready for distribution to small numbers of readers (because of limitations in the vigor of most printer engines to produce volume copies) or for further reproduction and subsequent mass distribution.

Desktop publishing places within the reach of the author most of the tools necessary to convey most concepts, thoughts, and ideas. Artwork can be scanned, created from scratch, purchased in ready-made form, or modified from existing images. Fonts, logos, and special characters and symbols can also be purchased or created using tools that are still unavailable to users of even the most sophisticated typesetting systems.

Even when the talents of the author and the capabilities of the system are not a perfect match, desktop publishing components can be used as the initial means to convert original thought into a form that can be better understood by others than can be produced with traditional word processing. By so doing, the work of an author who is a content expert, but who lacks a sense of design and a feel for aesthetics, can be refined by others who do have the necessary skills.

Desktop publishing has found quick acceptance in most areas of document production within business, industry, government, and education. It is a step beyond word processing, providing users with the capability to produce better-looking and more informationally potent documents.

The following is a list of printed materials currently produced using desktop publishing:

advertising literature	flow charts	posters
agendas	flyers	presentations
announcements	graphs	press releases
appointment books	greeting cards	price lists
booklets	indexes	product sheets
books	instructional materials	programs
brochures	instructions	proposals
bulletins	invitations	prospectuses
business cards	invoices	rate charts
business forms	journals	report covers
business plans	labels	reports
business presentations	leaflets	research papers
calendars	letterheads	resumes
catalogs	magazines	sales circulars
certificates	manuals	schedules
charts	maps	shopper guides
contracts	memos	signs
coupons	menus	slides
covers	name tags	specification sheets
cover sheets	newsletters	statements
curriculum materials	newspapers	storyboards
diplomas	notices	tabloids
directories	order forms	testing materials
documentation	packaging	tickets
errata sheets	pamphlets	title pages
fact sheets	planning materials	visual aids
financial statements	poetry	vue graphics

A FOOTHOLD IN THE GRAPHIC ARTS[1]

The graphic environments that Apple[2] has created for its family of Macintosh 32-bit computers have proven to be exceptionally good choices for professional graphic arts applications. It was not surprising that in the Spring of 1983 Compugraphic Corporation[3] announced the signing of a $20 million contract for the Macintosh XL (then Lisa) microcomputers. These microcomputers were to be sold as part of Compugraphic's Personal Composition System, ushering in the first relatively low-cost codeless typesetting system for the office. In mid-1985 Apple dropped the Macintosh XL from its product line, although it continued its commitment with Compugraphic.

The Compugraphic/Apple agreement was the initial step of both companies to make inroads into the automated office environment. The announcement was a milestone in the history of phototypesetting because it involved three companies, three technologies, and three or more distinct marketing benefits that were believed to be likely.

The three companies involved in the agreement were Compugraphic, its parent firm Agfa-Gevaert, and Apple Computer, Inc. The three principal technologies were Compugraphic's MCS (Modular Composition System) phototypesetters, Agfa's P-400 laser printer, and Apple's executive workstation, the Macintosh XL. With the signing of this agreement these companies, with their high-technology devices, became the initial strategists for defining the form in which high-quality image generation was likely to be executed in the automated office (and automated shop, automated studio, automated den, etc.).

Benefit One: Putting the "Graphic" in Compugraphic

The Macintosh XL emerged from its critical introduction as a winner (designwise if not saleswise) in the field of user-friendly multifunctional integrated executive computers. The PCS link provided it with the ability to use its native intelligence (standard bundled software supported by additional custom software written by Compugraphic) and natural manner (ergonomic design and mouse cursor controls) to compose full pages of type, as well as generate graphics, integrate them in their proper positions within documents, display them as they will be printed, file them, transmit them, and otherwise manipulate and edit graphics prior to sending them (in approximate order of their complexity and therefore their image quality) to a dot matrix printer, a letter-quality printer (sans graphics), a second-generation phototypesetter (sans graphics), a laser printer, or a digital phototypesetter.

It is probably the graphics capability of the Macintosh XL that most interested Compugraphic when the company was approached by Apple. Although it is known that considerable research activities, aside from any affiliation with Apple, have continued at Compugraphic in the area of graphic input devices and methods for generating logotypes, line art, and halftones, the Macintosh XL has, nonetheless, had an impact on Compugraphic's marketing strategy. The Macintosh XL is easier to use than almost any device yet available in the typesetting industry; being designed for the nonsophisticated user, who is usually the text or document originator. It has redefined the way in which a user's thoughts can be transformed into words.

[1]See Index and Resources for other Macintosh entries.

[2] Apple Computer, Inc.
20525 Mariani Avenue
Cupertino, CA 95014
(408) 996-1010

[3] Compugraphic Corporation
200 Ballardvale Street
Wilmington, MA 01887
(617) 658-5600

The integration of graphics with text long has been an objective of typesetting vendors, and more recently of manufacturers of office-automation and technical-publication equipment. The "marriage" of the MCS with the Macintosh XL brought together two technologies that had developed differently: in a philosophical sense (casual, unskilled user vs. dedicated, skilled user), in a functional sense (text originator vs. text processor), and even in a geographical sense (West Coast attitudes vs. East Coast attitudes). The interaction of these tech cultures has sensitized Compugraphic and other typesetting machine vendors to the need for easier user interfacing, and has also sensitized Apple to the need for higher-quality typographic imaging.

Benefit Two: The Fruit of Apple's Labor

The Apple name has become a household word, known to people in all age groups; Apple is accepted as the company that made the microcomputer a consumer item. Apple has also become the only formidable challenger to the IBM standard, making Apple a viable alternative for the business sector. In a marketplace occupied by literally hundreds of companies, Compugraphic's entry into the automated office was enhanced by Apple's name recognition, aggressive advertising and marketing campaigns, and reputation for third-party hardware and software development.

The Personal Composition System family, which included the Apple Macintosh XL and a variety of output device alternatives (including Compugraphic's EP 308 laser printer based on the Canon CX engine), was sold and supported exclusively by Compugraphic. The Macintosh XL-to-Afga P-400 laser printer system, which used Compugraphic's digitized typefaces, and had an output resolution of 406 by 391 dots per inch (dpi) and an output speed of 12 ISO-sized sheets per minute, was sold only in Europe.

Benefit Three: Shaking the Apple Tree

The use of considerably less sophisticated and less expensive microcomputers than the Macintosh XL for typesetting input is well established. Certainly no vendor of typesetting equipment can ignore this phenomenon. The Linotype Company[4] has introduced PostScript-compatible phototypesetters that serve as a high-quality output alternative for the Macintosh computer network. Linotype also offers products that directly support the IBM PC. AM Varityper[5] and Itek Corporation[6] have also signed agreements with IBM to become value-added retailers of the Personal Computer line.

It is believed that Compugraphic hoped to gain access into the local area network system called Appletalk. The Appletalk network is a low-cost ($50 per connection) twisted-pair system that links Apple computers (and optionally, computers from other manufacturers, IBM in particular) together in order to permit them to share both information and resources. The advantages of having an MCS in the office network are obvious, and will become essential in future office-automation scenarios.

Despite the strong initial predictions for success, the Compugraphic Personal Composition System ceased to be a viable product in 1986. The lack of compatibility with PostScript, with the standard Macintosh environment, and with other page-composition programs combined to make the Personal Composition System less attractive in terms of price, speed, and even ease of use.

A CLOSER LOOK AT APPLE'S MACINTOSH

The **Apple Macintosh** is unique among medium-cost microcomputer systems in its ability to provide user-friendly text and graphics integration. It is the first machine of its kind to combine many of the optimum qualities of a desktop

[4] Linotype Company
425 Oser Avenue
Hauppauge, NY 11788
(516) 434-2000

[5] AM Varityper
11 Mt. Pleasant Avenue
East Hanover, NJ 07936
(201) 887-8000

[6] Itek Graphix
Composition Systems Division
34 Cellu Drive
Nashua, NH 03063
(603) 889-1400

typesetting and graphics system with an easy-to-use human interface, consisting, in part, of a mouse and pull-down menus. One of the major factors that distinguishes the Macintosh from all other microcomputers of its class is its typographic capabilities.

Pack My Mac with Macintosh Typefaces

All of the typefaces that are resident on Apple's Macintosh word processing program, MacWrite, and graphics program, MacPaint, are designed after existing typefaces (FIG. 1). They are reasonable facsimilies of those typefaces. Although they lack commercial quality, the typefaces remain faithful to the standards after which they have been designed.

FIG. 1. A sampling of the various typefaces that are available in the original MacPaint and MacWrite programs. Note that the San Francisco typeface is no longer a part of the standard typeface repertoire.

A Selection of MacPaint and MacWrite Typefaces

New York (similar to Times Roman)
ABCDEFGHIJKLMNOPQRSTUVWXYZabcdefghijklmnopqrstuvwxyz

Geneva (similar to Helvetica Light)
ABCDEFGHIJKLMNOPQRSTUVWXYZabcdefghijklmnopqrstuvwxyz12345

Toronto (similar to Lubalin Graph Book)
ABCDEFGHIJKLMNOPQRSTUVWXYZabcdefghij

Monaco (similar to Avant Garde Condensed)
ABCDEFGHIJKLMNOPQRSTUVWXYZabcdefghijklmnopqrstuvwx

Chicago (similar to Cruz Tempor Medium)
ABCDEFGHIJKLMNOPQRSTUVWXYZabcdefghijklmnopqrs

Venice (similar to Zapf Chancery Med. Italic)
ABCDEFGHIJKLMNOPQRSTUVWXYZabcdefghijk

London (similar to Cloister Black)
ABCDEFGHIJKLMabcdefghijklmnopq

Athens (similar to City Medium)
ABCDEFGHIJKLMNOPabcdefghijklmnopqrs

San Francisco (similar to no other)
ABCDEFGHIJKLMNOPabcdefghijklmnop

An interesting typographic feature of the Macintosh is its built-in type family and size range capabilities. Using the Style menu, selected text can be displayed as plain, *italic*, underline, outline, shadow, or combinations thereof, such as **bold underline**, or *italic outline*. These changes are accomplished easily and immediately using either the mouse or the keyboard, without any coding or special procedures. The desired typographic choices can be "mouse-clicked" from the pull-down menus and all succeeding characters appear as selected. Using the mouse to indicate location, previously typed characters can be highlighted, and their typographic appearance can be changed by simply choosing new typographic information. In a similar way, type size can be altered from 9 point to 24 point in MacWrite, and 9 point to 72 point in MacPaint, as shown here:

9 point Times 12 point Times 24 point Times

Electronic Paste-Up

The integration of graphic images and text into whole-page documents is still an unreachable goal for most typesetting devices. The piecemeal assembly of strips of galley text along with illustrations, photographs, artwork, rules and borders, and other graphic images is still commonplace in the graphic arts. Just as MacWrite turns the Macintosh into a "typesetter," MacPaint turns it into a manual electronic page assembler. While other Macintosh software tools provide more sophisticated page assembly capabilities, MacPaint retains its usefulness by providing a full complement of artists' tools, giving the user the opportunity to create shapes and line drawings and combine them with type. Once combined, the editing capabilities permit great flexibility in moving, rearranging, cutting, pasting, and duplicating any part of the graphics and text displayed on the screen (FIG 2).

FIG. 2. Some of the character manipulations possible using MacPaint.

How About a Hand for the Mouse

The Macintosh's main feature is that it provides a natural, easy-to-learn, and easy-to-use interface between the user and the computer.

The accomplishment of a graphic and/or typographic objective can be achieved almost coincident with its creative inspiration. The process is completely codefree, and the results are immediate. The removal of the coding barrier (which the Xerox Star and Apple Lisa pioneered) will have a positive effect on the way in which creative artists produce their work in much the same way as word processing has moved text creation back to the thought originator (author).

MacWrite: A Word Processor with Typographic Capabilities

The role of the Macintosh as a typesetter for the general public is realized with MacWrite, which remains a *word processing program* combining traditional word-processing editing with some limited typographic functions. As such it is a cross between typewriting and typesetting, mixing the qualities of typographic point sizes and typefaces with typewriting line spacing and tabbing.

Chief among its limitations is the lack of horizontal and vertical spacing control in typographic units. This is an impediment to producing acceptable typographic results, even in consideration of the low-resolution nature of the character sets. Precise

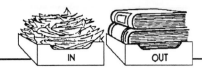

kerning is possible using the MacPaint program, but it is a time-consuming process, involving the manual repositioning of each character. The problem is further complicated by the fact that automatic hyphenation is not supported, which causes a further negative effect on the achievement of tight, uniform word spacing in justified lines. A number of programs produced specifically for page composition have, however, overcome these limitations.

As a general-purpose, self-contained publishing system, the Macintosh is unique, and literally defines its own genre. Yet its ease of use and user-friendliness provide an open stadium of opportunity for typographically unsophisticated users to experiment and to err. The potential of the situation is similar to the decline in typographic quality that followed the introduction of relatively inexpensive direct-input phototypesetters in the early 1970s. In an effort to make the machines easier to use and to place them in office and nontraditional environments, vendors deskilled the machines so that secretaries and other transient users could operate them. The result was that many errors of typographic style were committed (and continue to be committed) because of a lack of proper training and orientation. There are no safeguards to keep a typesetter or a Macintosh user from setting an entire job in italics or an unreadable typeface such as all capital blackletter (Macintoshes' London).

New Faces of the Future

Many of the typefaces provided with the original MacWrite program have been redesigned to correct for design flaws and otherwise improve their appearance. Users also may design their own typefaces using an Apple-supplied *font editor*. The font editor provides a design environment where users may paint each character on an enlarged matrix. As each character is built it is shown in actual size (FIGS. 3 to 6).

New Markets, New Opportunities

As a graphic production tool, the Macintosh is virtually without rival in its price range. Using its accompanying dot matrix or laser printer it permits the user to output virtually any image, with few limitations. This new ability packs personal publishing power into every Macintosh because the typographic and line-graphic capabilities are part of the system architecture.

Squeezing Out More Dots

The measure of quality of graphic images is the number of dots that can be packed into each vertical inch (sometimes expressed horizontally and vertically). The greater the concentration of dots, the finer the resolution of the image. The Macintosh screen has a resolution of 72 dpi. This conveniently corresponds to the conventional typographic conversion of 72 points to the inch. When output on the Imagewriter printer, the 72-points-to-the-inch resolution is maintained. The Imagewriter uses a standard resolution of 72 dpi, or 144 dots by 160 dots in high-resolution mode. In this mode, twice as many dots are printed across the page, and the print head passes over each line twice, with the second pass running over the line that has advanced one-half dot.

Because there need not be a strict relationship between screen display and output appearance, the Macintosh is an excellent candidate for driving more sophisticated output devices than a dot matrix or laser printer. True typeset output, in the range of 700 to 1000 dpi, is available through a number of trade typographers who will accept a Macintosh disk through the mail and return composed type within three or four

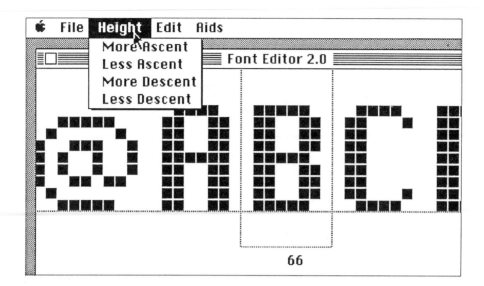

FIG. 3. The Font Editor provides a fat bit view of each character in the font. A pull-down menu provides control over the height of each character.

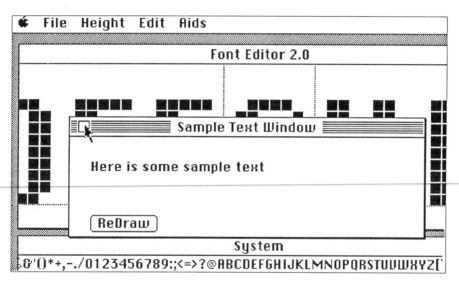

FIG. 4. As new characters are created they can be composed immediately in order to provide a proof for the designer.

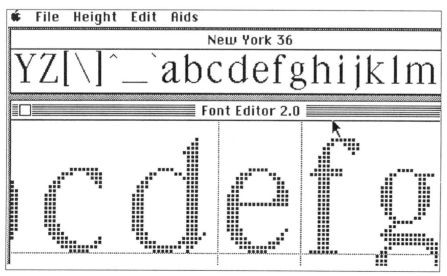

FIG. 5. The design screen can be rearranged by the user to provide whatever view of the typeface construction process is required.

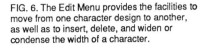

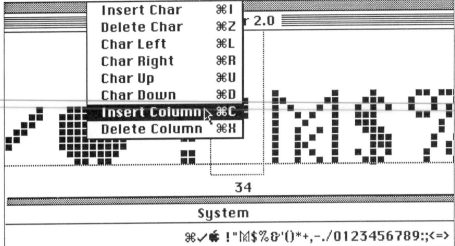

FIG. 6. The Edit Menu provides the facilities to move from one character design to another, as well as to insert, delete, and widen or condense the width of a character.

working days. Two such companies are George Lithograph[7] on the West Coast and Typeline[8] on the East Coast.

THE APPLE LASERWRITER PRINTER SYSTEM

The Apple LaserWriter System consists of at least four major components: The Macintosh, a highly customized Canon LBP-CX laser printer, the Adobe PostScript language, and a page-composition software package, such as the Aldus PageMaker program. A fifth component is the AppleTalk network connection, which permits multiple users to share the printer.

The Canon LBP-CX laser printer is the same engine that a number of other companies have chosen to Original Equipment Market (OEM). Among the most well known are Hewlett-Packard and Compugraphic. In each implementation of the laser printer, the basic machine specifications are the same (TABLE 1); however, each vendor has provided custom electronics to give its version of the machine specific capabilities. The Apple implementation is the most sophisticated yet, and provides the user with some typographic capabilities not presently available on most commercial typesetting systems. For this reason Apple has OEMed the device to other vendors, since it can be run through an RS-232C connection from a variety of computers. It is also the ideal proofing device for any phototypesetter that can accept PostScript input, such as the typesetters from The Linotype Company.

The design of the laser printer makes it particularly appealing for an office environment. It is whisper quiet, and requires virtually no maintenance since all of the high-failure components are housed in a user replaceable cartridge. The low-cost cartridges are changed after 100 to 3000 pages, depending upon the total image density printed. Although throughput is rated at eight pages per minute, complex pages might slow the machine to four to six pages per minute or even slower.

The Apple LaserWriter sets a milestone in the history of graphic arts imaging. Its small size, low cost (by graphic arts standards), high speed, reasonable resolution (300 dpi), graphic arts typefaces (licensed from the Mergenthaler typeface library and from the International Typeface Corporation), and plain paper imaging capabilities combine in a machine that literally anyone can use. It sets a new standard for office imaging quality, much in the same way that the typewriter did when it was introduced in the late nineteenth century.

7 George Lithograph
   650 Second Street
   San Francisco, CA 94107

8 Typeline
   170 State Street
   Teaneck, NJ 07666

TABLE 1. Original Equipment Manufacturer Specifications for the Canon LBP- CX Laser Beam Printer

Type: Desktop page printer.
Print Method: Electrophotographic recording with semiconductor laser beam.
Print Speed: 8 letter-size pages per minute.
Development Method: Dry monocomponent toner.
Paper Type:
    Cassette-Cut sheets: letter, legal, and other sizes. 64 g/m^2 (17 lb) to 80 g/m^2 (21 lb). Up to 100 sheets of 20 lb.
    Manual Feed-Envelope, postcard, business card, transparency, 60 g/m^2 (16 lb) to 128 g/m^2 (34 lb).
Vertical Dot Pitch: 300 (factory preset).
Warmup Time: Less than 2 minutes.
1st Printout Time: Less than 18 sec.
Noise Level: Less than 55 dB(A).
Power Requirement: 115 VAC, 60 Hz.
Power Consumption:
    Printing: Less than 0.8 KVA.
    Standby: Less than 0.3 KVA.
Dimensions: 475 mm (W) x 415 mm (D) x 290 mm (H).
    18.7" x 16.3" x 11.4"
Weight: 24.5 Kg (54 lb).
Interface: Serial video.

Source: Canon U.S.A. Inc., Laser Beam Printer Division, One Canon Plaza, Lake Success, NY 11042, (516) 488-6700. Specifications subject to change without notice.

In the heart of the laser printer is the PostScript interpreter, which converts instructions from the Macintosh internal instruction set, called QuickDraw, into instructions that direct the operation of the laser (FIG. 7). PostScript remains entirely transparent to the user, although it is possible to write instructions directly in PostScript by using the MacTerminal communications software. Direct access to PostScript, although not usually necessary, provides the user with the ability to produce typographic effects not currently supported by any Macintosh software, such as character rotations and special-effects imaging.

The actual electronics that Apple has added to the laser printer shell provide exceptional capabilities. The single-board electronics are controlled by a Motorola 68000 microprocessor running at 12 megahertz. There are 1.5 megabytes of RAM (random-access memory) for creation of the page image, and as a font cache and system buffer. An additional 0.5 megabyte of ROM (read-only memory) is used to store the PostScript language and the resident 13 typeface outlines. A second model of the LaserWriter, the LaserWriter Plus, was introduced in January, 1986, and has 1 megabyte of ROM.

The resident typefaces are the most popular typeface families in the world: Times Roman, Helvetica, and the typewriter face, Courier. The typeface images are true-cut versions of the originals, derived from the digital outlines supplied by Allied Linotype Company to Adobe Systems. The Times Roman family includes the regular weight, bold, italic, and bold italic. The Helvetica family includes the regular weight, oblique, bold, and bold oblique. The Courier family includes four variations, as well as a special symbols font. A single stored outline is used for the entire range of sizes. The LaserWriter Plus also includes ITC Avant Garde Book, Book demi; ITC Bookman light, light italic, demi, and demi

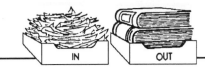

FIG. 7. The path by which instructions are
passed from the Macintosh to the laser printer.
Adapted from an internal Apple document
"Macintosh Imageserver Development
Conference."

The Apple LaserWriter
Imaging Model

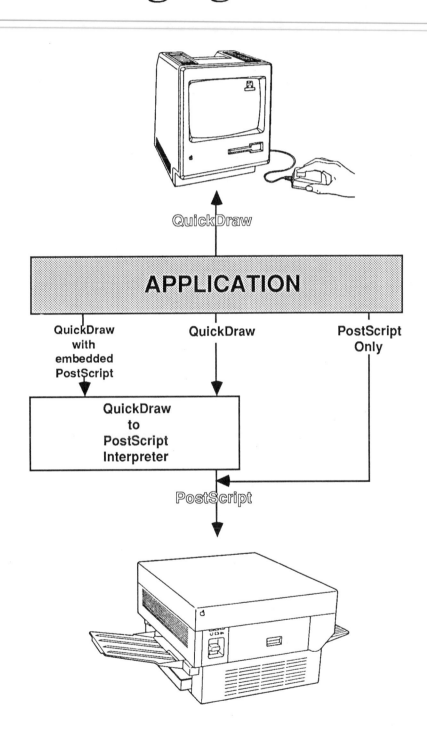

italic; New Century Schoolbook, italic, bold, and bold italic; Palatino, italic, bold, and bold italic; ITC Zapf Chancery medium italic; and ITC Zapf Dingbats. In addition, fonts from Adobe systems and other sources can be purchased separately and downloaded to the printer.

The LaserWriter uses two classes of typefaces. The first class, and highest quality, includes the resident typefaces that are burned in ROM. These can be augmented by downloadable typefaces, available in packaged sets (usually four to a disk) from other sources and stored in the printer's RAM for specific jobs. Each of these typefaces requires from 15K to 20K to store its outline. These fonts appear on the Macintosh screen in the approximate form, size, and width in which they will be printed. The second class of typefaces includes those that are normally resident on the Macintosh, and for which there are no character outlines stored on the laser printer. These native Macintosh typefaces—such as New York, Geneva, and Chicago—are sent to the laser printer as bit maps and are scaled and smoothed, but do not have the high resolution of the printer-resident outline designs. In some cases the user can opt to have certain LaserWriter typefaces substituted for certain native Macintosh typefaces.

Any font that exists on the LaserWriter in outline form can be manipulated according to any PostScript operation. PostScript treats each font as a graphical object, and any transformation that can be performed on an object can be performed on a font. Native Macintosh typefaces cannot be manipulated, however.

In order for an application to access the LaserWriter, assuming that all hardware connections have been completed, a QuickDraw-to-PostScript converter must be resident on the application disk, or the application must output PostScript commands directly. While PostScript can perform any operation that QuickDraw might send it, it is also capable of considerably more. It will be the task of third-party software designers to create applications that allow the Macintosh to access more of the power of PostScript. If the application is also to output to the Imagewriter dot matrix printer, it must output its commands in QuickDraw coding format.

POSTSCRIPT

PostScript, a trademark of Adobe Systems Inc.[9], is a simple, yet highly sophisticated, interpretive programming language providing an exceptionally effective means of integrating all aspects of page composition: type, line graphics, photographs, and all other manner of graphic images. It provides a software interface between document-creation programs and output devices that utilize raster imaging technology. It is the first language and imaging generation model that is both input (host machine) and output (printer device) independent. It can therefore use the same PostScript elements to output to a complete range of graphic printers, from low-resolution dot matrix to high-resolution laser imagers.

A page description written in PostScript is an executable program composed of various elements of a set of the PostScript language. PostScript, like other computer languages, is made up of variables and constants, operators and operands, syntax and semantics, and a collection of rules of usage. PostScript is generally transparent to the user, with its source code generated by a word processing program or other document processing application. The source code is in a form that can be processed by a PostScript interpreter, which translates it into a format which can be used to run a specific raster output device.

A PostScript file, which will embody the descriptors necessary for the printing of a document, is composed of two parts: a *prologue* and a *script*. The prologue precedes the processing of each document produced by a specific application program. It is a collection of definitions that translate the output of the application program to

9 Adobe Systems, Inc.
1870 Embarcadero Road, Suite 100
Palo Alto, CA 94303
(415) 852-0271

FIG. 8

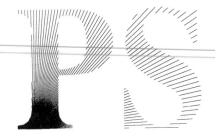

FIG. 9

FIG. 10

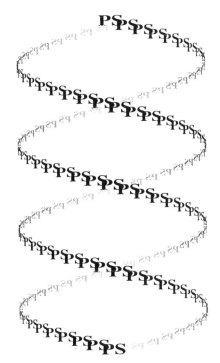

functions supported by PostScript, as well as provide primary setup commands. The prologue need only be written once, by the programmer, and is automatically sent as the front matter of every document output by the application program. The script is the actual description, in PostScript language, of the printed image (FIG. 8-18).

The PostScript Graphic Arts Model

The PostScript imaging model is fashioned after procedures used in the type-setting field and the greater graphic arts industry. In broad terms, it is as a precise methodology for applying minute marks of ink (in black, white, shades of gray, or color) on a page area referred to as the *current page*. The marks of ink can be designated to form character images, filled or outline shapes, lines, or halftones.

Conceptually, the PostScript model can be thought of like the procedures used by a screen printer: creating a stencil through which ink is forced to form images on a substrate. To form a single character, for example, the PostScript programmer would call a procedure to define the necessary stencil, or negative holes that would form the character outline, and then define a *source*, which would be passed through the stencil to form the image on the page.

Marks are placed on the page by using a set of *imaging operators*. The Fill operators image a defined area on the current page; the Stroke operators form lines of various weights on the current page; the Image operators paint gray scale renditions of scanned halftone representations of photographs on the current page; and finally, the Show operators paint character images onto the current page. Each of these operators has several associated arguments, which provide a hightened level of specificity.

Among the most important of the image-operator arguments is the *current path*, a description of a series of points (connected or disconnected), lines, and curves that together serve to describe shapes and their positions. The current path is constructed by applying path operators, such as Newpath, Moveto, Lineto, Curveto, Arc, Closepath, and others, which modify the path.

A page may be built of many layers of images. Only the most recently defined (or topmost) image will appear, however, because the "ink" is, in all cases, opaque, and obscures whatever is beneath it. After a page has been defined, it is printed on the output device through the execution of either the Showpage or Copypage operator. Showpage has the effect of clearing the current page after printing, while Copypage leaves the image of the current page intact for further use.

FIG. 11

How PostScript Attains Output-Device Independence

Path operators are designated to describe points on a page by means of referencing a Cartesian coordinate system. This grid of x and y coordinates is conceptually superimposed on the current page, describing points on and sometimes outside the page by specifying pairs of real numbers. The standard PostScript coordinate system, which uses 1/72-inch units, can be used to locate any point on the page area.

The great variety of output devices share no common coordinate system, either among themselves, or with the PostScript model. Their imagable areas, called *device space*, can vary greatly, and can even manifest different resolutions horizontally and vertically. Images specified in the PostScript environment are created within an ideal coordinate system called *user space*. PostScript incorporates an interpreter, which automatically converts points created in user space into corresponding points in the device space of the output printer. This process is transparent to the user and accounts for PostScript's device independence.

FIG. 12

Writing Simple PostScript Notation[10]

In almost all of its current implementations, the PostScript language remains transparent to the user. An application program such as MacWrite or MacDraw is used to construct a page, which is then invisibly translated by PostScript for imaging on the Apple Laser Printer. It is possible, however, to write directly in the PostScript language by communicating with the serial output device using MacTerminal.

Using the PostScript language to draw a straight line is one of the simplest activities to undertake. The specification must begin with the construction of a *path*, indicated in PostScript notation as *newpath*, which sets the current path to be empty. The Moveto operator is used to specify the x,y coordinate starting point of the line segment. All page locations are measured from the origin, which is located in the lower left-hand corner. The Lineto operator is used to draw the line from its origin to its lineto coordinates. A line of 400 units (of 1/72-inch) long would result from the following PostScript program, which is simply a series of graphic output operators:

FIG. 13

```
newpath

 100  390  moveto
 500  390  lineto
stroke
showpage
```

The Stroke operator paints the line along the trajectory indicated by the current path. The Showpage operator initiates the output processing of the image.

PostScript's native unit system of 1/72-inch, which is equivalent to one printers' point, can be converted easily to other unit measurements by defining a procedure. Defining PostScript units as inches and as centimeters is done as follows:

```
/inch {72 mul} def
```

```
/cm {28.3465 mul} def
```

Fonts used in PostScript may be specified as virtually any size. Sizes such as 6.12 point, 25.033 point, and 11.111 point are all acceptable sizes for PostScript processing. Fonts are referred to by name; a font name generally is composed of a combination of the font family name and the font face name. Each font character has two attributes: an *origin* and a *width*. The origin is positioned to the left of the

[10] Adapted from *POSTSCRIPT Cookbook, A Guide to Graphic Imaging*, Adobe Systems, 1984.

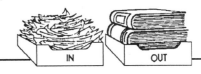

character's base line (an imaginary line upon which all characters sit). The width is generally equivalent to the horizontal dimension of the character plus a small amount of white space to either side.

To set a line of type it is necessary to select the typeface, scale it to size (it is stored at a unit value of 1), indicate the words to be set, and then give the instruction to set them. A single line of 12-point Times Roman type showing the words "Post-Script is transparent" would be written as follows:

```
/Times-Roman findfont 12 scalefont
setfont

300 500 moveto
(PostScript is transparent) show
showpage
```

Sizes and typefaces can be mixed easily, and in the interest of efficency, can be defined at the beginning of a program in order to reduce typing and simplify editing. To define a 9-point type as a *smallfont* and a 12-point type as a *normalfont,* the following would be typed:

defined at the beginning of a program in order to reduce typing and simplify editing.

```
/smallfont
    /Times-Roman findfont 9 scalefont def

/normalfont
    /Times-Roman findfont 12 scalefont def
```

Setting the words "PostScript is transparent" in 9-point would be accomplished as follows:

```
100 300 moveto
smallfont setfont
(PostScript is transparent) show
showpage
```

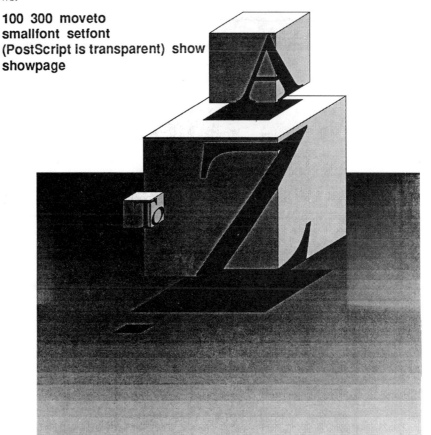

FIG. 14

Another PostScript descriptor that affects the appearance of fonts is the Makefont operator. Makefont uses a six-element matrix to describe various attributes of the font. The first and fourth elements of the matrix control scaling in the x and y dimensions. Altering these values can result in the creation of condensed or extended fonts. A 12-point Times Roman font on a 9-point body, resulting in a condensed 12-point font, would be specified as follows:

FIG. 15

/Times-Roman findfont [9 0 0 12 0 0] makefont

In a similar way, type fonts can be obliqued and backslanted. Additional typographic capabilities include setting type vertically; setting type in a circle; setting type in a spiral; setting type in reverse (on a black, tinted, halftone, pattern, or color background); setting type in outline form; setting type in a color, tint, pattern, or halftone; and defining a user-designed font.

Although the PostScript language provides almost limitless graphic freedom, accessing its power is, for most users, dependent upon the application software that is utilized. One method of providing a link between the page-layout capabilities of PostScript, the high-resolution output capability of the Apple Laser Printer, and the easy user interface provided by the Macintosh is the Aldus page-composition program.

FIG. 16

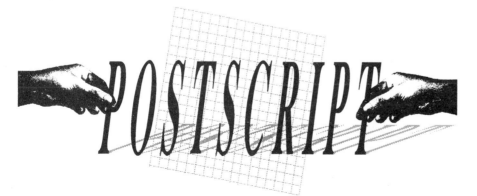

FIG. 17

FIG. 18

PC MACBRIDGE:
Sharing the Wealth of an Appletalk Network

From the beginning of the desktop publishing phenomenon, there has been the need for Macintosh and IBM personal computers to communicate in the same environment. Desktop publishers who use both kinds of computers have had to contend with the inconvenience of shuffling information between them and finding a workable method of sharing access to the LaserWriter. An answer to these problems is PC Mac-Bridge,[11] a hardware and software package that provides Appletalk connectivity and Macintosh resource access for the IBM PC or compatible.

Building the Bridge

The PC MacBridge card is a half-height Appletalk board that fits in any PC slot (except slot 8 of the PC/XT). The back of the card has a DB-9 Appletalk jack onto which an Appletalk connector is attached. The Appletalk cable is joined to another device in the network at any convenient node.

The system software can be configured for use on either two floppy drives or a hard disk. The PC MacBridge software supports access to the Appletalk network, as well as conversion of IBM PC text, data, and graphic files into PostScript form for printing on the LaserWriter or other PostScript-compatible device.

Optional software, published by Videx and Infosphere, provides network support for email and Macintosh hard disk sharing.

The Lay of the LAN

The main feature of the PC MacBridge package is the support for converting WordStar, Microsoft Word, MultiMate, and ASCII files into PostScript files for transmission over Appletalk.

Appletalk (FIG. 19) is Apple's proprietary local area network (LAN), which operates at a data transfer rate of 230,400 bits per second. The LAN is a type of network called a *serial bus*, meaning that devices are attached along a line, rather than in a circle, ring, or some other configuration.

As many as 32 devices can be connected to one Appletalk network at a distance of up to 1000 feet. Appletalk is built into the Macintosh and the LaserWriter, and is an option for the ImageWriter II. The Appletalk connector kit consists of the Appletalk connector box attached to a plug, for attaching to the printer port of a computer or the Appletalk port of a printer; a 2-meter length of cable; and a cable extender for joining lengths of cable. Attachments are simple, fast, and relatively inexpensive.

FIG. 19. An AppleTalk network consists of from 2 to 32 devices connected serially.

11 Tangent Technologies, Ltd.
   5720 Peachtree Parkway, Suite 100
   Norcross, GA 30092
   (404) 662-0366
A fully configured system also requires
Mail Center from Videx, Inc.
1105 NE Circle Blvd.
Corvallis, OR 97330
(503) 758-0521, and
MacServe from Infosphere, Inc.
4730 SW Macadam Ave.
Portland, OR 97201
(503) 226-3620

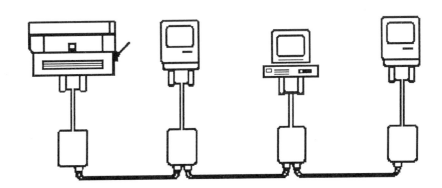

An Appletalk network essentially takes care of itself. Each device on the network identifies itself with a specific name, and messages are broadcast along the network bus, stopping only at the address for which they are intended. Devices only respond if the message is specifically addressed to them.

When the IBM PC is attached to the Appletalk network, it identifies itself as "IBM PC," although the name can be changed to one more meaningful, such as the name of its user. The PC can poll the network and seek the names of all devices that are on-line. This is the way by which the PC confirms the presence of a LaserWriter (FIG. 20).

LaserScript

LaserScript is a set of programs that convert certain word processing files, such as Microsoft Word, WordStar, or MultiMate, or plain ASCII files into PostScript form for printing on the Apple LaserWriter (FIG. 21).

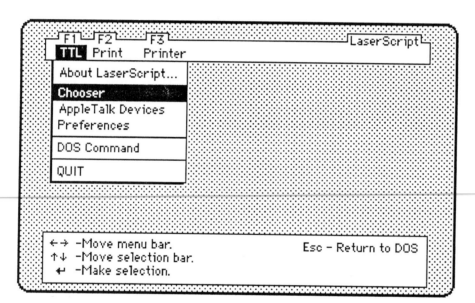

FIG. 20. The TTL (Tangent Technologies Ltd.) menu offers information about the program and the network environment.

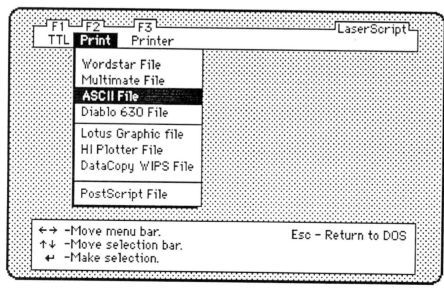

FIG. 21. The Print menu supports the selection of a file for conversion into PostScript. The PostScript file can be output on the Apple LaserWriter or other PostScript printer. Notice that user-written PostScript language files can also be processed.

The IBM PC can be part of a simple network composed of a single LaserWriter and single Macintosh, or it can be part of a more sophisticated network, with multiple printers, Macintoshes, and additional IBM PCs. Each device in the network has a name, which is used to identify it for incoming and outgoing data. Because there might be more than one AppleTalk printer in use, the "Choose Printer" option can be used to select which of the available printers will be accessed (FIG. 22). A test page can be sent to confirm that the printer is properly receiving data (FIG. 23), and the status of the selected printer can be checked in order to determine its availability and significant characteristics (FIG. 24).

For example, when a WordStar file is selected for printing on the LaserWriter, the user is prompted for information, including:

- The name of the WordStar source file. This is the name used to create the file originally.
- The name of the PostScript destination file. A temporary PostScript file is created during the conversion and printing process. The file is called ps.$$$, and can be from three to five times the size of the original WordStar file.
- Where the file will be printed. The system defaults to the "LaserWriter Via Appletalk" setting.
- The number of copies to be printed. The default is 1.
- The page orientation. Choices are "Portrait" or "Landscape," the default is "Portrait."
- The document scale. The default setting is 1.
- The paper feed requirement, either automatic or manual.

The LaserScript conversion process handles native WordStar commands, as well as special LaserScript character and page commands and the direct specification of PostScript.

The default font family for WordStar is Courier. The command ^PY is used to select Helvetica, and ^PW is used to select Times-Roman. Other fonts can be specified using PostScript programs provided in the operation manual.

Point sizes can be changed, but only two different sizes can be specified at any given time. The default normal size is 12 point (^PN), and the default alternate size is 16 point (^PA). The choice of default sizes can be changed using the ./char dot command. Respecification of the default font sizes does not automatically change the line spacing settings, which must be changed using the ./line dot command (FIG. 25).

Additional LaserScript commands are provided for formatting lines (centering, justifying, etc.), setting page margins, accessing special effects (strikethrough, underline, superscript, subscript, and special characters), setting tabs, and inserting graphics.

One of the most powerful capabilities of the LaserScript package is the specification of PostScript programs from within a word processing document. This feature provides users, who are familiar with writing PostScript programs, with the capability to compose pages far beyond the limits of conventional word processing. The command ./cmd indicates that the information that follows is to be sent directly to the LaserWriter's PostScript interpreter. The command ./file precedes the name of the file that is to be interpreted.

In addition to particular word processing files and regular ASCII text files, Laser-Script can convert files intended for a Diablo 630 Daisy wheel printer. The Diablo 630 is a popular printer manufactured by Diablo Systems, Inc., a Xerox company. The files are converted to a form compatible with the LaserWriter's Diablo 630 printer emulator which is normally available to applications through the printer's RS-232

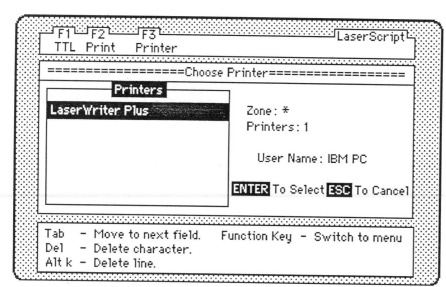

FIG. 22. The "Choose Printer" option displays a list of all on-line printers and supports the selection of the highlighted printer by pressing ENTER.

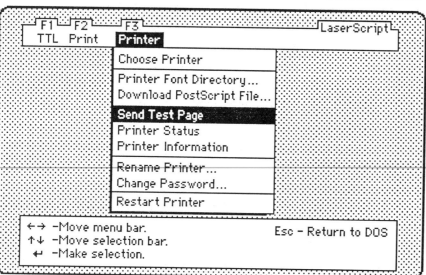

FIG. 23. The printer connection can be verified by sending a test page.

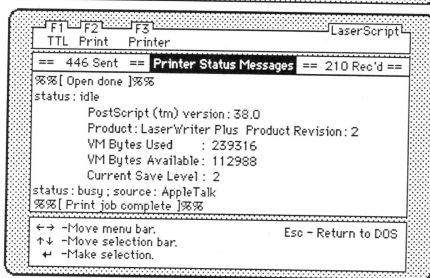

FIG. 24. The status of the printer can be checked in order to determine if it is available or is processing another job.

FIG. 25. PC MacBridge adds WordStar-like commands to control typographic and page-layout attributes. Similar commands are used to control other supported word processors.

Changing Type Style
Input

```
The Courier design is the LaserScript default font setting.
Characters can be changed to ^Bbold^B, ^Doblique^D, ^B^Dbold
oblique^B^D, and ^Sunderline^S. Courier characters are monospaced,
while other LaserWriter font characters are proportionally spaced.

^YHelvetica is a popular sans serif type design. It is available in
^Bbold^B, ^Doblique^D, and ^B^Dbold oblique^B^D variations.^Y

^WTimes Roman is a popular serif type design. It too is available in
^Bbold^B, ^Doblique^D, and ^B^Dbold oblique^B^D variations.^W
```

Changing Type Style
Output

The Courier design is the LaserScript default font setting. Characters can be changed to **bold**, *oblique*, ***bold oblique***, and <u>underline</u>. Courier characters are monospaced, while other LaserWriter font characters are proportionally spaced.

Helvetica is a popular sans serif type design. It is available in **bold**, *oblique*, and ***bold oblique*** variations.

Times Roman is a popular serif type design. It too is available in **bold**, *oblique*, and ***bold oblique*** variations.

Changing Point Size
Input

```
^WThe normal default point size is 12. ^AThe alternate is 16
point.^N

./char20 10
The point size has been respecified to 10 points for normal, and
^A20 points for the alternate size.^W
```

Changing Point Size
Output

The normal default point size is 12. The alternate is 16 point.

The point size has been respecified to 10 points for normal, and 20 points for the alternate size.

port. LaserScript allows access over AppleTalk. In order to use the Diablo 630 conversion program, the word processor or other software application must have the capability to "print to a file" with the intent of outputting to a Diablo 630. The "print file" is what is actually sent to the LaserWriter for output.

LaserGraph

PC MacBridge has capabilities to translate Lotus spreadsheet and graphic files into PostScript, as well as to develop charts and graphs for inclusion within word processing documents.

The LaserGraph Chart program can create bar, pie, and line charts with many options and design features. The charts can be output directly to the LaserWriter (or other PostScript output device) for proofing, manual paste-up with other documents, or as overhead transparencies.

Electronic Mail

Mail messages and file transfers can be communicated between IBM PCs and Macintoshes sharing the same AppleTalk network. The PC MacBridge enhancement card and the MailBox software make it possible for the IBM PC to send and receive electronic mail. The built-in AppleTalk circuitry and the Videx Mail Center software make it possible for the Macintosh to send and receive electronic mail.

The mail application appears differently on the two computers, although the functions are similar. The major differences are that the IBM PC version is not graphic, and cannot operate in the background. The PC menu offers choices for sending and receiving mail, checking who is on-line, and listing files that have been received (FIG. 26).

Electronic mail transfers are referred to as *packages*, and each transfer of a package is called a *transaction* (FIG. 27). Packages may be sent simultaneously to more than one receiver. A package contains the following components:

- The sender's name
- The destination name
- A time and date "postmark"
- A message and/or...
- One or more files

The message line is optional, and may merely describe the contents of the accompanying file(s) or be the entire substance of the package.

Mail can only be sent to users who are on-line. This information is displayed by using the "WHO Is ON-LINE" option. If no one is on-line, the message "No Mail users found" will appear.

For mail to be received by an IBM PC it must be in the Enable Receiver mode. In this mode it can receive mail unattended, with all transactions automatically saved to disk.

The Macintosh end of the mailbox is more elegant. The Mail Center program, which is a separate, additional-cost component of the PC MacBridge package, is composed of two parts. The first is the Mail Preferences desk accessory (FIG. 28), which is used to receive messages and files in background mode. The second is the Mail Center application program (FIG. 29), which is used to query the network for on-line users and to send messages and files to other users.

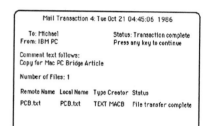

```
*** MailBox MAIN MENU Version 2.04 ***
     A. SEND Mail
     B. RECEIVE Mail
     C. Mail LOG
     D. Mail DIRECTORY
     E. WHO is ON-LINE
     F. RETURN TO DOS

     Enter Selection: A
```

FIG. 26. The PC MacBridge MailBox menu provides direct access to sending, receiving, and cataloging mail, as well as questioning the system for the presence of mail recipients.

```
     Mail Transaction 4: Tue Oct 21 04:45:06 1986

     To: Michael                  Status: Transaction complete
     From: IBM PC                 Press any key to continue

Comment text follows:
Copy for Mac PC Bridge Article

Number of Files: 1

Remote Name  Local Name  Type Creator  Status

PCB.txt      PCB.txt     TEXT MACB  File transfer complete
```

FIG. 27. A transaction screen shows pertinent information about each mail transmission.

FIG. 28. Two displays of the Videx Mail Center Mail Preferences desk accessory. The three icons in the dialog box on the left show that mail reception is open, the speaker is on, and the visual mail alert will be displayed in the upper right corner of the screen. The box on the right shows opposite settings: mail reception is off, the speaker is off, and there is no display of a mail message alert.

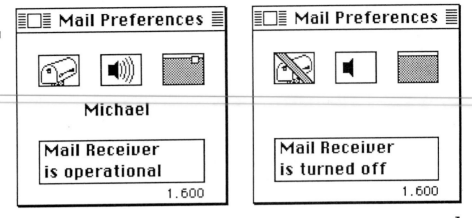

FIG. 29. The Videx Mail Center Application Program consists of three windows. Clicking in the line directly below the "On-Line" title results in a list of all on-line users. User names and message listings can be displayed as icons, as shown in the "On-Line" and "Send Log" windows, or as text, as shown in the "Receive Log" window.

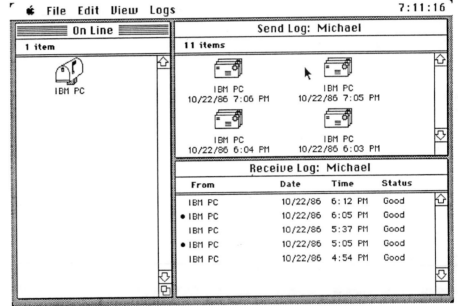

Each Macintosh must have its own copy of the Mail Center in order to be properly recognized on the network. Each Mail Center disk has a serial number identification, which makes it unique. Communication can only take place between Macintoshes having different serialized versions of the software.

A Mail Center user declares his presence on the network by opening the Mail Preferences desk accessory and eliminating the cross-out line from his mailbox icon. He can also adjust his speaker icon so that he is alerted when mail arrives, and specify where the visual mail alert will be displayed on his screen.

Mail is sent from the Mail Center Application window by clicking on the intended recipient's name or icon. A dialog box is displayed so that the sender can select files to send and add an optional message (FIG. 30). The mail is sent by clicking on the "Send Mail" box. The screen changes to an image of an envelope, with the name of the sender, receiver, and file(s) displayed (FIG. 31). If the recipient is an IBM PC, the "Mail Transaction" screen will be displayed at the receiving end (FIG. 27). If the recipient is another Macintosh, the computer will sound three ascending-scale tones in rapid succession, and/or display a small mailbox icon in a chosen corner of the screen.

Mail that has been sent can be reviewed by the sender by accessing the mail name in the "Send Log" (FIG. 32). The log entry shows who sent what to whom,

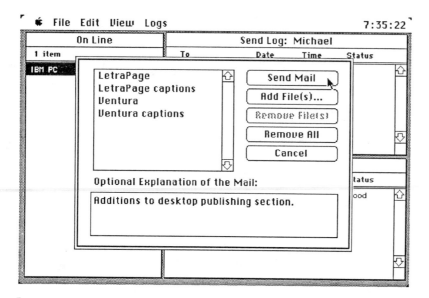

FIG. 30. Mail is sent by clicking on the recipient's name, as listed in the On-Line window. The result of that action is the display of a dialog box providing access to all available system files. As files are chosen, they are displayed in the package listing. The sender can add an optional message in the area at the bottom of the box. The mail is sent by clicking "Send Mail."

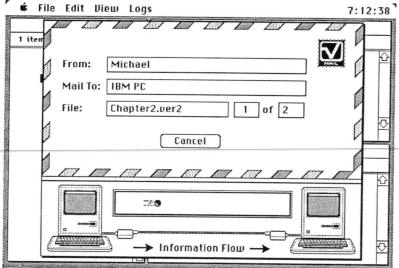

FIG. 31. A representation of an envelope is displayed during the mail transmission. An animated data bit travels between the two computers to verify that the message is being sent.

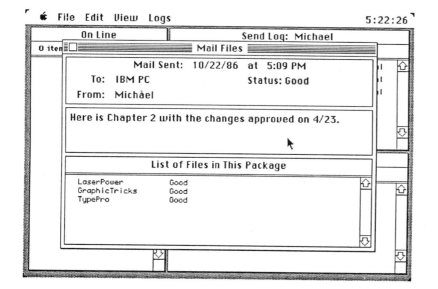

FIG. 32. The sender can review mail messages that have been sent by clicking on the message name listed in the "Send Log" window.

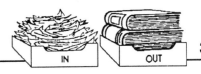

when, and with what transmission result. Mail that is received at a Macintosh will be listed in the "Receive Log." Listings that have not yet been read are preceded by a dot. The information available about each listing is identical to that displayed in the sender's "Send Log."

Macintosh Disk Sharing

Electronic mail is an effective way of sharing information, but in the PC Mac-Bridge environment it usually depends upon the coordinated efforts of at least two parties. If an IBM user is to receive mail, then he must have his computer configured to await a transmission. This requirement can hold needed files captive in a Macintosh until the systems can be properly set up. A better situation is to have shared files available on one or more hard disks. Such files can be accessed without the assistance of another network user. This is the intent of PC MacServe, a program component of PC MacBridge that works with the MacServe program.

PC MacServe provides AppleTalk access to one or more hard disks connected to one or more Macintoshes. Files can be read from, and written to, a hard disk, making it possible for authors to collaborate on articles, and for files destined for desktop publishing or professional typesetting to be processed through either kind of computer.

The PC MacServe screen is composed of these pull-down menus:

The TTL menu: Offers information about the software and the AppleTalk devices that are available on the network (FIG. 33).
The Files menu: Provides a choice of file listings on the MacServer or the IBM PC (FIG. 34).
The Volume menu: Provides access to the choice of Server (this is the same as the Chooser in the TTL menu), and the volume (a section of the hard disk) that is to be mounted (FIG. 35).
The Converter menu: Either does no conversion, or converts MacWrite TEXT files to ASCII so that they can be read by a PC word processor (FIG. 36).

Volumes are created on the Macintosh by the MacServe system administrator, a person who determines the names and sizes of the volumes, if they will be read-only or read/write, if they will be password protected, and if so, what the password(s) will be. When a "Volume Mount" request is made at the IBM PC, a list of available volumes is displayed. When a volume is selected, a listing of its contents is shown. If the Files menu is in the Macintosh position, files may be taken from the Macintosh hard disk. If the Files menu is in the Local DOS position, files may be transferred from the IBM PC to the Macintosh hard disk. Macintosh files that are selected for taking are renamed automatically to conform to DOS requirements, although the user has the option of renaming files in a more meaningful way. The Macintosh File window also shows the Macintosh File Type and Creator.

IBM PC files can be put on the Macintosh MacServer volume simply by selecting them. The file names are entered automatically.

ASCII file transfers are accomplished easily, although unnecessary control characters, such as line-feeds and carriage returns, are sometimes passed through. A Macintosh desk accessory called PC MacTxt™ from Tangent Technologies can correct most of these problems at the Macintosh end. Other conversion problems, such as handling data from spreadsheets, word processing documents, and databases, are dependent upon the software in use and the conversion utilities and built-in converters available within the application.

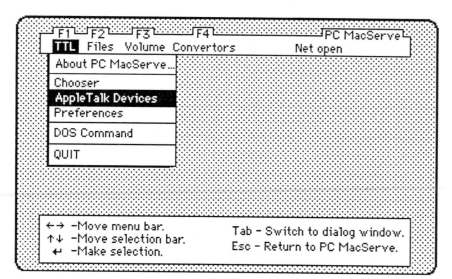

FIG. 33. The PC MacServe screen display and TTL functions are similar to those used in the LaserScript program.

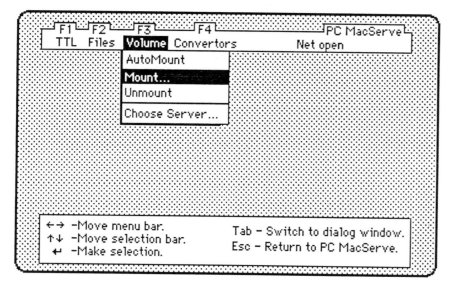

FIG. 34. The Files menu is used to set whether files will be taken from, or put on, the Macintosh hard disk.

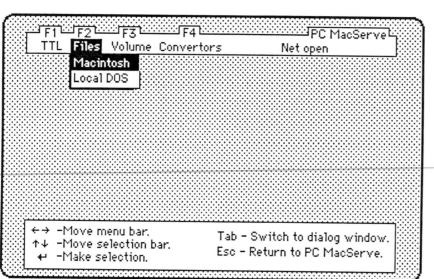

FIG. 35. The Volume menu provides access to MacServe volumes created on the Macintosh using Infosphere's MacServe program. The "AutoMount" selection mounts the volume that was last accessed. This feature can be useful if the user generally mounts the same volume during each session.

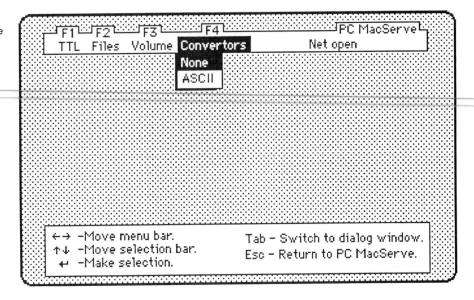

FIG. 36. In most cases, the conversion of data between an IBM PC and a Macintosh must take place within the application program itself. The PC MacServe conversion menu is limited to converting MacWrite files into ASCII for processing with an IBM PC word processor.

Creating the network volumes on the Macintosh is an easy process. Regardless of the way that the hard disk is partitioned, MacServe supports the creation of up to 16 of its own volumes. The MacServe system administrator gives each volume a name, a size (in K), and access attributes (FIG. 37). The attributes are:

- Automatic: Volumes specified as automatic will open each time the Macintosh host is booted.
- Locked: Volumes that are locked become read-only. This attribute is similar to using the write protect tab on a diskette.
- Network: Volumes specified as network are accessible to any user of the Apple-Talk network. If a volume is not tagged as network it is only available to the host Macintosh.
- Password: Volumes with password protection can be accessed only with the use of the proper password.

The system administrator has considerable flexibility in determining the characteristics of the volumes and of the system itself. Volumes can be removed, their attributes can be changed, and volume contents can be archived. The system can be configured with an optimum *cache size*, a reserved part of memory used to enhance performance. MacServe can also be turned off, can be set to stand alone (operating apart from AppleTalk), or can be set as a network server, which is its normal function. The system administrator can also temporarily downgrade his status to "Net user," disabling access to server functions, but retaining access to the network.

The MacServe desk accessory provides Macintosh users with access to all disks and print servers on the network (FIG. 38). Using the "Dialog" box, users can list the names of all available volumes, select them as either private (providing write access) or shared (read-only), and release them when they are finished.

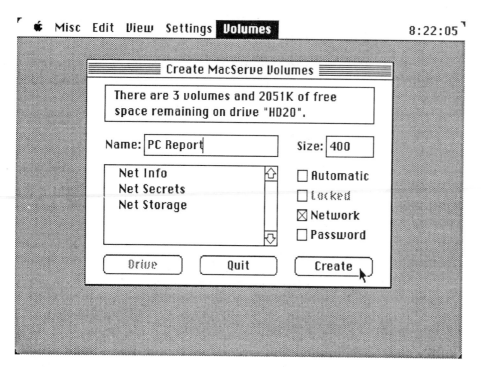

FIG. 37. MacServe volumes are easily created at the Macintosh.

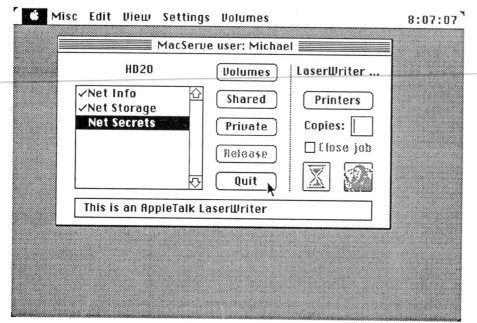

FIG. 38. This MacServe desk accessory is available to all Macintosh MacServe users on the network. Users can select which volumes they would like to use, as well as control certain ImageWriter II printer attributes, such as queuing, aborting, and setting the number of copies. InfoSphere has a separate program called LaserServe which provides spooling and other services for the LaserWriter.

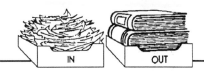

AppleWriter/LaserWriter Utilities:
Connecting a LaserWriter to the Apple II World

The considerable capabilities of the LaserWriter have attracted the interest of many third-party suppliers. A wide range of software and hardware companies, serving many different applications in many different professional fields, have found the Laser-Writer to be very worthy of support. Somewhat surprisingly, Apple's own Apple II microcomputers have not been so favored, at least not until the introduction of the Apple *II*GS.[12] A pioneer in this area has been Don Lancaster, an author and programmer who has devised software that works in concert with the AppleWriter 2.0 ProDOS word processing program on an Apple *II*e, *II*c, or *II*GS.

In essence, Lancaster has used the AppleWriter glossary and WPL (Word Processing Language) to provide fairly easy access to a broad selection of PostScript commands and routines. The user incorporates the commands and modifies and combines the routines to produce the required results.

Getting Started

The user copies his AppleWriter program onto Volume One of Lancaster's AppleWriter LaserWriter Utilities disks.[13] This copying makes the disk self-booting and automatically brings the user into AppleWriter upon start-up.

The actual connection of the computer to the laser printer depends on which model of the Apple II is being used. The Apple *II*e uses the Apple Super Serial card, while the *II*c can connect directly to the LaserWriter provided that the *II*c has the 3.5 ROM monitor installed. In either case, the computer serial cable connects to the RS-232C port on the LaserWriter, and communicates at 9600 baud. The Apple *II*GS can connect using the Super Serial card, or for other applications, can connect directly using AppleTalk.

Using the Utilities

Each of the five utilities disks can display a menu of options, providing direct access to a number of demonstration programs or leading the user to other capabilities. This is what the first menu looks like:

Don Lancaster's AppleWriter/LaserWriter Utilities Vol. I

A - Auto Diablo format	H - HIRES converter
B - Box and title rules	L - LGLOSS glossary
C - Change daisywheels	P - PGLOSS glossary
D - DIP ic pictorials	V - access to other volumes
E - Envelope printer	W - Wide print constants
F - Form letter manager	X - Exit to AppleWriter
G - Grids and rulers	Z - Zee tutorial help

Which? --->

---

[12] An Apple II can use the LaserWriter as a Diablo emulator without the need for specific LaserWriter software. Using a communications program and a serial card (or port in the case of the IIc), an Apple II can also communicate directly with the LaserWriter in PostScript. The Apple IIGS has an AppleTalk printer port.

[13] Synergetics
746 1st Street
PO Box 809
Thatcher, AZ 85552
(602) 428-4073

The user can quickly switch between the series of Utilities menus and the AppleWriter program.

The demonstration programs, which include routines for creating type in a circle and other special typographic effects, as well as producing practical applications such as business cards and disk labels, can be directly loaded into AppleWriter, and edited according to need. Although the utilities simplify the process of using a *IIe/IIc* for input, the user is still required to have a fundamental understanding of the PostScript language.

Some of the PostScript commands are available directly from the PGLOSS glossary (FIG. 39). An additional glossary, LGLOSS, contains LaserWriter/Diablo Emulation commands. Any of the glossary commands can be brought to the screen by pressing the Open-Apple key in combination with the glossary entry identity. For example, pressing Open-Apple-f (font inserter) results in the display of the Font Picker screen (FIG. 40). The user selects a font number and a horizontal and vertical point size which controls if the type is normal, expanded, or condensed). The result is a line of correctly written PostScript code automatically inserted in the AppleWriter document. Selecting typeface 14, with a horizontal point size of 14 and a vertical point size of 18 (18-point condensed) would result in the following line of PostScript code:

/AvantGarde-Demi findfont [14 0 0 18 0 0] makefont setfont

Automated procedures such as this make the Lancaster Utilities a valuable resource for Apple *IIe/IIc* users who need to access the capabilities of the LaserWriter.

PGLOSS PostScript Open-Apple Commands:

....

(') reset printer	(+) fix plus bug		
(A) arcto	(H) handfeed on	(O) -spare-	(V) vmsave
(a) arc	(h) handfeed off	(o) -spare-	(v) vm restore
(B) black	(I) init handshake	(P) prefeed on	(W) white
(b) begin	(i) initgraphics	(p) prefeed off	(w) linewidth
(C) showpage	(J) justify all	(Q) quit	(X) print stack
(c) copypage	(j) justify chars	(q) end of file	(x) stroke & save
(D) debugging delay	(K) clear	(R) repeat	(Y) -spare-
(d) do other volume	(k) closepath	(r) rlineto	(y) -spare-
(E) enlarge (scale)	(L) LGLOSS load	(S) show	(Z) -spare-
(e) erasepage	(l) lineto	(s) stroke	(z) tutorial
(F) fill	(M) makefont	(T) Translate	
(f) font inserter	(m) moveto	(t) twist (rotate)	(esc) insets escape
(G) gsave	(N) newpath	(U) userdict	(s0-s9) picks fonts
(g) grestore	(n) neg	(u) usertime	for justify
(0) print & debug	(1) prefix dr1	(2) prefix dr2	(3) set landscape

FIG. 39. The PostScript glossary provides a shorthand method for quickly and accurately writing PostScript procedures.

```
Font Picker:
.........................
Inserts font into current textfile position.

    13  Avant          0  Courier          29  Palatino
    14  Avant b         1  Courier b        30  Palatino b
    15  Avant i         2  Courier i        31  Palatino i
    16  Avant bi        3  Courier bi       32  Palatino bi

    17  Bookman         8  Helvetica         4  Times
    18  Bookmanb        9  Helvetica b       5  Times b
    19  Bookmani       10  Helvetica i       6  Times i
    20  Bookmanbi      11  Helvetica bi      7  Times bi

    25  Century        21  N Helvetica      12  Symbol
    26  Century b      22  N Helvetica b    33  Zapf Italic
    27  Century i      23  N Helvetica i    34  Zapf Dingbats
    28  Century bi     24  N Helvetica bi   99  Custom font

Which Font? --> 14
Horizontal points -> 14
Vertical points ---> 18
```

PAGEMAKER:
A Model for Desktop Publishing Software

PageMaker[14] is a program that integrates the operations commonly required in the paste-up or page make-up stages of offset lithographic reproduction. It is an electronic means by which the user can accurately specify the placement of text and graphics. The visual assembly of one or a series of pages is executed directly on the Macintosh screen using a set of screen tools that are analogous to those used in the physical assembly of galleys of type and line illustrations.

The PageMaker concept covers those publishing jobs typical of an office environment; that is, jobs with a relatively small number of pages done on an occasional basis. Such jobs usually require the use of outside typesetting services, requiring significant cost, as well as producing the delays inherent in sending work out of the office. Although a word processing program, such as MacWrite, is superior to others in the respect that it can integrate graphics with text, PageMaker extends that capability by providing a means of producing pages with headlines, boxed text, and columns of varying widths.

PageMaker is not a word processor itself; however it does allow for entering and editing text. It was designed primarily to take text produced with a Macintosh word processor, such as *MacWrite* or *Word*, and graphics produced with a graphics program, such as *MacPaint* or *MacDraw*, and position them on a page according to the visual judgment of the user. Using PageMaker the user can make use of a wide variety of software, using each for its most helpful features, and then integrate the various outcomes into a finished, printed product.

PageMaker can retain the formatting instructions (type size, typeface, type variation) that have been selected for MacWrite documents, as well as use standard Macintosh Cut and Paste commands used with the Clipboard (a part of memory reserved for cut and paste operations) and Scrapbook (a desk accessory which can store a number of graphic images). MacPaint and MacDraw graphics can be cut, moved, stretched, deleted, and cropped.

[14] Aldus Corporation
11 First Avenue South
Seattle, WA 98104
(206) 622-5500

Additional features were added to the Macintosh version of PageMaker in late 1986 making it functionally identical to the PC PageMaker version 1.0 release. See the description of PC PageMaker for a listing of the enhancements.

What the System Looks Like

PageMaker runs on an Apple Macintosh with a minimum of 512K and outputs to either the Apple ImageWriter or LaserWriter printer. In the latter case the output is of typeset quality, although either device produces output suitable for reproduction. True typeset quality can be obtained by printing the final pages to a PostScript version of the Allied Linotype 100 or 300 phototypesetters.

The PageMaker screen, with the publication window in place, resembles a paste-up board with a sheet of paper affixed to the center (FIG. 41). A toolbox sits upon the board in a convenient location chosen by the user, although it can be removed temporarily. The toolbox holds tools for locating graphic elements, cropping artwork, and drawing straight lines, boxes, round-cornered rectangles, circles, and ovals. Scroll bars along the right edge and bottom of the screen (which can be hidden if the user is so inclined) control the area of the layout surface that is visible. The bottom left section of the screen shows a line of page icons which indicate the number of pages in the publication. The page currently visible is highlighted. Additional controls under the Windows menu allow display of the page at actual size, reduced to fit, 200 percent enlargement, and 70 percent and 50 percent reductions (FIG. 42).

The paste-up page is surrounded by a work area. A number of paste-up elements can be placed, temporarily on this periphery prior to placement on the page. This setup is convenient for getting a visual impression of the collective elements that will constitute a layout.

Assembling a Page

The various elements of a page must be created using the appropriate word processing or graphics software. Each item that will be used is selected from a PageMaker dialog box, which is displayed by clicking the "Place" selection from the File menu. This box lists all of the compatible files available on the disk that is in the active drive. Double-clicking on a selection causes that item to be read into memory and appear in the publication window as an icon, indicating that it is either a graphic or text.

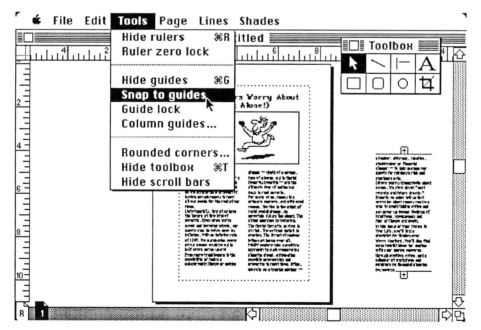

FIG. 41. The PageMaker desktop provides a work environment adaptable to the individual preferences of the user.

FIG. 42. The active page can be viewed in a number of different magnifications, providing either a number of close-up views of a particular page portion, or a reduced view showing the entire page.

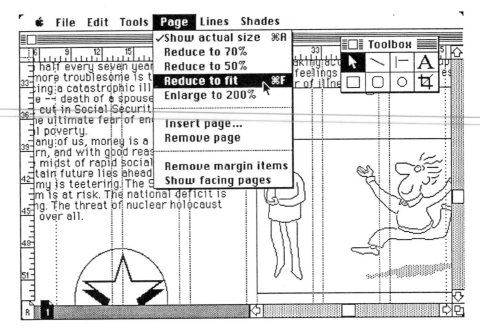

It can be positioned immediately in its exact or approximate position on the page, or can be placed in the margin area until it is needed. All of the items necessary for a page can be selected and handled in this way.

At any point in the page creation process the user may receive help from a fully documented Help window, which is accessed from the Apple icon menu, located on the extreme left of the screen. Information about all of the tools and menu items is available.

When the PageMaker program is loaded, it displays its menu bar across the top of the screen and a blank gray desktop below. To begin a new page the user selects "New..." from the File menu and the desktop changes to the page assembly environment. The new page is titled "Untitled," a name which PageMaker will not accept for disk storage. When the layout is ready to be saved the user will be prompted for a title by which to save it on disk. If the publication already exists, it is brought to the screen by selecting "Open." The "Open" command presents a dialog box with the names of all of the publication files presently available. The required file is selected by double-clicking its name or single-clicking its name and then clicking on the "Open" button.

The size of the page and its margins are specified by selecting "Page Setup" from the File menu. The paper choices are US letter, US legal, or international A4, B4, and tabloid sizes. The orientation of the images can be either *tall* (the normal output format, with the top line printed right reading at the top of the page), *tall adjusted* (used to compensate for the correct proportion of graphics for Imagewriter only), or *wide* (with text running sideways, starting with the first line printed from the right bottom of the page).

The measurement system of choice—either inches, millimeters, or points and picas—can be selected from the "Preferences" dialog box accessed from the Edit menu (FIG. 43). The margin settings for the inside, outside, top, and bottom then may be specified. The inside margin is next to the binding and can be adjusted to compensate for the loss of page area as a result of the binding.

The Place command, as just described, is the means by which each element is copied off the disk for placement. When it is executed, a dialog box is presented showing a listing of all of the text and graphic files that can be accessed directly by Page-

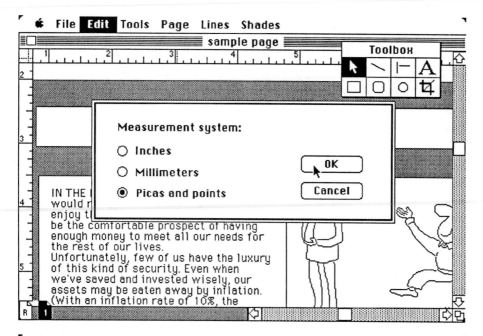

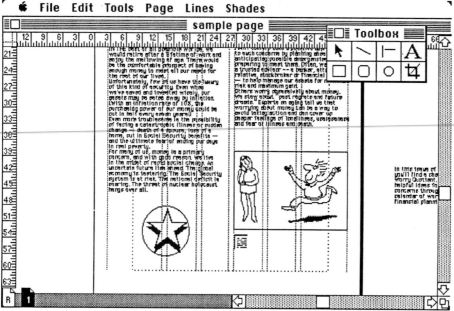

Maker. When a text file is selected, the cursor changes shape to that of the "galley flow" icon (FIG. 44). This icon is positioned on the page layout in the upper left-hand corner of the column (or in another starting position) where the text is to be placed. The starting position is activated by clicking the mouse, then the column of text flows onto the page. The text extends either to its limit or a page boundary. The text selection now displayed retains two column markers, which provide further placement flexibility. These "Column Top" and "Column Bottom" icons appear as thin lines, with a small box located in the center; above the top line and below the bottom line. Pressing in the top box will drag the starting position of the column up or down within the column. Pressing on the bottom box will release the end of column marker to make the column shorter. If the column is made shorter or the text did not originally fit in

READYSETGO:
Interactive Page Makeup

If a measure of elegance is simplicity, then the ReadySetGo[15] interactive page-makeup program from Manhattan Graphics is elegant.

ReadySetGo was developed by Martin Rosenberg and Kenneth Abbott, principals in a trade typesetting and printing house in New York City. They were among the first to realize the typesetting and graphics potential of the Macintosh and develop a product to exploit it.

ReadySetGo uses the simple concept of *blocks* as the elements from which all pages are constructed. A page element may be one of four block varieties: a *text block* for copy, a *picture block* for illustrations, a *frame block* for ruled boxes, or a *solid box* for rules and solid window areas (FIG. 46).

The ReadySetGo work area is a grid marked off in 1-inch increments. In the original version of the program pages were discrete files, and a file could only contain a single page. A multiple-page publication would, therefore, consist of a series of files. Later versions of the program overcame that restriction.

The physical boundaries of a page are selected from the "Page Setup" option of the File menu. It provides access to a variety of common paper sizes, as well as either a tall or wide paper orientation.

The creation of a page begins with the selection of a block from the Create menu. Each new block is always 1 inch square and automatically appears on the grid 1 inch down and 1 inch from the left. Each block, regardless of its type, has a number of attributes that make it flexible enough to meet the great variety of designs found in page layouts. The most immediate attributes are those that move the block and change its shape. Movement is accomplished by placing the mouse pointer within the upper horizontal frame and dragging the block to a new position. The new position should mark the correct placement of the upper left corner of the block, since placing the mouse pointer in the lower right corner of the frame will resize it to fit any needed column, window, line, or other rectangularly shaped element.

Once a block is positioned, its screen location and other descriptive specifications can be called to the screen by choosing the *Modify* selection from the Edit menu. The block specification display shows the exact linear position of the block in inches. New values can be input in order to accurately move the block quickly around the page. Additional modification choices exist for each different block type (FIG. 47).

When a block is active—and only one block may be active at a time—its outline appears as black. This makes it readily visible on the screen. When a different block is selected, the previously selected block's outline changes to gray. Blocks can be positioned alongside of, on top of, or overlapping one another. A block of type, for example, might be positioned over a frame block. The relative front/back position of blocks occupying the same physical location is controlled by the "Send Behind" selection from the Special menu. This selection brings the block directly beneath the topmost block to the surface, and places the previously fully visible block underneath.

The text block is the most flexible of all block types. As with most other text-oriented Macintosh programs, characters can be composed in a variety of sizes, typefaces, and styles. In addition to the seven sizes listed in the Size menu, the user can type in an unlisted size by selecting "Other" from the Size menu.

The line measure for the text is determined by the horizontal dimension of the block, and the column depth is determined by the vertical dimension. Characters are input in realtime, transferred through the Clipboard, or brought in as text files.

[15] Manhattan Graphics
401 Columbus Avenue
Valhalla, NY 10595
(800) 634-3463
(914) 769-2800 (in New York)

As text is input it automatically fills the line measure according to the justification setting (left, right, center, justified) chosen from the Block Specification menu. Multiple size, typeface, and style changes are possible within a text block, but only one justification and line spacing (single, single and one-half, and double) setting may be operative.

After text has been input, the block may be moved or resized. Text automatically readjusts to fit the new dimensions. If the block is resized to a shape too small for the text, only a portion will be displayed, but the remainder will still be intact when the block is either enlarged or the text is resized downward.

The Macintosh screen provides only a window on the page. Moving around the page landscape is accomplished by using the "Show Page" option from the Special menu (FIG. 48). "Show Page" displays a miniature dummy of the page, indicating block positions in relation to the Macintosh window. The window, which appears on the Show Page display as a rectangular dotted line, can be dragged by using the mouse pointer in order to display another portion of the page.

Pictures, or graphics, are carried on the page within *picture* blocks. Picture blocks are distinctive in that when they are created they have an "X" across their centers to indicate that they are empty. Pictures are placed within these blocks by transferring images through the Clipboard or the Scrapbook. In the case of the Scrapbook, an image would be drawn, painted, and/or scanned prior to using ReadySetGo, and then copied into the Scrapbook. In ReadySetGo the picture block would be created, the Scrapbook opened, the image copied, the Scrapbook closed, the picture block selected, and the image pasted. Resizing picture blocks can result in reducing, enlarging, or distorting artwork.

Since the selection, placement, and sizing of various combinations of blocks serves to define the geography of the page layout, ReadySetGo provides the options of saving either the entire page, or just the layout. If only the layout is saved, it can be filled in at some future time. If the entire page is saved, it can be edited and revised. Pages can be printed on either the ImageWriter or the LaserWriter.

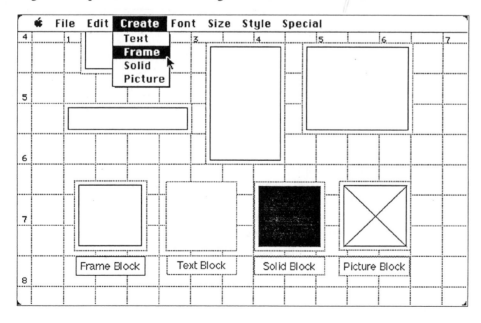

FIG. 46. In truly modular form, all components of the ReadySetGo page are composed of one of the basic building blocks: frame, text, solid, or picture.

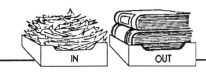
FIG. 47. Each building block can be modified by making changes to its specification menu. Each menu presents options related to the specific personality of its associated block. The Text Block Specification menu shown here, for example, shows not only the exact location of the block (an attribute common to all blocks), but also the settings for justification, line spacing, and tabs.

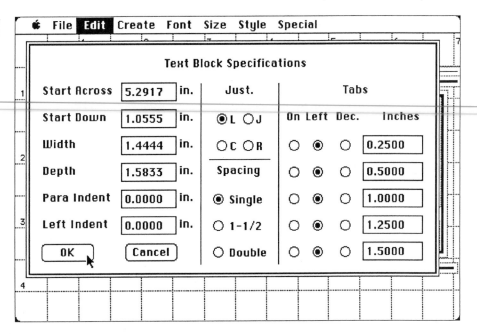

FIG. 48. The Show Page capability serves both to display a dummy of the entire layout and to facilitate movement around the page.

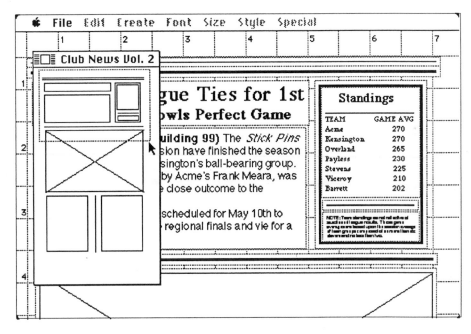

READY,SET,GO! 3:
Batch Page Processing

An example of the rapidly increasing sophistication of desktop publishing software is the Ready,Set,Go! (RSG) program series.[16] Version 1.0 was released in January of 1985, coinciding with the announcement of the Apple LaserWriter. A second-generation product, version 2.0, was shipped in September of 1985, followed by the upgraded version 2.1 in February of 1986. Version 3.0, released in November of 1986, marks a major improvement, providing more professional, powerful capabilities. Exclusive marketing rights to the program were purchased by Letraset in January, 1987.

A Third Time Around the Block

The heart of RSG 3 is still the *block*, the rectangularly shaped compartment used to hold text or graphics. Blocks are initially defined by free-hand placement on the page, although text blocks can be repeated automatically on any number of successive pages. The arrangement of blocks is aided by a user-definable grid (FIG. 49), which assists in placement as well as design. One of a number of standard system grids (FIG. 50) also can be used, or the grid can be completely hidden from view.

Text blocks are strung together by use of the Linker tool (the lightening bolt). After a number of text blocks have been drawn, the Linker is clicked in each block to indicate the order of text flow (FIG. 51). When pages are added to a publication, they can be specified to link automatically with the last block on the previous page, or to stand independently (FIG. 52).

Text is made to flow between blocks by first inserting the I-beam tool in the starting block, and then selecting "Get Text" from the File menu. If the file is being imported from a Macintosh word processor, such as MacWrite or Microsoft Word, the text will retain all of its character-based attributes, such as font, size, and style, that were originally assigned. If the imported file is plain ASCII, the text will take on the properties preselected in the Font and Style menus. Text also can be entered manually, and hyphenation and justification can take place in real time.

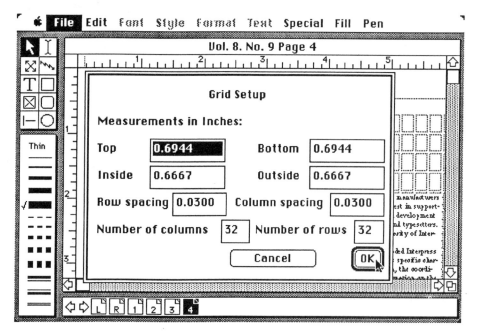

FIG. 49. Ready,Set,Go! 3 has a newly designed user interface, with a Toolbox and Rule Selection window along the left side. The page layout area can be divided into a user-specified positioning guide by using the "Grid Setup" dialog box.

16 Letraset USA
40 Eisenhower Drive
Paramus, NJ 07653
(201) 845-6100

FIG. 50. The program provides eight common grid rulings. The page shown behind the "Design Grid" dialog box (reduced to fit) is one of five views that the user can select. Other views are double-page spreads, actual size, 70 percent size, and 50 percent size.

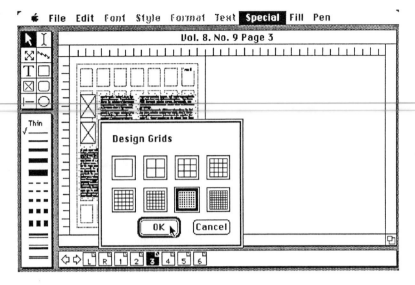

FIG. 51. The Linker tool is clicked in successive text blocks to assign the order of text flow. A double-click in the last text block indicates that it is the end of the text chain.

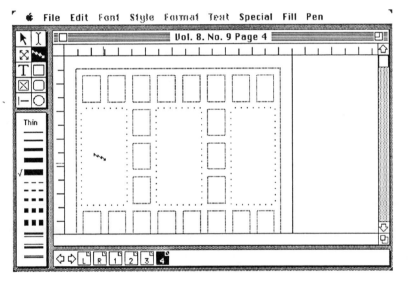

FIG. 52. Any number of pages can be inserted at any time, in any publication. The pages can be specified to link only within themselves, globally with other pages in the publication, or not at all.

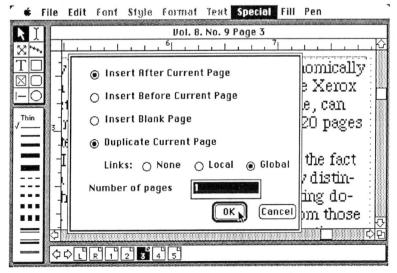

As one block fills with text, the remainder of text is automatically channeled into the next linked block. If excess text exists, it is indicated by short, solid, right-angle lines in the bottom right corner of the final block (FIG. 53).

All block elements have specification sheets for exact page positioning and the control and selection of certain associated characteristics. The "Text Block Specification" sheet (FIG. 54) displays the position of the block origin, as drawn by the user, and its width and depth. These values can be changed directly on the sheet. The block also can be tagged as "PostScript" or "Run Around." A "PostScript" block contains actual PostScript notation that will be interpreted as a program by the PostScript output device. This option is very useful for producing graphic effects that are not obtainable directly with RSG 3, such as type set in a circle. The "Run Around" option makes the text block reform to accommodate a graphic block that appears within its boundaries.

Graphic blocks are drawn using the "X-in-a-box" tool. Their size can be adjusted precisely by using the on-screen ruler in combination with the grid, or by using the "Picture Block Specification" sheet (FIG. 55). This sheet permits the control of the size of the graphic and also its proportionality. The increment system in use—either inches, centimeters, or points and picas, can be changed for this and all other specifications by using the "Preferences" selection in the Special menu.

A graphic block is selected by clicking the Cropping tool (NSEW arrows) anywhere within its borders. The block takes on a patterned background, and a graphic is chosen by selecting "Get Picture" from the File menu. The graphic then appears in the block and is cropped by moving it within the boundaries of the block outline (FIG. 56A, B, C). After the graphic is placed, the block size and graphic size can be adjusted to suit the layout.

Text, pictures, and other graphic object blocks, such as rules, rectangles, round-cornered rectangles, and ovals, can be placed on all, some, or most of the pages of a publication. They are indicated on the left- and right-hand master pages, accessible by clicking on the L or R page icon on the bottom of the screen. Master pages also can hold page numbers, and date and time information tags.

The specification of repetitive text blocks on master pages makes it possible to handle files in batch mode, rather than page by page. RSG 3 has no stated page limitation, other than the confines of the disk in use. Page number icons, scrolled horizontally across the bottom of the screen, are one of the program's methods of changing pages.

Typographic Refinements

RSG 3 uses algorithmic and exception word dictionary hyphenation methods to display hyphenated and justified text very quickly. Built-in kerning pair tables are accessed when more than one character is highlighted and the "Kerning" option is selected. The kerning pair values are based on the font's resource file, as defined by Adobe Systems. If the font does not have an associated kerning file, then no character adjustment takes place.

An individual character can be kerned by selecting it and choosing "Kerning" from the Format menu (FIG. 57). The user is prompted for the number of points the character is to be moved to the left. An alternative method of executing shift movements, involving a variation in space between characters (horizontally) or lines (vertically), can be accomplished by selecting the affected characters and holding the command key in combination with the up, down, left, or right arrow on the Mac Plus keyboard. Characters are moved in one-point increments in the selected direction.

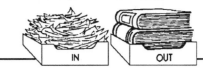

FIG. 53. When excess text remains in the last block of a linked series, a small corner marker appears as a warning.

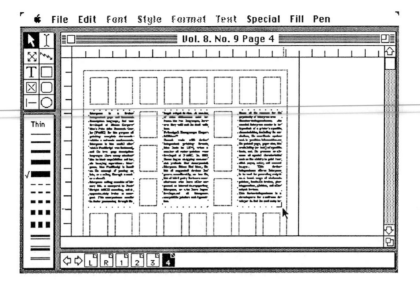

FIG. 54. Precise placement information about text blocks appears in the "Text Block Specification" dialog box.

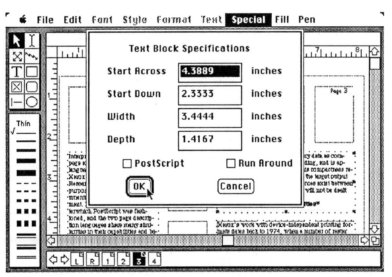

FIG. 55. The "Picture Block Specification" dialog box supports the reassignment of block dimensions, picture size, and picture proportions.

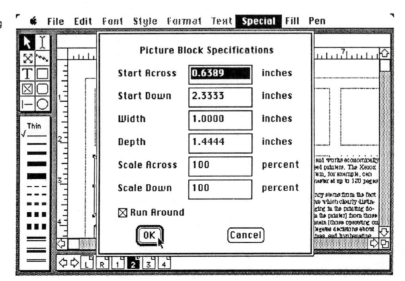

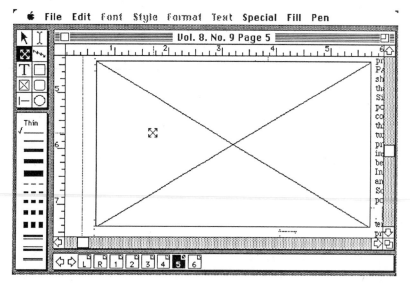

FIG. 56A. Picture blocks are easily identified by their large X. The Cropping tool appears on the left of this block.

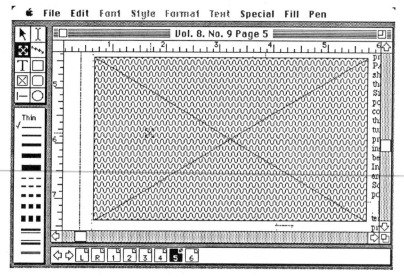

FIG. 56B. Clicking the Cropping tool in a picture block creates a patterned background, making the block active for receiving a graphic image.

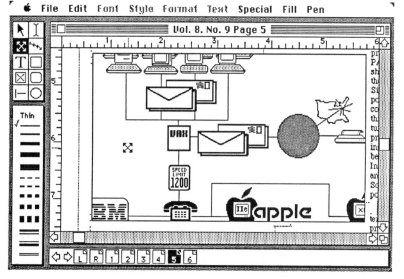

FIG. 56C. A graphic is selected, and immediately appears in the block along with the Cropping tool. The tool is used to position the graphic within the block area. The "Picture Block Specification" dialog box can be used to change the dimensions or proportion of the graphic, or the size of the picture block itself. The block size also can be changed directly on the layout work surface.

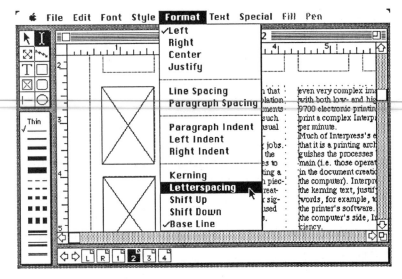

FIG. 57. A number of typographic controls are available in the Format menu. Character- and line-fit changes can be activated either by menu selection or direct keyboard control.

The line spacing increment defaults to an automatic value based on the chosen point size. The user can specify a different value for all or part of a given article.

Paragraph spacing can be adjusted in one-point increments, and a paragraph indent can be specified. The left paragraph indent affects all lines except the first, and the right indent affects every line.

Additional Features

RSG 3 adds more than 35 new features. Among them are:

- The "Put Text" option can be used to export formatted text out of RSG 3 for use in another application.
- Characters can be set in condensed or expanded form.
- The program supports multiple levels of Undo.
- More than one publication can be open at a time.
- Graphics can be copied in a group, and entire pages can be lifted from one publication and placed in another.
- A whole page can be copied to the Clipboard.
- Point sizes as large as 127 point can be set.
- A built-in real-time spell-checker can be activated.
- Global search and replace can be used to modify an unlimited number of linked blocks.
- A single text block can have any mix of typographic attributes, including hyphenated/unhyphenated, justified, flush left, flush right, and centered, in alternate type faces, styles, sizes, and line spacing values.

LASER AUTHOR:
Midground Between WP and DP

As the sophistication of both word processing and desktop publishing software increases, there is a narrowing of the gap between the pure forms of either one. Word processing programs are moving toward page composition and graphic integration, while desktop publishing programs are gaining increased text processing and handling capabilities. About midway on the continuum of capabilities between these two forms is Laser Author,[17] a word processor with automatic typographic formatting features.

The premise behind Laser Author is that authors produce different kinds of documents, each of which requires different formatting. The formatting process might, in certain complex cases, involve a considerable amount of time and effort, and detract from the prime objective of any author, namely putting thoughts into words. Laser Author provides the tools to easily assign predefined appearance values (formats) to blocks of text. Individual format descriptions are called *styles*, and a group of styles for any one document design are saved as *stationery*.

Laser Authorship

Laser Author adheres well to the Macintosh user interface, and the basic word processing functions perform predictably. The program's main departure from the realm of word processing is the use of the Style editor (FIG. 58), which allows the user to define the appearance attributes for sections of text. These attributes include, among others:

- Margins and tabs
- Justification mode (left, right, center, justified)
- Font
- Fixed spacing (interlinear, above, and below)
- Character fit (normal, add space, subtract space)
- Style variation (bold, italic, etc.)
- Indentions

The author names a style according to any logical divisions appropriate for a document, and assigns them to one of three menus: Heading, Paragraph, or Text. Some possible document divisions for a few popular kinds of work are shown in Table 2.

Any text block can be assigned any existing style. In order to make the assignment, the I-beam cursor is placed anywhere in the block. The style is selected from one of the style assignment menus, or by the use of a command key sequence as defined during the style creation process. The style editor can be used at any time to modify any of the format variables.

Frames

Frames are defined rectangular areas that can be assigned to either text or graphics. Frames can be placed within other frames, and text frames can be self-generated and linked together with a stream of text.

A frame is created by selecting "Make a frame" from the Page menu. A dialog box appears (FIG. 59) presenting the frame options. The frame is composed by first indicating its upper left corner and then dragging the mouse. Digital read-outs are presented to show the position and the size of the frame. Both the text and the graphic frames are composed of a move bar along the top for repositioning, and a grow handle in the lower right for re-sizing. Only the text frame includes the I-beam cursor for text insertion. Text that is pasted or typed into a frame can be assigned any style definition.

TABLE 2. Document Divisions

Report
- —Title
- —Author Information
- —Table of Contents
- —Abstract
- —Major Head
- —Text
- —Minor Head
- —Footnotes
- —Summary

Book
- —Title
- —List of Other Books By the Author
- —Copyright Notice
- —Dedication
- —Preface
- —Acknowledgements
- —Table of Contents
- —List of Illustrations
- —List of Figures
- —Introduction
- —Major Heading
- —Text
- —Subordinate Heading
- —Second Subordinate Heading
- —Appendices
- —Index
- —Colophon (production notes)

Correspondence
- —Letterhead
- —Date
- —Addressee
- —Text
- —Closing

---

[17] Firebird Licensees, Inc.
P.O. Box 49
Ramsey, NJ 07446
(201) 444-5700

Graphics are positioned in a graphic frame by copying from the Macintosh Scrapbook. The paste operation can be either *scaled*, to fit the dimensions of the frame, or *clipped*, to retain the original graphic dimensions and being cropped if the frame is smaller than the image. If the graphic is clipped, it can be moved within the frame until it is properly displayed.

Frames are a part of the page layout, which is saved as Stationery. In addition to defining the text elements of a report, for example, an illustration could be saved in a graphic frame and appear in position on a standardized document.

Additional Features

Laser Author has a number of somewhat unique capabilities that serve the needs of professional authors. Because one of the most critical aspects of good typography is proper character fit, Laser Author provides the means to both add and subtract inter-character spacing. Individual character pair fit can be adjusted by positioning the I-beam cursor between the characters and pressing the Control key and comma to kern, or the Control key and period to letterspace (FIG. 60A).

An unusual capability is the facility to type both a superscript and a subscript with the same character. This process is accomplished with a series of command key sequences (FIG. 60B). Also rare is the overstrike function, whereby two or more characters can be overstruck (FIG. 60C).

At any point during an editing session a listing of document statistics can be displayed (FIG. 61). These statistics show such things as the length of the document in pages, words, lines, and characters, and the amount of time spent working on the document (currently and previously). All of this information is helpful to professional writers.

FIG. 58. The Style editor provides considerable control over the typographic appearance of a text block.

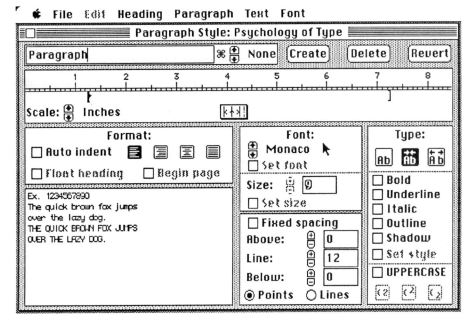

🍎 File Edit Search Page Heading Paragraph Text

Psychology of Type

The Psycholog~~y and Mechanics of~~
Type Legibilit~~y~~

INTRODUCTION

Choose frame contents:
⦿ Text   ☐ Allow continuation frames
○ Graphics

Attach frame to:
○ Paragraph
⦿ Page/Frame

[OK]   [Cancel]

The legibi~~lity~~   which it can
be comprehend~~ed~~   se from a
reader is a me~~ans~~   es of type are
assembled int~~o~~   properties
relative to co~~mprehension~~   bles of
readability are governed by the typographer, whereas the problems of
legibility are assigned to the designer. [1]
    In typographic circles there is the question of how, when speaking of a
printed piece, one can separate the legibility of the type face from the
readability of the material. Realistically one can not. The legibility of a type
face, roman or sans serif, italic or bold, is just as much a factor in
readability as line length, leading, and spacing. In other words, too long a
~~line length, wide leading, and open spacing can ruin the legibility of a type face~~

Page 1   Words 176

FIG. 59. Frames are easily constructed, positioned, and sized. They can be nested, overlapped, or placed side by side.

🍎 File Edit Search Page Heading Paragraph Text   3:22:55

Characterfit

Buying into the Future

with Available Technology   normal

Buying into the Future

with Available Technology   kerned

Page 1   Words 14

FIG. 60A. Minute spacing adjustments between characters can be controlled manually, on an individual character pair basis, or overall by using the Style editor.

🍎 File Edit Search Page Heading Paragraph Text   3:25:54

Untitled 15.17.29

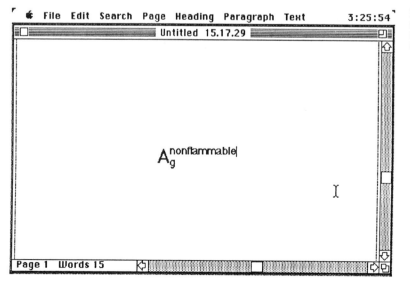

$A_g^{\text{nonflammable}}$

Page 1   Words 15

FIG. 60B. Difficult typographic effects, such as combined subscript and superscript and multiple character overstrikes, are accomplished easily in Laser Author.

FIG. 61. A number of useful job statistics are always available.

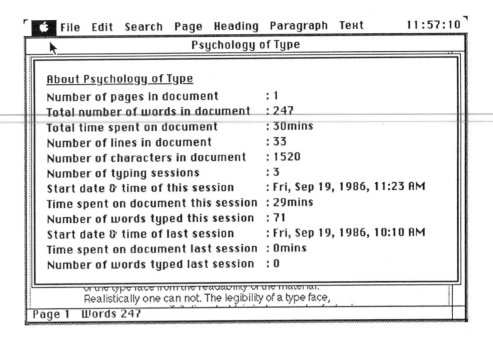

File   Edit   Search   Page   Heading   Paragraph   Text   11:57:10

Psychology of Type

About Psychology of Type

Number of pages in document	: 1
Total number of words in document	: 247
Total time spent on document	: 30mins
Number of lines in document	: 33
Number of characters in document	: 1520
Number of typing sessions	: 3
Start date & time of this session	: Fri, Sep 19, 1986, 11:23 AM
Time spent on document this session	: 29mins
Number of words typed this session	: 71
Start date & time of last session	: Fri, Sep 19, 1986, 10:10 AM
Time spent on document last session	: 0mins
Number of words typed last session	: 0

of the type face from the readability of the material.
Realistically one can not. The legibility of a type face,

Page 1   Words 247

DTI DISPLAY AD SYSTEM:
Professional Typesetting of Advertisements

Display advertisements, such as appear in the telephone yellow pages and shoppers' guides, newspapers and magazines, tabloids and sales circulars, and newsletters and brochures, constitute a particularly complex and time-consuming form of typesetting. They are characterized by a high-frequency rate of typeface, type size, line space, and line measure changes. For conventional typesetting systems, that translates into a considerable amount of coding, and therefore a high coding-to-text ratio. The high coding overhead makes ad typesetting more expensive, not only because of the additional time required, but also because of the higher skill level required of the keyboard operator.

The highly visual nature of the Macintosh makes it a particularly good environment for ad make-up. Since the orientation is toward advertisements, which are usually small parts of a page, the size of the Macintosh screen is not a drawback. A number of Macintosh programs, such as MacWrite, MacPaint, and MacDraw, provide limited capabilities to produce ad typography output on either an ImageWriter or a LaserWriter.

In the realm of professional typesetting, the threshold of image quality is in the range of 800 to 1000 dpi. At this time the most economical way of achieving that resolution is with a phototypesetting machine. A professional software package called the DTI Display Ad System[18] outputs ads composed on the Macintosh to the Compugraphic 8400, 8600, and other high-speed digital typesetters.

The DTI Display Ad System provides all of the tools and capabilities necessary to create display ads up to 69 picas, 11 points wide by 20 15/16 inches deep, which is larger than a tabloid newspaper page. Each ad is saved as a separate file.

The procedure for creating an ad begins with the selection of the ad width (FIG. 62), which may be specified in either picas or inches. The picas selection results in a full-screen display of available sizes, in whole picas and points (FIG. 63). The depth is specified by selecting either "Picas Long" or "Inches Long" from the Adsize menu.

[18] Digital Technology International
500 West 1200 South
Orem, UT 84058
(801) 226-2984

Requires a Macintosh with a minimum of 512K. This software is priced for the professional typesetting market.

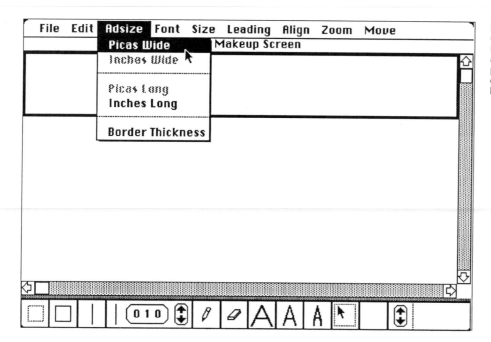

FIG. 62. The DTI Display Ad System screen is divided into three major parts: a series of menus along the top to specify such things as ad dimensions and typographic identity and position; the main window work area for composing the ad; and the tools along the bottom of the screen.

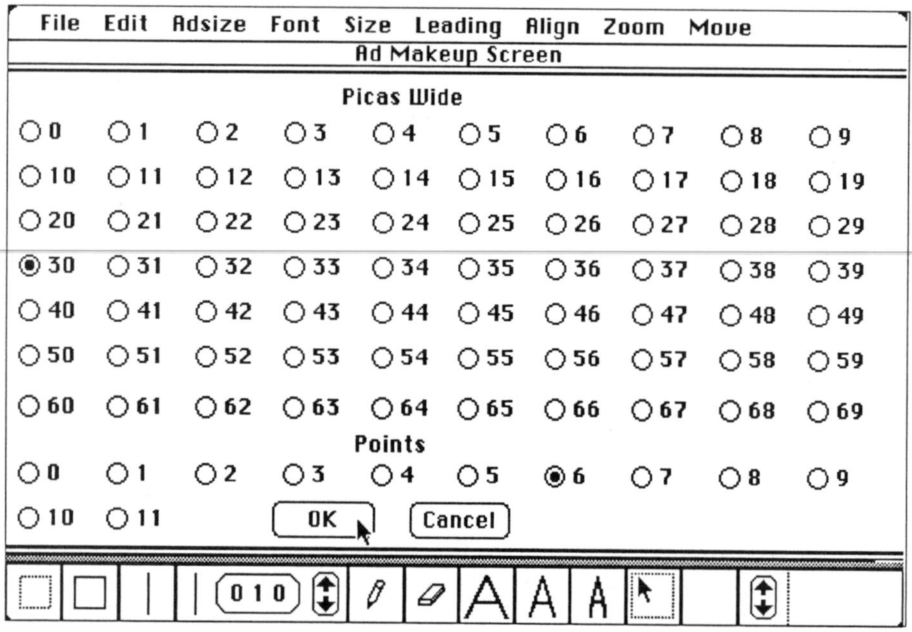

FIG. 63. The specification of ad size, in picas/points or inches/fractions, is accomplished from menus such as this.

The rule weight for lines and borders is set by clicking in the numeric window in the fourth position from the left along the bottom of the screen. Clicking in the arrow areas, either up for a heavier weight line or down for a narrower one, results in an instant representative line display to the immediate left of the numeric window. The ad border is created in the operative rule weight by selecting "Border Thickness" from the Adsize menu (FIG. 62).

The text for the ad is input at a single time (although additions may be made later) by choosing the "Master Text" selection from the Edit menu. This selection provides an editing window into which the copy is keyboarded. Each element of the ad is separated by the accent key (located in the upper left of the Macintosh keyboard), which is displayed as a vertical bar (FIG. 64). When all of the copy has been input, the

FIG. 64. Text elements are separated by a delimiter which the program uses to isolate each text segment for individual treatment. During the text creation process all of the normal Macintosh editing options (copy, cut, paste, etc.) are available.

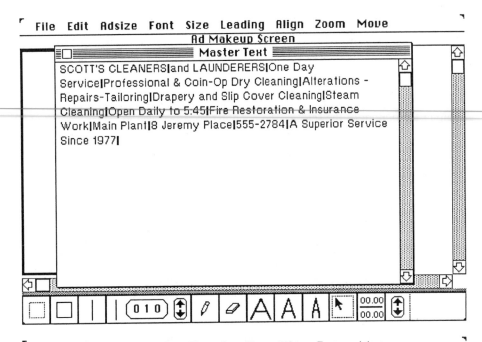

FIG. 65. Copy is brought onto the screen by creating individual windows for each text element.

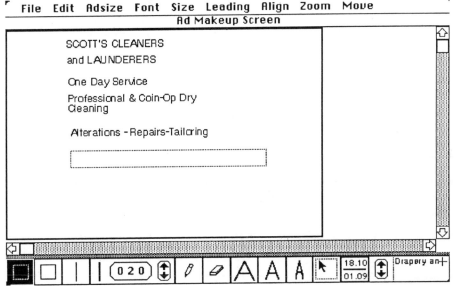

text window is closed by clicking in the close box (the small square in the upper left of the text window).

In order to position the text within the ad it is necessary to create a line measure box for each text element. This task is accomplished by clicking in the Set Measure box (the first box on the left of the bottom Tool menu). The Set Measure tool appears in the ad area as a cross-hair, which expands into a dotted line window when the mouse button is held and the mouse is dragged. The size of the window is displayed in the second window from the right along the bottom of the screen, with the width in picas and points in the top half, and the depth in picas and points in the bottom.

After the first line measure box has been created, the first element of the text automatically appears in the Copy box, which is located in the extreme right lower corner of the screen (FIG. 65). The cross-hair is clicked over the element to transfer it into the awaiting measure window. The next text element is brought into the display by clicking on the down arrow within the Copy box. The procedure is repeated either immediately, or at such time as is required, until all of the elements appear within the ad.

Activating an element, in order to specify its typographic identification, is done by clicking on the Mode box, which is located immediately to the right of the series of A's along the bottom of the screen. The resulting arrow is used to select the text element that will be typographically altered. After an element is selected, its dotted-line window reappears. The contents of the highlighted window can be resized (FIG. 66), the typeface can be changed (FIG. 67), its line spacing can be respecified; the element can be realigned with other elements; or the element can be moved with a grabber hand (look for the grabber in FIG. 68).

The pencil tool in the bottom menu can be used to create line graphics, which will not appear in the typeset output, but which serve to help the layout person reserve space for the manual paste-up of artwork, logotypes, and photographs (FIG. 68). The eraser tool is used to remove unwanted images from the ad area.

Ads that extend beyond the viewing area of the Macintosh screen can be scrolled using the horizontal and vertical scroll bars, or the entire ad can be reduced by using the Zoom menu. The "Show Attributes" option from the Zoom menu displays the font, point size, and line spacing value for the highlighted text window (FIG. 69).

The box and line tools in the bottom tool menu are fairly self-explanatory. After a box or line has been created, double-clicking in the respective tool window will cause the just-created shape to be copied. In this way parallel lines, grids, and other shapes can be constructed.

The three A tools are used to change the character width of text within a selected window. Successive clicking in the narrow A causes the text to be set narrower, while clicking in the expanded A causes the text to be set wider. Clicking in the middle A returns the selection to its normal set width.

From the File menu the ad can be saved and then printed either to the ImageWriter for proofing, or to the typesetter for final output.

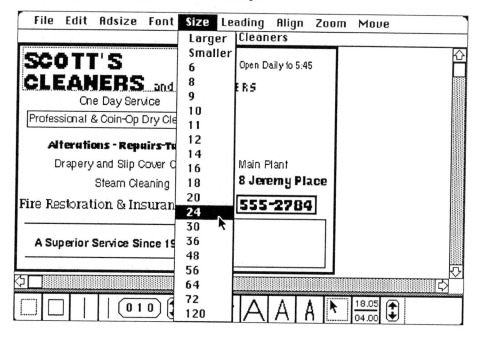

FIG. 66. A wide range of sizes may be assigned to text elements.

FIG. 67. Typefaces, which are available on the output device are listed in the Font menu. DTI provides representative screen fonts to match the font repertoire on the output phototype-setter.

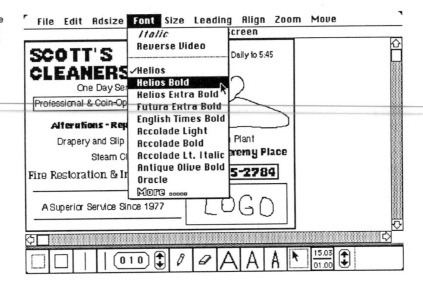

FIG. 68. Line graphics are added to indicate space reserved for later manual insertion of artwork, logos, or photographs.

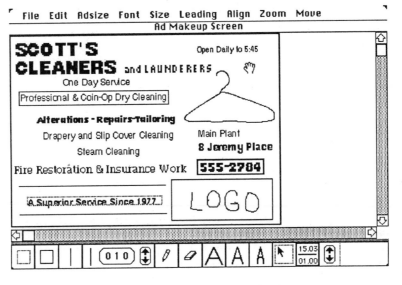

FIG. 69. The typographic attributes of any text element may be determined by first selecting the element, and then choosing the Show Attributes option from the Zoom menu.

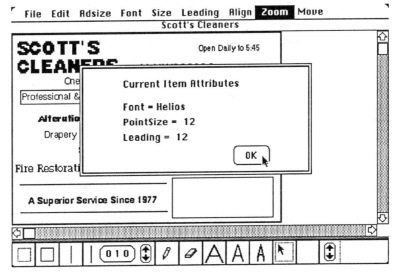

MacPublisher:
Personal Publishing on a Desktop

The publishing process has always been somewhat of an enigma to most people. How something gets published, when it is in publishable form, and when the act of publication actually occurs, are often mysteries. Even those people familiar with the publishing process see great variation in the ways in which author's ideas are ultimately converted into ink on paper.

In simple terms there are six basic steps in the publishing process:

- The origination of a message.
- The generation of text and graphic images to communicate the message.
- The design and assembly of text and graphics into a functional form (usually pages).
- The conversion of the composed forms into a reproduction master(s).
- The mass reproduction of the master(s) into copies.
- The distribution of the copies to public or private audiences.

In many publishing environments these steps are further divided into specific functions related to the editing, production, manufacturing, promotion, and distribution of a wide variety of different kinds of publication work. The notion of *self-publishing*, however, is not new, and dates back, in fact, to the printer/scholars of the earliest days of printing. Self-publishing, in one form or another, has existed throughout the history of literacy.

The idea that the entire publishing process could take place within the confines of an individual's desk is a new concept. Desktop publishing has been made possible by smaller, more powerful computers, notably the Macintosh; smaller, more powerful and capable composition devices, notably the Apple LaserWriter; and smaller, and increasingly less expensive photocopiers. The cinchpin holding such systems together is powerful, easy-to-use software, such as *MacPublisher*.[19]

MacPublisher is designed around the premise that all publications are composed of articles (words) and pictures (graphics). Words may be composed using any of the Macintosh word processing programs and brought into the MacPublisher environment via the Clipboard. Graphics may be created using any Macintosh paint or drawing program and carried into the MacPublisher environment via either the Clipboard or the Scrapbook.

The MacPublisher publication creation routine treats each page as a *dummy*, a block-shaped representation indicating all of the various elements of a page (FIG. 70). The dummy is displayed at 44 percent of the actual page size, and alternately can be displayed in *minipage* form (FIG. 71) showing more page detail.

A page can be designed within the column limitations (one-third page, one-half page, two-thirds page, or full page) imposed by the program. Articles and pictures can be positioned in compliance with column specifications, or the "Free-form" option can be invoked, allowing the placement of an element in any position on the page.

An article is created by selecting "New Article" from the Edit menu. The user is then prompted for a name, that becomes not only the ID tag by which the article will be identified on the dummy, but also the title for its entry in the automatic page index generator (FIG. 71). While the article is being composed, all of the standard Macintosh editing tools are available. The typographic and justification descriptors, such as typeface, size, style, column width, and line orientation, also can be invoked at any time after the article is opened. These assignments apply to the entire section of the article; that is, a single word of italic could not be specified without the entire section being converted to italic.

[19] Boston Software Publishers, Inc.
1260 Boylston Street
Boston, MA 02132
(617) 267-4747

Runs on either a 128K or 512K Macintosh.

FIG. 70. The MacPublisher desktop includes a creative area to the left for inputting articles and taking pictures, and a layout board on the right for assembling pages.

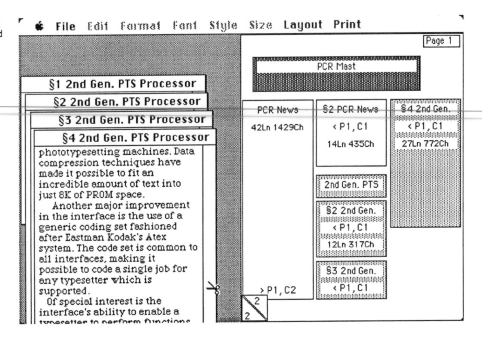

FIG. 71. The dummy page can be converted to a minipage by invoking the proper selection from the Layout menu. Automatic index generation is easily accomplished through the use of a menu selection. The index contains the title of the article and its page and column location.

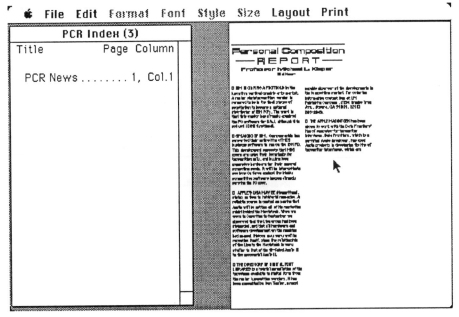

Page items that are repetitive from one issue of a publication to another are saved in a folder of *standing elements*. Common standing elements might be mastheads, logotypes, copyright indicia, staff listings, running heads, or folios.

The article can be printed directly at either same size, 133 percent, 150 percent, or 200 percent. These enlargements are provided so that the user can use an Image-Writer printer like a typesetter, and have the output photographically reduced in order to increase its effective resolution.

When an article has been completed, it is cut from its article status using the scissors icon and lifted onto the dummy. The dummy might contain, at the user's option, an invisible grid onto which the article would be snapped, or the page might allow for free-form positioning. When the article appears on the dummy it is displayed with its name, length in lines and characters, and an indication if the article continues on another page and in another column, or if it originated in another page or another column.

One of the most impressive features of MacPublisher is its *ruler*, a transparent tool that can measure in either lines of type, inches, or pixels. It can be used in a number of ways, depending upon how the user chooses to work. In its primary function, the ruler is positioned on the dummy, and a point of depth is clicked using the mouse. The depth at that location then appears in a small box, and a dotted line simultaneously appears in the Open Article window, indicating where the copy would have to be cut in order to fit on the page (FIG. 72).

It is obvious that not all articles will fit within a single column or portion of a column, and will need to be broken into smaller segments. MacPublisher handles lengthy text in a very interesting manner. Using the ruler and scissors, the article can be cut to fit any available space precisely . The remainder, or *carryover*, becomes section 2 of the same article name. The article may be cut in as many sections as needed. Each section can be handled as a separate typographic entity; therefore, a single headline, for example, can be a section unto itself, and set larger and bolder.

Pictures are brought into the MacPublisher environment by copying them onto the Clipboard and then selecting the camera (FIG. 73). Using the Clipboard size selector, the MacPublisher "Format" options, and the camera cropping capability, the picture then can be properly sized. When it is satisfactorily framed, the camera is positioned over it and snapped by clicking the mouse. After a brief flash, the user is prompted for the name of the picture. The picture then can be cut instantly and lifted onto the page dummy.

Output may be directed to either the ImageWriter or the LaserWriter.

In mid-1986 a new version of the program, MacPublisher II was released, with many enhancements including pages sizes up to 21" x 28", kerning, depth justification, and repeating elements.

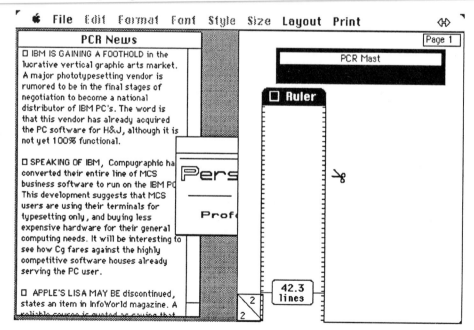

FIG. 72. The MacPublisher ruler is a transparent measuring device which accurately displays page depth in either lines, inches, or pixels.

FIG. 73. Pictures are cropped and converted into MacPublisher manipulable images through the use of the camera.

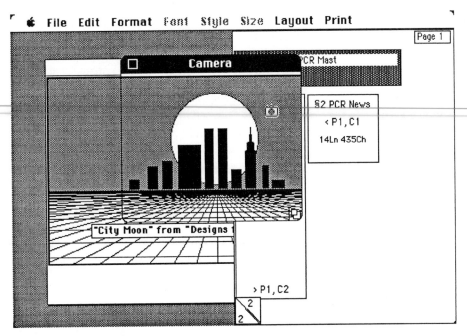

MacPublisher III:
Two Steps Beyond MacPublisher

Many of the software tools available to desktop publishers are distinguished by the fact that they have matured almost as fast as the market has grown. Users have told software publishers what enhancements they would like to see in their products, and publishers have shown sensitivity to the capabilities of competitive products, and the need for innovation, creativity, and the implementation of large system functionality. MacPublisher III[20] is a good example of such a product.

MacPublisher III was developed in response to Letraset USA's decision to enter the desktop publishing market. Letraset, known for its Instant Lettering dry transfer process, considered computerized page assembly as an electronic extension of the typographic and design freedom that it pioneered. It purchased Boston Software Publishers Inc. and the rights to the MacPublisher series, MacIndexer, and Mac-Hy-phen in 1986.

Prior to its public introduction, Letraset returned the program, tentatively named LetraPage, to its developer, and purchased worldwide marketing rights to ReadySet-Go! 3. MacPublisher III was released independently in early 1987.

The Improved MacPublisher

MacPublisher III is completely redesigned, with an improved user interface. Significant features include:

- Editing directly on the layout page with the text tool.
- Drawing directly on the layout page using any of the five graphic tools for creating rules, boxes, and circles/ovals.
- Cropping graphic images in a variety of different shapes.
- Placing text and graphic elements with precision, using Spec Sheets.
- Automatically kerning ill-fitting character pairs with a built-in kerning pair table, as well as manually adjusting character fit by operator intervention.
- Designing graphic backgrounds and designs using a flexible Graphics Palette.

20 Boston Publishing Systems
  1260 Boylston St.
  Boston, MA 02215
  (617) 267-4747

- Hyphenating text using the built-in 96,000-word dictionary, or manual or discretionary hyphenation methods.
- Setting pages to any of 20 different sizes.
- Adjusting page boundaries and columns, and utilizing a layout grid and snap-to guides.
- Interactively resizing any item on the page layout.
- Viewing a page in sizes ranging from 44 percent to 900 percent.
- Creating automatic page numbers, continuation lines, and a publication table of contents.
- Creating a publication with up to 1024 pages, 1024 text article entries, and 1024 pictures. Each text and picture element is maintained independent of the publication and can be used in other issues.
- Reading MacWrite, MacPaint, MacDraw (PICT), and Microsoft Word files directly from disk.
- Outputting individual pages as a MacPublisher picture, a MacDraw PICT file, a MacPaint document, or a PostScript file. PostScript files can be telecommunicated to a typesetting service for output on a high-resolution phototypesetter. A telecommunications desk accessory called Newswire is included with the program.

Making an Issue

MacPublisher III (MP III) publications are called issues, and they consist of from 1 to 1024 pages composed of articles (text) and pictures (graphics). As each article and picture is created, it appears in its own window (FIG. 74).

The maximum size of an issue is determined by available disk space. The actual MP III issue document does not contain all of the articles and pictures of which it is composed, but information on how to assemble text and graphic files that are available on the mounted disk(s) or hard disk. Because the items that compose an issue remain independent of it, they can be used again in other issues. This feature can be a significant timesaver, especially for elements that are created within MP III and have no basis in a word processing or graphic program environment. It also means that text

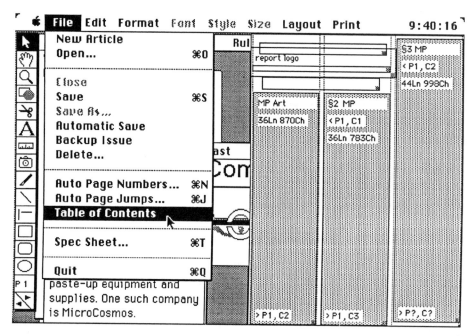

FIG. 74. The File menu provides access to existing text and graphics, and to the creation of new articles. Among the other features that are accessible from this menu are an "Automatic Save" option, which saves the issue to disk at regular intervals; dialog boxes for specifying automatic page numbering and page jumps (i.e. "continued on page x"); an automatic Table of Contents generator; and "Spec Sheets" for selected articles or pictures. The right side of the screen shows the dummy page view.

files which have been modified from within the MP III program can be reused in their updated form in the word processing program of their origin.

An MP III article is a standard Macintosh Text file. It can vary in length from a single word for a headline to up to 32K. Text can be imported from other sources or can be composed in real time, either directly on the MaxiPage full-size layout (FIG. 75), or in an article window. Text imported from MacWrite and Word will retain font style information (bold, italic, etc.) but will be stripped of the actual font and size parameters. The font, style, size, and justification of text within an article can be changed, although it cannot be altered for individual characters or words. If a heading with an article must be set in bold, for example, then the article must be cut before and after the heading. The cut sections of an article are called *carryovers*, and each carryover can have its own typographic treatment.

Articles are saved automatically, and named Text-1, Text-2, etc., or whatever name the user chooses. The placement of article windows is accomplished in the same manner as in MacPublisher, namely by clicking the scissors in the article's title bar and moving the article onto the layout.

FIG. 75. The MaxiPage is a full-sized representation of the articles and pictures. The MaxiPage provides the clearest view of how the page will appear when it is printed. Items can be moved, text can be character-fit, pictures can be resized, and much more, all directly on the page.

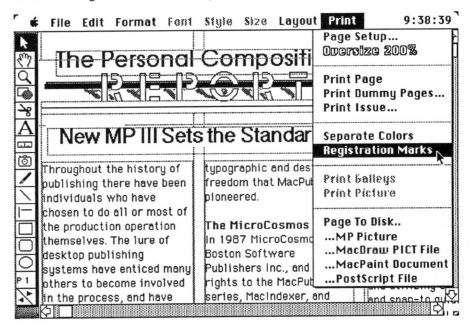

Typographic Controls

MP III provides precise controls for altering character fit. Individual character pair spacing (kerning) can be manually or automatically adjusted. A built-in dictionary of 137 kerning pairs is used, and the amount of kerning (negative or positive) conforms to a system default or to a user-specified uniform number of points. Kerning also can be specified for individual character pairs by selecting the Text tool, clicking the pointer between the pair of letters, and pressing command and the "<" to kern closer, or the ">" to kern farther away. The results of the kerning operation are visible on the MaxiPage. Character spacing also can be modified within entire articles by selecting the condensed or extended form from the Style menu.

Interlinear spacing can be modified in single- or multiple-point increments by selecting the "Add Leading" or "Remove Leading" option from the Style menu. Other methods used to accomplish the same end include choosing the "Spec Sheet" from the

File menu and modifying the leading entry, or pressing Shift and clicking in the article's block. The necessary number of points then is typed into the "Leading" check box.

Each article maintains a "Type Spec Sheet" (FIG. 76) with detailed information. Similar "Spec Sheets" are available for pictures, layout pages, and the Camera. The "Type Spec Sheet" provides direct control over an article's format (justification), size (number of lines and characters), and placement (page number).

Working with Pictures

MP III pictures are any graphic document: a ruled line, a bit-mapped image, or a MacDraw PICT file. When a graphic is opened it appears in its own picture window in full-size view. The picture can be resized by using the width and depth boxes in the "Spec Sheet" or the Format menu. Pictures that have been assembled on a page can be resized in position by dragging the small gray square called a *sizer*.

Pictures also can be created through the use of the Camera (FIG. 77). In order to use the Camera, the graphic first must be copied to the Clipboard. When the Camera tool is selected, the Clipboard automatically opens and the Camera appears as a frame around it. The Camera frame size is changed by any of a number of methods in order to capture the required section of the graphic (crop it), or to change its size or scale it to fit. When the correct dimensions have been set, the pointer, which takes on the appearance of a miniature camera, is positioned anywhere in the Camera window. When the mouse is clicked, the Camera snaps the picture and a momentary flash appears on the screen. The picture then appears in its own window.

Each picture, like each article, has its own "Spec Sheet" (FIG. 78). A "Picture Spec Sheet" shows the name of the picture, its page location, scaling values, color (for use with the ImageWriter II), and if it is to repeat on successive pages. If the picture originated as a MacPaint document, then it can be reverted to its original size if need be.

MP III treats line and pattern graphics as pictures, and has a very flexible Graphics Palette (FIG. 79) for the design of graphic elements such as pen lines, borders,

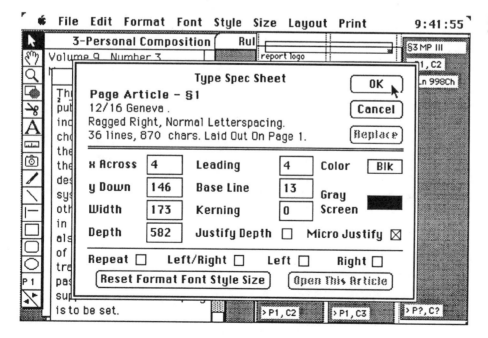

FIG. 76. Significant typographic information on each article is kept in the "Type Spec Sheet."

FIG. 77. The Camera frame appears over the Clipboard in order to copy all or part of its contents.

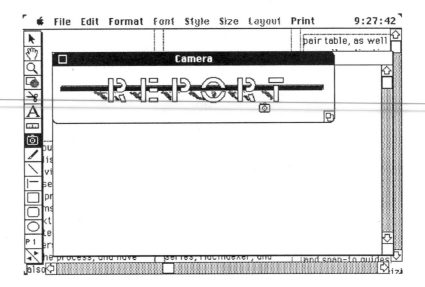

FIG. 78. The "Picture Spec Sheet" shows the exact size and location of the picture. All of the displayed values can be changed to suit particular needs. Movement of the picture on any of the page views automatically changes the values stored in the "Spec Sheet."

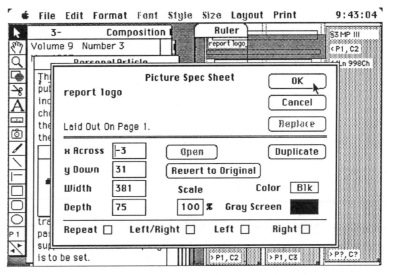

FIG. 79. The Graphics Palette provides a flexible tool for creating tint areas, borders, rules, and other graphic effects.

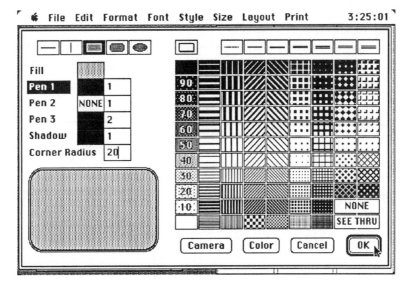

and fill shapes. The graphics are object oriented rather than bit-mapped, meaning that they retain their graphic identities despite a change in their size. Object-oriented graphics also have the advantage of occupying less memory than an equivalent sized bit-mapped image.

Tools along the left side of the MP III screen provide direct access to the designs created using the Graphics Palette. Drawing tools are available for creating diagonal lines, horizontal and vertical lines, straight- and round-corner rectangles, and circles and ovals.

Assembling an Issue

Articles and pictures are assembled on a layout page by:

- Opening their respective windows
- Selecting the Scissors tool from the toolbox
- Clicking on the item's title bar
- Dragging the item's outline onto the layout page
- Releasing the mouse button

The layout page can be viewed in three different ways: either as a full-size page representation (MaxiPage), a miniature full-screen detailed view (MiniPage; FIG. 80), or a miniature page showing individual items as blocks (Dummy Page). An item's position or size on any of the page representations can be changed by dragging the item or using the item's sizer box. Very precise placement can be controlled by using the item's "Spec Sheet." Any item can be deleted, replaced, aligned, edited, resized, or selected as a repeating element on succeeding pages.

The items on a page conform to predetermined margins and columns. Margins can be set to alternate automatically for right- and left-hand pages, and can, like all specifications, be indicated in inches, centimeters, or picas. As many as 48 columns can be specified for a page, with a minimum recommended separation of 8 points. Items can be specified to snap-to the columns, or columns can be used as a visual grid, with items arranged in free form.

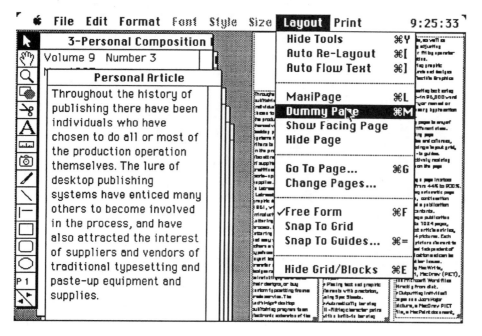

FIG. 80. The MiniPage, shown beneath the Layout menu, provides a miniature view of the page. Articles appear stacked on the left.

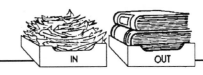

Items can be stacked in order to achieve special graphic and typographic effects. When items are stacked, they receive special treatment. For example:

- When an article is stacked with a picture, the pointer selects the article first.
- When a picture is stacked with a picture, the pointer selects the picture that was created first.
- When an article is stacked with an article, the pointer selects the article that was created first.

Up to nine items may be stacked. Items deep in the stack may be selected by clicking on an item in the stack and pressing the numeric key corresponding to its stack position. For example, to select the item that is fifth in the stack, click on the top item in the stack, press and release the "5" key, and click on the stack again.

Printing

MP III provides some useful and unique printing options. Pages can be printed in 200 percent Oversize format, making it possible for users to reduce the printed output 50 percent on a copier or repro camera and effectively double the resolution. The option also can print a double-sized original as four pieces that can be joined together to form a poster. Registration marks can be printed to aid in assembling the quadrants.

Single pages, a range of pages, and the entire issue can be specified in one or more copies. Dummy pages, for planning an issue and making marginal notations, can be printed singly, in a range, or in total. Additionally, open articles can be printed in galley format, in the font, style, size, and format selected.

STYLO-FORMATTER:
Code-based Input for Phototypesetting

Macintosh applications tend to conform to the basic Macintosh philosophy of providing a consistent user interface—highly visual and innately intuitive. This tendency has held true for virtually all of the typographic composition programs that have been introduced. A notable exception to this rule is Stylo-Formatter,[21] a code-based input system devised specifically for output to the Allied Linotype CRTronic phototypesetter.

Stylo-Formatter works in conjunction with Macintosh word processing programs, such as MacWrite. It interprets typesetting codes that have been embedded within text into a screen representation of the typeset output (which also may be printed as a hardcopy proof), as well as a correctly coded file for transmission to a CRTronic typesetter.

The typesetting codes are of two varieties: *comma* and *backslash*. The reason for using the Comma commands is to retain compatibility with Stylo-Software's Stylo-Graph word processing software. The Comma commands are interpreted by the Stylo-Formatter program into forms for presentation on the screen, the Apple ImageWriter printer, or the typesetter. The Comma command syntax requires that each command be on its own line at the extreme left, and that it begin, obviously, with a comma.

For example, the specification of a line length of 35 picas and a line spacing (*leading*) of 12 points would be written as:

,ll35/
,ld/12

[21] Stylo-Software, Inc.
161 Vine Street
Reno, NV 89503
(702) 322-1884

Notice that numbers before the slash indicate picas and those after the slash indicate points. A line length of 18 picas and 10 points would be written as:

,ll18/10.

The Backslash commands are less restrictive. They may be placed anywhere within a line of text, either individually or in groups. Each command begins and ends with a backslash and contains a mnemonic code, and sometimes a value. A type size of 10 points using font number 2 would be written as:

\sz/10\\f2\.

While the Comma and Backslash commands are acted upon by Stylo-Formatter, native CRTronic typesetting commands can be passed right through the input stream without being converted by the program. Although this capability somewhat negates the benefits of using Stylo-Formatter, it does offer a further degree of flexibility to those familiar with writing standard CRTronic coding. These Pass commands are enclosed between sets of backslashes containing delimiters beginning with a greater than sign and ending with a less than sign. The CRTronic command to fill a line with a specified character, for example, would be written as:

\>J,char<\.

A major advantage of the coding nature of the Stylo-Formatter program is that text can be input using virtually any computer, and then transfered to the Macintosh through telecommunication or hardwire connection. The Macintosh then serves the function of a typesetting preview terminal, providing a soft proof of the job prior to committing it to typeset output.

Within the Macintosh environment there are a number of programs that are appropriate for text input (FIG. 81). CE Software's MockWrite,[22] which installs as a desk accessory, is useful either for the original input of text, or for the correction of text while Stylo-Formatter is active.

```
 File   Edit   Search   Format   Font   Style

═══════════════ Graphic Dimensions Ad ═══════════════
,ll28/
,ld/26
\sz/24\
,DEFONT 1,Helvetica-Bold
,DEFONT 2,Helvetica
,ce 2
\f1\Microtypesetting
Information Center
,ld/10
\sz/10\
\f2\Graphic Dimensions carries the largest selection of books, reports,
and other information covering the rapidly developing area of typesetting
via personal computer.
\em\Our \f1\Personal Composition Report (PCR)\f2\ provides up-to-the-
minute news of new, innovative, and helpful developments in the use of
personal computers, both as input devices for traditional
phototypesetting output, and as components in desktop publishing
systems, with dot matrix, plotter, and laser printer output. An
annual subscription of 10 issues is only $50/year.
```

FIG. 81. Input for the Stylo-Formatter program may be created using any word processing program, either within the Macintosh environment, or imported from another source. This lack of dependence on the Macintosh for the creation of coded text greatly expands the flexibility of the program.

[22] CE Software
801-73rd Street
Des Moines, IA 50312
(515) 224-1995

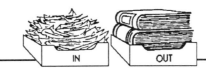

The Stylo-Formatter screen provides two pull-down menus: File and Options (FIG. 82). The Options menu has only one choice, "List," to display a listing of all of the available text files and make a selection (FIG. 83).

After a file has been chosen, it is processed using the File menu options (FIG. 82). These choices include:

- View: Displays a representation of how the job will appear when typeset (FIG. 84).
- Printer: Activates the ImageWriter, producing a hardcopy proof of the pseudotypesetter screen.
- Typesetter: Sends the encoded file to the LCI communications port of the CRTronic. This port is a CRTronic option and requires a specially constructed cable in order to support the use of the Macintosh.
- Typeprint: Produces a hardcopy of the encoded file with the actual CRTronic codes as it will be output to the typesetter (FIG. 85).
- Typeview: Displays the interpreted encoded file as it will be seen by the CRTronic.
- Translation: Sends a translation file to the CRTronic in advance of any encoded text files.
- Quit: Exits the program and returns the user to the Macintosh desktop.

The use of the Stylo-Formatter program does not presume that the user has an Allied Linotype CRTronic within his environment. A number of typesetting shops using the Stylo-Type setup can accept telecommunications or compatible media for output processing. In addition, Stylo-Software offers a typesetting service called Type/Net, which specifically supports this configuration.

FIG. 82. The Stylo-Formatter File menu presents the options for outputting either the translated or nontranslated version of the file to the screen, ImageWriter, or typesetter.

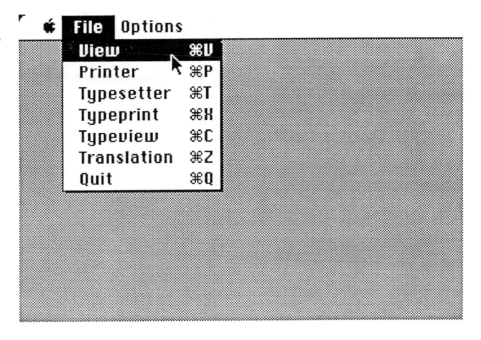

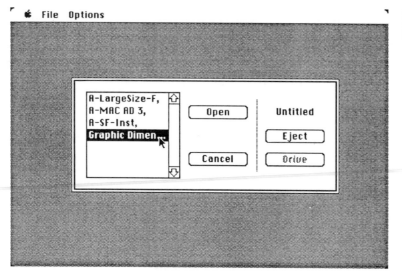

FIG. 83. The selection of the Options *List* choice displays a listing of all of the available text files.

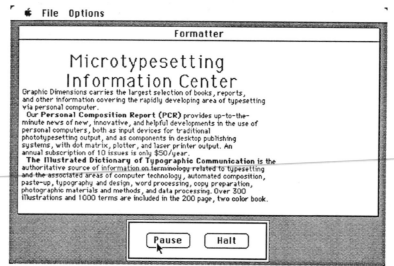

FIG. 84. The translated text file is displayed in representative type styles and sizes, showing how the CRTronic will output it. As the file is converted it scrolls up the screen. It may be momentarily stopped by clicking on the Pause button, or cancelled by clicking on the Halt button.

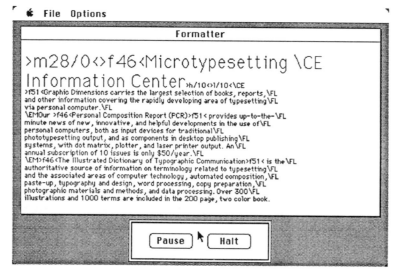

FIG. 85. This screen, displayed by selecting *Typeview*, shows the file as it will be seen by the CRTronic. Comma and Backslash commands have been converted into CRTronic codes.

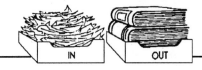

MICROSOFT WORD:
A Typographic Workslate

A survey printed in the June, 1985, issue of *Today's Office* magazine reported that 96 percent of the responding readership specified word processing as one of their major microcomputer applications. It is not surprising since there are literally hundreds of word processing software packages available to support that need, with many aimed at the specific writing needs of particular groups, such as mathematicians, scientists, engineers, script writers, and music composers.

There are, in many cases, only subtle differences in the capabilities and approach used in one word processing package compared to another. All have editing, file maintenance, and printing features which support the transfer of information from the mind of the originator to the surface of the printed page. It is in the realm of Macintosh word processing software where the differences are more apparent, and in the example of Microsoft's Word,[23] where the differences are more significant.

Word's functionality in a typesetting environment is related to its ease of use, design as a typographic workslate, and compatibility with a variety of output devices.

The document-creation process is facilitated by such built-in capabilities as the *glossary.* Using the glossary the user can define a word, a character, or a phrase to be an often-used text passage of almost any length (so long as it fits on the disk). A glossary entry is created by first typing the entry in the document and transferring it to the Clipboard, by either copying it or cutting it. Next, the "Show Glossary" option is selected from the Edit menu. The glossary window is displayed (FIG. 86), and the glossary entry name is typed. The Clipboard contents are then appended to the entry by selecting the "Paste" option from the Edit menu. The glossary entry name then appears in the right-hand side of the glossary window.

The glossary entry is used by typing it where required. It is expanded from its abbreviated form to its full text form by pressing the Command-Backspace keys.

Word provides the user with the option of constructing documents in the measurement system that is most appropriate for the application. In the case of typesetting, Word offers increments in points, with the ruler, and all screen measurement displays reflecting that unit system (FIGS. 87 through 89).

FIG. 86. The glossary window displays a listing of all glossary entries on the right side. The chosen glossary entry, in this case *rsg*, displays its resultant glossary string directly below itself.

[23] Microsoft Corporation
10700 Northrup Way
P.O. Box 97200
Bellevue, WA 98009

Allied Linotype uses the IBM version of Word with its Series 200 personal computer based typesetting system, which outputs to either the Linotron 101 or 202.

 File   Edit   Search   Character   Paragraph   Document

ReadySetGo File

Glossary

varieties: a *te...* ...ns, a *frame*

block for rule... ...dow areas

(Figure 1).

Name in Glossary:

rsg

ReadySetGo

page
footnote
cr
rsg

The Read... ...ch

increments. Pa... ...a single

page. A multip... ...eries of files.

The physical boundaries of a page are selected from the Page Setup option of the File menu. It provides access to a variety of common paper sizes, as well as either a tall or wide paper orientation.

The creation of a page begins with the selection of a block from the *create* menu. Each new block is always one inch square, and automatically

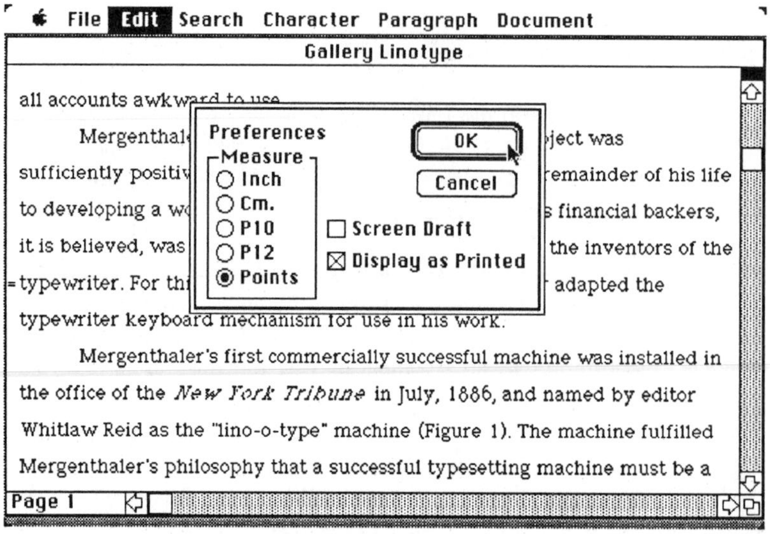

File Edit Search Character Paragraph Document

Gallery Linotype

all accounts awkward to use.

Mergenthal[   ]ject was
sufficiently positiv[   ]remainder of his life
to developing a w[   ]s financial backers,
it is believed, was[   ]the inventors of the
typewriter. For th[   ]adapted the
typewriter keyboard mechanism for use in his work.

Mergenthaler's first commercially successful machine was installed in
the office of the *New York Tribune* in July, 1886, and named by editor
Whitlaw Reid as the "lino-o-type" machine (Figure 1). The machine fulfilled
Mergenthaler's philosophy that a successful typesetting machine must be a

Preferences
— Measure —
○ Inch
○ Cm.
○ P10
○ P12
⦿ Points

[OK]
[Cancel]

☐ Screen Draft
☒ Display as Printed

Page 1

FIG. 87. The Preferences menu allows the
user to specify the unit system that is most
convenient for the application at hand.

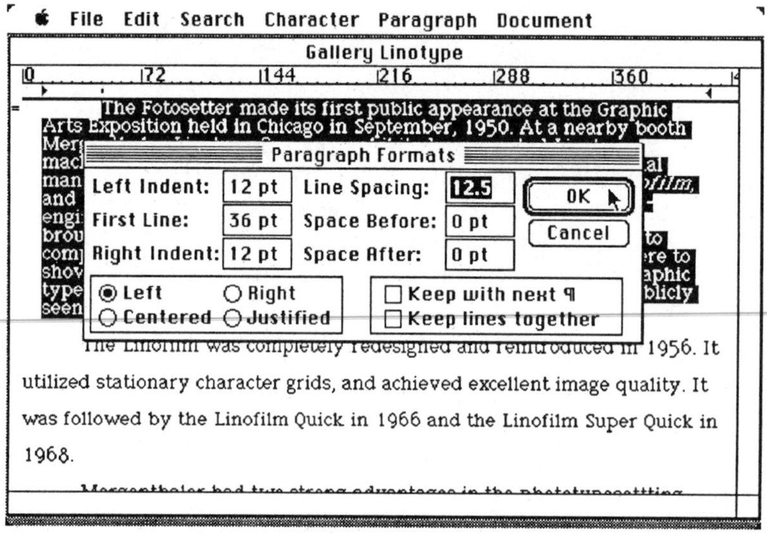

File Edit Search Character Paragraph Document

Gallery Linotype

|0 |72 |144 |216 |288 |360

The Fotosetter made its first public appearance at the Graphic
Arts Exposition held in Chicago in September, 1950. At a nearby booth

Paragraph Formats

Left Indent: 12 pt   Line Spacing: 12.5   [OK]
First Line: 36 pt   Space Before: 0 pt   [Cancel]
Right Indent: 12 pt   Space After: 0 pt

⦿ Left   ○ Right   ☐ Keep with next ¶
○ Centered   ○ Justified   ☐ Keep lines together

The Linofilm was completely redesigned and reintroduced in 1956. It
utilized stationary character grids, and achieved excellent image quality. It
was followed by the Linofilm Quick in 1966 and the Linofilm Super Quick in
1968.

FIG. 88. The Paragraph Format window
displays all of its values in the chosen unit
system, in this case points.

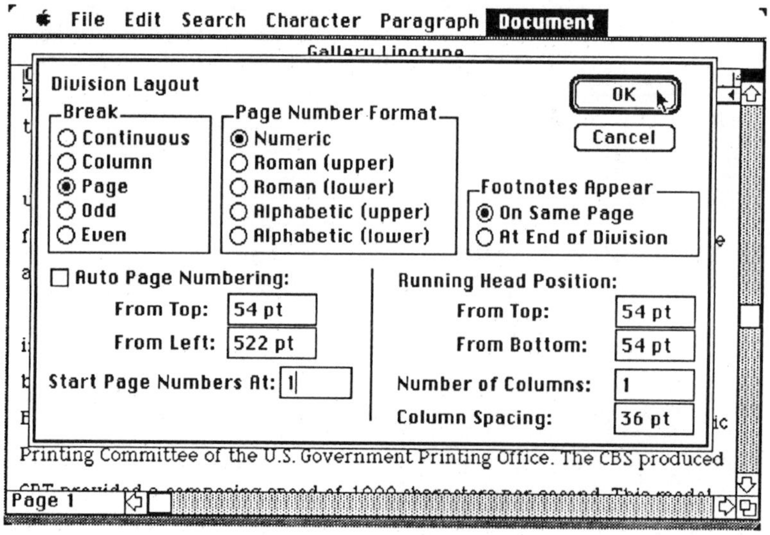

File Edit Search Character Paragraph Document

Gallery Linotype

Division Layout   [OK]

— Break —   — Page Number Format —
○ Continuous   ⦿ Numeric   [Cancel]
○ Column   ○ Roman (upper)
⦿ Page   ○ Roman (lower)   — Footnotes Appear —
○ Odd   ○ Alphabetic (upper)   ⦿ On Same Page
○ Even   ○ Alphabetic (lower)   ○ At End of Division

☐ Auto Page Numbering: Running Head Position:
   From Top: 54 pt   From Top: 54 pt
   From Left: 522 pt   From Bottom: 54 pt
Start Page Numbers At: 1   Number of Columns: 1
                                          Column Spacing: 36 pt

Printing Committee of the U.S. Government Printing Office. The CBS produced

Page 1

FIG. 89. The Division Layout window provides
the means of specifying a variety of page
description items.

The Word screen can support up to four open documents on the desktop at one time. Text can be moved freely from one document to another. Optionally, two documents can be viewed simultaneously, with split windows within each one, making it possible to see two separate sections of the documents.

The document merge capability, used most often for creating form letters, can be used in a typesetting context for creating repetitive forms, and formats requiring the insertion of variable information. The merge operation requires two documents: the main document, which contains the special variable field names as well as the fixed text, and the merge document, which contains the variable data (FIG. 90).

The main document encloses the merge fields in special double brackets. The first field always defines the name of the merge document and is identified by the label *DATA*. Other fields are embedded within the main document in their expected sequential positions. The merge document is composed of the variable data records, with each record field separated by commas, and ended by pressing the Return key.

The first data field in the merge document is the *header record*. It lists the actual names of the fields into which the variable information will be placed. The merge function supports a number of instructions about how to handle certain information, or where to look for specific information. One of the instructions, DATA, has already been mentioned. Others include the means of prompting the user for information at the time of printing, merging entire documents within the main document, and printing all records within a single document. Conditional instructions, such as printing a record only if it conforms to specific operators, are also supported.

The overall appearance of documents produced using Word can vary greatly, not only from document to document, but also from one section of a document to another. Word handles these intradocument design variations through the use of *divisions*. A division is a portion of a document that has a single design or layout identity. The Division Layout menu (FIG. 89) provides the capability of accomplishing any of the following: changing the page number style (from numeric to Roman, for example), changing the position of a page number, changing the number of columns on a page, changing the sequence of page numbering, changing the position of a running head, changing the numbering or placement of footnotes, or changing the way a division breaks a page.

Word's suitability as front-end software for typesetting already has been proven with Allied Linotype's selection for use in its typesetting systems. A version of Word with hyphenation and justification capability is also available.

FIG. 90. Word's merge capability makes it possible to combine repetitive, though variable, information within a static format description.

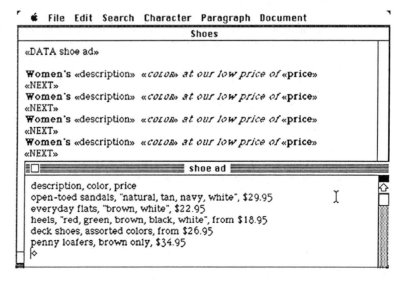

FONTASTIC:
Creating and Editing Macintosh Fonts

In typographic terms, most typewriters are flawed by their inherent limitations of type style, size, and proportionality. Typesetting machines, on the other hand, are usually supported by large libraries of professional typeface designs, created or commissioned by the typesetter vendor or offered by a third-party supplier. The sale of typefaces is a big business, with literally thousands of styles available to meet a wide variety of communication needs. The Macintosh is unique in that not only does it support the use of a number of typefaces, variations, and sizes, but it also supports the means for the user to create custom designs. Apple provides a font editor, which has been circulated through user groups, the Apple University Consortium, and on-line information services such as CompuServe and local and national bulletin boards. Although limited in capability, the Apple Font Editor has been used by software developers and users to create a significant number of new typefaces for sale and public-domain distribution.

A professional Macintosh font editor has been created by Altsys Corporation. Called the *FONTastic*[24] font editor, and written by Kevin Crowder and Jim Von Ehr, it provides an easy means to create new fonts, modify existing fonts, and edit either.

FONTastic provides complete control over the physical space delimiters of each character (FIG. 91). Movable guidelines control the precise location of the character baseline, ascent and descent delimiters, origin, and width. Characters can be drawn with blank space between the origin and the start of the character to create a looser character fit. This blank space is called *offset*. If the character begins to the left of the origin, which would cause it to overlap with its preceding character, the effect is a tighter fitting character, which is *kerned*.

A Macintosh font can be composed of up to 255 characters, to a maximum size of 32K. An exceptionally large font might exceed the 32K limit and need to be broken into two smaller fonts: for example, capitals and numbers in one font, and lower case, punctuation, and special characters in the other. Large font editing might also require the use of a 512K Macintosh in order to utilize FONTastic's "Undo," "Cut," and "Paste" capabilities.

Upon startup, FONTastic displays its Font Selection window (FIG. 92). This window is used to specify which font will be edited, copied into the system, removed, or

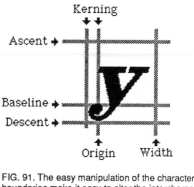

Character Boundaries

FIG. 91. The easy manipulation of the character boundaries make it easy to alter the intercharacter spacing of a font.

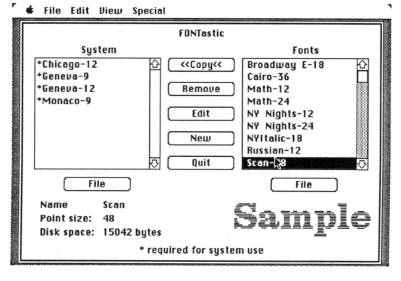

FIG. 92. The Font Selection window provides access to previously created fonts, as well as the option to create a new design.

[24] Altsys Corporation
720 Avenue F, Suite 108
Plano, TX 75074
(214) 424-4888
MCI Mail: ALTSYS (271-8914)

A demonstration version of FONTastic is provided in Softstrip form in the Cauzin section of Chapter 6.

created. A font also can be opened directly from the Macintosh desktop by simply double-clicking on it. When an existing font is chosen, the program displays its name, point size, byte size, and a true-size type specimen. If an existing font is to be edited, it is selected along with an accompanying click in the Edit box.

After a font is opened, the System View, comprised of a grid of the available character identities and a sample of composition, is displayed (FIG. 93). Characters that have not been defined appear on the grid as small boxes. The View menu provides the choice of seeing the font either system wide, with all character identities displayed, or in actual view, with the defined characters displayed in the grid. An individual character is presented for editing by selecting it and either choosing "Open" from the File menu or simply double-clicking it.

FIG. 93. The FONTastic System View displays the entire Macintosh standard character set. The actual character identities of members of the particular font being processed are displayed by selecting "actual" from the View menu.

The Character Edit Window (FIG. 94) is composed of many parts. The major portion of the window displays an enlarged pixel map of the character. The actual representation of the character is displayed in a smaller window in the upper left. Along the left edge are a number of drawing tools: a hand to move a character larger than the editing box, a four-way arrow to move the character within the editing box, a pencil to turn pixels on or off, line and box tools to draw straight lines and rectangular boxes, and an eraser to remove large portions of a character. Shortcuts are available to make any tool function as a scrolling hand, or to cause a tool to move in a horizontal or vertical direction only.

The character guidelines appear as arrows and bars along the left-hand and bottom edges of the main character window. The grid that surrounds each screen pixel can be turned on or off using the "Grid" option from the View menu. All of the standard Macintosh editing commands are available, making it possible to cut characters (remove them from the file), paste them (reassign them to a new character identity), and copy them (duplicate their images in other character identities).

A powerful capability of FONTastic is the Styling feature (FIG. 95). With this menu the user can alter the character to be bold, italic, underlined, outlined, shadowed, condensed, expanded, inverted, or a combination thereof. Once the style command has been invoked, it cannot be undone except by using the "Undo" or "Revert" commands.

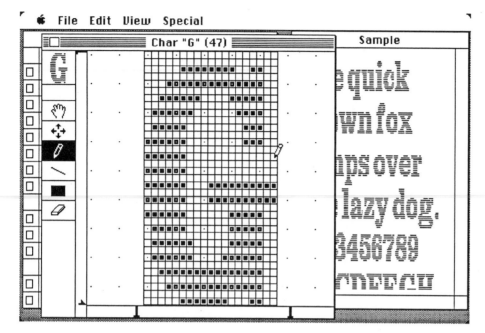

FIG. 94. The actual character designing process takes place in the Character Edit Window. Changes to the selected character are reflected immediately both in the actual size sample in the upper left-hand box of the window, as well as in the Sample window on the right.

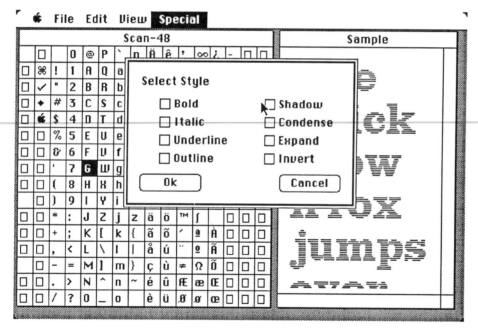

FIG. 95. The Select Style menu supports the immediate redesign of an active character into a completely different design variation.

An entire font also can be scaled horizontally and/or vertically to produce an expanded or condensed typeface (FIG. 96).

A major change added to version 2.0 is a bit-level cut and paste capability. Characters and other images can be cut from MacPaint and inserted into a new font, or vice-versa. Additionally, a new tool has been added: the dashed selection rectangle. It is used to mark an area of a character for cut and paste operations.

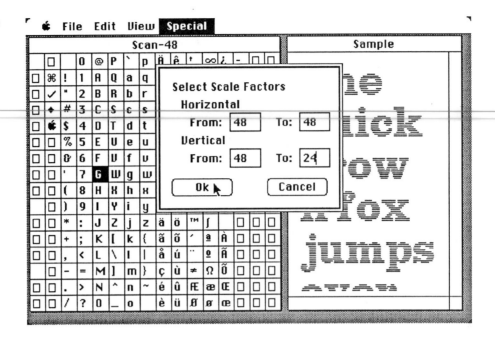

FIG. 96. The Scaling menu provides a simple means of creating a condensed or expanded font.

FONTOGRAPHER:
High Resolution Fonts for PostScript Printers

There is considerable debate today as to what the true attributes of typographic characters are. It has been suggested by professional typesetting craftspeople, as exemplified by a position paper published by the Typographer's International Association (TIA) in the winter of 1986, that the major determinant of typographic quality is a character resolution of at least 1000 dpi. Although the 1000 dpi threshold generally has been accepted in the trade as equivalent to *graphic arts quality*, it is undeniable that lower-resolution typefaces (in the range of 240 to 600 dpi) have found general acceptance for a wide variety of applications, from correspondence and business reports, to invitations and newspaper pages. It is obvious that even lower- resolution type is capable of conveying information effectively and providing most of the benefits of the best typographic composition, namely *compaction, aesthetics,* and *readability*.

Historically there has been a virtual monopoly on the design and production of typeface designs for machine setting. Typesetting vendors have developed elaborate organizations to generate typeface designs in suitable forms (metallic, photographic, or digital) for their machines. Such complicated and precise production activities have restricted end-users from participating in the process of converting typographic drawings into usable typographic fonts.

The Apple Macintosh/LaserWriter/Linotype Linotronic 100/300 combination is one of the first to allow the user to break from a strict dependency upon a single manufacturer to supply type fonts. Not only have third-party suppliers entered the marketplace with inexpensive laser fonts, but powerful tools, such as the Altsys Fontographer,[25] have put the means of font production into the hands of the end-user. Just as the general availability of personal computers spawned countless computer programs (some of which have had an overwhelmingly positive impact on the usefulness of computers in general), the availability of font-development tools will stimulate greatly the production of more (if not better) laser-printer and typesetter fonts.

[25] Altsys Corporation
720 Avenue F, Suite 108
Plano, TX 75074
(214) 424-4888
MCI Mail: ALTSYS (271-8914)
Minimum configuration requires a Macintosh with 512K.

Although the 300 dpi resolution of the LaserWriter is relatively low compared to the 1000+ dpi resolution of digital typesetters, it is relatively high compared to the 72 dpi (and lower) resolution of the ubiquitous dot matrix printer. Font design for correspondence-size characters, composed on a 9-x-9 matrix for an Epson dot matrix printer, for example, provides a coarse area of 81 dots which can be turned on and off. The design possibilities are fairly limited. A 72-point display character designed at 300 dpi resolution, however, provides up to 90,000 dots which can be turned on and off to define its shape. At this resolution, character designs can be truly representative of the intent of their creators.

The design of the characters is just one part of the process of preparing a font for use. Each character, which initially takes a full-screen representative form on the Macintosh, must be interpreted into a form usable by the output device, as well as a form usable by application software. Each font, therefore, must have two forms: the laser font form and the screen font form.

How easy it is to execute a character design is dependent upon the functionality of the font-design software. In the case of Fontographer, characters are composed of line segments, each of which can be edited. The line segment drawings of each character in a font automatically are translated into PostScript notation, in order to download them to the LaserWriter, Linotronic, or another PostScript-compatible device. The font drawings are also translated into bitmap form so that they can be displayed on the Macintosh screen in representative form when selected from within an application program.

The Fontographer Environment

Fontographer provides a microenvironment for type design, adapting trade methods and procedures in a user-friendly application. Although Fontographer will not design aesthetically pleasing characters automatically, it does provide an easy-to-use palette upon which to draw. At any point during the creation of an individual character, one or more characters can be sent to the LaserWriter for proofing, in order to give the user immediate feedback. Although Fontographer fonts can be used on the Linotype Linotronic 100 and 300 PostScript models, this discussion only deals with the use of the LaserWriter, which is a helpful tool for proofing, and for final output of newly created characters.

The Apple LaserWriter is very flexible in that it can support three different kinds of fonts: *Bitmaps*, which are a matrix of dots, some on, some off; *outlines*, which are composed of lines and curves defining the outline of a character; and *algorithmically defined fonts*, which are character drawings defined by a computer program.

The Fontographer drawing board is composed of three layers, or planes. One plane contains the typographic reference lines (ascender, descender, baseline, and mean line); the second contains drawn or scanned images for tracing; and the third contains the lines and curves used to draw the actual character definition. The line and curve segments are used to form character outlines, which are automatically interpreted into screen bitmap characters and algorithmically defined LaserWriter characters. The same fonts that are created for LaserWriter use can be used on other PostScript-compatible output devices.

The LaserWriter contains a number of resident fonts, which are burned in ROM and are unalterable by the user. A limited amount of RAM is provided for downloading additional fonts, either third-party or user created. The complexity of the font designs determines exactly how many fonts may be downloaded. Downloaded fonts may be either *permanent* or *transient*. Permanent fonts are downloaded only once, and remain in memory until power is interrupted (i.e., the LaserWriter is turned off). Transient fonts are downloaded as needed, each time a document requiring them is printed. They stay in memory only as long as they are actually in use. Since transient fonts use the same memory again and again, their number might be quite large.

The language resident within the LaserWriter that makes font drawing possible is Adobe Corporation's PostScript page-description language. PostScript is able to describe almost any picture as a program, and it treats typographic characters as *pictures*. Typographic pictures are composed of geometric primitives: either straight lines or *Bezier curves*. A Bezier curve is a kind of curve that has one or more control points along its path which can be moved in order to create a nonuniform curvature. Such control is necessary to generate complex designs, which are typical of typographic characters.

When a curve point is selected during the drawing process, the Bezier control points (BCPs) appear as small pluses (+). Moving the pluses can result in radically different curves, as shown in FIG. 97. Each curve point has two BCPs, one on each side. The BCPs are connected by an imaginary line that runs directly through the curve point. Each BCP may slide along the imaginary line, keeping the slope of the curve point the same, or either BCP may be used as a handle to manipulate the curve point slope.

FIG. 97. Movement of the Bezier control points (indicated by the plus symbols), can result in radically different curves, although only two curve points (as indicated by the small open circles) have been selected.

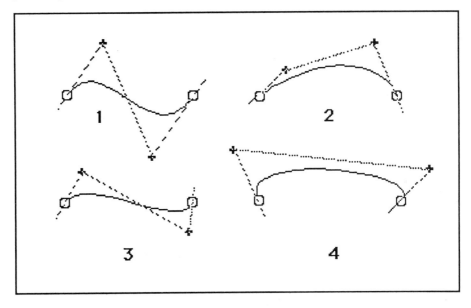

Another important property of Bezier curves is the fact that they ensure smooth connections at the endpoints of the curve. The juncture at which a curve joins another line segment is called a *tangent join*, and accurate connections are necessary for well-executed character designs.

The construction of characters out of line segments must take into account a number of considerations peculiar to PostScript. Among them are:

- Character outlines are made up of *paths*. A path is a series of line or curve segments, which may be connected or disconnected. A path may be either open or closed. An *open path* is one in which the last segment does not connect with the first. A *closed path* has the last segment connected to the first.
- A character may have disconnected closed paths, such as the letter i, where the dot is a disconnected segment.
- A character design may be composed of either an open or a closed path, but not both. In most cases, the character is constructed of a single closed path, which then would be filled solid during the composition process.

• Certain characters, such as O and Q are composed of both an inside and an outside path. If both outlines were filled in, the resultant characters would be completely solid circles. PostScript offers two solutions for this problem. One is the *nonzero winding number* fill technique, which requires that one path be defined in a clockwise direction, and the other in a counterclockwise direction. The second is the *even-odd* fill technique, wherein a ray is drawn from any one point in any direction, and the number of path segments that the ray crosses are counted. If the number is odd, the point is inside; if the number is even, the point is outside.

Fontographer characters are composed of points: corner points, curve points, and tangent points (FIG. 98). *Corner points* can be used to construct paths composed of straight line segments, to join straight lines to curves at an angle, or to join two curves at a cusp. *Curve points* join curves to curves. Finally, *tangent points* join line segments to curves. The tangency of points is ensured by an automatic calculation of the slope of each point.

FIG. 98. Three different point types are used in the construction of Fontographer characters.

Using Fontographer

The font creation process begins with an assignment of the initial font characteristics, including the size of the ascent and the size of the descent. These values default to 800 and 200 respectively. The values are the number of units, a measurement system arbitrarily set by Fontographer. A third characteristic is the stroke width, which sets the specification of the width for open (nonfilled) paths.

A set of tools is provided by Fontographer to simplify character design (FIG. 99). The Effects menu provides the means of mathematically altering one or more characters. *Scale* can be used to make a character condensed or expanded; *flip horizontal* and *flip vertical* flips the point about its center of gravity, or a character about the base-point; *rotate* moves the point about its center of gravity, or a character about the base-point, a positive or negative number of degrees; *skew* creates oblique characters, such as italics and special effects; and *move* causes all selected points, or the entire character, to move in a horizontal or vertical direction.

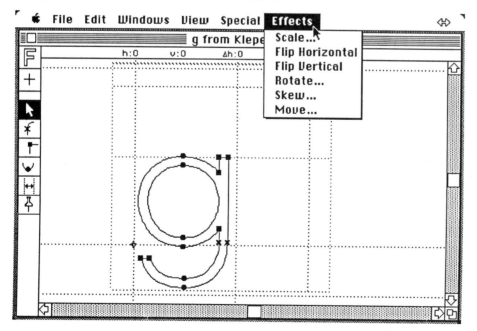

FIG. 99. The main Fontographer window provides many tools along the left side of the screen. Starting from the top the tool functions are: Plane selector, Horizontal and/or vertical movement lock, Selector, Tangent point, Corner point, Curve point, Character width adjustment, and Base point position. The Effects menu also is shown.

The x-height (the upper limit for lower-case characters) is set by selecting the guideline plane (clicking in the plane-selector tool twice) and drawing a line using the corner point tool. Other reference lines can be added to the guideline plane according to individual design requirements.

Characters are drawn by selecting the foreground plane and a drawing tool (corner, curve, or tangent). Exact horizontal and vertical positions are displayed directly above the drawing area, providing very accurate positioning despite the relatively low resolution of the display (as compared to that of the LaserWriter). The scrollable screen area encompasses a maximum em-square area of -8000 to +8000 units in both horizontal and vertical directions, a drawing area well beyond the needs of most users. Successive points are added to build the required character shape. Each point can be manipulated in almost any way, and points can be added or removed. The undo command is eight layers deep, meaning that up to the last eight editing operations can be undone or redone.

The screen image can be enlarged, and the corner, curve, and tangent points can be hidden to judge the design more effectively. In addition, the movement of the mouse can be constrained to move a point only horizontally or vertically, and can be *demagnified*, so that the mouse effectively is slowed to half speed to move more precisely.

After the character has been completed, the width line, located to the right of the character, is moved to the left by selecting the width-setting tool from the menu and dragging the width line with the mouse. This action ensures that each character receives a horizontal escapement relative to its true width.

The character width can be tested and adjusted, if necessary, by displaying up to three characters using the Character Metrics window (FIG. 100). The window permits respecification of the character origin and width, and, although limited to screen resolution, can reduce the number of printer proofing cycles required.

Characters or an entire font can be tested by instructing the program to automatically convert the character outlines into PostScript notation and send the sample to the LaserWriter. The size, position, and composition of the sample sheet is dependent upon a sample document supplied with the program. The sample document can be modified or completely rewritten by the user so that character combinations and sizes most useful to the user can be proofed.

FIG. 100. The Character Metrics window shows up to three characters in context. Each character's origin and width can be dynamically adjusted. Any changes made in the window are reflected elsewhere in the character's attributes.

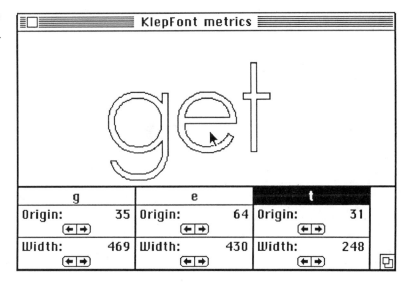

After a font has been designed and successfully tested, the screen font bitmaps are generated by selecting the "Generate Bitmaps..." option from the File menu. Up to 12 different bitmap sizes can be generated, in a range of sizes from 1 to 127 points. The user is prompted for a point size and font size information, including the ascent, descent, and leading values. Default values for each of these parameters are suggested by the program. When the values are correct, clicking the "OK" button starts the bitmap font-generation process. As the process proceeds, the character number being generated is displayed on the screen.

After the bitmap fonts have been created, they can be edited by using the Fontographer companion program, *Fontastic*. Fontastic, which is included with the Fontographer package (and is also available separately), is a Macintosh screen font editor. Fontastic comes with a Switcher document, which automatically installs both Fontographer and Fontastic upon startup, thus providing the user with immediate access to both programs. Fontastic also can be used to install the newly created screen fonts into a Macintosh System file for use within an application. Fontographer fonts are compatible with all current applications programs.

In order for a font created by the Fontographer (or any nonresident font) to be used, it first must be downloaded into the LaserWriter. Fontographer comes with a program called LW Download, which makes this procedure quite easy. Running the program results in a File Selection window listing all PostScript fonts available on a given disk. Clicking on the required file sends it to the printer, after which it is immediately ready to use.

The PostScript files produced by Fontographer are editable text files, which can be read by programs such as Microsoft Word and Apple's MacWrite. Modified PS files cannot be read back into Fontographer, but the PS files themselves can be used by other programs that process PostScript. Anyone attempting to learn to write in PostScript notation would advance their training considerably by discovering how PostScript describes various shapes drawn on the Fontographer screen.

The Fontographer font design environment (FIG. 101) offers the user of a Macintosh-based desktop publishing or typesetting system a powerful and easy-to-use font development system the likes of which has never been available to end-users of any composition system. It assuredly will have a large impact on the availability of fonts for Macintosh users, and set a benchmark for font-development systems for other pc-based typesetting systems.

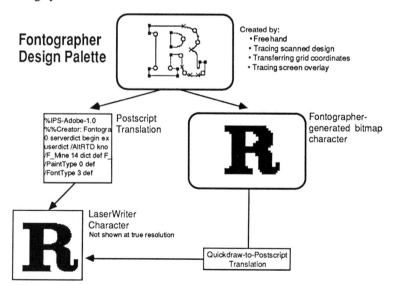

FIG. 101. The Fontographer character-development system reduces the process of creating PostScript character descriptions and Macintosh screen fonts to the one-step operation of drawing characters composed of lines and curves.

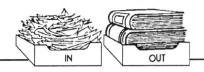

LaserWorks:
An Image Laboratory for PostScript Printers

The graphic manipulations that the PostScript language affords to users are many, varied, and exceptionally powerful. Unfortunately, the only way to access all of these capabilities is by actually writing in the PostScript language itself. For most people, the complexities of writing programs are sufficiently intimidating to completely discourage any attempt.

What is necessary is a software interface that shields the user from PostScript, yet provides an easy means for accessing many of its features. Such a program is LaserWorks,[26] a graphic environment for the creation of fonts, symbols, and special characters.

The main LaserWorks screen (FIG. 102) provides the major tools for drawing characters. Up to 256 characters and/or graphics (images) may be created for each font, with individual image identities selected by using the CHAR window. Images are drawn in the Edit window (with or without the use of the alignment grid), and are always created by first selecting the Moveto tool (the Rollerskate icon), then positioning the Moveto cursor at the starting point and clicking the mouse. The cursor position is displayed in the X and Y coordinate windows, allowing for exact placement of image points.

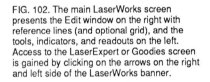

FIG. 102. The main LaserWorks screen presents the Edit window on the right with reference lines (and optional grid), and the tools, indicators, and readouts on the left. Access to the LaserExpert or Goodies screen is gained by clicking on the arrows on the right and left side of the LaserWorks banner.

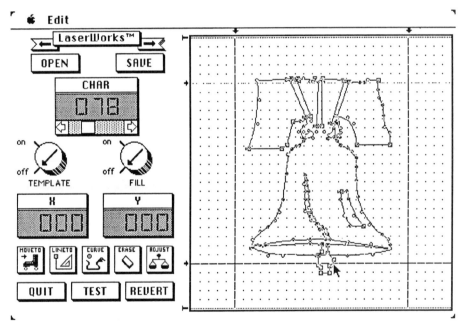

Images are composed of line and curve segments, which are joined to form a path. Each path must begin and end at the Moveto arrow, although the program will add it automatically if the user forgets. The Lineto and Curve tools are used to create image elements, which can be removed using the Erase tool or repositioned using the Adjust tool.

Curves are controlled through the use of control points, which are small circles that appear close to, but do not touch, the curve. Each one of these points can be moved independently in order to control the shape of the curve.

At any point during the creation of an image it can be proofed on the Laser-Writer (or other PostScript output device) by clicking on the Test button. The image is proofed in four sizes (9, 18, 36, and 72 points) using a default-proofing file (which

26 EDO Communications Inc.
63 Arnold Way
West Hartford, CT 06119
(203) 233-5850

Requires an Apple Macintosh 512K or greater and an Apple LaserWriter.

can be modified by the user). Additional proof layouts can be accessed by using the numeric keys in combination with the Test button.

Images are initially created out of line segments; however, during printing PostScript will use these segments as an outline and fill them in solid within their boundaries. Activating the Fill Switch will demonstrate how PostScript will handle this procedure. PostScript uses the *reverse direction rule* when it encounters one path within another, such as the counter space within a letter a. This rule states that the inner path must be created in the opposite direction from the initial path, or the image will fill in completely solid.

The normal Macintosh editing capabilities are always available. Image segments can be cleared, cut, copied, or pasted. In addition, the image can be reverted back to its last permanent state. On-screen help is fully available for each and every program capability.

The guide lines within the Edit window can be adjusted to accommodate the design and the width of the image. The arrow markers attached to each line can be grabbed and dragged using the mouse.

Simplifying the Image-Creation Process

Although the free-hand creation of images might be appropriate for those users who are skilled in design, most users will appreciate the capability of using *templates*. A template is a picture or a picture part that resides in the Macintosh Scrapbook. It can be created using any application that supports the Scrapbook, and most applications do. Additionally, scanned images, such as from MacVision, can be placed in the scrapbook and used as a template.

There are two major benefits in converting an existing scrapbook image into a LaserWorks image. The first is that it can be used as part of a font, accessible directly from the keyboard. The second, and most important, is that it can be output on the LaserWriter, or other PostScript output device, at a higher resolution.

The Scrapbook exists as a desk accessory. Pictures are copied from the scrapbook using the "Copy" option from the Edit menu, and displayed in the Edit window by turning on the Template Switch. The LaserWorks path-creation tools (Moveto, Lineto, and Curve) are used then to trace over the template.

The fonts that appear on the Macintosh screen (screen fonts) also can be used as templates for creating higher-resolution images. The screen fonts, which are stored in the System file, are opened using the CHAR Window's "Open" option. Characters then are individually selected, displayed as a template, and traced, and the image paths are saved. A character chart of the font graphically indicates which images have been converted into PostScript form by showing a circled character.

Creating a Laser Dictionary

A Laser Dictionary is a set of all of the PostScript formulas derived from a set of images created in the LaserWorks environment, which the LaserWriter (or other compatible device) will keep in memory at any one time. A Laser Dictionary can be composed of an entire font or just a single image.

A Laser Dictionary is created by clicking on the SAVE button. The user then is prompted for a name for the dictionary. This name also is used for the font. If the dictionary coincides with an existing screen font, then the name must match exactly. If the screen font does not exist yet, it will need to be named to match the dictionary name when it is created.

The Laser Dictionary is loaded by using the LaserExpert functions (FIG. 103). The LaserExpert Window is accessed by clicking on the left side of the LaserWorks banner. The "DOWNLOAD LASER DICT" option presents a display of all available Laser Dictionaries. The user selects the one that is needed, and it is downloaded to the LaserWriter. The LaserWriter produces a Confirmation Page to show that the download was successful. The downloading function can be accessed directly from the Macintosh Finder, so LaserWorks does not have to be open to download fonts.

FIG. 103. Entire fonts, or collections of images, can be tested, altered, and installed by using the LaserExpert screen.

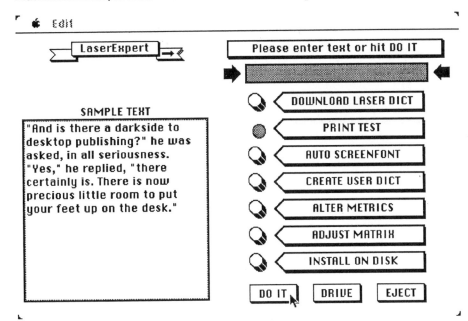

Fonts can be tested by selecting the PRINT TEST button. The user is prompted for the name of the screen font associated with the downloaded font that presently resides in the LaserWriter. Because the name must match that of the downloaded font, it appears by default and is selected by clicking on the DO IT button. Next the user is prompted for a point size, from 1 to 127. Text is typed and appears in the SAMPLE TEXT window. The sample text is printed by clicking on the DO IT button.

If a screen font representation of a Laser Dictionary image does not exist, it can be created automatically by using the "AUTO SCREENFONT" option. Screen fonts can be any size up to 127 points. They can be installed in application programs by using Apple's Font/Desk Accessory Mover or by using the "INSTALL ON DISK" option within LaserExpert.

The "ALTER METRICS" and "ADJUST MATRIX" options are used to fine-tune the fit of the characters, as well as their size on the screen.

Graphic Manipulation

The images that are created in the Edit window can be altered by using the Goodies window (FIG. 104). The Goodies window is accessed by clicking on the right side of the LaserWorks banner.

The Goodies environment is a graphic laboratory where an individual character or an entire font can be modified (depending upon the setting of the WORKING switch). The available functions are:

- Translate—The entire image can be picked up and moved anywhere within the Edit window.

- Rotate—The image can be rotated left or right to any degree mark.
- Mirror—The image attributes can be reversed and duplicated in an adjacent quadrant.
- Reverse—The image path direction can be changed. This function is helpful if the reverse direction rule was not heeded during the creation of the image.
- Flip—The image can be flipped either horizontally or vertically.
- Italic—The image can be italicized up to 30 degrees to the left (backslant) or the right.
- Weight—The image weight can be increased or reduced from light to bold in 5 percent increments across the entire character by using Shift-Weight, or simply across the x-axis by selecting Weight alone.
- Peak—The top or bottom of the image can be expanded to create a perspective effect.
- Parts—Repetitive elements of an image design can be saved in a Parts Pad for use in the creation of other images. Separate parts dictionaries can be created.
- Pick—Elements of an image are identified as "parts" with this function.

By exiting and re-entering the mirror, italic, weight, or peak options a character can undergo unlimited changes.

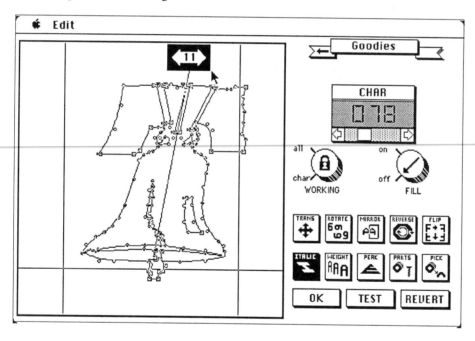

FIG. 104. An amazing array of graphic effects can be achieved by using tools in the Goodies window. Here the Liberty Bell image, character number 78, has been italicized 11 degrees. The OK button is used to make graphic modifications permanent (unaffected by the Revert command).

JUSTTEXT:
Code-Oriented Control of PostScript Features

Although visually captivating, the WYSIWYG screen displays, which are characteristic of the Macintosh environment, often are limiting in their ability to implement the power of PostScript output devices, such as the Apple LaserWriter. Programs that provide a WYSIWYG user interface must interpret the size, position, orientation, and other graphic descriptors of all elements on a page into a coded form which the output device can process. The WYSIWYG interface shields the user from the necessity of writing codes while, at the same time, restricts access to capabilities that the software has not implemented as yet.

It was for this reason that William Bates wrote the JustText[27] program. Bates, an author and a producer of books, wanted to use the LaserWriter to produce fully composed pages, but found that none of the available software met his criteria for producing attractive pages. Being familiar with the typesetting process, Bates wrote a word processor (FIG. 105) that supports the inclusion of typesetting commands to control those elements which are important for quality typesetting. He also built in multiple-window capability, as well as a filter to eliminate unnecessary data from imported text files. Although JustText is not WYSIWYG, it does support the Macintosh user interface, i.e., the Clipboard, Desk Accessories, Cut, Paste, and Undo.

FIG. 105. The JustText editor shows all of the typesetting commands placed between sets of braces, as well as PostScript notation and normal text. The file in the active window can be converted entirely into PostScript and edited in the PostScript language.

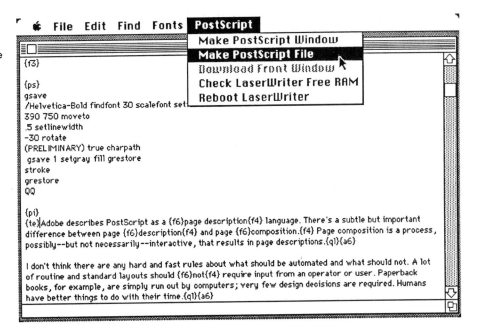

JustText files are plain seven-bit ASCII text. As such they can be created with most word and text processors, and communicated easily over a modem or from a serial connection with another computer. JustText uses a mnemonic coding system that encloses typesetting commands, and sometimes a value, within a set of delimiters (braces). Prior to, or coincident with, printing, JustText converts its codes into PostScript, which can be processed directly by the LaserWriter or other compatible devices.

Although JustText does not implement all of the capabilities of PostScript, it does support the command {ps} which passes PostScript commands directly through JustText text files. By using this command a user can have access to all of the power residing within a PostScript output device.

[27] Knowledge Engineering
G.P.O. Box 2139
New York, NY 10116
(212) 473-0095

Minimum 512K Macintosh required.

The Typographic Basics

In the JustText environment, the LaserWriter is a typesetting machine. It can be used to create entire pages of text and graphics, or to produce traditional galleys of type, which will be assembled by hand into pages. Regardless of what level of sophistication will be employed, there are four commands that are absolutely essential: point size, font, line spacing, and line measure.

Point size is written as {p_}, where the value following the p can be up to 255 points (3.5 inches). Larger sizes can be set by editing the resulting PostScript file.

Fonts are chosen by number, and each of the LaserWriter and LaserWriter Plus fonts has specific assignments. The command {f_}, is used to specify the font number, such as {f4}, for Times Roman.

The line spacing command is {l_}. Just as on a phototypesetting machine, specifying a line spacing value that is less than the point size will result in overlapping lines. Without a preview of an improper code choice, in such a case, might require multiple passes to get the needed result. It is, therefore, best to remember to change the line spacing whenever the point size is changed. Some coding errors, such as a missing delimiter, are trapped prior to printing.

The line measure can be specified in a number of ways. PostScript describes a page in terms of a Cartesian coordinate system: the x-axis, measured in points, runs along the bottom of a page, and the y-axis, also measured in points, runs vertically along the left edge (FIG. 106). The beginning point, (0,0), is at the bottom left corner, and the top left point (of an 11-inch-high page) is at point (0,792) (11 inches x 72 points/inch = 792 points). Any position on the page (JustText can access any size page that a PostScript printer can produce) can be specified as x,y coordinates. Specifying a line measure can be accomplished by either moving to a specific location {xy_,_} and specifying a line measure {m_}, or more easily, by specifying column information {c_,_,_,_,_}, which indicates the column number, and its top, left, bottom, and right page coordinates.

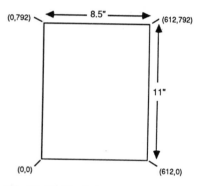

FIG. 106. The PostScript page area is specified in point increments with the origin at the lower left corner.

Line-ending decisions can be invoked manually, such as for quadding (quad left {ql}, quad right {qr}, and quad center {qc}), and force justification ({fj}). Line breaks are made through justification using stored width values, and word breaks are made through hyphenation using a set of rules from the TEX typesetting system. If the rules are not sufficient to make the word-break decision, a user-alterable exception word dictionary is consulted. The exception word dictionary is a normal text file named *Hyphenation Dictionary*.

Discretionary hyphens ({-}) can be embedded within text (one per word) to indicate the preferred hyphenation point. A word that is preceded by a discretionary hyphen will not be considered for hyphenation.

Typographic Niceties

Although the similarities between typesetting and typewriting are obvious, the differences are, to some minds, less remarkable. JustText automatically compensates for some of these seemingly subtle differences. For example:

- Multiple word spaces, such as between sentences or at the beginning of a paragraph, are removed.
- Ligatures for the two-letter combinations of fi and fl are automatically substituted.
- Double hyphens automatically are converted to an em dash. The em dash ({ed}) and en dash ({nd}) also may be manually inserted.
- Quotation marks are correctly interpreted into the proper typographic style.

In addition there are codes to expand and condense any style type; directly access trademark and copyright symbols; produce true fractions, subscripts, and superscripts; insert fixed spaces (thin, en, em); automatically leader across a column or page; manually or automatically kern; indent left, right, both, and hanging, and to align text; create tables, boxes, and rules; and automatically wrap text around artwork.

Coding Efficiency

JustText provides a number of commands that automate the production of certain kinds of typographic effects. The "Drop Cap" command ({dcn_}) is a good example. This simple command takes as input the number of text lines of height that the cap is to be set, along with the specification of the cap itself (FIG. 107). If, for example, a paragraph was to begin with the letter H and stand four lines of text tall, the code would be indicated simply as {dc4H}. In such a case, a code-intensive system is more efficient than a WYSIWYG system.

FIG. 107. The Drop Cap command is a simple, yet very powerful, method of producing a very effective paragraph opening. This example was created using MacDraw, for illustrative purposes only. The actual drop cap produced by JustText is considerably more uniform in typographic form.

Bold drop cap equivalent in size to the height of the specified number of lines.

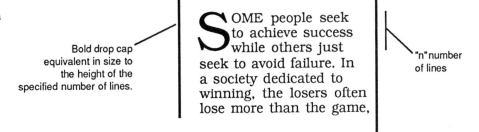

"n" number of lines

Other Capabilities

In addition to the more than 70 commands that JustText supports, the package also includes a set of programs called LaserTools. The LaserTools programs convert MacPaint (FIG. 108), Thunderscan, or MacVision files into PostScript form so that they can be included with JustText files. The tools also support the repositioning (according to PostScript x and y coordinates), scaling, rotating, and cropping of files.

Since JustText represents the needs of a knowledgeable author who must produce his own type, it continues to undergo refinement and improvement. William Bates says about his program, "This is not a consumer product, and may never be. I'm not sure professional-quality graphics arts production can be 'made simple.' I think of the Macintosh user interface as something akin to an automatic transmission on a car. For a lot of people—perhaps the majority of people—it's fine. But there are a few people who need and want the level of control that a stick shift provides. This system (JustText) is for people who must have a lot of control over the LaserWriter, and care that extra percent about the quality of their output."

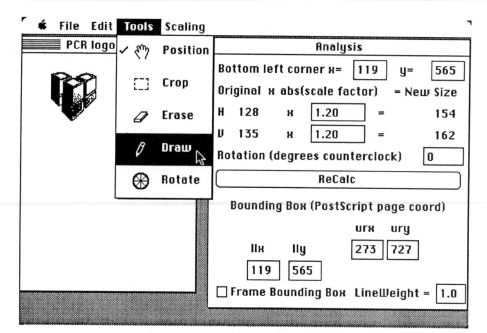

FIG. 108. The MacPaint-to-PostScript LaserTool is one of three programs that provides the means to alter files and convert them to PostScript so as to improve their appearance and make them compatible with JustText.

MEASUREUP:
A Publishing Tool for Test Material Production

Desktop publishing programs are malleable tools. They can be shaped to fit comfortably into the hands of many diverse professionals. The software products that provide the means to compose pages are suitably flexible to meet the needs of people producing a wide range of materials, from accounting practices through zoological expeditions. Certain publishing activities, however, have special requirements that are not adequately met with general-purpose desktop publishing products. One such activity is test production.

Tests are especially difficult to produce because they often must be published in many different versions. Although each version can draw on the same pool of questions, the questions must be arranged and renumbered manually, and a separate answer key must be produced for each version. In addition, unlike most materials that are published only once, tests usually are modified and used again. The needs of the test producer are sufficiently different for there to be a software product that blends desktop publishing with test generation. The first such product is measureUP,[28] a flexible test question database.

A Test of Strength

The measureUP program is easy to use despite its many capabilities. It consists of two main programs, or *modules*, although other compatible programs will be forthcoming. First is the Questions module, which is used to create and maintain test question files. Second is the Design module, which is used to design, format, and generate tests.

From the moment a question is input, measureUP begins to keep track of it (FIG. 109). Questions are kept in files according to subjects, called *objectives* . An objective can hold from 1 to 999 questions. As questions are added to an objective, their sequence number automatically is incremented by one. Each question maintains an iden-

[28] Logic eXtension Resources
9651 Business Center Drive, Suite C
Rancho Cucamonga, CA 91730
(714) 980-0046

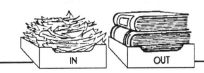

FIG. 109. The measureUP questions module provides text and graphics editing for the quick and efficient creation of questions and responses.

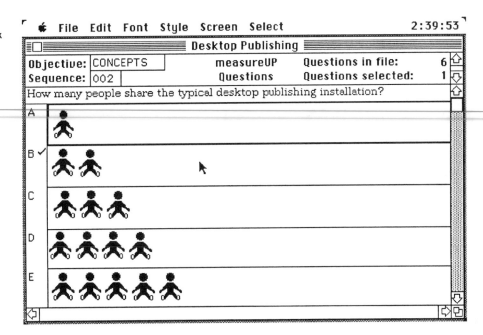

tity composed of the objective name followed by the sequence number. The fifth question in the Animals Objective, for example, would be designated as *ANIMALS005*.

The question itself consists of two parts: the *stem*, which is the actual question, and the *alternatives*, which are the answer choices. There can be up to five alternatives for a multiple-choice format or two for a true/false format. The question also can be free form, in which case only the question stem box is filled in.

In its default mode, measureUP displays a single line for the stem and a single line for each of five alternatives, labeled A-E in the answer box along the left margin. The size of each entry box can be expanded by placing the cursor on its bottom line and dragging the line downward. Each entry box is independent and may contain graphics as well as text. The font, style, and size of text within each box is also independently alterable.

The correct response is indicated by clicking the mouse pointer in the appropriate area of the answer box. The measureUP database can independently scramble the response alternatives to produce up to nine different test versions, in addition to the original. It produces a separate answer key for each, maintaining absolute accuracy.

Each question carries with it a set of statistics accessible by selecting *Show Statistics* from the Screen menu (FIG. 110). The statistics include:

- A history of the test question administration
- The date the question was created or last modified
- A note if it is o.k. to scramble the alternatives to produce different versions
- A note if the question should be numbered (not all entries need to be actual test questions)
- A note if the question is linked to a companion question that must always appear with it in a test
- Key words referring to the question (used to select test items in a future version of the program)
- Notes about the question
- Prescriptive measures recommended for someone who answers incorrectly. A version of the test can be printed with the answers and the prescriptions as a remedial tool.

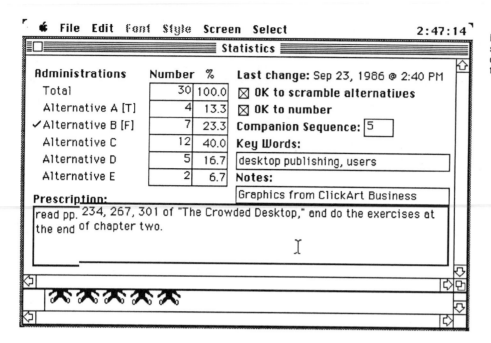

FIG. 110. Each question has an accompanying statistics page, which can be used, among other things, to set the criteria by which questions are to be included in tests.

The Question of Pictures

Graphic images can be imported to the measureUP environment from any standard Macintosh source by using the Clipboard. The measureUP database can be used with Switcher; that is, it can share the Macintosh with one or more additional applications programs for easier transfer of graphics. An image from MacPaint, MacDraw, or FullPaint, for example, can be copied to the Clipboard and pasted into a measureUP stem or alternative box. A collection of images also can be saved in the system Scrapbook and then copied and pasted into measureUP.

The graphics of measureUP are transparent, and can be positioned anywhere within a stem or alternative box (FIG. 111). Text can be seen through a graphic, providing great flexibility in the manner in which words and pictures are displayed. When a graphic is selected, the cursor changes to an image of a hand, which permits movement of the graphic anywhere within the box. If a portion of the graphic is outside the box, the "Trim Picture" option can be used to clip and remove the invisible portions. Graphics also can be resized by selecting the "Scale Picture" option, which prompts the user for a horizontal and vertical scaling factor to change the size or the proportion of the image.

Scanned images from hardware devices such as MacVision also can be used. This capability is quite helpful for integrating existing training materials and instructional aids into measureUP tests without the need to redraw them.

The entries in measureUP need not all conform to the question/alternative format. An illustration, with text, can be created as a nonnumbered entry to serve as a reference for a series of questions. Additionally, a stem box can be expanded to full page to serve as a cover for a test, or reduced for a graphic heading, testee information area, or whatever is required.

Designing the Test...Testing the Design

A test is composed of selected questions and nonnumbered items from one or more objectives. The Design module screen consists of four windows (FIG. 112). The

FIG. 114. Text and graphics that will be repeated on the top or bottom of each page is assembled in the same way as test questions. Note the hand icon that is used to position the graphic anywhere in the header/footer area.

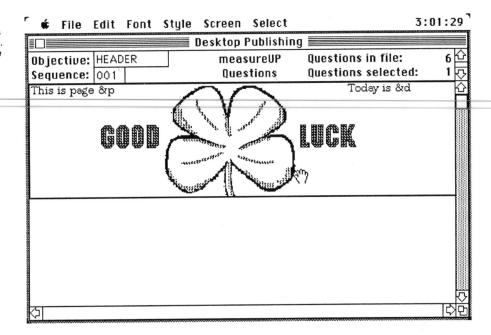

Reaching Beyond the Test

The measureUP database has both an import and an export utility to bring test item information in from other sources or to send it out. The export format supports sending question data to measureUP itself, in order to create subsets of existing question files. Additionally, text data can be exported for mail merge, or to the Clipboard, or as a text file.

The elements of a question item are independently exportable. They are chosen in a manner similar to the way in which tests are constructed. Two panels are presented, one for the question parts and the other for the output fields.

Data that is destined for mail merge is formatted with tabs delimiting each field and a return ending each record. The first record contains the field names in order of their exportation, followed by the text edit fields enclosed in quotations.

Data that will be sent to either the Clipboard or to a text file has fields ending with a return and records ending with two returns.

The importation of question data can come from existing measureUP files, or from mail merge. The mail merge import format takes a file of data containing text fields delimited by a tab or a comma and records terminated with a return, and adds them to an existing question file. The first record must contain the valid field names that measureUP will use to identify and process the incoming data.

MACINTOSH GRAPHIC ACCESSORIES

The Macintosh graphic environment has spawned a number of products and programs that enhance its usefulness as a typesetter and as an imagesetter. Following is a representative sampling of the diversity of items presently available.

ClickArt

The ClickArt[29] family of products is based on the concept of the clip art libraries that have been marketed in the graphic arts industry for many years. Clip art is artwork on a wide variety of subjects that is printed on glossy paper and can be cut (or copied) and pasted-up with text and other graphic elements. The availability of clip art frees printers and graphic arts professionals from having to create particular images for inclusion in their work. In much the same way, the ClickArt image libraries relieve the Macintosh user from the time-consuming process of drawing complex line art and typographic images. Unlike clip art, which is supplied in static form on paper, ClickArt images are stored on disk and can be modified, without restriction, using a Macintosh paint program.

ClickArt can be utilized with MacPaint or MacWrite, or through the use of the Macintosh Scrapbook and Clipboard, with numerous other programs. In most instances the images will be selected and edited (if desired) in the MacPaint environment. In most instances the procedure will be as follows:

1. The MacPaint program will be loaded.
2. The Untitled file that appears on startup will be closed.
3. One of the ClickArt files will be opened. Each file is listed according to the general category of art it contains.
4. The opened file appears on the screen. The image can be used in whole or in part.
5. After the image has been selected and modified (if necessary), it can be added to another MacPaint file or to another program file, by saving it in the Scrapbook (a collection of Macintosh images accessible to almost any program at any time), or by cutting or copying the image and pasting it into another application (i.e. using the Clipboard).

The first ClickArt disk contained images of a very general nature. Subsequent editions have focused on particular graphic needs, such as those related to publications work and display lettering. The general topics and the specific image descriptions follow.

FIG. 115. ClickArt Personal Graphics.

ClickArt Personal Graphics (FIGS. 115, 116)

People: presidents, Al & Jimmy, celebrities, famous people, tennis/running, skier/football, rain/chef, cartoons.
Animals: gorilla, cats, egret.
Stuff: little guys, bigger guys, wine & beer, good guys, Americana, arrows, more little guys.

ClickArt Publications (FIG. 117)

Column Formats: Format Two, Format Three.
Alphabets: stencil letters, French manuscript.

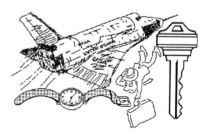

[29] T/Maker Graphics Company
2115 Landings Drive
Mountain View, CA 94043
(415) 962-0195

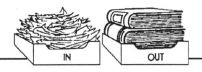

Headings: phrases, Columns-2, Columns-3.
Backdrops: around town, displays.
People: literaries, cartoons.
Maps: USA map, Europe/USA
Borders: borders 1, borders 2.
Misc.: desk items, calendar, dingbats, abodes.

ClickArt Business Graphics (FIG. 118)

Abstract Logos
Arrows
Chart Templates
Logos Large
Logos Medium
Logos Oblique Large
Logos Oblique Medium
Logos Small
News Heads
People Symbols
Symbols
Transportation

FIG. 116. Additional illustrations from ClickArt Personal Graphics.

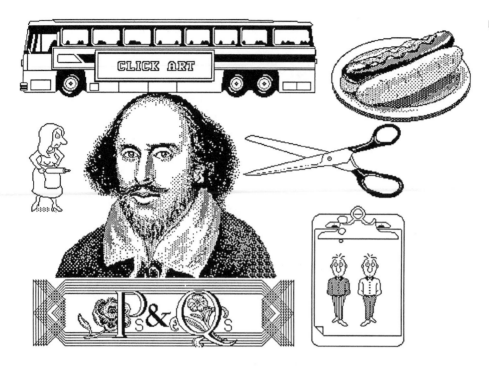

FIG. 117. ClickArt Publications.

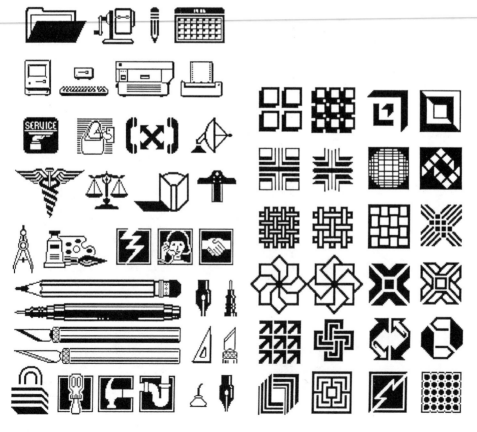

FIG. 118. ClickArt Business Symbols I (left),
ClickArt Business Abstract Logos (right).

MAC THE KNIFE

Mac the Knife[30] is a series of disks comprising a collection of over 400 clip art images that cover such general subjects as sports, the office, international icons, corporate symbols, animals, borders, and more (FIG. 119). Although each disk is unprotected and users are encouraged to use only their back-up copy, each file is meant to be used in a read-only mode. That is, a file is opened, and one or more images are copied from it for insertion into a MacPaint document, leaving the original file intact.

When a file is opened, it automatically repaints the texture pallette on the bottom of the MacPaint screen. There are literally hundreds of new patterns provided.

Three new fonts are included on Mac the Knife Volume 1: Manhattan, which is a modified version of New York, Mos Eisley, which provides space theme icons, and Hollywood, which is an art deco design with Hollywood-style icons. Each font can be installed on any Macintosh disk using the Font Mover program. Mac the Knife, Volume 2 is a collection of over 24 fonts including scripts, decorative display faces, and practical text fonts.

FIG. 119. A selection of graphic images composed from Mac The Knife Volume I.

---

[30] Miles Computing, Inc.
7136 Haskell Avenue Suite 212
Van Nuys, CA 91406
(818) 994-7901

McPic!

McPic!³¹ is another clip art collection; however, it differs from others in both its
repertoire of images and in its method of use. Most Macintosh clip art images are created by their publishers using MacPaint, and therefore are sold as collections of MacPaint files. While this approach is generally satisfactory and does, in fact, provide an
easy route to graphic editing, Magnum has chosen instead to provide its image collections in the form of individual Macintosh scrapbooks.

The Macintosh scrapbook is a desk accessory, a small utility program that is
available to the user at any time, merely by clicking on the Apple icon and highlighting it. Each disk has its own scrapbook, which can be used to move images between applications. The scrapbook images are stored in a file called Scrapbook File, a
file which is normally held in the disk's system folder. The System Folder is visible
on the Macintosh desktop after a disk is inserted. In order to specify one of the McPic!
files as a replacement scrapbook, it merely is necessary to change the name of the existing scrapbook, copy the required MacPic! file onto the disk, and rename it "Scrapbook
File."

There are 12 McPic! scrapbooks comprising 130 ready-to-use images. Among
them are:

Animal Scrapbook File: Eagle, fish school, kitten, dog, mouse, butterfly, unicorn,
    tiger heads, lion head, elephant, stallion, mare's head.
Astrology Scrapbook File: Capricorn, Aquarius, Pisces, Aries, Taurus, Gemini,
    Cancer, Leo, Virgo, Libra, Scorpio, Sagittarius.
Business Scrapbook File: Visa and Mastercard, stopwatch, telephone, computer and
    disk, USA map, world globe, stamp and envelopes, banner, file cabinet,
    newspaper, microphone, city skyline (night). (FIG. 120).

FIG. 120. Illustrations from the McPic! Business Scrapbook (above) with two variations (left).

Fun Scrapbook File: illusion box, eight ball, four aces, light bulb, megaphone,
    feet/paw/shoe/finger prints, crystal ball, musical notes, guitar,
    hamburger/fries/shake, target, cannon.

³¹ Magnum Software
21115 Devonshire Street, Suite 337
Chatsworth, CA 91311
(818) 700-0510

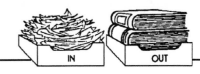
Holiday Scrapbook File: birthday cake, firecracker, American flag, turkey, pumpkin, black cat, snowman, snow flake, Santa Claus, box and bow, rabbit, champagne bottle/glass, Valentine heart.

Home Scrapbook File: big house, house in snow, two houses, three houses, pencil, mail box, note pad, umbrella, coffee cup, books, push pin.

Money Scrapbook File: dollar bill, roll of bills, various coins, stacks of coins, bag of coins, glass piggy bank.

Nature Scrapbook File: olive tree, pine tree, palm tree, two roses, orchid, rain cloud, sun, moon and star.

People Scrapbook File: nine human heads, eight male cartoon heads, four female cartoon heads, four men, three women, four children, wizard and alien, exotic woman, baby, clown, lips, kiss imprint, dancing couple, eye.

Sports Scrapbook File: basketball, tennis ball, soccer ball, golf ball, football, football player, sail boat.

Symbol Scrapbook File: hand thumbs up, pointing hand (man), pointing hand (woman), hour glass, scissors, stars and fleur de lis, cigarette, skeleton key, padlock, two arrows left, three arrows right, sword, first place ribbon, comedy/tragedy masks. (FIG. 121).

FIG. 121. Illustrations from the McPic! Symbol Scrapbook. The bottom row of faces was modified using FullPaint.

Transportation Scrapbook File: VW bug, VW van, sport coupe (two views), car (three views), truck (3/4 view), jet plane, two motorcycles.

DrawArt

DrawArt[32] is a collection of images created with MacDraw rather than MacPaint. MacDraw defines shapes by their attributes. It is object-oriented rather than bitmap-oriented. Because of this method of production, the images can be independently or collectively resized, repositioned, reshaped, or edited. Patterns can be changed, added, or removed; line widths can be modified; and portions of graphics can be combined in new ways (FIGS. 122 and 123). When DrawArt graphics are output on a LaserWriter, each element of each design is interpreted as a PostScript shape, which means that DrawArt graphics maintain high resolution despite an alteration in size.

Scale

Fill Pattern

Line Width (thick)

Pen Pattern

Expand and Condense

FIG. 123. A selection from the DrawArt Media folder.

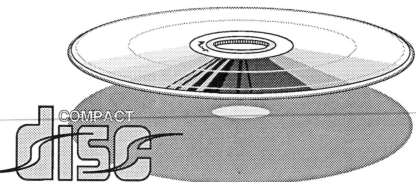
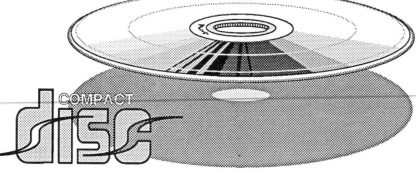

Shadow: Duplicate, Fill Black, and Send to Back

Reflection: Flip Vertical

Chicago font

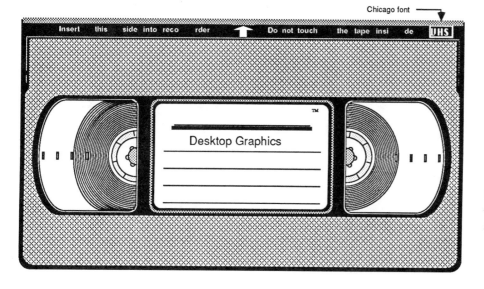

Reshape (Distort)

FIG. 122. DrawArt lettering variations.

[32] Desktop Graphics
400 Country Drive
Suite H
Dover, DE 19901
(302) 736-9098

SOFTFORMS

The Macintosh is a valuable graphic arts tool, both because of the things it can do, and the way in which it can do them. A simple example is the generation of a business form, composed of rules of various weights, type of various styles and sizes, and graphics of various sorts, such as line art and logos. A number of Macintosh software packages makes this creative process fast and easy.

For those who would rather buy business forms already composed and alter them to suit their needs, there are a number of off-the-shelf packages designed specifically for user customization. One such package, called SoftForms, Volume 1,[33] contains 23 commonly used business and personal-use forms created as MacPaint data files (FIG. 124). These forms include an employment application, weekly reminder, customer invoice, time & materials invoice, monthly calendar, things to do list, follow-up memo, purchase order, routing form, telephone memo, credit application, payment reminder, call report, speed memo, inventory report form, receiving record, 3-column

FIG. 124. SoftForms provides a library of common business and personal forms alterable to suit individual needs.

WHILE YOU WERE OUT

TO:_____

NAME _____

COMPANY_____

PHONE _____

TELEPHONED	URGENT
CAME BY	PLEASE CALL
PERSONAL	WILL CALL BACK
RETURNED YOUR CALL	

Please take action

Date	To

☐ Note and file
☐ Note and return
☐ Return with more information

TO:

JOB INVOICE

No:_____

Phone	Date of Order
Order Taken By	Customer's Order #
Job Name – Number	
Job Location	
Job Phone	Starting Date

Terms:_____

QTY	MATERIALS	PRICE	AMOUNT	DESCRIPTION OF WORK

WEEKLY RE

MONDAY

1 ☐ _____
2 ☐ _____
3 ☐ _____

CALL REPORT   SALESMAN__

COMPANY_____ PHONE____

ADDRESS_____

CITY_____ STATE_____

TALKED TO:_____ POSITION_____

COMMENTS: _____

DATE OF CALL: _____

☐ BY TELEPHONE   ☐ PE

33 Artsci, 5547 Satsuma Ave.
   North Hollywood, CA 91601
   (818) 985-2922.

accounting paper, graph paper, credit card recordkeeper, bank account recordkeeper, balance checkbook form, and speed gram. Forms can be modified using the MacPaint graphic tools and printed on the ImageWriter or LaserWriter. Multiple copies can be produced using either a photocopier or standard offset lithographic reproduction.

MacPaint, like most Macintosh software, supports the integration of text and graphics produced with other applications. A drawing created in MacDraw, for example, could be combined with a piece of clip art, and then positioned in a SoftForms form. By means of the Clipboard and Scrapbook, elements produced through a variety of methods could be reassembled according to particular needs (FIG. 125).

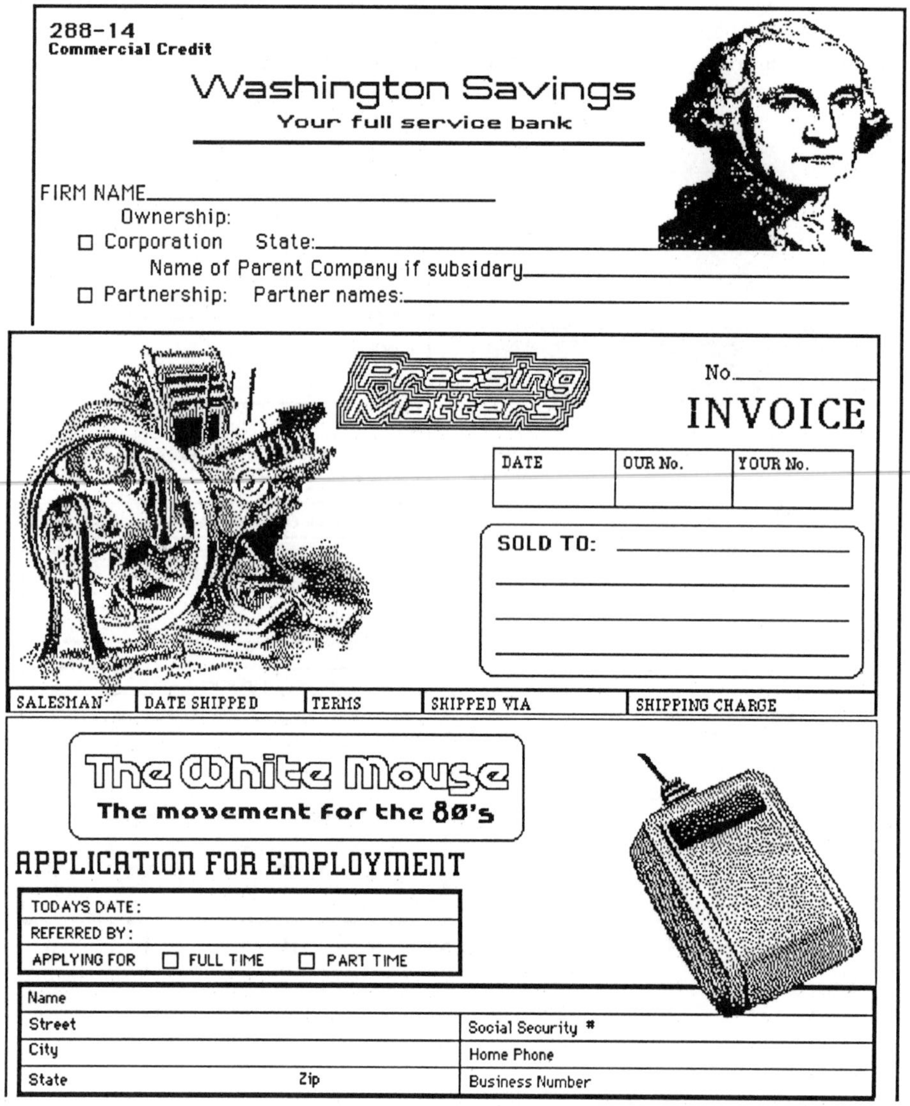

FIG. 125. Forms can be customized using a variety of Macintosh clip art packages or user-drawn artwork.

SPRINGBOARD

Art a la Mac I and II

Springboard Software, Inc
7808 Creekridge Circle
Minneapolis, MI 55435

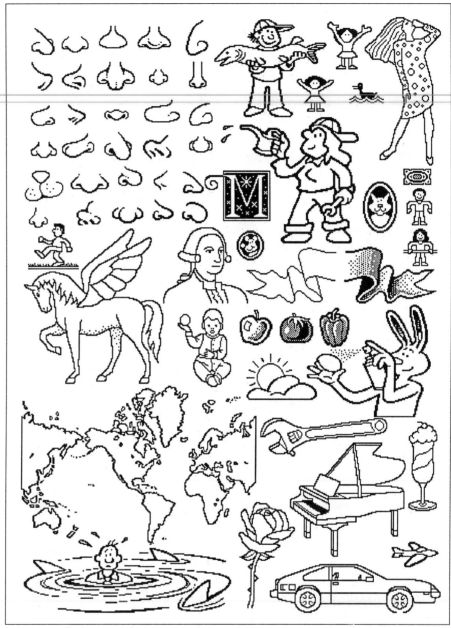

REALART

Electric Cottage Industries
PO Box 217
Spooner, WI 54801-0217

big buck

AD TECHS

AdTechs
7220 Old Kent Road
Amarillo, TX 79109
(806) 353-7063

atlas girl

sewing

ring round

MACMEMORIES

ImageWorld, Inc.
PO Box 10415
Eugene, OR 97440

MatMacBook

Electronic Publisher, Inc
210 South Marietta Street
Excelsior Springs, MO 64024
(816) 637-7233

camera

diver

butcher

produce

smARTmouse

Pleasant Graphic Ware
PO Box 506
Pleasant Hill, OR 97455
(503) 741-1401

animals

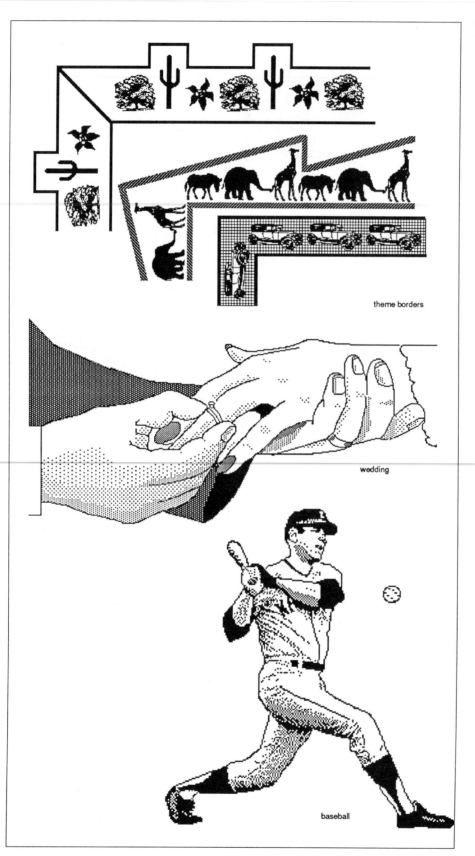

theme borders

wedding

baseball

MAC ART

compuCRAFT
PO Box 3155
Englewood, CO 80155
(303) 850-7472

DESKTOP ART

Dynamic Graphics, Inc.
6000 N. Forest Park Drive
Peoria, IL 61614-3592
(309) 688-8800

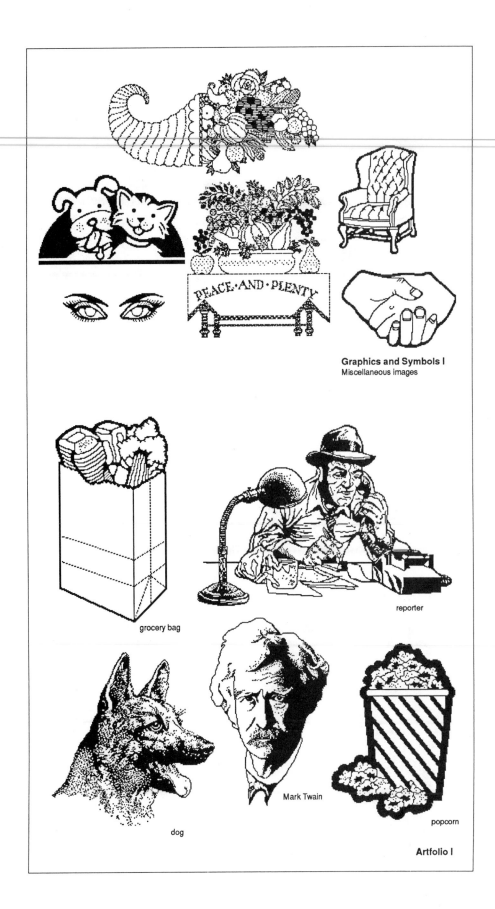

PEACE·AND·PLENTY

Graphics and Symbols I
Miscellaneous images

grocery bag

reporter

dog

Mark Twain

popcorn

Artfolio I

DESKTOP ART
(continued from page 105)

Four Seasons I
miscellaneous images

Sports I
miscellaneous images

CONGRATULATIONS GRADS

Education I
miscellaneous images

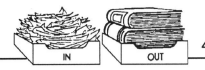

AAH Graphics

A.A.H. Computer Graphic Productions
PO Box 4508
Santa Clara, CA 95054

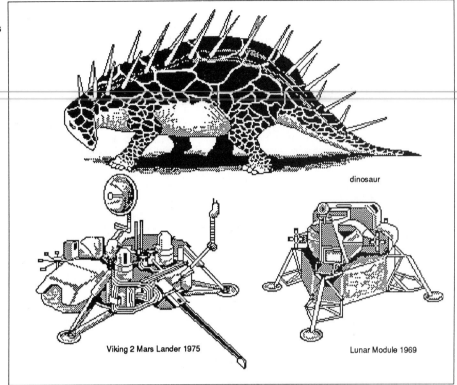

dinosaur

Viking 2 Mars Lander 1975

Lunar Module 1969

ArtBase

Computer Graphic Services
815 Princess Ave.
Vancouver, B.C., V6A 3E5
(604) 255-8077

FLUENT FONTS AND FLUENT LASER FONTS

Fluent Fonts[34] is a two-disk collection providing both decorative and functional fonts (FIG. 126). Specific applications include a font for architecture, ASCII encoding, astrobiology, astrology, electronics, mathematics, chemistry, and meteorology. Language fonts include Cyrillic (Russian and Ukrainian), Czech (Slovak and Serbo-Croatian), Greek, Hebrew (actual Hebrew as well as a romanized version), and Polish. A number of unusual decorative designs, borders, and initials makes the collection particularly useful, as well as unusually attractive.

The user's manual is very helpful, not only in describing how best to use the fonts, but also in explaining how the Apple ImageWriter and LaserWriter use them. In the case of the ImageWriter, the best high-quality printing is achieved when a font twice the size of the font being used is installed in the system. The Fluent Fonts manual describes it as follows: "When High Quality is selected in programs like MacWrite, Word, MacDraw, and ReadySetGo, and the Mac is trying to print Easy Street-9 (the 9 point Easy Street font) it first looks for Easy Street-18. If it finds Easy Street-18 it will overlap the dots with two passes of the print head, giving a 9-point font with the resolution of 18 point. The dots do not get smaller, they just get closer together. If the Mac cannot find Easy Street-18, it will print two passes of Easy Street-9, with the second slightly offset. The exception to this method is selecting Final Print in MacPaint, which does not have a High Quality mode. Print Final makes two passes which smooth the jagged edges."

In the case of the LaserWriter, Fluent Fonts have been designed to be compatible, so that jagged edges are minimized. The smoothing routines that are built into the LaserWriter usually are activated in the "Page Setup" portion of most programs, although in the case of MacPaint they are invoked automatically when "Print Final" is selected.

FIG. 126. Casady Fluent Fonts.

Script AaBbCcDdEeFfGgHh

Easy Street AaBbCcDdEeFfGgHhIiJjKkLlMmNnOo

El Camino AaBbCcDdEeFf

Calligraphy AaBbCcDdEe

MAZEL TOV ABCDEFGHIJKLMNOPQRST

OLD WEST ABC

CANTERBURY ABCDEF

IMAGES

Fluent Fonts Sampler from Casady Company

[34] Casady Company
P. O. Box 223779
Carmel, CA 93921
(408) 646-4660
(800) 331-4321

Fluent Laser Fonts[34] are a collection of auto-downloadable display and book faces in PostScript form (FIG. 127). The fonts are provided with the screen representations and printer installation software.

The number of fonts that can be downloaded to the LaserWriter or LaserWriter Plus is somewhat limited, particularly if the fonts are to remain permanently in memory (until the power is turned off). If the fonts are only to remain in memory temporarily, a greater number can be used. The maximum number of fonts that can be used at one time is a function of the application software in use, the complexity of the fonts, and the available RAM in the LaserWriter.

FIG. 127. A selection of Fluent Laser display and book fonts.

Prelude Script

Prelude Bold Slant

Right Bank

Ritz

Ritz Italic

ABCDEFGHIJKLMNOPQRS
abcdefghijklmnopqrstuv
1234567890`~!@#$%^&*(){}:"?

Ritz Condensed

ABCDEFGHIJKLMNOPQRSTUVWXYZ
abcdefghijklmnopqrstuvwxyz
1234567890`~!@#$%^&*()+{}:"<>?,./;'[=]¡™£¢"

Calligraphy

ABCDEFGHIJKLMNOPQRST
abcdefghijklmnopqrstuvwxyz
1234567890`~!@#$%^&*()+{}:"<>?,./;'[=]¡™£¢

Regency Script

ABCDEFGHIJKLMNOPQRSTUV
abcdefghijklmnopqrstuvwxyz
1234567890`~!@#$%^&*()+{}:"<>?,./;'[=]`¡™£¢

Bodoni

ABCDEFGHIJKLMNOPQRSTUVWXY
abcdefghijklmnopqrstuvwxyz
1234567890`~!@#$%^&*()+{}:"<>?,¡™£¢

Bodoni Italic

ABCDEFGHIJKLMNOPQRSTUVWX
abcdefghijklmnopqrstuvwxyz
1234567890~!@#$%^&*()+{}:"<>?,¡™£

Bodoni Bold

ABCDEFGHIJKLMNOPQRSTUVW
abcdefghijklmnopqrstuvwxyz
1234567890`~!@#$%^&*()+{}:"/;'`™

Bodoni Bold Italic

ABCDEFGHIJKLMNOPQRSTUVWX
abcdefghijklmnopqrstuvwxyz
1234567890`~!@#$%^&()+{}:/;'™£¢*

Sans Serif

ABCDEFGHIJKLMNOPQRSTUVWXYZ
abcdefghijklmnopqrstuvwxyz
1234567890`~!@#$%^&*()+{}:"<>?,./;'[=]`™£

Sans Serif Book

ABCDEFGHIJKLMNOPQRSTUVWXY
abcdefghijklmnopqrstuvwxyz
1234567890`~!@#$%^&*()+{}:"<>?,./;'[=]`

Sans Serif Demi Bold

ABCDEFGHIJKLMNOPQRSTUVWX
abcdefghijklmnopqrstuvwxyz
1234567890`~!@#$%^&*()+{}:'[=]`™£¢

Sans Serif Italic

ABCDEFGHIJKLMNOPQRSTUVWXY
abcdefghijklmnopqrstuvwxyz
1234567890`~!@#$%^&*()+{}:"<>?,./;'[=]`™

Monterey

ABCDEFGHIJKLMNOPQRSTUVWXY
abcdefghijklmnopqrstuvwxyz
1234567890`~!@#$%^&*()+{}:"<>?,./;'[=]

Monterey Italic

ABCDEFGHIJKLMNOPQRSTUVWXY
abcdefghijklmnopqrstuvwxyz
1234567890`~!@#$%^&*()+{}:"<>?¡™£¢

Monterey Medium

ABCDEFGHIJKLMNOPQRSTUV
abcdefghijklmnopqrstuvwxyz
1234567890`~!@#$%^&,./;'[=]`¡™

Monterey Bold

ABCDEFGHIJKLMNOPQRSTU
abcdefghijklmnopqrstuvwxyz
1234567890`~!@#$%^&?=]`¡™£¢

Monterey Bold Italic

ABCDEFGHIJKLMNOPQRSTU
abcdefghijklmnopqrstuvwxyz
1234567890`~!@#$%^&?¡™£¢"

ULTRA FONTS AND LASER FONTS

UltraFonts[35] is available in two versions: one a collection of general-use and graphic fonts, and the other a Technical and Business Set (FIG. 128).

A quality of both collections is the addition of special characters that extend the audience and the special uses to which the fonts may be applied. The general-use fonts include the accents necessary for writing in over 30 languages. Printer's spaces (em, en, and thin spaces), proportional numbers, and bullets also are provided, along with a font for creating borders in any application program.

[35] Century Software
2306 Cotner Avenue
Los Angeles, CA 90064
(213) 829-4436

The Technical and Business Set contains fonts for constructing the symbol and typographic requirements of such specialized fields as astronomy, astrology, chemistry, chess, law, mathematics, medicine, meteorology, petroleum engineering, philately, physics, and religion. The fonts provide the tools to easily produce multilevel equations, chess boards, data processing forms, square roots, strike-outs (text with a line through it), filled boxes and circles, map legends, chemical formulas, and much more.

Having chosen to specialize in the area of symbology for technical and professional applications, Century Software also offers a font-design service in which they will design type styles, pictures, logos, even signatures on a custom basis. For further information about this service contact Michael Mace, Director of Marketing.

LaserFonts (FIG. 129) are a developing series of downloadable fonts for the LaserWriter and LaserWriter Plus. These fonts which are noncopy-protected, include bold, italic, condensed, and expanded variations. Each low-cost package includes the downloadable fonts, the Macintosh screen fonts, and an installer program.

FIG. 128. A selection of Century Software's UltraFonts.

Neosho Bold

ABCDEFGHIJKLMNOPQRSTUV
abcdefghijklmnopqrstuvwxyz
1234567890=+!@#$%&*("""");:'

FIG. 129. A showing of some of the fonts from the LaserFonts library.

Trent

ABCDEFGHIJKLMNOPQRSTUV
abcdefghijklmnopqrstuvwxyz
1234567890=+!@#$%*("""");:"",.,.?

Thin Trent

ABCDEFGHIJKLMNOPQRSTUVWXYZ
abcdefghijklmnopqrstuvwxyz
1234567890=+!@#$%*("""");:"",.,.?/

Fat Trent

ABCDEFGHIJKLMNOPQ
abcdefghijklmnopqrstuvwxyz
1234567890=+!@#$%*("

Extra Light Williamette

ABCDEFGHIJKLMNOPQRSTUVW
abcdefghijklmnopqrstuvwxyz
1234567890=+!@#$%*("""");:"",.,.?/

Thin Times

ABCDEFGHIJKLMNOPQRSTUVWXYZ
abcdefghijklmnopqrstuvwxyz
1234567890=+!@#$%^&*({[]});:'"<>,.?/

Devoll

ABCDEFGHIJKLMNOPQRSTU
abcdefghijklmnopqrstuvwxyz
1234567890-+!@#$%&*("""");:'",.,.?/

Congo

ABCDEFGHIJKLMNOPQRSTUV
abcdefghijklmnopqrstuvwxyz
1234567890=+!@#$%&*("'''');:'',.

Cumberland

ABCDEFGHIJKLMNOPQRSTUV
abcdefghijklmnopqrstuvwx
1234567890=+!@#$%&*("""");:"',.,.?

Thames

ABCDEFGHIJKLMNOPQRSTUV
abcdefghijklmnopqrstuvwxyz
1234567890=+!@#$%&*("""");:"',.,.?

Spokane

ABCDEFGHIJKLMNOPQRSTUVW
abcdefghijklmnopqrstuvwxyz
1234567890=+!@#$%&*("""");:"',.

Manistee Bold

ABCDEFGHIJKLMNOPQRSTUV
abcdefghijklmnopqrstuvwxyz
1234567890=+!@#$%&*("""");:'

Columbia

ABCDEFGHIJKLMNOPQRSTU
abcdefghijklmnopqrstuvw
1234567890=+!@#$%&*("""");:"',.,

PROFESSIONAL TYPE FONTS

The Professional Type Font[36] series from Kensington consists of two collections, each with two disks: one for text sizes, and the other for display sizes.

It was the aim of the designers of these collections to be as true as possible to existing typographic designs, even if it meant breaking from Macintosh conventions to do so. In traditional type design, the proportions of the characters usually are redrawn for different sizes or size ranges of the font. The Macintosh works differently. If the letter e is 10 pixels wide in Font X at 12 point, then it must be 20 pixels wide in Font X at 24 point. To have followed this rule in the creation of these fonts would have led to a compromise in the quality of the typefaces as representative of "true cut" versions of the originals.

The Kensington approach is to draw each character proportional to its actual design width, without regard for the size relationship required on the Macintosh. The result of this approach is twofold. First, the range of sizes maintain a design integrity unequalled in other Macintosh typeface collections. This is one way in which the fonts earn the designation *professional*. Second, because the font size relationships do not conform to Macintosh specifications, the high-quality printing mode can prove troublesome with the Kensington fonts. Because the Macintosh will look for the size double of the operative font size to achieve higher-image resolution, it will be fed improper information from the Kensington designs. The solution to this predicament is to either remove the double size font from the disk, or not use the high-quality print function. Kensington states that its designs are sufficiently dense that the high-quality printing mode is not necessary to achieve satisfactory results.

The Kensington Professional Type Fonts are based upon designs considered to be standard in the typesetting industry. They include the following:

Professional Type Fonts Name	Similar To
Beta Italic	Lubalin Italic
Epsilon	Optima
Eta Medium	Eurostile Medium
Kappa Bold	City Bold
Lambda (FIG. 130)	Greetings Monotone
Nu Black	Bolt Bold
Omega	Transmission
Omicron Bold	Futura Bold
Rho SemiBold	Times Roman Bold
Sigma	Helvetica
Sigma Bold	Helvetica Bold
Theta	Astra
Zeta Bold	Stop

[36] Kensington Microware Ltd.
251 Park Avenue South
New York, NY 10010
(212) 475-5200

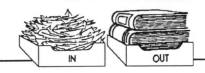
FIG. 130. A font selection from the Kensington Professional Type Fonts collection for the Apple ImageWriter.

Lambda

Available in 18, 24, 36, and 48 point sizes

abcdefghijklmno

pqrstuvwxyz

ABCDEFGHIJKLM

NOPQRSTUVWXYZ

1234567890

.,:!$&*()+[];:'"""◇?/

FONT CREATIONS

The Font Creations[37] Volume One disk is one of many custom designed typeface collections by a number of software companies and independent designers. This assortment of typefaces was created using the Apple font editor based on an artist's conception of which typefaces would be particularly useful in complementing the typefaces supplied with each Macintosh system. The typefaces are named *Art Deco*, a heavily contrasted thick and thin design; *Centura*, a stencil-like design; *Circus*, a bold, rounded stem design; *Palo Alto*, a computer-like design; and *Wall Street*, a simple, lightweight upright design (FIG. 131).

Each of the typefaces, in a range of sizes from 9 point to 36 point, may be installed on Macintosh application programs, such as MacPaint and MacWrite in addition to, or in place of, existing typefaces. The storage requirements of typefaces are significant, and most users (those without hard disks) must carefully select the typefaces and sizes they are most likely to use. The Macintosh Font Mover utility provides an easy means of installing typefaces.

A single typeface design, regardless of whether it is a native Macintosh design or one from a third party, can use the built-in font selections from the Style menu to produce a range of variations. These appearance modifications include altering the basic character design to appear in any two of the following ways: bold, italic, underline, outline, shadow, and of course, plain text.

[37] Font Creations
 Box 36
 Newton, MA 02164

FIG. 131. Font Creations bitmap type designs with variations.

CLICKART LETTERS

ClickArt Letters is another of the ClickArt series of programs available from T/Maker Graphics Company.[38]

Typefaces: Berkeley, Boston-LC, Boston-UC, Boston-Numbers, Cambridge, New Haven-Italic, Rio, Stanford, Tampico.

Fonts: Basel-48 (point), Boston-48, Calgary-36, Cambridge-36, Dallas-8, Fargo-48, Houston-36, New Haven-24, New Haven-36, Oxford-36, Plymouth-36, Quebec-48, Sydney-24, Vegas-48. (FIG. 132)

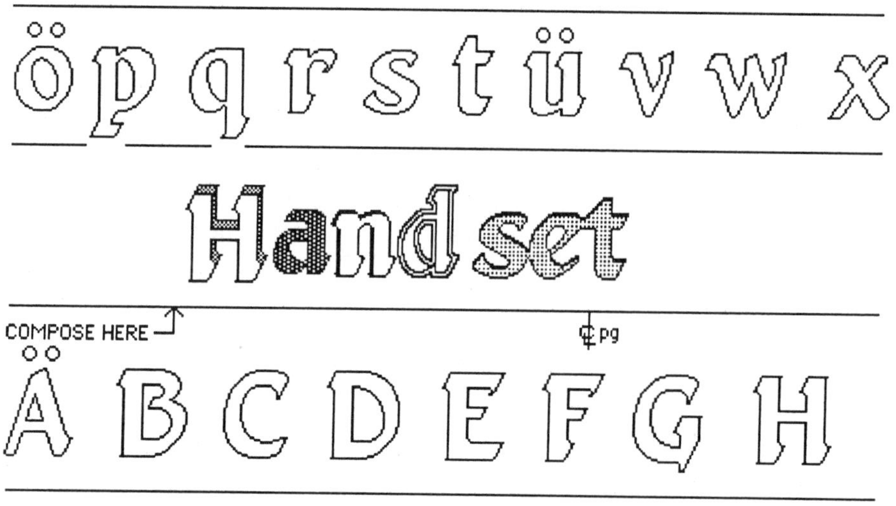

FIG. 132. ClickArt Letters bitmap typefaces are supplied as MacPaint documents (left) and as fonts (below).

Oxford
Vegas
New Haven
Boston
Basel

[38] T/Maker Graphics Company
2115 Landings Drive
Mountain View, CA 94043
(415) 962-0195

ADOBE SYSTEMS INCORPORATED

Adobe Systems[39] occupies a unique position within the graphic imaging industry in that it is the publisher of both the PostScript page description language, and a large collection of typefaces that are compatible with PostScript output devices.

PostScript typefaces are resident in the ROM in every Apple LaserWriter. They include typefaces that are licensed from the Mergenthaler[40] and International Typeface[41] Libraries. Nonresident Adobe typefaces can be purchased separately and downloaded to the LaserWriter's RAM. Specimens of LaserWriter and LaserWriter Plus typefaces and additional Adobe downloadable typefaces are shown in FIGS. 133 and 134.

FIG. 133. Adobe type faces resident in the Apple LaserWriter (first four) and LaserWriter Plus (all fonts) are among the most popular designs in use today.

Times Roman

ABCDEFGHIJKLMNOPQRSTUVWXYZ
abcdefghijklmnopqrstuvwxyz"'-<>,.?
1234567890`~!@#$%^&*()_=+{}[]:;/|\

Helvetica

ABCDEFGHIJKLMNOPQRSTUVWXYZ
abcdefghijklmnopqrstuvwxyz"'-<>,.?
1234567890`~!@#$%^&*()_=+{}[]:;/|\

Courier

ABCDEFGHIJKLMNOPQRSTUVWXYZ
abcdefghijklmnopqrstuvwxyz"'-
1234567890`~!@#$%^&*()_=+{}[]:;

Symbol

ΑΒΧΔΕΦΓΗΙϑΚΛΜΝΟΠΘΡΣΤΥςΩΞΨΖ
αβχδεφγηιφκλμνοπθρστυϖωξψζ∀э–<>,.?
1234567890 ̃!≅#∃%⊥&*()_=+{}[]:;/|∴ ℑ

Bookman

ABCDEFGHIJKLMNOPQRSTUVWXYZ
abcdefghijklmnopqrstuvwxyz"'-<>,.?
1234567890`~!@#$%^&*()_=+{}[]:;/|\

[39] Adobe Systems, Inc.
1870 Embarcadero Road
Palo Alto, CA 94303
(415) 852-0271

[40] International Typeface Corporation
2 Dag Hammarskjold Plaza
New York, NY 10017
(212) 371-0699

[41] Mergenthaler Typeface Library
Linotype
425 Oser Avenue
Hauppauge, NY 11788
(516) 424-2000

Helvetica Narrow

ABCDEFGHIJKLMNOPQRSTUVWXYZ
abcdefghijklmnopqrstuvwxyz'"-<>,.?
1234567890`~!@#$%^&*()_=+{}[]:;/|\

Palatino

ABCDEFGHIJKLMNOPQRSTUVWXYZ
abcdefghijklmnopqrstuvwxyz'"-<>,.?
1234567890`~!@#$%^&*()_=+{}[]:;/ | \ `¡™£¢

Avant Garde

ABCDEFGHIJKLMNOPQRSTUVWXYZ
abcdefghijklmnopqrstuvwxyz'"-<>,.?
1234567890`~!@#$%^&*()_=+{}():;/ | \

New Century Schoolbook

ABCDEFGHIJKLMNOPQRSTUVWXY
abcdefghijklmnopqrstuvwxyz'"-<>,.?
1234567890`~!@#$%^&*()_=+{}[]:;/|\`¡™

ITC Zapf Chancery

ABCDEFGHIJKLMNOPQRSTUVWXYZ
abcdefghijklmnopqrstuvwxyz'"-<>,.?
1234567890`~!@#$%^&*()_=+{}[]:;/|\`¡™£

ITC Zapf Dingbats

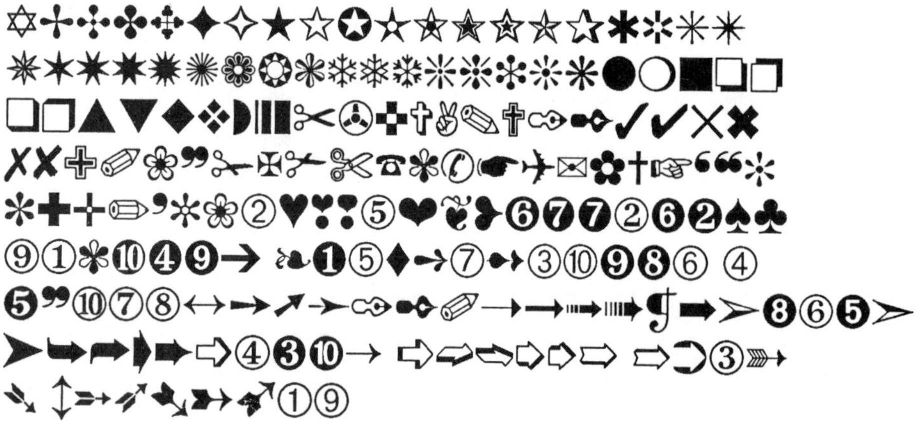

FIG. 134. A variety of downloadable type faces from the Adobe library. Additional type designs are released on a regular basis.

Optima®
ABCDEFGHIJKLMabcdefghijklmnopqrstuv

ITC Souvenir® Light
ABCDEFGHIJKLMabcdefghijklmnopqrstu

ITC Lubalin Graph® Book
ABCDEFGHIJKLMabcdefghijklmnopqr

ITC Garamond® Light
ABCDEFGHIJKLMabcdefghijklmnopqrstuv

ITC American Typewriter® Medium
ABCDEFGHIJKLMabcdefghijklmnop

ITC Benguiat® Book
ABCDEFGHIJKLMabcdefghijklmnopqr

Glypha®
ABCDEFGHIJKLMabcdefghijklmnopqr

Helvetica® Condensed Light
ABCDEFGHIJKLabcdefghijklmnopqrstuvwxyz

ITC Galliard® Roman
ABCDEFGHIJKLMabcdefghijklmnopq

Trump Mediæval®
ABCDEFGHIJKLMabcdefghijklmnopq

Helvetica® Light
ABCDEFGHIJKLMabcdefghijklmnopqrst

ITC Machine®
ABCDEFGHIJKLMNOPQRSTUVWXYZ1234567890¢?!£

ITC Korinna® Regular
ABCDEFGHIJKLMabcdefghijklmnopqr

Melior®
ABCDEFGHIJKLMabcdefghijklmnopqrst

Goudy Old Style
ABCDEFGHIJKLMabcdefghijklmnopqrstuv

ITC New Baskerville® Roman
ABCDEFGHIJKLMabcdefghijklmnopqrstu

The Adobe Typeface Package

Volumes are sold in packages supporting from one to five printers. A volume from the Adobe typeface library usually consists of two disks: A Font Initializer and Screen Fonts. After fonts have been initialized on a printer, they work only on that printer. Initialized fonts can be copied and shared with whomever has access to the target printer, but can not be used with any other output device. A multi-printer typeface package can be initialized on up to five different printers.

Installing Adobe Fonts

Although Adobe fonts can be used with any PostScript output device, this description will be limited to the use of the LaserWriter.

Adobe fonts cannot be used until they have been initialized. Uninitialized and initialized fonts can be recognized on the Macintosh desktop by the appearance of their icon (FIG. 135). The initialization process retains the original font file.

The Font Initializer disk contains the Font Initializer program. The first program phase consists of polling the AppleTalk network to detect the presence of all available printers (FIG. 136). A printer is choosen, and a listing of the uninitialized fonts appears, along with a new set of options (FIG. 137). An individual or a group of fonts are selected, and the Initialize button is activated. The user is prompted for the location of the disk to be used to save the initialized fonts. The initialization process takes place, and the program is exited. Although fonts can only be initialized for a specific printer, they can be reinitialized on the same printer if the need arises.

Before   **After**

TrumpMedRom.pre   TrumpMedRom

FIG. 135. An uninitialized font icon on the left and an initialized font icon on the right.

Using Adobe Fonts

In order to use the initialized fonts they must be accompanied by a matching set of screen fonts. Screen fonts are installed using the Apple Font/DA Mover program (FIG. 138). The program adds the screen display versions of the fonts to Macintosh System disks.

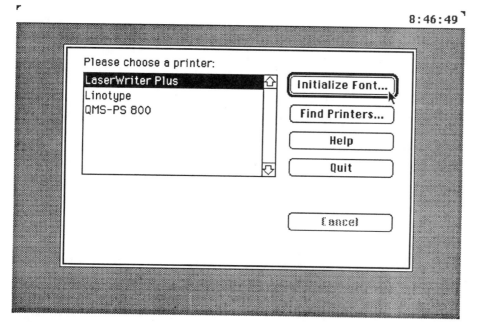

FIG. 136. Font packages can be initialized for one printer only.

FIG. 137. The initialization process takes a matter of minutes and consists of the user selecting the fonts and choosing "initialize."

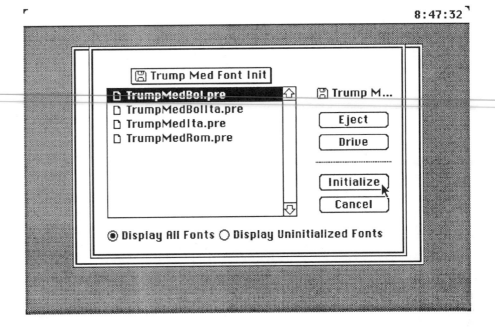

FIG. 138. Screen fonts are copied onto a Macintosh System disk by using the Apple Font/DA Mover.

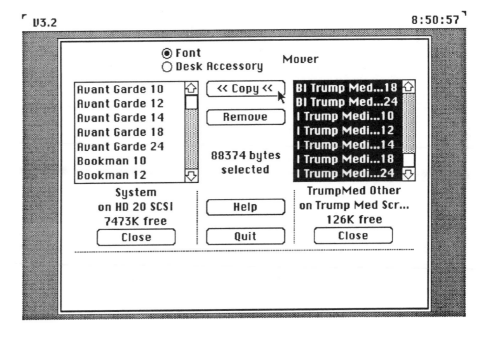

Adobe provides a screen font version for each of the LaserWriter fonts in a library package. The screen fonts have been carefully tuned to properly represent proper character spacing. For highest display clarity each of these screen fonts should be copied to the System disk. This is usually no problem for a system equipped with a hard disk, but can cause disk space problems for smaller media configurations. An alternative is to copy only one or two point sizes of each font, or to copy only the *Plain* font, and use the Style menu of the application to select Bold and Italic variations.

Screen fonts are selectable from the pull-down font menus of applications that use the System disk for startup.

Printer fonts are downloaded in one of two ways, either automatically or manually. Many Macintosh applications will download fonts to the printer without user intervention. When an application requires a font that is not resident in the printer it searches the on-line disks for the font file and downloads it. Because fonts require a considerable amount of the printer's RAM, a font is automatically deleted after its document has been processed, or at the end of its text block in the case of PageMaker.

Fonts can be manually downloaded using the Font Downloader program provided with the Adobe Systems Typeface Package (FIG. 139). Both manually and automatically downloaded fonts can reside in the printer at the same time.

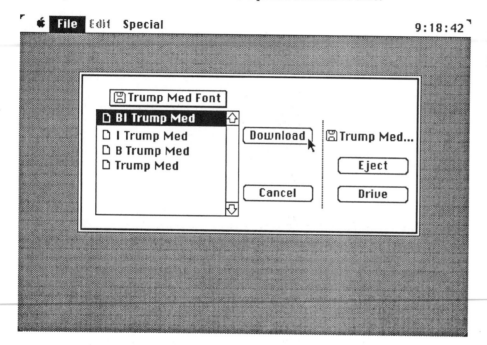

FIG. 139. Fonts can be manually downloaded to the LaserWriter by using the Font Downloader program provided by Adobe. The program can also be used to send PostScript files to the printer.

PAINTMATE

PaintMate[42] is a low-cost graphic input device that facilitates the transfer of three-dimensional objects and two-dimensional pictures into the MacPaint environment. PaintMate is a reflective acrylic plate that is hung at an angle before the Macintosh screen (FIG. 140). Any object that is properly illuminated below it is reflected onto the plate, presenting an image that appears superimposed on the Macintosh screen. The image then can be traced or painted using the MacPaint tools.

FIG. 140. The PaintMate.

[42] Hoglund Tri-ordinate Corporation
343 Snyder Avenue
Berkeley Heights, NJ 07922
(201) 464-0205

CLICKART EFFECTS

ClickArt Effects[43] provides four special graphic tools which are not a part of the MacPaint program. These special effects—rotation, slant, perspective, and distortion—are of particular usefulness in the creation of special effect lettering, greatly enhancing the typographic flexibility of the Macintosh (FIG. 141).

ClickArt Effects installs as a part of the MacPaint program, available by pulling down the Apple menu on the extreme upper left of the screen. When selected, Effects presents four icons: a wheel, representing rotation; the Leaning Tower of Pisa, representing slant; a road, representing perspective; and hands twisting a sheet of paper, representing distortion. The normal MacPaint document window appears to the right of the icons. A tool is selected, and the area that is to be altered is enclosed in a Selection Rectangle (or marquee). An activation arrow then appears, which provides the user with the power to alter the rectangle according to the characteristics of the chosen tool.

FIG. 141. Graphic manipulations produced using ClickArt Effects.

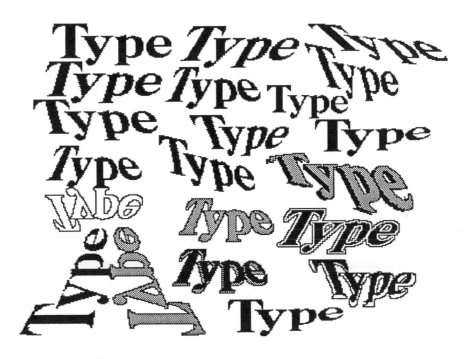

IMAGE SCANNING DEVICES

The visual nature of the Macintosh has been creatively developed by a number of companies making devices that can capture a two- or three-dimensional image and display it on the Macintosh screen. These devices create a bitmapped image that can be edited pixel by pixel and incorporated with text or other graphics for a wide range of applications. The possible uses extend to almost any application for which a graphic representation is useful. Among the possibilities are:

Business and Industry
Product illustrations
Employee photo records
Personnel security identification (graphic reproduction of face, fingerprints, etc.)
Prototype development

43 T/Maker Graphics Company
2115 Landings Drive
Mountain View, CA 94043
(415) 962-0195

Parts cataloging
Component call outs
Product development
Competitive analysis of products (side-by-side comparisons)
Product design and modification
Production of charts and graphs
Illustration of report covers

Advertising
Ad layouts
Point-of-purchase displays
Package designs
Storyboarding
Cartooning
Graphic design
Typographic experimentation

Education and Training
Capture of images from textbooks and guides
Visual recordings of experiments
Real-time capture of scientific investigations
Time-lapse recordings

Personal Uses
Family archives and records
Creation of titling and decorative screens for slide and video presentations

MacVision

MacVision[44] (FIG. 142) is a small (5 inches long x 7 inches wide x 2 inches deep) interface device that permits the attachment of either a video camera, video cassette recorder (VCR), videodisc player, or video output of another computer to the Macintosh modem or printer port. Any device that uses an RS-170 video output may be used. The input device connects to MacVision through an RCA-type jack, and a built-in cable connects to the Macintosh. MacVision derives its power from the Macintosh 128K, or 512K. The Macintosh Plus requires a separate power source. Two controls on the top of the unit are provided in order to adjust the image: a brightness dial and a contrast dial. Additional control can be obtained through image adjustments that might be a part of the image-sensing device in use. The brightness adjustment on a video camera, for example, can be manipulated in order to alter the appearance of an image on the Macintosh screen.

The quality of the image that the Macvision, or any similar system, is able to capture, is a function of at least two variables. The first is the host imaging system, which most functionally, will be a video camera (FIG. 143). The camera might be black--and-white or color, and might be a simple surveillance-type camera or a sophisticated professional model. The most significant feature of the camera might be its optics, and most particularly, its ability to focus at close range. The second variable is the lighting. Because Macvision basically is analyzing each incoming pixel as being either on or off (black or white), the lighting can be critical in differentiating shapes, textures, and details. Through the use of a video switch box it is possible to attach a TV set or video monitor in order to examine the image that the camera is "seeing." Previewing the input is helpful in determining that the best possible image has been captured.

[44] Koala Technologies Corporation
Division of PTI Industries
269 Mt. Hermon Road
Scotts Valley, CA 95066
(800) 223-3022

FIG. 142. The MacVision control unit, as digitized by MacVision. The dial on the left controls brightness, while the dial on the right controls contrast.

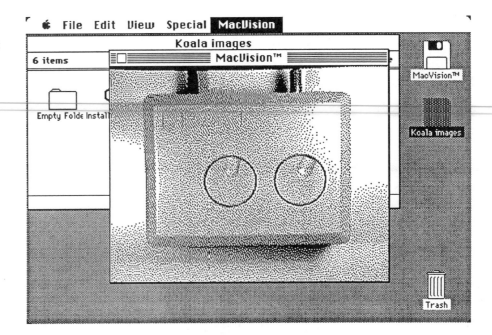

FIG. 143. MacVision's signature as scanned with a video camera. High-contrast images, such as black type on a white background, are easiest to digitize because they are basically composed of the two light states that MacVision can sense most easily.

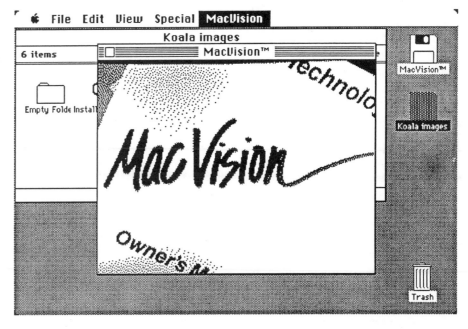

On the software side, MacVision installs on any applications disk as a desk accessory. It is therefore available at any time by pulling down the ever-present Apple icon menu with the mouse, and clicking on the MacVision selection. To install Mac-Vision the user simply turns on the Macintosh, inserts the applications disk onto which MacVision is to be installed, and then inserts the MacVision disk. The "Install MacVision" icon is dragged onto the application disk desktop whereupon it is copied. The user then double-clicks on the new Install MacVision icon and, in a matter of seconds, the MacVision program is available on the applications disk.

When the MacVision desk accessory is opened, it provides the user with a number of options. The first is a calibration procedure for the MacVision hardware and the incoming video signal (FIG. 144). This adjustment is optional since the image is

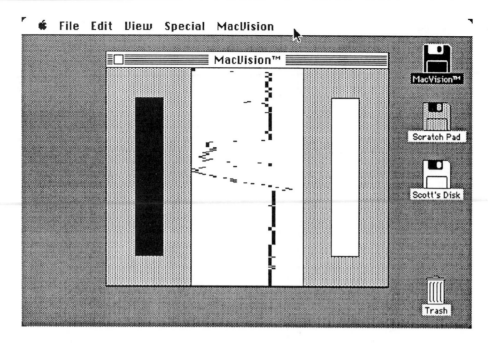

File Edit View Special MacVision

FIG. 144. The MacVision scanning adjustment can be set to optimize the incoming video signal for each "shot."

scanned fast enough on the Macintosh screen to make real-time compensation possible through visual inspection. The MacVision "Adjust" selection provides the means to optimize the brightness and contrast controls, leaving the final determination of image quality to personal interpretation. To adjust the incoming video signal, the brightness control is turned to its maximum clockwise position and the contrast control is turned to its maximum counterclockwise position. The Adjust screen shows a black vertical bar on the left and a white vertical bar on the right. Shades of gray are represented by an irregular line running down the middle of the screen. The optimum brightness setting is achieved by turning the brightness control counterclockwise until the outermost part of the irregular line touches the left edge of the center panel of the Adjust screen. The contrast setting is made with a similar, though opposite, procedure.

The Scanning Process

The actual scanning process is initiated by selecting "Scan Window" from the MacVision menu. The window that is produced is scanned continuously at the rate of one scan every five seconds from the left side to the right. Any change in the brightness, contrast, focus, or movement of the object is reflected almost immediately in the image appearance on the screen.

When an acceptable image appears within the window, a click of the mouse freezes the scan at the end of its sweep across the screen. Double-clicking on the mouse stops the scan immediately, even if it has only partially completed its movement. The scanning process can be reactivated by pulling down the MacVision menu and reselecting the "Scan Window" option.

The captured window image can be saved by using the normal Edit menu. The complete window can be saved, or any portion can be isolated and carried on the Clipboard for insertion in another application. This feature is especially useful when using MacPaint. At any point during the creation of a MacPaint file, the MacVision system can be activated, an illustration or object scanned, the required portion of an image cut, and the result immediately placed within the MacPaint work (FIGS. 145 through 148).

FIG. 145. Scanned images can be brought into the MacPaint environment for editing and for use with other images and typographic treatments.

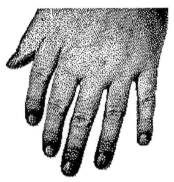

FIG. 146. The tools provided in MacPaint make it possible to create a new version of graphic reality.

FIG. 147. Complex typographic forms can be scanned in and composed into words. The Altsys FONTastic program supports the creation of fonts composed of MacPaint-drawn (and therefore MacVision-scanned) images.

FIG. 148. Clip art and copyright free art collections can be scanned in easily, edited, and incorporated into artistic creations.

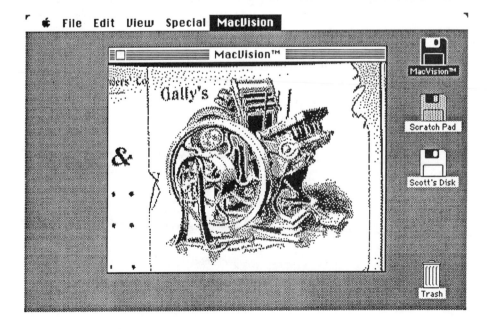

Capturing an image in the MacVision window is fast; however, speed might be sacrificed in order to scan the entire Macintosh screen. This operation is activated by selecting the "Scan Screen" option from the MacVision menu. A screen scan takes about 22 seconds and can be stopped using the mouse in the same way as it is in the window scan procedure.

The full-screen scan can be saved on disk by selecting the "Save Screen" option from the MacVision menu. The screen is saved automatically under the name SCREEN 0, or some successive number. It is not possible to give the image a specific name until the user returns to the Macintosh desktop and renames the generically labeled file.

The window image and the screen image can be printed in a number of ways. Each is supported directly on the MacVision menu with specific selection options. A saved screen image occupying an identifiable file on the Macintosh desktop can be printed by highlighting it and selecting "Print" from the File menu. Either the screen or window images also can be printed from within an application, such as MacPaint, by using the printing procedures of the application.

The image that MacVision, or any similar device, can capture is limited to the screen resolution of the Macintosh. All printed pictures, or halftones, are composed of patterns of tiny dots, and the halftone process simulates gray scaling by varying the size of the dots, while maintaining a specific number of dots, or horizontal scan lines, per inch. Since a Macintosh pixel can be only one of two colors—entirely black, or entirely white—it is difficult to express shades of gray, or any image that is not high contrast; composed entirely of black and white components (FIG. 149).

MacVision compensates to some degree for this inherent deficiency. With a properly illuminated subject—that is, one in which the light and dark areas are satisfactorily lit and the middle tones are present in a visible gradient—MacVision will scatter the pixels in such a way as to suggest gray scaling. Experimentation with lighting effects can dramatically alter the appearance of a human subject or inanimate object. Koala suggests that three-dimensional subjects be illuminated with three light sources. The first is the *key light,* which is the main source of illumination. It is placed in proximity to the subject or at an angle to it. Its function is to clearly differentiate the subject from its background. The second is the *fill light,* which is placed away from the subject and serves to illuminate the subject in order to differentiate its shape by providing gray scale tones. The third is the *high light,* which, as its name implies, is placed above or in front of the subject in order to provide further indication of tonal differences.

An accessory program for use with MacVision, called MoreVision, provides a menu of scanning options in order to achieve halftone, outline, zebra, and other special effects.

FIG. 149. The multiple gray tones of a photograph are reduced to a limited number of black-and-white patterns.

MAGIC

Printed pictures are composed of minute dots of various sizes, which the eye perceives as gradations of tone. These pictures, called halftones (FIG. 150), are photomechanically or photoelectronically converted from continuous shades of gray to patterns of dots. The greater the number of shades of gray (i.e. the greater the number of steps in the gray scale), the greater the detail possible in the reproduction. Computer-generated graphics also are composed of very small dots, called *picture elements*; abbreviated *pixels* or *pels*. In the case of the Macintosh, the screen is madeup of a mosiac of 512 by 342 square, uniformly sized dots, with each dot representing only one of two possible states: completely on (black) or completely off (white). Arranging those dots to best present a scanned graphic image is partly dependent upon the skilled eye of the operator, but mostly dependent upon the video interface used to interpret the incoming video signals. The MAGIC (*MA*cintosh *G*raphics *I*nput *C*ontroller) Video Digitizer[45] is one of the most flexible methods of converting flat artwork and three-dimensional objects into representative screen patterns.

The MAGIC system provides a number of ways to capture an image. In addition to a high-contrast, black-and-white picture, the following options are available:

- An edges-only image, providing an outline of tonal areas
- A gray-scale picture, providing tonal control
- An inverted picture of any kind, with black and white reversed
- A flopped picture of any kind, with right and left reversed (useful for printing T-shirts)

The video source can be a standard video camera, either with its own power supply or connected through a video cassette recorder (VCR). The camera can be mounted on a copy stand for digitizing flat artwork and small three-dimensional objects, or mounted on a tripod for shooting larger objects and scenes. Prerecorded images on the VCR also can be used as input.

FIG. 150. All printed photographs are made up of tiny variously sized dots, which give the illusion of shades of gray.

Photograph courtesy of Apple Computer, Inc.

[45] New Image Technology, Inc.
10300 Greenbelt Road
Seabrook, MD 20706
(301) 464-3100.

The MAGIC screen (FIG. 151) provides a number of tools useful for the manipulation and alteration of the video signal. Running down the left side of the screen are a number of commands and settings that control the image capture process before, during, and after its execution. Here are what these selections provide:

Quit (151-1): Exits the MAGIC environment and returns the user to the Macintosh desktop.

Print (151-2): Prints either the screen buffer or a MacPaint file in either final or draft mode, in either full or half size.

ClrWindow (151-3): Clears the focus window (main blank area in the center of the screen) to the desktop pattern.

ClrWindow Box (151-13) (The small box in the upper right of the larger ClrWindow box): Used to turn off all focus scan buttons.

Review (151-4): Used to select from previously saved MacPaint files and display them in full screen mode.

Scale Set (151-5): Used to define a window into which a reviewed or patterned picture will be read.

Scale Box (Ruler Control) (151-14) The small box in the upper left side of the Scale box: Used to turn the precision 1/8 inch rulers on and off.

MacPaint (151-6): Provides quick access to the MacPaint program. All MAGIC captured images are saved as MacPaint-compatible files that can be edited and included in other Macintosh application programs.

Pattern Sav/Get (151-7): "Save" saves the current pattern settings (pattern bar and pattern matrix) to disk. "Get" retrieves a previously saved set of patterns.

Show Pict (151-8): Removes the control screen to show the fully scanned image.

Fast Focus (151-9): Initiates a fast scan of the video target within the control screen.

Full Focus (151-10): Initiates a full screen focus on the entire screen.

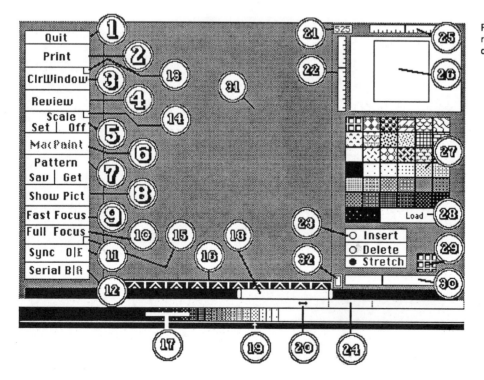

FIGURE 151. The MAGIC screen provides a rich environment for the graphic manipulation of scanned images.

Sync E/O (151-11): Reverses the odd and even line synchronization of the video signal, enabling the use of even inexpensive video cameras.

Serial A/B (151-12): Selects Macintosh serial port A or B (printer or modem).

Other items are: (151-15) Full Focus Box, which takes a full screen black and white picture; (151-19) Last Pattern Bar Click, which shows where the last Pattern Bar click was; (151-21) 525/625 Lines, which selects between U.S. and European line video signal standards; (151-24) Overlap Indicator, which shows the amount of pattern overlap (blend); (151-26) Focus Pan Control, which is used to move the Fast Focus window around in the full screen capture area; (151-27) Pattern Matrix, which includes the available patterns for substituting on the pattern bar; (151-28) Load, which is used to load pattern matrix from a MacPaint file; (151-29) Selected Pattern Box, which shows the currently selected pattern; and (151-31) Focus Window, which is the picture display area.

A black-and-white picture (FIG. 152) is created by clicking and holding the mouse button on the CutBar (151-18). An image immediately begins to appear on the screen. Sliding the CutBar left (whiter) or right (blacker) changes the picture's contrast, and therefore its acceptability. The CutBar setting can be adjusted to produce a normal black-and-white picture, an inverted black-and-white picture (FIG. 153), or an outline picture. By clicking in the Fast Focus box, the picture is continuously captured until the mouse button is clicked.

After the image has been captured successfully, it can be repositioned on the screen using the Screen Positioning Controls. The Vertical (151-22) and Horizontal (151-25) Pan slide controls move the exposed picture within the full screen capture area until the required image area is displayed. Pictures are saved by hitting the "S" key, which results in the display of a standard Macintosh Savefile dialog box.

A patterned picture (FIG. 154) is taken by repeating the initial process for capturing a black-and-white picture. The program is provided with a number of stock pattern bars, supporting 5-level, 20-level, and 38- level patterns. Pattern bars assign specific patterns to different ranges of light intensities. A pattern bar is loaded by selecting "Get" under the word "Pattern" (151-7). The Pattern bar (151-17) is editable.

FIGURE 152. The MAGIC black and white picture is a high contrast graphic rendition of a scanned image. What is white in the original appears white, what is black in the original appears black, with no shades of gray in between.

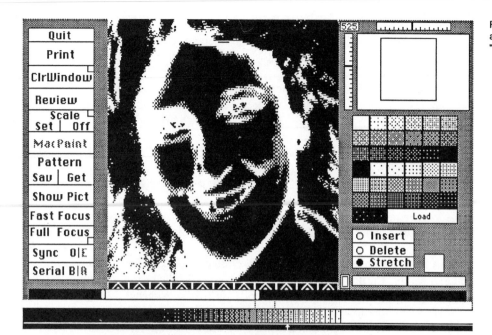

FIGURE 153. A contrast reversal may be achieved by using the cut bar or pressing the "I" key to invert the pixel values.

FIGURE 154. A patterned picture is composed of a series of patterns (as shown in the pattern bar) associated with various levels of light as they are interpreted by the video interface.

Brightness is controlled by sliding patterns back and forth, and contrast is controlled by stretching and compressing them (151-23). Clicking on the Slide bar (151-20) causes the picture to fill with patterns. Adjusting the pattern bar results in immediate changes in the patterns displayed on the screen. The Blend bar (151-30) is used to control the overlap of adjacent patterns. Moving it to the right makes the patterns blend together with only gradual differences between tonal areas. Moving to the left makes the differences more pronounced.

An Edges Only picture (FIG. 155) is, perhaps, the easiest variety to produce since it requires little more than clicking in the Edges Only box (151-32). The result is an outlined picture, in which areas normally filled with patterns are displayed as white.

FIGURE 155. The Edges Only picture ignores the active pattern set, substituting white and surrounding each mock pattern area with a black outline.

The fineness of the outline is controlled by moving the Blend bar, which should be set at zero to start.

A series of Focus Scan Buttons (151-16) are turned on or off to control which vertical areas of the Focus window will be scanned. These buttons are useful for increasing the refresh rate of the scanning process, or for comparing two picture-taking methods side-by-side.

The MAGIC software disk includes a program that allows users of the Hewlett-Packard Laserjet to print MAGIC and other MacPaint files at resolutions of up to 300 dots per inch. After the HP Laser program has been loaded, the user is prompted for the name of the MacPaint file. The user then hits a "1" to print the file at 75 dots per inch (dpi), a "2" for 100 dpi, a "3" for 150 dpi, or a "4" for 300 dpi.

MICROTEK:
High Resolution Scanning

A concern regarding the WYSIWYG nature of any computer publishing system is how accurately the system's screen can display a representation of the final printed output. The closer the match between the screen resolution of the front end, and the printer resolution at the back end, the higher the degree of WYSIWYGishness (whizzie-wig-ish-ness). In general in the realm of desktop and electronic publishing, the more accurate the depiction on the screen, the more efficient and productive the system.

In its initial release, the Macintosh and the ImageWriter represented the near-perfect match of screen and printer resolution. What was displayed on the screen was what was printed on the ImageWriter dot matrix printer. The introduction of the Laser-Writer, with more than four times the resolution of the ImageWriter, drastically changed the screen-to-printer relationship and actually made the Macintosh less WYSIWYGish.

Present economics preclude the possibility of producing a display screen that matches the relatively high resolution of a device such as the LaserWriter. However, the resolution of the display screen should not impede the input and manipulation of

[46] Microtek Laboratories Inc.
16901 South Western Ave.
Gardena, CA 90247
(213) 321-2121

graphic images at the full resolution that the output device is capable of printing. In the case of MacVision, MAGIC, and other video digitizers, the screen resolution of the Macintosh determines the final printed resolution. This situation is fine for the Image-Writer, but is deficient for the LaserWriter. In order for the LaserWriter to work most efficiently, it requires an image-scanning system that can address images at its full 300 dpi resolution.

Fortunately, there are compact desktop scanners that operate at the compatible 300 dpi resolution. A popular model for use with the Macintosh, as well as the Apple *II+*, *II*e, and *II*GS and the IBM PC, is the Microtek MS-300A.[46] This scanner, which uses a stationary CCD (Charge Coupled Device) sensor array, can be used to scan photographs, line art, and graphics, as well as optionally perform OCR (Optical Character Recognition).

How the Scanner Works

The Microtek MS-300A scanner is a tabletop device that uses a feed roller assembly to pass the original document relatively quickly (9.9 seconds for an 8 1/2 x 11 inch page) by its image-sensing field. Two scanning modes are used: one for *line art*, which processes imagery composed entirely of black-and-white, and one for *halftones*, which processes imagery composed of shades of gray. The software, called Versa-Scan, provides the ability to mix the two modes, based on document requirements, as well as to control resolution, contrast, brightness, and gray-scale settings.

During imaging, a bitmap of the original image is produced on the basis of readings taken at the scan window. As each minute section of the document is scanned, logic within the scanner is used to determine how the image is to be interpreted. In the case of black-and-white copy, a black area will result in a dot and a white area will result in none. In the case of a photograph, a shade of gray is interpreted as a pattern of dots, simulating the gray-scale effect used in offset lithographic reproduction photography.

Making the Macintosh Connection

Connecting the scanner to the Macintosh is a simple matter. With the power off on both devices, a cable, supplied with the system, is attached to the serial port on the scanner and to the modem port on the Macintosh (FIG. 156). When the scanner is turned on, it goes through a brief self-test of its principal components and assemblies. If all is well, the READY light illuminates after about six seconds.

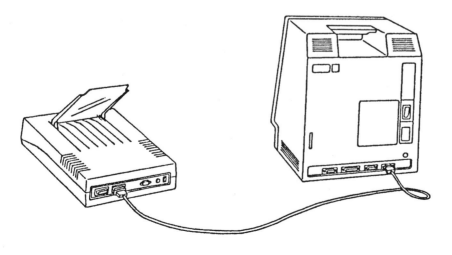

FIG. 156. The Microtek scanner attaches to the Macintosh in a matter of minutes.

When the VersaScan software is loaded, it results in the display of the Welcome screen (FIG. 157). At this point the user has four choices: to scan an image, to change the scanning parameters, to process a stored image, or to return to the Macintosh desktop.

FIG. 157. The VersaScan Welcome screen offers the user immediate access to the major functions of the program.

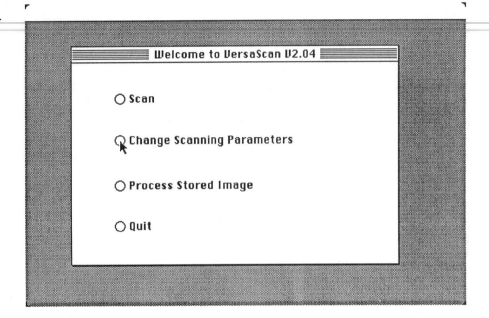

Scanning Line Art

Although the physical scanning operation is automatic, the preparatory steps are manual. Just as a photographer using a manually adjustable camera must set the lens aperture and time, the scanner user must evaluate the characteristics of his document and make the appropriate adjustments on the Scanner Settings screen (FIG. 158). Set-

FIG. 158. The Scanner Settings screen is used primarily to indicate the location of the image(s) that will be scanned. During the scanning process the paper transport quickly moves beyond those portions of the image that are not to be processed.

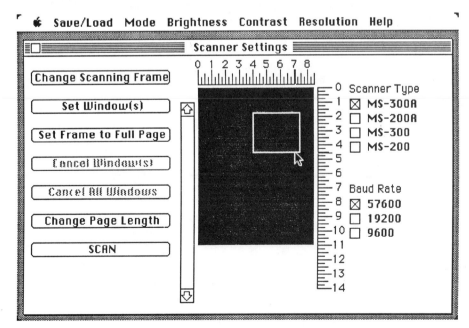

tings for common types of images can be saved and recalled as needed. An often-used setting can be installed so that it automatically loads each time the program is run.

Scanned images are notoriously large, and quickly consume disk space. Although images as large as 8 1/2 x 14 inches can be scanned, such a large image would be quite cumbersome. At an uncompressed data density of 300 x 300 dpi (90,000 bits per square inch), a full page of scanned data would greatly exceed the capacity of an 800K disk. Since there is no need to scan margin area or unwanted imagery, a scanning window is indicated in the incremented area in the center of the Scanner Settings screen. The window restricts the areas (up to four) that will be scanned (either as line art, halftones, or a mix of both kinds).

The Brightness and Contrast menu settings are used to establish a threshold value for the scanning process itself. This threshold is a numeric value based on the amount of light reaching the scanner sensor. When the amount of light is determined to be below the threshold value, a data bit, represented as a black dot, is sent to the Macintosh. When the amount of light is determined to be above the threshold value, a white dot results.

Scanning Photographs

Photographs present a special problem in scanning since conventional halftone techniques represent tones by using dots of various sizes. In a digital scanning device, all of the dots are the same size. The effect of shading is accomplished by grouping dots into square units called *grains*. The Microtek scanner provides grains composed of 2, 3, 4, 5, 6, and 8 dots square (FIG. 158A).

Small grain sizes are useful for capturing picture details. Because they are composed of so few bits, however, they are very limited in the gray scale range they can produce. A 2 x 2 grain, for example, has only 4 dot positions that can be filled, resulting in a 5 step gray scale, from completely white to completely black. An 8 x 8 grain, on the other hand, can produce 33 gray levels, resulting in more shades but less detail (FIG. 158B). Grain size has no effect in Line Art mode.

The Contrast setting provides 14 increments, ranging from ''no adjustment'' (step 7), to +24 percent or −24 percent. Adjusting the contrast upward lightens the overall contrast of the image, whereas a downward adjustment has the opposite effect.

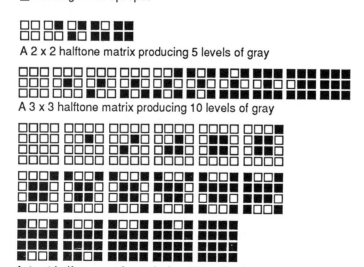

■ A single 300 dpi spot

A 2 x 2 halftone matrix producing 5 levels of gray

A 3 x 3 halftone matrix producing 10 levels of gray

A 4 x 4 halftone matrix producing 17 levels of gray

FIG. 158A. The halftone effect is achieved by generating patterns out of small mosiacs of dot blocks called *grains*.

FIG. 158B. A comparison of the same half-tone area scanned with a 2 × 2 grain and an 8 × 8 grain.

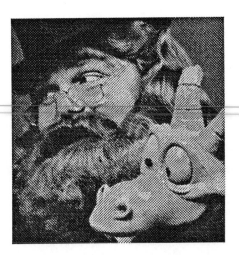

Photograph courtesy of Eastman Kodak Company

The Resolution setting is dependent on the final output size of the scanned image. Since the size of individual dots cannot be changed, a reduction in the size of an image is achieved by eliminating dots at regular intervals during the transmission of the data bits to the Macintosh. The Resolution menu offers the following choices:

Setting	Resolution	Size
0	300 dpi	Full
1	285 dpi	95%
2	270 dpi	90%
3	255 dpi	85%
4	240 dpi	80%
5	225 dpi	75%
6	210 dpi	70%
7	200 dpi	66%
8	180 dpi	60%
9	165 dpi	55%
10	150 dpi	50%
11	135 dpi	45%
12	120 dpi	40%
13	100 dpi	33%
14	90 dpi	30%
15	75 dpi	25%

Editing Scanned Images

Each image is scanned directly into memory, and is visible in one of three viewing forms almost immediately. The first is the RealBits form, which is the program default. In this mode each scanned bit is represented by one screen bit. Because there are about four times as many scanned bits as screen bits, only a portion of the image will be displayed at one time, except if the scan was reasonably small. Scroll bars along the right and bottom of the screen are used to move to other areas of the image.

The second form is FatBits, wherein each scanned bit is represented by sixteen (4 x 4) screen bits. A small portion of the screen is used to show what the FatBits section looks like in RealBits form (FIG. 158C). The FatBits mode greatly magnifies the image and makes image dot editing easier. Editing capabilities include turning individual dots on or off, or painting or erasing small areas.

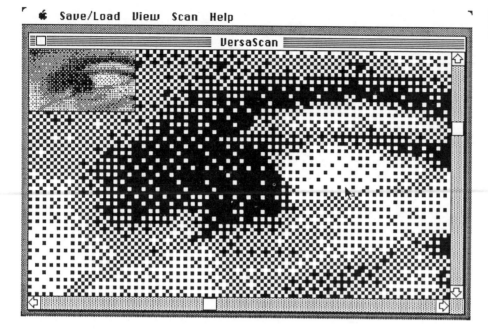

FIG. 158C. The FatBits screen provides an immediate, although limited, editing environment for minor corrections.

The final viewing form is ShowPage, wherein the entire scanned image in memory is displayed in reduced size. In this mode the user can indicate which portion of the image is to appear in the RealBits display (a quick way of moving around a large image), what the contour and size of a MacPaint image format will be (576 pixels by 720 pixels), and what the dimensions of a PostScript Area will be for images which are to be saved as PostScript files.

Scanned material (or portions thereof) can be saved as MacPaint files and edited in the MacPaint program. This capability provides a complete set of editing tools for scanned images. In order to modify a 300-dpi image, the original image is saved as a normal VersaScan file. After the MacPaint editing of a portion of the image has been completed, the normal VersaScan file is loaded back into the VersaScan window. When the edited MacPaint file is reloaded, it is automatically pasted into the position it originally occupied.

Placing Scanned Images on a Page

Scanned images can be saved in any of five different formats, depending on how they will be used. Normal VersaScan files are saved in either *compressed* or *noncompressed* form. Compression techniques are very effective for line art scans. These techniques can reduce the size of files by an average of 90 percent because such images are composed of scan line portions where the image is either all black or all white. In halftone scans, the variation of black and white is much more random, and halftones do not compress very efficiently, if at all. In fact, attempting to compress a halftone image can result in a file larger in size than the original.

The *MacPaint* format is used to import sections of a scanned image into the Mac-Paint program. The edited file can be pasted back into either a compressed or noncompressed file residing within the VersaScan window environment.

Images, or sections of images, that are destined to be printed directly on the Laser-Writer are saved in *PostScript* format. A file called PostScript.dump is provided by Microtek to enable such files to be printed directly. Very large images—those greater than a single Macintosh disk—are saved using the *Gray PostScript* format. This format

saves a full-page image, either line art or halftone, in compressed form. The data compression achieved is about 75 percent. When the image is printed, it exhibits a distinctive texture (hence the name "gray") because it is reconstructed using a limited set of dot patterns.

Noncompressed images can be used directly in Aldus PageMaker. The images are placed just like MacPaint images, and appear on the Macintosh screen in a somewhat mottled form. Halftone images can be cropped, but do not respond well to resizing. Line art images can be cropped and/or resized; however, resizing will result in a change in resolution.

ABATON:
Extending the Utility of the Scanning Process

Although the scanning process solves the problem of capturing images at 300 dpi, it also creates the problem of working with (relatively) high-resolution images. Helping to meet that need is the Abaton[47] Scan 300 digitizer, which is based on the Microtek scanning engine. The Scan 300 provides virtually all of the functionality of the Microtek VersaScan software, as well as a number of software features that aid the user in editing scanned images immediately after they are received by the Macintosh.

The Abaton software, called *C-Scan*, supports the scanning of up to five images (in separate screen windows) to either disk or memory. The images can be cut and pasted from window to window, forming new images, or copied to the system Clipboard and Scrapbook for transfer to other applications. Images also can be printed immediately for proofing, along with a caption line or system generated ID tag.

The Scanning Control screen (FIG. 158D) offers three sliding knobs along the left side. These knobs control the Halftone, Contrast, and Brightness settings. The scan mode is selected, as well as alternate mode zones if both halftone and line art areas are to be scanned.

The actual area to be scanned is indicated on the page facsimile by drawing with the mouse. As the scan area is designated, its size is displayed. The output size is

FIG. 158D. The Abaton Scan 300 Scanning Control screen provides easy access to the entire collection of scanning functions.

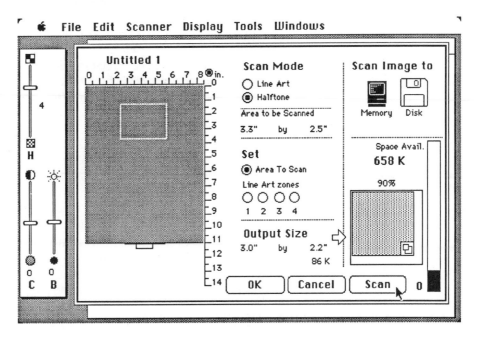

[47] Abaton Technology Corporation
1526 Cloverfield Blvd.
Santa Monica, CA 90404
(818) 905-9399

specified by dragging the corner of the Size window up from its lower right corner. As the window is moved, its size is displayed both as inches (or optionally centimeters) and as a percentage of the finished size.

A bar graph along the right side of the screen shows how much memory the scan will require. The scanning process is initiated by clicking in the Scan box. Within ten seconds the scanning begins. A progress display appears on the Macintosh screen to show what percentage of the scan has been completed (a function also performed by the VersaScan software). The scanned image then appears in a window (FIG. 158E).

FIG. 158E. As soon as the scanning process is complete, the scanned image appears in Screenbits mode. It can be edited immediately using a selection of tools similar to those in MacPaint.

Working with Multiple Images

The ability to have several scanned image windows open simultaneously is very useful, not only for editing, but also for making quick visual comparisons of the same original image scanned with different settings. Tools for drawing (pencil), indicating a work area (selection box), scrolling (hand), and painting or erasing (paintbrush), are all accessible from the Tools menu. When a part of an image is transferred by use of the selection box and the copy (cut)/paste commands from the Edit menu, it can be pasted over an existing image, or it can be handled as a *transparent* image, allowing the existing image to show through.

Additional scan windows are opened by selecting "New" from the File menu. This selection not only opens a window (named "Untitled x" by the system), but brings the user to the Scanning Control screen. If the same scanning settings are to be used, the scan can commence immediately. If changes need to be made, the user makes the necessary modifications and begins the scan. This process can be repeated for up to five original scannings, or previously scanned images. Regular MacPaint files, can also be opened and manipulated in any of the five windows (FIG. 158F). Entire window contents or selected areas (indicated by use of the Selection Box tool) can be saved as separate files.

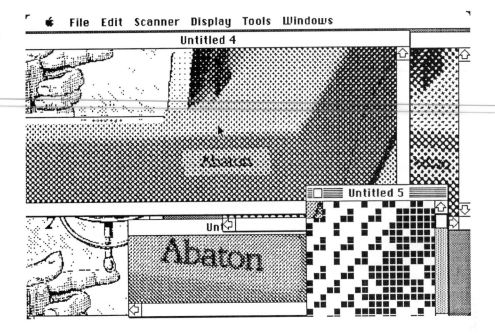

Maintaining Resolution

The objective of scanning images at 300 dpi is to maintain that resolution when the image is transferred to an application and eventually printed. When a portion of a scanned image is copied and pasted within the Scan 300 environment, it maintains its same size and resolution. Like the VersaScan software, an image can be viewed in Reduced to Fit (ShowPage), Screenbits (RealBits), and Fatbits modes. Additionally, it can be displayed in the 300 Dots Per Inch mode, where the scanned image is displayed at the size at which it will be printed on a 300-dpi printer, such as the LaserWriter. Because the screen display does not match this resolution, the image will be unclear; however, all of the editing tools can still be used. Areas cut or copied from images displayed in the Reduced to Fit or 300 Dots Per Inch modes are maintained at 300 dpi on the Macintosh Clipboard. Areas cut or copied from images displayed in the Screen Bits mode are saved on the Clipboard at 72 dpi.

Working with MacPaint, MacDraw, and PageMaker

MacPaint. Scanned images can be saved directly as MacPaint files at the normal Macintosh screen resolution of 72 dpi. Images saved in this way measure 8 inches wide by 10 inches tall as measured from the upper left corner of the scanned image window. The image can remain in MacPaint format and can be used in any way in which a normal MacPaint document would be used. It also can be brought back into the Scan 300 environment and pasted into a 300-dpi image. When it is, the MacPaint image essentially shrinks to about one-quarter (72/300) its size.

Images also can be created in MacPaint and brought into the Scan 300 environment expressly for combining with a scanned image.

MacDraw. Scanned images can be transferred to MacDraw at the full 300-dpi resolution by using the Clipboard and Scrapbook. As long as the images are copied at 300 dpi, using either the Reduced to Fit or 300 Dots Per Inch modes, they will print at that resolution. The display of the images on the screen, however, will be somewhat mottled looking.

PageMaker. There are three ways in which Scan 300 images can be incorporated into PageMaker documents.

1. Images saved as MacPaint documents can be used like any other MacPaint document. The image at 100 percent will appear at the screen resolution of 72 dpi. In order to achieve 300 dpi, the image will need to be proportionately reduced to 24 percent, and then printed at 96 percent. This method is not only awkward, but limits the size of the reduced image to 2 inches wide by 2 1/2 inches high.
2. Images saved to the Clipboard or Scrapbook by the method described for MacDraw, will also work with PageMaker.
3. PageMaker version 1.2 and beyond can use noncompressed format images directly. Because 300-dpi noncompressed images are so large, however, a PageMaker publication containing many such images might need to be broken into smaller publications. The LaserWriter also requires additional time—five minutes or more—to print pages with several such images.

Optical Character Recognition

In late 1986 Abaton introduced two new scanners: The Scan 300/SF, a lower-cost roller-fed optical scanner, and the Scan 300/FB, a flat-bed scanner. The flat-bed design makes the device useful for scanning rigid, fragile, or oversized documents or artwork. Coincident with the release of these machines was an optional system that extends the scanning capability to include intelligent recognition of text characters. The Abaton ACR (Abaton Character Reader) consists of software for the Macintosh along with a 5 1/4" Abaton TurboDrive (FIG. 158G).

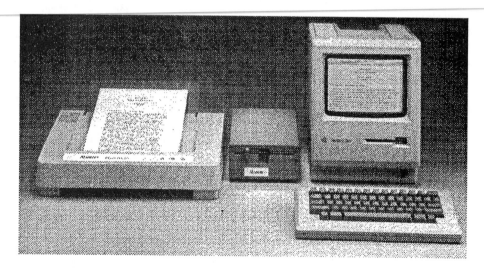

FIG. 158G. The Abaton Character Reader System. Scanned from a color photograph.

The reader is simple to use. Sheets of text from almost any normally spaced typewriter or printer are inserted into the scanner, the characters are read by the TurboDrive, and are sent to the Macintosh screen in a format compatible with most word processing programs. The system can recognize and preserve boldface and underlined words, further reducing the amount of text that needs retyping or reformatting.

The ACR uses a "topological analysis" method making it possible to read mixed sizes and typefaces simultaneously. Sizes as small as six point can be read accurately.

Some of the common fonts that the system can read are:

Courier	Brougham
Pica	Titan
Elite	Esteem Pica
Prestige Pica	Esteem Elite
Prestige Elite	Copy Elite
Letter Gothic	Pearl Elite
OCR-B	Universal Elite
Bookface Academic	Universal Pica
Prestige Renown/Style	and Vintage

The Benefit for Desktop Publishers

The first practical publishing application for OCR was in the newspaper field. Prior to the widespread use of personal computers and editing terminals, reporters keyboarded their stories on typewriters. The typewritten copy then had to be rekeyboarded in order to be set in type, an undesirable duplication of effort. OCR machines, although expensive at the time, made it possible to machine-read typewritten pages. It also made it possible to automate the editorial process without forcing significant changes in the way in which reporters worked. Eventually the introduction of sophisticated electronic newspaper editorial systems, with the advantages of on-screen editing and networking, negated the advantages of OCR scanning.

For the desktop publisher, OCR capability is yet another means of processing text. It makes it possible to take text that has been printed on another computer system, locally or remotely, and quickly, easily, and inexpensively enter it into the Macintosh. This capability can provide compatibility between unlike systems, using a storage medium (typed pages) that is inexpensive, easily duplicated, and most importantly, human-readable.

✍ Production Notes

This chapter was produced by the author entirely on the Apple Macintosh, and output on the Apple LaserWriter Plus. The PostScript examples, which were manually pasted in position, are the sole exception.

The text was prepared using Microsoft Word. Spelling was checked using Target Software's MacLightening. Pages were assembled using PageMaker 1.2 following a layout designed by Jaclyn Saunders of TAB Books. Illustrations were prepared using MacPaint, MacDraw, or FullPaint. Digitized images were produced using the MacVision system or the Microtek scanner with the Abaton C-Scan software.

Pages were imaged on Hammermill's Laser Plus paper.

—*MLK*

THE IBM DESKTOP PUBLISHING ALTERNATIVES

One of the most significant characteristics of desktop publishing software is that it usually cannot stand alone in providing powerful publishing capabilities to its users. In general, desktop publishing programs are *integrative*, combining text, graphics, and images created using a wide variety of programs. Popular personal computers, for which there are a large number of software products available, are, therefore, prime targets for the development of desktop publishing software.

Software Support for the IBM PC

Since its introduction in 1981, the IBM PC has developed rapidly in terms of models, capabilities, third-party add-ons, and most importantly, software. Presently, software is available for the IBM PC to accomplish virtually any business-related computing function.

Personal computers in general, and the IBM PC in particular, have a chameleon-like quality, taking on a new appearance and new functionality on the basis of perceived need, creative programming, and skillful hardware design. The evolution of dedicated word processors into equally powerful personal computer implementations is a good example. Over time, the flexibility of a personal computer, coupled with software rivaling that of a dedicated word processing system, has virtually eliminated the market for single-purpose word processors.

Desktop publishing systems, unlike word processors, originated on personal computers. The fact is significant not only because personal computer hardware had reached the level of sophistication to support such a complex task, but also because the programmers of desktop publishing applications were very much aware of all of the supportive software available for accomplishing the publishing task on a personal computer.

Since desktop publishing programs are integrative in nature, the elements that they integrate are almost as significant as the methods and procedures used by the integrating program itself. In the realm of the IBM PC, there are many powerful word tools for:

- Creating text
- Organizing thoughts in outline form
- Checking text for spelling and grammar errors
- Communicating text to and from a remote location
- Optically reading text

There are powerful graphics tools for:

- Creating artwork
- Digitizing line art
- Tracing artwork
- Scanning photographs
- Generating graphs and charts

There are powerful database tools for:

- Organizing information
- Generating lists, directories, and reports
- Retrieving relevant data

There are powerful utility programs for:

- Modifying the attributes of text files
- Searching and retrieving information from text files
- Compressing and expanding file sizes
- Creating keyboarding shortcuts (macros, glossaries, etc.)

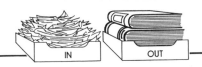

In short, supportive desktop publishing software for the IBM PC environment is readily available.

The Hardware Side

When the Apple Macintosh was introduced, its potential as a page-composition device was obvious, and its evolution into a desktop publishing system was inevitable. The IBM PC, on the other hand, was not designed as a graphic environment (which a desktop publishing system must have for WYSIWYG), and in its native state, it lacked the display, memory, mouse, and processing speed necessary for a reasonable implementation. The availability of advanced models, such as the PC/AT and the PC/RT, as well as enhancements for the PC and PC/XT, to a large degree have overcome these deficiencies. As the hardware matured, so did the market. In the summer of 1986, IBM formalized its involvement with electronic publishing by forming a division to market and support personal computer systems and page printers designed specifically for this application.

MICROSOFT WINDOWS:
Desktop Publishing and Environmental Control

A significant characteristic of desktop publishing is the need to funnel the output from a number of different computer-related activities into one application. It's something like cooking fresh alphabet soup: the vegetables come from a farm, the noodles from a bakery, and the beef from a butcher. The various raw materials are processed and combined, and the result is neither one of them nor all of them, but something completely different.

It is a reasonable expectation that at some point in the near future all or most computer printed output will meet the present appearance criteria for desktop published materials. When it does, the capabilities of today's desktop publishing products will be completely integrated into all kinds of software applications. Until this situation becomes a reality, however, the difficulty of moving, editing, manipulating, and combining text, data, graphics, and scanned images remains a significant and continual series of hurdles.

In most computer environments, the ease of file movement is dependent upon the barriers imposed by the disk operating system and the file export/import limitations inherent in the applications software. Fortunately, most desktop publishing programs have implemented user interfaces that are much friendlier than the unadorned, native disk operating system under which they run. Although not all users find DOS commands to be cryptic, confusing, and sometimes just inconvenient and awkward, few users would protest a layer of cushy software to insulate them from DOS.

One of the most popular DOS insulation programs for the IBM PC is Microsoft Windows from Microsoft Corporation.[48] Windows is an extension of DOS that provides the following benefits:

- Easier access to DOS commands
- Plain-English specification of DOS commands
- Simultaneous operation of more than one software application
- User sizable, positionable, and selectable graphic screen windows
- Iconographic representation of closed but active windows
- System-supported desk accessories
- Mouse or keyboard activation
- Drop-down menus, clipboard, control panel, and more

[48]Microsoft Corporation
10700 Northup Way
Box 97200
Bellevue, WA 98009-9717

A View of Windows

Windows fulfills the role of a system administrator, simplifying the flow of text and graphic information from a number of different and varied sources into, in this case, a desktop publishing program. Although many desktop publishing programs not specifically written to run with Windows are compatible, some, such as PageMaker PC, require the Windows environment.

As a system administrator, Windows provides programs under its care with a number of advantages:

- Windows provides a uniform, easy-to-learn, and easy-to-use shell, which enhances the use and functionality of the applications programs it supports.
- Windows handles the interface between an application and various system resources, such as printers and port assignments.
- Windows offers optional Paint and Write programs, which fully conform to the environment specification and are compatible with other applications.
- Windows manages available memory, making it possible to work with more applications than can fit into RAM at one time. It does so by automatically loading particular applications as they are needed, without quitting any of them.
- Windows can provide a view of the entire processing environment at one time, or use the entire screen for a single application.

A Walk through Windows

Windows is easy to use, especially with a mouse. Although the keyboard can be used to perform all functions, a mouse is much more efficient. For purposes of this discussion, only the mouse movements will be described.

Windows opens to reveal the MS-DOS Executive window, which displays a list of files on the logged disk and icons representing all of the attached disk drives. DOS functions, such as changing directories, formatting disks, and renaming files, are all accessible from drop-down menus in this window. Applications are run by highlighting them with the mouse arrow then clicking.

A typical window consists of many parts, all of which are relatively obvious, especially to an Apple Macintosh user (FIG. 159). The major window attributes are:

Resizing. The window can be resized by a number of methods to fill all or part of the screen. As additional windows are opened, they are automatically tiled so that at least a partial view of all open windows remains.

Scrolling. The contents of a window can be scrolled horizontally and vertically by using the scroll bars along the bottom and right sides.

Moving. An entire window can be repositioned by pointing to the middle of the title bar and clicking the mouse. The mouse pointer changes to an icon that can be dragged to a new location.

Zooming. Windows can be zoomed to fill the whole screen and dezoomed to occupy their original size. The "Zoom" command is selected from the System menu, which is a part of each window. Other options included in the System menu are "Size," "Move," "Icon" (to convert the window into an icon along the bottom of the screen), and "Close."

Out One Window and in the Next

Information is moved from window to window through the use of the Clipboard. The Clipboard is a holding area for text or graphics that is cut or copied from an application. The Clipboard is used automatically when Cut or Copy operations are specified, although some programs cannot take advantage of it.

FIG. 159. A typical Windows window consists of compartments to manipulate contents and appearance.

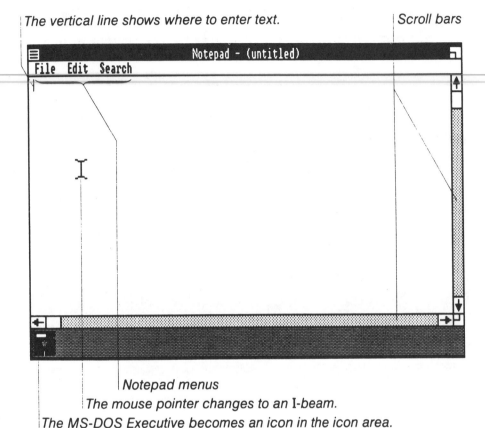

The vertical line shows where to enter text.   *Scroll bars*

Notepad menus
The mouse pointer changes to an I-*beam.*
The MS-DOS Executive becomes an icon in the icon area.

The contents of the Clipboard can be viewed by running CLIPBRD.EXE from the MS-DOS Executive window. The contents of the Clipboard can be inserted into a window by selecting an insertion point with the mouse, and selecting ''Paste'' from the Window System menu.

Windows and Other Housekeeping Chores

One of the main reasons for a programmer to select Windows as the environment for his application is the fact that it manages the flow of information between both software and hardware (FIG. 160). It simplifies the installation, selection, and set-up of printers, for example—a concern for all authors of desktop publishing programs. Additionally, Windows has a built-in spooler to queue files to the printer in the background without seriously interrupting the use of open applications.

Windows is unable to anticipate the needs of all IBM PC applications, so it uses Program Information Files (PIF) to modify itself. PIFs for popular applications are included with the program on the Utility Disk. When Windows encounters an application for which it doesn't have a PIF, it uses a set of defaults. A user can create a PIF (FIG. 161) for any application that does not run properly or work in the most efficient manner.

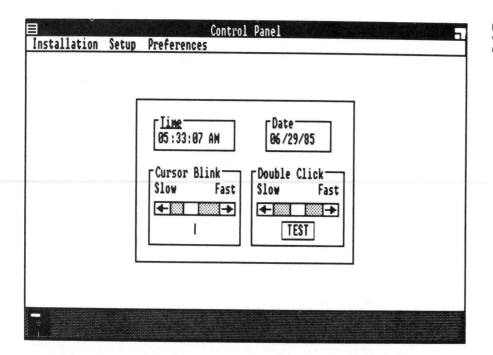

FIG. 160. The Windows Control Panel provides access to many system capabilities and resources.

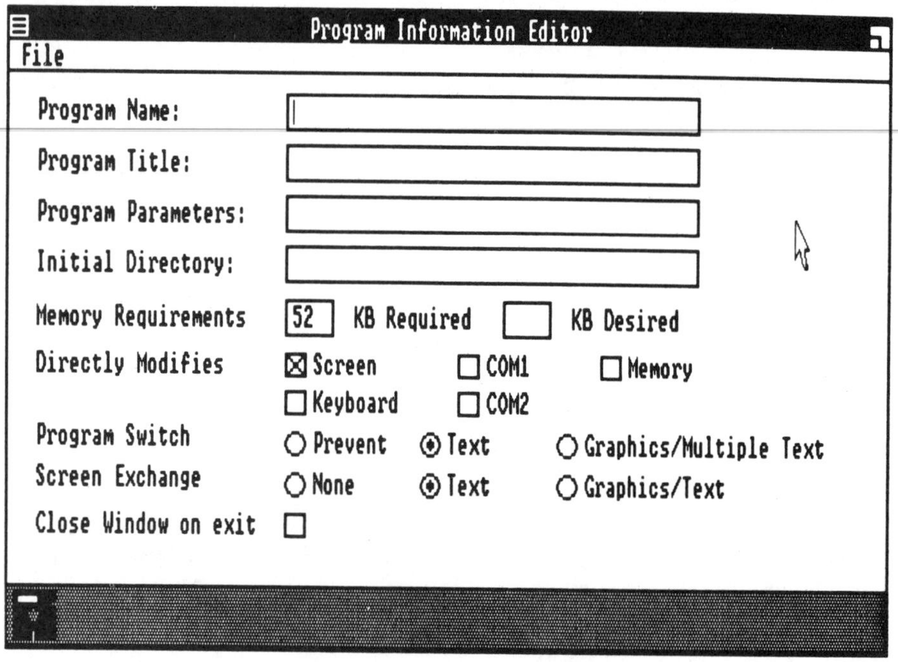

FIG. 161. The Program Information File editor offers the user the means to customize the installation of applications that Windows does not handle well with its default settings.

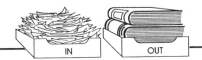
CLICKART PERSONAL PUBLISHER: Implementing a Macintosh-like Desktop Publishing Environment on an IBM PC

The desktop publishing market came into being by the coincidence of a number of developments that took place within and around the planning, design, and manufacture of the Apple Macintosh computer. The Macintosh, itself a responsive medium-resolution graphics environment, presented a particularly good opportunity for use as a graphic arts workstation. This fact, the 300-dpi resolution of the LaserWriter, the flexibility of the PostScript page-description language, the design intricacies of the printer-resident Mergenthaler typefaces, and the ease of use of software such as PageMaker have combined to define what desktop publishing is all about.

The rapid growth of the desktop publishing movement has been fueled by the recognition that such powerful capabilities are needed by individuals in many diverse fields of endeavor. While the desktop publishing path is open to any Macintosh user with the need and the financial resources, IBM PC users have had relatively few low-cost options. The native IBM PC environment does not provide graphics or a mouse, and lacks the processing speed to be responsive to the demands of WYSIWYG publishing, such as rapidly displaying changes in typographic attributes.

One of the first low-cost desktop publishing solutions for IBM PC users is ClickArt Personal Publisher.[49] The objective of Personal Publisher is to present the user with a Macintoshlike environment with a minimum of additional hardware. Owners of a color monitor are required to have an IBM Standard Color Graphics Adapter, while monochrome users must have a Hercules Graphics Card. The use of either the Microsoft or Mouse Systems mouse is optional, although quite advantageous. A minimum of 512K of memory is required. The basic program supports output to a number of dot matrix printers. Output drivers for laser printers, such as the HP LaserJet, the Apple Laser-Writer, and other PostScript-compatible printers, are available at additional cost.

A Look at the Desktop

The use of pull-down menus, icons, dialog boxes, and mouse support all contribute to emulating the Macintosh-type environment (FIG. 162). Text and graphics can be combined on the screen and printed essentially as they appear. Text files can be composed using a standard word processor (in ASCII form) and are limited in size to 5K,

FIG. 162. The ClickArt Personal Publisher File menu provides access to file management resources. The text that appears on the screen was typed directly into the program and has not yet received typographic attributes.

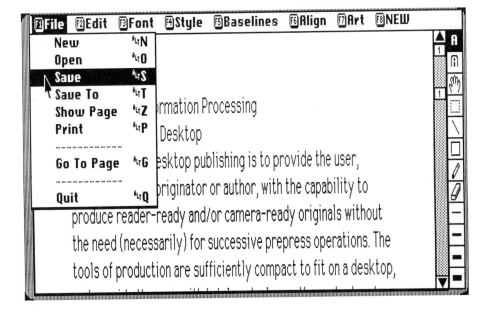

[49]Software Publishing Corp.
1901 Landings Drive
Mountain View, CA 94039
(415) 962-8910

the size of the system Clipboard. Text also can be generated directly in the Personal Publisher program, although the screen display sometimes lags behind the currently typed characters. After text has been input, it can be selected (by positioning an I-beam pointer), and cut, copied, pasted, inserted, or deleted in a manner similar to standard Macintosh procedures.

The Personal Publisher provides the means to compose preexisting graphics, rather than require the user to create them from scratch. The graphic creation tools that the program does provide are limited to drawing lines and boxes. A collection of clip art images, converted from T/Maker's Macintosh ClickArt series, is included as an introductory premium. Graphic images also can be created using graphic programs, such as GEM Draw or PC Paintbrush, and imported using the SnapShot (screen capture) utility. Screens captured in this way must be processed using the Snap2Art utility to convert them into a form that Personal Publisher can use.

Creating a Page

The program is started by loading the mouse driver program or indicating that no mouse will be used by typing **nomouse**, in which case all mouse movements default to keyboard operations. After the program is loaded, an I-beam pointer appears on the work surface. When the I-beam is moved to the top or side menu, it changes to a pointer, which can be used to make menu selections. Menus can be selected from the keyboard by using function keys F1 through F8, as indicated by the small square beside each menu name, or the user can choose to click the mouse button.

The program is started from the DOS prompt by typing **Publish.** The File menu is selected by either pressing function key F1, or pointing to it with the mouse and clicking. The "New" option is selected by either pointing to it with the mouse and clicking, or using the Down Arrow and the Return keys. All mouse and keyboard selection procedures work in a similar way.

A new file is saved automatically under the default name of *New*, although the user, of course, may change that name. The system also appends the filename extension *.PUB* to identify the file as a publication. The current page number appears in the elevator box along the right side of the screen.

Text is brought into the environment by selecting the "Get Text" option from the Edit menu (FIG. 163). The I-beam pointer is positioned in the location in which the text

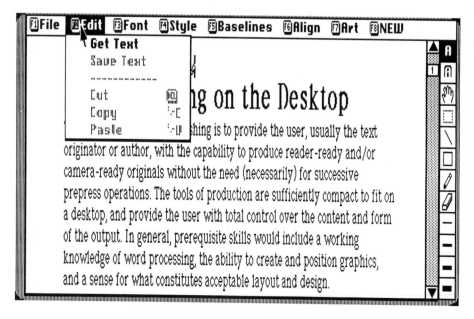

FIG. 163. The Edit menu is used to bring in text blocks, save text blocks, or delete, duplicate, or move text.

is to flow, and then the "Paste" option from the same menu is selected. Text flows within the confines of the current page, and any excess text moves to the text overflow buffer.

Text that is created within the Personal Publisher program can be saved by first highlighting it and then selecting the "Save Text" option from the Edit menu. The program automatically appends the file extension *.TXT* to the file. All hard carriage returns are saved with the file, but none of the typographic formatting information, such as font and style, is.

Font, style, and size descriptors are added to text by first highlighting a particular text string and then selecting the typographic identifiers that are needed (FIGS. 164 and 165). The text then takes on those attributes as quickly as the system can update the screen.

FIG. 164. Lines of text that will undergo font assignment or respecification are highlighted first. The current font selection is indicated with a check mark.

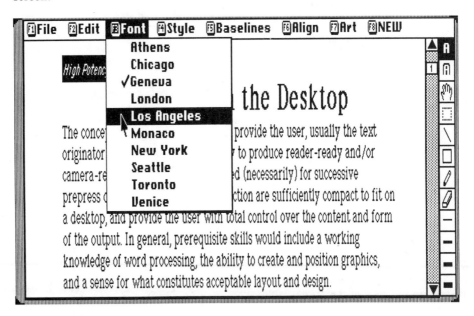

FIG. 165. Style specification is limited to bold, italic, or normal. Bold and italic styles may not be combined.

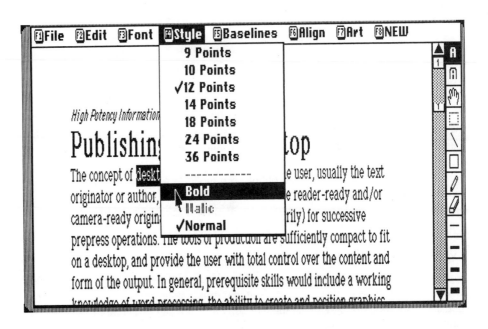

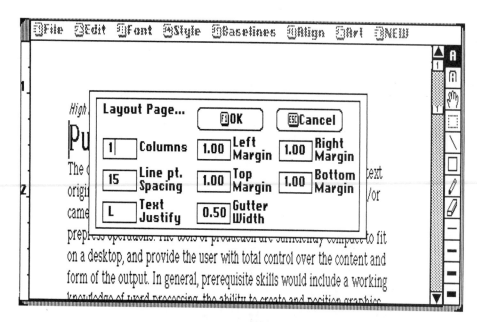

FIG. 166. The Layout Page Query box, accessible from the Baselines menu, provides control over major page attributes, which can be carried through the entire publication.

The overall layout of the page, including the number of columns (there may be up to four), the text justification, and the margins, may be changed at any time by selecting the "Layout" option from the Baselines menu (FIG. 166). The values that are input for the current page are carried to all subsequent pages unless they are changed later in the publication. The line space increment specification which appears in the query box is the minimum value that will be used. The program automatically adjusts for the spacing of larger sizes.

The Baseline menu also is used to adjust the line spacing of single and multiple lines. Selecting one of the "Adjust" options causes the program to display the baseline of each line of text on the screen. The text changes to a gray color, indicating that it cannot be edited. The arrow is positioned on the reference line that is to be processed. In the case of the "Adjust Single" option (FIG. 167), for example, selection causes actions to affect only the selected baseline (indicated by selection boxes at both ends and in the middle). Possible actions include moving the baseline up or down, changing its length, or changing the alignment (centered, left, right) of the text that sits upon it.

An entire column can be adjusted by selecting a single line from within the column and selecting the "Adjust Column" option from the Baselines menu. The "Adjust Above" and "Adjust Below" options affect the baselines on the columns either above or below the selected baseline.

A companion menu to Baselines is Align. In order to use most of the options in the Align menu, the user must first select the baselines that will be processed. The Align menu (FIG. 168), supports the means by which text-line orientation (left, right, center, justify) is changed, text is wrapped around graphics, and rulers (in 1/4-inch increments) are displayed.

"PictureWrap," an Align menu option, is a mode in which text is forced to flow around the square outline of a graphic. When "PictureWrap" is off (no check mark appears beside its name in the menu) text will flow through the graphic rather than around it.

Working with Graphics

T/Maker has an established record as a Macintosh software publisher, and the company has been able to convert all of its font and graphics libraries for use in Personal Publisher. Additionally, any PC graphic or screen image can be captured by using the SnapShot and Snap2Art utility programs.

FIG. 167. The Baselines menu offers flexible control over the interlinear fit of individual lines and entire columns.

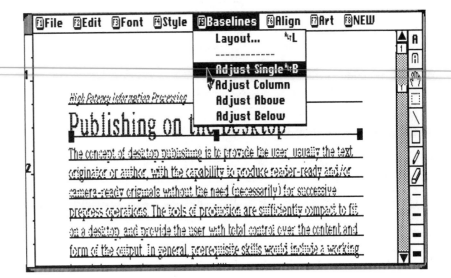

FIG. 168. The Align menu is used to change the orientation of the characters on a single line, a column, or an entire page.

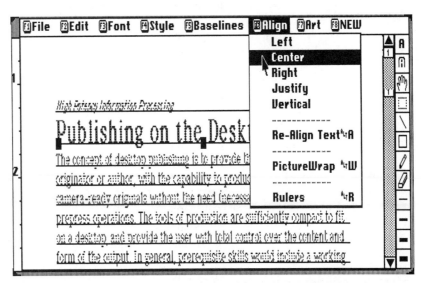

FIG. 169. The Art menu provides access to importing, exporting, and editing art.

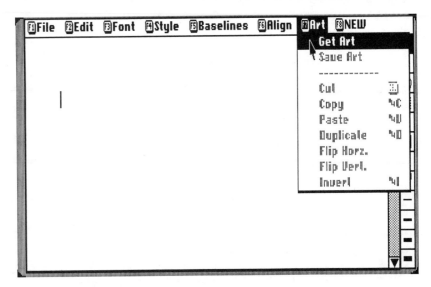

The Art menu (FIG. 169) is the means by which graphics are selected, stored, copied, moved, erased, flipped, or inverted. The "Get Art" option brings up a query box listing only those files that have the *.ART* file name extension. After the file has ben selected, the Hand tool appears on the screen in order for the user to indicate where the upper left-hand corner of the graphic will be placed. Keyboard users press the F10 key to stamp the graphic into position, and make adjustments to the now visible position by moving the hand. Pressing the F10 key a second time locks the graphic in place.

The tools along the right side of the screen are for graphic purposes, with the exception of the top tool, the Text tool. The Text tool allows the user to input, erase, move, copy, modify, and align text on the text plane. The selection of any of the remaining tools will place the user in a state of *graphic transparency*, graying the text on the text plane. The graphic tools have the following functions:

- *Graphics Text:* Presents characters as graphic images rather than as editable characters. Characters created using this option can be erased partially or totally, inverted, flipped, duplicated, and even saved as .ART.
- *Hand Tool:* Used to move a graphic area that has been selected with the Selection-Rectangle.
- *Selection-Rectangle:* Provides the user with the capability of marking graphic areas that may be moved, cut, copied, duplicated, inverted, or PictureWrapped.
- *Straight-Line Tool:* Used to draw a line between two defined points. The width of the line can be changed by selecting one of the alternative line widths at the bottom of the Tool menu.
- *Box-Drawing Tool:* Used to draw boxes and rectangles. The width of the box line can be changed as in the case of the Straight-Line tool.
- *Pencil Tool:* Used for freehand drawing and for touching up minor mistakes in graphics.
- *Eraser Tool:* Used to erase portions of a graphic.

The work window within which text and graphics are composed only shows a portion of the page—one-quarter page for CGA users, one-half for Hercules Monochrome users. A representation of an entire page can be displayed by selecting the "Show Page" option from the File menu (FIG. 170). Although the program specification provides for handling up to 99 pages, the program's speed and responsiveness make it more appropriate for small publications such as newsletters and brochures.

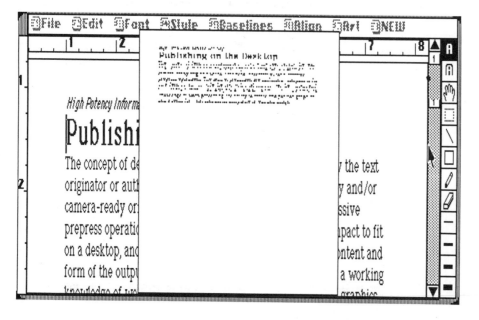

FIG. 170. The "Show Page" option, accessible from the File menu, displays a reduced-size representation of the current page.

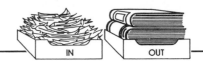
DO-IT:
Simulating a Paste-up Board

One of the most significant societal changes that personal computers have brought about is the general availability of powerful computing tools for the nonprofessional. Reasonably priced computer hardware and software have provided amateur astronomers, stockbrokers, rocket builders, genealogists, and many others with the means of emulating traditionally professional roles, and attaining remarkably professional results. This observation is equally valid in the area of the graphic arts, where do-it-yourself typesetting and publishing is a growing phenomenon.

The integration of various publishing tasks into a microenvironment has been achieved in the DO-IT program.[50] The program name might be derived from *DO-IT yourself,* in that all of the various aspects of assembling publication-quality pages are available to the user.

The DO-IT philosophy is that if you have ever laid out a brochure, or created an ad, or designed a newsletter, then you already know how to DO-IT. The DO-IT screen essentially becomes an automated art board, where all of the various page-processing activities are carried out.

The DO-IT screen is partitioned into three areas: a palette of tools and options, a work area for positioning text and graphic elements, and a message area for viewing system messages and prompts (FIG. 171). Movement on the art board screen is accomplished by use of either the cursor control keys (the ''+'' key activates gross movements and the ''-'' key activates fine movements), or an optional mouse (FIG. 172). The Return key or any of the the mouse buttons become the DO-IT switches, causing the selected item to be processed.

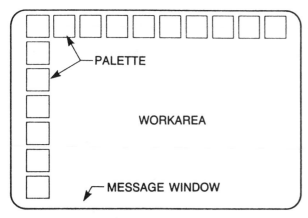

FIG. 171. The DO-IT screen area is divided into three parts: the Palette, for tools, organizers, and supplies; the Work Area, for the actual layout of text; and the Message Window, for system prompts and messages.

[50]Studio Software
17862-C Fitch
Irvine, CA 92714
(714) 471-0131

Requires an IBM PC with hard disk, 512K RAM, math co-processor, Hercules monochrome graphics card, two serial ports, and a TTL monitor.

FIG. 172. There are two devices that can be used to activate program functions: the mouse and the cursor keypad.

The DO-IT icons which adorn the desktop are divided into three categories: organizers, supplies, and tools (FIG. 173). Organizers are items used to reduce the clutter on the screen, supplies are consumable items related to a job, and tools are items that accomplish specific tasks, such as drawing lines or resizing artwork.

FIG. 173. The DO-IT icons fall into three categories: organizers, supplies, and tools.

ORGANIZERS

Since your WORKAREA can only hold so many items at a time, you have a variety of ORGANIZERS which allow you to store tools and supplies in an effective manner. DO-IT provides you with:

THE TOOLBOX—stores tools you are not using.

THE FLOPPY—keeps documents you want to save.

THE TRASH CAN—contains items you may wish to throw away.

THE CLIPBOARD—temporarily stores information for later use.

THE BOOK—contains forms so you can customize your system.

SUPPLIES

DO-IT has very special supplies which are key to your saving time and money.

BOARDS—allow you to store and retrieve your work easily.

DOCUMENTS—contain the text to be included in a layout.

TYPE SPECS—contains instructions on how to print the text.

TOOLS

Many TOOLS in the DO-IT system are already familiar to you. Yet with DO-IT's tools, you can do things that were impossible with the old-fashioned way of doing layouts. For example, you'll never have to erase lines again. With DO-IT, you can move them around, stretch them, or pick them up and throw them away! DO-IT's tools include:

BLUE PENCIL – used to draw non-reproducible lines.

RULERS – three are provided depending on the kind of measurement you need (English, Metric and Printer's).

T-SQUARE – used for precise alignment.

MAGNIFYING GLASS – allows for a closer look at your work.

STAT CAMERA – used to make duplicate copies.

SPRAY FIX – allows you to protect against alteration.

LUCEY – allows for proportionate resizing.

RULING PEN – used to create rules and borders.

STRETCH – used to expand or shrink items you've drawn.

SCANNER – used with the Magnifying Glass to scan your work.

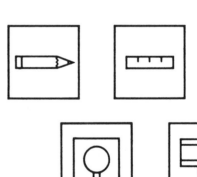

Central to the DO-IT methodology is the concept of *elements*. Elements are the building blocks, created with the Blue Pencil tool, into which text is positioned. The elements can be moved, stretched, shrunk, duplicated, or deleted. The elements for a series of like pages, or volumes of a publication, can be saved for future use.

When the system is started, all of DO-IT's resources are stored in organizers along the left side of the screen (FIG. 174). In order to open or activate an icon, the cursor is placed within its boundaries and the DO-IT key or mouse button is activated. The icon then appears in reverse video. The cursor then can be moved to a new location to indicate the next processing step. In the case of the Toolbox, moving the cursor to the work area and activating DO-IT causes the display of the Toolbox contents. The user selects the assortment of tools necessary for the job at hand by moving individual tools into empty frames along the top of the screen. A tool is moved by selecting it, moving its upper left-hand corner to an empty frame, and activating DO-IT. After tool selection is complete, the Toolbox is returned to its frame by selecting the work area, dragging its corner to the empty Toolbox frame, and activating DO-IT.

FIG. 174. The Toolbox is opened by selecting the Toolbox icon (highlighted), moving the cursor into the work area, and activating DO-IT.

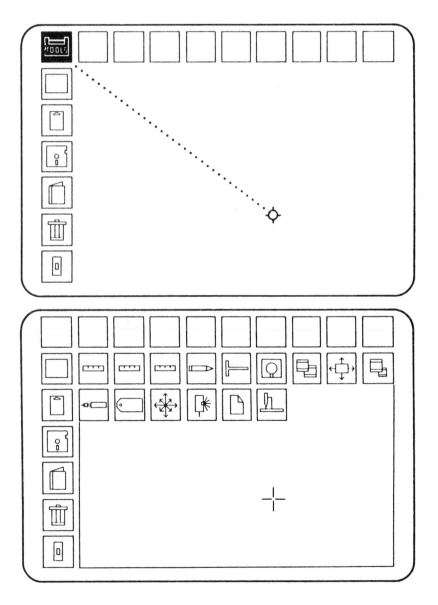

All actions within DO-IT conform to the following basic mode of operation. Select an item by placing the cursor on it, activate DO-IT, move the cursor to a target area, and activate DO-IT again. In the normal course of producing a job, the next task would be to work on a drawing board. In DO-IT, this step is accomplished by selecting the Board icon, moving the cursor to the work area, and activating DO-IT. Rulers along the bottom and right-hand sides of the board can be positioned by selecting the ruler (English, metric, or printer's), positioning the cursor at the intended horizontal and vertical zero point, then activating DO-IT. As each icon is highlighted, a message appears at the bottom of the screen, confirming its selection.

The elements are created by using the Blue Pencil. Similarly shaped or sized elements are duplicated using the Stat Camera. Unwanted elements are dragged to the Trash Can and disposed.

Accurate positioning of elements is done by selecting both the Blue Pencil and the T-Square (FIG. 175). The T-Square guides extend onto the Ruler scale, making the precise sizing of elements possible despite the relatively small size of the screen.

The Tag tool is used to attach an identifying name to both elements and boards. Tags can be inserted, accepted, replaced, or rejected within the Message Window.

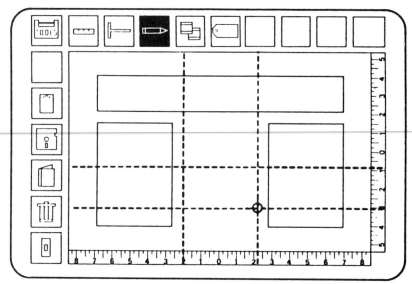

FIG. 175. Elements can be drawn accurately by using the Blue Pencil in combination with the T-Square and the Ruler.

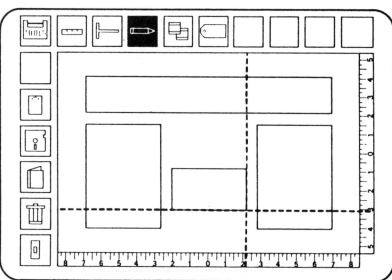

Boards that will be used for repetitive work can be saved on disk by positioning the cursor on an empty area of the board, activating DO-IT, moving the upper left corner of the board to the Floppy icon frame, and again activating DO-IT. When a work session is completed, the environment is shut down by selecting the Switchoff icon and selecting an exit mode (Save & Exit, Save & Return, Exit-No Save, or Take Out Trash).

Text that is to be placed on a DO-IT page is prepared using a standard word processing program. In order for DO-IT to be able to process such files, it automatically creates a copy and then translates the duplicate file into a form it can use. It is sensitive to differences between typewritten and typeset copy, such as the need for only one space between sentences in typesetting. As the translation takes place, each converted line is displayed in the Message Window. When the file has been completely read, the text can be displayed in the work area and edited, if necessary (FIG. 176).

Each portion of text has been labeled with a callout indicating its typographic treatment (FIG. 177). These callouts are typed when the copy is created in the word processing program. The callouts can be seen preceding each copy block (FIG. 176) and can be

FIG. 176. Text that has been prepared in a word processing program and translated into the DO-IT format can be edited prior to the layout step.

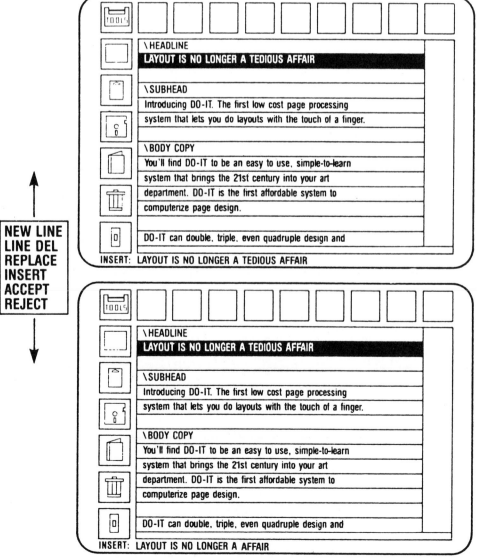

NEW LINE
LINE DEL
REPLACE
INSERT
ACCEPT
REJECT

edited as needed. The Type Specs, which also can be edited, are kept in the Book icon and can be opened on top of organizers and supplies using a DO-IT capability called *layering*.

Type Specs are applied to various elements by selecting the Type Spec icon, moving the cursor to within the boundary of an element, then activating DO-IT. The element then takes on the typographic characteristics of the Type Spec sheet.

Text is laid out in position on the board by selecting the Text icon, moving the cursor to the first element, then activating DO-IT. Successive text blocks are filled in the same way. Because of the size of the screen, only headline text appears in readable form. Body copy appears in greeked-in form, showing the space it will occupy, but not the actual characters of which it is composed. Small areas of the screen, however, can be zoomed-in by using the Magnifying Glass tool.

Printing a job is accomplished by opening the Toolbox and moving the icon of the output device to an empty frame. With the icon highlighted, the cursor is moved to an unused portion of the board and DO-IT is activated. User prompts appropriate

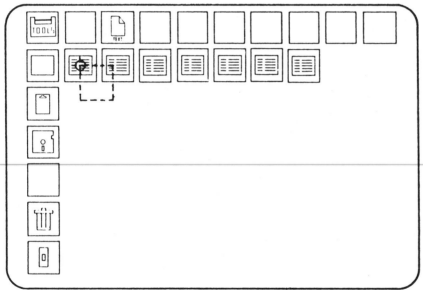

FIG. 177. The Type Spec sheet indicates the typographic attributes of each of the callouts. The sheets can be edited to conform both to specific job requirements, as well as to any limitations (number of typefaces, range of sizes, etc.) inherent in the output device.

TYPE SPEC CALLOUT	PG 1 - BASIC ADJUSTMENTS TYPE FACE	POINT SIZE	LEADING LINE	LEADING PARA	LINE SETTING
HEADLINE	SERIES 90 BOLD	72.0	.0	.0	CENTER
SUBHEAD	SERIES 90 BOLD	54.0	.0	6.0	CENTER
SUB EMPHASIS	SERIES 50 ITALIC	16.0	2.0	.0	CENTER
BODY COPY	SERIES 50 BOOK	14.0	1.0	5.0	JUSTIFY
SUBHEAD 2	SERIES 90 BOLD	54.0	.0	6.0	CENTER
BODY EMPHASIS TWO	SERIES 90 ITALIC	12.0	.0	.0	JUSTIFY
FOOTNOTE	SERIES 90 BOOK	5.0	.0	.0	JUSTIFY
CAPTION	SERIES 90 BOLD	5.0	.0	.0	CENTER

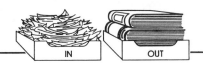
for the particular output device are displayed in the Message window. DO-IT supports the use of dot matrix and laser printers, as well as plotters and phototypesetters.

FRONT PAGE:
Page Assembly: *Doing-It* Better

Software products sometimes take on a life of their own. They undergo refinement, and sometimes evolve through entire generations of change. Such is the story of Studio Software's DO-IT, which was reintroduced as FrontPage[51] in late 1986.

FrontPage addresses many of the performance concerns about DO-IT, while retaining the same basic user interface (FIG. 178). The major changes are these:

- Text can be mixed with graphics. Among the graphics packages supported are:
    Lotus 1-2-3/Symphony
    Freelance
    Graphwriter
    ChartMaster
    PC-Paint
    Sound Presentations
    AutoCAD
    VersaCad
    P-CAD
    Any graphics program generating HPGL or Metafile formats.
- Support of scanners (as an additional cost-option).
- Support of a wider range of graphic cards and monitors.
- Support of a wider range of output devices (some at additional cost), including laser printers and typesetters.
- 60 variations per typespec (12 entries per typespec plus 5 typefaces per entry) as compared to 8 for DO-IT.
- The addition of four new tools:
    Rubylith; for creating tint blocks or windows for artwork.
    White Out; for covering areas of the page that are not to print.
    Typewriter; for editing text directly on the screen.
    Freehand Pen; for drawing point-to-point graphics.

FIG. 178. The screen appearance of the FrontPage desktop publishing program is very similar to its predecessor, DO-IT (Courtesy of Studio Software Corporation).

[51]Studio Software Corporation
17862-C Fitch,
Irvine, CA 92714
(714) 474-0131
(800) 821-7816 (nationally)
(800) 221-3806 (in California)

SCLASERPLUS:
A Code-Based Approach to Automated Page Processing

A common characteristic of desktop publishing software is that the text and graphic components of a target publication usually are composed separately, using a word processing and a graphics program. The reason is quite understandable: dedicated text- and image-creation programs are better able to handle the specific requirements of the development stage of authorship and art production. The desktop publishing software provides the capability to combine text and graphics into finished page format.

The creative process, however, is not a simple linear progression. Thoughts, ideas, and circumstances all can change and significantly influence the content and form of the publication up to the moment when it is output. For this reason, most desktop publishing programs provide at least a limited means of text editing.

In time, desktop publishing programs will incorporate more powerful text-editing capabilities, and conversely, word processing programs will incorporate some degree of graphic integration capability. In each case, the goal is the same: to provide the user with better communication tools.

The scLASERplus program[52] is one of the first attempts to provide a desktop publishing environment built around a word processing program (scWRITERplus). Unlike the WYSIWYG approach that typifies other desktop publishing programs, scLASERplus uses a command-driven system composed of a proprietary formatting language using plain English.

The Software Components

The scLASERplus package is composed of four parts: one to compose the text, one to create special symbols, one to capture graphic screen images, and one to translate coded text into a form that can be interpreted by the HP LaserJet (or LaserJet Plus) printer. The first three components are independent, and are combined by the use of the fourth at the time of printing.

While the scWRITERplus program is a fully functional word processor (also available as a separate product), any word processor or text editor that can produce a standard DOS ASCII text file can be used for input. The benefits of using the scWRITERplus program are that it provides a relatively uncomplicated editing window (FIG. 179) and

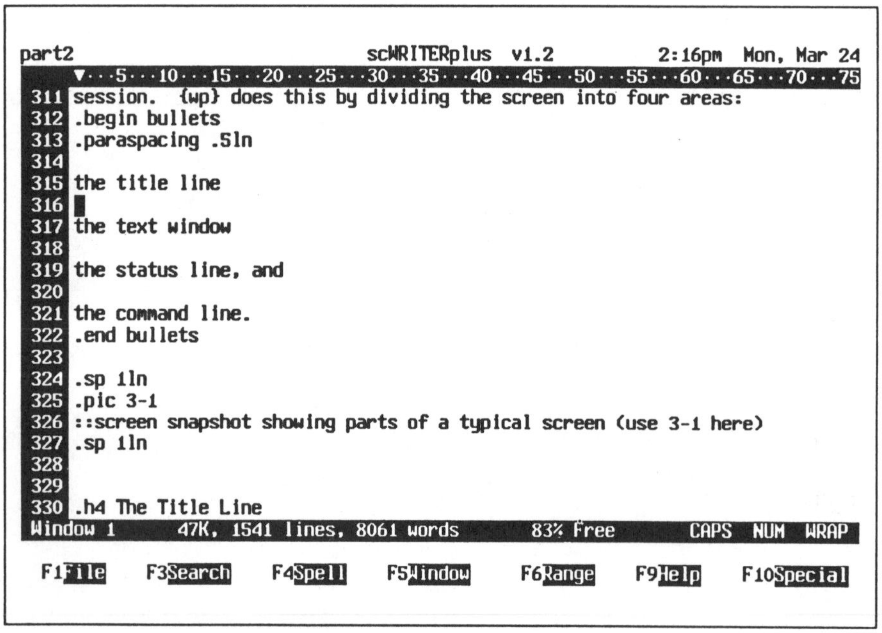

```
part2                    scWRITERplus  v1.2        2:16pm  Mon, Mar 24
    ▼··5···10···15···20···25···30···35···40···45···50···55···60···65···70···75
311 session.  {wp} does this by dividing the screen into four areas:
312 .begin bullets
313 .paraspacing .5ln
314
315 the title line
316 █
317 the text window
318
319 the status line, and
320
321 the command line.
322 .end bullets
323
324 .sp 1ln
325 .pic 3-1
326 ::screen snapshot showing parts of a typical screen (use 3-1 here)
327 .sp 1ln
328
329
330 .h4 The Title Line
Window 1      47K, 1541 lines, 8061 words       83% Free    CAPS  NUM  WRAP

  F1 File   F3 Search   F4 Spell   F5 Window   F6 Range   F9 Help   F10 Special
```

FIG. 179. The scWRITERplus screen is the place where formatted text and graphic definitions are integrated for single-pass printing.

[52]Graham Software Corporation
212 King Street West
Toronto, Ontario, Canada M5H 1K5
(416) 591-9131
or Four King Place
Kingwood, TX 77339
(713) 359-1024

IBM PC system requirements include 256K or more of RAM, at least two double-sided floppy disk drives, DOS Version 2.0 or later, and a serial or parallel adaptor, depending on the type of interface available on the LaserJet or LaserJet Plus printer.

an integrated 50,000 word spelling checker, and is free of menus, control keys, and command structures. Major functions are listed along the bottom of the screen and are activated by pressing and holding the required function key. The result is the display of a number of appropriate options.

Writing Page Instructions

A text file is formatted for typographic appearance and pagination through the use of three types of instructions: *functions, dot commands,* and *environments.*

A function is an instruction used within a paragraph to change the appearance of a string of text, or to insert the contents of a variable. A variable is a named string of text. The proper form for a function is:

{name of the function__optional parameters}

The proper form for indicating a line of italic text would be written as:

{it This line will print in italics.}

Dot commands usually are used for specifying the layout appearance of a document, such as its line spacing, margins, or section headings. Dot commands must always occupy a line of their own, and take the following form:

.commandname__parameters

The proper form for indicating a 1-inch left margin and a 2-inch right margin would be:

.margin left=1in right=2in

Environments are text blocks composed of one or more paragraphs. An environment would be used to enclose a block of text within a box, or to indent an entire paragraph. The specification of an environment always starts with the word *begin,* and always ends with the word *end.* Environments take the following form:

.begin *environment__parameters*
insert block of text here
.end *environment*

The proper form for indicating a 3/4-inch indent would be:

.begin in 0.75in
This is text that will appear indented 3/4 inch from the left margin when the paragraph is printed. The command is active until the "end" command is invoked.
.end in

Both functions and dot commands can be used within environments. Environments can be embedded one within another.

The scLASERplus program provides output control commensurate with the smallest increment obtainable on the LaserJet printer, i.e. in units of 1/300 inch. The thinnest line obtainable would be written as: .line thick=1. When no unit of measure is specified, as in this example, the unit value defaults to 1/300 inch. Other units that may be used are inches (in), centimeters (cm), millimeters (mm), points (pt), and picas (pc).

Units relative to the size of the type in use also may be used. These units are the *em space* (em); *en space* (en); *three-to-the-em space* (el); *line* (ln), which is equivalent to 1.2 ems (the size of the type plus 20 percent); *space* (sp), which is the width of a space; and *figure* (fg), which is the width of a zero.

Specifying the Page Layout

The page-layout commands define the general layout of the pages. The parameters and their defaults are:

Parameter	Default Value
Page length	11 inches
Page width	8.5 inches
Printing offset	0.1 inches
Left margin	1.25 inches
Right margin	1.25 inches
Top margin	1.75 inches
Bottom margin	1.75 inches
Header margin	1.25 inches
Footer margin	1.25 inches
Width of gutter	0.25 inches
Columns per page	1
Page headers	none
Page footers	none

Only those parameters that are not appropriate for a particular job need to be changed. The following list shows how some of the page layout parameters would be indicated:

Specification	Meaning
.pagesize width=7in length=10in	a 7-×-10-inch page
.pagecol 2	2 columns
.margin gutter=0.75in	3/4-inch column separation
.head/{page}/	page numbers printed at the center of each page head
.set WIDOWFLAG=0	turn on widow elimination
.newpage	force a new page
.newpage even	skip to the next even-numbered page

Controlling Text Layout

The scLASERplus program offers considerable control over the arrangement of text on the page. This control covers such concerns as character spacing, line spacing, paragraph spacing, indentation, filling, justification, and hyphenation. A few of these capabilities are explained here.

Horizontal Spacing. The fit of characters in a line is calculated according to the length of the line, the size of the type, and the width of the characters. The word spacing that is used is relative to the size of the current fonts. This size value may be increased or decreased to print words closer together or farther apart. The command takes the following form: .charspacing n. The n value is specified in units of 1/300th of an inch, and may be a positive (increases word space) or negative (decreases word space) number.

Vertical Spacing. Vertical spacing controls the line spacing of text within paragraphs, the amount of space between paragraphs, and the addition of a variable amount of line spacing at any user-specified location, such as before or after an illustration.

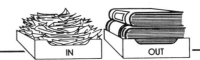

Typical commands would include the following:

Command	Meaning
.linespacing 0.166in	a line space value of 1/6 inch
.paraspacing 1ln	sets the space between paragraphs to 1 line
.sp -1in	space up 1 inch

Text Orientation. The line endings of text prepared in the scWRITERplus program generally do not bear any relationship to the actual LaserJet output, since screen character widths are far different from laser printer character widths. Sometimes, as in the setting of poetry, an author wants the lines on the screen to appear in print as they appear on the screen. The scLASERplus program provides for this need with the *".nofill"* command, which processes lines as if they were individual paragraphs. The normal mode is *Fill*, which is indicated as **.fill**.

Lines of text may be justified in any of four different ways: Left (*.just left*), Right (*.just right*), Center (*.just center*), and Full (*.just full*). A form of the Justification mode may be activated for single lines, paragraph blocks, or environments.

In the Full Justification mode, the program automatically activates its Hyphenation command. The scLASERplus program uses tables to determine how a word that is too long to fit at the end of a line should be broken. Hyphenation can be activated for other justification modes by using the command, .hyphen *n*, where *n* is a number from 0 to 10 indicating how much hyphenation is required. When the value is set at 0, no hyphenation is done, whereas when the value is set at 10, the program hyphenates whenever possible.

Controlling Text Appearance

There are a number of commands that allow access to the typographic capabilities of the LaserJet. These commands control the selection of the typeface, type size, and type design variations (bold, italic, etc.). Selection of a typeface is dependent upon which typefaces are available on the font cartridge or which have been downloaded into the laser printer's RAM. The command specification is .typeface *typeface*, where the typeface name is one of the list of acceptable identities. If the name specified by the user is not available on the laser printer, the Formatter program substitutes whatever font is closest.

The type-size specification is limited to the actual sizes of the fonts mounted on the laser printer relative to the size of the current font. To change to the next smaller available type size, the command .smalltext is used. Conversely, increasing to the next largest size would be accomplished with the .largetext command. The "Change Size" command takes precedence over a change in typeface. In other words, if a larger italic font is requested, but the only larger font is roman, the Formatter will use the larger roman font.

The LaserJet cannot print a bold or italic version of a normal type design unless that variation is available on the font cartridge or in downloaded form. The *".shadowtext"* command, however, is a means of creating a boldface variation mechanically by printing each character twice. The resultant characters are not as sharp as a true bold rendition, but the command can be applied to any typeface. Accessing an available boldface type is done with the *".boldtext"* command, and accessing an available italic type is done with the *".italtext"* command.

Automating Text Components

The Formatter program is very effective in converting lists of information into orderly, easy-to-read text. It can convert a list into a numbered, bulleted, or dual-column form using either the *".begin list"* (numbered list), *".begin bullets,"* or *".begin points"* (dual-column) commands. The following example illustrates the coding and resultant output for a short numbered list.

—Source File—
The following is a list hierarchy created automatically by the
scLASERplus Formatter program.
.begin list
Advantages of the scLASERplus program.
.begin list
        Any ASCII text editor can be used.
        .begin list
                Compatible input can be created on other computers.
                scWRITERplus program is included with the package.
        .end list
        Complex tables can be created automatically.
        Degrees of hyphenation are obtainable.
.end list
Disadvantages of the scLASERplus program
.begin list
        Pages can not be previewed in advance of printing.
        Graphic snapshots can not be pixel edited.
.end list

—Formatted Result—

The following is a list hierarchy created automatically by the
scLASERplus Formatter program.
    1. Advantages of the scLASERplus program.
       a. Any ASCII text editor can be used.
          i. Compatible input can be created on other computers.
         ii. scWRITERplus program is included with the package.
       b. Complex tables can be created automatically.
       c. Degrees of hyphenation are obtainable.
    2. Disadvantages of the scLASERplus program
       a. Pages can not be previewed in advance of printing.
       b. Graphic snapshots can not be pixel edited.

Text can be placed within a regular or a shaded box by use of the *".begin box"* or *".begin box style=shade"* commands. The Formatter automatically draws a box around the indicated block of text.

The "Table" command has a variety of formats for creating tables with many different features. The basic beginning command is .begin table *width1, width2,...*, where the width values indicate the relative widths of the columns. This is an example of a simple table specification:

—Source File—
.begin table 1,1,1
        Living Room   18 feet   24 feet
        Kitchen   12 feet   16 feet
        Master Bedroom   19 feet   16 feet
—Formatted Result—

Living Room	18 feet	24 feet
Kitchen	12 feet	16 feet
Master Bedroom	19 feet	16 feet

A number of attributes can be respecified to improve the appearance of the table. Among them are:

Column Widths: The column-width notation can indicate the relative widths of the columns, as well as the number of columns. To indicate that column 1 is to be twice as wide as columns 2 and 3, the command would be written as: .begin table 2,1,1

Column Justification: Items within columns can be justified independently (left, right, center, or full) with the use of the "just=" parameter. A table with columns justified left, center, and center would be indicated as: .begin table 2,1,1 just=l,c,c

Text Style: The font variation of each column of information can be specified as either regular text (x), boldface (b), or italic (i). A three-column table with the first column bold and the remaining columns in regular text would be indicated as: .begin table 2,1,1 just=l,c,c text=b,x,x

Shaded Columns: Any or all columns can be shaded by use of the "shade=" parameter. If a column is to be shaded, its relative position is indicated by a y for "yes." If the column is to remain unshaded, its relative position is occupied by an n for "no." If only column one were to be shaded, the coding would appear as: .begin table 2,1,1 just=l,c,c text=b,x,x shade=y,n,n. A shaded row is indicated by using the shade environment, i.e., .begin shade and .end shade.

Lines: A table normally consists of all horizontal and vertical lines separating columns and rows. Using the "lines=" parameter, however, particular lines can be specified according to the following options:

all	draws border and all horizontal and vertical lines
border	draws border only
vert	draws vertical lines only
horiz	draws horizontal lines only
border+vert	draws border and vertical lines
border+horiz	draws border plus horizontal lines
none	draws no lines

A table specified by the commands .begin table 2,1,1 just=l,c,c text=b,x,x shade=y,n,n would appear like this:

Living Room	18 feet	24 feet
Kitchen	12 feet	16 feet
Master Bedroom	19 feet	16 feet

Working within the Programming Environment

The scLASERplus program provides the user with many features to customize the Formatter in order to meet individual needs. These features include the specification of variables, expressions, literals, functions, and macros. The use of these features are reserved for advanced users, and an explanation of their implementation is beyond the scope of this book. A number of these features, however, have been preprogrammed into templates, which address specific formatting needs. The scLASERplus package includes templates for creating office memos, standard business letters, mail merge/form letters, and two report formats with automatic generation of table of contents and index.

Templates are called by the Formatter when it sees that the command .include *template* appears at the beginning of the source file. By processing the macro commands in the template, the Formatter is able to interpret properly the set of commands peculiar to the template. The memo1 template, for example, automatically inserts the heading "MEMORANDUM," and arranges the names of the originator and addressees, the date, the subject, and the memo text.

Working with Graphics

The scLASERplus program has three major ways of dealing with graphic integration: icons, snapshots, and business graphics. The icon creation process is used to create special characters, symbols, and logos that are not a part of the normal laser printer character repertoire or the small set of prepared icons supplied with the program. Snapshots are graphic screens of any program image captured on disk for integration within an scLASERplus document. Business graphics are charts and graphs composed within the text-creation environment, sometimes consisting, in part, of icons.

The Use of Icons. A variety of icons supplied with the program produce simple shapes (square, circle, triangle, etc.), business marks (trademark, copyright, etc.), keycaps (right arrow, shift, space, etc.), and miscellaneous forms (star, heart, checkmark, etc.). A defined icon is included within text by enclosing its name within braces. The star icon, for example, would be specified as {star}.

An icon editor (FIG. 180) is supplied with the program for those users who have an IBM-compatible standard graphics card. The icon editor is used to modify existing icons, as well as to create new ones. The dots within the icon editor frame are turned on or off to form the pattern representing the icon shape. A number of tools are available to aid in the drawing and editing process. The completed icon is saved in a library of associated images.

Screen Graphics. A program supplied with the scLASERplus package is the Snapshot Utility. In use, the utility is loaded into memory where it resides without interfering with other programs. When a screen from any other program, such as a paint, spreadsheet, or business graphics program, needs to be captured, the Shift-PrtSc key combination is pressed and an image of the screen is created in the snapshot buffer. A number of snapshots can be held in memory, depending upon the amount of memory available in the computer system and the characteristics of the screens being captured. When the buffer is full, the computer beeps to indicate that it cannot hold another picture. At this point, the application software must be exited, and the user must return to DOS and type **SNAPSHOT.** The snapshot program senses that undeveloped pictures reside in its buffer, and the user is prompted for names for each picture, one by one. The program saves the pictures with a ''.PIC'' file extension.

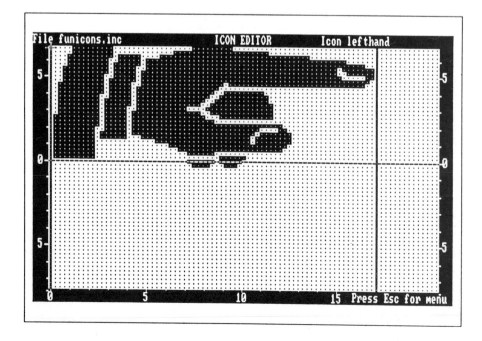

FIG. 180. The Icon editor is used to draw small graphic images, which can be integrated within text and used for pictographic purposes within business charts.

Pictures are included within documents by using the "Picture" command followed by the name of the picture (without the ".PIC" file extension) like this: .picture *name*

Business Graphics. A special set of commands must be requested to produce graphs and charts. For this purpose, the command .include graphics must be input at the beginning of the text file.

There are many forms of graphs and charts that can be created; however, only one simple example of a bar chart will be shown here. A bar chart is created using the command .begin hbarchart max=*max*. *Max* is the largest number that will be plotted. The scLASERplus program needs this number in order to properly scale the bars. Here is an example that results in an uncomplicated bar chart:

```
.—Source File—

center {bo APRIL ADVERTISING REVENUE BY CATEGORY}
.center {it in thousands of dollars}
.sp
.begin hbarchart max=500
    {bo Automotive:}  352
    .plot 352
    {bo Electronics:}  175
    .plot 175
    {bo Dairy:}  500
    .plot 500
.end hbarchart

.—Formatted Result—
```

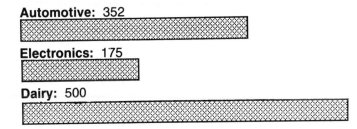

APRIL ADVERTISING REVENUE BY CATEGORY
in thousands of dollars

Automotive: 352

Electronics: 175

Dairy: 500

Other graphic variations include cluster bar charts (using different shadings for each bar in a cluster), pictographs (using icons to represent statistical data), vertical bar charts, and chart enhancements including scales, labels, multiple plots, legends, patterns, etc.

An additional, and rather unique, graphic capability is the generation of bar codes, which are used for scanning product information. The three bar-code symbologies are the Industrial 2 of 5, the Interleaved 2 of 5, and the 3 of 9 code. Each of these can be produced in any of three sizes.

XEROX VENTURA PUBLISHER:
Automating All Phases of Document Production

The desktop publishing process, like the traditional page-composition process, deals with both the content and the form of documents. In a typical typesetting environment, control passes from originators to production personnel, whose skills, technologies, and schedules have significant impact on the final publication. The desktop publishers knows no such restrictions; he is free to control the entire process, from organizing thoughts to distributing finished publications.

The intimate relationship of content and form is the basis of a remarkable desktop publishing program called Ventura Publisher being marketed exclusively by Xerox Corporation.[53] The package was created by four former employees of Digital Research Incorporated (DRI)—John Meyer, Don Heiskell, Lee Lorenzen, and John Grant,—and runs on the IBM PC, XT, and AT, and other compatible MS-DOS computers.

The premise of the program is that individual elements of text, such as headlines, lead paragraphs, and body copy, all can be identified with *tags*, created within the customer's word processor, within the Ventura Publisher environment, or both. Each tag can be defined in any number of different ways by including it within a *style sheet*. By changing the style sheet, a publication can take on a dramatically different appearance.

This separation of typographic descriptors from the structural content of a document is the basis of generic coding. By identifying elements by their function within a document rather than by their printed appearance, coding is generally faster, easier to comprehend, and considerably more flexible in terms of design decisions (either before, during, or after text creation).

The Preliminaries

The program is virtually self-installing, with user input limited to a series of selections related to the location of the hard disk and the choice of mouse, graphics card, and printer.

The program is run by typing **VP** at the DOS prompt. The program takes from 5 seconds to 1 minute to load, depending on the computer in use.

Once upon the Desktop

The main screen (FIG. 181) is Macintoshlike. The menus that run horizontally along the top are activated by moving the mouse arrow to the vicinity of their names. The

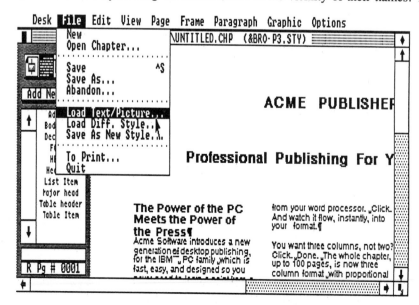

FIG. 181. The Xerox Ventura Publisher desktop represents a user-friendly object-oriented user interface.

[53]Xerox Corporation
P.O.B. 24
Rochester, NY 14692
800-TEAM-XRX

menu then drops down, without the need to press the mouse button (as generally must be done). When the required menu choice is highlighted, the mouse button is pressed. Regardless of the mouse in use or the number of buttons on the mouse, Ventura uses only the left mouse button to activate commands.

Unless a Xerox (or competitive) full-page display is installed, the main work area window shows only a portion of a page, although the View menu offers the options of seeing the page in reduced or 2X sizes (FIG. 182). Window controls are available for horizontal and vertical scrolling, changing the size of the window, changing the location of the window, and growing the window from a reduced size back to full screen.

A major part of the main screen is the *Sidebar,* composed of the Assignment List, Current Selection Box, and Function Selector. The Assignment List displays the choices available in the Function Selector. There are four main Ventura functions: ''Frame Setting'' (to create text and graphic compartments), ''Paragraph Tagging'' (to assign tags to text elements), ''Text Edit'' (to assign typographic attributes and perform word processing functions), and ''Graphic Drawing'' (to draw lines, circles, and rectangles). In the case of the ''Paragraph Tagging'' function, for example, the Assignment List shows the names of the items that can be assigned to selected text passages on the screen. As an item is selected from the Assignment List, its name appears in the Current Selection Box. If a paragraph is selected in the screen area, for example, and the ''firstpar'' item is selected from the Assignment List, the paragraph will take on whatever typographic attributes have been defined for that item. Multiple items on the screen can be processed simultaneously by holding the Shift key while selecting the items.

The Function Selector, which is located in the upper left-hand corner above the Current Selection Box, is used to switch between the four major program activities. In the ''Frame Setting'' mode, a list of text, line art, and image files can be built in the Assignment List by selecting them through the use of the ''Load Text/Picture'' option in the File menu. Selected (highlighted) files can be placed on full-size pages (within defined columns on the area known as the *underlying page*), or within user-drawn regions called *frames* (which sit on top of the underlying page). When the file is placed on an underlying page (which is itself a frame), any excess text is carried automatically to the next consecutive page. When text is placed in a frame, any excess must be assigned manually, and only to a frame on a succeeding column or page. To place text, the page or frame must be selected first. Selection of a page or frame is confirmed by the appearance of small square handles at each corner and center.

FIG. 182. A page can be viewed either at normal or twice size (with only a portion appearing in the work window), or reduced to fit (as shown).

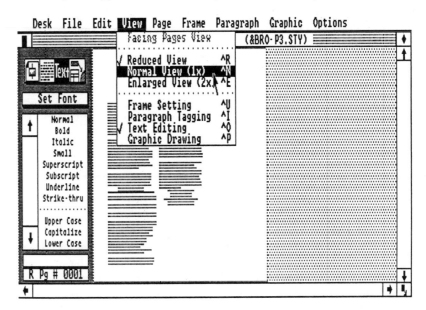

The Frame Game

A frame can serve a number of purposes. It can be used to hold text, graphics (line art), or pictures (scanned images), as well as to define the overall page layout for columns and other repeating elements. Extensive menu choices provide considerable flexibility in defining the frame attributes (FIGS. 183 through 186).

A frame is created by first selecting "Frame Setting" from the Function Selector. The "Add New Frame" button is activated and the cursor changes to a corner mark with the initials *FR*, indicating that it is in the frame creation mode. To form a frame, the mouse pointer is positioned on the page at its upper left starting point. The mouse button is held down and, as the mouse is dragged, a frame is formed. A frame consists of an outline border and small square selection points in each corner and in the middle of each side. After the frame is formed, the mouse cursor reverts to a crosshair, which can be used to move or resize the frame. Clicking and holding the mouse button inside the frame results in the display of a hand, which is used to reposition the entire frame. Clicking and holding the mouse button on top of any of the square points results in increasing or reducing the size or changing the proportion of the frame.

The size and the proportion of the frame also can be changed, according to specific numeric values, by filling in information in the "Sizing and Scaling" option in the Frame menu (FIG. 185). If the content of a frame is a picture, it can be resized to fit the frame or to maintain its original aspect ratio (relationship of height to width). Picture images can be cropped by holding the Control key in combination with the mouse button and moving the picture around underneath the frame opening.

A picture frame that is placed over a text frame will cause the text to automatically reflow around it (if the "Text Flow Around" option from the Frame menu is activated). The reflowed text normally follows the horizontal and vertical boundaries of the frame, although with manual intervention, the text can be made to follow an irregular runaround (FIGS. 187 and 188).

In most cases, frames are invisible compartments that hold printable contents. Frame outlines do not print; however, they can have a border, a background, or both. The background can be a pattern or a color, depending on the output device.

Captions can be added to frames, and the frame/caption pair is maintained as a single entity. A caption is linked to a frame when the frame is moved, copied, cut, or pasted. The program maintains intelligent counters for figures, tables, and chapters. These elements are updated when captioned frames are added, deleted, or moved. For example, when a picture frame is moved to another page, all figure numbers on affected pages are updated automatically.

Frames can be replicated on multiple pages by using either a cut and paste method or the "Repeating Frame" feature. For example, a frame containing a scanned company logo that will be repeated can be specified for right pages only, left pages only, or both left and right (FIG. 186). A repeated frame also can be hidden and its space used for other page assets.

Special frames for headers and footers are created automatically under menu selection. They are specified for left- or right-hand page placement. Their placement on the left, right, or center of the page also must be indicated. The header or footer may include a page number, a chapter number, and a tagged item such as a section head from copy located in the chapter.

Columns within a frame or the last page of a text file can be balanced automatically in terms of their vertical placement. The objective of balancing pages is to have both columns of a page be of equal length. Page balance is affected by "Widow and Orphan" control as well as the "Keep With Next" option. The "Widow and Orphan" control allows the user to specify the minimum number of isolated lines at the top (widow) or at the bottom (orphan). The minimum is in the range of one to five lines. The "Keep With Next" option links paragraphs so that they always will appear together on a page.

FIG. 183. The Frame menu provides access to a number of dialog boxes controlling the attributes of frames.

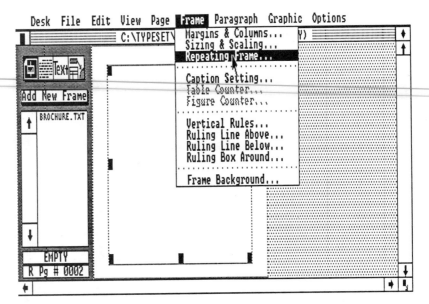

FIG. 184. Column and margin settings can be specified with great accuracy for both right- and left-hand pages.

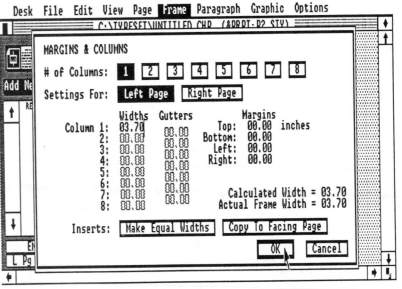

FIG. 185. As a frame is drawn on the screen, its numeric values are recorded. These values are displayed when this dialog box is viewed. Changes to these values are reflected in the frame when it is redisplayed.

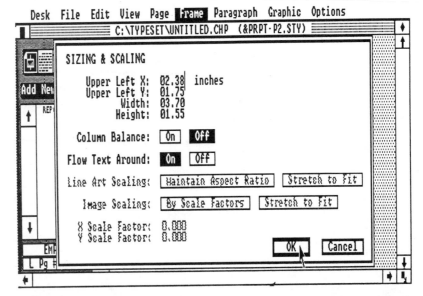

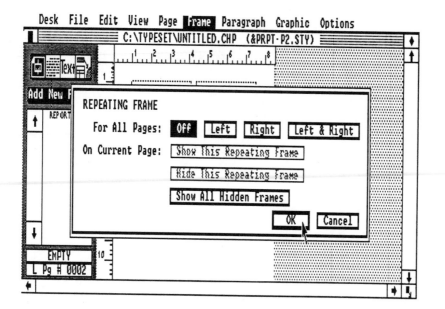

FIG. 186. Frames may be repeated on any or all pages in a publication. Repeated frames are useful for creating columns or repeating a company logo on all or most pages of a document.

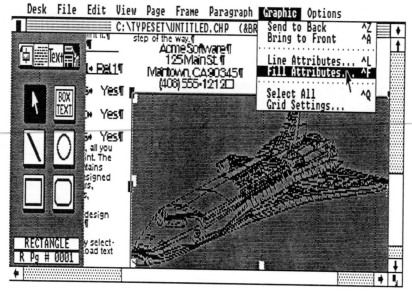

FIG. 187. Graphics and scanned images are placed in frames, which are rectangular. The graphic drawing tools can be used to add a background tint (as shown), add text callouts and labels, add a border, or add lines.

FIG. 188. Text can be made to run around a graphic by inserting invisible frames on top of the graphic image.

trip really began in September last year when Gerry won first prize in a raffle at the ch Rush-Presbyterian-St. Luke's Medical Center holds every year. The prize was two ro Hong Kong on United Air- Hong Kong and return, but at the same time, Unite nd ten nights in the Hong gotten its routes and equipment from Pan America Hyatt Hotel. Analyzing received authority to fly to o od fortune, tions or between points in the concluded On February 10th, United ve wanted authority, and on February more than began putting our trip togeth ten days in on March 2nd and returne We entered seven countries, traveled over 25,000 miles on four a 0 Kodachrome® slides, almost 200 Kodacolor® prints, and 5 1/2 hours of color and sound

The flow of text also is controlled by a text *break*. A break can be inserted to force text to start on a new line (line break), to start at the top of a new page (page break), or to start at the top of the next left- or right-hand page (page break before/until left/right). A nonbreak command can be inserted within a paragraph to ensure that it always will be kept intact on a page.

The Tag Commands

Tags are the formats that define the typographic appearance of paragraphs (FIG. 189). A tag may contain information on the font, line spacing, alignment (quadding), breaks, tabs, ruling line characteristics, and special affects (paragraph openings composed of a dropped capital letter or a bullet). A set of tags, the underlying page layout, and its accompanying margin and column settings comprise a *style sheet*. The program provides the user with a number of style sheets that have been designed by professional typographers.

The available Tag options include the following:

Font. This option specifies the choice of typeface, type size, style (light, medium, italic, etc.), color (dependent on the capabilities of the output device), up/down shift, and kerning (FIG. 190).

Alignment. This option determines the manner by which text lines up with a column. Specifications include alignment (left, right, center, justified), the minimum word space (a user-supplied value multiplied by the value of the normal word space), the overall width of the paragraph (either conforming to the column or the complete frame), an opening line indent or hanging indent, the option of having the indent be equal to the length of the last line of the preceding paragraph, and the specification of a fixed indentation (FIG. 191).

Spacing. This option sets the spacing above and below tagged paragraphs, between paragraphs of a single tag, and between lines (line spacing) of a paragraph. To maintain base alignment between lines in adjacent columns, the "Vertical Snap" option can be selected. "Vertical Snap" activates an invisible grid, which uses the spacing value set by the "Body Text Inter-Line" spacing. It forces the first line of a paragraph to conform to this grid. Additional snap-to capabilities are provided for "Column Snap," which forces frames to align with the sides of column guides, and "Line Snap," which forces frames to align with the body text on the underlying page (FIG. 192).

Tabs. Up to 16 tabs can be set, with tab contents specified as left, right, center, or decimal. Each tab can be displayed as open space or as a leader character. The choice and spacing of the leader character is the decision of the user (FIG. 193).

Ruling Lines. There are three menus dealing with the use of lines: one for lines above, one for lines below, and one for lines around a paragraph. Each line can be specified in terms of width, color, pattern, and spacing (FIG. 194).

Tag Revisions. Menus are provided to add, delete, and rename tags.

Making Book on It

Although Ventura Publisher can manage up to 64 chapters, with up to 100 pages per chapter, the efficiency of working with such an enormous file is beyond the comprehension of most people. Even a significantly smaller publication becomes more manageable by being broken into sections or chapters. The program supports this method of working by offering a "Multi-Chapter" option, which provides for the specification of separate files into one discrete publication. The page, chapter, table, and figure notations all are updated automatically to reflect the assembly of the component parts.

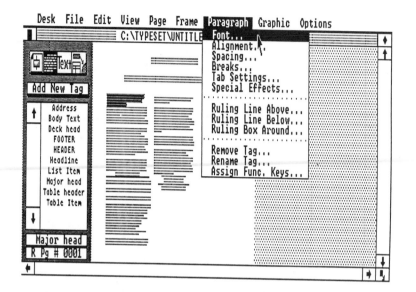

FIG. 189. The Paragraph menu provides access to the typographic attributes of the tags.

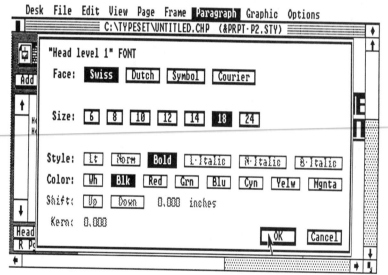

FIG. 190. These are the font attributes for the "Head Level 1" tag.

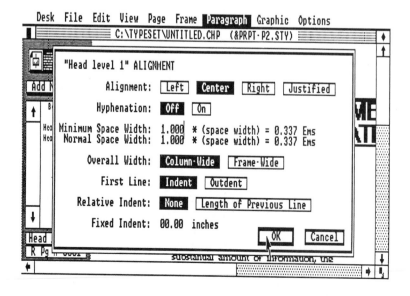

FIG. 191. The Alignment dialog box provides control over the fit of the tagged text. When text is read into the program, it is hyphenated automatically using a hyphenation algorithm as well as one or more user-created exception-word dictionaries.

FIG. 192. The spacing attributes control the amount of space between lines and paragraphs.

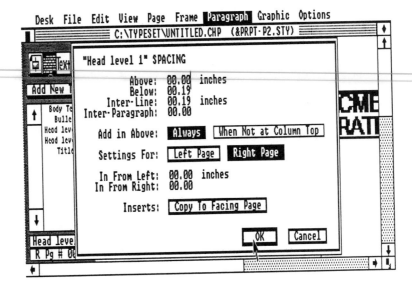

FIG. 193. Up to 16 tabs can be set, with text alignment and leadering alterable for each tab.

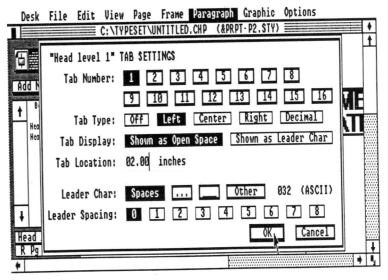

FIG. 194. Ruling lines can be specified as part of a tag in order to separate text blocks.

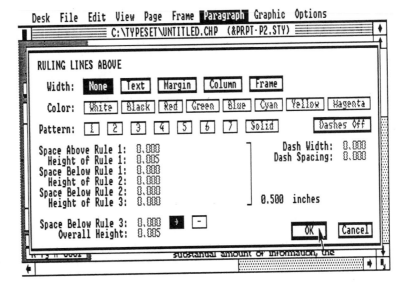

During the course of specifying a multipart publication, the program also can generate a Table of Contents and an Index automatically. The Table of Contents is created on the basis of tagged text, such as Chapter Heads and Sub Headlines, and their page numbers. The Table of Contents is an ordinary text file that can be processed like any ASCII file within Ventura Publisher. The Index is generated on the basis of words marked during the preparation of the publication using the ''Insert/Edit Index'' option. Words and phrases so marked are identified by the user as either primary ''index'' or ''see'' or ''see also'' items. The Index also is compiled into a text file, reflecting a number of user choices, such as turning on the ''Letter Headings'' so that each alphabetic section is preceded by the appropriate letter, selecting the punctuation that will be used to detail index references, and choosing the text that will be used for ''See'' and ''See also'' citations.

The output options include a variety of printers and typesetters. Dot matrix printers include the Epson MX-80 and FX-80. Laser printers include the Xerox 4045 and 4020, the Hewlett-Packard LaserJet and LaserJet+, the Tall Tree JLaser card, and PostScript laser printers and phototypesetters. Interpress devices such as the Xerox 9720, 8700, 4050, 3700, and 8000CP also will be supported.

PAGEMAKER PC:
Classic Desktop Publishing for the PC

Aldus PageMaker[54] is the program that most effectively has defined and shaped the character of desktop publishing. The original version, introduced in 1985, was the linchpin that held together the Macintosh and the LaserWriter as a single-station electronic publishing system. This hardware and software combination provided page make-up capabilities that had only been available on systems costing many tens of thousands of dollars.

Both the IBM PC and the enhanced version 2.0 of the Macintosh PageMaker program were introduced in early 1987. The programs share 80 percent of their core code, with the remaining 20 percent addressing peculiarities in the different systems. A user who is familiar with one version can transfer his skills easily to the other. (See Macintosh PageMaker section earlier in this book.) Likewise, pages prepared on one system can be transferred to the other, with no loss of data or functionality.

Hardware Requirements

A critical requirement for any WYSIWYG program is performance. PageMaker PC, therefore, runs best on an IBM PC AT or compatible. Minimum hardware includes 512K RAM, a 10Mbyte hard disk, an IBM Enhanced Graphics Adapter or Hercules Graphics Card, and a Windows-compatible mouse-pointing device. If the PC AT hardware supports Microsoft Windows, it most likely will run PageMaker.

Printer support is provided for all Windows-compatible printers including:

- Hewlett-Packard LaserJet
- Hewlett-Packard LaserJet Plus
- AST Research TurboLaser
- PostScript-compatible devices:
    Apple LaserWriter
    Apple LaserWriter Plus
    QMS P800
    Texas Instruments OmniLaser Series 2000
    Linotype Linotronic 100
    Linotype Linotronic 300

[54]Aldus Corporation
411 First Avenue South, Suite 200
Seattle, WA 98104
(206) 622-5500

Software Requirements

PageMaker PC operates in a graphic, Macintoshlike environment supported by Microsoft Windows. Windows features drop-down menus, icons, dialog boxes, tiling, a clipboard, multitasking, and of course, windows. The screen appearance of both the Macintosh and IBM PC versions is very similar.

PageMaker PC can handle files from a large variety of programs, using its own import filters for text and graphics. Among the programs initially supported are:

- Word Processing:
  - Word Perfect
  - Microsoft Word
  - MultiMate
  - WordStar 2000
  - WordStar 3.3
  - XyWrite III
- IBM Revisable-Form-Text DCA format:
  - Microsoft Windows Write
  - IBM Displaywrite 3
  - Volkswriter 3
  - Samna Word
- ASCII text files from any program producing a text-only file
- Spreadsheet reports in ASCII format
- Database reports in ASCII format
- Bitmap Graphics:
  - Windows Paint
  - PC Paintbrush
  - Mouse Systems' PC Paint
- Object-oriented Graphics:
  - Lotus 1-2-3
  - Symphony
  - Micrografx Windows DRAW!
  - In*a*Vision
- Graphics exchange via Windows clipboard

The Added Features List

The Macintosh version of the program was used as a platform for building enhanced features into version 1.0 of PageMaker PC. These enhancements address such general issues as ease of use, professional typographic control, page-composition attributes, direct PostScript language support, true WYSIWYG, and improved printing.

Among the typographic control enhancements are the following.

Hyphenation. Three modes of hyphenation are available to the PageMaker user: automatic, prompted, and manual. Automatic hyphenation control is based on a 90,000-word dictionary compiled by Houghton-Mifflin Company. The user can add up to 1,000 additional words. The prompted Hyphenation mode highlights words that are not included in the dictionary and prompts the user for the correct hyphenation point. Soft, or *discretionary*, hyphens can be inserted directly through keyboarding.

Kerning. Two forms of kerning are available: automatic and manual. The Automatic mode uses the predefined kerning pairs that are determined by the font manufacturer for specific output devices, such as those supporting PostScript. Manual kerning (negative increments) and letterspacing (positive increments) are obtainable through keyboard control.

Word Spacing. The interword spacing of an entire justified PageMaker story file can be set for maximum, minimum, and optimum word space limits. The word spaces in ragged text can be set for a looser or tighter appearance.

Letterspacing. An intercharacter spacing increment can be set for justified text throughout an entire PageMaker story. Letterspacing is used only if the maximum word space is exceeded, in order to justify a line.

Paragraph Spacing. The amount of space preceding and following a paragraph can be set in half-point increments.

Additional Type Styles. Strike thru, small caps, and all caps have been added to the type style choices. Uppercase and lowercase text can be changed to all caps, yet retain the original case properties for respecification.

Typographic Fixed Spaces. The traditional printers' fixed spaces, em space, en space, and thin space are supported.

Leader Tabs. Leader-filled tabs composed of either thin-space periods, dashes, underlines, or up to two user-defined characters can be used.

Among the page composition enhancements are the following.

Expanded Publication Size. Files can hold up to 128 pages. When used with the program's four-digit numbering capacity, the total combined publication size is up to 9999 pages.

Interactive Facing Pages. Double-page spreads can be displayed for each of the program's five interactive page-viewing sizes. Each page may use up to 40 nonprinting ruler guides for positioning, measuring, and aligning.

Added Line Styles. Half-point and reverse line rules have been added to the Line menu.

Column Width Resizing. Columns can be resized while text is present. Text immediately reflows to fill the new column width.

Full Story Editing. The program now deals with full stories rather than with individual column segments. Text editing can be initiated from column to column and page to page.

Select All. An entire story or all objects on a page can be selected with a single command. Selecting an entire story makes it possible to change its typographic parameters in one operation. Selecting an entire page makes it possible to copy a page to another publication easily.

Among the advanced graphic enhancements are the following.

Placement of PostScript. PostScript graphic files can be placed on a PageMaker page, with an outline box displaying the image's exact output dimensions. Using this feature, PageMaker pages can be integrated with other PageMaker pages.

High-Resolution Scanner Support. Scanned images from a variety of manufacturers, including Microtek, Abaton, DEST, and Datacopy, can be placed, displayed, scaled, cropped, and printed. Aldus has engineered the Tag Image File Format to ensure that scanned images conform to its structure and can be integrated into PageMaker documents.

Among the display enhancements are the following.

Improved WYSIWYG. The line endings displayed on the screen are exact representations of those that are printed. The screen representation of all rulers, line styles, and graphic objects also has been improved.

Hand-Scrolling of Cropped Graphics. Graphics that have been cut or cropped can be repositioned by scrolling the object within its given space.

Among the printing enhancements are the following.

Print Spooling for Laser Printers. Microsoft Windows supports a print spooler as part of its operating environment. PageMaker 2.0 for the Macintosh uses the Adobe/Apple print spooling protocol requiring a hard disk.

Printer-Specific Scaling. PageMaker determines the optimum enlargement or reduction size for bitmap graphics, based on the resolution of the printer. This optimum calculation can improve the appearance of screened or patterned areas.

Other Printer Support. Additional features include crop marks, reverse older printing, automatic tiling, and user-specified paper sizes as supported by the printer.

The following 12 pages reveal some of the extraordinary capabilities of desktop publishing. For an international competition of work done with PageMaker, Aldus received over 2000 entries. The work of several finalists is shown here.

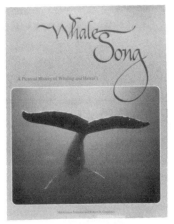

Robert Goodman
Honolulu, HI

Tom Hamilton
Sacramento, CA

Frank Stapleton
Emeryville, CA

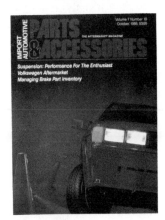

Bob Lee
Los Angeles, CA

Victoria Pecsok
Honolulu, HI

Martin Safir
North Hollywood, CA

The Lahaina Whaling Museum

*T*he helmeted figurehead suspended over the entrance to the Lahaina Whaling Museum has a most unusual past, for it was carved to grace the bowsprit of the wooden square-rigger *Carthaginian* in the 1966 epic film "Hawaii" and its 1970 sequel, "The Hawaiians."

The *Carthaginian* was built in 1923 in Denmark, christened the *Wandia of Skæhavn*. She spent decades plying the Baltic as a sea-going produce cart, trundling fresh fruits and vegetables from port to port. The Hollywood magic makers washed out the last of the faint aroma of bananas and set to work transforming her into a nineteenth-century whaler. After the filming, she was purchased by the Lahaina Restoration Foundation, and retired comfortably to Lahaina's harbor as a reminder of Maui's whaling past.

On Easter Sunday 1972, with a crowd of hundreds of well-wishers on hand, the *Carthaginian* prepared to sail to Honolulu for drydocking. There was a heavy swell in the roadstead that morning, and the engine coughed just as the ship neared the reef. Seconds later, it was over. A coral head had holed her wormy hull, and she rapidly took on water. All efforts to save her failed, and a piece of Maui's history was gone forever.

A souvenir hunter armed with a chain saw took an inflatable boat out to the listing wreck and, with a great smoky roar, sliced off her figurehead, floated it to shore, and made plans to sell it to a Mainland collector. Rick Ralston matched the offer, and added the promise that he would keep the figurehead on display in Lahaina.

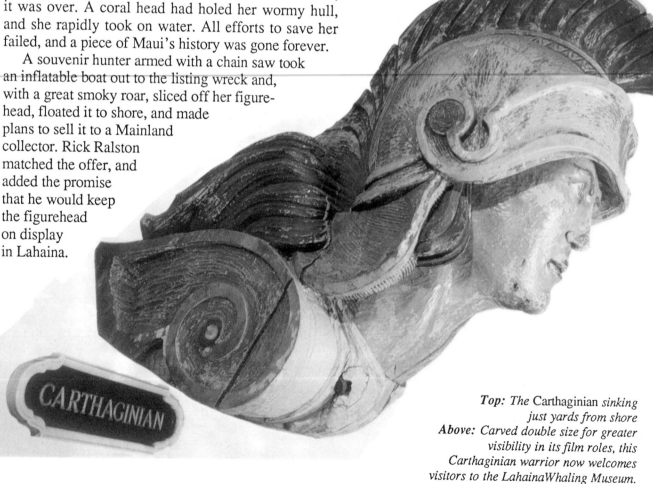

Top: The Carthaginian *sinking just yards from shore*
Above: *Carved double size for greater visibility in its film roles, this Carthaginian warrior now welcomes visitors to the LahainaWhaling Museum.*

The story behind the Lahaina Whaling Museum is the story of one man's urge to collect and to share.

Rick Ralston, the founder of Crazy Shirts, is a successful Island businessman. And, far more than that, he is also an artist, connoiseur, consummate perfectionist, eclectic collector and a guardian of the past. A number of historic homes in Hawai'i facing the "progress" of imminent demolition owe their preservation and restoration to Ralston. Today, these same homes are filled with period antiques, and Ralston's Crazy Shirts factory headquarters and shops are decorated with other fruits of his collecting —cigar store Indians, pressed-steel toys, working jukeboxes and nickleodeons, and Hawaiiana. One Crazy Shirts shop on Kaua'i, in 1890 a plantation General Store, still sells chilled Cokes—in green glass bottles—for a nickel. (They cost him 50¢!)

During Ralston's first visit to Lahaina in 1964, he fell in love with the historic town and its century-old whaling seaport atmosphere. It was then that he began collecting whaling artifacts from the 1800s—a collection assembled over the next twenty years both here in Hawai'i and on trips back to the old Yankee whaling centers of Nantucket, New Bedford and Mystic. The growing collection found its way into displays in Lahaina, until sheer numbers mandated a permanent home. Ralston then contacted conservator Mildred Valentine and architect Robert Herlinger, and charged them with designing a whaling and maritime museum for Lahaina's Front Street. The result, the Lahaina Whaling Museum, is free to the public, and celebrates more than a half-century of Maui's past. Built right on the ocean, it faces Lahaina Roads where the old whaleships anchored, and is just a few doors down from the long forgotten site of the notorious and uproarious "Whale Fluke's Inn," where merriment abounded—both downstairs and up.

WhaleSong was created under commission from the Lahaina Whaling Museum, and is dedicated to sharing the fascinating story of Hawai'i's whaling past, and present. Profits from the sale of the book will support grants in Hawaii for marine mammal research and education.

Top left: Rick Ralston, creator of the Museum.
Bottom left: A popular attraction for photographers ("Stand right there next to him, Edna, and hold onto his harpoon!"), Elmo Gates welcomes visitors to the picturesque Lahaina Whaling Museum at 865 Front Street. Harpooneer Gates was carved by famed Maui sculptor, Reems Mitchell.

Tips For Using The Weather Check And Flight Plan Forms

Refer to the Weather Check and Flight Plan forms below as you read these tips.

1 Complete pilot's name, aircraft information and planned launch site.

2 Determine for what stations/locations you will want weather data (sequence reports, terminal forecasts, and winds aloft forecasts including desired altitudes) and write in the identifiers for each. It is a good idea to "bracket" the area you plan to fly in with weather information.

3 Use the map to sketch out the general weather pattern (synoptic situation) as the weather briefer describes it and note the valid time of the weather information.

4 Sequence (hourly) surface weather reports are recorded here.

5 Terminal forecasts that are applicable to your flying area are placed here.

6 Winds aloft forecasts at various altitudes are entered here.

7 Ask for any NOTAMS, pilot reports (PIREPs), and other significant (hazardous) weather and record it in this area.

8 The Pilots Weather "GO or NO GO" Checklist is used to make sure that you have received and reviewed all of the important weather information.

9 Using the weather information you can now confirm your planned launch area, select a proposed landing area and estimate your flight time. Along with listing the field elevation, calculate the density altitude.

10 Gross weight calculation can be made here.

11 Consult the balloon owner's manual performance charts and determine expected envelope temperature during the planned flight.

12 This block is for recording notes on the expected flight path, planned manuevers, planned instruction, or other appropriate data.

13 This area provides a place to make notes on altitude considerations, noting sensitive areas such as restricted airspace, obstructions, congested areas and landowner caution and/or red zones. Appropriate charts and maps of the planned flying area should be consulted and used in preparing the notes for this section of the flight plan.

14 Radio frequencies you may need can be listed here.

15 Important phone numbers for **both** pilot and crew are placed here. *Be sure the crew has a copy of the numbers.*

16 Your actual launch, landing, and flight time recorded.

17 At the conclusion of your flight record the fuel consumption and time for each tank.

A copy of the Flight Plan should be provided to the recovery crew in advance of your flight to assist them in their planning and recovery operations.

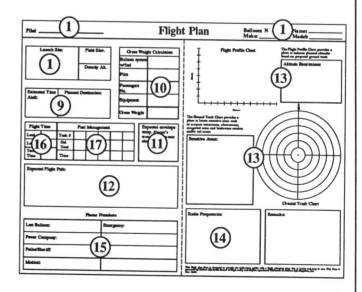

Weather Check

Date & Time _____

Sunrise/Sunset _____

FSS Phone Number _____

General Weather Pattern

Terminal Forecasts

Station					

Winds Aloft Forecasts

Station	Alt.	Alt.	Alt.	Alt.

Significant Weather/Notams

Station		

Other Data:

To Convert to Greenwich Mean Time (Zulu)

EST+5	EDT+4
CST+6	CDT+5
MST+7	MDT+6
PST+8	PDT+7

Pilots Weather "GO or NO GO" Checklist

Synopsis & Area Weather	Winds Aloft Forecast	Stability Index - Lifted and K Index
Adverse weather, including Sigmets/Airmets	Temperature/Dew Point spread (Fog)	Notams
Forecast Weather	Radar Summary	

Sequence Reports

Station	Sky & Visibility	Temp	Dew Pt	Wind	Altimeter

A R T   S U P P L Y

Table of Contents

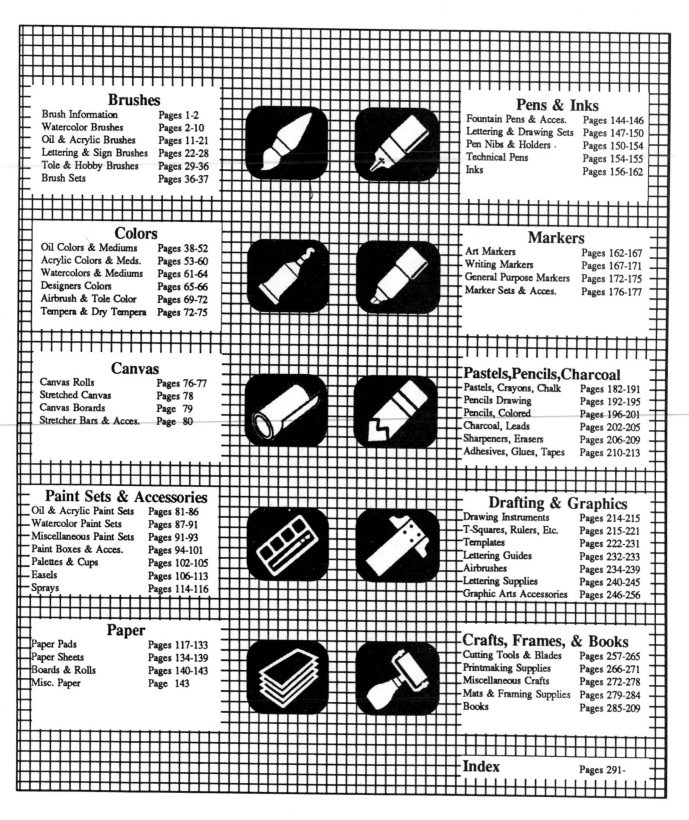

Airbrush Sets (Paasche)

These sets offer the widest possible range and application capabilities available. They come complete with an airbrush and the needed accessories to easily convert them to 3 different sizes. Also included in the sets are appropriate bottle assemblies, metal color cups, air hose with couplings, hanger wrenches, airbrush lessons booklet and parts sheets. Refer to the following section for "Airbrush Parts & Accessories". (Qty = Each)

Order No.	Item
PAHSET	H Airbrush Set
PAVLSET	VL Airbrush Set

Designaire Marker Spray Kit (Eberhard Faber)

For airbrush techniques using Design Art Markers. Easy color changes - just change markers. Nothing to mix or spill. Set contains one marker, one can of propellant, and one hose and nozzle unit. (Qty = Each)

Order No.	Item
EF3345	Designaire Marker Spray Kit

Air Force Compressors

"The leading source for silent portable air." These compressors feature extremely quiet performance, double quiet suspension and lightweight, rugged construction. They are unwelded, to allow for servicing, have a modified valve plate assembly to maintain constant pressure build-up and eliminate overheating, adjustable, air regulator, automatic on/off pressure lever, line pressure gauge, tank pressure gauge, safety relief valve, flexible rubber air hoses and a one-year warranty. (Qty = Each)

Model AF1: 4 airbrush capacity, 1/3 hp @ 3500 RPM, 2.11 CFM, 400 Watts/4.5 AMPS, PSI Starts @ 80, Stops @ 110, Tank Size=4 liters, Weight=46 lbs., Noise Level=40 db

Order No.	Item
AF1	1/3 hp Compressor

Model AF3: 1 airbrush capacity, 1/6 hp @ 3500 RPM, .80 CFM, 154 Watts/1.99 AMPS, PSI Starts @ 60, Stops @ 90, Tank Size=1 liter. Weight=33 lbs., Noise Level=20 db

Order No.	Item
AF3	1/6 hp Compressor

Model AF4: 8 to 10 airbrush capacity, 1 hp @ 3500 RPM, 4.50 CFM, 800 Watts/9.8 AMPS, PSI Starts @88, Stops @ 120, Tank Size=24 liters, Weight=100 lbs., Noise Level=50 db

Order No.	Item
AF4	1 hp Compressor

AF1

AF3

AF4

Badger Compressors

Model 180-1 1/12 H.P. portable oil-less diaphragm-type compressor has internal bleed, allowing use with any make airbrush. Develops 25 PSI at 1.0 cfm. Compact, lightweight and quiet, can be carried easily. Model 180-11 is the same as Model 180-1 with the added feature of automatic shutoff which will automatically stop the air flow from the compressor to the spray gun when the spray trigger is released and divert it out an escape valve. Model 180-22, 1/8 H.P., oil-less piston compressor with air regulator and gauge. Will operate up to 3 airbrushes. Delivers .8 cfm at 40 PSI. May be operated by foot switch (opt.). (Qty = Each)

Order No.	Item
BA180-1	1/12 H.P. Compressor
BA180-11	1/12 H.P. Compressor with Automatic Shutoff
BA180-22	1/8 H.P. Compressor

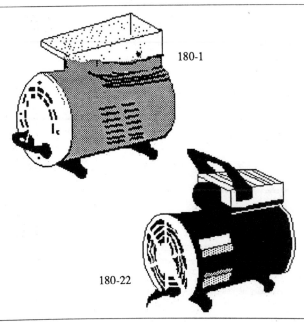

180-1

180-22

Shock Absorbers

Tokico America, Inc. has released a catalog spotlighting its full line of gas pressurized shock absorbers and sus-

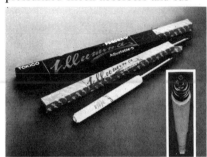

pension products. The 20-page catalog includes four-color photography and illustrations. **Tokico America, Inc.** Circle 156.

Alfa Romeo

Alfa Ricambi has stocked a complete selection of replacement suspension components for the earliest Alfa Romeo 150 series through the latest 119 Milano. Alfa Ricambi also stocks Koni-Spica and F&S shock absorbers and a line of aftermarket performance equipment including adjustable upper A-arms, springs and sway bars. Most components are in stock and ready for same-day shipment. **Alfa Ricambi**. Circle 157.

Expanded Line

GMP, Inc. has released a new line of suspension components to upgrade the suspension for 1985 and on Volkswagen Golf, Jetta, GTI and GLI. The

kit includes anti-sway bars front and rear; front bottom and rear stress bars; and specially-wound springs to lower to right height for the sporty look. **GMP, Inc.** Circle 162.

Anti-Sway Bars

Sway-A-Way Corp. has released front and rear anti-sway bars for the Volkswagen air cooled bus. The front bar is a direct replacement for the factory bar. The rear strut is clamped to the torsion tube housing with specially designed stainless steel clamps. Sway-A-Way reports that the ground control package will reduce sway by approximately 25%. According to the company, all hardware is grade 5 or better. **Sway-A-Way Corp.** Circle 163.

Mercedes-Benz

Dinan Engineering has expanded its performance suspension products to include Mercedes-Benz as well as BMW. The Mercedes-Benz suspension

also includes a unique camber adjustable crossmember like the one shown. This crossmember ensures accurate wheel alignment, even after the car has been lowered. **Dinan Engineering**. Circle 164

Suspension Packages

Neumann Distributing is offering a variety of suspension packages and sway bars. The line features precision machining, fine heli-arc welding, baked powder-paint coatings, and clear, illustrated, easy-to-read instructions. The line is designed for such Volkswagen models as the Rabbit, Scirocco, Golf, and Jetta. Individual products are also available including upper strut tiebars, springs, and lower strut tie-bars. **Neumann Distributing**. Circle 169.

Dropped Spindle

Western Chassis is offering dropped spindles for the S-10 pickup, 2WD Blazer 1/2 ton pickup, and 2WD Blazer 1973 to 1986. The company reports that the S-10 spindle will also fit the 1980 and later mid-size GM cars. The

spindles have been manufactured from the highest quality ductile iron and machined to exacting specifications for easy bolt-on operation. Installation can take place without the need for cutting or welding. **Western Chassis**. Circle 179.

Porsche

Weltmeister is offering a line of sway bars for the Porsche 911, 912, 930, 914, 924, 944, and 928. The sway bars can be adjusted by using a sliding clamp and loosening and adjusting one bolt. They utilize load-resistant Poly-Graphite bushings. The

bars themselves are made of heat-treated aircraft alloy steel formed on a computer bender for uniformity. In addition, the company is offering springs for the Porsche 914, 924, 928, and 944. The springs are cold wound and feature high-tensile strength chrome silicon alloy steel. The springs are heat-treated to prevent spring sag. **Weltmeister**. Circle 170.

IAPA

Rolling Back Odometer Tampering

By Tim Runner

ODOMETER TAMPERING is a major area of crooked used car deception. In one way or another, each of us pays for these crimes, even if we never buy a used car or truck. You may be surprised to learn that odometer roll back crimes cost the public billions of dollars each year.

The list of people and companies charged with odometer tampering reads like a who's who. It includes car dealers, car rental companies, fleet operators, along with thousands of individual owners. One recent report presented at the National Odometer Enforcement Association conference claimed that in state, 50% of all leased cars modified odometers. This amounted to over 2 million vehicles showing false low mileage readings. They estimate the total annual national loss due to odometer tampering to be $4 billion.

Many factors have contributed to the common occurrence of odometer tampering. One of the biggest factors is the fact that car makers have failed to make their products very tamper resistant. It is still very easy to roll back the odometers on most new cars. A knowledgeable person can do the deed in a matter of minutes. Even the new cars equipped with digital odometers are not that tough to modify. For example, the speedometer cable or digital pickup cable can be disconnected.

The rewards can be so great that people are tempted to modify their odometer readings. On most car leases, there is a penalty for exceeding a certain number of miles during the course of the lease. These fees can easily exceed ten cents per mile. This adds up to a savings of $1,000 for rolling back the odometer on a car that has exceeded the mileage allowance by 10,000 miles.

Another major contributor to the

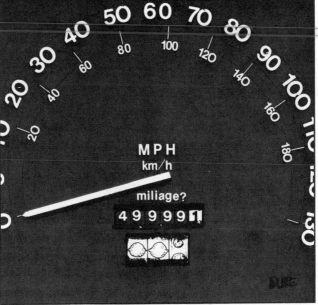

ILLUSTRATION BY KELLY DUKE

tampering problem has been lax enforcement of the existing laws. Most convicted odometer tamperers have their hands slapped with a fine and a couple years of probation. This is beginning to change. For example, in one recent case in Alexandria, VA, the grand jury found that an individual had gone into the business of buying high mileage used Cadillacs, adjusting the odometers on these cars, and reselling them at a tidy profit. This individual has been charged with 21 counts of odometer tampering, 17 counts of interstate transportation of altered securities, and 4 counts of using false Social Security numbers. He faces the possibility of years in prison and hundreds of thousands of dollars in fines if convicted of all charges. I guess he needed the false Social Security Numbers to shelter his big profits.

In Baltimore, three people were recently convicted of an odometer roll back program. One of the three was ordered to pay over $200,000 in restitution and spend two years in prison. The second crook, a used-car dealer, was ordered to pay $51,000 and spend two months in prison. The third criminal, a son, was ordered to pay $2,000 and put on probation. The scheme was very simple. The used-car dealer purchased high mileage cars and then had their odometers "adjusted" by one of his salesmen or his son.

These are but a few examples of the many enforcement cases going on today. Sadly, these cases are just the tip of the iceberg. What we need is a nationwide program to stop this expensive crime once and for all. There are a number of steps that need to be taken immediately to save us all billions of dollars:

First, we need a nationwide database of all cars and trucks in use. This database should include all pertinent information about the car including its registered owner, the mileage at the time of purchase, the odometer reading submitted the last time the car license was renewed, the Vehicle Identification Number (VIN), and the engine serial number. This data base could help reduce car thefts by making it easier to keep track of cars crossing state lines.

Second, the manufacturers must produce odometers that are tougher to change. The current "tamper proof" odometers are a joke. Almost anyone can learn to roll them back. The on board computers could be used to maintain a mileage log which could be checked by a dealer. The data could be kept in a computer memory chip having a self-contained backup power battery so that simply disconnecting the car's battery would not invalidate the data.

Third, the public must be made aware of the problem and how to detect high mileage cars. The pros use many tricks to spot the trade-ins having suspiciously low odometer readings.

Fourth, the lease companies must be made to use realistic mileage penalties in their leases so customers will not be so tempted to have odometers rolled back.

This problem will not go away by itself. We need to attack it head on to reduce the rampant odometer frauds occurring every day.

IAPA

SCS Implements ICOMLAC Proposal

Although the Soil Survey Staff completed the full text in 1970 and distributed it internationally, *Soil Taxonomy* was not published until 1975 and this final version contained only minor changes. Even at the time of publication, classification of soils of the tropics was recognized as less than satisfactory due to general lack of comprehensive data and an incomplete knowledge concerning distribution of these soils. During the 1970s, soil survey programs were initiated in many countries and now there is more information available on soils of intertropical areas. The United States Department of Agriculture's Soil Conservation Service (USDA/SCS) recognized that *Soil Taxonomy* must be continuously updated as knowledge is gained in order for it to be a viable system. *Soil Taxonomy* is constructed in such a way that changes can be made without drastic revisions in the basic concepts or the general framework of the system.

By 1975, many people thought Alfisols and Ultisols in the intertropical areas were too narrowly defined among the many soils classified in Oxic subgroups. There was a general opinion that while some subgroups could be improved, there was a concomitant need for new ones. These ideas were communicated to SCS and also voiced at several international meetings. Operational mechanisms to coordinate such a task presented a problem and SCS decided this effort must be lead by a person of wide and varied experience with these soils. Additionally, it must be soil scientists of intertropical areas who should take the leadership for providing inputs to refine the system as they would best know the problems and constraints. The SCS was fortunate to obtain the services of F.R. Moormann, a soil scientist at the International Institute of Tropical Agriculture in Ibadan, Nigeria. Moormann who has a lifetime of experience in the tropics had earlier collaborated in the development of *Soil Taxonomy*. During March 1975, Moormann was invited to become the chairman of an international committee specifically responsible for refining part of *Soil Taxonomy*. He introduced the now famous *Circular Letters* for communicating with as many soil scientists as possible, and these have since been compiled as the Soil Management Support Services Technical Monograph 8. Many interested persons responded to the *Circular Letters* and in 1978, the informal group became known as the International Committee on Low Activity Clay

(ICOMLAC) which was the forerunner of eight other International Committees or ICOMs.

In 1979, the Soil Management Support Services (SMSS) was created and then asked to coordinate the work of the ICOMs. Through a contract with the University of Puerto Rico, the Agency for International Development (AID) funded the First International Soil Classification Workshop held in Brazil during 1976 to facilitate the work of ICOMLAC. This first workshop was the forerunner of workshops organized to support the work of other ICOMs. To date, SMSS and the University of Puerto Rico have organized eight workshops funded by AID and other sponsors.

> ▟▟ ICOMLAC has generated considerable interest in *Soil Taxonomy* and made a tremendous contribution to refinement of the system. More importantly, ICOMLAC has brought soil scientists from many corners of the world together to work and contribute to increasing our knowledge about soils of the tropics. ▛▛

International Collaboration

ICOMLAC has generated considerable interest in *Soil Taxonomy* and made a tremendous contribution to refinement of the system. More importantly, ICOMLAC has brought soil scientists from many corners of the world together to work and contribute to increasing our knowledge about soils of the tropics. Thus, the final proposal of ICOMLAC is a major accomplishment. However, during the ten years it took to develop, test, and validate the proposal, ICOMLAC also made contributions in other fields of Soil Science. New concepts were developed, methods of soil analysis were designed and tested, other classification systems were reviewed, and the soils literature was searched. There were contributions by many persons: P. Segalen of France, R. Tavernier and C. Sys of Belgium, W.G.

Sombroek and J. Bennema of Holland, R. Dudal and R. Pecrot of the Food and Agricultural Organization (FAO), S. Paramanathan of Malaysia, M.N. Camargo and his staff in Brazil, J.A. Comerma and R. Schargel of Venezuela, S. Panichapong and the Soil Survey Staff of Thailand, and countless contributors from more than forty countries.

The early years of ICOMLAC work received guidance and support from G. D. Smith, the "father of *Soil Taxonomy*." Since 1975 and until his death in 1981, many meetings were held at the University of Ghent, Belgium. Smith had many long discussions with R. Tavernier concerning each *Circular Letter* published by Moormann. Moormann often made special trips to Ghent to discuss his proposals and the responses of Smith and Tavernier to the *Circular Letters*. At the Ghent meetings, some of the basic concepts of the ICOMLAC Proposal were developed just like the terminology of *Soil Taxonomy*.

Also noteworthy to mention was the dedication of F.H. Beinroth of the University of Puerto Rico. It was through Beinroth's initiative that AID provided funds to organize the International Soil Classification Workshops; and he managed all the workshops in a most skillful manner. Support was also provided by T.S. Gill of AID, who saw the significance and importance of these International Soil Classification Workshops. Through Gill's commitment the workshops and SMSS materialized. Finally, the contributions of J. McClelland, K.W. Flach, and W. Johnson are recognized for their foresight to establish the committee in 1975.

History of the Kandic Horizon

ICOMLAC introduced the KANDIC Horizon based on a proposal by H. Eswaran. "Kandites" is a mineralogical term used to group the kaolinitic family of minerals such as kaolinite, halloysite, dickite, and nacrite. The intent was to confine this horizon to soils dominated by kaolinitic mineralogy with subordinate amounts of iron oxyhydrates. Soils of the kandic horizon presented the most problems in identification of the argillic horizon.

The concept of the kandic horizon evolved slowly. There were those who wished to bring all these soils into the Order Oxisols, whereas others preferred

ICOMLAC Chairman F. R. Moormann stands in front of a Kandiudult at the First International Soil Classification Workshop held in Brazil during 1976.

just a minor modification to the definition of argillic horizon to accommodate such soils. Those emphasizing genesis did not like the concept as they could not visualize the landscape relationships; and the other extreme were a few who wished to completely eliminate the concept of argillic horizon which was defined as an illuvial horizon. There was also dissatisfaction over the current split between Ultisols and Alfisols, and through ICOMLAC, the use of Cation-Exchange Capacity (CEC) was proposed to make this distinction; this proposal would have paralleled the Ferralsols and Ferrisols of the Belgian soil classification system where base saturation is employed only at a lower level.

It was indeed a difficult task to sieve through all the diverse opinions and many times tempers flared at the workshops. However, compromise was the name of the game--compromise not in the sense of give-and-take but rather based on hard facts. Chairman Moormann was very adamant about this. By the IVth International Soil Classification Workshop in Rwanda during 1981, many of the initial questions had been resolved. Meanwhile, the International Committee on Oxisols (ICOMOX) was already operational with Chairman Eswaran then of the University of Ghent in Belgium, and this introduced a new dimension to ICOMLAC discussions because ICOMOX was formed when SCS realized the Order Oxisols would be most affected by changes being considered by ICOMLAC. About 1979, a group in France lead by Segalen was working to develop a new French classi-

fication. The French approach was radical in a sense; however, many of their concepts were important for the discussions by ICOMLAC and ICOMOX. After the 1981 Rwanda Workshop, ICOMLAC activities lessened allowing ICOMOX to develop preliminary proposals. S.W. Buol, Professor of Soils at North Carolina State University, accepted the chair of the ICOMOX when the appointment of Eswaran as Program Leader of SMSS prevented him from continuing as the committee chairman. Buol's experience with South American soils provided a valuable addition to proposals and refinement of the Oxisols.

The consequences of proposed changes on the classification of soils in the U.S. was an important consideration during this period. In the early stages of ICOMLAC discussions, this in fact was a deterrent to many of the proposals. However, as SCS, the universities, and U.S. soil scientists became more familiar with the proposals, they began to appreciate the new rationale and there were fewer objections to them. The ICOMLAC proposals were discussed at the Work Planning Conferences of the National Cooperative Soil Survey (NCSS). Soil scientists of the U.S. gradually contributed to refine the proposals.

In November 1983, a special meeting was held in Washington D.C. and Moormann, Buol, Eswaran, J.M. Kimble, R.W. Fenwick, T.D. Cook, R.L. Guthrie, and R.W. Arnold attended this meeting to review the entire ICOMLAC Proposal. The decision to submit the proposal for international testing was made. The draft proposal was sent to all collaborators by mid-1984, and by mid-1985 the chairman had received most of the responses. Concurrently, ICOMOX was also progressing with its proposals. On 10 February 1986, J. Witty, Fenwick, Cook, and Eswaran reviewed the ICOMLAC Proposal once more and made final changes.

Introduction of the "kandic horizon" reduces many difficulties encountered in application of the definition of argillic horizon. The new taxa provides a more logical place in *Soil Taxonomy* for many soils of intertropical areas that have properties transitional to Oxisols. Because of the introduction of the kandi taxa in Alfisols and Ultisols, the Order Oxisols becomes a more homogeneous class. Introduction of these taxa will enhance the quality of *Soil Taxonomy* to serve the purpose of making and interpreting soil surveys.

Description and Definition of the Kandic Horizon

The following descriptions and definitions of the kandic horizon are excerpts from the *National Soil Taxonomy Handbook* Issue No. VIII, April 1986, Part 615, Amendments to *Soil Taxonomy.*

The textural differentiation in pedons with kandic horizons may result from one or more processes acting simultaneously or sequentially, affecting surface horizons, subsurface horizons, or both. These processes are not all clearly understood, although the most important ones can be summarized as follows.

1. Clay eluviation and illuviation

In some soils, it is often difficult to find clear evidence, even by micromorphological analysis, that the higher clay content in the B horizon is a result of accumulation by illuviation of layer silicate clays. Specifically, clay skins (cutans) may be completely absent, or they may be present only at depths below the control section used in classification. In other soils, clay skins may have been destroyed by biological activity or pedoturbation processes. High concentrations and strong activity of soil fauna in soils of tropical and subtropical areas where kandic horizons are common, may cause the partial or total disappearance of clay skins over time and to a considerable depth.

Many of the soils with kandic horizons that have probably formed by illuvial processes occur on stable geomorphic surfaces. On stable surfaces, the illuviation process may no longer be operative, or at least acting so slowly that mixing by soil organisms is more rapid than the formation of clay skins. Under these conditions, clay skins may be found in some pedons but not in other nearby pedons which otherwise have similar morphology. Even within the same horizon of a single pedon, some peds may have clay skins while others do not.

2. Clay destruction in the epipedon

Weathering of layer silicates may lead to a relative loss of clay in soils. The loss is usually greatest in the upper horizons where weathering processes are most intense. Elimination of bases and some silica is enhanced by high surface soil temperatures in well-drained soils with high rates of leaching. Because this process affects surface horizons more than subsoil horizons, a vertical textural differentiation may result. This may also

Haskell puts pep in reps! Evans Paint Colormaster™ Program promises big sales

Manufacturers' Representatives are a real specialty for John Haskell. After years of exposure to representatives and their way of doing business, Haskell is finding it very helpful for clients to understand and properly utilize Representatives.

The paint industry traditionally shuns reps in favor of company sales personnel. Evans Paints developed a new sales approach and was about to introduce the Colormaster ™ program through a company sales group. John Haskell presented the case for Manufacturers' Representatives and the Colormaster™ program became a representative driven one.

The results speak for themselves according to Chuck Duff, Chief Operating Officer of Evans, **"It is too soon to tell if we are**

The new Colormaster™ program was carefully constructed to broaden the market postion of Evans Paints. With the support of a trained, experienced force of Manufacturers' Representatives Evans is off to a flying start.

going to meet our revenue goals, but our first goal of getting to the customer to make a presentation is definitely in sight. The reps have performed better than any company group I have ever seen. We are moving forward at an acceler- ating pace. John Haskell told us to 'get feet on the street--professional feet'. Our Colormaster™ Representatives are certainly doing the job."

Experience and exposure are important for a consultant. A knowledge of Manufacturers' Representatives is one example of the broad market exposure Haskell brings to clients.

Selling-the-System for ERA

One of the major challenges facing Manufacturers' Representatives is keeping the Representative System alive and well. Two years ago, the Electronic Representative Association, a 2000 member firm trade association asked John Haskell to get involved with marketing the services of Manufacturers' Representatives.

Ray Hall, the Executive Director of ERA comments, **"John Haskell has effectively become our 'Vice President of Marketing.' He has taken our STS program and given it definition and direction...We have an active, aggressive program which John works to keep on target. His new manual, '*The 20 Minute Marketing Plan*' is going to help our members organize their marketing efforts--we see bottom line results, now!"**

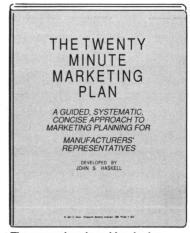

THE TWENTY
MINUTE
MARKETING
PLAN

A GUIDED, SYSTEMATIC, CONCISE APPROACH TO MARKETING PLANNING FOR

MANUFACTURERS' REPRESENTATIVES

DEVELOPED BY
JOHN S. HASKELL

The manual and workbook give every user a Marketing Consultant at his or her finger tips.

Industrial Division scores for Zephyr

In August of 1985 John Haskell was retained by Zephyr Manufacturing, a prominent maker of aerospace tools. Haskell was assigned the development of a marketing plan for a new Industrial Division. Zephyr's engineering skills had made it a leader in drilling technology in aerospace materials. Many years earlier Zephyr engineers had developed a line of screwdriver bits for industry. No real marketing or sales effort had been put behind these fine products.

Working with Zephyr's sales management group, John Haskell led the planning program. Now over a year later Bernie Kersulis, Zephyr Vice President comments, **"We are firmly established in the Industrial market. Our screwdriver bit line is achieving significant levels of sales. Our rep force has established distribution and we are looking at new products to sell into the industrial market. All of the volume from this division brings us extra profit as our primary business is still aerospace.**

"We recently asked John Haskell to come back to work with us on our 1987 plans. I can think of no better recommendation."

This catalog, trade ad and flyer are the keystones of the Zephyr program. Working with Zephyr's agency we were able to develop a complete set of sales tools which got the new representative groups excited and motivated. The tools are visible evidence of Zephyr Manufacturing's commitment to the industrial market.

ELECTRONIC PUBLISHING CAPABILITIES ON A PERSONAL COMPUTER

There is no clear delineation as to where desktop publishing ends and electronic publishing begins. Larger publishing systems such as Xyvision, Interleaf (FIG. 195), Texet, and Kodak KEEPS are distinguished by their more robust hardware (larger display screens, more RAM, more on-line storage, etc.), as well as their more sophisticated software (halftone processing, automatic pagination, index generation, document orientation, etc.)

Desktop vs. Electronic Publishing

One of the more obvious observations that can be made concerning computer technology is that, over time, costs decrease and capabilities increase. It is, therefore, a virtual certainty that the technological *trickle-down effect*, whereby features found on expensive electronic publishing systems are implemented on personal computers, will be strongly felt in the realm of desktop publishing. The following areas are likely to reflect this growing technological sophistication.

- *Display Screens:* A high-resolution display showing at least a standard letter-size page will become standard. Larger displays will show two such pages, side by side, or all or most of a publication in reduced size.
- *Data Storage:* Low- to moderate-cost removable media storage devices will make the processing of large documents practical, as well as efficient.
- *Font, Art, and Photo Storage:* Low-cost CD-ROM and laser disk technology will make the distribution and use of large font, artwork, and photographic libraries cost-effective for disk publishers and users alike. On-line service centers will

FIG. 195. The Interleaf TPS-2000 Technical Publishing System incorporates a scanner for input and a laser printer for output. Scanned graphics can be edited on the screen and incorporated into finished documents. The system also supports interfaces to several phototypesetters for output of camera-ready text and graphics (Courtesy of Interleaf).

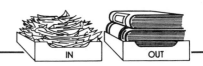

provide images from vast libraries on a per-image basis or by subscription. Custom graphic services also will be available through telecommunication channels.

- *Networks:* Local area networks will bring publishing resources to groups, as well as to individuals. Such configurations will support the distribution of effort, with specialists performing various parts of the publishing process. Such a scenario is counter to the perception of desktop publishing as a personal endeavor; however, the use of a network would not preclude an individual from performing all aspects of the publishing process himself.
- *Multitasking:* Computers will have sufficient processing power to perform two or more operations simultaneously. As a result, the user will never be waiting for the system to complete a task before he can do some useful work.
- *Image Processing:* Virtually any image, in black-and-white or color, will be able to be converted into digital form. Digitized images will be able to be edited, manipulated, and combined.
- *Printing:* Output will be in high resolution, on plain paper (laser graphic quality), in sizes appropriate for efficient page imposition. Color output will become an economic reality.
- *Finishing:* In-line binding equipment will yield a finished publication, reader ready.

Publishing and Printing

The publishing process always has been characterized by its complex nature and, of course, by its intimate association with the printing process. The term *publishing* generally is understood to encompass both the activities leading to the printing of a book, a newspaper, or other work, as well as to the activities surrounding its release to the public.

The extension of the expression of creative thought, from mere word processed input to totally composed reader-ready pages, has resulted in a change in the relationship between page assembly and printing. There is a clear separation between the tools, systems, and capabilities available to the desktop publisher and the printing processes and methods used to convert original pages into multiple copies. Despite the availability of quality Xerographic duplicators, much work is still produced using high-speed, high-quality offset presses.

The printing process is considered essential for many different kinds of work that many emanate from the desktop publisher. Critical job characteristics for which traditional offset printing would be most practical would include:

- Jobs requiring multiple colors
- Jobs involving a large number of pages and a large number of copies
- Jobs requiring large finished sheet sizes
- Jobs having process color
- Jobs having images composed of fine detail
- Jobs having fine halftone screens
- Jobs requiring specialty papers

While computer companies work to extend their capabilities further into the publishing production cycle, traditional printing equipment manufacturers are pushing back their capabilities, from the reproduction of finished pages to the creation and manipulation of information. For example, A.B. Dick, an established manufacturer and vendor of offset duplicators and associated products, markets the InPrint System,[55] a personal computer based publishing system with large system features. The system supports the production of offset printing masters, in addition to laser-printed pages. The printing masters are paper-based plates that are used on offset duplicators to produce thousands of copies.

[55]A.B. Dick
5700 West Touhy Avenue
Chicago, IL 60648
(312) 647-8800

Chapter 12

Output Devices:
Desktop and
Full-Sized Typesetters

*A variety of output options
ranging from compact plain paper laser printers,
producing near-typeset output,
to professional phototypesetting machines,
producing high-resolution images.*

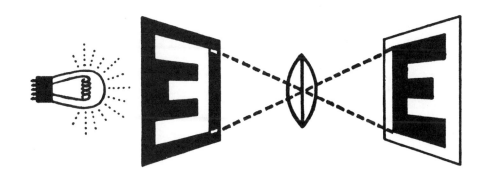

ALMOST EVERY ADVERTISEMENT EVER PRINTED FOR PHOTOTYPESETTING MACHINES HAS been devoid of one key element: a photographic processor. It is as if vendors are somehow suggesting that finished phototypeset output exits the machine ready to use, with no postprocessing development necessary. Of course, the reality is that phototypesetting machines expose the light-sensitive materials, and photographic processing machines convert them into visible, environmentally stable images.

Phototypeset images, while high in quality, have the disadvantage of requiring relatively expensive machines and silver-based photographic materials to process them. Furthermore, in the case of nonRC (resin-coated) materials, the image life of the materials is limited, and requires special handling and storage procedures. Perhaps most significant, in terms of its usefulness in an office or nontraditional graphic arts environment, is the fact that photographic materials cannot be circulated like ordinary paper documents. They usually do not conform to standard business size (8 1/2 × 11 inches); they usually do not accept the use of ballpoint pens or pencils (and markers sometimes smudge); they do not always lay flat (they are prone to curling); they do not always retain a highly visible image (the image can fade, the background can darken or discolor); and they can have an odor because of their retention of processing chemicals.

The solution to the problem is an easy conversion from the phototypeset version on photographic material to an electrostatic version on plain paper. This conversion is accomplished by reproducing the typeset material on a plain paper copier and circulating the copy rather than the original. This method maintains, to a reasonable degree, the image quality of phototypesetting, while carrying it on a medium that is inexpensive, transportable, and compatible with all known office procedures.

Relatively new to the microcomputer market are laser printers, which combine the speed and functionality of an electrostatic plain paper copier with the imaging precision of a laser. Although the image resolution of these machines (generally 240 to 300 dots per inch) does not favorably compare with that of phototypeset output (1000 to 5000—dots per inch), there is a definite market for such machines.

Setting the quality issue aside, the advantages of laser printers over phototypesetters are many. First, the cost is usually less. How significant this cost differential will be, and for how long, is unknown at present. Second, the laser printer is fast—as fast or faster than many phototypesetting machines. Third, the laser printer is capable of combining text and graphics in position. This feature is usually found on only the more expensive phototypesetting systems. Fourth, the laser printer produces finished media, ready for distribution in whatever (reasonable) quantity is required. The phototypesetter, on the other hand, produces one copy, which usually must undergo a number of assembly stages prior to reproduction. Fifth, the laser printer is quiet, making virtually no noise other than its fan. The phototypesetting machine, depending upon its vintage and the technology employed, might be quite noisy. Sixth, the laser printer is small and compact, usually occupying a portion of a tabletop. Most phototypesetters are relatively large, usually about the same bulk as a refrigerator. Seventh, the laser printer can be controlled by relatively untrained operators; its coding requirements usually are transparent. The phototypesetter requires trained operators who are aware of all of the specialized codes required. Eighth, the laser printer is entering the market as a companion for the personal computer and is compatible with many common hardware and software configurations. The phototypesetter is adaptable to personal computer input, but not to the extent that laser printers are. Ninth, the potential market for laser printers includes almost anyone who uses a personal computer and needs some form of printed output. Phototypesetting is still reserved for specialized high-quality output.

HP LASERJET: Emulating the Daisy Wheel Printer

The laser printer traditionally has been used in large offices to print significant volumes of information at high speed, and at high cost. Office systems usually have configured such devices on a network, supporting 50 or more users, and resulting in a cost per user that approached an acceptable level. The availability of a laser printer within the price range of a personal computer user was first accomplished in 1984 by Hewlett-Packard. This company's LaserJet Printer supports output from almost any computer.

The LaserJet (FIG. 1) incorporates the technology that Canon, the Japanese photocopier company, developed for its line of inexpensive plain paper copiers. These copiers use a disposable cartridge containing the most service-prone components: the toner, the developer, the drum, and the light receptor. Canon devised a laser-print engine that used the copier design in combination with a semiconductor laser, rotating multifaceted mirror, and focusing optics. The result is the Canon LBP-CX, which was introduced at the 1983 Fall Comdex show. The HP LaserJet printer uses this LBP-CX design as its core, in addition to HP's own interface and formatter.

The HP interface electronics support the use of a personal computer through an RS-232C serial connection. Data is transmitted from the computer at rates of up to 9600 baud. When the data reaches the LaserJet, it is passed through character-generation circuitry (designed by HP) which contains the dot patterns for 182 characters, including the standard ASCII character set and some special characters required for certain European languages. Additional character sets representing italic, boldface, and proportionally spaced fonts are available in the form of plug-in ROM cartridges.

After the electronic signals are coverted into dot patterns representing characters and other graphic symbols, they enter circuitry that changes them into electrical impulses which control the laser. The laser beam is reflected off of a six-faceted mirror, which spins at a rate of 5600 revolutions per minute, onto the copier drum (FIG. 2).

FIG. 1. The LaserJet shown with the HP 150 touchscreen personal computer. Access to font changes and other output parameters is controllable from word processing programs using escape sequences (Courtesy of Hewlett-Packard).

The image is developed through an electrostatic process (FIG. 3) and is output on plain paper at the rate of eight pages per minute.

The LaserJet provides three output modes: print, which is used for standard document printing, and two graphic modes—portrait and landscape. The print mode supports the highest resolution attainable on the printer: 300 dots per inch. The resolution of the graphic mode is dependent upon the display resolution of the computer in use—anywhere from 75 to 300 dots per inch (FIG. 4).

In its standard configuration, the LaserJet produces characters that would be classified as "letter quality." The technology used in the system, however, has been applied to more typographically oriented output, making such devices reasonable alternatives to phototypesetting machines.

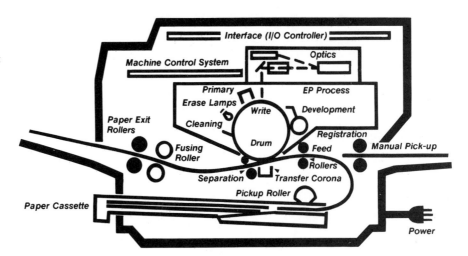

FIG. 2. A diagram of the interworkings of the HP LaserJet printer. In many respects, it resembles a tabletop plain paper copier (Courtesy of Hewlett-Packard).

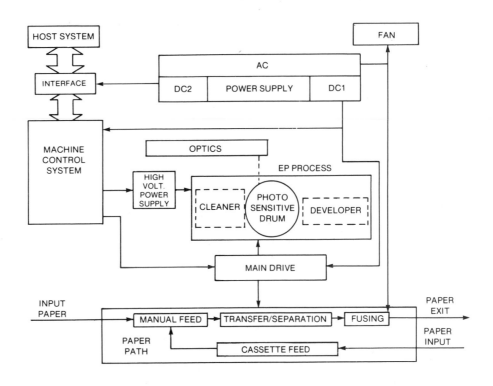

An Improved LaserJet

In the fall of 1985, Hewlett-Packard introduced the LaserJet Plus, an enhanced version of the company's laser printer with more memory and additional capabilities. It was offered in addition to the original LaserJet model, with upgrade kits available for existing users who wanted the advanced features.

The most significant improvement in the printer is the memory upgrade, increased to 512K, 395K of which is available to the user (six times that of the LaserJet). The additional memory provides support for downloadable fonts; the storage of up to 32 macros (combinations of escape sequences accessible by a command shorthand); the printing of rules, patterns, and various shades of gray; and support for full-page raster graphics at 150 dpi (one-third page at 300 dpi).

Other significant improvements are the specification of imaging in dot increments, the addition of a Centronics parallel interface option (to reduce the amount of time necessary for communicating graphic information), a data-transfer indicator; the addition of a reset button on the control panel, and the addition of seven more internal fonts.

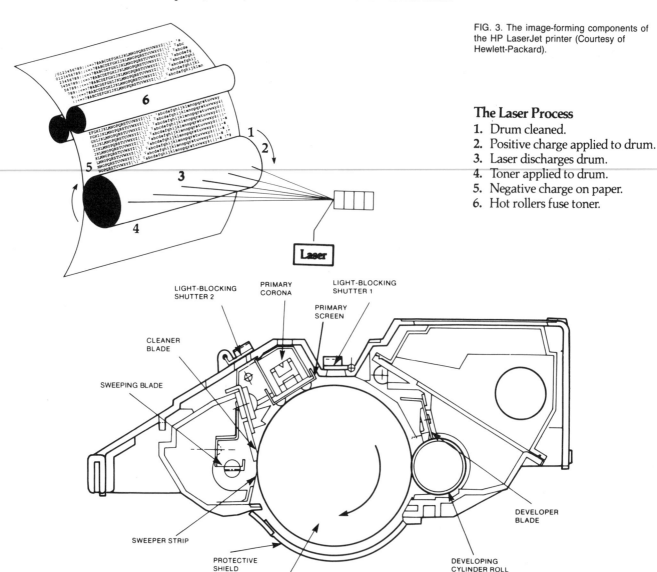

FIG. 3. The image-forming components of the HP LaserJet printer (Courtesy of Hewlett-Packard).

The Laser Process
1. Drum cleaned.
2. Positive charge applied to drum.
3. Laser discharges drum.
4. Toner applied to drum.
5. Negative charge on paper.
6. Hot rollers fuse toner.

FIG. 4. A sample page of output from the HP LaserJet printer (Courtesy of Hewlett-Packard).

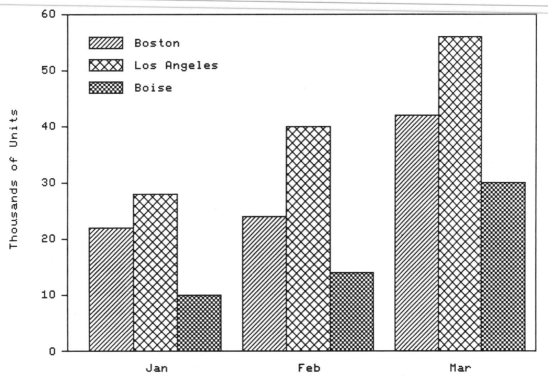

First Quarter Sales

1984 Sales

Office	Jan	Feb	Mar	Apr	May	Jun	Jul	Aug	Sep	Oct	Nov	Dec
Boston	22	24	43	50	48	53	59	60	11	9	10	12
Boise	10	14	31	28	32	28	24	20	28	24	26	32
L.A.	29	40	55	54	60	56	71	53	74	63	69	84
Phoenix	6	8	10	9	11	13	11	12	17	14	16	19
Portland	9	11	12	14	15	17	18	20	21	23	24	26
SFO	14	16	20	19	23	27	23	25	35	30	33	40
San Diego	7	8	11	10	12	14	12	13	18	16	17	21
Seattle	4	5	6	6	7	8	7	8	11	9	10	12
Total	101	118	174	175	194	217	202	210	214	188	205	246

Graphics and text printed on the Hewlett-Packard LaserJet printer

COMPUGRAPHIC EP 308:
Implementing Phototypesetter Functionality

While typographic versatility is incorporated to varying degrees in many low-cost laser printers, a complete implementation of graphic arts composition was released by Compugraphic Corporation, in the form of its no longer marketed Personal Composition System/EP 308 (FIG. 5).

Using the previously mentioned Canon laser engine, Compugraphic wrote proprietary software that allowed the user to create documents composed of text and graphics and manipulate directly on the PCS terminal, which was actually an Apple Macintosh XL computer. The combination of PCS software and the high-resolution XL screen provided a "what-you-see-is-what-you-get" environment, with codeless typesetting and full composition capabilities.

Compugraphic provides the EP 308 with storage capacity of up to 25 fonts online, outputting at the rate of eight pages per minute. The output resolution is 300 dots by 300 dots, which when utilized with typefaces of graphic arts quality is more than adequate for most office communications, as well as a wide variety of more general purposes (FIG. 6).

The EP 308, which is still sold, was Compugraphic's plain paper alternative to two high-speed digital phototypesetters—the Compugraphic 8400 and 8600—which also were supported by the Personal Composition System workstation.

The PCS supported the complete integration of a wide range of graphic images— charts, graphs, free-hand drawings, and clip art—which could be created on the screen and merged with a range of typeface styles and sizes. Using the mouse-activated pull-down menus, the operator made typographic choices without the burden of specifying

FIG. 5. The Compugraphic Personal Composition System/EP 308 combined the Apple Macintosh XL and the Canon Laser Printer with proprietary Compugraphic software and hardware to produce a complete tabletop publishing system (Courtesy of Compugraphic Corporation).

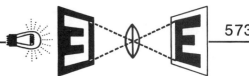

FIG. 6. A sample page of output from the EP 308 shows the clarity of type definition obtainable, as well as the mixing of multiple type styles and sizes and the integration of text with graphics.

codes to accomplish particular composition tasks. For example, the specification of the line spacing value merely required the operator to slide an indicator, under mouse control, along a continuum between loose and tight. The appropriateness of the choice was apparent to the operator immediately by visual inspection of the text.

B u l l e t i n

To: All Branch Managers

From: T.R. Martin, senior vice president

Subject: Typographic Communication

As you know, corporate headquarters has directed all administrators to expedite internal communications by limiting all messages to a single page.

This requirement can best be met by using newly developed typographic composition systems instead of typewriter style printers.

Typographic composition not only saves space but also enables you to create publisher quality documents as easily as you currently produce wordprocessor output. This gives you several important benefits:

1. More easily read materials that will be understood immediately and remembered longer.

2. Professional quality and credibility.

3. Unlimited mixing of sizes and styles for highlights and subheadings.

4. Easy creation of charts, tables and other attention getting graphics.

In addition, typographic communications copy compaction saves money because typeset copy occupies approximately half the space required for

typewriter style text. That means paper, postage and handling costs can be cut by as much as 50 percent. The graph below illustrates these important benefits.

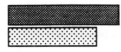 Reading speed increased by 27% over typewriting

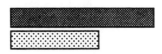 65.6% found typographic communication more **persuasive** than typewriting

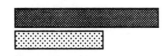 66.7% found typographic communication more **credible** than typewriting

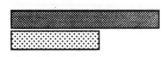 **Readability** increased by 69.6% over typewriting

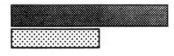 78.7% found typographic communication more **professional** than typewriting

For further details about this new form of office communication, please call Compugraphic Corporation at (617) 658-5600.

The use of prepared artwork, or clip art, also was supported by the system. Shipped with each Personal Composition System was a copy of the Art Department, a graphics library published by Business & Professional Software, Inc.[1] This product provided over 300 ready-to-use illustrations and figures that could be modified (resized, selectively shaded, grouped, cut and combined, etc.) and incorporated into documents. The Art Department provided the PCS user with 12 general categories of illustrations:

1. *Maps and Flags.* A map of the world and a map of the United States are included. The map of the United States can be broken down into the component states. There is also a library of national flags and generic renderings of urban, suburban, and rural landscapes.

2. *An Extended Alphabet.* Letters are treated as graphic images rather than as immutable word processing characters, and therefore can be resized, reshaped, and shaded.

3. *Arrows and Accent Characters.* These elements provide a graphic means of presenting relationships and emphasizing textual remarks.

4. *The Business Environment.* Included in this category are symbols for various methods of communication, economic indicators, office equipment and furniture, modes of transportation, types of industries (i.e., retail, wholesale, service, and government), job functions, and people at work in various poses (i.e., talking, writing, on the phone, etc.).

5. *Decorative Elements.* These include various borders and other elements similar to typographer's symbols.

[1]Business & Professional Software, Inc.
143 Binney Street
Cambridge, MA 02142
(617) 491-3377
(800) DIALBPS

The Art Department is also available for the Apple Macintosh XL exclusive of the Compugraphic Personal Composition System.

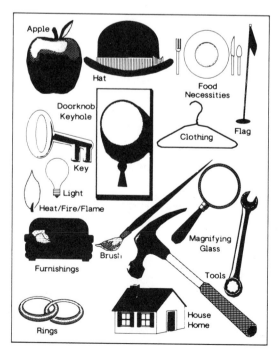

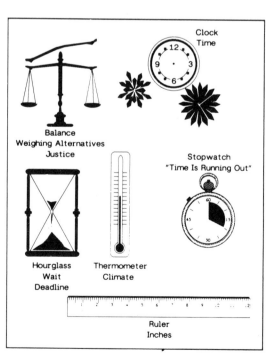

FIG. 7. Two sample categories from the Art Department, a library of graphic images that could be combined flexibly with text on the Compugraphic Personal Composition System.

6. *Demographics.* These images symbolize age, income, personal attributes, geographical areas, the media, lifestyles, occupations, and possessions.

7. *Dotted Lines and Shapes.* These elements are useful for the creation of business forms and charts.

8. *Everyday Objects.* This category includes drawings of objects and concepts associated with the home and outdoors, including those related to living standards, travel, and recreation.

9. *People and Other Living Things.* These elements include symbolic and pictorial representations (FIG. 7).

10. *Standard Graphs and Axes.* These images replicate common graph paper rulings.

11. *Standard Forms.* These elements include business form "templates" such as calendars, invoices, and statements.

12. *Symbolic Images.* This category includes images representative of idioms and abstractions (i.e. time and thinking), as well as generic traffic signs.

UTILITY PROGRAMS
LASERSTART: Marrying an Apple Macintosh to an HP LaserJet

When typesetting was a manual process, the issue of compatibility related to a concern that type was all of the same height, and that it could be used on a printing press without extraordinary preparation. Since that time, more than a century ago, typesetting machinery has become considerably more complex, and so has the problem of compatibility.

The use of personal computers, and their companion laser printer output devices for typesetting and personal publishing presents a new set of incompatibilities. The printer must be driven according to its set of specific requirements; the personal computer must have the necessary hardware to connect to the printer; and the software must be written to run on the computer and to drive the particular printer.

The linchpin that holds together the computer and the printer is the software. The software is the means by which input at the computer is translated into the stream of codes necessary to activate the built-in capabilities of the printer. Good software can overcome the apparent incompatibility of equipment that was never intended to be used together. A case in point is the Laserstart[2] application software, which permits the Apple Macintosh to be used with the Hewlett-Packard LaserJet laser printer.

The Laserstart program provides the means of modifying applications, such as word processing and drawing, as well as other kinds of programs, to output to the LaserJet. The modification process is quite simple (FIG. 8). The Laserstart disk is booted, and the port (modem or printer), transmission speed (1200 to 19,200 baud), and printer (LaserJet or the Apple ImageWriter) are selected. The Laserstart disk is ejected, the application disk to be converted is inserted, and the "Modify Disk" selection is chosen. The entire process takes less than one minute. The Laserstart package also contains a printer cable (identical to the ImageWriter cable), which connects directly to the LaserJet.

The Laserstart program does not turn the LaserJet into an Apple LaserWriter. It does, however, provide the means of outputting Macintosh pages in higher resolution, with greater dot definition, and of course, with greater speed.

The Macintosh has three basic types of printing output: Draft, Standard, and High. Only Standard and High support the printing of graphics and text together. The inherent capabilities of the LaserJet limit the total page area that can be used for graphics, and if exceeded, might run the graphics onto a subsequent page.

[2]SoftStyle
7192 Kalanianaole Highway, Suite 205
Honolulu, HA 96825
(808) 396-6368

When the Laserstart modification is made to an applications disk, a desk accessory item is added to the Apple menu. This item, called "Print Adjustment" (FIG. 9), provides the user with control over the number of copies to be printed, as well as a choice of typefaces for Draft printing.

In the Draft mode, the Macintosh ignores any graphics, and processes only the ASCII text characters. The Draft mode permits users to take advantage of available LaserJet font cartridges and print text in true 300-dpi quality. In order to do so, however, the user must work with Macintosh fonts that closely approximate the size and fit of those available on the font cartridge.

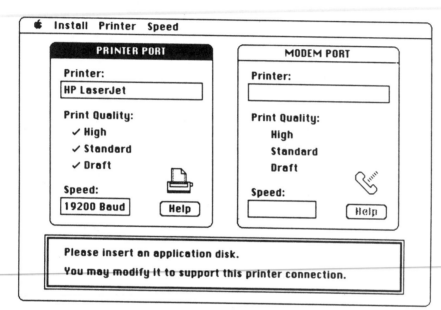

FIG. 8. The Laserstart Install screen provides easy access to the selectable printer attributes.

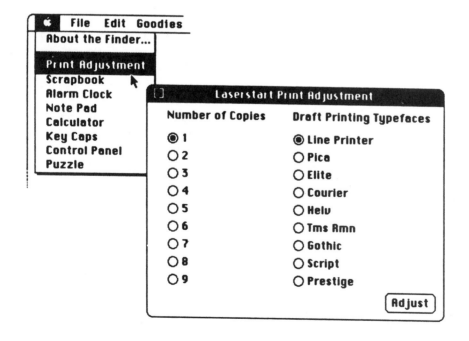

FIG. 9. The Print Adjustment desk accessory is added to each Laserstart-modified applications disk. It can be selected at any time from any application, to choose the copy count and the draft mode typeface.

JETSET: Creating a Laser Printer Control Environment

Like a phototypesetter, a laser printer has a set of built-in capabilities that control the selection, sizing, and positioning of typographic elements on a page or length of galley material. As for a phototypesetter, the determination of how easily these functions are accessed depends upon the capabilities of the front-end system that is driving the particular output device. The software resident in the input station—be it an expensive, sophisticated, dedicated typesetting terminal or a generic personal computer—essentially establishes the rules for the form the input must take to access the corresponding output on the typesetter. Generally speaking, the more powerful the software, the easier it is to control the typographic capabilities of the output device.

Laser printers, such as Hewlett-Packard's LaserJet, are designed to be used with a variety of personal computers and software applications. For these reasons, as well as others, HP provides access to its LaserJet printer functions through a series of escape code sequences, which can be input from almost any ASCII keyboard. While these codes are unique from codes required for any other personal computer application, they are also cumbersome to use and to remember. For example, a code sequence to output a passage indented 10 characters and in the Line Printer Light typeface would require the following codes:

$$<esc>E<esc>\&l10<esc>(8U<esc>(s0p\ 16.66h85v0s-1bT<esc>\&a10L.$$

When the overhead of format codes is high relative to the number of alphanumeric characters, the inputting process becomes burdensome and possibly difficult. Typesetting trade customs dictate that customers purchasing typesetting output composed of mathematical, scientific, medical, or other complex matter be assessed a penalty cost of X percent, in order for the typesetter to recover the additional time required for such keystroke-dependent work. Professional typesetters who specialize in such work have found many methods to help automate the process and reduce the complexity of the coding. These solutions include special-purpose hardware and software, as well as formatting and coding storage and retrieval techniques utilizing keyboard enhancers and accessory keypads.

A software solution to the escape code complexity inherent in the LaserJet is the JetSet program from Datamate.[3] This program, consisting basically of two parts, allows the user to create input using any word processing program, and then output the file to the LaserJet without the use of any escape codes.

The first part of the JetSet package is the SetLaser program (FIG. 10), which provides menu control of all of the available LaserJet capabilities. Its initial function is

[3]Datamate Company
4135 S. 100E. Avenue, Suite 128
Tulsa, OK 74146
(918) 664-7276
(800) 262-7276

Works with IBM PCs and compatibles. An HP 150 version is available.

FIG. 10. The JetSet SetLaser menu provides easy access to all of the built-in features of the Hewlett-Packard HP 2686A laser printer.

```
Format HP Laser Jet printer         Copyright 1984 Datamate Company Tulsa OK
  1   Reset printer to default values    20   End of line wraparound ON
  2   Portrait mode                      21   End of line wraparound OFF
  3   Landscape mode                     22   Perforation skip mode ON
  4   Feed from manual slot              23   Perforation skip mode OFF
  5   Feed envelope                      24   Number of copies (1-99)
  6   Feed from cassette                 25   Display functions mode ON
  7   Select typeface 0 - 8              26   Display functions mode OFF
  8   Set top margin                     27   Set stroke weight (-1 to 7)
  9   Set MAX lines per page             28   Courier Medium Portrait
 10   Set TEXT lines per page            29   Courier Medium Landscape
 11   Set left margin                    30   Courier Bold
 12   Set right margin                   31   Courier Light
 13   Clear margins                      32   Landscape Line Printer Light
 14   6 lines per inch                   33   Helv Bold
 15   8 lines per inch                   34   Tms Rmn Medium
 16   Set lines per inch                 35   Tms Rmn Bold
 17   Set VMI in 1/48 inch (0-126)       36   Tms Rmn Italic
 18   Set Horiz MI 1/120 inch (0-126)    37   Tms Rmn light 8 point
 19   Set line termination mode (0-3)

Enter function code
Font : PRIMARY  98 changes font affected (PRIMARY/SECONDARY) 97 = Test Pattern
```

to reset the LaserJet to its default settings of the Courier Medium typeface, 6 lines per inch, 60 text lines per page, and a left margin of zero. This operation is accomplished by selecting item 1. When an item is selected, an asterisk appears beside its number. The purpose of the menu is to set the LaserJet easily and quickly without the use of any coding. The program automatically creates a text file with all of the necessary escape codes and sends it directly to the printer. Settings also can be saved on disk for reuse. The program also can be used to output a built-in test file to verify the settings or to confirm that the printer is operating properly.

After the laser printer settings have been made and communicated to the printer through a direct cable connection, the text file can be output by using the MS-DOS "Print" command or the JetSet companion program, Runoff.

The Runoff program is a text formatter that works in conjunction with the Set-Laser program and the user's word processing program. It converts simplified embedded codes that control printer functions into the escape code sequences the printer requires. The embedded codes (FIG. 11) control the type style, margin settings, tabbing, and other formatting requirements.

A function code consists of a period and a two-letter lowercase mnemonic, and sometimes a numeric or alphabetic value. The code must appear on a line of its own, and must begin with a period in column 1. The function code lines do not add to the length of the printed page since they are removed by the Runoff processor after they have been translated.

FIG. 11. These Runoff function codes can be embedded within any text file to replace the cryptic escape code sequences required by the LaserJet. The Runoff program automatically translates these dot commands into the LaserJet's native command set.

.bm	*value*	bottom margin in lines from top margin
.cc	*value*	number of copies of each page (1-99)
.cf		cassette feed paper (default mode)
.cm		clear margins
.ct		clear tabs
.dm	*value*	display a message while running
.dt		print the date (.i.e. 09-08-1984)
.ef		envelope feed
.fa	*value*	set type face indicator character to *value*
		for *value* use digits on **RUNOFF** menu
.hm	*value*	set horizontal motion index in 1/120 inch
.in	*value*	input a line from keyboard. For *value* enter message you
		wish to display on screen (i.e. **Enter Customer Name**)
.li	*value*	set lines per inch at 1,2,3,4,6,8,12,16,24,or 48
.lm	*value*	set left margin column (spacing varies with typeface)
.mf		manual feed paper
.of		open file for input lines (RUNOFF will ask for
		name of file when running)
.pg		page (force end of this page)
.pl	*value*	page length in lines (actual form size)
		NOTE: whenever you use .pl, it resets your tabs
		and margins to the default values - *so use .pl first!*
.re		read the next line from input file
.rb		ring bell (sound audible tone)
.rm	*value*	right margin column
.rs		reset printer to default *value*s
.tb	*value1, value2*	set tab of character column *value1* at *value2* inches
.ti		time (print time .i.e. 12:14:00)
.tm	*value*	set top margin in lines
.vm	*value*	set vertical motion index in 1/48 inch

After a text file has been created, it is saved in the normal way. Datamate suggests that the file be given the extension. *ROF* to identify it as a file containing Runoff commands.

Before the file is printed, the LaserSet program is run in order to initialize the printer. The LaserSet menu is cleared from the screen by pressing the Return key twice. Next Runoff is executed, resulting in a new menu (FIG. 12). The user is prompted for the name of the file to be printed. After the file name has been input and the Return key pressed, the file is translated and sent to the LaserJet for output.

Additional capabilities let the user pause during printing to input variable information, such as a name or dollar amount. Documents also can be created specifically for merging with variable information by using the *.re* command, which instructs Runoff to accept the next line of input from a previously specified input file. The *.cc* command is another useful feature, which prompts the user for the number of output copies that are needed.

FIG. 12. The Runoff screen prompts the user for the name of the file that is to be output to the printer.

```
RUNOFF Copyright 1984 Brad Jensen
All rights reserved.
918 664 7276

Loading fonts

  0 Courier Medium
  1 Landscape Courier Medium
  2 Courier Bold
  3 Courier Light Italic
  4 Landscape Line Printer Light
  5 Helv Bold
  6 Tms Rmn Medium
  7 Tms Rmn Bold
  8 Tms Rmn Italic
  9 Tms Rmn light 8 point

Fonts are loaded

File to print on laser printer:
```

LASERCONTROL:
Changing and Controlling a Laser Printer's Personality

Despite the availability of relatively low-cost direct-input phototypesetting machines, dot matrix and daisywheel printers have remained the "typesetting" methods of choice for hundreds of thousands of people. Not only are they good enough for many categories of work, but they are undeniably the least expensive methods of presenting uniformly legible images on paper.

Therefore, it is not particularly surprising that laser printers that emulate such output are very popular. They offer faster output, multiple type styles, and the capability to include line graphics.

Word processing, database, spreadsheet, and other programs, which contain printer drivers for dot matrix and daisywheel printers, do not necessarily provide printer drivers for laser printers. This lack presents something of a dilemma for the user. Will the acquisition of a laser printer necessitate buying a new complement of software to support it? In some cases, newer software will provide the means to access capabilities in the laser printer that previously were unanticipated. In other cases, the existing software can be used with vendor-supplied printer updates. Yet other cases can be handled with the use of utility programs, which not only bridge the gap between a software application and output device, but also provide the means to control and manipulate the appearance of the output.

In order to use any existing software package effectively with the Hewlett-Packard LaserJet, it would be necessary to convert the printer codes that a particular application program outputs into codes understood by the LaserJet. The ability to emulate the most popular line printers would ensure the compatibility of the LaserJet with virtually any IBM PC program. This ability is exactly what LaserControl[4] has. It emulates the Epson MX-80 (with GrafTrax Plus), Diablo 630, NEC 5510/7710, and Qume Sprint V, as well as lets the LaserJet perform in its native mode.

LaserControl is available in three implementations. LaserControl 100 is a software program that uses the serial port on a PC. LaserControl 200 is a printed circuit card, which occupies a slot in the computer, utilizes the parallel port, and processes output 25 to 35 percent faster. LaserControl 300 is a stand-alone box that supports virtually any computer, using either parallel or serial output. The 300 can support CP/M computers, minicomputers, mainframes, multiuser systems, local area networks, and dedicated workstations and word processors.

LaserControl 100 is a set of programs consisting of software shells that create the LaserControl environment, as well as special emulations for certain daisywheel and dot matrix printers. The necessary shells are copied onto any of a user's boot disks (or installed on a hard disk), and are autoexec'ed upon start-up.

An appropriate LaserControl 100 shell is chosen, depending upon whether the Laser-Jet is connected to the computer's COM1 or COM2 serial output port. With a parallel printer emulator installed, LaserControl will divert output destined for the parallel port, convert the printer codes into a form LaserJet can process, and send it all out the chosen serial port. All of these operations take place automatically.

The only input required from the user is the creation of one or more settings sheets. These sheets specify such things as what printer is to be emulated, how many copies of each page are to be printed, which fonts will be used, and how the page will be laid out.

Settings sheets are defined by the user by running the LaserControl program, which results in the display of the Main menu (FIG. 13). The numeric keypad (with the Num-lock key turned off) is used to move among selections and to make choices. After a settings sheet has been defined, it can be saved and utilized for one or more applications. The setting sheet can be activated immediately by selecting the ''GO'' option, which sends the selected parameters to the LaserJet and puts it in a ready state.

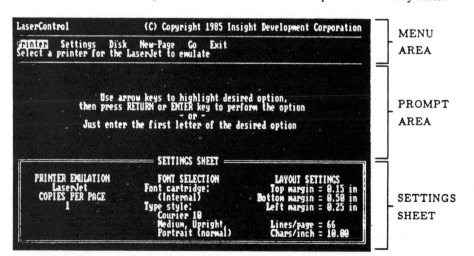

FIG. 13. The LaserControl menu is divided into three parts: the Menu area, where major selections are made; the Prompt area, where helpful messages are displayed; and the Settings Sheet, where particular application parameters are displayed.

[4]Insight Development Corporation
2005 Vine Street
Berkeley, CA 94709
(405) 527-8646

Runs on IBM PCs and compatibles, as well as the Texas Instruments PC family.

The LaserControl shells, as well as a particular settings sheet, can be placed into an *auto.exec file*, which is a text file containing programs that are to be booted upon start-up. The computer interprets them just as if the user had keyboarded in the instructions to run the particular programs. After the LaserControl programs have been activated, applications programs such as word processors, spreadsheets, and databases are utilized in their normal modes. When the "print" option from within the application is selected, the LaserControl program transparently translates the output, diverts it, and sends it to the LaserJet.

PHOTOTYPESETTER GALLERY

As of the start of this decade, the number of phototypesetting machines in use totaled well over 100,000 units. Almost all of the units were utilized by professional typesetting services or in-plant facilities, and approximately 90 percent of the units were classified as *second-generation phototypesetters*; that is, machines using spinning disc technology with negative character images held on film strips, drums, grids, turrets, or discs (FIG. 14).

FIG. 14. A variety of image masters used in second-generation spinning-disc phototypesetters: from left to right, a glass disc, a glass turret, and a glass matrix grid. Other material used to make image masters include clear plastic and thick base film (Courtesy of Eastman Kodak Co.).

A great number of those machines have been replaced or upgraded, and the aftermarket has presented numerous opportunities for inventive individuals and small companies to develop ways of using microcomputers to drive these older machines. Although not all of the machines presented in this section have stimulated such third-party support, most have. This developing market promises to offer considerably more support for an increased number of phototypesetters, as well as provide significant technological enhancements to expand the capabilities of these typesetters greatly.

Despite the fact that older phototypesetters have been replaced by faster, easier to operate, and more powerful models, they retain the ability to produce attractive typographic composition in a variety of sizes and typefaces. Few people are able to tell whether their newspapers, books, or magazines were produced with high- or low-technology equipment. Although technology has created more efficient ways of producing similar output, the economic benefits of retaining the older means of production have ensured that such machines will continue to retain some value and utility.

The useful life of an operational phototypesetter is almost impossible to estimate since it will be sold and resold until it is no longer usable. A brief history has shown that, with each production reincarnation, the machine can achieve greater capability.

The microcomputer has compensated for its deficiencies and has created new markets for older technology.

In brief, harnessing a microcomputer to an older phototypesetter can offer some or all of the following advantages:

- Full-screen editing with a word processor or text editor
- Storage and retrieval of information on floppy or hard disk
- Telecommunication of remote data
- Spell-checking, grammar-checking, and other editorial aids
- Hard-copy proofing on an inexpensive plain paper printer
- Sorting, indexing and other text utilities
- Database creation and report generation
- General business capabilities (i.e. general ledger, payroll, etc.)

Profile: Allied Linotype

Linotype,[5] formerly the Mergenthaler Linotype Company, is the oldest of the mainline phototypesetting vendors. The company was begun by Ottmar Mergenthaler, who was born in Germany in 1854 and achieved a modest reputation at a very young age for his innate mechanical ability. He was known in his village by the nickname ''cleverhead,'' and earned local notoriety for fixing the village church tower clock, which had been broken for years. He was apprenticed to his Uncle Louis, a watchmaker, and having learned his skills quickly, emigrated to America in 1872. He found employment with a cousin living in Washington, D.C., and become a partner in his model-making business.

The partners made models of inventions as required by the patent office. It was in the modelmaking shop that Ottmar became acquainted with typesetting and set out to solve some of the problems with the Moore and Clephane machine (1877). He succeeded, and the resulting Rotary Impression Machine was patented in 1879. It used piano keys for inputting, and by all accounts was awkward to use.

Mergenthaler's involvement in this typesetting project was sufficiently positive to influence him to devote the remainder of his life to developing a working mechanical typesetter. One of his financial backers, it is believed, was a close friend of Latham Sholes, one of the inventors of the typewriter. It is speculated that, for this reason, Mergenthaler adapted the typewriter keyboard mechanism for use in his work.

Mergenthaler's first commercially successful machine was installed in the office of the *New York Tribune* in July 1886, and named by editor Whitelaw Reid as the *lino-o-type* machine (FIG. 15). The machine fulfilled Mergenthaler's philosophy that a successful typesetting machine must be a single device that could be operated by a single person. He saw many benefits in having the entire process of character assembly, justification, casting, and distribution under the control of one operator. This concept remains today in the design and engineering of direct-entry phototypesetters and desktop publishing systems.

The Mergenthaler Linotype Company's involvement in phototypesetting was not to come until the late 1940s, and was instigated more by competitive pressure than by internal planning. The Mergenthaler Company's chief rival in the linecaster business was the Intertype Company. Its president, Neal Dow Becker, recognized that the growing popularity of the offset lithographic printing process presented marketing opportunities for a compatible typesetting process, and he set his engineers on a project to convert a linecasting machine into a phototypesetter. The project got off to a slow start until Becker, on a European visit in 1936, was approached with the idea of using a photographic-bearing matrix. Upon his return, he gave Intertype Chief Engineer Herman Freund the job of building a machine that would use circulating photomats.

Freund and his staff worked for 11 years converting the basic linecaster into a phototypesetter. They worked from the beginning with the Eastman Kodak Company, which

[5]Linotype
425 Oser Avenue
Hauppauge, NY 11788
(516) 434-2000

ultimately designed the lens system and devised a special Kodalith film (Type 3). The result, announced in 1948, was the Intertype Fotosetter (FIG. 16).

The Fotosetter made its first public appearance at the Graphic Arts Exposition held in Chicago in September 1950. At a nearby booth, Mergenthaler Linotype Company exhibited a converted Linotype machine using ebonite matrices, which were assembled in the usual manner and then photographed. The machine was called the Linofilm, and it was quickly recalled (during the show) to the factory for re-engineering. Accounts differ as to why the Linofilm machine was brought to the show at all. Some say that the machine was meant to compete against the Fotosetter; others suggest that it was only there to show how foolish it was to use recirculating matrices in a photographic typesetter. Regardless of the intention, the machine was never seen again publicly.

FIG. 15. The Linotype machine retained its distinctive form through numerous models. This machine, the Elektron, was one of the last produced and was sold as "the world's most productive linecaster." The tape-operated model was capable of producing 15 newspaper lines per minute—slow in terms of phototypesetter speed (Courtesy of The Linotype Company).

The Linofilm was completely redesigned and reintroduced in 1956. It used stationary character grids and achieved excellent image quality. It was followed by the Linofilm Quick in 1966 and the Linofilm Super Quick in 1968.

FIG. 16. The Intertype Fotosetter was built on the skeleton of a hot-metal linecasting machine. The circulating brass matrices had negative film images mounted through their sides, and were presented for photographing before the camera unit mounted to the left.

Linotype had two strong advantages in the phototypesetting market: first, it had a large base of installed linecaster customers, and second it had a large and impressive typeface library. By building phototypesetters with nearly identical linecaster typefaces, customers found it easier to make the transition from hot-metal typesetting to phototypesetting.

Linotype's major second-generation phototypesetting line through the 1970s was the V-I-P (Variable Input Phototypesetter). When it was introduced in 1970, the machine (FIG. 17) supported up to six 96-character film font segments mounted on a rotating drum. Fonts were classified as either A-range, from 6 point to 24 point, or B-range, from 12 point to 48 point (larger for extended range models). B-range fonts were twice as long as A-range fonts, and so a drum could be *dressed* with as few as three B fonts, or as many as six A fonts, or a combination thereof. Many models were built, differing in output speed, input media (punched tape or floppy disk), size range, and typeface capacity (FIG. 18).

FIG. 17. The V-I-P was a particularly popular product in trade and commercial typesetting establishments. It is shown here with the MVP Editing System, which was introduced in 1976 (Courtesy of The Linotype Company).

FIG. 18. The optical path of the three-drum V-I-P. Characters were scanned across the photographic material by the movement of the rotating mirror (Courtesy of The Linotype Company).

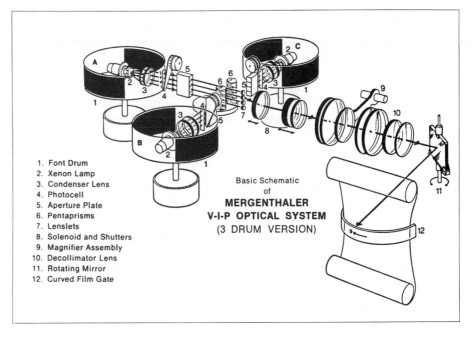

1. Font Drum
2. Xenon Lamp
3. Condenser Lens
4. Photocell
5. Aperture Plate
6. Pentaprisms
7. Lenslets
8. Solenoid and Shutters
9. Magnifier Assembly
10. Decollimator Lens
11. Rotating Mirror
12. Curved Film Gate

Basic Schematic
of
**MERGENTHALER
V-I-P OPTICAL SYSTEM**
(3 DRUM VERSION)

The Linocomp was Linotype's first entry into direct-input phototypesetting (FIG. 19). Available in two models that differed basically in the number of point sizes available on-line, the machine used four separate film strips mounted on a spinning drum. Line editing was limited to a 32-character floating display, although the machine had an optional punched tape reader/punch, which could record keystrokes for later replay or read tape produced off-line.

The Linocomp 2 was wedded to a Linoscreen 300 editing terminal, as used in the MVP system, and introduced as the Linoterm (FIG. 20). The front end provided the needed editing capability, as well as access to storage and retrieval.

Linotype produced a great number of other typesetting models, including a series of Linotron third-generation phototypesetters. The line began in 1967 with the Model 1010, which was a joint effort with Columbia Broadcasting System's Laboratories under a contract issued by the Electronic Printing Committee of the U.S. Government Printing Office. The CBS-produced CRT provided a composing speed of 1000 characters per second. This model was followed by the 505 (1968), 303 (1974), 606 (1975), 404 (1978), 202 (1978, FIG. 21) and 101 (1984). A series of tabletop moving-head CRT typesetters, the CRTronics, were introduced in 1980 (FIG. 22).

In 1979, Linotype made typesetting history by introducing a typesetter that combined laser imaging, digital fonts, and nonsilver dry output. Because of this combination of features, Linotype labeled the machine the first member of the fifth generation of phototypesetters. In concept, the Omnitech 2000 (FIG. 23) fulfilled the major need of typesetting users: quality page-oriented composition on silverless paper. In reality, however, the machine did not live up to its expectations, and was replaced with a standard photo material model, the Omnitech 2100.

FIG. 19. The Mergenthaler Linocomp required manual lens changes in order to achieve changes in point size (Courtesy of The Linotype Company).

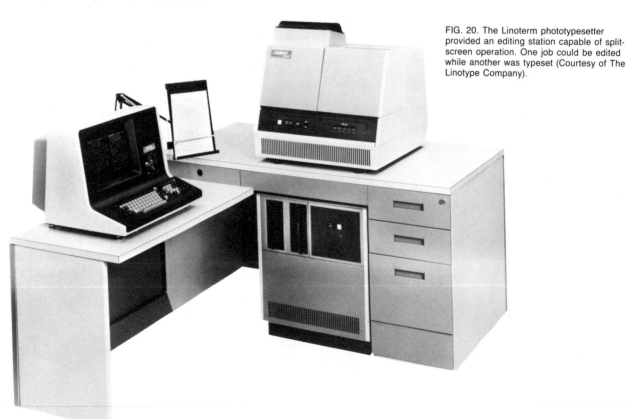

FIG. 20. The Linoterm phototypesetter provided an editing station capable of split-screen operation. One job could be edited while another was typeset (Courtesy of The Linotype Company).

FIG. 21. The Linotron 202 is an all-electronic system, with the only moving parts being those associated with the transport of photographic material (Courtesy of The Linotype Company).

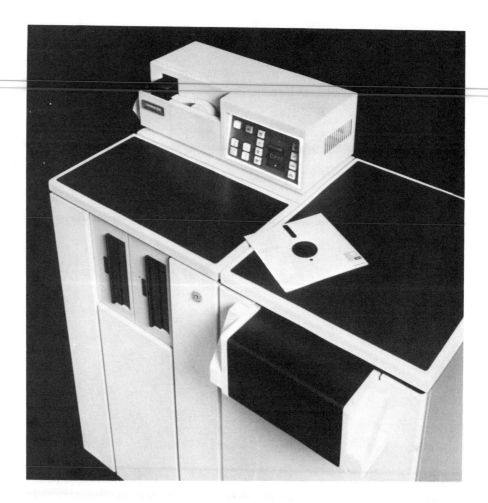

FIG. 22. The CRTronic typesetter line combines a detached keyboard, positionable CRT, dual disk drives, and compact CRT photo unit in one tabletop package. Designed and manufactured in Germany, it shares the distinction, with all Linotype typesetters, of being made outside of the United States (Courtesy of The Linotype Company).

Linotype has aggressively pursued formal product development using personal computers. The company offers at least two systems, the Series 100 and Series 200, which utilize Apple Macintoshes, and IBM PCs, respectively. The Linotronic 300 (FIG. 24)—a high-quality, wide-measure laser typesetter—provides an optional PostScript driver, which makes it compatible with all Apple Macintosh-produced documents, without the addition of typesetting codes.

FIG. 23. Using a liquid toner and specially treated electrographic paper, the Omnitech 2000 offered the first promise of high-quality, inexpensive, nonsilver typesetting. Problems with the system, as well as lackluster market response, resulted in the discontinuation of the product (Courtesy of The Linotype Company).

FIG. 24. The Linotronic 300 provides extremely accurate imaging with point sizes from 1 to 186 in 1/10-point increments, condensing and expanding capability from 50 to 500 percent in 1 percent increments, forward/reverse slanting from 0 to 45 degrees in 1-degree increments, a resolution of up to 2540 scan lines per inch. and speeds of up to 200 lines per minute. The model 300P is Postscript-compatible, accepting Apple Macintosh files directly (Courtesy of The Linotype Company).

Profile: Compugraphic Corporation

The history of Compugraphic actually began with the invention of the first commercially successful second-generation phototypesetter: the Photon 200. The prototype for the Photon (FIG. 25) was invented in France in 1946 by Rene Higonnet and Louis Moyroud and was financed by American businessman William Garth Jr. Garth was at that time the president of the Lithomat Corporation, a manufacturer of presensitized offset plates. It was Garth's intention that the marketing of a phototypesetting device would stimulate interest in the offset printing process, and therefore increase his sales of offset printing plates.

Garth's involvement with the phototypesetting venture gradually changed to a full commitment, and he changed the name of Lithomat to Photon, in order to devote his full-time energies to the development of phototypesetting technology. Garth served as president of Photon throughout its most productive years. He left in 1960, along with Ellis Hanson, and formed Compugraphic in order to manufacture special-purpose computers for use in the printing industry.

Compugraphic's first phototypesetters were introduced in 1968. The CG 2961 was a text machine operated with a punched tape and having a point-size range of 5 1/2 to 12 and two 90-character type styles. It operated at 25 lines per minute and accepted both justified and unjustified tape. It was followed by a succession of similar machines that provided more type styles, greater point-size ranges, and higher speeds. The CG 2961 was joined in 1968 by the CG 7200 (FIG. 26), a direct entry keyboard display phototypesetter with one of two point-size ranges: 14 to 72 point, or 30 to 120 point. Four type styles of 102 characters each could be accessed to produce headlines and display composition.

Compugraphic greatly expanded the market for phototypesetting in 1971 by introducing the CompuWriter I (FIG. 27). This machine was the first low-cost direct-entry phototypesetter. It provided either manual or automatic justification of lines. It successfully challenged the reigning office-composition device of the day, the IBM Selectric Composer (FIGS. 28 AND 29), eliminating the need for two-typing justification and greatly expanding the complement of typographic capabilities available to both the professional and nonprofessional user.

FIG. 25. The original Photon breadboard model built by Louis Moyroud and Rene Higonnet to prove the feasibility of a spinning-disc phototypesetter (Courtesy of Louis Moyroud).

[6]Compugraphic Corporation
200 Ballardvale Street
Wilmington, MA 01887
(617) 658-5600

The CompuWriter was instrumental in establishing direct-entry phototypesetting as a legitimate means of typesetting production. A single user could control the input and output of a self-contained, automated typesetting device. It became the model for a succession of machines from Compugraphic, as well as from its competitors. Among the more significant machines in the Compugraphic product family have been:

- *The ACM 9000* (1970): The precursor of the CompuWriter, this machine combined direct-entry phototypesetting with tape operation. It featured eight type styles in 12 sizes, at an output rate of approximately 20 lines per minute (FIG. 30).
- *The CompuWriter Jr.* (1973): This machine was basically the same as the CompuWriter I except that all of the character widths conformed to a standard fixed-unit system. Unlike the other CompuWriters, which utilized a plug or a card to store width values, the Jr. series had the width values permanently wired into the machine.

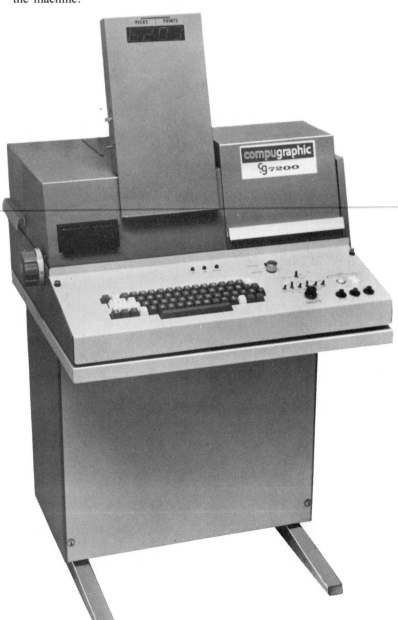

FIG. 26. Among the very earliest Compugraphic type-setters, the CG 7200 fulfilled a role in phototypesetting similar to that which the Ludlow machine, a manually operated hot-metal caster for display type, fulfilled in a hot-metal typesetting environment. While the Ludlow was the companion to the text-producing linecasting machine, the CG 7200 was the companion to the text-producing CG 2961 and others of its kind (Courtesy of Compugraphic Corporation).

- *The CompuWriter II* (1973): Designed for more complex text and limited display composition, it supported the interline mixing of four type styles in two sizes, from 5 1/2 to 24 point. It also introduced the automatic insertion of leaders, rules, and blank space.
- *The MagSet* (1973): An option offered for the CompuWriter I, II, and Jr., this it provided the means to record keyboarded data on magnetic cassettes with 85,000-character capacity. The recorded data could be played back, edited, and typeset.

FIG. 27. The CompuWriter I popularized phototypesetting by reducing its price and complexity (Courtesy of Compugraphic Corporation.

FIG. 28. The IBM Selectric Composer was a typographic implementation of typewriter technology. This photograph of the magnetic tape version of the machine (MT SC) was the precursor of the word processor (Courtesy of International Business Machines, Inc.).

- *The VideoSetter I and II* (1973): These were high-speed CRT typesetters with 12 type styles, 14 point sizes, and speeds exceeding 450 lines per minute. Unlike most CRT typesetters, the character images in the VideoSetters were held on film grids and converted into video signals.
- *The CompuTape I and II* (1974): These machines were high-speed punched tape operated phototypesetters with four type styles. They were capable of accepting a wide variety of input modes.
- *The CompuWriter IV* (1974): Designed for text and display, it featured eight type styles in 12 sizes. Additional capabilities included automatic insertion of leaders and rules, tabbing, and intercharacter space reduction.
- *The Unified Composer* (1974): This machine was a copy processing, editing, and magnetic disk storage terminal for six-level tape operation (FIG. 31).
- *The ExecuWriter I and II* (1974): The first truly tabletop typesetter, it produced justified composition in sizes ranging from 6 to 12 point in one or two type styles. A display version of the machine, providing a point size range of 12 to 42 point with two duplex styles, was also available.

FIG. 29. A selection of type elements used in the IBM Selectric Composer system. Any change in point size or type style necessitated a manual change of the element (Courtesy of International Business Machines, Inc.).

- *The CompuWriter II Jr.* (1975): This machine was a duplicate of the CompuWriter II, with the exception that the Jr. version incorporated a fixed 18-unit system for all type styles.
- *The CompuWriter 48* (1975): This machine provided eight point sizes and four type styles.
- *The CompuWriter 88* (1975): This machine provided eight point sizes and eight type styles. Do you detect some logic to the product numbering system?
- *The Unisetter* (1975): This was a high-speed (80 lines per minute) tape operated phototypesetter with eight type styles and 12 sizes (FIG. 32).
- *The VideoSetter Universal* (1975): This machine offered ultra high speed tape operation at over 400 lines per minute. It also supported unlimited mixing of 96 type styles in 73 sizes (5 to 72 point).
- *The TrendSetter 8000* (1977): This machine featured a built-in drive for mini disks produced by the MDT 350 terminal (1977). It was a RAM-based programmable machine with 8 type styles and 12 point sizes.
- *The EditWriter 7500* (1977): Believed to be the most popular phototypesetting machine in history, it provided an integrated keyboard screen, disk drive, and photo unit all in one direct-entry machine (FIG. 33). It was considered by Compugraphic to be the ultimate replacement for the matured CompuWriter line, and

FIG. 30. The ACM (Area Composition Machine) 9000 provided a direct-entry keyboard (DEK) as well as punched tape input. This combination of input methods made it possible to utilize off-line paper tape perforators, as well as operate the machine on-line. An optional perforated tape punch was available so that input produced on the DEK could be captured and reused. The ACM 9000 also had the distinction of being the only phototypesetter that accomplished character escapement by moving the photographic paper from side to side (Courtesy of Compugraphic Corporation).

FIG. 31. The Unified Composer automatically justified and hyphenated data input through perforated six-level tape and displayed a facsimile of the line breaks on the terminal screen. A classified ad program automatically stored and sorted 100 ad categories (Courtesy of Compugraphic Corporation).

FIG. 32. The Unisetter utilized a hard-wired program that supported automatic justification, tabbing, quadding, rules, and leaders. Character unit widths were stored on PROM cards plugged into the front of the machine, to the upper center and right part of the base (Courtesy of Compugraphic Corporation).

FIG. 33. The EditWriter, referred to as the photographic word processor, offered considerable text-editing and typographic capabilities. Although the machine is no longer produced, Compugraphic sells and supports remanufactured units (Courtesy of Compugraphic Corporation).

FIG. 34. The MCS 100 provides a "cluster" of four on-line workstations that share a common database. In the center is the MCS Preview, which displays a soft copy of the typeset page as it will appear when output. The MCS 8400 digital phototypesetter is shown in the lower left (Courtesy of Compugraphic Corporation).

featured eight type styles, 12 sizes, and a speed of 17 lines per minute. It was the first direct-entry typesetter to provide independent foreground and background processing, with dual CPUs operating out of ROM. The front-end editing unit had 48K of ROM plus 8K of RAM, while the photo unit had 32K of ROM and 4K of RAM. The rejustification speed at the editing screen was rated at 50 characters per second. Enhancements and additions to the EditWriter family included:

The EditWriter 7700 (1978): A higher speed photo unit (50 lines per minute), sufficient to support more than one keyboard (i.e., offline keyboards).

The EditWriter 2750 (1978): The front-end portion of the EditWriter without the photo unit. Served as a stand-alone, off-line input station.

The EditWriter 1750 (1978): A low-cost off-line input station without character-width counting capability.

The EditWriter 7900 (1978): A stand-alone high-speed photo unit providing speeds of 50 lines per minute and therefore capable of supporting more than one off-line keyboard. Capable of accepting input from any EditWriter product.

The EditWriter II (1980): A RAM-based version of the EditWriter. Provided options for a line printer, font ruling, communication, and autokerning.

The EditWriter 7770 (1980): A high-speed version of the EditWriter with a full 70-pica line measure. Offered the full EditWriter II capabilities.

- *The MCS (Modular Composition System)* (1981): This is a complete line of products engineered to fit together in a wide variety of ways to suit a wide variety of user needs (FIG. 34). Output alternatives (original specifications) include:

MCS 8212: A second-generation photo-mechanical typesetter with 12 type styles, a size range of 5 to 36 point, a 70-pica line length, and a speed of 30 lines per minute.

MCS 8400: A third-generation moving CRT tube imaging system with 16 type styles on-line, a size range of 5 to 72 points, a 70-pica line length, and a speed of 150 lines per minute.

MCS 8600: A third-generation stationary CRT tube imaging system with 100 type styles on-line, a size range of 5 to 96 point, a line length of 68 picas, and a speed of 300 lines per minute.

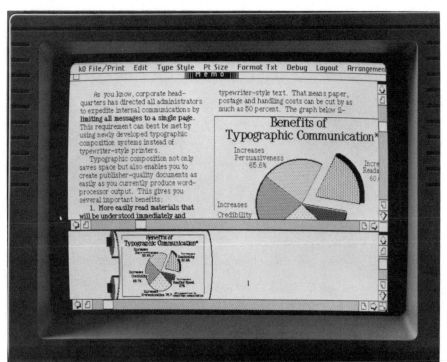

FIG. 35. The screen of the Compugraphic Personal Composition System Macintosh XL, showing representative type styles, in relative sizes and position, along with integrated graphics. The Compugraphic Compose II software works compatibly with the Lisa 7/7 Office System programs (Courtesy of Compugraphic Corporation).

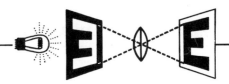

Compugraphic's model 9600 laser phototypesetter offers either Postscript or Interpress compatibility, making it a high-end option for desktop and electronic publishing.

Because of Compugraphic's preeminent position within the typesetting industry, there has been considerable support from third-party vendors for interfaces, software, and other devices to make it possible to use microcomputers for typesetting input to various Compugraphic typesetters. Compugraphic itself was the first typesetting vendor to offer a product, the Personal Composition System (FIG. 35), that utilized a microcomputer as an integrated front-end device. The PCS combined an Apple Macintosh XL with either an MCS 8400 digital typesetter or an EP-308 (Canon LBP-CX) laser printer to provide the first codeless typesetting system.

Profile: AM VariTyper

VariTyper began its involvement in the typesetting industry with the production of a direct-impression typesetter modeled after the Hammond typewriter of 1884. Many models of the machine were designed, all of which were known as VariTypers (FIG. 36). In 1957, the company was acquired by the Addressograph Multigraph Corporation, which changed its name to AM International in 1979.

VariTyper's first entry in the phototypesetting field was the AM 725, which was manufactured by Photon, the originator of second-generation phototypesetting. There were four other models in the 700 series, which basically differed in typographic capability and technological sophistication (FIGS. 37 and 38).

VariTyper widened its market considerably with the introduction of the Comp/Set 500 (FIG. 39), their first direct-entry phototypesetter. The Comp/Set 500 combined a CRT display with limited editing, along with a phototypesetting output device. The use of a zoom lens (FIG. 40) provided a range from 5 1/2 points up to either 24, 36, or 74 points, depending upon the particular model. Output speed was rated at 17 newspaper lines per minute. The Comp/Set line matured to include higher speed models, the addition of either paper tape or floppy disk recording, and off-line terminals. These machines have been well supported by manufacturers of computer-to-typesetter interface devices.

The Comp/Set was superceded by the Comp/Edit line (FIG. 41), which provided more editing capabilities, a wider line length (70 picas), 16 type styles, 138 type sizes, and 16 inches of reverse line spacing. The Comp/Edit, which was introduced with a 40-line display screen and an 8K buffer, was compatible with the AMtext 425 word processor. It was one of the first to provide such media compatibility with word processing.

FIG. 36. The VariTyper 720 Composing Machine provided semicircular snap-in fonts with two faces available at one time. The VariTyper typeface library included more than 1000 selections (Courtesy of AM VariTyper).

[7]AM VariTyper
11 Mt. Pleasant Avenue
East Hanover, NJ 07936
(201) 887-8000

FIG. 37. The AM 748 contained its own built-in minicomputer. It accepted six-, seven-, or eight-channel punched paper tape, and could store recurring commands or entire job formats in memory (Courtesy of AM VariTyper).

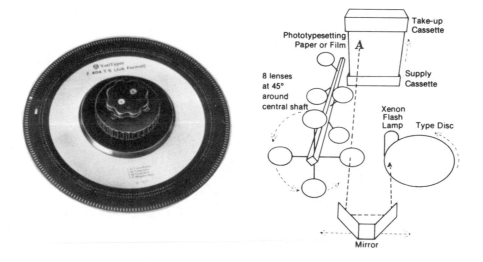

FIG. 38. One type disc in the AM 748 carried four type styles of 112 characters each. Any of the eight lenses could be substituted manually without the use of tools (Courtesy of AM VariTyper).

FIG. 39. The Comp/Set was the first VariTyper product to combine input and output in a single integrated machine. As the operator completed a line, it was typeset immediately. Editing was limited to the line that was being input (Courtesy of AM VariTyper).

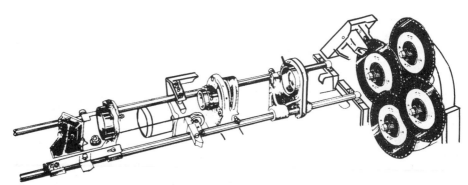

FIG. 40. The optical assembly used in the model 4500 is similar to that used in the entire Comp/Set line. Here four type discs are used before the zoom lens system to produce a total of 1120 on-line fonts (16 type styles × 70 type sizes). (Courtesy of AM VariTyper).

FIG. 41. The Comp/Edit phototypesetter was the embodiment of the natural progression of the Comp/Set line: more speed (starting at 50 lines per minute), more fonts (2200), and more editing capability (Courtesy of AM VariTyper).

VariTyper presently offers a number of options that allow users to link IBM and other microcomputers to their Comp/Edit second- and third-generation phototypesetters.

Profile: Itek Composition Systems

Itek Graphic Products introduced its first phototypesetting machine on August 12, 1976, at a press showing at MIT. As a manufacturer of printing and prepress equipment for the in-plant and small commercial printing market, Itek saw the need for a phototypesetting device to complete its product offerings, in order to become a single-source vendor. The Quadritek 1200 (FIG. 42), provided a compact integrated typesetting machine with CRT, zoom lens photo unit, and dual tape cassette for record and storage capability.

Among the more unique features of the Quadritek typesetter series is a segmented font system, which allowed the user to dress the machine with four fonts (hence the name *Quad*) of his choice. This feature is in contrast to the more conventional type dressing technique used on most typesetters, whereby two or more typefaces are held on a single disc or film strip.

The Quadritek was designed to fit primarily into the office environment, fulfilling the typesetting needs of an internal printing department in a small, medium, or large company. As such, its keyboard was designed for secretarial use, and therefore needed to be less intimidating than other typesetting keyboards. The em and en space characters, for example, were renamed to Full Space (FS), and Half Space (HS), and mnemonic code sequences were used rather than dedicated keys. The use of tape cassettes provided the means of capturing keystrokes and performing limited editing functions.

FIG. 42. The Quadritek 1201 was the floppy disk version of the original model 1200. The 1200 utilized dual magnetic tape cassette drives located between the keyboard and CRT. The floppy disks provided up to 492,544 characters of storage in up to 300 files. The character capacity of the tape cassette version was 17,024 characters (Courtesy of Itek Composition Systems).

[8]Itek Composition Systems
34 Cellu Drive
Nashua, NH 03063
(603) 889-1400

The Quadritek 1200 was the first, and for quite some time the only, software-controlled direct-input phototypesetter. Because of its programmability, it grew in ways other machines could not. In 1980, Itek introduced the Quad Quick package, a series of program formats for composing a wide variety of typesetting work. The objective of the package was to make the operator and the machine immediately productive so that the capabilities of the phototypesetter would not go unused while an operator-in-training discovered what the machine could do. Even experienced operators do not always approach similar jobs in a systematic way. As a result, they sometimes extend the time required to produce work since they need to replan and rekeyboard similar formats again and again.

Just as user-generated software helped to speed the growth of the microcomputer market, the Quadritek's development was enhanced by two enterprising users in Palo Alto, California. David Kilbridge and his associate, Russell Mills, partners in Abra Type,[9] rewrote the typesetter operating software (TOS) for the Quadritek 1210 and 1211 (low- and high-range floppy disk models). Their program, TygerTOS, overcame many of the apparent shortcomings of TOS (FIG. 43). According to Mills, ''. . . we felt hampered by various oversights and inefficiencies in Itek's TOS.''

FIG. 43. The TygerTOS display screen offered more information than the standard Quadritek display (Courtesy of Abra Type).

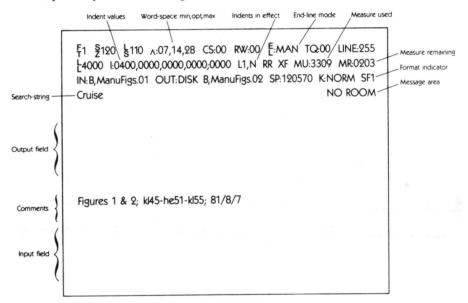

[9]Abra Type
450 Ramona Street
Palo Alto, CA 94301
(415) 326-1347

In essence, the TygerTOS program consisted of four additional commands, the reassignment of ten commands, and the replacement of two.

Although the program did not achieve spectacular success, it did stimulate interest among other Quadritek owners to try to utilize the computer power of their typesetting machines. M.J. Benningfield, a printer from Texas, had a need for a business computer, and reasoned that the Quadritek had many untapped capabilities. Having had some contact with Kilbridge and Mills, Benningfield was able to develop a version of the BASIC programming language that he could utilize on his Quadritek. He sold his rights to the program, named Quad Basic, to Itek in June of 1981.

Quad Basic was an interpreter program that utilized the BASIC programming language common to most popular business/personal computers. Using this package, the user of a Quadritek (cassette tape or floppy model) could convert the typesetter into a user-programmable computer. The program was compatible with any Quadritek typesetter having at least 16K RAM. At such a level, the program provided 8K of user program space. The memory capacity at the time was up to 72K.

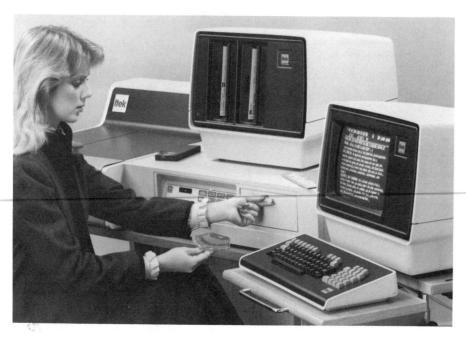

FIG. 44.(a) The Quadritek 1600 provided a modular approach to a small, clustered system design. Note the font segment that the operator is placing inside the font-mounting compartment. (b) The components of the modular system each contain their own microprocessor to ensure system integrity (Courtesy of Itek Composition Systems).

(a)

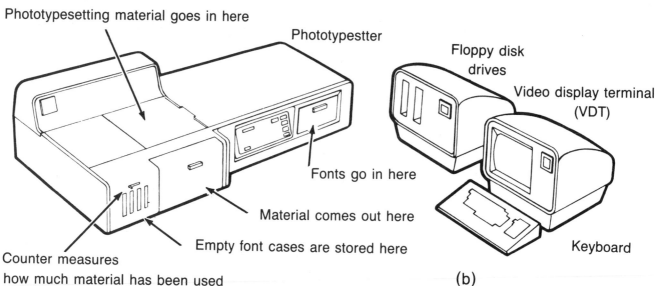

Phototypesetting material goes in here

Phototypestter

Floppy disk drives

Video display terminal (VDT)

Fonts go in here

Material comes out here

Empty font cases are stored here

Counter measures how much material has been used

Keyboard

(b)

The Quadritek 1200 series underwent a number of upgrades, including an extended point size (Quadritek 1210), floppy disk drives (Quadritek 1201), and the Data Communications Interface (DCI, released in 1978). It was replaced in 1981 by the Quadritek 1400/1600 series, which was a modular design. The 1400/1600 series were disk and font compatible with the original Quadriteks, and were a major R&D project for four years.

The Quadritek 1400/1600 consisted of four modules, the keyboard, the video display terminal, the floppy disk drives, and the typesetter (FIG. 44). These modules formed a "distributed architecture" with each component housing its own microprocessor, thus permitting the separate and simultaneous operation of each device. The system operating program was a modification of a foreground/background editing program called I-Jet, which previously had been released for the original Quadritek. A typesetting queue holding up to nine prioritized jobs freed the operator of frequent monitoring of the typesetter status.

The photo unit was of the same second-generation design as the model 1200, with some notable differences. First, in terms of speed, the model 1400 was twice as fast as the 1200 (bringing its speed up to the range of 25 lines per minute). The model 1600 was four times as fast as the 1200, or about 50 lines per minute. The 1400 and 1600 model designations were for the low-range versions, setting from 5 1/2 to 12 points, in 1/2-point increments, and 13 to 36 points in whole-point increments. The 1410 (FIG. 45) and 1610 models were the high-range versions, setting all the way up to 74 points.

The central processor, within the floppy disk cabinet, was capable of supporting more than one terminal, thus providing shared access to disk-bound data. The processor also served to queue jobs to the typesetter.

The real significance of these two machines was not their typesetting capabilities, but their status as early members of a new breed of business machines. These machines incorporated typesetting as a product or a by-product of other business activities, such as word processing, and use the components of the system to support other business activities, such as inventory, accounting, and payroll. These business capabilities were

FIG. 45. The Quadritek 1410 shown with the optional preview screen. The preview screen provides a soft electronic copy of how the job will appear when typeset. Note that the typesetting terminal shows the job with typesetting codes embedded within the text (Courtesy of Itek Composition Systems).

made possible by the addition of an optional CP/M operating system. CP/M made it possible to run MicroPro's WordStar word processing program, as well as other off-the-shelf software, without modification. The optional QuadTran program enabled a user to translate text and data files from CP/M to Quadritek (TOS) files for typesetting. Quadritek files also could be translated to CP/M for use in CP/M programs.

In 1982, the Quadritek 2100 and 2200 were introduced, replacing preceding models and integrating minidisk drives into the CRT cabinet (FIG. 46). A full range of CP/M-based packages—including WordStar, SpellStar, MailMerge, DataStar, SuperSort, Calc-Star, QuadTran, and Basic-80—were sold and supported by Itek. Two line-printer options, a dot matrix and a daisy wheel, were offered to support typesetting proofing, as well as word processing and other business applications.

Itek's entry into third-generation digital typesetting came in 1983 with the release of the Digitek (FIG. 47). The Digitek formed characters by displaying them as arrays of Light Emitting Diodes transmitted through a bundle of fiberoptic strands. The terminal retained CP/M compatibility, as well as optional data communication and preview screen capabilities. At a speed of 160 newspaper lines per minute, it could typeset a 12-page annual report in less than 10 minutes.

A more powerful Digitek, the 3000, was introduced in 1985. It offered character-modification capability, as well as direct control by an IBM XT or AT with the use of the PTW (Personal Typesetting Workstation) program (FIG. 48).

The PTW utilizes a codeless WYSIWYG display with fully interactive menus, prompts, and on-line help. Over 100 fonts can be on-line, and up to 128 typefaces can be used in a single job. The program supports 150 automatic kerning pairs per typeface, as well as up to 40 MB of hard disk storage. The H & J speed is rated at 6000 characters per second (among the fastest available), and a 50,000-word spell-checking and hyphenation dictionary is standard.

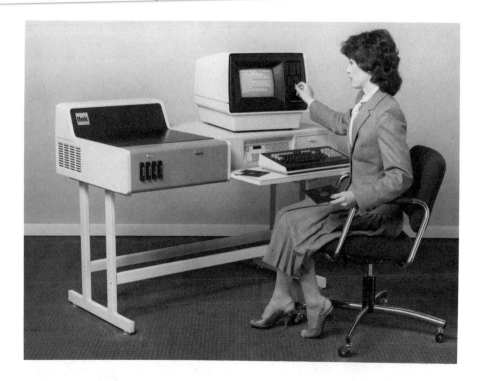

FIG. 46. The Quadritek 2100/2200 series consolidated the disk drives and controller within the terminal enclosure. Mini disks (DD/DS) provided a combined storage capacity of 654K with as many as 566 files (Courtesy of Itek Composition Systems).

FIG. 47. The Digitek digital phototypesetter utilizes a unique LED/fiberoptic imaging system. The input workstation has been combined with the Quadritek 2110 to form a new product, the Quadritek 2500. The 2500 provides users with an upward compatibility to Digitek output (Courtesy of Itek Composition Systems).

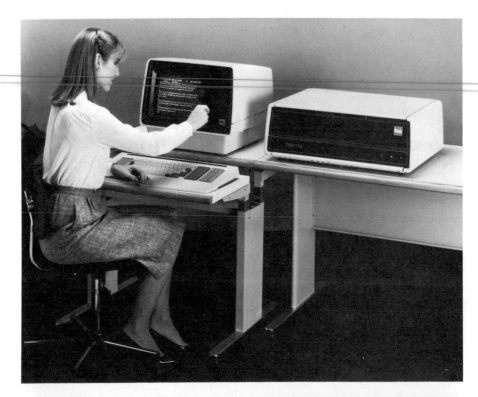

FIG. 48. The Personal Typesetting Workstation displays jobs in correct proportion and style representation (roman, italic, bold, and bold italic), but at a 14 percent larger than usual size. The system continuously counts characters at 6000 characters per second, regardless of cursor motion. As a result of this speed, the copy is always justified (Courtesy of Itek Composition Systems).

ACCESSORY PRODUCTS AND DEVICES
COMPUWRITER PRODUCTIVITY PAK

This concept links Compugraphic's no longer manufactured CompuWriter IV (model B), CompuWriter 48, and CompuWriter 88 with the company's lowest cost Modular Composition System (MCS) front end, and the MCS 5. The MCS 5 provides disk storage, full-screen editing, and simplified copyfitting capabilities to a feature-limited direct-entry phototypesetter.

The CW Productivity Pak[10] includes 256K of memory, special operating software, a cable, and an interface board for the CompuWriter. The interface does not override the CompuWriter's keyboarding capabilities, so one operator can use the MCS 5 to input a job while another sets type on the output unit.

MICROSETTER TYPESETTER INTERFACES

The MicroSetter system[11] originally was designed specifically for Apple II and *IIe* microcomputers interfaced to Compugraphic CompuWriter models Jr., I, or II. Using almost any commercially available word processing package—ScreenWriter II, Apple Writer II, and WordStar are recommended—the user will be able to store, edit, format, and recall typesetting jobs. New interface models have been created for the Compugraphic EditWriter and ExecuWriter, as well as the AM Comp/Set and Comp/Edit (FIG. 49). These models are not limited to the use of any specific microcomputer for input.

The MicroSetter CompuWriter package consists of an easily installed hardware interface and six software programs that enhanced its use. They are:

- *On-line Composing:* This program simulates the character unit counting apparatus on the CompuWriter and provides automatic justification off-line.
- *Edit:* This program allows editing of text previously prepared by using the on-line composing program. At this point, a spell-checking program could be utilized.
- *Auto Format:* This program allows the user to embed typesetting codes directly into text files prepared using a commercial word processing package. Using the Insert Space function, for example, would involve keyboarding IS in the appropriate place. The program also allows for the use of fixed indents by specifying a number of thin spaces to be set at the beginning of each line.

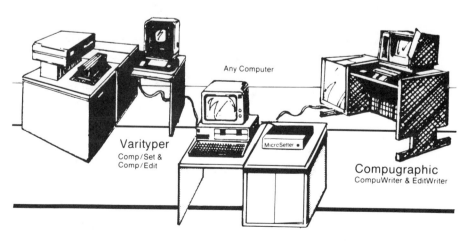

Any Computer

Varityper
Comp/Set &
Comp/Edit

MicroSetter

Compugraphic
CompuWriter & EditWriter

FIG. 49. The MicroSetter interface is part of a line of interfaces that marry a word processor or computer directly to one of a number of second-generation phototypesetters (Courtesy of TeleTypesetting Company).

[10]Compugraphic Corporation
200 Ballardvale Street
Wilmington, MA 01887
(617) 658-5600

[11]TeleTypesetting Co.
244 Nickels Arcade
Ann Arbor, MI 48104

- *Print:* This program provides an opportunity to send completed text files to a thermal, dot matrix, or letter-quality printer for proofing. This option helps to eliminate unpleasant surprises caused by typographical errors or improper coding procedures.
- *Send to Typesetter:* This program sends completed text files directly to the CompuWriter.
- *Customize:* This option permits the user to change information on the MicroSetter program disk to conform to user requirements. One application is to change keys on the Apple to produce particular characters on the typesetter.

The MicroSetter system requires a 48K Apple II or *II*e, one disk drive, a printer (helpful but not essential), and a word processing program.

Newer models support the use of the Apple Macintosh for WYSIWYG typesetting with a wide variety of phototypesetters.

WordSet:
Word Processor-Based Input for Phototypesetting

WordSet[12] is a specialized hardware and software package for the generation of typeset output using a conventional computer-based word processing system, as well as output using an AM VariTyper Comp/Edit phototypesetter. It was devised for the professional writer and clerical personnel, rather than for trade typesetting use, and was actually designed for the Ingle Company to prepare pay-television guides nationwide. It is CP/M-based and uses MicroPro's Wordstar as its word processing software. Typesetting codes are added using either a comma precedence code, such as *,A2* to indicate the typeface located on type disc A, position 2, or for another set of commands, a dollar-sign mnemonic, such as *$ LL* to indicate line length.

After a file is prepared, it is sent to the typesetter. First the computer must be told to direct its flow of data to the typesetter, rather than to the printer. This process is easily accomplished using CP/M commands. Second, the typesetter must be initialized to accept telecommunicated data. When both systems are ready, the file is sent from the computer to the typesetter, where it is stored on disk and then typeset.

The WordSet system requires modification of the CP/M operating system and the word processing software, as well as additional hardware and hardware interfaces. System Interface Consultants, Inc., provides complete installation, as well as operator training.

microCOMPOSER-X:
Microcomputer-to-Typesetter Interfaces

The microCOMPOSER-X[13] is an improved model (the *X* stands for extended) of the original microCOMPOSER, which will continue to be manufactured. The X model retains all of the capabilities of the previous model, adding a new command set that provides for hanging indents, ragged right and left columns, and the automatic insertion of paragraph indents and quad lefts at the end of paragraphs. Also provided is a typesetting queue, which allows the user to list a series of jobs to be typeset without further operator intervention, and to typeset the actual processing time at the end of each file.

The microCOMPOSER systems are available for all CompuWriters, Juniors through CompuWriter IV; as well as for UniSetters, ACM 9000, CompuTapes, and EditWriters. The systems are available for a wide variety of computers.

[12]System Interface Consultants, Inc.
1900 Avenue of the Stars
Suite 1455
Century City, CA 90067
(213) 556-0807

[13]Cybertext Corporation
702 Jefferson Avenue
Ashland, OR 97520
(503) 482-0290

PHOENIX COMMUNICATIONS INTERFACE
for Dissimilar Devices

The PCI[14] is a stand-alone interface that facilitates communication between dissimilar devices, such as word processors, typesetters, microcomputers, OCRs, terminals, and large computer systems. The unit is able to send as well as receive data, and can be configured with any of a number of communications protocols.

Code-translation tables are prepared on the equipment communicating with the PCI and are sent before the main text is. A search and replace capability within the PCI scans incoming data and converts it to the appropriate codes expected by the receiving device. This function effectively gives the user the ability to capture original keystrokes input on a word processor or other computerized equipment, and to send the data to an in-house typesetter without rekeyboarding.

Typesetters presently supported include the Linotype Linoterm, VIP, 202, Omnitech, CRTronic; the Compugraphic EditWriter, 8400, 8600, 4961, CompuWriter IV and Jr., TrendSetter, UniSetter, VideoSetter; the Autologic Micro V, APS-5; the AM VariTyper Comp/Set; and others. The PCI is compatible with any word processor or microcomputer that uses RS-232C communications using TTY or 2780/3780 Bisync.

CW/CI INTERFACES
for the Compugraphic CompuWriters

The CW/CI interface[15] is from the company that makes telecommunications interfaces for typesetting vendors, including Compugraphic, Linotype, and Autologic. The CW/CI, for the CompuWriter I, II, and Jr., can be used with any microcomputer, small business computer, word processor, or large data processor, provided that the computer can drive a printer and be translated by the interface. The unit permits the use of any word processing software, either on-line or from remote systems over normal telephone lines, with the use of an optional direct-connect auto-answer modem. The interface has a built-in pagination program for automatic typesetting of complete pages of single-column text or tabular data, including headers and footers and automatic page numbering.

Installation consists of connecting five wires from the interface plug onto connections behind the control panel of the CompuWriter. Soldering is not necessary, and the CompuWriter remains usable directly from its keyboard. Activation of the interface is accomplished by sending $com from the remote input device.

The base price for the CW/CI includes the interface with RS-232C serial communications and Centronics-compatible parallel communications input; 2K byte locally loaded translation table memory; format memory, consisting of 16 user definable/selectable formats of 32 characters each, stringable and usable with standard CompuWriter operation; pagination program, including automatic positioning of headers, footers, and folios, user-definable copy depth in points, and auto-sequencing of folio including beginning page number; installation and operating manual; and basic translation table. A modem package that includes all of these features, is also available. A bisynchronous package for communication with IBM and various Wang WP configurations is available at extra cost.

MICROTYPE
Apple-to-VariTyper Comp/Set Interface

The MicroType system[16] can be configured in a number of ways to utilize the typesetting capabilities of the AM VariTyper Comp/Set and Comp/Edit phototypesetters. The total system consists of an Apple *IIe*, the MicroType software program, the

[14] Phoenix Service Co., Inc.
117 Kay Court
Hurst, TX 76053
(817) 268-5254

[15] G.O. Graphics
179 Bedford Street
Lexington, MA 02173
(617) 861-7757

[16] Data Transfer Corp.
P.O. Box 68
Hillsboro, OR 97123
(503) 649-4975

Series 1000 Computer Interface, and the Parallel Interface Port. The specialized software translates computer codes into a form acceptable to the typesetter, and provides for user-defined mnemonic codes for frequently used formats.

The system can be purchased without the Apple if the user already has one, and also will support other microcomputers (contact DTC for a current list). In order for the Comp/Set to accept incoming data, it must be equipped with an interface port, such as DTC's Parallel Interface Port (PIP). Similarly, the Comp/Edit must have a GPI port for the same purpose.

QS CALL
Communications System for the VariTyper Comp/Set

The QS CALL system[17] interfaces with the AM VariTyper Comp/Set phototypesetter. The general-purpose package includes customized software, which controls both the AM interface and telecommunications. This menu-driven communications package permits the user to set up characteristics of a client's system, catalog it, and use it by referring to its name and number. Text can be received from both asynchronous and synchronous systems, and can be stored on disk pending typesetting. Files so stored can be transferred to the typesetter buffer or onto an AM diskette using QS SAM, another software package. QS SAM offers the user a mnemonics file for typesetting code translation, which can be devised for a variety of typesetting requirements (different jobs or clients).

AX UNIVERSAL
Interface to Translate PC Input into TTS

The AX Universal Interface[18] supports almost any microcomputer and its word processing software. It has its own internal microprocessor, which translates all keystrokes into their proper TTS codes and sends them on to the typesetter. Contact First Main for a list of typesetters supported.

COMPAX

The Compax interface[18] supports all models of CompuWriter and standard ASCII input from virtually any computer supporting parallel printer output (Centronics, Diablo, or Epson). The unit installs in 10 minutes and includes a comprehensive user manual.

EL CID (THE COMPUTER INTERFACE DEVICE)
Any Computer/Any Software/Typesetter Interface

This compact interface drives a number of typesetters, including but not limited to all models of the Compugraphic CompuWriter, EditWriter, and VariTyper Comp/Set. Installation takes about 10 minutes with no tools, no soldering, no wire-cutting, and no modification of any kind by the typesetter. The EL CID[19] can be used with almost any computer, from micro to mainframe, that uses the industry standard RS-232C (x-on, x-off protocol) or Centronics standard parallel (FIG. 50). Users retain their choice of word processing software using a simple scheme of mnemonics to access typesetter keyboard characters and functions.

The interface is microprocessor-controlled and utilizes a softswitch that allows the operator to turn the unit on or off under software control, without leaving his seat at the computer terminal. The unit features built-in hardware diagnostics and switch-selectable baud rates.

[17]Quality Software, Inc.
60 Lewis Street
Newton, MA 02158
(617) 965-2231

[18]First Main Computer Systems, Inc.
P.O. Box 795
Bedford, TX 76021
(817) 540-2491

[19]Baseline Inc.
3800 Monroe Avenue
Pittsford, NY 14534
(716) 385-6149

FIG. 50. The major external components of the EL CID serial interface.

Anatomy of an Interface

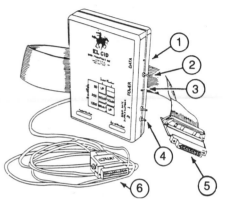

Although it is inside EL CID where all of the electronic magic happens, there is much to learn about the outside of EL CID as well. Illustrated to the right is the serial version of the EL CID interface. Among its more interesting features are:
1. The DATA LIGHT blinks as data passes through the interface. It is very helpful in verifying that the computer is transmitting information properly.
2. The DATA SWITCH sets EL CID to match the RS-232 wiring scheme used by the computer. Although RS-232 is considered a standard, cables are often wired according to manufacturer's preferences. This switch makes EL CID a truly universal serial device.

3. The POWER LIGHT confirms that EL CID is receiving power from its host typesetter. The low power components used in EL CID draw a very small amount of current.
4. The BAUD RATE SWITCHES permit the user to set the transmission rate of characters from 110 baud to 1200 baud.
5. The TYPESETTER CONNECTOR (varies with model) easily plugs into the typesetter without the use of any tools, wire cutting, soldering, or permanent modification to the typesetter.
6. The COMPUTER CONNECTOR plugs directly into the port on the computer.

INFORMATION DESIGN 1000
Computer-to-Typesetter Interface

The Information Design Series 1000 Interface[20] is a means of linking input from most micro, mini, and mainframe computers, as well as word processing systems to the AM Comp/Set or Comp/Edit.

The unit is Bell 103A-type modem compatible, and has switch-selectable baud rates from 110 to 9600. No operator intervention is required.

The device also can be used to generate AM-compatible media (diskettes) by using the record/playback capability of the phototypesetter. By so doing, downloaded jobs can be kept on diskette for future editing and typesetting, thereby increasing system efficiency.

The Series 1000 uses a standard RS-232C cable, which connects to AM typesetters that have installed the optional General Purpose Interface Port.

APP/COMP
Apple-to-Comp/Set Interface

The APP/COMP interface[21] is one solution to the shortcomings of the AM VariTyper Comp/Set 500, 503, and 504. The APP/COMP uses a standard Apple II or II+ microcomputer with a modified word processing program. No modification is necessary to either the Apple or the Comp/Set. Literally thousands of additional programs are available for use on the Apple, including a number of other word processors and business applications.

COMPTRECK WP2
CompuWriter Interface

Here is an approach to using any model of the CompuWriter as an output device with an on-line microcomputer, with a major difference. Unlike the other systems that typically use an Apple or TRS-80, the Comptreck system[22] uses a custom-designed computer, the Versat 1, which the company describes as a word processor capable of running a phototypesetter. The Versat also can be used to run business applications software, telecommunications, and multitasking and multiuser capabilities.

Comptreck claims that by using its system, CompuWriter owners can have capabilities "equal to or better than the MCS, EditWriter or Comp/Edit systems."

[20]Information Design
P.O. Box 68
Hillsboro, OR 97123
(503) 649-4975

[21]Robert J. Sehnert & Associates
1644 S. Garden Street
Palatine, IL 60067
(312) 359-5793

[22]Comptreck
4115 Jackson Road
Ann Arbor, MI 48103

EDITERM 90
Radio Shack-to-Typesetter Interfaces

The Editerm 90 system[23] uses the Radio Shack TRS-80 (unmodified) with special interfaces to drive the Compugraphic 8600, Editwriter 75/7700, and the Linotype VIP, Linoscreen 7000, Mycrotek, Omnitek, CRTronic, and the Linotron 202. The Editerm 90 features full editing capabilities, large video screen, disk storage, optional hardcopy printer, telephone communications, and paper tape to disk coversion.

Keyboarding is simplified by use of the Universal Translation Program (UTP), which is a code-substitution table that allows the user to avoid learning cumbersome typesetting codes. Any operator can simplify input coding by not having to key typeset codes in the data file. Anywhere a machine command or repetitive blocks of copy are required an operator simply types target strings (a mnemonic designator such as **, +a, or /bd/,) of up to four characters in length.

The standard program will accept up to 99 translation strings, which are stored on disk. Before the data files created by the operator are output to the typesetter, the formats are called from disk and loaded into the terminal's memory. As the data file is sent to the typesetter, the UTP automatically and instantly substitutes the entire format (up to 254 characters) for the four-letter callout.

Systems can be configured in a variety of ways. A system to drive the VIP, for example, would consist of a microcomputer, monitor, keyboard, two disk drives, typesetter driver software and hardware, interface cable, Bell Code error checking, and Bell Code suppression software for output to a printer.

SPECIALIZED SUPPORT HARDWARE

SWITCH & MUX
Specialized System Apparatus

The Switch & Mux[24] Company makes an entire line of products, some which make it possible to connect multiple personal computers (up to eight) to a phototypesetter (or a printer) via a single modem.

Serial 2 to 1. This is a manual switch box used to connect two personal computers to a serial device such as a modem, printer, or typesetter.

Serial 5 to 1. This is a manual switch box used to connect five personal computers to a serial device.

System Expander. This is an automatic multiplexer used to connect eight serial devices to one. It has a unique printing feature that allows the transmitting devices to run a serial printer at the same time they are sending data to a system, modem, or typesetter. It is compatible with the Compugraphic 8600 and others that have serial capability.

Parallel 2 to 1. A manual switch box used to connect two personal computers to a single printer, it is compatible with the Centronics, Okidata, NEC, and Epson printers.

Serial Automux. This is an automatic multiplexer used to link two personal computers to a serial printer automatically.

Converter I. This device connects a personal computer directly to a Compugraphic 8600, Videosetter, Unisetter, or Universal.

Model 1004. This manual switch box is used to connect three systems to a Compugraphic Videosetter, Unisetter, or Universal. It is compatible with the Converter I.

Model 1005. This manual switch box is used to connect three systems to a Compugraphic 8600 typesetter. It is compatible with the Converter I.

The Splitter. These newswire serial modems can drive eight systems simultaneously. The Splitter has a unique port that allows channel #1 to communicate with an Associated Press Electronic Carbon modem.

">[23]Marcus Computer Services Inc.
   243 Riverside Drive
   Suite 1002
   New York, NY 10025
   (212) 678-0406

[24]Switch & Mux, Inc.
   10 Oakridge Avenue
   Merrimack, NH 03054
   (603) 424-4161

Chapter 13

Typesetting Decisions

Bringing typesetting operations in-house.

MAJOR CONSIDERATIONS

Armed with the conviction that phototypesetting is the logical output alternative for some, all, or most files created on your microcomputer system, sooner or later you will be faced with these two major decisions:

- At what point do I know if I have enough typesetting work to support my own typesetting equipment?
- Should I invest in my own typesetting equipment? If so, should I buy new or used equipment?

The answer to the first question cannot be derived easily from a simple formula, although there have been a number of "rules of thumb" presented over the years which suggest that when the value of outside purchases reaches x dollars per month it is time to bring typesetting production in-house. Regardless of what this magic figure might be, the decision to establish typesetting internally for personal or business publishing is very much tied to other considerations, some of which have been briefly mentioned earlier in this book.

Control. One of the most significant advantages of having a captive typesetting operation is the benefit of having immediate access and direct control over all aspects of its production. The setting of priorities and the scheduling of jobs are totally under the control of a single dedicated user or a small group of users with a single common objective.

Turnaround Time. Even when dealing with a good outside typesetting service supplying excellent delivery, the user must deal with a time factor in getting data to the service (either electronically or physically) and getting it back again (either by mail or by messenger). The availability of a captive typesetting system enables immediate response and processing. For certain categories of work, these abilities can eliminate hours or days of waiting.

Confidentiality. When data is sent to an outside typesetting service, there is no way to ensure absolute security. When the job is typeset in-house, the people who process it are the people who wrote and produced it. The job does not leave the confines of its creative environment. Although trade typesetters abide by a code of ethics and are professional in their handling of clients' work, it is almost impossible not to have workers examining the job during the normal course of processing. For most categories of work, this situation might be of no real significance; however, in those cases where it is, this factor alone can be persuasive enough to justify a captive typesetting system.

Alteration Cycles. The nature of the data in question might be such that the data is subject to frequent changes prior to final typesetting. Typesetting services charge a penalty for author's alterations made following the first typesetting pass. Not only does each successive pass add to the cost of the job, sending it back and forth adds to the time necessary to produce it.

Redundant Labor. Some typesetting services build in a labor factor for proofreading and for making a final check of typographic coding and stylistic formatting. This function is usually compatible with the job of content and form editing performed internally.

Convenience. Having a typesetting system on standby, ready to perform, is a convenience that cannot be quantified easily. It makes deadlines easier to live with and easier to attain. It makes last-minute changes and alterations easier to accommodate and produce. Also, perhaps most importantly of all, it encourages, rather than deters, users from making necessary changes which, under other production circumstances, would be "too much trouble" or too time-consuming.

METHODOLOGY

Given that the reasons to purchase a typesetting system are rational and are justifiable in terms of cost, the second set of decisions deals with the question of how a system should be acquired. There is no single answer to this question, only suggested strategies and guidelines, which deal mainly with coming to understand exactly what your typesetting needs are (and will be in the foreseeable future) and what equipment is available to meet those needs.

The methodology that follows was used first in the book *How to Build a Basic Typesetting System,*[1] and is presented in an abridged form. It is a logical approach to analyzing and specifying typesetting needs for virtually any kind of installation. Some steps can be skipped, depending upon the complexity of the system being contemplated, as well as the size and sophistication of the organization considering it.

Step 1: Planning

A successful project begins with thoughtful planning. There are 15 elements in this plan, each of which will need to be quantified in terms of estimated time.

- *Investigating System Options*—This step involves becoming familiar with the elements that comprise a typesetting system, their functions, and their relationships with other parts of the system. This step includes a study of major vendor product lines.
- *Evaluating Equipment Compatibility*—This step involves determining how the typesetting equipment will interrelate with computer elements presently in place.
- *Defining System Requirements*—This step involves specifying the exact components that comprise the microtypesetting system. A diagram should be generated to show how each element relates to another, and also to indicate which elements already exist and which need to be purchased.
- *Gaining Management Approval*—The previous steps are usually sufficient to generate a project proposal worthy of presentation to upper management, fellow associates, or merely to satisfy your own personal needs.
- *Developing the Project*—Following approval by the appropriate sanctioning body, the typesetting research project is specified, which usually will consist of an organizational and departmental needs analysis. The Typesetting Needs Analysis will include a listing of departments or organizational units, job descriptions of currently produced work, listings of current typesetting costs for such work, the frequency of revision, the percent of revision, and whether or not it is likely that the job can be produced in-house. The design should support the quantification of data for easy data analysis.
- *Gathering Data*—This step involves the actual collection of data according to the criteria listed in the last step. It may consist of an historical analysis of previously typeset jobs, a current compilation as jobs are presently generated, or a combination of both. Regardless of how it is executed, it must present a clear picture of the characteristics of the kinds of jobs that are being typeset.
- *Analyzing Data*—A study of the data should lead to a set of conclusions as to the nature of the typesetting needs of the organization or individual. These needs should be prioritized in terms of their relative importance.

[1]Michael L. Kleper
© 1979, Graphic Dimensions
8 Frederick Road
Pittsford, NY 14534

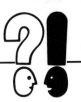

- *Invoking the Decision-Making Process*—The study, along with the preliminary investigation, should provide sufficient information to generate a series of recommendations concerning the optimum typesetting system configuration.
- *Reporting to Management*—The recommendations (system architecture, functionality, projected expense/savings, etc.) are presented to the decision-making body for analysis, discussion, and approval.
- *Searching for Employees/Interviewing*—Depending upon the size and complexity of the anticipated typesetting system, it may be necessary to hire new employees. The human resource is critical for a well-run, efficient, and profitable typesetting operation. This process should be conducted with extreme care and careful consideration.
- *Planning the Preinstallation*—Floor plans should be drawn and discussions with contractors undertaken.
- *Preparing the Site*—The site must be adequately prepared in terms of electrical, plumbing (for the processor), if necessary and environmental (temperature, relative humidity control) factors. Likewise, work surfaces, seating, lighting, storage, and other ergonomic considerations must be well-planned.
- *Installing the System*—Equipment is properly located, set up, and tested. All connections with local and remote microcomputers, word processors, terminals, etc. are thoroughly tested. A burn-in period is conducted while the vendor representative is on-site.
- *Training*—All staff who will use the system are presented with hands-on training using sample jobs that are representative of those commonly produced.
- *Breaking-in the System*—A user log is maintained during the warranty period (and preferably beyond) listing all of the problems, mishaps, and unexplained occurrences that befall the system.

Step 2: Operation

The addition of phototypesetting capabilities to a microcomputer system requires a number of procedural changes, which, taken together, will have a direct impact on the entire system of text preparation. Even when the use of phototypesetting is considered as an internal service, rather than as an outside business, it is necessary to pay attention to these areas:

- *Ordering Materials and Supplies*—It is the nature of photographic materials that they have a limited shelf life, and that they work best when used before their expiration date. Stock rotation, proper storage (in a controlled environment), and inventory rotation procedures are necessary components of even a superficial quality-control program.
- *Maintaining the System*—The proper functioning of the typesetting system is a concern from day one. A method of providing prompt service, be it a service contract or use of vendor or independent service contractors, must be determined from the very beginning. A service log should be kept, indicating the date, symptoms, and remedy for each service call. By keeping adequate records, recurring and associated problems can be identified. Likewise, uncomplicated servicing can be performed in-house after the proper servicing procedures have been recorded.

Some vendors offer spare parts kits for various models of their phototypesetters. These kits include a selection of the most vulnerable parts of the system, and are generally good insurance against expensive downtime. Some parts, such as IC chips, motors, filters, etc., are available from normal supply channels, the critical factor being absolute identification of the part in question. Vendors usually renumber parts with their own part number, making identification (cross-referencing) difficult or impossible. Some vendors have been known to supply cross-referencing information along with their spare parts kits. Other sources of such information generally come from other users or from organized user groups.

- *Managing Files*—Keeping track of the location and status of each job file is of obvious importance. It requires care in establishing a procedure whereby each job is properly identified as to whether or not it has been edited, proofed, hyphenated and/or justified (prior to typesetting in some systems), embedded with typesetting codes, and approved for typesetting, as well as has completed one or more passes through the typesetter and achieved archival status.

- *Record Keeping*—Getting the best results from a typesetting system is closely related to understanding exactly how well the system is functioning. Areas of concern include a measure of total system uptime; categorical service, coding, operator, or material problems; throughput measurements in terms of total characters, average processing time, etc.; the tracking and determination of cause of textual output errors; the productivity levels of individual operators; a comparison of the actual ratio to the optimum ratio of input keyboards to the phototypesetter; a measure of material consumption; and a cross-index of computer file names and typesetter file names.

- *Housekeeping*—Typesetting systems are very prone to contamination by dust and dirt. Since most phototypesetters use some sort of optical system in order to form characters, any foreign matter that crosses the optical path will cause a degradation in the quality of the output. This decrease in quality is usually a very gradual process, and the inexperienced user might not even notice that it has occurred until he compares a current output sample to one produced when the system was set up. This problem can be reduced by having adequate air filtration equipment in the environment, as well as by following a regular schedule of typesetter air filter changes. When using second-generation phototypesetters, the image masters (film strips, grids, disks, or wedges) can be cleaned using approved anhydrous cleaners, lint-free wipes, and great care following a prescribed procedure.

- *Controlling Quality*—Maintaining consistent quality output is of prime importance. The characters the typesetting system produces must remain sharp, dense (in contrast), and precisely aligned. It is beyond the scope of this book to suggest how to set up a full quality-control system, yet some formalized quality control must be implemented. Any quality-control system has, as its objective, maintaining consistent output as measured against a standard. The standard is usually an output sample that had been generated when the system was new and tuned by the service engineer to account for all variables in the environment (electronic, electrical, mechanical, chemical, and physical). Maintaining quality might be as simple as making an optical comparison between the standard and current output samples. The two can be compared side by side, or, as is more common, a square can be cut out of the center of the "standard," forming a window in which the current sample can be viewed.

More complex procedures utilize densitometric measurements, which are precise readings of the density of the black-silver images on the photographic paper, and high-power magnification devices, which aid in seeing changes in the formation of character shapes. Regardless of how it is monitored, some quality-control procedure must be used on a regular basis. This need can become very obvious, as when a large job produced 6 months previously requires minor changes, and the weight of the same characters produced today does not match

those produced originally. Keep in mind that quality-control procedures can suggest that the system has somehow changed; however, determining what has happened and how it can be corrected, might be beyond the deductive capabilities of the system operator.

- *Storing Output*—The ultimate use of phototypesetter output is usually as part of a paste-up or mechanical, which will undergo various photomechanical operations before appearing on the printed page. Since few phototypesetters are capable of complete page assembly, which would include artwork, photographs, borders, background tints, etc., these additional elements must be added manually. This process appreciably adds to the cost of producing typeset pages, and it is therefore advantageous to maintain these assembled components in storage should they be needed again in the future.

  There are four basic considerations to keep in mind when devising a storage (and retrieval) system. First, how will jobs be labeled for quick and easy identification? Second, what kind of cabinetry or storage furniture will provide the best protection and easiest access? Third, what particular selection of materials will best withstand the passage of time? Fourth, what atmospheric conditions will prolong the life of stored materials?

  To briefly answer each of these questions, first, a job envelope containing the parts of the job should be labeled by whatever naming convention has been adopted for file management or job tracking. Job envelopes are usually preprinted with specific production information as well. Large, empty, rigid graphic arts film boxes are frequently used in addition to job envelopes, or sometimes in place of them. Second, the envelopes are best stored flat; therefore, the furniture should provide multiple shallow drawers or shelves. Third, certain kinds of phototypesetting papers, called *stabilization,* have limited image lives. Long-term storage (beyond 6 months) of such processed paper is often futile, as it routinely will fade or discolor. Resin-coated papers or reproduction copies (photostats or photomechanical transfer sheets) provide the longest lasting images. Wax has been shown to be a good adhesive for archival storage. When properly applied and stored, it retains its tack and slideability characteristics. Fourth, the storage environment should be cool, dry, and softly lit. The storage area should be away from direct contact with heat vents, steam pipes, windows, sinks, etc.

- *Proofing*—The quality of the output from a phototypesetter is not only measured in terms of its physical conformance with a prescribed appearance standard, but also by the accuracy of its form and content. Typographical errors (typically misspellings) and typographical coding errors (such as failure to change point size or line spacing) easily can be the cause of multiple passes through the phototypesetter. A means of eliminating, or at least reducing, these errors is by using "proofing" procedures prior to entering the typesetting cycle. Proofing might be as simple as generating a line printer copy of the file for proofreading, or, depending upon the sophistication of the system, might consist of a soft display (preview) of the job as it will appear when typeset (FIG. 1). In any event, the purpose of the proofing step is to catch errors before they are typeset. In those cases where the author is self-publishing and self-typesetting, another individual should be employed to do the proofreading.

- *Considering Author's Alterations*[2]—There seems to be some dynamic force that compels authors to change copy once they see it in typeset form. It might be that the author realizes that his words have reached their ultimate and final form, or perhaps, the passage of time has created some new thoughts and altered some old ones. Regardless, author's alterations (A.A.s) are a certain part of the typesetting process. Even if the typesetting system can deliver an accurate and timely

[2]Taken from Michael L. Kleper
How To Build A BASIC Typesetting System
Rochester, NY (1979)

product, there is absolutely no guarantee that external forces will not react adversely and return the product for massive revision. Knowledge of these possibilities suggests that a well-planned phototypesetting system must make adequate allowance for frequent revisions.

FIG. 1. The soft display preview screens used as part of many phototypesetting systems can save many passes through the phototypesetter output unit. This display, shown with the Linotype Linotronic 300 laser typesetter, is the Typeview 300 (Courtesy of The Linotype Company).

Chapter 14

Typesetting Business Applications

Personal computer programs for the efficient operation of a typesetting operation.

DETERMINING TYPESETTING COSTS

Any business, whether it exists to provide typesetting services to others or to provide them to itself in the process of performing services or making a product, must know its true costs in order to effectively compete and efficiently perform. Budgeted hourly cost systems, such as those promoted by the Printing Industries of America (PIA), National Association of Printers and Lithographers (NAPL), and many graphic arts consultants, give managers a valid approach to distributing overhead expenses on a prorated basis to each cost center. These systems are very helpful in providing management with information that can be useful in making decisions relative to product mix, manufacture versus purchase, equipment purchase, expansion or retrenchment, and, ultimately, the prices to charge (or charge back).

Budgeted Hourly Costs. A computer program for the IBM PC, which was written in part by a trade typographer, addresses the problems of cost, not only for typesetting, but also for all aspects of a graphic arts operation. The Budgeted Hourly Costs for the Graphic Arts Industry software from Target Associates, Inc.[1] is a menu-driven program that accurately takes all costs into account for operations of up to 40 cost centers and 100 employees.

The program is designed to make the best use of the IBM function keys, with particular options chosen by using one of those keys. The Main menu presents the following choices:

BUDGETED HOURLY COSTS		FUNCTION KEYS
	<F1>	GENERAL COMPANY INFORMATION
	<F2>	EMPLOYEE PAYROLL INFORMATION
WHICH SECTION WOULD YOU LIKE	<F3>	COST CENTER INFORMATION
TO ACCESS? PRESS <F>UNCTION KEY	<F9>	ANALYZE DATA & PRINT OVERALL REPORTS
	<F10>	QUIT PROGRAM

In order for the program to provide meaningful information, the user must input numerous details concerning the company's costs (FIG. 1). These items enumerate such things as rent, insurance, utilities, and advertising.

The factors associated with employees, such as their names, the number of hours they work, the type of labor (direct or indirect), and the division of their time among the various cost centers, are input within the Employee Payroll Information section. Employees, like cost centers, are identified by number and verified by the program by name.

Defining a cost center requires the exact specification of the premises and equipment, the utilities usage, the average production statistics, and the employee assignments. The cost center information verification for a typesetting operation is shown in FIG. 2.

[1]Target Associates, Inc.
461 Park Avenue South
New York, NY 10016
(212) 889-2464

After all financial and production data has been input, the program analyzes it and produces any or all of the following reports:

- Employee distribution of labor
- All-inclusive cost-center allocations for all cost centers
- All-inclusive cost-center allocations for one cost center
- Direct/indirect dollar allocations for all cost centers (company totals)
- Direct/indirect dollar allocations summary by cost center

FIG. 1. The information profile of a company includes specific items in the general categories of premises, utilities, insurance, non-production, and vehicle costs.

```
******************************
    GENERAL COMPANY INFORMATION
           VERIFICATION
******************************


PREMISES INFORMATION

ANNUAL RENT.......................................    9600.00
TOTAL SQUARE FEET.................................    1100.00
MORTGAGE/LOAN $...................................       0.00
REAL ESTATE/OCCUP TAX.............................       0.00


UTILITIES

ANNUAL ELECTRICITY................................    3000.00
COST PER KWH......................................       0.0500
HEAT/AIR CONDITIONING.............................       0.00
OTHER.............................................     100.00


INSURANCE

FIRE INSURANCE....................................     325.00
CONTENT INSURANCE.................................     630.00
CONTENT INS RATE/$1000............................       2.75
OTHER.............................................       0.00


NON-PRODUCTION ITEMS

DEPREC/FIXED ASSET & LEASE $......................     255.00
REPAIRS/SVC CONTRACT $............................     100.00
TELEPHONE.........................................    2400.00
SALES COSTS.......................................    5000.00
ADVERTISING/PROMOTION.............................    1500.00
OFFICE SUPPLIES/EXPENSES..........................     600.00
MAINTENANCE/CLEANING..............................     210.00
OTHER.............................................       0.00
BAD DEBT EXPENSE..................................    4200.00


VEHICLE COSTS

DEPRECIATION/LEASE $..............................    4800.00
MAINTENANCE/UPKEEP................................    1200.00
```

The Employee Distribution of Labor report lists all of the employees and their fractional allocation of time, both in terms of the cost centers in which they function, and the type of labor they perform (and the extent to which they perform it).

The All Inclusive Cost Center Allocation report breaks down the expense into various categories and distributes it among the various individual cost centers (FIG. 3). This report thus provides an overall picture of how a single cost center carries the burden of fixed company expenses.

The Direct/Indirect Dollar Allocation Summary by Cost Center report lists the cost per hour for each cost center. These are, perhaps, the most meaningful figures, since they are the basis for setting the prices that will be quoted to customers.

By adjusting any of the costs, such as adding or deleting employees or entire cost centers, it is possible to input a number of various management scenarios without the risk of actual implementation. This "what if" capability can provide a powerful tool for aggressive, innovative management.

FIG. 2. A cost center is defined according to how it accounts for its share of company expenses.

```
*******************************************
        COST CENTER INFORMATION VERIFICATION

              COST CENTER NO.   3
                 TYPESETTING
*******************************************

NAME...................................... TYPESETTING

PREMISES AND EQUIPMENT
# SQUARE FEET..............................     700.00
REPLACEMENT VALUE/EQUIPMENT................   35000.00
DIRECT SUPPLIES/EXPENSES...................   29000.00
DEPRECIATION COST/EQUIP....................    6000.00
LEASE/LOAN $...............................       0.00
SVC CONTRACT/REPAIR $......................    1500.00


ELECTRICITY
# HP/MOTORS................................       0.00
# WATTS/OTHER..............................       3.80

PRODUCTION INFORMATION
# PRODUCTION UNITS.........................       2.00
PRODUCTION HOURS AVAIL.....................    1670.00
EST % SALEABLE PRODUCTION HRS..............      80.00
TOTAL # EMPLOYEES..........................       2.00

EMPLOYEE # 1
  SOLOMON, D.
  % TIME THIS COST CNTR..... 100
EMPLOYEE # 2
  BROWN, M.
  % TIME THIS COST CNTR..... 100
```

```
****************************************
ALL INCLUSIVE COST CENTER ALLOCATIONS
          COST CENTER NO.  3
              TYPESETTING
****************************************
```

	DIRECT COST	INDIRECT COST	TOTAL COST
RENT/PREMISES	6109.09	-1359.97	4749.12
UTILITIES	0.25	1339.63	1339.88
INSURANCE	96.25	215.51	311.76
LABOR	26253.09	19233.69	45486.78
MACHINERY, EQUIPMENT & SUPPLIES	36500.00	0.00	36500.00
NON-PRODUCTION CATEGORIES & VEHICLE(S)	0.00	10092.46	10092.46
TOTALS	68958.69	29521.31	98480.00

```
================================================
  1336.00  TOTAL PRODUCTION HOURS (ADJUSTED)
    73.71  COST OF OPERATION PER HOUR/ENTIRE COST CENTER
    36.86  COST OF OPERATION PER HOUR PER PRODUCTION UNIT
================================================
```

FIG. 3. The cost center report shows how its particular expenses are computed to reach a production-per-hour cost rate.

BILLING FOR TYPESETTING AND RELATED SERVICES

A typesetting operation is a business. Whether it exists to serve many clients, a few clients, a single organization, or a single individual, it must justify its existence according to some measure of economic worth. The value of the products (typeset galleys, custom typography, display typesetting, paste-ups, mechanicals, etc.) and services (designing, editing, proofreading, etc.) provided by a typesetter must be estimated accurately in order to establish a reasonable and competitive pricing structure.

It is the nature of the typesetting process, as a manufacturing operation, that every job is custom-made. There can be no standing inventory of typeset jobs waiting for customers, no generic typeset job that will suit a variety of needs. Because every job is different and produced to order, no job can be produced until an estimate of its production cost can be generated. A good estimating system is crucial to the survival of a typesetting operation in a highly competitive marketplace.

Typebill. Computerized estimating systems also do not exist in pure, generic forms. Estimating is a very personalized process, reflecting the complex ways in which individuals and management teams run their companies. Many variables come to play in determining costs and establishing pricing. A company must account accurately for such things as the cost of equipment, materials, and supplies; salaries, wages, bonuses, and benefits; heat, light, water, and rent; administrative and sales support; maintenance, repair, and replacement; transportation and delivery; advertising and promotion; entertainment and hospitality; and so on. Adapting an off-the-shelf estimating program to function in concert with the intricacies of a particular typesetting operation is often difficult, and sometimes totally impossible.

The observation that every estimating system requires customization has led to a unique experiment on the part of The National Composition Association,[2] a division of the Printing Industries of America. The National Composition Association distributes a massive estimating system written by Professor William Birkett of the Rochester Institute of Technology. For a modest reproduction fee, the buyer receives the program, which is composed of multiple disks (or printed program listings), for either Apple II CP/M or the IBM PC. The program is a full-fledged operating estimating system, incorporating all phases of printing production. The real costs are incurred if, and when, the buyer decides to have the program customized to suit his individual needs.

Understanding costs is the first step to the profitable operation of a typesetting installation. Monitoring costs and restructuring the pricing schedule to reflect changes are ongoing activities that ultimately result in a profit or a loss for the business. In this realm, microcomputers are very helpful in tracking day-to-day operations and in developing a picture of how daily transactions have an impact on profitability.

A program written specifically for the production of typographic service invoicing and business activity reporting, is Typebill[3] for the Apple II family of microcomputers. Typebill is a menu-driven program that batch-processes invoices, and records and computes jobs according to job classifications useful to shop management.

In a normal work session, the user is presented first with the Main menu (FIG. 4). Initial setup of the program consists of inputting information about pricing, invoice numbering, taxables, and the invoicing period (FIG. 5). The hourly rates and flat prices only need to be input when the program is first run, or as changes arise (FIG. 6).

To input billing information for a customer, his account first must be set up. This process is accomplished by selecting menu choice 6, "Edit Customer File" (FIG. 7). From the Customer File menu, customers can be added, deleted, or listed on the printer. Only basic information is required to establish the customer account (FIG. 8), after which each customer is identified by his customer number.

[2]The National Composition Association
  1730 North Lynn Street
  Arlington, VA 22209
  (703) 527-6000

[3]Typographic Consultation Service
  360 East 72nd Street
  New York, NY 10021
  (212) 221-6273
  (212) 734-6285

Returning to the Main menu (FIG. 4), the user has the option (Number 2) of using the program as a typographic pricing calculator, with none of the transactions recorded, or actually entering live data into a customer's data file (Number 1). Selecting option 1 prompts the operator for the customer number (FIG. 9). If the number has been recorded previously, the name of the customer is displayed on the screen. The user then is presented with prompts that describe the identity and nature of the work performed. After this information has been completed, the calculation portion of the program is presented. This screen (FIG. 10) is the same one that is displayed when option 2 is selected.

```
            PROGRAM MENU

    <1> CALCULATE & PRINT INVOICES

    <2> ESTIMATE/CALCULATE ONLY

    <3> CONFIGURE

    <4> GENERATE REPORTS

    <5> MAKE DISK BACK-UP COPY

    <6> EDIT CUSTOMER FILE

    <7> END PROGRAM
```

FIG. 4. The Typebill Main menu provides a listing of the main features of the program. The documentation suggests many ways the user can extend the functionality of the program to suit specific needs.

```
    ENTER THE NUMBER OF YOUR
    CHOICE AND PRESS 'RETURN':   2
```

```
            CONFIGURE

    <1> RATES/PRICES

    <2> INVOICE NUMBERING & FORM STYLE

    <3> TAXABLES

    <4> RESET FOR NEW MONTH

    <5> RESET FOR NEW FISCAL YEAR

    <6> END CONFIGURE

        ENTER THE NUMBER OF YOUR

        CHOICE AND PRESS 'RETURN'
```

FIG. 5. The Configuration menu is used to input new pricing or calendar information.

On the Calculation screen, the user is prompted for the original number of hours and the additional author's alterations necessary for completing the text and display composition, and the mechanical art. Flat charges for proofing, creative services, shipping, and performing additional services also are added. When the user verifies that all entries are correct, the bottom line of totals is computed instantly.

After each invoice is computed, the user is prompted for the input of another invoice. After all invoices for the session have been completed, the batch is printed. Either plain paper (FIG. 11), or custom forms, available from Typographic Consultation Service, can be used. In either case, the invoices fold to fit a standard business window envelope.

FIG. 6. The pricing schedule is updated easily at any time. Costs not listed here can be entered manually on each invoice.

```
            CURRENT RATES/PRICES


    <1> TEXT COMPOSITION:    33.00

    <2> MECHANICAL ART:      20.49

    <3> PROOFS (A):           7.75

    <4> PROOFS (B):           0.00

    <5> PROOFS (C):           0.00

    <6> DATE CHANGED: JULY 20, 1985



ENTER NUMBER OF ITEM TO CHANGE
ENTER 'O' IF ALL CORRECT         ?
```

FIG. 7. The Customer File menu provides access to the Customer database.

```
            CUSTOMER FILE


        <1> ADD CUSTOMER

        <2> CHANGE CUSTOMER

        <3> RETURN TO MAIN MENU

        <4> PRINT CUSTOMER LIST

        <5> END PROGRAM


ENTER THE NUMBER OF YOUR CHOICE
AND PRESS 'RETURN':
```

At any time reports can be generated to show either month-to-date or year-to-date sales summaries or sales analyses. The Sales Summary report (FIG. 12) shows the sales activity from different customer classifications, and in various categories of work. The determination of the classifications are totally the decision of the user. The Typebill documentation suggests classifications such as ad agencies, art studios, printers, and publishers. Sales categories are used to indicate which of up to six sales personnel is responsible for the sale.

The Sales Analysis report (FIG. 13) shows, both in dollars and as a percentage of the total, which area of activity has generated the most income.

```
NEW CUSTOMER NUMBER: 3

  NAME: Tried & True Software

  ATTN: Paul Oslow

  ADDR: 20433 Plymouth Highway

  CITY: Riverton

STATE: MA     ZIP: 01677

TAX RATE: 7.25

P.O. REQUIRED (Y/N)? Y

TELEPHONE NO. 454-3200

ALL CORRECT (Y/N)?                    Y
```

FIG. 8. Establishing a customer on the system is quick and easy, since only the essential information is required.

```
ENTER CUSTOMER NUMBER: 3
CUSTOMER: Tried & True Software

INVOICE DATE

  MONTH: FEBRUARY     DAY: 16


CUSTOMER P.O./JOB NUMBER: 86-1503

JOB TITLE: MORRIS BOOK

TYPE SHOP JOB #: 40-311

CLASSIFICATION CODE: A5

  ALL CORRECT (Y/N)?                  Y
```

FIG. 9. Entering information for the production of an invoice begins with the identification of the customer by number. It is followed by information that identifies the job both to the customer and for internal accounting.

Both of these reports provide a good picture of the production generated by the typesetting system. Other helpful information that would be of use in operating a typesetting facility is not provided by Typebill. For example, a conscientious manager also would be interested in knowing:

- The productivity of individual operators in terms of chargeable hours, number of keystrokes, number of jobs completed, etc.
- The productivity of individual typesetting machines in terms of hours in use against total capacity.
- The consumption of materials on a per job basis, and as a monthly total.
- The straight time and overtime totals for individual operators and individual jobs, and collectively for all operators and all jobs.
- The derivation of input for typesetting—from dedicated keyboards, from word processors, from microcomputers, etc.
- The method by which input reaches typesetting—on-line keyboarding, compatible media, media translation, telecommunication, etc.
- An analysis of estimated time versus actual production time.
- An analysis of the profitability of certain categories of work—straight text, tabular, runarounds, display, etc.

FIG. 10. The calculation portion of the program computes the invoice totals in real time.

```
TEXT COMPOSITION        MECHANICAL ART
OR:52.3    AA:14.2      OR:21.9   AA:3.4

DISPLAY                 PROOFS  (A)
OR:7.6     AA:1.2       OR:8.4    AA:2.2

PROOFS  (B)             PROOFS  (C)
OR:        AA:          OR:       AA:

CREATIVE SERVICES       SHIPPING CHARGES
>>>   248.00            >>>   45.00

OTHER SERVICES  (1)     OTHER SERVICES  (2)
>>>   175.00            >>>
------------------------------------------
INVOICE LEGEND FOR OTHER SERVICES:
1. COVER DESIGN

2.
==========================================
S/TOT 3271.84   TX 159.73    TOT 3431.57

ALL CORRECT (Y/N)?   Y
```

FIG. 11. The actual invoice reflects all of the information previously keyboarded. Notice that invoice items need not be restricted to typesetting and related charges. Subsequent operations, such as printing, binding, etc., may be included also, as might preceding operations, such as editorial assistance, job planning, etc.

```
                                                I N V O I C E


        FIRST AVENUE DESIGNERS                    FEBRUARY 5, 1984
        ATTN: FREDDY FURST
        111 FIRST AVENUE                          ACCT #: 1
        NEW YORK, NY 10111



        JOB TITLE: BOOKLETS

        OUR JOB NO. 10011         YOUR JOB/P.O. NO. 123/ABCD
  =================================================================


     TEXT COMPOSITION                            ORIGINAL       220.25
                                                 REVISIONS       61.67


     DISPLAY HEADLINE SETTING                    ORIGINAL        32.75
                                                 REVISIONS       11.50


     MECHANICAL ARTWORK                          ORIGINAL       299.52
                                                 REVISIONS       68.64


     REPRODUCTION AND/OR READING PROOFS          ORIGINAL        88.76
                                                 REVISIONS       16.02


     CREATIVE: LAYOUT, TYPE SPEC, ILLUSTRATION, ETC.            135.00


     PRINTING PER ESTIMATE                                      129.80


     ADDITIONAL HALFTONE                                         19.75


     DELIVERY AND/OR SHIPPING & HANDLING                         22.20



                                              SUB-TOTAL        1105.86

                                              SALES TAX          65.24

     INVOICE NO.                                 TOTAL         1171.10
        3001
```

FIG. 12. The Sales Summary report may be generated for either month-to-month or year-to-year.

```
                                      YEAR TO DATE AS OF FEBRUARY 8


        SALES  SUMMARY  REPORT



     CUSTOMER CLASS
                                         DOLLARS    PERCENT
                                         ----------  -------
           GROUP 'A'                     1920.72     54.90
           GROUP 'B'                     1295.07     37.00
           GROUP 'C'                        0.00      0.00
           GROUP 'D'                      280.32      8.00
                                         ----------  -------
              SUB-TOTAL                   3496.11    100.00
                                         ----------
              SALES TAX                    120.77
                                         ==========
                 TOTAL                    3616.88



     SALES CATEGORIES

           CATEGORY 1                     921.58     26.30
           CATEGORY 2                     339.39      9.70
           CATEGORY 3                    1129.28     32.30
           CATEGORY 4                       0.00      0.00
           CATEGORY 5                       0.00      0.00
           CATEGORY 6                    1105.86     31.60
                                         ----------  -------
              SUB-TOTAL                   3496.11    100.00
                                         ----------
              SALES TAX                    120.77
                                         ==========
                 TOTAL                    3616.88


     -------------------------------------------------------

     7 JOBS BILLED      /    AVG. INVOICE: $499.44 (W/O TAX)
```

FIG. 13. The Sales Analysis report provides an overview of the revenues generated by each component of production.

```
                    MONTH TO DATE AS OF FEBRUARY 8


        SALES  ANALYSIS



   SALES IN DOLLARS


        TEXT COMPOSITION              458.12         29.40%
        DISPLAY COMPOSITION            89.60          5.70%
                                    ------------     -------
             COMP SUB-TOTAL:         547.72         35.10%

   MECHANICAL ART                    511.68         32.80%

   PROOFS-- 'A' & 'B'                122.90          7.80%
   PROOFS-- 'C'                       13.92           .8%
                                    ------------     -------
           PROOFS SUB-TOTAL:         136.82          8.70%

   CREATIVE SERVICES                 135.00          8.60%

   OTHER SERVICES (1)                172.60         11.00%

   OTHER SERVICES (2)                 19.75          1.20%

   SHIPPING CHARGES                   33.90          2.10%

                                    ==========      ======
                 TOTAL:             1557.47         100.00


   UNIT SALES


        TEXT COMPOSITION HOURS          5.2

        MECHANICAL ART HOURS            8.2

        PROOFS-- 'A'                   10

        PROOFS-- 'B'                    4

        PROOFS-- 'C'                   12
```

Chapter 15

Desktop Publishing and Typesetting User Applications

Successful uses of personal computer typesetting technology.

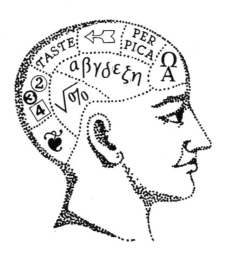

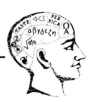

APPLICATIONS USING
A COMPUTER-TO-TYPESETTER INTERFACE

A trade organization uses their interface to typeset name badges for a convention using a report feature of their microcomputer database program. The report is passed through the interface to the typesetter.

A college produces its student newspaper using their interface and multiple microcomputers.

A university newspaper uses its interface to typeset news gathered from computer terminals connected by a campus-wide network.

A college uses its interface to provide typesetting training to hundreds of students through remote input. From dormitories, the library, the computer center, or any terminal or microcomputer able to access the network, students produce typesetting jobs which completely control the full range of commands, characters, and media entry available on the typesetter.

A directory publisher gathers entries from numerous part-time cottage laborers through telecommunications, merges them in his database, and then uses his interface to typeset multiple variations of the database information.

A quick printer accepts over-the-counter submission of diskettes for processing on his compatible microcomputer. He adds all necessary typesetting codes and then sends the files, through his interface, to his typesetter.

A word processing service offers its customers the alternative of typeset output by adding typesetting codes to files, and then sending them from the word processor through the interface to the typesetter.

A commercial printer accepts precoded manuscripts from customers. The media sometimes needs to be converted to a format readable by the printer's microcomputer. It is then processed through the interface to be typeset.

A typesetting service receives jobs via telecommunications on a dedicated microcomputer system supported by a hard disk. Communication with the system is available 24 hours a day, from anywhere in the world. Customers upload their files, some of which have typesetting codes in place, others which don't. At regular intervals the most recent jobs are written on floppy disks, carried to another computer, checked for the presence of typesetting codes, then sent, through the interface, to the typesetter. Completed jobs are mailed back to the customer.

A self-publisher prepares his manuscripts using a popular word processor, uses a companion spell-checking program, then sends his files through the interface to the typesetter.

A weekly newspaper supplies all of its reporters with portable computers. As reporters return from the field they connect their computers directly to the interface to typeset their stories.

An in-plant printer uses the organization's electronic mail system to receive files. Typesetting codes are added locally and the files are sent, through the interface, to be typeset. Completed jobs are reproduced and returned through normal internal company mail channels.

A consultant writes his monthly newsletter on his portable computer as he travels, inserts typesetting commands just prior to typesetting, and then sends his files through the interface to be typeset. He pastes-up his output and reproduces it electrostatically.

A real estate cooperative accepts listings over a dedicated computer network, channels all files to one worker who sends the daily listings, through the interface, preceded by a single line of codes which converts all output into the required format on the typesetter.

A small typesetter copes with peak production periods by providing work-at-home temporaries with portable computers. After the work has been keyboarded the media is returned to the shop where it is sent, from a dedicated microcomputer, through the interface, to be typeset.

A walk-in graphic services center provides a number of different microcomputers, switch-selectable to the interface, which users can rent at an hourly rate, paying for typesetting on a per foot basis.

A printer writes programs in BASIC to produce sequentially numbered listings for lengthy price lists. The output is sent directly through the interface for typesetting.

A free-lance graphic artist produces text and display type for clients' jobs using her portable computer, and sending the files, through the interface, to the typesetter.

A linguist publishes specialized books, using a microcomputer for text and graphics generation. Text is processed through the interface to the typesetter. Graphics are produced directly on the dot matrix printer and combined with the typeset output. The resulting mechanical art is photographically reproduced for offset duplication.

A teacher uses his school's computer lab to instruct printing students in the procedures used on create typesetting input. A computer on a cart is then wheeled into the printing lab where it is connected to the interface, and the jobs are then sent on to the typesetter.

A specialty printer prepares a run of labels using formats which he has created in his word processing program. Variable input concerning customer information is all that need be keyboarded. The batch of jobs is then sent on through the interface for typesetting.

A typesetter receives customer files which have been sent as electronic mail on an information utility computer system, which is accessible from any telephone. The jobs are downloaded from the remote computer to the typesetter's computer system. Jobs which don't have typesetting codes are appropriately edited, and then all jobs are sent, through the interface, to the typesetter.

A printer receives jobs from customers who send them directly from their computers to the printer's computer. The printer first establishes voice communication, receiving all job specifications and instructions, and then switches to modem processing. The job is then sent, through the interface, to the typesetter.

A building supply manufacturer generates product reports on their mainframe, sends them to their microcomputer, formats them for typesetting and sends them, through the interface, for typesetting. A typesetter performs editing (spell and grammar checking) as a value-added service to customers' files. The files are then sent on, through the interface, to the typesetter.

A large directory publisher takes in typewritten copy, scans it on an optical character reader (OCR), and sends the scanned data on-line, through the interface, to the typesetter.

APPLICATIONS USING MEDIA CONVERSION

A homeowner's association prepares an annual listing of its members using a database program that writes its report to disk. This disk is converted to a typesetter-compatible form, and the output is produced in the form of a member directory and reproduced in quantity.

An advertising agency keyboards clients' copy on an IBM-compatible computer and sends the disks to an out-of-town typesetting service. The disks are converted, and they and the resultant type are returned by next-day parcel delivery.

Computer magazine personnel prepare all copy using IBM PCs. They use two different typesetting services, selecting which to use on the basis of how close to deadline they are. One service converts the media into a form readable by its typesetter, while the other reads the disk directly on an IBM PC that is on-line with its typesetting system.

A small college keyboards its catalog information on a number of Apple *IIe* computers. The disks are converted by a typesetting service into a form readable by a Varityper Comp/Edit 5810.

A word processing service bureau sends a number of disks from various word processors to a typesetting service for conversion to both typesetter format, for files destined for typesetting, and to other word processing formats to make them readable by other word processing machines in the company.

A paper supply house with offices in six cities sends its word processing disks (produced on six dissimilar systems) to a typesetting service for the production of its monthly catalog. The disks are converted to one format, which is readable by the typesetter's front-end system. The files then are sorted, merged, and composed.

A designer and manufacturer of telephone systems produces its documentation on networked microcomputers. The personnel download files to disks, which are sent to a typesetting service for conversion. The output is produced in the form of microfilm for use by their field engineers.

A graphic designer keyboards client work on his CP/M system, which is equipped with 8-inch disk drives. The disks are brought to a typesetter with a VariTyper Comp/Edit, which uses the CP/M option. The information is converted on the typesetter from CP/M format to Comp/Edit readable form.

A small printer keyboards all of this customer's work on an Osborne I computer. He carries his CP/M disks to a neighboring typesetting service, where they are converted to Itek Quadritek format.

A self-publisher of children's books embeds data call codes in her files to indicate such major text divisions as chapters, headings, and liner notes. Her DEC Rainbow disks are converted to VariTyper Comp/Edit format. The embedded data call codes are converted on the typesetter into strings of typesetter commands.

A magazine writer based in South America sends his Kaypro IV disks to his publisher in New York City. His disks are edited on similar Kaypros in the New York City office and then converted in-house, directly on the Kaypro, into Compugraphic MCS disk format. The MCS disks are sent to an internal typesetting department, where they are processed on a Compugraphic MCS 8400.

A bus company produces its schedule by keyboarding the information into its Lanier word processor. Using embedded mnemonic codes, its typesetting service is able to convert the word processing media into proper format for use on the company's Mergenthaler CRTronic typesetter.

A weekly newspaper converts disks from a variety of different microcomputers, all of which use the CP/M operating system. The disks are all converted to a common format readable by the Compugraphic EditWriter 7700.

A stockbroker produces a weekly newsletter by producing text on his Radio Shack Model 2000 and then dropping off his disk at a typesetting service in the same building. The disk is converted to the Compugraphic MCS format and the type is set on the MCS 8600. The original disk and the type are returned within 24 hours.

The electronic engineering department of a large university produces the proceedings of its annual seminar program on a Xerox 820 II computer. The disks are sent to a media conversion service and returned in IBM PC format. They are then sent to the university graphic reproduction facility, where an IBM PC is connected to a VariTyper Comp/Edit 6400 typesetter via a null modem.

A multinational bank, which had annually produced its personnel manual on a Wang word processor and output it on a daisywheel printer, sends its disks to a typesetting service for conversion to a form readable by a front-end system driving a Linotype 202. The typeset version of the manual requires less than half of the paper used in the nontypeset edition.

APPLICATIONS USING TELECOMMUNICATIONS

A banquet and party house composes menus for special events on its Apple Macintosh. The type and graphics are telecommunicated to a service bureau, which reformats them as necessary and outputs them on an Apple LaserWriter. The completed menus are returned by courier within 24 hours.

A management organization for a minor league baseball team composes player profiles, team information, and game schedules on its Kaypro 4. Personnel use the built-in Kaypro modem to send the information to an out-of-town printer, who adds the necessary typesetting codes, converts the data into type, and combines it with photographs and artwork into a baseball program.

A large bookstore chain uses electronic mail to poll its stores concerning book sales. The reports are combined and edited, and a finished report is telecommunicated to a central reproduction facility, where it is formatted for laser printer output. The laser-printed pages are reproduced on a high-volume Xerographic duplicator, and distributed by hand delivery to corporate executives.

A manufacturer of electronic components uses an Epson computer to compose information regarding additions to its product line. The information is telecommunicated to the company's printer, who adds typesetting codes, sets the type, and composes pages. The pages are printed, collated, stuffed in envelopes, and since the printer maintains the mailing list for the electronics company, mailed to wholesalers and dealers.

A consulting firm for small businesses prepares all of its client reports using IBM PCs and XTs on a local area network. Completed reports are telecommunicated to a nearby quick printing shop, where they are printed out on an HP LaserJet printer, and reproduced.

A multistore computer equipment and office supply business issues a monthly newsletter composed, primarily, of editorial contributions from store managers. Each store manager uses his computer equipment (either IBM or Kaypro) to telecommunicate the information to the main office, where it is edited and formatted. The completed text is output on an HP LaserJet printer, photocopied, and distributed.

An oriental rug dealer regularly receives detailed descriptions of rare and expensive rugs that are available from members of a dealers' association. These descriptions are electronically communicated through a bulletin board system, which is located at the association's headquarters. He edits the telecommunicated information, prints it on his Apple LaserWriter, and sends notices to his customers.

A large construction company receives lengthy construction project information from its representatives in the state capital via telecommunications. The data is captured on an AT&T computer, edited, and revised into a number of versions for various subcontractors. Each version is printed using a QMS laser printer.

A nationwide employment service keeps its clients' resumes and job qualifications on a database accessible from any number of the Cordata PCs located in satellite offices. Copies of job candidates' portfolios are downloaded from the database to individual placement counselors, who print them out on a Cordata laser printer.

A chain of quick printing shops accept IBM format disks over-the-counter. The shop personnel telecommunicate customer files, along with specific formatting instructions, to a remote central typesetting facility, where they are processed. The files are returned by next-day parcel service to the shop. At the quick print shop, the type usually is assembled into pages and reproduced.

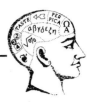

USER PROFILES

LaserWriter Produces a Newspaper

The publisher of a twice-monthly business newspaper is using Apple MacWrite, MacDraw, and MacPaint with three Macintosh computers and a LaserWriter printer to produce between 24 and 28 pages of type and graphics per issue.

Tom Oat, who previously had produced his *Business Fortnightly of Rhode Island* newspaper by sending his microcomputer disks out to a typesetting service, considers his present typesetting capabilities as more than sufficient. In an interview printed in *Publisher's Auxiliary*, Oat observed that "We're a healthy tabloid. Even if we were a weekly, it would still work just fine."

Pages are imaged on 8 1/2-×-11-inch 70-pound coated stock, which is a particularly receptive surface for the LaserWriter toner. The thickness of the sheet also resists wax bleed through.

Oat rates the Macintosh publishing system highest on its ease of use. He received delivery of his LaserWriter on a Friday, set it up, tried it out, and produced his first issue by Tuesday. He also rates the LaserWriter high on reliability. Despite repeated sessions of 12- to 15-hour nonstop use, the printer performs flawlessly.

PC Printer Replaces Typesetter

A letter-quality printer has replaced a Compugraphic CompuWriter phototypesetter for the production of galleys at the *Barron County News-Shield* in Barron, Wisconsin. According to a story published in *Publisher's Auxiliary,* the equipment consists of one TRS-80 Model 4 microcomputer, two Model 4P portable computers. Super-SCRIPSIT word processing software, and a DWP510 letter-quality printer. The equipment is used to produce the weekly newspaper at a time savings of about 30 hours per issue, and a cost savings of about $1200 in silver-based materials.

A 10-point proportionally spaced bold type wheel is used to produce the body copy on plain paper. It is then reduced 82 percent on a Canon reduction copier using a high-quality, 20-pound copy paper. Headlines are produced on the CompuWriter, and are pasted up with the photocopied galleys.

According to publisher Jim Bell, reader acceptance of the new typesetting system was favorable. "Not too many people noticed the change; we didn't hear any negative comments and one person said, 'Hey, what did you do to the paper this week—it seems easier to read!' "

Data Conversion Using TIMESAVER 10

A typesetting house in Texas uses a CCI front-end system driving two Mergenthaler 202 digital phototypesetters. Information is input into the CCI system through a number of methods, including telecommunications, cable connections to microcomputers, streamer cassettes, and 9-track mag tape, and, of course, keyboarding.

The telecommunications process might involve a direct transfer of a client's information to one of the company's IBM-compatible computers, which is then communicated to the CCI system. Another telecommunications method is the telecommunication of data directly to one of the CCI ports.

Client data usually is keyboarded using MultiMate or WordStar word processing programs, and must be converted into ASCII for telecommunications. Word processing codes that have equivalent representations in the typesetting realm, such as centering and italicizing, can be converted directly into meaningful typesetting codes. The Timesaver 10 program is used for these purposes. Even complicated tabular work is handled in this fashion. "In these cases we capture every keystroke and control character, instead of the standard word processing stripping. Using the search and replace capability in the Timesaver 10, we convert the customers codes to relevant typesetting codes."

When noncompatible disks are supplied by customers, the type shop sends them out to a computer service for conversion to MS-DOS or PC-DOS. The process usually takes no more than one hour at a cost of $5 to $7 per disk.

The use of a microcomputer, the Timesaver 10 software, and the services of the disk conversion shop provide this typesetting service with the same capabilities provided by expensive dedicated conversion and translation equipment.

How a Microcomputer Magazine Uses Microcomputers for Typesetting

Bob Embry, Senior Editor of *Personal Computer Age*[1] (The Definitive Journal for the IBM Personal Computer User), uses IBM PCs exclusively in the preparation of copy for his magazine. "Since we're an IBM Personal Computer magazine and our office is heavily populated with the beasts, we long ago decided to use IBM PCs for typesetting preparation in addition to all other purposes, regardless of additional efficiencies we might gain using different equipment for typesetting."

In addition to the hardware decision, Embry chose the Volkswriter word processing program for the processing of editorial material. "VW is easy to learn and use. While it lacks the versatility of, say, WordStar, VW is plenty adequate for massaging editorial text." Special Volkswriter control characters are embedded in stories and are globally replaced with typesetting codes. The Volkswriter ASCII text is converted into typesetting format just prior to telecommunicating the text to a typesetting service.

All files that are sent for typesetting must be in an acceptable form prior to transmission. The training provided to Embry and his associates to accomplish this task consisted primarily of several pages of coding equivalencies, prepared specifically for their application. "We still have no typeset conversion handbook—there hasn't been time to write one, and the necessity seems marginal in a small but very busy organization."

Completely processed text contains special codes that will be interpreted by either the telecommunications interface or the typesetter. The typesetter-specific codes control such parameters as type style, type size, line spacing, and line measure. As an example, the following line might be entered at the beginning of a story:

###$FFa1$SZ10$PL11$ LL1306

The codes have the following meanings:

###	Flags the human operator to indicate that this is a new file.
$FFa1	Signals the typesetter to activate font position a1, which happens to be a Garamond Roman face. Position a2 accesses Garamond Italic, position a3 accesses Garamond Bold, etc.
$SZ10	Sets the type size at 10 points.
$PL11	Sets the primary line spacing value to 11 points. The magazine never uses the secondary line spacing feature.
$ LL1306	Sets the line length (measure) at 13 picas and 6 points.

The dollar sign serves as the precedence code indicating that the characters which follow are to be treated as commands rather than as settable text. "A number of custom codes were programmed by I/OCR (the typesetting service) into Shaffstall's (telecommunication converter) lookup conversion table dedicated to us to accommodate Volkswriter's particular format commands. The custom conversion code *a, for instance, is converted at I/OCR to a Compugraphic control code meaning 'Do a line wrap here and indent the new paragraph one em space.' *b means 'Do a line wrap here and resume setting at the left margin.' These asterisk codes we globally strip into our text in place of the carriage return symbols indicated on our screens by VW. Other codes must be globally swapped to control italics, boldface, and other special print effects."

[1]Personal Computer Age
8138 Foothill Boulevard
Sunland, CA 91040
(818) 352-7811
The Source: TCP914

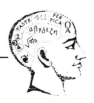

The typesetting and character data is transmitted from the magazine office over voice-grade telephone lines using a Hayes Smartmodem. A modem at the typesetting service relays the signal to a Shaffstall MediaComm protocol converter. This device receives ASCII text, control characters, and special control characters devised for the magazine by the typesetting service. These special typesetting control characters are stored in a custom look-up table stored within the Shaffstall. The converter, while on-line, converts the code into EBCDIC Compugraphic typesetter coding and stores it on floppy disk in a Vector Graphic microcomputer. The information then is transferred to the typesetting system, where it is inspected and processed.

The results of the typesetting conversion are long lengths of typeset galleys. I/OCR also provides the magazine with same-size photocopies of the galleys for use as markup proofs.

Embry cautions potential users of this kind of text conversion to use it only if the volume justifies it. He considers the cost of in-house training and in-house code conversion to be significant and suggests that "these costs can only represent a direct reduction over manual typesetting when volumes are high enough to economically outweigh the relatively fixed costs of the conversion infrastructure." He also recognizes that there are a number of ancillary savings that are difficult to quantify:

- Turnaround time can be much faster.
- Galley proofreading requirements can be minimal.
- No layout art time is expended stripping in corrected type necessitated by typesetter keyboarding errors, since there aren't any.

The biggest drawback to doing in-house coding for typesetting is coping with operator errors. "What's greatly needed is 'preview' software that modifies the WP text in real-time or near real-time to a graphic representation of its typeset result."

Artistic Letter Design Using an Apple Macintosh

A course entitled "Art of the Book," taught by Howard Gralla at Yale University, got student Gideon Rose interested in letter design and printing. Rose sought a way of combining the classical beauty of traditional letterforms and the crispness of letterpress printing with contemporary computer design capabilities. As a class project, he used his Apple Macintosh and the MacPaint program to design a Greek alphabet (FIG. 1), which was to become part of a limited-edition book.

In order to transform his letter designs into functional relief printing plates, Rose traced the designs, which he printed on his ImageWriter printer, onto individual linoleum blocks. He then carefully cut around each letter so that only the character image was raised.

For his small run of books, he used a Vandercook SP-15 proof press. The Greek characters were printed individually in color. The text was composed by hand using foundry type, and printed in black. The completed pages (FIG. 2), created by the union of very old and very new technologies, are quite impressive.

Processing Input for Financial Printing

A financial printer in downtown Manhattan accepts typesetting input from its clients. Most of the information is created on dedicated word processing equipment and must be transmitted to the printer in the form of plain ASCII text. Magnetic media also can be processed, and depending upon the disk format, can be converted in-house or through a disk-conversion service.

No matter how the information is received, the sensitive nature of financial work demands that clients also submit a hardcopy of the file content. The hardcopy both serves as a check on the accuracy of the communication or conversion process and gives the proofreaders a standard to compare to the processed copy. The hardcopy also is used by the printer's production personnel for marking up the copy, since clients do not embed any typesetting codes in their word processing files.

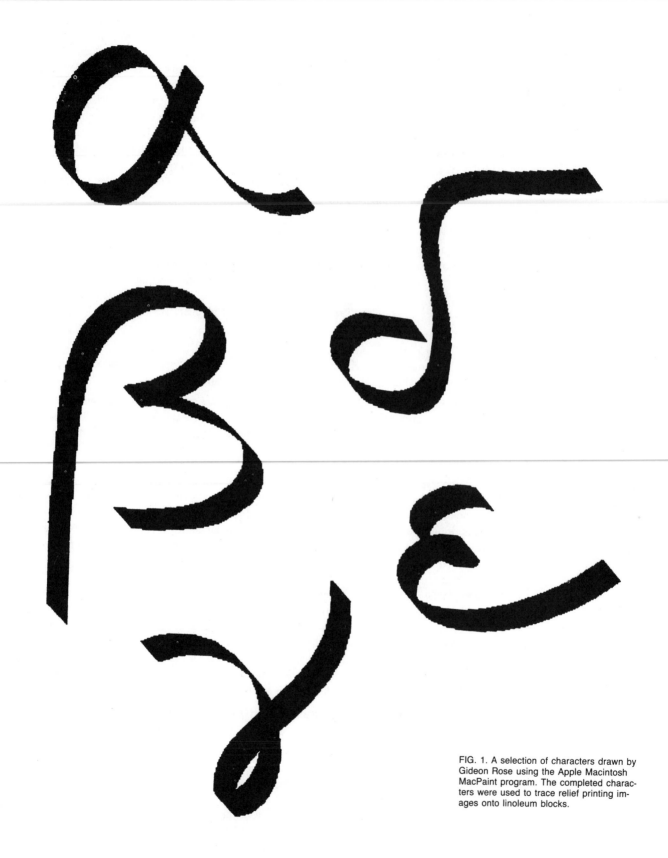

FIG. 1. A selection of characters drawn by Gideon Rose using the Apple Macintosh MacPaint program. The completed characters were used to trace relief printing images onto linoleum blocks.

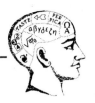

IN 480 B.C. XERXES INVADED GREECE with a huge force. The Greeks, deciding to make an eventual stand at the northern pass of Thermopylae, sent a small advance force ahead under the command of Leonidas, king of Sparta. When Xerxes attacked the Greeks defended their position heroically, and the Persian king was stymied until a Greek traitor showed him a secret route around the pass. Told by runners of his impending doom, Leonidas permitted his troops to leave as they liked; nearly alone, the Spartans stayed. Knowing they had no chance of victory, they fought for honor and for Greece until they were overwhelmed. Two of the 300 Spartans, Eurytus and Aristodemus, suffering from temporary blindness, had been sent home by Leonidas to recuperate. Hearing what the Persians had done, Eurytus called his servant to help him with his armor and lead him to the battle. Plunging into the middle, he was immediately killed. An epitaph was inscribed over the dead. It ran: 'Go tell the Spartans, you who read. We took their orders, and are dead.'

Alpha
Beta
Gamma
Delta
Epsilon
Zeta
Eta
Theta
Iota
Kappa
Lambda
Mu
Nu
Xi
Omicron
Pi
Rho
Sigma
Tau
Upsilon
Phi
Chi
Psi
Omega

FIG. 2. A page from Gideon Rose's *Greek Originals: A Modern Interpretation of a Classical Alphabet with Occasional Sketches of the Unique Hellenic Character*. The typeface used for the text is Perpetua.

Financial printers, in general, provide all of the graphic reproduction services needed by their clients, from setting the type to printing the work. The major clients of financial printers are law firms, corporations, and underwriters. The clients' expectations are that the typeset copy will be processed accurately and quickly.

Sending Files for Typesetting Via an Information Utility

Users of CompuServe, an on-line information service providing news, programs and programming, and electronic messaging, can mail text produced on their personal computer directly from their home or office to Cimarron Graphics, a typesetting service. Cimarron maintains an account on CompuServe (user I.D. [70130,161]), and regularly downloads client mail to its personal computer system for processing through its phototypesetter.

The service is disk-compatible with the IBM PC and PC/XT using MicroPro's WordStar, and therefore can accept such media directly through normal postal channels.

The service requires that the user embed all of the necessary typesetting codes; however, for complex work, such as tabular material, charts, and tables, Cimarron will add or modify the coding for an hourly charge plus the per-character typesetting charge. Rates are based upon the number of characters typeset, using the following scale (subject to change without notice):

10,000 char or less	$4.00/thousand
10,001 to 49,999 char	$3.00/thousand
50,000 char & over	$2.00/thousand

(minimum charge $30.00)

Cimarron[2] also maintains its own computer bulletin board (BBS), with 300- or 1200-baud service. Users may download their files directly between the hours of 7:00 A.M. and 7:00 P.M. Central time, thus saving the CompuServe connect time charges, but accruing any long distance telephone charges. On-line help concerning the operation of the service is available to new users.

Promising savings of one-third to one-half, Cimarron returns typeset material on a continuous roll of typesetting paper, ready for layout and paste-up.

Excess Typesetter Capacity Sold to PC Users

The Chronicle of Higher Education[3] makes use of excess capacity on its typesetting system by providing services to other publications. In almost all cases, the input for typesetting is composed on personal computers, most notably IBM PCs, Apple IIs, and various Radio Shack models. IBM clients tend to use XyWrite II to compose their text, while other clients use such popular word processing programs as WordStar, AppleWriter II, and PerfectWriter. Approximately half of all clients do their own coding, and many depend upon the production services of *The Chronicle* for the finished paste-up of their pages.

The typesetting system consists of an Atex front-end supported by a DEC PDP 11/34, and a Linotype Linotron 202 phototypesetter. The PDP 11/34 supports three dial-in lines (two 1200-baud, and one 300-baud), which are the paths through which most input is received. The service also can support the processing of compatible media in either IBM or CP/M format. Such media is read on an IBM PC, which is within the typesetting environment, and then sent either via hard-wire connection or telecommunication to the Atex system.

According to Greg Steinke, associate production manager, the amount of training required by clients varies greatly. Some clients produce entire newspapers and magazines, while others produce simple pamphlets and brochures. Not only does the nature

[2]Cimarron Graphics BBS
(214) 691-5092

[3]The Chronicle of Higher Education
1255 23rd Street NW, Suite 785
Washington, D.C. 20037

of the typeset product vary, but so do the degree of typesetting coding that clients want to do and the degree of page completion that they want delivered. The pricing structure is based upon all of these factors.

Newsletters Produced
from Files Telecommunicated to Copy Shop

J. Fields, a writer and Computerland store manager from Honolulu, Hawaii, produces two computer club newsletters using a variety of computer equipment and software.

One of his computers, an Apple II that he calls "Elwood," is set up as an electronic mail system. Computer club members telecommunicate their articles to Fields via Elwood, which saves all incoming files on disk. As a deadline approaches, Fields transfers the files to an Osborne, again via modem, where he edits them using Word-Star. He strings enough files together to create the contents for an entire issue of a newsletter, and then edits the text as a single file.

Editing and spell-checking are simplified with the use of Spellguard and Grammatik. The global Search and Replace function in WordStar is useful for cleaning up the text in order to prepare it for typesetting. Double spaces and extra carriage returns are removed, and a check is made to search for the presence of any troublesome control characters.

The edited copy is sent via an Amcall modem and software from the Osborne to a typesetting service at the Copy Center of Honolulu. An associate stops by the center a day or two later to give final approval for the copy. Any necessary corrections are made, and the newletters are printed with 24 hours.

Consultant Produces Newsletter
with Help from Keyboard Macros

David Farris, the publisher of *University R&D*[4], does all of his own typesetting input using his Apple II+ with the ScreenWriter II word processor. His rationale for doing so is quite simple: "Since I need to keyboard it during the editing process, why pay someone to do it again?"

Farris has stored all of the repetitive typesetting commands in macro files on his library diskette. The macros are specific for different typesetting formats required in the production of his newsletter (FIG. 3) such as the production of headlines, subheads, and text. When he types CTRL-**F**, for example, the following string of commands appears on his computer screen, and is embedded within his text:

$PS12$LS13$FT84$SS9$LL13.06$KO$QLL

Not only does the macro capability free Farris from remembering a long set of typesetting commands, but it ensures consistent and error-free coding.

When approximately 10,000 characters of text are prepared (Farris uses the character count feature of ScreenWriter II to determine the number of characters that have been keyed in), he sends the file to his typesetting service at 300-baud, using an Apple Cat II modem. The typesetter charges $3.50 per 1000 characters approximately one-half the charge for both the keyboarding and printing.

[4]University R&D
P.O. Box 9802-677
Austin, TX

FIG. 3. A page from one of the early issues of *University R&D* typeset through telecommunications.

VOLUME 1   NUMBER 6   ISSN 0739-3164   JUNE   1984

A Multidisciplinary Approach to Information Systems Research

By Gad Ariav et al, Center for Research on Information Systems Research, NYU Graduate School of Business Administration.

The development of computer-based information systems has had a dramatic impact on business during the last three decades. The government estimates that half of all U.S. workers are in the 'knowledge industry'; their jobs involve significant information processing. While the study of information systems is often considered an applied field, it is more of an underlying management discipline. Managers, no matter what their specialty, process information, make decisions and take action. In a business school, finance, marketing, economics, production and most other areas all share a common bond of information processing.

Underlying Disciplines:

The field of information systems extends across a number of areas and systems research must encompass topics ranging from organization and management to applied mathematics. NYU has based its research program on three underlying disciplines:

Behavioral Science - questions of how organizations are structured and managed, the flow of information, individual perceptions, decision making and the behavior of individuals, groups and organizations, and the use of information and systems.

Computer Science - especially database design and formal systems for describing and representing knowledge; issues in the design and performance of combinations of hardware and software; the development and integration of different aspects of technology.

Applied Mathematics - approaches to the optimization of decision problems, particularly decisions supported by computer-based applications; also the optimization of aspects of information systems and systems development.

Multidisciplinary Research:

Given the broad nature of the information

Continued On Page 3

New Technology Enterprises Development Center Announced at UT Arlington

The University of Texas at Arlington has founded a Technology Enterprise Development Center in its College of Engineering to aid small businesses in the Dallas-Forth Worth, Texas area.
Funded by the Small Business Administration, the TEDC is the first technology-based Small Business Development Center in the United States. It is unique in that it provides owners and operators of small businesses throughout North Texas with current technical information and engineering expertise, in addition to business-related assistance. The services are of a type that small businesses could not otherwise afford and that are often critical to the success of a business in the rapidly evolving high technology marketplace.

UT Arlington is one of a growing number of universities that are recognizing the importance of small businesses that provide technology-based products and services in economic growth and job creation. It believes that the success of this segment of the economy is extremely important to the country as a whole, and has special significance to the Dallas-Fort Worth area that the University serves.

The TEDC provides individualized, confidential counselling for owners and operators of small businesses who require technical information or engineering assistance. The Center utilizes members of the faculty of the UTA College of Engineering, technologists from area industries, and members of SBA volunteer groups such as SCORE and ACE.

Continued On Page 3

RESEARCH OPPORTUNITIES

Field Assessment Techniques for Determination of Impacts of Organophosphate Pesticides on Avian Wildlife Populations

Three field studies have been conducted during the past year aimed at assessing the effects of organophosphate insecticides on wild bird populations. Two of these studies occurred in the northern Puget Sound region of Washington State and the third in Gainesville, Florida. The research conducted in Washington involved large-scale field studies on agricultural plots while the Florida study was conducted on a golf course to assess effects of a chemical being registered for use in such areas.

Field procedures included corridor bird censusing, avian reproductive behavior and success monitoring, bird sample collections, carcass searching and soil, water and vegitation sampling. The monitoring or reproductive behavior and success involved manual and electronic monitoring of starling (Sturnus vulgaris) nest boxes, visual monitoring of natural bird nests, visual monitoring of duck broods, and manual and automated radiotelemetry monitoring of breeding female ducks.

Laboratory procedures involved the determination of brain acetylcholinesterase activity levels in carcasses and bird samples. The contents of some crops of collected birds were analyzed by gas chromatography to assess exposure to pesticides. Soil, water and vegitation samples were analyzed for pesticide residues to assess field exposure patterns.

THE UNIVERSITY/INDUSTRY R&D CONNECTION

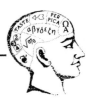

Software Output Services: A Service Bureau for Laser Printing

When Maggie Lovaas and Jim Lindner got their first look at the Apple LaserWriter, they realized that its high-quality output represented both an upgrade for conventional office printer output and an alternative for phototypeset output. With their technical backgrounds in computers and printing systems, they formed a company, Software Output Services (SOS),[5] to bring high-quality LaserWriter laser printing to users of IBM PCs and compatibles, as well as Apple Macintoshes, on a per-page basis.

SOS acts as a service bureau, taking in a diversity of file types and converting them through custom and off-the-shelf software into a form that can be processed by the LaserWriter. For IBM files, this process can involve multiple translation steps and sometimes manual intervention to add or correct formatting information. Even in the case of files prepared on a Macintosh, there can be numerous details that need correction (from changing from the ImageWriter fonts to LaserWriter fonts to redefining paragraph indents). Despite the fact that most laser printers can simply be plugged into personal computer ports, the layout requirements of complex pages require specialized software, and sometimes specialized knowledge, in order to take full advantage of the printer's capabilities.

Most of the work that SOS attracts is from businesses which need to upgrade their graphic image (FIGS. 4 AND 5). A typical mix of jobs includes business presentations, newsletters, direct-mail pieces, proposals, menus, flyers, pamphlets, brochures, business forms, and academic theses. Were it not for the SOS service with its conversion technology and modest pricing, most of these jobs would remain in typewritten form.

In addition to *single-page mastering*—that is, producing a single master page on the LaserWriter for reproduction on a plain paper copier or offset duplicator—many clients opt to have the LaserWriter produce their final copies. Preprinted paper stock with a customer's logo or other graphic treatment can be fed directly into the LaserWriter and imaged at up to eight pages per minute.

A number of SOS clients use the service in place of phototypesetting. At a cost that is from 60 percent to 95 percent less than professional typesetting services, many people have found that the convenience and savings of LaserWriter output more than compensate for the lower character resolution. Feedback from the customers of SOS clients who switched from phototypesetting to laser printer output suggests that the general public is not aware of any differences in image quality.

The combination of the right software tools, along with expertise and experience, has led to the availability of SOS franchises through quick printing shops across the country. Users of a variety of computers are able to bring their disks to a franchise, select an output style from a book of samples, and have their finished pages and media returned to them within a few days.

[5]Software Output Services
  12 East 46th Street
  New York, NY 10017
  (212) 697-4450

SOS also provides 35mm color slide production from IBM PC input

FIG. 4. A page prepared on the Apple Macintosh using MacWrite and printed on the ImageWriter dot matrix printer (left) as compared to the same file processed on the SOS LaserWriter (right). Because the page on the right is more attractive and easier to read, it is more likely to get read, and therefore, more likely to produce results.

OPPORTUNITIES FOR GIVING

Gifts may be made to support the 1985-86 program and operating budgets of the Nature Park as outlined on the previous page. Specific gifts can also be made to develop individual elements of the Nature Park programs such as the following:

NATIONAL LECTURE PROGRAM

. Underwrite a block of lectures for schools in your area.
Cost per lecture: $ 250

. Contribute to the lecture program promotional brochure.
Total cost of 10,000 brochures: $ 2,000

NATURE PARK PROGRAM

. Contribute to the costs of production
of the Nature Park Manual.
2500 copies: $10,000

EDUCATION CAMPAIGN

Networking Campaign
. Underwrite a reception in your area.
Cost of invitations, catering
and transportation for the
Nature Park presentation team: $ 2,500

. Volunteer facilities for a reception in your area.

Film Production

. Contribute to the costs of production of the film.
Total production costs: $30,000

. Underwrite a set of copies of the film which can
be distributed to the schools of your choice.
10 videocassettes: $ 250

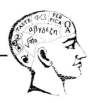

OPPORTUNITIES FOR GIVING

Gifts may be made to support the 1985-86 program and operating budgets of the Nature Park as outlined on the previous page. Specific gifts can also be made to develop individual elements of the Nature Park programs such as the following:

NATIONAL LECTURE PROGRAM

. Underwrite a block of lectures for schools in your area.
Cost per lecture: $ 250

. Contribute to the lecture program promotional brochure.
Total cost of 10,000 brochures: $ 2,000

NATURE PARK PROGRAM

. Contribute to the costs of production
of the Nature Park Manual.
2500 copies: $10,000

EDUCATION CAMPAIGN

Networking Campaign
. Underwrite a reception in your area.
Cost of invitations, catering
and transportation for the
Nature Park presentation team: $ 2,500

. Volunteer facilities for a reception in your area.

Film Production

. Contribute to the costs of production of the film.
Total production costs: $30,000

. Underwrite a set of copies of the film which can
be distributed to the schools of your choice.
10 videocassettes: $ 250

	1	3.	4	5	7
1					
2	Jerry's Pie Factory				
3	Dough Made in 1984				
4	Fiscal 1984 (Ending March 31, 1984)				
5		1st Quarter 84	2nd Quarter 84	3rd Quarter 84	4th Quarter 84
6	Income				
7	Cake Division	$10	$7,89		
8	Pie Division		$11.14	$.99	$234,567,789
9	Doughnut Division			$.78	
10	Miscelaneous	$5		$123.56	$.99
11					
12	Total Income	$15	$19.03	$125.33	$234,567,789.99
13	Cost of Goods Sold				
14	Baking Costs	345345	345345	3453	5675
15					
16					
17	Baking Profits	$5675	$56757	$5675675	$5676
18					
19					
20	What I payed to my Bakers				
21	Cupcakers Salaries	$13815	$19231	$56756	$80080
22	Piemakers Salaries	8215	9919	8987	899
23	Cakemakers Salaries	25668	29077	345	96
24	Travel and Entertainment to Conventions	2132	3968	69678	45
25	Insurance	1332	1187	2446	645
26	Legal and Accounting	2575	470	89	5645
27	Flour bills	6157	6996	435	74
28	Baking Magazines	2467275	765467458	89667	76
29	Pie Promotions	442562447	676	255	8
30	Miscellaneous	3233375	45845	6785687	5888888
31					
32	Total G&A	$448322991	$765584827	$7014345	$266655552256
33	Operating Income	($448317316)	$4567	$2636462236	$262534623
34	Interesting Expenses - net	2669	6738	262356226	25565666
35	Net Income (all the dough)	($448319985)	($21171)	$2610227O010	$2363879597

FIG. 5. Spreadsheet information from Microsoft's Multiplan is easier to read in laser-printed form (on following page). The LaserWriter also provides the option to set the percentage of reproduction size at the time of printing.

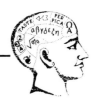

Jerry's Pie Factory

Dough Made in 1984

Fiscal 1984 (Ending March 31, 1984)	1st Quarter 84	2nd Quarter 84	3rd Quarter 84	4th Quarter 84
Income				
Cake Division	$10	$7.89	$125.33	$234,567,789
Pie Division		$11.14	$234,567,789.99	$.99
Doughnut Division	$5		$.78	
Miscelaneous			$123.56	$.99
Total Income	$15	$19.03		
Cost of Goods Sold				
Baking Costs	345345	345345	3453	5675
Baking Profits	$5675	$56757	$5675675	$5676
What I payed to my Bakers				
Cupcakers Salaries	$13815	$19231	$56756	$80080
Piemakers Saleries	8215	9919	8987	899
Cakemakers Saleries	25668	29077	345	96
Travel and Entertainment to Conventions	2132	3968	69678	45
Insurance	1332	1187	2446	645
Legal and Accounting	2575	470	89	5645
Flour bills	6157	6996	435	74
Baking Magazines	2467275	765467458	89667	76
Pie Promotions	442562447	676	255	5
Miscelaneous	3233375	45845	6785687	5888888
Total G&A	$448322991	$765584827	$70143345	$26665555256
Operating Income	($448317316)	$4567	$2636462626236	$26254623
Interesting Expenses - net	2669	6738	262356226	25666666
Net Income (all the dough)	($448319985)	($2171)	$26102270010	$23687957

Alphagraphics Printshops of the Future

One of the few valid measures of the usefulness of a technology is the degree to which it is accessible to a user. It is with this concept in mind that Alphagraphics Printshops Of The Future devised LazerGraphics, the first system to bring Apple Macintosh and LaserWriter access to customers on a walk-in, fee-for-service basis (FIG. 6).

Alphagraphics is the national franchisor of over 120 rapid copying and printing stores throughout the Sunbelt. It now requires all new shops to install, as a standard configuration, at least two Apple Macintoshes and a LaserWriter laser printer. The company's goal is eventually to have this basic equipment in all of its shops.

The service is promoted as a means for individuals to impress their boss, and for companies to upgrade their graphic image. First-time customers are entitled to a 10-minute demonstration and up to 2 hours of free system use. Thereafter, the costs are based on an hourly use for the Macintosh and a per-page cost for the LaserWriter.

Although the LazerGraphics approach emphasizes self-service, AlphaGraphics provides custom laser typesetting and layout services for those who need it.

FIG. 6. Rodger Ford, the founder and president of AlphaGraphics Printshops Of The Future, standing beside Maryanne Gargiulo and the LazerGraphics workstation (Apple Macintosh). (Courtesy of AlphaGraphics Printshops Of The Future.)

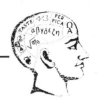

The Prometheus Products' In-House Publishing Experience

During the development of Prometheus Products' ProModem 1200M,[7] the technology for producing technical documentation improved dramatically. The initial draft of the ProCom-M manual, detailing the operation of both the modem and communications software for the Apple Macintosh, was written using WordStar on an IBM PC. Screen dumps from the Macintosh were printed on the Apple ImageWriter dot matrix printer, reduced on a Kodak Ektaprint copier, and pasted up with the WordStar output. The production time for the first edition of the manual was appproximately 2 months (FIG. 7).

The availability of the Apple LaserWriter, with its attendant quality and speed capabilities, prompted Prometheus Chairman Tom McShane to seek a way of converting the existing documentation into a totally Macintosh-compatible form. He was able to convert all of the WordStar files to Macintosh Microsoft Word format by using the MacLink program,[8] which converts word processing and spreadsheet files created on an IBM PC into Macintosh compatible form. According to McShane, ''The transfer from WordStar to Word was perfect.''

The transfer and reconstitution of the manual involved placing the text files, Word, MacPaint, ProCom-M, and Apple's application integrator called ''Switcher'' together on a Quark 10mb hard disk. Switcher is a program that allows the user to partition a 512K Macintosh into as many as four 128K computers, allowing the instantaneous ''switching'' from one program to another. From the ProCom-M program, a number of series of screen shots were made. The Macintosh provides a simple means of automatically creating a MacPaint-editable file of any display that appears on the screen. The screens were viewed in MacPaint, reduced in size, and pasted into the Word file. Although reduced screen shots printed on the ImageWriter usually are distorted, those output to the LaserWriter are not.

The turnaround time of the ProModem 1200M manual produced using the Macintosh and LaserWriter was less than 2 weeks. Not only was it easier to produce and faster to assemble, but it significantly improved in aesthetic quality, while reducing in bulk and therefore in reproduction and distribution costs (FIG. 8).

An interesting aside to the manual production story is the unexpected versatility and impressive usefulness of the ProModem 1200M (FIG. 9) in a typesetting environment. The modem offers many features that are either not available or are prohibitably expensive when purchased from other sources. Chief among them are:

- *Password security.* The communications buffer within the modem provides three options concerning the use of passwords. The first level requires no password. The second level requires the caller to enter his correct password before gaining access to the system. The third level requires the caller to enter his password correctly, at which time the modem hangs up the telephone and redials the caller to confirm that he has a legitimate right to access the system.
- *Multipurpose buffer.* Up to 512K of RAM is available, serving a number of uses. The buffer is independent of the host computer and functions under the control of its own microprocessor. Some of these applications are:

   A store and forward message system. The memory capacity of the modem makes it a powerful stand-alone device, even with the Macintosh turned off or totally disconnected. The modem is capable of answering the telephone and recording text while unattended, as well as automatically dialing a series of numbers and transmitting prespecified files. Because the modem has its own built-in clock calendar (which is quickly set from the Macintosh's built-in clock), it can initiate these operations according to preprogrammed instructions, and also datestamp incoming messages for later identification.

[7]Prometheus Products Inc.
4545 Cushing Parkway
Fremont, CA 94538
(415) 490-2370

[8]DataViz
16 Winfield Street
Norwalk, CT 06855
(203) 866-4944

A printer buffer. A portion of the modem memory can be used to buffer the line printer so as to return the Macintosh for user input while printing is taking place.

Telephone directory. A listing of predefined names and numbers can be stored within the modem. The telephone directory is stored in 2K of battery-backed CMOS memory, which is not prone to loss from power failure. Additional directory listings may be stored in RAM.

- *The alphanumeric display.* An optional display consisting of 12 LED characters provides the user with messages concerning the operating status of the modem, the time and date, the status of the current call, the duration of a completed call, and the presence of messages in the buffer.

FIG. 7.(a) Original PROCOM-M manual page.

```
CHAPTER 1:  QUICK-START


CHAPTER 1:  QUICK-START

This chapter is designed to show you in a few short steps
how to get started using PROCOM-M communications software.
We'll first boot the software, then ADD a name and telephone
number to the dialing directory and automatically DIAL the
telephone number.  With PROCOM-M, telecommunications is not
only at your fingertips, it's as easy as the click of a
mouse.

1.0  POWERING-UP WITH PROCOM-M

After connecting your modem to the Macintosh, you are ready
to power up PROCOM-M communications software and begin using
it for all of your communications needs.  First, check to
make sure that you have received the following:

     1.   One 3 1/2 inch disk containing PROCOM-M
          Communications Software.

     2.   One PROCOM-M Owner's Manual.


To boot PROCOM-M:

     1.   First, insert the 3 1/2 inch disk into the
          Macintosh disk drive.

     2.   Turn the Macintosh ON.  You will hear a small
          "beep", then see a "Welcome to PROCOM-M"
          message. Wait a few seconds and you will see the
          following Macintosh Finders Window·
```

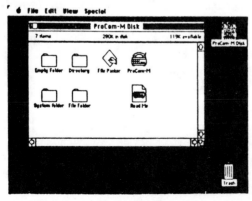

```
                    FINDER'S WINDOW
```

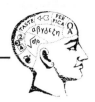
- *Multifunction call connection.* The modem has the capability of adapting itself to the dialing requirements of the telephone line to which it is connected. It defaults to tone dialing, but automatically converts to pulse dialing if required. Before dialing, it awaits positive dial-tone detection so as to increase the chances of successful connection. The ProCom-M software allows the user to switch between data and voice communications in order to facilitate the communication of instructions or other information.

Since the modem can function independent of its host computer, the operator of a typesetting service could utilize the host for a variety of different purposes without the fear of losing any incoming calls. He could also program the modem to call customers' computers (assuming they were in Await Call mode) at night when rates are low to confirm that their jobs were received and processed satisfactorily.

FIG. 7b. The PROCOM-M manual page produced on the LaserWriter.

CHAPTER 1: QUICK-START

This chapter is designed to show you in a few short steps how to get started using PROCOM-M communications software. Any 1200/300 intelligent, modem (such as a ProModem 1200 or Hayes Smartmodem 1200 (or compatible) may be used successfully with PROCOM-M. In this QUICK-START, we will first boot the software, then ADD a name and telephone number to the dialing directory and automatically DIAL the telephone number. With PROCOM-M, telecommunications is not only at your fingertips, it's as easy as the click of a mouse.

1.0 POWERING-UP WITH PROCOM-M

After connecting your modem to the Macintosh, you are ready to power up PROCOM-M communications software and begin using it for all of your communications needs. First, check to make sure that you have received the following:

    1. One 3 1/2 inch disk containing PROCOM-M Communications Software.

    2. One PROCOM-M Owner's Manual.

To boot PROCOM-M:

    1. First, insert the 3 1/2 inch disk into the Macintosh disk drive.

    2. Turn the Macintosh ON. You will hear a small "beep", then see a "Welcome to PROCOM-M" message. Wait a few seconds and you will see the following Macintosh Finders Window:

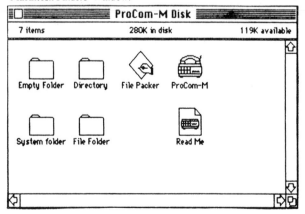

FINDER'S WINDOW

FIG. 8. The Prometheus Promodem 1200M with PROCOM-M communications software for the Macintosh (Courtesy Prometheus Products Inc.).

Appendix

Helpful Sources
of Information

Where to look for more information.

COMPUTER-TO-TYPESETTER INTERFACES

THE INTERFACE
Arman Publishing, P.O. Box 785, Ormond Beach, FL 32074, (904) 673-5576
    An inexpensive on-line interface for the Comp/Set phototypesetter and Tandy computers.

EL CID
Baseline of New York Inc., 3800 Monroe Ave., Pittsford, NY 14534, (716) 385-6149

MICRO COMPOSER
Cybertext Corp., 702 Jefferson Ave., Ashland, OR 97520, (503) 482-0733
    A line of computer-to-phototypesetter interfaces supporting the most popular typesetter models.

MICROTYPE SERIES 1000
Data Transfer Corp., P.O. Box 68, Hillsboro, OR 97123, (503) 649-4975
    A system consisting of an Apple IIe, MicroType software, the Series 1000 Computer Interface, and a parallel interface port. Connects to the AM Comp/Set or Comp/Edit.

TYPESETTER INTERFACES
G.O. Graphics, 18 Ray Ave., Burlington, MA 01803, (617) 229-8900

TEXT-TO-TYPE
Gem Business Systems, Ltd., 380 North Bdwy., Jericho, NY 11753, (516) 681-6666
    A hardware/software system that converts word processing codes produced on the Vector 4/30 with the Memorite word processing program into typesetter-compatible form.

COMP/SET AND COMP/EDIT INTERFACES
Independent Technical Services, 727 Grousewood Place, Victoria, BC V9C 2X6, (604) 474-4939
    Model Comp/300: On-line interface for the AM Comp/Set phototypesetter, program level 23 or greater. Unidirectional parallel data transfer only.
    Model Comp/3000: On-line interface for the AM Comp/Set. Available as unidirectional, or optionally, bidirectional. Serial data transfer speeds of up to 19,200 baud.
    Model Comp/300 E: On-line interface for the AM Comp/Edit; Unidirectional parallel data transfer only.
    Model Comp/5000: A bidirectional Comp/Edit interface with two I/O ports. The unit can receive data at up to 9600 baud.

SERIES 1000
Information Design, P.O. Box 68, Hillsboro, OR 97123
    Telecommunications device for AM Comp/Set or Comp/Edit that takes in data from word processing and data processing machines.

PHOTOTYPESETTER INTERFACES
Phoenix Service Co., Inc., 117 Kay Court, Hurst, TX 76053, (817) 268-5254

PC-001

Switch & Mux, Inc., 579 D.W. Hwy., Merrimack, NH 03054, (603) 424-4161

A plug-in card for the IBM PC that permits the direct connection of a number of different Compugraphic phototypesetters.

Phototypesetter Interfaces

Teletypesetting Co., 210 Nickels Arcade, Ann Arbor, MI 48104, (313) 761-7664

The Universal Interface

Xitron, 1428 East Ellsworth Rd., Ann Arbor, MI 48104, (313) 971-8530

A multiported data communicating device for connecting front-end systems, mainframe computers, personal computers, or word processors to phototypesetters.

Hyperset

Xitron, 1428 East Ellsworth Rd., Ann Arbor, MI 48104, (313) 971-8530

An expansion card for the IBM PC that supports the direct connection of the computer to typesetters or laser printers. Pop-up windows provide system monitoring information.

SOFTWARE
Business

Apple II

Touch Type

Kinko's Academic Courseware, 4141 State St., Santa Barbara, CA 93110, (800) 235-6919

A program for the beginner and advanced typist. Features include percentage accuracy reports, custom lessons, lesson selector, speed testing, multilevel typing games, and variable on-screen help messages.

Type To Learn

Sunburst Communications, 39 Washington Ave., Pleasantville, NY 10570-9971, (800) 431-1934

A keyboard instruction program using a language-based approach to teach accurate and efficient typing. Lessons include spelling practice, composition, grammar, and punctuation. An extensive student record-keeping system includes data on accuracy and speed goals. An optional gradebook disk can be used to keep track of an entire class of students.

Apple II, IBM PC

AccuTouch

Keyboard Productivity, Inc., 4676 Admiralty Way, Suite 419, Marina Del Ray, CA 90292, (213) 827-7616

A professional typing instruction program.

Apple IIGS

Visualizer IIGS

PBI Software Inc., 1155B-H Chess Dr., Foster City, CA 94404, (415) 349-8765

A program for creating graphs from AppleWorks spreadsheet files, standard DIF files, or files produced within Visualizer. The program makes use of the IIGS environment, supporting pull-down menus, mouse selections, windows, and super high resolution mode (640×200 pixels). Graph types include pie, 3-D pie, point/line, area, high-low, scatter, and five kinds of bar charts. Statistical analyses, including regression, mean, and standard deviation, can be performed on data.

Other features include the creation and placement of text anywhere on the screen, automatic scaling and labeling of X and Y axes, palette of over 130 colors; chart overlay over any background picture, and more.

Apple Macintosh

MACTYPE

Palantir Software, 12777 Jones Rd., Houston, TX 77070, (800) 368-3797

A typing instruction and improvement program that monitors student progress and provides encouragement by automatically printing a certificate of achievement when a student reaches a threshold typing rate. Both QWERTY and Dvorak keyboards are supported.

POWER PAGE

Magic Software, 121 W. Mission St., Bellevue, NE 68005, (800) 342-6243

A program that combines drawing, word processing, and database applications into a flexible spreadsheet format. Unlike traditional spreadsheets that are constrained by row and column placement, Power Page lets data and drawing cells be placed anywhere on a page. Cell types include calculated, text, data, solid, graph, pie, graphic, and PICT.

A built-in programming language called Script provides 22 commands that can control every aspect of the program. Script can be used to do such things as prompt the user for input, print a page at defined intervals, or start one Script program form within another.

IBM PC

FREELANCE PLUS

Lotus Development Corp., 55 Cambridge Pky., Cambridge, MA 02142
(800) 345-1043

A charting and presentation graphics program compatible with Lotus 1-2-3 and Symphony. It uses the standard Lotus user interface for the production of charts, diagrams, freehand drawings, symbols, and maps. Features include:

- Creation and editing of pie, bar, column, line, and scatter charts from imported or directly entered data
- File export to Lotus Manuscript, Studio Software's Front Page, and others
- Predefined templates for easier chart creation
- Object-oriented graphic elements that can be formed into complex images
- Graphic creation capabilities, including freehand drawing, fill patterns, grids, rulers, zoom, and rotation
- The ability to edit or redesign any image from the symbol library of almost 500 pictures
- Ability to direct output to a long list of dot-matrix and laser printers, plotters, film recorders, and video presentation systems

GRAPH-IN-THE-BOX

New England Software, Greenwich Office Park 3, Greenwich, CT 06831,
(800) 633-2252

A memory-resident program that can convert numbers from spreadsheets, databases, programming languages, or word processing files into instant graphs.

Business Applications

Apple Macintosh

DOCUMENT MODELER

The Model Office Co., Inc., 49 Wellington St. E., Toronto, CN M5E 1G9,
(416) 860-1033

A sophisticated interactive document merge program designed primarily for customizing mailings and reports.

CP/M, MS-DOS, PC-DOS

SUNTYPE CLASSIFIED SYSTEM

SunType Publishing Systems, P.O. Box 3262, Berkeley, CA 94703

A complete classified ad-entry, typesetting, and billing program.

IBM PC

COPYFIT

The Data Group of America, 3912 Reservoir Blvd. NE., Minneapolis, MN 55421, (612) 788-5729

A menu-driven program for the calculation of the optimum point-size and line-spacing values for a given number of characters and a given area. The program includes width values for 60 popular fonts from the Compugraphic, Varityper, and Mergenthaler typeface libraries, in 16 sizes ranging from 6 to 14 points. Width tables can be edited and new user-written tables can be added. Supported layout shapes include rectangles, triangles, parallelograms, trapezoids, circles, and rectangularly shaped runarounds and wrap-arounds.

LETTERS ON-LINE

Power Up, 2929 Campus Dr., San Mateo, CA 94403, (800) 851-2917

A large collection of standard business letters that can be of use in personal publishing situations. The letters can be saved as text files and used with most word processing programs. Personal letters can be added to the collection, and any letter can be located by category or key word search. Categories include accounting and collection, employers and employees, general business transactions, sales and good will, legal affairs, shipping and ordering, personal affairs, etc.

NAMER

The Salinon Corp., 7430 Greenville Ave., Dallas, TX 75231, (800) 722-0054

A specialized program for developing names for products, services, companies, books, magazines, songs, projects, clubs, and practically anything else. The menu-driven program can generate hundreds of possibilities according to user-selected criteria, such as the number of letters, the connotations that parts of the name are to have, and more.

Essentially, three types of names can be created: 1) Totally new names that have no specific meaning but are pronounceable, such as "tendix." 2) New names formed from Greek, Latin, or English root parts. Such parts have a meaning and can be combined to express a particular message, such as "AutoDoc." 3) New names composed of existing words grouped together, such as "Munchy Crunchy Malted Cookies."

The program uses the Adaptive Learning Method to control the generation of new names. The user can select the starting, middle, and ending letter pairs, fixed characters at the beginning and end of the name, the length of the name, the number and placement of the vowels and consonants, etc. As the program generates names, it prompts the user for a rating from 1 to 9. Based on the user input, the program automatically adapts or modifies its name-generating tables and rules to create names more in line with the requirements of the user.

POWER TOOLS FOR PUBLISHING

Interlink, P.O. Box 207, Berrien Springs, MI 49103, (616) 473-3103

Two programs for use in a publishing environment: Advertising Billing and Circulation Management. The Advertising Billing program features computation of newspaper discounts, unit and inch charges, sales summaries by category, service fees for overdue accounts, advertising agency billing, 24-month historical review, and more. The Circulation Management program features automatic USPS package (bundle) scheme, USPS Form 3541 totals, automatic renewal notices, gift subscription tracking, home plus vacation addressing, and more.

PUBLISHER'S SOFTWARE
Publisher Control Systems, Inc., 141 1/2 S. Main St., Shawano, WI 54166, (715) 526-6547

A library of software products developed to assist the publisher in computerizing his operations. Programs include Accounts Receivable/Billing, Subscription Management, Classified Ad/Billing, Ad Scheduling, General Ledger, Accounts Payable, and Payroll.

IBM PC, Apple, others
TYPESETTING ESTIMATING PROGRAMS
Noguska Industries, P.O. Box 1004, Fostoria, OH 44830, (419) 435-1844

A series of typesetting job-costing and pricing programs running on a variety of different personal computers.

Itek
PRINTER'S PARTNER
Itek, 400 Amherst St., Nashua, NH 03063, (603) 881-8448

Estimating program for calculating typesetting and other standard printing charges. The program runs on the Quadritek front-end terminal.

MS-DOS
TYPESETTING ESTIMATING TEMPLATES
Kathryn N. Makuta/WP Assoc., 15 Ideal Dr., RD 1, Cheswick, PA 15024

A series of spreadsheet overlays in Lotus 1-2-3 and Perfect Calc format for doing typesetting price-estimating.

NorthStar Advantage
MATCHBOOK
William Kircher & Assoc., 1101 14th St., NW., Washington, DC 20005, (202) 371-0700

A series of three programs: 1) JobJacket, a program designed to track jobs from their creation through their production to final billing. 2) Artime, a program that keeps track of all time billable against a specific job. It also records specific categories of time, like design, layout, mechanical, sick leave, and vacation, etc. 3) Controller, a program that provides complete accounting capabilities, including Accounts Receivable, Accounts Payable, Cash Receipts, and Cash Disbursements.

MATCHMARK
William Kircher & Assoc., 1101 14th St., NW., Washington, DC 20005, (202) 371-0700

A series of programs that serve the needs of a small- to medium-sized dedicated publications operation. The series consists of: 1) MatchWord, a word processing program especially suited to the production of books, manuals, newsletters, reports, and newspapers. 2) CountDown, a character-counting program that processes files created with MatchWord to produce accurate character castoff information. With known column width, type style, type size, and line-spacing, the exact space requirements can be determined. 3) ThumbNail, a graphic layout program that aids the user in positioning artwork, photographs, and text. 4) MatchSpec, a program that can add necessary typesetter codes automatically into files produced with the MatchWord program. 5) Match-Link, a communications program for the transmission of prepared and coded text to a typesetting service or to others involved in text preparation and/or processing.

TRS-80/III, IV
TYPOGRAPHER'S COST & BILLING SYS.
LTcap, Inc., 102 Oak Bluff Dr., Palm Harbor, FL 33563, (813) 937-8209
A typesetting management program.

Business Forms

Apple Macintosh
BUSINESS FORMS 1
Computer Aide, 1063 Silver Tip Way, Sunnyvale, CA 94086, (408) 984-2558
A single-disk collection of common business forms. To obtain a copy, send a $10 donation along with a blank disk and a stamped, self-addressed envelope.

DRAWFORMS
Desktop Graphics, 400 Country Dr., Suite H, Dover, DE 19901, (302) 736-9098
A collection of predesigned business forms in Macintosh MacDraw format. The forms, which can be edited to suit individual needs, include an employment application, attendance record, cash report, credit memo, debit memo, delivery receipt, inventory record, invoice, ledger card, organization chart, packing list, proposal, purchase order, quotation, sales slip, service call, speed memo, things to do, work order, and many more.

FILEMAKER PLUS TEMPLATES
Forethought, Inc., 250 Sobrante Way, Sunnyvale, CA 94086, (408) 737-7070
A set of templates for FileMaker Plus that are designed to be printed on NEBS Computer Forms. The templates' package includes six files that work with over ten of NEBS' most popular preprinted forms. Purchasers can print their data onto a variety of forms, including invoices, purchase orders, proposals, accounts payable checks, mailing lables, postcards, and rotary file cards.

FORMDESIGN
Clearview Software, P.O. Box 3294, Providence, RI 02906, (401) 351-1930
A specialized program with some unique forms design tools such as the Table tool, for generating columns and rows, and the Comb tool, for creating strings of boxes for the insertion of alphanumeric characters. The complete design palette contains tools for producing practically all of the elements common to standard business forms.
An accessory program, FormMerge, makes the forms created with FormDesign live. Data can be entered and maintained in a database. The program supports lookup fields, for the automatic insertion of a product name on the basis of its product code; computed fields, for column totals, percentages, and averages; and special fields, for page numbering, dating, and serializing.

MACFORMS
Desktop Graphics, 400 Country Dr., Suite H, Dover, DE 19901, (302) 736-9098
A collection of predesigned business forms encompassing the areas of accounting, financial management, purchasing, materials management, personnel, time management, and sales and project management.

MEGAFORM

Megahaus Corp., 5703 Oberlin Dr., San Diego, CA 92121, (619) 450-1230

An integrated program for designing, storing, retrieving, compiling, and processing all sorts of business and personal forms. A useful tool for business applications as well as the desktop publishing of business forms. Graphic images can be designed using MacPaint and/or MacDraw and assembled using the program's graphic tools. Forms can be designed intelligently so that relationships between columns and rows can be computed on an individual and range-of-forms basis. Form completion can be done directly by keyboard, or by automatic insertion from a database (Megahaus MegaFiler).

SILICON PRESS

Silicon Beach Software, P.O. Box 261430, San Diego, CA 92126, (619) 695-6956

A special-function printing utility for a Macintosh with 512K or more of RAM. The program simplifies the production of repetitive labels, cards, stickers, etc. Variable information can be combined with fixed text and graphics by merging data from most database programs, or by creating the merge file directly. The program supports the ImageWriter I and II (in color), as well as the LaserWriter.

IBM PC

FORMWORX

Analytx International Inc., 1365 Massachusetts Ave., Arlington, MA 02174, (800) 992-0085

A program developed for the design of custom forms and data sheets. Capabilities include provision for lines, type sizes, shadings, arrowheads, and more. Forms can be processed and printed on any of nearly 100 different printers.

POWERFORM

The 'Puter Group, 1717 W. Beltline Hwy., Madison, WI 53713, (608) 273-1803

An inexpensive program for users of the Compugraphic MCS-8400 phototypesetter that provides the benefits of a preview screen on any IBM-compatible computer. As characters are input with their associated typographic parameters, they are displayed on the PC screen in a form approximating their final typeset appearance.

CHARTS UNLIMITED

Graphware, Inc., P.O. Box 373, Middletown, OH 45042, (513) 424-6733

A graphics/text processor for creating, editing, and printing flow charts, organization charts, floor plans, Gantt charts, and more.

FORMATION

PBT Software, 1750 Leffingwell N.E., Grand Rapids, MI 49505, (616) 363-4067

A forms creation program supporting boxes (shaded, unshaded, with no visible right end, or no visible bottom), lines, and type (pica, elite, condensed, italics, superscript, or subscript). Any of the attributes may be combined in any way. Variable form information is entered as a screen prompt, and presented to the user at the time of form completion. Existing data from a dBASE file or BASIC program can be combined with a form file to produce a form-oriented report, directory, or other document.

FORMEASY

GDI, 41 Calafia Ct., San Rafael, CA 94903, (415) 492-8618

A forms-generation program for output on the Cordata/H-P LaserJet/LaserJet Plus.

FORMMAKER I

FormMaker Software, Inc., 4362 Midmost Dr., Suite A, Mobile, AL 36609, (205) 342-0583

A program for the IBM PC/XT/AT and laser printers such as the QMS Lasergrafix 800 that supports the on-screen creation of complex forms.

FORMS

Polaris Software, 613 W. Valley Pky., Escondido, CA 92025, (619) 743-7800

A forms-creation program that works with most word processing programs.

FORMS ON-FILE

Power Up, 2929 Campus Dr., San Mateo, CA 94403, (800) 851-2917

A collection of 100 business forms grouped by category. Each form can be personalized, and any text on the form can be changed. Also included are dozens of blank, ruled templates that can be used to design custom forms. Three type sizes are available, although no ruling capability is provided in the program.

FORMSET

Orbit Enterprises, Inc., 799 Roosevelt Rd., Bldg. 6, Suite 1, Glen Ellyn, IL 60137, (312) 469-3405

This program requires a word processor or text editor to create ASCII files with embedded FormSet English-like commands. FormSet compiles the ASCII file, producing a new file that can control the H-P LaserJet Plus printer.

Forms are composed of text, boxes, lines, and patterns. Instructions consist of a command word, such as BLOCk, BOLD, HORIzontal, and SETGray, followed by appropriate parameters and delimiters.

Forms can be saved on disk, printed directly on the printer, or downloaded to the printer as a standing form. Once the form is resident in the printer's memory, it can be combined with merged information from other applications and printed all at once.

FORMTOOL

Bloc Development Corp., 1301 Dade Blvd., Miami Beach, FL 33139, (800) 624-2063

A forms-creation and -editing system for outputting to an IBM-compatible dot matrix printer or the Hewlett-Packard Laser printer.

IPRINT

Indigo Software Ltd., 1568 Carling Ave., Suite 22, Ottawa, ONT K1Z 7M5, (613) 728-0016

An electronic forms program outputting to the Hewlett-Packard LaserJet. The mouse-driven program supports the composition of electronic forms with user-created logos and graphics (through the use of PCPaint).

IBM PC, Apple Macintosh

FORMEASY

Graphics Development Int'l., 41 Calafia Ct., San Rafael, CA 94903, (415) 492-8618

A combination word processor/desktop publisher/forms generator. Features include context-sensitive help screens, preview and zoom functions, free-hand drawing, logo creation, a library of standing forms, graphics/data merge, and the capability to import/export database information.

IBM PC, HP 3000

LASERSOFT

Business Systems Int., 20942 Osborne St., Canoga Park, CA 91304, (818) 998-7227

A program for the HP 3000 and IBM PC that supports the composition of complex business forms. Data from an application program can be merged with a previously constructed form for simultaneous printing on any of a number of different laser printers. Forms are designed by inputting the page coordinates, indicating the start and stop locations of lines and nonchanging text. The coordinate values are derived by the user by making a rough sketch of the form on a supplied grid. Features include: single-user and multiuser versions, menu-driven user interface, on-line testing and set-up of laser printer, editing and revision of existing forms, automatic box duplication (horizontally and vertically), and adjustment of text in micro increments (1/720 inch).

IBM PC, Apple Macintosh

LABLMAKR.PC2

ETS Center, 35026-A S. Turtle, Willoughby, OH 44094, (216) 946-8479

A label program for output to a dot matrix printer. Over 50 ready-to-use formats are included for producing file cards, post cards, tickets, audio and video cassette labels, rotary index cards, diskette labels, name badges, index tabs, table tents, and more. Form sizes range from 1/2 inch to any height, and up to 8 inches wide. Prints from 1 to 999 labels in five different type sizes, from subscript to 1/3 inch high. Other features include sequential numbering, sideways printing, saving to disk, redefining printer type, and on-screen editing.

MS-DOS

BAR-CODE

ETS Center, 35026-A S. Turtle, Willoughby, OH 44094, (216) 946-8479

A menu-driven program for printing Code 39 (3 of 9) bar codes on labels and standard stocks using a dot matrix printer. On-line help is provided in lieu of a manual.

Wang OIS, 130, 140, 145

PULSA PRICE-A-I-D

Intergraphics, Inc., 106-A S. Columbus St., Alexandria, VA 22314, (800) 368-3342

A price list development program for typesetting applications using the Wang OIS 130, 140, or 145 system.

CAD

Apple Macintosh

MGMSTATION

Upgrade Technologies, 23011 Moulton Pky., Bldg. C1, Laguna Hills, CA 92653, (714) 951-7332

A professional CAD program with extensive drawing tools, cross-hatching, complex variation of text, dimensioning with tolerances, symbol library creation, mirror imaging, translation and rotation, zooming, splining, and coordinate measuring.

Clip Art

Apple II

CLIPCAPTURE

Clipcapture, 477 Windridge Dr., Racine, WI 53402, (800) 628-2828

A program to create graphics usable in Springboard's The Newsroom or Broderbund Software's Print Shop. Features include creating original clip art from any hi-res picture, converting part of any hi-res picture or Newsroom photo into a Print Shop graphic, and integrating over 185 public-domain Print Shop graphics into Newsroom format.

DAVKAGRAPHICS I

Davka Corp., 845 N. Michigan Ave., Suite 843, Chicago, IL 60611, (312) 944-4070

A collection of over 60 Jewish symbols and pictures for use with Broderbund Software's The Print Shop and Print Shop Companion. The library includes graphics representing the Torah, commandments, candles, synagogue, bar/bat mitzvah, ark, menorah, and many others.

DAVKAGRAPHICS II

Davka Corp., 845 N. Michigan Ave., Suite 843, Chicago, IL 60611, (312) 944-4070

A collection of over 75 Jewish symbols, as well as holiday, event, and place pictures compatible with Broderbund Software's The Print Shop and Print Shop Companion. Graphics include a scroll, shofar, Chanukah, wine cups, Moses, sages, David & Goliath, and many more.

PRINT SHOP COMPANION/LIBRARIES

Broderbund Software, 17 Paul Dr., San Rafael, CA 94903, (415) 479-1185

A collection of graphics, along with an enhanced graphic editor for use with the original Print Shop program. The Print Shop Libraries are additional ready-to-use graphic designs grouped by subject. Both are for use with the Apple II and a dot matrix printer.

Apple Macintosh

3D CLIP OBJECT DISKS

Enabling Technologies, 600 S. Dearborn, #1304, Chicago, IL 60605, (312) 427-0386

A collection of images for Easy3D and Pro3D use. Categories include desktop publishing, anatomy, and transportation.

500 MENU PATTERNS FOR MACPAINT

FingerTip Software, P.O. Box 4917, Long Beach, CA 90804, (213) 498-8064

A collection of 500 patterns for MacPaint to augment the 38 provided with that program.

ART A LA MAC VOLUME 1, 2

Springboard Software, Inc., 7808 Creekridge Cir., Minneapolis, MN 55435, (612) 944-3912

Volume 1: People and Places. Over 600 pieces of clip art including buildings, faces, fantasy, fun, historical items, kids, maps, men, sports, women, and workers.

Volume 2: Variety Pack. Over 600 pieces of clip art featuring alphabets, astrology, borders, holidays, monsters, music, plants, religion, space, vehicles, and miscellaneous.

ART PORTFOLIO; THE CARD SHOPPE

Axlon, Inc., 1287 Lawrence Station Rd., Sunnyvale, CA 94089, (408) 747-1900

The Art Portfolio is a collection of over 120 pieces of clip art arranged in 12 categories. The Card Shoppe contains drawings and materials for making greeting cards.

CLIP 1

Frazier, Peper & Assoc., P.O. Box 3019, Santa Cruz, CA 95063, (408) 476-2358

A collection of clip-art illustrations and drawings in MacPaint format.

DAVKAGRAPHICS FOR THE MACINTOSH

Davka Corp., 845 N. Michigan Ave., Suite 843, Chicago, IL 60611, (312) 944-4070

A collection of Jewish-oriented MacPaint documents organized in the following categories: Torah, Bar/Bat Mitzvah, Sabbath, Signs, People, Holidays, Symbols, and Israel. A Hebrew type font is also included.

DESKTOP ART
Dynamic Graphics, Inc., 6000 N. Forest Park Dr., Peoria, IL 61656-9979,
(800) 255-8800

A collection of prepared artwork in MacPaint, FullPaint, and MacDraw document
formats from a company with a well-established reputation in the graphic arts for prepared clip art. Themed packages include Sports, Education, Four Seasons, Artfolio,
Graphics & Symbols, and more. Dynamic Graphics also publishes a desktop graphics
newsletter providing information on design techniques and developments in desktop
publishing.

DIGIT-ART
Image Club Graphics, 2828 19 St. N.E., Calgary, Alberta T2E 6Y9, (403) 250-1969

Multidisk collections of MacDraw-compatible graphics featuring borders, symbols,
dingbats, sports, food, forms, and decorative fonts.

DRAWART VOLUME TWO
Desktop Graphics, 400 Country Dr., Suite H, Dover, DE 19901, (302) 736-9098

A collection of more than 300 images drawn in MacDraw (object-oriented) format. Categories include Business, People, Communication, Borders, Leisure, Office,
Typefaces, Nations, Money, Food, Sports, Transportation, and Home and Holidays.

EZ GRAPHIX
AdTechs, 7220 Old Kent Rd., Amarillo, TX 79109, (806) 353-7063

A clip-art collection in MacPaint format of over 950 images covering commercial
and business themes. Categories include Agriculture, Aircraft, Animals, Auto Repair,
Beverages, Boats, Buildings, Carpet, Cars, Clothing, Contractors, Doors, Electronics,
Fans, Fences, Fireplaces, Flags, Flowers, Food, Furniture, Glass, Insects, Medical,
Motorcycles, Moving, Music, Office, Optical, People, Photographer, Plumbing,
Printers, Religious, Rental, Security, Service Station, Sewing, Signs, Sports, Telephone,
Tires, Trailers, Travel, Trucks, Vacuum, Welding, Window Coverings, and Windows.

GAZETTE LIBRARY, PAINT
International Datawares Inc., 2278 Trade Zone Blvd., San Jose, CA 95131,
(408) 262-6660

A collection of public-domain, shareware, and copyrighted MacPaint documents
distributed with permission, organized into useful categories. The images are available
at no cost other than a charge for duplication, media, postage, and handling.

GRAPHIC BYTES SERIES
A.A.H. Computer Graphic Prod., P.O. Box 4508, Santa Clara, CA 95054

A collection of graphics in MacPaint format for those in need of fantasy, science
fiction, and horror images. The finely detailed images in the Dinosaur-Bytes and Sky-
Bytes volumes also are suitable for educational purposes.

IMAGES
Matrix Advocates Co., P.O. Box 1238, Bricktown, NJ 08723, (201) 899-4739

A set of over 200 designs and illustrations in MacPaint format. Also included are
a page and screen ruler and a 360-degree compass.

JAPANESE CLIP ART SCROLLS 1 & 2
Enzan-Hoshigumi Co. Ltd., 150 W. Acton Rd., Stow, MA 01775, Tokyo, 151 Japan

A collection of more than 360 Japanese theme images in MacPaint format. Scroll
1 is named Heaven, and contains the following pages of images: Primaevus, Sumeru,

Shinsen, Characters, Mandalas, Sengai, Sennin, Yokai, Kigan, Geino, Reiju, Matsuri, Dec Art, Pic Chars, and four Japanese fonts. Scroll 2 is called Earth, and contains the following pages of images: Ukiyoe, Hokusai, Fuji, Samurai, Ink Brush, Motifs, Symbols, Kankon, Kano, Kacho, Jomon, three Japanese calligraphic kana fonts, and one regular kana font.

Each collection is handsomely packaged in a uniquely Japanese holder. A lengthy annotated guide accompanies each set.

MAC-ART LIBRARY

CompuCraft, 6818 S. Magnolia Ct., Englewood, CO 80112, (303) 850-7472

A multiple-volume collection of MacPaint images designed for the desktop publisher and graphic artist. Image categories include Sports, Animals, Tools, Geography, Flowers/Trees/Plants, Signs/Symbols/Borders, Transportation, Greeting Card Art, On the Farm, Buildings, and In the Kitchen.

MACANATOMY

MacMedic Publications, Inc., 5805 Westheimer, Houston, TX 77057-5616, (713) 977-2655

An electronic atlas of the human anatomy drawn by Dr. Robert Davis, M.D., F.A.C.S. presented in MacPaint format. Diagrams can be modified and can be merged with text. Volume 1 includes the Head and Neck, Abdomen and Pelvis, and the GI Tract; Volume 2 includes the Heart and Lungs, Thoracic Cavity, and Nervous System; Volume 3 includes the Upper and Lower Limb; and Volume 4 includes the Bones and Joints, and Cross Sections. Volumes are available singly or as a set.

MACART FOR BUSINESS

Wiley Professional Software, 605 Third Ave., New York, NY 10158, (212) 850-6788

A collection of clip art specifically for use in business situations.

MACATLAS

Micro:Maps, P.O. Box 1353, Morristown, NJ 07960

A collection of presentation-quality map templates in MacPaint and MacDraw format consisting of MacAtlas USA, MacAtlas World, and MacAtlas Counties (USA).

MACBITS

MacPoint, 5704 Harper, Chicago, IL 60637, (312) 955-1954

A three-disk set containing a complete collection of Macintosh system icons in a range of sizes, covering MacPaint, the desktop, popular applications, the system, and common symbols. These images are useful for software authors, reviewers, and publishers.

MACINSHOTS PHOTO ALBUMS

Design Loft, Inc., P.O. Box 1650, Palo Alto, CA 94302, (415) 493-9500

A set of MacPaint clip-art collections of photographic images.

MACMATBOOK

Electronic Publisher, Inc., 210 S. Marietta St., Excelsior Springs, MO 64024, (816) 637-7233

A series of clip-art volumes created in MacPaint format and available for use in the PictureBase pictorial database. The professionally designed libraries include categories covering hardware, people, the arts, animals, food, potpourri, nature, transportation, seasonal, buildings, children, and sports.

MacMemories

Imageworld Inc., P.O. Box 10415, Eugene, OR 97440, (503) 485-0395

An extensive collection of turn-of-the-century copyright-free scanned images for the Macintosh. The multidisk set of clip art is compatible with any program that can process MacPaint files. Images can be copied, modified, and customized according to need. Titles include Seasons and Holidays; Art Nouveau; Silhouettes and Shadows; Apples of Our Eye; Attention Grabbers; Butcher, Baker, and Candlestick Maker; Fish, Fur, and Fowl; Memory Lane; Tools, Machines, and Merchandise; Twig, Leaf, Root, and Flower; Wheels, Hulls, Rails, and Wings; and Wild, Wild West.

MacMemories Blue Ribbon Set

ImageWorld, Inc., P.O. Box 10415, Eugene, OR 97440, (800) 457-6633

A collection of clip art in MacPaint or Picture Base format with a holiday theme. Images include Borders and Frames, Christmas and Winter, Food and Feasting, Music and Dance, Divine Images—We Are One, and The Blue Ribbon Image Book.

Magnetic Art Portfolio

Magnetic Arts, 215 Bridgeway, Sausalito, CA 94965, (415) 331-5069

A collection of hand-drawn MacPaint images by professional graphic artist Adele Aldridge. Portfolios include Erotica, Faces, Hands, Landscapes, Portraits of the Beatles, Portraits of Prince, Portraits of the 49ers, and Romantic Images.

Optical Illusions

ArtBase, 815 Princess Ave., Vancouver, BC V6A 3E5, (604) 255-8077

A collection of over 50 of the most famous optical illusions in MacPaint format. The accompanying manual includes information on biological design, the optical pathway, physiological similarities, cognitive illusions, ambiguous figures, the hindrance of memory, visual contexts, brightness as a variable, afterimages, and moiré patterns.

RealArt

Electric Cottage Ind., P.O. Box 217, Spooner, WI 54801-0217

A collection of digital artwork featuring nature themes.

smArt mouse

Pleasant Graphic Ware, P.O. Box 506, Pleasant Hill, OR 97455, (503) 741-1401

A collection of over 100 graphics in MacPaint format covering a wide variety of subjects, including Oriental themes, aviation, animals, cartoons, people, time, etc.

Soft Palette Clip Art; Borders

Decision Science Software, Inc., P.O. Box 7876, Austin, TX 78713, (512) 926-4527

Clip Art is a collection of more than 300 images and paint patterns for MacPaint. Borders is a collection of decorative outlines and frame enclosures in MacPaint format.

Student Atlas Series

Kinko's Academic Courseware, 4141 State St., Santa Barbara, CA 93110, (800) 235-6919

A series of maps in MacPaint format covering state counties, state borders, major cities, and continents.

SunShine Graphics Library

SunShine, P.O. Box 4351, Austin, TX 78765, (512) 453-2334

A large collection of low-cost MacPaint-format graphics, including these specialized topics: Mayan Ruins: Oriental Designs I & II; Visions from the Rubaiyat I & II;

Anatomical Drawings; Art Nouveau Borders I & II; Flowers and Plants; Decorative Full-Page Patterns; Fanciful Animals; Full-Page Floral Wallpaper Patterns I & II, Erotic Drawings; Elaborate Antique Borders I & II; Weird Stuff I & II; Decorative Antique Panels; Floral Patterns from Weaving; Pictorial Borders; The Age of Knights; Flower and Animal Fantasies; American Indians; Pictorial Borders from Nature; The Wonderful World of Insects; A Treasury of Large Mammals; A Treasury of Birds; Creatures of the Sea; Beautiful Women; and Nudes.

IBM PC

Fontasy Art Folders

Prosoft, 7248 Bellaire Ave., North Hollywood, CA 91603, (818) 765-4444

A diverse and expansive collection of artwork for use with the Fontasy program. Volumes include Holiday and Party; Sports, Recreation, and Music; Advertising Attention Getters; Food and Cooking; Animals and Plants; and Home and Office.

PC Quik-Art

PC Quik-Art, 50 Gaines School Rd., Athens, GA 30605, (404) 354-1911

A large collection of clip art from the copyrighted files of SCW Services, Inc. (a Scripps Howard Company). These are the same images supplied to newspaper and magazine publishers. Images are compatible with PC Paintbrush (Z-Soft), Fontrix or Printrix (Data Transforms). Images are available on a monthly subscription basis (200 clips), or quarterly on CD ROM. Formats are available ranging from the 640-×-200 CGA to the 1280-×-800 Wyse mode. Clip file categories include general advertising themes (crowds at sales, grand opening sales, etc.), service-specific art (ethnic foods, florists, etc.), seasonal sale themes (Valentine's Day, back to school, etc.), headings (emblems, alphabets, etc.), equipment/items/people (coins, farm equipment, etc.), borders, fashions, recreation (sporting activities, holidays, etc.), cartoons (animals, beach scenes, etc.), and ad tools.

Windows Clip Art Collection

Micrografx, Inc., 1820 N. Greenville Ave., Richardson, TX 75081, (214) 234-1769

A collection of over 500 object-based images held on five diskettes. The symbol libraries and artistic images are compatible with Microsoft Windows applications such as Aldus PageMaker, Micrografx Windows Draw and In*A*Vision, Microsoft Windows Write, and Palantir's Filer.

Communications

AM Comp/Edit

Comp/5000 Software

Independent Technical Services, 727 Grousewood Pl., Victoria, BC V9C 2X6, (604) 474-4939

Menu-driven telecommunications software for the AM VariTyper Comp/Edit phototypesetter, providing full bidirectional communication. All typesetting machine functions can be accessed through the use of mnemonic coding. The use of four types of file-transfer protocols make it possible to communicate with almost any microcomputer in use.

Apple IIGS, *IIe, IIc*

ASCII Express MouseTalk

United Software Ind., 8399 Topanga Canyon Blvd., Canoga Park, CA 91304, (818) 887-5800

A mouse- or keyboard-controlled telecommunications program with a user interface similar to that of the Macintosh. A central feature of the program is a built-in full-screen editor, making it possible to create files for transmission while still on-line, or edit them immediately after their reception. Files from disk can be opened and read at the current cursor position, making it possible to combine a number of files. Text can be selected with the mouse and cut, copied, pasted, cleared, copied to a file, copied to the printer, or filled to the limit of the margin settings. Other editor features are forward or reverse string searching, finding the next occurrence, reverting to the last saved version, and printing the entire contents of the editor.

On-line sessions can be saved for automatic log-on to remote systems. Session elements consist of the telephone number, baud rate, data word format, and all other system settings. Macros can be defined to control MouseTalk's interaction with the host computer. Categories of macros control the movement of text, the transfer of data, the relationship of macro strings (branching, macro decision-making), and communications control commands.

A number of terminal emulators are included, making it possible for MouseTalk to display text on the Apple as if it were a different computer terminal. This capability increases the likelihood that the Apple will be able to display the correct screen format properly.

Apple Macintosh

CAUZIN SOFTSTRIPS

Cauzin Systems, Inc., 835 S. Main St., Waterbury, CT 06706, (203) 573-0150

Machine-readable data strips that can be read by the Cauzin hand-operated reader. Stripper software can be used by Macintosh, Apple II, and IBM PC users to produce their own softstrips via a dot matrix printer. Softstrip text files can be transferred easily between computers using Softstrip readers without the concern for disk formats.

The Laser Stripper is a Softstrip program that supports the printing of Softstrips on the Apple LaserWriter printer. Use of the laser printer allows more data to be printed per strip than with the use of a dot matrix printer.

A number of free programs are provided by Cauzin Systems to support desktop publishing. Such programs aid in the transfer of information from word processing programs to page-composition programs.

INBOX FOR THE MAC

THINK Technologies, Inc., 420 Bedford St., Lexington, MA 02173, (617) 863-5590

A desktop communications program that provides electronic mail and other communications services to Macintosh networks of up to 100 users. InBox permits users to create, send, and receive memos, messages, and files. It supports the transmission of entire PageMaker documents over AppleTalk.

MOUSE EXCHANGE BBS

Dreams of the Phoenix, P.O. Box 10273, Jacksonville, FL 32247, (904) 396-6952

An inexpensive remote bulletin board system that supports user names, passwords, private electronic mail, public news, and file uploads and downloads (in ASCII or XMODEM).

MAC.TRANSFER

Southeastern Software, 7743 Briarwood Dr., New Orleans, LA 70128, (504) 246-8438

A set of two programs, one for the Apple II computers and the other for the Macintosh, created for the purpose of moving data between them. Word processing and other standard ASCII text files can be listed, sent, or received, and Applesoft programs can be converted to text file form for transfer. The transfer operation can be performed by transmitting over telephone lines, directly connecting modems that are in proximity, or directly connecting the computers through their serial ports.

IBM PC

CARBON COPY

Meridian Technology, 1101 Dove St., Newport Beach, CA 92660, (714) 476-2224

A program that makes it possible to run an IBM PC remotely. When the program links two computers, their screens and keyboards are linked as one. Any keystroke entered on either PC is displayed, in proper position, on both systems. Anything that could be done sitting in front of one computer also can be processed at the remote computer, except of course changing a floppy disk.

FIDO BBS CO 10.1

Public Brand Software, P.O. Box 51478, Indianapolis, IN 46251, (800) IBM-DISK

A full-featured remote bulletin board system with the unique ability to pass on messages to other FIDO boards across the nation. This feature turns on at night and automatically contacts other FIDO boards to pass data. This capability can be disabled to use the system as a single-node electronic mail service.

GAMMAFAX

Gammalink, 2452 Embarcadero Way, Palo Alto, CA 94303, (415) 856-7421

A communications program that supports the transmission and reception of information stored on a PC to Group III facsimile machines. Text and graphics on the PC are converted into facsimile format and sent at 9,600 baud over telephone lines to an awaiting facsimile machine anywhere in the world.

PERSONAL TYPOGRAPHY SYSTEM

Compugraphic Corp., 200 Ballardvale St., Wilmington, MA 01887, (617) 658-5600

An option for the Compugraphic MCS typesetting system that provides disk conversion and communications capabilities using an IBM PC.

RBBS/RBBS SUPPORT CO2a/b.5/3.5

Public Brand Software, P.O. Box 51478, Indianapolis, IN 46251, (800) IBM-DISK

A complete remote bulletin board system providing password protection, messaging, bulletins, file uploading and downloading, conferencing, and more. A Hayes or Hayes-compatible modem is required.

SYNCRA

Eastman Communications, 1099 Jay St., Rochester, NY 14650, (716) 464-5555

A program offering PC-to-PC communications compatibility, and the option of communicating with other models of IBM and DEC host computers that are also running SYNCRA software. SYNCRA lets the user package one or more computer files into batches that are sent over telephone lines (or other communications channels) to another computer running SYNCRA. Files are validated as they are sent. The receiving computer unpackages the transmission and applies error-checking to ensure that the data is complete and intact.

SYNCRA compresses the files that it sends in order to save transmission time (and cost). Each compressed file has an accompanying control file that carries information unique to its contents. The control file is used to ensure the accuracy of the transmission process. After files are received, they are converted into a usable form.

Among the program's features are auto restart at the point of error (rather than at the beginning of the file); transmission of fixed- and variable-length records; asynchronous and bisynchronous operation; unattended operation; ASCII-to-EBCDIC conversion (sending and receiving computers can be of different types); operator status displays before, during, and after transmission; autocalling on dial-up lines; transmission of coded and noncoded information including source, text, object code, video scans, digitized photographs, and other materials; and password protection of files.

Design

Apple II

816/PAINT
Baudville, 1001 Medical Pk. Dr. S.E., Grand Rapids, MI 49506, (616) 957-3060

A graphics program that is compatible with all Apple high-resolution graphics modes, including that of the IIGS. Features include scaling, stretching, painting, full-scale editing, color cycle animating and printing to the ImageWriter II or LaserWriter.

Apple Macintosh

ADOBE ILLUSTRATOR
Adobe Systems Inc., 1870 Embarcadero Rd., Palo Alto, CA 94303, (415) 852-0271

An exceptionally powerful art production program for producing high-quality line art and illustrations, such as logos, drawings, technical illustrations, maps, designs, and type characters. A gray background template can be created by electronically scanning in artwork, or it can be generated from an existing MacPaint file. The template is used as a guide for tracing. Original drawings also can be created from scratch. The curves, lines, and text created with the program are generated as PostScript, compatible with any PostScript output device.

The program is significant in that it is not based on bitmaps, but rather powerful pen tools that create lines and shapes to the maximum resolution of the output device.

Tools have the following names: scroll hand, drawing, text, rectangle, circle, cut, scale, rotate, reflect, shear, and page.

The drawing or any part of the drawing, including text, can be rotated to any angle, scaled, skewed, and manipulated to create special effects.

Objects can be moved or changed, and the multilevel zoom control (6.25% to 1600%) makes it possible to attain the most helpful view.

COMIC STRIP FACTORY
MacNifty Central, 6860 Shingle Creek Pky., Suite 110, Minneapolis, MN 55430, (612) 566-0221

A program that converts MacPaint bitmap graphics into object-oriented elements, which can be multilayered. Elements can be used to create comic strips or composed pages.

DESK DESIGN
Manhattan Graphics, 163 Varick St., New York, NY 10013, (212) 989-6442

A Macintosh accessory program for the ReadySetGo page-composition program that includes a selection of preformatted templates supporting the creation of advertisements, brochures, fact sheets, forms, newsletters, letterheads, and more.

LASERPAINT
LaserWare Inc., P.O. Box 668, San Rafael, CA 94915, (800) 367-6898

A combination graphics and text environment designed to create professional camera-ready artwork for the designer. Its three major modules—Drawing, Painting, and Writing—combine the functions of pen, brush, and typesetting.

Drawing capabilities include full-resolution line drawing; pattern and screen fill-in; circles, squares, arcs, curves, and spirals; shape-masking; custom dashed lines, line joining, and line capping; and line widths from hairline to fatline (1 to 99 pixels).

Painting capabilities include full-resolution bitmaps, air brushing, and automatic creation of custom screens and artwork.

Writing capabilities include negative and positive leading adjustment; full kerning control; multistyle, multisize, multifont; text runaround inside or around any picture; and text following any defined path.

One strength of LaserPaint is its ability to create color separations with registration marks, and overlays with instructions for the printer.

PAGEMAKER PORTFOLIOS
Aldus Corp., 411 First Ave. S., Suite 200, Seattle, WA 98104, (206) 622-5500

A series of design models presented as PageMaker templates. The collection includes Newsletters, Brochures and Flyers, Manuals, Catalogs and Price Lists, and Corporate Communications.

THE GRAPHIC ARTIST
Progressive Computer Applic., 2002 McAuliffe Dr., Rockville, MD 20851, (301) 340-8398

A program combining computer-aided design and desktop publishing. Features include: business graphics generation, spreadsheet for data manipulation, word processing, adjustable intercharacter and interline spacing, rotation of text and graphics to any whole degree, 256 drawing layers, and basic drawing elements (circle, box, line, etc.).

IBM PC

WINDOWS "DRAW!"
Micrografx, Inc., 1820 N. Greenville Ave., Richardson, TX 75081, (214) 234-1769

An object-oriented drawing package for producing newsletters, brochures, proposals, flowcharts, organization charts, illustrations, and other documents. Includes Microsoft Windows runtime so that the Windows program is not required. Graphics can be merged from Lotus 1-2-3 and Symphony.

A library of predefined symbols is provided. The user also can create his own symbols and store them in a personal library. Additional symbol libraries are available from Micrografx.

Other features include: WYSIWYG drawing and editing; mouse or light pen input; a 34-×-34-inch drawing area; cut-and-paste text and graphics from other applications; in excess of 5,000 symbols per drawing; output-device independence; comprehensive undo; 11 drawing modes (arc, ellipse, freehand, horizontal/vertical, jointed line, line, pie, polygon, rounded rectangle, rectangle, and text); 7 alignment options; combine and break-apart symbols; flipping; rotation of symbols and text; multiple-page views; variable zoom; interruptable redraw; rulers and grids; variety of line styles, widths, and colors; variety of patterns, hatches, and colors for fills; 15 user-selectable point sizes; 7 different fonts with 4 attributes (bold, strike out, italic, and underline); and more.

IBM PC, Apple *IIe/IIc*

GRID DESIGNER
Power Up, 2929 Campus Dr., San Mateo, CA 94403, (800) 851-2917

A collection of gridded paper templates including 24 varieties of standard quadrille graph paper, 12 varieties of accountant's paper, 6 scales of quadratic coordinate paper, 7 time grids, and 3 kinds of ruled paper. Custom grids can be created using single, double, bold, dashed, or dotted lines in intervals of 1/16, 1/12, or 1/10 inch.

Editorial

Apple II

PROTEUS
Research Design Assoc., P.O. Box 848, Stony Brook, NY 11790, (516) 928-5700

A prewriting tool providing a number of ways for an author to organize thoughts and ideas prior to beginning a writing assignment. The Freewriting section forces the writer to write as quickly as possible about the subject. The Looping section provides the opportunity to expand on a topic input in the Freewriting section. The Listing section prompts the writer for outline entries. The 5 W's section prompts the writer with who, what, where, when, and why questions. Finally, the Cubing section forces the writer to analyze, compare, contrast, and define concepts and topics. A completed Proteus session can be saved as a DOS 3.3 text file and edited with a word processing program.

SENSIBLE SPELLER

Sensible Software, Inc., 210 S. Woodward, Birmingham, MI 48011, (313) 258-5566

A spell-checking program using an 80,000-word main dictionary available for DOS 3.3 or ProDOS. It suggests the correct spelling of words that it does not recognize. In addition to the main dictionary, specialized dictionaries are available for technical areas such as life sciences (anatomy, biology, medicine, psychology) and physical sciences (astronomy, aviation, electronics, engineering, geology, math, meterology, mineralogy, optics, photography, physics), as well as business, computers, chemistry, military science, nautical science, and others. Additional special dictionaries include Stedman's Medical Dictionary and Black's Law Dictionary.

Apple IIe/IIc

MULTISCRIBE

StyleWare, Inc., 6427 Hillcroft, Houston, TX 77081, (800) 233-4088

A Macintosh-like word processor that provides a wide range of character sizes, styles, and text-formatting options. A font editor is included to give the user the option of creating custom fonts.

Apple Macintosh

MACGAS

EnterSet, 410 Townsend, San Francisco, CA 94107, (415) 543-7644

MacGAS (Glossary And Spellchecker) includes two dictionaries, a glossary, a thesaurus, and a word look-up feature, all of which are available as a desk accessory at any time and from any application. Features include batch checking of large documents, interactive checking (as you type), user dictionaries, specialized dictionaries, and more.

MACINDEXER

Boston Software Publishers Inc., 1260 Boylston St., Boston, MA 02215, (617) 267-4747

A desk accessory program for the Apple Macintosh that simplifies the generation of document indices by allowing the user to flag keywords in a MacWrite or Microsoft Word file. The resultant index alphabetizes the keywords and their page numbers, and creates a file that can be edited and included in the document.

MACLIGHTENING

Target Software Inc., 14206 S.W., 136th St., Miami, FL 33186, (800) 622-5483

A spelling and grammar checker that installs as a desk accessory, and works with over 90 percent of all Macintosh software, including most desktop publishing programs. The spell-checker can work either interactively as text is being typed, or in batch mode after text has been input. In interactive mode, the Macintosh will beep whenever a word is typed that is not in the 80,000-word Merriam *Webster's Ninth New Collegiate Dictionary*. Optional reference materials include Merriam Webster's 45,000-word thesaurus, 35,000-word legal dictionary, and 28,000-word medical dictionary.

MacLightening provides an analysis of the spell-checking process, displaying the number of words checked, the number misspelled, the average word length, and the length of the longest word. A listing of misspelled words is used to check against the dictionary. Correctly spelled words can be added to the dictionary easily. A phonetic utility is provided to find words that sound like a selected word. If the correct word is located in the dictionary, it can be pasted automatically in place of the misspelled word.

MacProof

ALP Systems, Inc., 190 W. 800 N., Provo, UT 84604, (800) 354-5656

An automated proofreading program that checks spelling, punctuation, capitalization, double words, style, sexist language, racist expressions, confused words, vague words and phrases, overworked phrases and expressions, and document structure.

MacSpec

LM Software, P.O. Box 93, Belmont, CA 94002-0093, (415) 594-0627

A special-purpose word processor and text editor designed for the creation of specifications. It uses a hierarchical scheme to organize information and automatically generate section headings into a table of contents. Information generated using other Macintosh applications can be cut and pasted into MacSpec documents, and MacSpec documents can be processed further using other word processing programs. Features include graphics support, flexible numbering schemes, odd and even page headers and footers, subscripts and superscripts, document preview, and flexible character-attribute assignment.

MindWrite

MindWork Software, P.O. Box 222280, Carmel, CA 93922, (800) 367-4334

A word processing program with integrated outlining capabilities. Thoughts, ideas, concepts, and other document content is maintained in an editable hierarchy of subordinate relationships. As many windows as are needed can be opened and displayed in a variety of split-screen modes.

Different levels of the outline can be assigned specific typographic treatments, making the program suitable for publishing as well as for text creation.

A unique accumulating Clipboard maintains text and graphics that have been cut or copied. Anything on the Clipboard can be retrieved and placed within a document.

Graphics can be imported from MacPaint, MacDraw, and other Macintosh graphic programs. Graphics can be resized and reproportioned.

Time and date stamping is maintained for each paragraph, making it possible to search for information according to the time it was created.

Document statistics are available, including the number of characters, words, and paragraphs. The average word length is calculated automatically.

Information can be sorted alphabetically or numerically, in ascending or descending order. Paragraph labels can be identified with diamonds, section numbers, or bullets. A table of contents can be generated automatically, with a user-selected level of detail. It can be edited and formatted as necessary.

Personal ResumeWriter

Bootware Software Company, Inc., 5856 Parkmor Rd., Calabasas, CA 91302, (818) 880-4877

A desktop publishing document-creation program for producing customized resumes. The user types the resume information into customized windows, and the program performs the rest. Information can be retained in a database form for producing various resume versions. The program also includes Tip screens that provide suggestions for writing a resume.

SCRIPTWRITER
American Intelliware, 350 Crenshaw Blvd., Torrance, CA 90504, (213) 533-4040

A word processing program specifically for the professional writer who needs to produce letters, outlines, treatments, formatted screenplays, and dual-column scripts. It supports the importation of MacWrite and Word files; multiple windows; automatic file backup with variable timing; header and footer options; global search for words, scenes, and page numbers; interchangeable keyboard/mouse control; on-screen screenplay formatting palette; automatic scene numbering; automatic setup and placement of scenes, character names, stage direction, and dialogue; automatic "continued" and "more;" automatic pagination; synchronized dual columns; intercolumn editing; interfacing with Storyboarder; and more.

SPELLSWELL
Green, Johnson Inc., 321 Alvarado, Suite H, Monterey, CA 93940, (408) 375-2828

A spell-checking and proofreading program for any plain-text document, as well as MacWrite 4.5, Microsoft Word 1.0 and 1.05, Microsoft Works, Living Videotext More and ThinkTank, and Lotus Jazz documents. Features include both a small (40,000-word) and large (93,000-word) dictionary; automatic word replacement; homonym (similar sounding words) checking; and detection of proper nouns that are not capitalized, incorrect forms of abbreviations, double words, words missing apostrophes, words that appear incorrectly hyphenated, and words and sentences missing spaces. The user can both add and delete words from the main dictionary, as well as create individual document dictionaries.

TOOLS FOR WRITERS
Kinko's Academic Courseware, 4141 State St., Santa Barbara, CA 93110, (800) 235-6919

An inexpensive program that performs the following checks and diagnostic tests on writing samples: average sentence length, word frequency in alphabetic order and frequency order, vague word finder, Be finder, subordination finder, spelling problems finder, duplicate word finder, and article use checker.

A series of eight lessons also are included: Writing Stronger Paragraphs; Focusing on your Topic; Eliminating Weak Verbs; Avoiding Vague Words; Cleaning Your Writing of Extra, Empty Words; Using Strong Verbs; and Writing More Interesting Sentences.

VOILA!
Target Software Inc., 14206 S.W. 136th St., Miami, FL 33186, (800) 622-5483

A desk accessory outliner that can be used in combination with a word processing program to organize thoughts, ideas, and presentations. Elements can be sorted, expanded, collapsed, moved, or deleted. Headlines can include graphics as well as text. Basic word processing functions can be performed, and lengthy entries can be made under each headline and subheadline.

Text and headlines can be rearranged using either command keys, command arrows, or the Hand Icon. Type specifications can be assigned to all or various parts of an outline. Options can control a selected headline, all elements of the same level, or all elements of a selected family (all elements under one headline). Files can be saved either as outlines or text only. In "text-only" form, files can be read by most word processing programs.

A powerful capability is the ability to convert any document into an outline by simply highlighting the text within the word processing window and pasting it into the Viola! window.

WORD 3.0 FOR MACINTOSH

Microsoft Corp., 16011 NE 36th Way, Redmond, WA 98073-9717, (206) 882-8080

The first significant upgrade of Word since its introduction. Significant improvements include:

- Improved Performance—Scrolling, saving, and printing operations have been optimized by advanced computer algorithms.
- Integrated Outlining—The framework of a document can be created using any number of headings and subheadings and then converted into a regular document.
- Style Sheets—Stored sets of instructions detailing combinations of character and paragraph formats can be maintained for a variety of often-used formats.
- Page Preview—One or two full pages can be examined in the exact form they will take when printed. Interactive commands include the ability to place page numbers and adjust margins, headers, and footers.
- Flexible Menus—The appearance of menus can be adjusted to suit the needs of the user. The Short Menus option is for the novice, presenting only the basic word processing options. Full Menus includes the full range of commands, as well as user customization to add or remove options.
- Quick-Switch—A single command key that can switch a user to a companion program such as Microsoft Excel, MacPaint, or MacDraw in order to easily import text, graphics, formatted numerical tables, and equations.
- Document Interchange—Utilities are included to interchange documents with the IBM DCA, MacWrite, Microsoft Works and Word (MS-DOS), Plain Text, and Rich Text Format (RTF), used by Microsoft Windows.
- Column Manipulation—Columns can be moved, deleted, sorted, and mathematically processed using +, −, ×, /, and % operators.
- Desktop Publishing—Text and graphics can be arranged in independent or snaking columns. PostScript commands can be embedded.
- Spelling Corrector—An 80,000-word dictionary checks spelling and suggests alternatives for spelling errors.
- Indexing and Table of Contents—Notations inserted within a document can be used to generate a multilevel index or table of contents.

Apple Macintosh, Amiga, MS-DOS

DOUG CLAPP'S WORD TOOLS

Aegis Development, 2210 Wilshire Blvd., Santa Monica, CA 90403, (213) 306-0735

A style and punctuation program featuring word, sentence, paragraph, space, and blanks counting; sorted word list generation; grade-level analysis; display of average paragraph and word length; and ''suspect'' phrase search and suggested replacement.

CP/M

ELECTRA-FIND

O'Neill Software, P.O. Box 26111, San Francisco, CA 94126, (415) 398-2255

A program that can retrieve, extract, and collect information stored in text files. Among the capabilities of the menu-driven program are searching for lists of items; searching using AND, OR, and NOT; searching phonetically; searching with wildcards; searching by exclusion; searching for case-sensitive context; searching for words, phrases, characters, control codes, and degrees of indentation; searching multiple files and disks; searching databases, spreadsheets, word processing files, and binary files; converting non-ASCII code to ASCII code; and retrieving sentences, paragraphs, control codes, fixed-length records, lines of code, footnotes, quotations, hyphenated words, underlined words, delimited text.

CP/M, PC-DOS, TRSDOS
ELECTRIC WEBSTER

Cornucopia Software, Inc., P.O. Box 6111, Albany, CA 94706, (415) 524-8098

A sophisticated document proofing program that processes at the rate of approximately 15 seconds per page. The 50,000-word dictionary is user-expandable. Features include context display of suspect words; automatic insertion of discretionary hyphens (exceptionally useful in a typesetting environment); grammar and style checking for 22 different types of errors; document analysis displaying average phrase, sentence, and paragraph lengths; and a readability rating.

IBM PC
COMPARERITE

JURISoft Inc., 336 Harvard St., Cambridge, MA 02139, (800) 262-5656

A program that quickly scans the contents of two drafts of a document and displays the differences between them, either on the screen or in printed form. The user maintains control over how the differences will be shown, as bold, underlined, italic, in quotes or brackets, or as endnotes. Using the appropriate equipment, the differences can be shown in color.

The redlined version of the two drafts is a compilation of both, showing the differences appearing in one draft in one graphic treatment, and the differences in the other draft in another.

CompareRite supports a number of word processors, as well as works with standard ASCII text files. The program can run directly from the DOS prompt, or under menu control. The menu provides easy specification of the files to be compared, the manner by which additions and deletions to the first draft are to be displayed, the name of the newly created output file, and user-defined printer options.

DOCUMAX

Signum Microsystems, 120 Mountain Ave., Bloomfield, CT 06002, (203) 726-1911

A full-text search and retrieval program for researching and managing computerized documents. The program helps a user to locate information quickly and easily. Features include searching for arbitrary phrases within several documents at the same time; using FlexSearch to overlook misspellings or find phrases containing extraneous characters; gathering information on any group of phrases from several documents into a single file, which is automatically indexed; compressing text by about 50% to double the disk storage and the speed of text transmission by modem; and cutting and pasting across several files to quickly create preliminary drafts from existing text.

FORCOMMENT

Broderbund Software, 17 Paul Dr., San Rafael, CA 94903-2101, (415) 479-1700

A review processor for the in-file addition of notes, comments, and suggested revisions to a document. The program works with files created by WordStar, MultiMate, and WordPerfect, as well as with ASCII files from other word processors, spreadsheets, or databases.

MINDREADER

Businessoft, Inc., 703 Giddings Ave., Annapolis, MD 21401, (800) 843-6964

A word processing program that incorporates artificial intelligence to anticipate the words that the user will type. As soon as the program has enough letters (usually two) to guess what word is wanted, it displays the choices on the screen. If one of the displayed choices is correct, the user selects it. The program provides for changing suffix and tense, making the word form plural, and adding -ing. A spell checker is included as well as a set of desk accessories for scheduling personal meetings, keeping a diary, incorporating math, automatically addressing letters, etc.

RED PENCIL

Capsule Codeworks, 9024 132nd Pl. SE, Renton, WA 98056, (206) 235-7099

A special-purpose program for adding editing marks and comments to an author's manuscript via computer, using standard marks of correction and notation. Files must be in ASCII form or else be WordStar document files. The use of Red Pencil preserves the author's original file while including editorial emendations. When the corrected manuscript has been finalized, the Red Pencil notations are merged with the original document automatically, producing a clean copy ready for the publication process.

RIGHTWRITER

DecisionWare Inc., 2033 Wood St., Suite 218, Sarasota, FL 33577, (813) 952-9211

A grammar and style checking program that uses advanced artificial intelligence technology to analyze text. The program is compatible with most word processors, and inserts messages directly into text to indicate possible errors and to suggest improvements. The program can detect such errors as wordy phrases, weak sentences, and overused words. It also will recognize the use of cliches, redundant phrases, slang, passive voice, and jargon. Version 2.0 uses over 2,200 rules and a 45,000-word dictionary to make recommendations. A readability index, based on the D.O.D. standard Flesch-Kincaid formula, is automatically calculated and presented as a reading grade level number. Text statistics, such as number of words, average sentence length, and longest and shortest sentence length, also are calculated automatically.

WORDSTAR PROFESSIONAL RELEASE 4

MicroPro Intl. Corp., 33 San Pablo Ave., San Rafael, CA 94903, (415) 499-1200

An updated version of the standard word processing program for personal computers. Over 125 enhancements have been made, including an on-line 220,000-word thesaurus; line and box drawing; programmable macros; an Undo command; 14-function calculator; 87,000-word spell-checking dictionary; improved laser printer support; multiple-printer access; print to ASCII; case conversion; Index Every Word command; support for full-page screen monitors; and suppress file types from directory.

WRITER'S PROOFREADER

Thorn EMI, P.O. Box 16549, Irvine, CA 92714, (800) 225-8327

A program that works in concert with a number of popular word processors to check spelling, locate similar words, find homonyms, check reading level, revise text, count words (as well as sentences and characters), and check for redundancy.

IBM PC, Apple *IIe, IIc,* IIGS

WORDPERFECT

WordPerfect Corp., 288 W. Center St., Orem, UT 84057, (801) 225-5000

A word processing program with a full complement of writing tools, including macro capability, automatically numbered footnotes, data merging, spell-checking, flexible block moves, automatic date insertion, file management utilities, hyphenation, automatic pagination, widow/orphan control, word counting, and more.

MS-DOS

PRD+

Productivity Software Intl., 1220 Bdwy., New York, NY 10001, (212) 967-8666

A productivity enhancement product that lets the user of an MS-DOS computer predefine a set of abbreviations. The abbreviations then are replaced with full text as they are typed. This personal shorthand can reduce keyboarding errors inherent in scientific, medical, technical, and foreign language typesetting.

Tandy
SARDINE

Traveling Software, Inc., 19310 N. Creek Pky., Bothell, WA 98011, (800) 343-8080

The first electronic pocket dictionary for portable battery-operated computers. Available as a 33,000-word Random House American Dictionary on 3 1/2-inch disk, or a 7,000-word plug-in ROM chip. The list on ROM consists of often-used and frequently misspelled words compiled by Wang Laboratories lexicographers. The ROM version includes the T-Word word processor. The disk version is designed for use with Traveling Software's Ultimate ROM II.

File Management

Apple Macintosh
FILEMAKER PLUS

Forethought, Inc., 250 Sobrante Way, Sunnyvale, CA 94086, (800) MACWARE

A powerful database and forms-management system that offers flexible database publishing capabilities. Forms are created using any Macintosh fonts and user-created, commercial, or scanned graphics. Forms can contain computed fields, automatic look-up, automatic data insertion, and preset values. File information can be imported or exported using many different file formats, including BASIC, text, and SYLK. Reports and summary information can be compiled from one or more forms. Forms and reports can take on a professional appearance. Output can be directed to any Apple printer.

MEGAFILER

Megahaus Corp., 5703 Oberlin Dr., San Diego, CA 92121, (619) 450-1230

A file-management system with the distinct advantage of printing its reports to the printer (ImageWriter or LaserWriter), a document file (on disk), the screen, or the system clipboard. This flexibility makes the use of database-bound information more accessible for desktop publishing purposes. Information processed with the program also can be sent to the Megahaus MegaForm program for further data processing and image enhancement.

IBM PC
NAMEPRO

Computer Mgmt. Corp., 2424 Exbourne Ct., Walnut Creek, CA 94596, (415) 930-8075

A database program for categorizing, sorting, and printing names, addresses, and other information in a personal black-book format. Almost any printer can be used to produce reports as mailing labels, Rolodex cards (2 sizes), 8 1/2-×-11-inch pages, or imposed pocket-sized book pages. Files can be both imported and exported. File imports can be from Borland's Sidekick, mail merge programs, Data Interchange File (DIF), System Data Format (SDF), or a standard word processing format. File exports support the creation of a directory for the Sidekick telephone directory and word processing, SDF, and DIF formats.

The package includes a vinyl cover and page templates for the assembly of a personal little black book that can be carried in a pocket.

Font Creation

Apple II
FONT DOWNLOADER

Micro Ware, 1342 B Rt. 23, Butler, NJ 07405, (201) 838-9027

A program that permits the user to download custom fonts to a number of different dot matrix printers.

Apple III

CUSTOMFONT

Swenson Assoc. Inc., 45 Newbury St., Boston, MA 02116, (617) 267-3632

A printer program for character, symbol, and font design, plus graphics.

Apple Macintosh

FONTASTIC PLUS

Altsys Corp., 720 Ave. F, Suite 108, Plano, TX 75074, (214) 424-4888

An advanced version of FONTastic including the following enhancements:
- Professional typographic features, including kerning and fractional character spacing for more attractive letterspacing.
- Ability to create logos and custom bitmap characters for the ImageWriter and screen from scanned art or existing fonts. Two drawing planes allow the user to create logos and composite fonts by tracing over background scanned art or existing fonts. The user can assign these logos and fonts to a custom keyboard mapping and use them in any standard Macintosh software application for screen display and printing.
- Multiple-size fatbits in $2\times$, $4\times$, and $8\times$ magnification to improve character visualization. Characters and logos can be scaled up to 127 points.
- Ability to rotate, flip, and scale selected portions of letters.
- Ability to cut and paste images between multiple windows.
- Four levels of undo for easy correction of editing errors.

FONTOGRAPHER VERSION 2.0

Altsys, 720 Ave. F, Suite 108, Plano, TX 75074, (214) 424-4888

A program upgrade providing kerned fonts and simplified logo creation. Additional features include display of the actual characters in the font overview window, instant generation of sample characters, auto screen scrolling, and simplified disk protection.

IBM PC

FONTGEN

VS Software, Inc., 2101 S. Bdwy., Little Rock, AR 72206, (501) 376-2083

A font editor and font generator for Cordata (Corona) and HP LaserJet Plus printers. It supports the design of complete fonts, logos, symbols, and special characters.

FontGen supports the editing of user-produced fonts, as well as those released by VS Software. Among the typefaces published by VS are HLV (similar to Helvetica), OPT (similar to Optima), ORN (a collection of ornamental faces), PCF (fixed-space typewriter faces in regular and landscape formats), BKM (similar to Bookman), CNT (similar to Century), GMS (Greek, mathematical, and scientific), and more. Each font package provides a variety of styles (medium, demi-bold, bold, italic, etc.) and a range of sizes.

The font editor has a number of design tools to create or alter lines, circles, and ellipses; center, reverse, fill, merge, combine, or move characters; and more. An existing font can be enlarged, reduced, compressed, expanded, obliqued, rotated, or emboldened.

The FontGen editing window defaults to a 48-$\times$-48-pixel frame. The editing cursor can be moved to any coordinates and turned on or off. A status line near the bottom of the screen displays the row and column position, as well as the name of the font in the editor work files and the name of the font in memory.

Both portrait and landscape fonts can be created, with the word **PORT** or **LAND** shown on the screen to indicate the orientation. A series of letters appears along the bottom of the screen signifying the available tools and graphic maneuvers.

Word processor print drivers are available for Microsoft Word 3.0, Word Perfect 4.1, and WordStar 2000.

FONTGEN IV PLUS
VS Software, 2101 S. Bdwy., Little Rock, AR 72216-9990, (501) 376-2083

A faster, more flexible, and more powerful version of FontGen. Additional features include mouse and graphic tablet support; WYSIWYG display capability, and expanded compatibility with laser printers, word processors, and desktop publishing programs.

POEMS FONT EDITOR
Poems, 509 Marin St., Thousand Oaks, CA 91360, (805) 373-1919

A font editor that can be used to produce fonts for laser printers with downloadable font capability like the Cordata (Corona) LP300 and the Hewlett-Packard LaserJet Plus. Features include mouse support, character previewing, inbound conversion of Fontrix fonts (an extra-cost option), and automatic transforms for emboldening, slanting, and scaling.

TYPESETTER II FONT EDITOR
DataArts Software, P.O. Box 1613, Troy, NY 12181, (518) 273-3053

A typeface editing system for dot matrix printing.

Greeting Cards

Apple Macintosh
MISSION "GREETINGS" IMPOSSIBLE
Computer Poet Corp., P.O. Box 7707, Incline Village, NV 89450, (702) 831-8800

A program to produce customized greeting cards. The kit includes special tractor-feed paper and envelopes.

THE PRINT SHOP MAC
Broderbund Software, 17 Paul Dr., San Rafael, CA 94903-2101, (415) 479-1700

A version of the original The Print Shop enhanced to make use of the graphic capabilities of the Macintosh. Graphic images can be created in MacPaint. Clip art from other programs also can be used as is, or modified using The Print Shop's built-in Graphic Editor. Graphic elements can be moved and replaced as needed. Additional fonts can be added using Apple's Font/DA Mover. The Macintosh screen shows an exact representation of how the card, banner, sign, stationery, etc. will look when printed.

YOUR'S TRULY
Looking Glass Software, 5221 Central Ave. #205, Richmond, CA 94804, (800) 643-0800

A greeting card production package featuring over 30 greetings and 10 designs. Cards can be personalized automatically from a user list, and custom greetings can be inserted. Additional greeting designs, paper and envelopes, and colored ribbons are available separately and at additional cost.

Apple Macintosh, Apple II, IBM PC, Atari ST, Amiga
Your Personal Poet
Door Openers, Inc., 775 E. Greg St., Sparks, NV 89431, (800) 422-7638

A unique menu-driven program that prompts the user for personal information in order to create personalized greeting rhymes for Christmas, Birthdays, Mothers Day, Valentines, Thank You, I Love You, I Miss You, Weddings, Risque, Sexy, and more.

Image Creation

Apple II
Flying Colors
The Computer Colorworks, 3030 Bridgeway, Suite 201, Sausalito, CA 94965, (415) 331-3022

An inexpensive graphics/drawing program.

GraphicMaster, MicroTypographer
Tid Bit Software, P.O. Box 5579, Santa Barbara, CA 93108, (805) 969-5834

Programs for the preparation of visual presentations.

Graphics Expander Volume I
Springboard Software, Inc., 7808 Creekridge Cir., Minneapolis, MN 55435, (612) 944-3915

A graphics library and drawing and editing toolkit for users of Broderbund Software's The Print Shop program. This program lets users convert high-resolution pictures into usable graphics, create graphics using Koala's Koala Pad, flip graphics, magnify graphics, add text in a variety of sizes and styles, and recover easily from mistakes.

Apple IIGS
DeluxePaint
Electronic Arts, 1820 Gateway Dr., San Mateo, CA 94404, (415) 571-7171

A sophisticated feature-laden paint program that exploits the graphic capabilities of the Apple IIGS. Users mix colors from a palette of 4,096, setting hue, saturation, and value. Colors can be shifted, replaced, blended, shaded, cycled (to produce an animation effect), and otherwise altered in an almost limitless variety of ways.

Tools include a set of brushes, although any part of the screen can be converted into a brush. An extensive menu of brush options also is provided. Other tools are the dotted freehand; continuous freehand; straight line; curve; fill; airbrush; unfilled/filled rectangle, circle, ellipse, and polygon; brush selector (to capture part of the screen as a brush); text; grid; symmetry (mirror effect); magnify; zoom (in magnified mode); undo; and clear.

Pictures can be drawn on either or both of two planes, with images swapped or combined between them. Stencils can be used to prevent certain areas of a picture from being affected by the application of graphic treatments. A picture also can be locked so that additional painting adheres only to its foreground.

Resolution on the Apple IIGS RGB monitor is sufficiently high to produce an image suitable for professional slide-making.

Paintworks Plus
Activision, Inc., P.O. Box 7287, Mountain View, CA 94039, (800) 227-9759

A paint and animation program with a user interface similar to MacPaint, but with 4,096 colors, any 16 of which can be accessed at one time. Mouse-selectable and

-controllable tools are available for moving any part of the screen image, adding type, filling areas, spray-painting, painting with a brush (in a variety of sizes), drawing with a pencil, making straight or angled lines, erasing, and making filled or outlined squares, rectangles, circles, ovals, and free-form shapes.

Colors are mixed using the Color Palette Dialog Box. Sliders along five vertical bars control the mixture of red, green, and blue, and the lightness and darkness of the color. Each of the bars displays 16 variations of the selected color. Collections of custom-mixed colors can be saved as reusable palettes. Up to 128 palettes can be retained.

Colors can be searched and replaced using a color-search option. Screen areas can be selected for color substitution of the palette color complement. Pixel editing can be accomplished by using Fat Bits magnification.

A series of Paintworks pictures can be animated by saving successive motion frames on a disk, using the Compress command, and indicating an animation timing interval. The animated sequence is run from within Paintworks by using the Show option from the Goodies menu.

Paintworks Plus pictures can be combined with Activision's Writer's choice Elite to produce greeting cards, newsletters, illustrated manuscripts, business proposals and reports, and other documents that benefit from color illustration.

Apple Macintosh
ACCESSORY PAK 1
Silicon Beach Software, Inc., P.O. Box 261430, San Diego, CA 92126, (619) 695-6956

A collection of graphic tools for the Macintosh, including Paint Cutter, which permits the user to copy all or part of a MacPaint or MacDraw document to the Clipboard, to the Scrapbook, or to a separate file. Up to four documents can be open at one time, and areas can be copied freely between them. In addition, areas within the Selection Rectangle can be inverted, flipped horizontally or vertically, and rotated. Also included are the MacPaint Rulers Desk Accessory, which provides a choice of increments and can be positioned next to the MacPaint window or within the MacPaint document, the Screen Saver program, which blanks the Macintosh screen after a predefined number of minutes of nonuse, and more.

COMIC WORKS
Mindscape, Inc., 3444 Dundee Rd., Northbrook, IL 60062

A combination paint, draw and page-layout program especially designed for the production of comic strips, greeting cards, and newsletters. The program combines bit mapped graphics with object-oriented graphics. It is capable of freely combining text (both bit mapped and PostScript) and graphics anywhere on the page. Among the features are progressive flow airbrushing, art import and export, custom panel and balloon shapes, custom-designed comic book fonts, automatic greeting card impositioning, flexible poster printing, a library of comic art, and more.

CRICKET DRAW
Cricket Software, 3508 Market St., Philadelphia, PA 19104, (800) 345-8112

A drawing program that introduces advanced PostScript capabilities such as placing text along an arbitrary path, tilting objects, selectively filling objects, shading borders and text, producing text shadows, and washing objects with fountain tinting.

CRICKET GRAPH
Cricket Software, 3508 Market St., Philadelphia, PA 19104, (800) 345-8112

A professional color graphics presentation/desktop publishing program that permits users of Excel, Jazz, and other software packages to create high-quality color presentation graphics quickly using Switcher, the ImageWriter II, or any of a number of other color printers. High-resolution color slides also can be created using a number of different film recorders.

DRAFTING SKETCH-TO-SCALE PLUS

Williams AG Products, 8282 S. Memorial, Suite 118, Tulsa, OK 74133, (918) 252-7477

Two- and three-dimensional scale drawings with screen overlays for producing MacDraw and MacDraft drawings in any of 16 different scales.

EASY3D

Enabling Technologies, Inc., 600 S. Dearborn St., Chicago, IL 60605, (312) 427-0386

A program that can be used to create two-dimensional and three-dimensional solid and shaded objects, and manipulate and view them from any angle or perspective with varying lighting effects. Features include compatibility with MacPaint, MacDraw, Videoworks, PageMaker, LaserWriter, and ImageWriter; full rotation, orientation, and scaling; merge, clone, and outline objects; simultaneous four-view; four independent light sources; variable perspective; and shaded surface embossing.

FULLPAINT

Ann Arbor Softworks, Inc., 308 1/2 S. State St., Ann Arbor, MI 48104, (313) 996-3838

A replacement program for MacPaint that offers the ability to have up to four windows open at one time; three different screen-viewing options; horizontal and vertical rulers in inches, centimeters, pixels, or picas; editable brush shapes; free rotation of images; and skew, distort, and perspective options.

GLUE

Solutions, Inc., P.O. Box 989, Montpelier, VT 05602, (802) 229-0368

A unique utility program for capturing images in programs that create information, such as Jazz, Excel, or MacProject, and copying the images into programs that compose documents, such as MacDraw, ReadySetGo, or PageMaker. The program consists of the ImageSaver and the Viewer. The ImageSaver is like a camera, which photographs one or more pages of an application and saves it to disk, to the Clipboard, or to the Scrapbook. Saved images can be examined using the Viewer. Images can be modified using MacPaint and can be converted into MacPaint documents. Image-Saved documents can be utilized in desktop publishing applications and also can be transferred as binary files over telephone lines to other Macintosh users.

GRAPHICWORKS

Mindscape, Inc., 3444 Dundee Rd., Northbrook, IL 60062

GraphicWorks is a repackaged version of ComicWorks with a special template library developed especially for desktop publishing. Templates include a newsletter, a greeting card, a restaurant menu, disk labels, tickets, a product sheet, advertisements, a flyer, a business report, and a variety of business forms.

Document pages are composed of one or more panels, each of which may contain one or more easels for graphics and one or more balloons for text. Up to 64 easels and/or balloons can be held in each panel. A significant feature of the program is the capability to mix bitmap graphics and LaserWriter fonts on the same page.

Version 1.1 includes the following enhancements:

- High-resolution drawing from 72 to thousands of dots per inch
- TIFF support for high-resolution scanned images
- Integrated color printing capabilities
- PICT file-format output, compatible with PageMaker and other programs
- Importation of PICT files from the Clipboard
- On-screen rulers
- Tools for rotation, perspective, skew, and distort
- User-defined font sizes

GRAY PAINT

Macnifty Central, 6860 Shingle Creek Pky., Minneapolis, MN 55430, (800) 328-0184

Special-effects software to modify scanned images created with Thunderscan or MacVision. The program features tools for drawing and designing, allowing up to 64 levels of gray for any one pixel. Up to 16 levels of fat bits (ultra fat bits) are obtainable.

GRIDMAKER

Folkstone Design, Inc., P.O. Box 86982, North Vancouver, BC V7L 4P6, (604) 986-8060

A perspective grid construction set for the creation of a variety of three-dimensional drawings. The use of a grid simplifies the drawing of perspectives, such as views of boxes or interiors of rooms. A grid can be built around three axes using pitch, yaw, and roll. Both the size and the shape of the grid can be changed. A grid is saved and/or cut and pasted into another application, most usually MacDraw. After the grid has been imported to MacDraw, it may be drawn on, modified, and/or printed.

MAC-A-MUG PRO

Shaherazam, P.O. Box 26731, Milwaukee, WI 53226, (414) 442-7503

A program for the creation of composite human faces, such as are generated by law enforcement agencies on the basis of eye-witness descriptions. Facial features can be scrolled, selected, and altered with a variety of tools. Individual faces can be saved and assembled with other faces using MacPaint. Other features include the addition of scars and blemishes, facial hair, age lines, wrinkles, articles of clothing, jewelry, and glasses.

MAC3D

Challenger Software, 18350 Kedzie Ave., Homewood, IL 60430, (312) 957-3475

A two- and three-dimensional graphics and solids modeling package that can create and manipulate complex graphic objects from a number of viewing perspectives. The graphics can be used as artwork, architectural models, illustrations, technical drawings, etc.

Mac3D is object-oriented, working in a three-dimensional space called the "World." The World is described in terms of a large XYZ Cartesian coordinate system. At a 1:1 scale, the cube is approximately 19 feet on a side, with enough space to represent over 5,800 full-scale models of the Macintosh.

Objects are drawn using 24 original tools, as well as 18 custom tools. Objects are viewed by using the Camera, which can be moved around the world or a particular object to present any required view. Objects can be moved, combined, resized, reshaped, duplicated, rotated, filled, shaded, glued, unglued, grouped, ungrouped, beveled, rounded, exploded, and made either translucent of opaque.

Any two-dimensional object can be extruded (like pushing dough through a cookie cutter) to form a three-dimensional object. The exceptions are the arc and curve objects.

Objects can be combined with other Macintosh applications through the use of the Clipboard or Scrapbook. Images also can be saved in PICT format and opened by other applications that support it, such as MacDraw and PageMaker.

MAC CALLIGRAPHY

Enzan-Hoshigumi Co., Ltd., 150 W. Acton Rd., Stow, MA 01775

A program that simulates the basics of Japanese brush calligraphy. The interaction between absorbent paper and wet ink is created on the Macintosh screen by the selection of the brush and the control of the mouse. Ink flows when the mouse button is held. A "tail" is formed on a character stroke by setting a time delay to follow the release of the mouse button. Tools consist of five touch selections, a touch editor, six brush sizes, five shades of black ink and a white ink, a gray ink underlay switch, a selection rectangle, a full-page view area, and more.

Hand-rendered word processing is possible using familiar Macintosh cut and paste techniques.

The unusual wooden box packaging includes a number of different kinds of traditional Japanese papers for experimentation using real ink and brush.

MapMaker

Select Micro Systems, 2717 Crescent Dr., Yorktown Heights, NY 10598, (914) 245-4670

A map-creation package consisting of one program disk and three data disks. The program can generate customized full-page maps of U.S. States, States by County, Major Metropolitan Areas, and the World by Country with useful demographic and population data. Data files provided include statistics on state income (population, number of households, percent with incomes of x, and housing values), population statistics (land areas, number of families, number of persons per square mile, population growth, population ages, and work force distribution), state retail statistics (number of retail establishments, types of stores, store payrolls, employees, etc.), county population statistics, and world population statistics.

Such maps are useful for business, education, and desktop publishing. Data files from spreadsheets and database applications can be imported, and the information can be linked to a map. MacPaint documents can be imported as maps, and MapMaker maps can be exported as MacPaint documents.

SuperPaint

Silicon Beach Software, Inc., P.O. Box 261430, San Diego, CA 92126, (619) 695-6956

An advanced graphics-creation program incorporating both bitmap and object-oriented images. Features include full-screen editing, multiple windows, three levels of magnification, use of LaserWriter fonts, and LaserBits, an editing mode for 300 dpi images.

A paint layer and a draw layer appear on the screen at one time. Images from either layer can be moved to the other in order to take advantage of the tools and capabilities available.

Color can be assigned to objects using the Color Palette. Colors are assigned to an object's fill patterns and line patterns. Output is to the Apple ImageWriter II or other color-capable printer.

Documents can be saved in SuperPaint, MacPaint, PICT, or StartupScreen form. Images also can be saved to the Clipboard and to the Scrapbook, making SuperPaint images compatible with most other Macintosh applications.

Portions of the Paint layer can be selected with the Selection Rectangle tool and converted, with the LaserBits option, from 72 dpi to 300 dpi. LaserBit objects print at the full resolution of the LaserWriter. LaserBit objects can be edited using all of the SuperPaint editing tools. Although there is no limit to the number of LaserBit objects that can be included in a SuperPaint document (depending upon available disk space), the functional limit of the size of a LaserBit object is restricted to $2 \times 2\ 1/2$ inches because of the fact that a LaserBit object is four times as big as a Paint image, and must still fit within the 8-$\times$-10-inch image area of the SuperPaint drawing surface.

Z-3D

Computer Graphics Center, Inc., 140 University Ave., Palo Alto, CA 94301, (415) 325-3111

A three-dimensional drawing program featuring shadowing; multiple vantage points; multiple light sources; viewing as wire frames or opaque surfaces, with hidden line removal and perspective and shading; and multiple fonts.

Atari

PAGE DESIGNER

Xlent Software, P.O. Box 5228, Springfield, VA 22150

A program for the Atari 400/800/XL/XE that supports the integration of graphics and text using a variety of fonts.

CP/M, MS-DOS

PRINTMASTER

PeopleTalk Associates, Inc., P.O. Box 863652-A, Plano, TX 75086, (800)-PT BOOKS

A graphics program with a library of over 100 graphic images for any CP/M and most MS-DOS computers. Supports many dot matrix printers.

IBM PC

DR. HALO II

Media Cybernetics, Inc., 7050 Carroll Ave., Takoma Park, MD 20912, (800) 446-HALO

A program that supports the merging of text from a user's word processor with graphics created in the Dr. Halo program.

ICON BUILDER

White Sciences Inc., P.O. Box 24756, Tempe, AZ 85282, (602) 967-8257

A program that supports the creation of icons using graphic-tablet, digitizer, or keyboard input. Icons, graphics, charts, graphs, logos, etc. can be combined with word processing files for creating technical documentation and other specialized applications.

THE PRINTING PRESS

Power Up, 2929 Campus Dr., San Mateo, CA 94403, (800) 851-2917

A program that supports a graphics dot matrix printer and provides for the creation and printing of letterheads, greeting cards, posters, invitations, etc. The menu-driven program offers over 100 clip art images (each in three different sizes), 11 background patterns, 11 border designs, and 8 type styles (each in two sizes with outline, solid, three-dimensional, and textured options). Original images also can be created using the graphics editor.

PUBLISHER'S PAINTBRUSH

ZSoft Corp., 1950 Spectrum Cir., Marietta, GA 30067, (404) 980-1950

A paint program for modifying 300 dpi scanned images.

TURBO PAINT GR 12.0

Public Brand Software, P.O. Box 51478, Indianapolis, IN 46251, (800) IBM-DISK

A paint program with circle, ellipse, arc, line, rubberband, triangle, square, box, hexagon, freehand, fill, pattern, undo, fatbits, and text capabilities. Requirements are 256K, color graphics card, and a Mouse Systems or Microsoft-compatible mouse.

Kaypro CP/M

FRANK-ART

Frank-Art, P.O. Box 12282, Boulder, CO 80303-2697, (800) 621-8385

A graphics and typesetting program that outputs to a wide variety of dot matrix printers.

SCS-DRAW

Second City Software, P.O. Box 267960, Chicago, IL 60626, (312) 577-7680

A program that supports the creation of graphics and their integration with text.

Language

Any

POSTSCRIPT LANGUAGE

Adobe Systems Inc., 1870 Embarcadero Rd., Palo Alto, CA 94303, (415) 852-0271

A powerful page-description language that provides the bridge between composition software packages and a variety of raster-image output devices.

Math & Science

Apple II

TEKDRAW

Computer Aided Instructional Sys., P.O. Box 177, Holly, MI 48442

A graphic-design program for the creation of technical and mechanical drawings, circuit boards, schematics, certificates, graphs, curves, and more. Symbols, which are parts of image collections called *symbol sheets,* are positioned on the high-resolution screen using keyboard or joystick control. Symbols can be moved, erased, rotated, and printed on the screen. Original shapes and designs can be created by using the Draw, Plot, Pencil Erase, and Circles programs. Using the Text Writer, alphanumerics can be added to the screen diagram.

The package also includes 14 predrawn screen formats, consisting of graphs, borders, and screen divisions. Five utility programs also are included for decoding ASCII, converting HGR screens, reading memory locations, recalling pictures from memory, and printing drawings.

Apple Macintosh

DAYTON MATH FONTS

Plugh, Inc., 595 Royal Springs, Springboro, OH 45066, (513) 748-2423

Special bit-mapped math fonts, including mathematical symbols, Greek and Roman alphabets, fractions, summations, and more.

MATHWRITER

Cooke Publications, P.O. Box 4448, Ithaca, NY 14852

An intelligent full-screen editor for the typesetting of complex mathematical equations, which are assembled in WYSIWYG form using the mouse and a user-customized palette of symbols. Equations can be combined with text and also can be cut and pasted into other Macintosh applications.

DEC, Prime, IBM, Sun, Apollo, UNIX

SCRIBE

Unilogic, Commerce Ct., Four Station Square-240, Pittsburgh, PA 15219-1119, (412) 281-5959

Software specifically designed for the intermixing of text, graphics, special characters, and mathematical equations. Output can be on a range of devices, from letter-quality typewriters to phototypesetters and laser printers.

Media Conversion

IBM PC

DATACHANGE

DataChange Inc., 6075 Atlantic Blvd., Norcross, GA 30071, (404) 441-1332

A program that uses an IBM PC to read, write, and convert word processing disks for other word processing systems, phototypesetters, and data processors. The software has the capability of producing Compugraphic MCS-compatible disks directly.

WORD FOR WORD

MasterSoft, 4621 N. 16th St., Phoenix, AZ 85016, (602) 277-0900

A word processor file-conversion utility that makes a direct translation of word processing documents from one format to another. The program supports over 130 different conversions and produces a mirror image of the converted document. Supported word processors include WordStar, Volkswriter, IBM Writing Assistant, WordPerfect, pfs:Write, and MultiMate.

Converted documents retain such special functions and formats as underlining, boldface, margins, headers, footers, and columns. Full conversions can be initiated only if both the source and the target word processor have the features implemented.

The program operates in either interactive or batch mode, and can produce a special type of file that can be telecommunicated between IBM PCs which are both running Word for Word.

Although the program is 99 to 100 percent accurate when working with word processors with like features, the user can request that the system display a report of any nonconverted items.

Any of the supported word processor file types can be converted to either ASCII or EBCDIC format for communication to another system. In either format, the special features of the word processor, such as underlining and margins, are stripped out. Only the COM.FORMAT, which is unique to Word for Word, will retain such information.

XENO-DISK

Vertex Systems, Inc., 6022 W. Pico Blvd., Los Angeles, CA 90035, (213) 938-0857

A program for the IBM PC that supports the reading, writing, and reformatting of over 130 different disks, including Compugraphic.

Printer Control

Apple II

FACELIFT 2

Companion Software, Inc., P.O. Box 480741, Los Angeles, CA 90048, (800) 628-0304

A utility program for Epson dot matrix printers and compatibles featuring a set of custom typefaces, a mini word processor, and a keyboard program to pass characters directly to the printer.

ULTRAFORM

Cascade Micro Software Inc., P.O. Box 18039, Seattle, WA 98118

A typesetting package with a sophisticated editor designed for dot matrix output.

Apple Macintosh

HP LASER PRINTER UTILITY

New Image Technology, 10300 Greenbelt Rd., #104, Seabrook, MD 20706, (301) 464-3100

A utility program to enable Macintosh users to print MacPaint files on Hewlett-Packard's 2686A LaserJet printer.

LASERSERVE

Infosphere, Inc., 4730 SW Macadam Ave., Portland, OR 97201, (503) 226-3620

Personal service software that spools up to 16 printing jobs to the LaserWriter with queue ordering and individual job control. A priority service option lets the user move important jobs to the front of the queue. Jobs also can be spooled to more than one printer, removed from the queue, or rearranged. The status of the queue can be displayed, to show if a job is ready to print, has priority status, is starting to print, is printing, or is closing. The status of the printer also can be displayed, to show which printer is working, which job is being printed, and what the printer is doing.

LASERSPEED

THINK Technologies, Inc., 420 Bedford St., Lexington, MA 02173, (617) 863-5595

A utility program to SPOOL (Simultaneous Peripheral Operations On-Line) documents in the background to an AppleTalk-based printer, thus releasing the Macintosh for use in the foreground. The program is composed of two parts: the spooler itself and a desk accessory to control it. The features of the program include use with any normal Macintosh application; control of queue sequencing, document removal, and printer halting; compatibility with PageMaker, MacWrite, Word, Excel, MacPaint, More, InBox, and other programs; spooling to any mounted volume; automatic crash protection; optional display of the printer status; accumulated spooling for printing at a future time; and compatibility with downloadable fonts.

LASERSPOOL

Mac America, 18032-C Lemon Dr., Yorba Linda, CA 92686, (714) 779-2922

A utility program for the Macintosh 512E and Plus that can spool files to the Laser-Writer and LaserWriter Plus. Multiple files may be spooled, releasing the computer to do additional work. A desk accessory is provided to monitor the printer and check on the status of jobs in the print queue.

SUPERLASERSPOOL

SuperMac Software, 950 N. Rengstorff Ave., Mountain View, CA 94043, (415) 964-8884

A printer spooler that optimizes the use of an AppleTalk-connected printer such as the LaserWriter and AppleTalk-compatible ImageWriter. Documents are spooled to the printer in the background while the user maintains use of the Macintosh in the foreground. For example, a four-page ReadySetGo 3.0 document that takes 6.5 minutes without a spooler takes only 6 seconds using SuperLaserSpool. Printer controls include changing the queue order, accessing on-line help, specifying the disk volume destination, deleting documents from the queue, pausing the printer, deinstalling the spooler, displaying the printer status, and setting the user network priority.

Atari

MEGAFONT II PLUS

Xlent Software, P.O. Box 5228, Springfield, VA 22150

A printer utility for the Atari 400/800 that permits files to be printed in any of approximately a dozen different fonts on a variety of dot matrix printers.

TYPESETTER

DataArts Software, P.O. Box 1613, Troy, NY 12181, (518) 273-3053

A low-cost program that includes four type styles, although additional fonts are available at additional cost. A variety of dot matrix printers are supported.

Burroughs B20.B25

MICRO IMAGE PRINTING SYSTEM

Gregory Publishing Co., 333 Cobalt Dr. #107, Sunnyvale, CA 94086, (415) 875-8358

A program that supports the use of Burroughs B20/B25 word processing files on the HP LaserJet printer.

IBM PC

LASERSCRIPT/PLUS

Tangent Technologies, Ltd., 5720 Peachtree Pkwy., Norcross, GA 30092, (404) 662-0366

A program that generates PostScript-formatted files from specific IBM PC applications such as WordStar, Lotus 1-2-3, DisplayWrite 3, MultiMate, and more. The PostScript files then can be output on any PostScript printer, such as the Apple Laser-Writer or Linotype Linotronic L100 or L300 phototypesetters.

CANSET

Orbit Enterprises, Inc., P.O. Box 2875-CX, Glen Ellyn, IL 60138, (312) 469-3405

A setup utility for users of the Canon LBP-A1/A2 printers that controls font selection, margins, line spacing, number of copies, and most other printer features. Distributed as shareware.

EASY LASER

Acorn Plus Inc., 4219 W. Olive Ave., Burbank, CA 91505, (213) 876-5237

A memory-resident, menu-driven program for embedding commands to control the operation of the HP LaserJet and LaserJet+. The program works with most word processors, accessible at any point in which a printer command is to be inserted. Pressing ALT-= results in the display of the Easy Laser menu. Commands for line position, indentation, column position, font selection, justification, ragged edge, line height, page frame, macros, and submenu are obtained by using one of the function keys. Other user-selectable commands include tabs, underline, superscript, subscript, repeat character, text graphics (line, rectangle, gray scale, and patterns), and nonprinting comments. The package also includes a tutorial disk.

FANCYWORD

Softcraft, Inc., 222 State St., Madison, WI 53703, (800) 351-0500

An accessory program for Microsoft Word that adds typographic capabilities to a dot matrix or laser printer.

LASERJET UTILITIES UP 5.0

Public Brand Software, P.O. Box 51478, Indianapolis, IN 46251, (800) IBM-DISK

A collection of programs providing the capability to print envelopes; print Epson-compatible graphics; manipulate fonts with cartridges A, B, D, E via a pop-up menu; and download a graphics character set.

LASER PRESS

Award Software Inc., 236 N. Santa Cruz Ave., Los Gatos, CA 95030, (408) 395-2773

A printer-control program for the HP LaserJet that supports commands users insert within word processing files. Such commands can control spacing between characters and words, center and justify lines, create multiple columns, kern characters, flow text around picture windows, and allow logic-based hyphenation.

LASER PRINT

Janus Assoc., 50 Commonwealth Ave., Boston, MA 02116, (617) 236-1892

A program for the IBM PC and HP LaserJet combination that permits access to LaserJet capabilities through the use of 100 short, easily learned, wordlike commands which are embedded into text files. The program works with any word processing editor, spreadsheet, or other application package.

LETTRIX

Hammerlab Corp., 938 Chapel St., New Haven, CT 06510, (800) 351-4500

A program for IBM PCs outputting to dot matrix printers that supports both the output of a wide variety of supplied typefaces, as well as the design of custom faces. The memory-resident program provides proportional spacing, microjustification, and the addition of InLine commands, which allow sophisticated printer formatting from within a word processor, database, or spreadsheet.

MICROLASER

Cybertext Corp., 702 Jefferson Ave., Ashland, OR 97520, (503) 482-0733

A PostScript-compatible output program that uses the Compugraphic MCS code set for input. Files produced for the MCS can be sent to a PostScript laser printer or to the MCS phototypesetter with no difference in output other than resolution.

PC EM-U-PRINT

Koch Software Industries, 11 W. College Dr., Bldg. G, Arlington Heights, IL 60004, (312) 398-5440

A program that supports the printing, to a Hewlett-Packard LaserJet, of files from most applications packages used on an IBM PC.

PIZAZZ

Application Techniques Inc., 10 Lomar Pk. Dr., Pepperell, MA 01463, (617) 433-5201

A memory-resident program that supports the insertion of a graphics screen image in a word processing or graphics program.

PRINTKEY

Northwest Software, 12469 E. Olive Ave., Spokane, WA 99216, (509) 928-2361

A memory-resident printer utility program that generates the actual hexadecimal formatting codes used by virtually all printers. Using the manual that accompanies a printer, the user can set up the program to support any printer feature, including special formatting, graphics, and color.

PRINTMERGE

Polaris Software, 310 Via Vera Cruz, Suite 205, San Marcos, CA 92069, (619) 471-0922

A printer-control program for the IBM PC and HP 150 that prints WordStar and ASCII print files on an HP LaserJet.

PRINTRIX

Data Transforms Inc., 616 Washington St., Denver, CO 80203, (303) 832-1501

A program for automatic typographic formatting of ASCII text files prepared on a word processor and output on a dot matrix or laser printer. The program can be used as a command line processor, wherein a text file and a layout file can be processed automatically in a batch file, or it can be used as a typical software package, working from a menu.

PRINTWORKS FOR LASERS
SoftStyle, 7192 Kalanianaole Hwy., Honolulu, HI 96825, (808) 396-6368

A memory-resident pop-up menu program for controlling the Hewlett-Packard LaserJet. With one or two keystrokes the user can select font type, style, size, weight, pitch, spacing, margins, page size, lines per inch, multiple copies, sideways printing, etc. The program coexists with other memory-resident software, as well as supports most software applications.

THE NICEPRINT SYSTEM
Spies Laboratories, 13904 Crenshaw Blvd., Gardena, CA 90249, (213) 538-8166

A memory-resident program that intercepts print commands from any application, and outputs near-letter-quality characters on a graphic dot matrix printer. The program includes seven fonts: a roman, sans serif, orator large, script, old English, and computer designs. NicePrint commands can be inserted within word processing documents to mix character styles.

Also included in the program package is TwistPrint, a utility that twists wide-line widths 90 degrees in order to print down the length of a page.

WORD PROCESSOR TOOL KIT
VS Software, 2101 S. Bdwy., Little Rock, AR 72216-9990, (501) 376-2083

A set of printer drivers for popular word processing programs that make it possible to use VS Software laser printer fonts, or fonts, logos, and signatures created with the FontGen font editor.

IBM PC, Victor 9000
MEGATYPE
SoftSet Assoc., 318 Harvard St., Brookline, MA 02146, (617) 739-0707

A dot matrix printer lettering system.

Kaypro CP/M
FONTSTAR
Central Computer Products, 330 Central Ave., Fillmore, CA 93015, (805) 524-4189

A program for certain dot matrix printers that supports the output of documents in any of 16 preprogrammed type styles. A utility is included for the creation of user-designed typefaces.

Publishing

Apple *II*e, *II*c, IIGS
SPRINGBOARD PUBLISHER
Springboard Software, Inc., 7808 Creekridge Cir., Minneapolis, MN 55435, (612) 944-3915

A desktop publishing program for the Apple II series that includes an optional Laser-Writer driver. Program features include text editing; master page formats; complete integration of text and graphics; multiple-column pages; multiple-width pages; multiple-page documents; importation of text and graphic files; multiple type styles and sizes; line spacing and letterspacing; justification options; an extensive graphics library; freehand drawing; and a graphics tool box.

Apple IIGS
GRAPHICWRITER
DataPak Software, Inc., 14011 Ventura Blvd. #507, Sherman Oaks, CA 91423, (818) 905-6419

A publishing package with a Macintosh-like interface, full word processing capabilities, color-separation capability, color layout display, object-oriented graphics, cut/copy/paste, headers and footers, and paint tools.

Apple Macintosh

MacInTax

SoftView Inc., 4820 Adohr Ln., Suite F, Camarillo, CA 93010, (800) MACNTAX

A tax-computation program that displays a representation of tax forms on the screen; calculates and links forms; interfaces with spreadsheets, accounting programs, and databases; and prints completed forms ready for signature and mailing. The completed forms are approved by the IRS for submission.

MacPublisher II

Boston Software Publishers Inc., 1260 Boylston St., Boston, MA 02215, (617) 267-4747

An enhancement of MacPublisher featuring over 40 improvements, including Maxipage, actual size page layout, zoompage 2-9X size, repeating master elements, style changes within a line, automatic page numbering, automatic continuation lines, resizing of pictures, proportional scaling of pictures, direct access to Mac-Write/MacDraw/MacPaint files, type specification sheet, view facing pages, snap-to guides, three types of rulers, kerning pairs table, manual kerning, depth justification, and more.

The program works in concert with many Macintosh applications, as well as accessory programs from Boston Software for generating an index (MacIndexer), inserting prepared artwork (Designs for MacPublishing), and automatically inserting discretionary hyphens (Mac-Hy-phen). The NewsWire desk accessory for sending and receiving ASCII text files also is included with the program. Files received from remote locations can be inserted into MacPublisher publications immediately.

MacSMARTS

Cognition Technology Corp., 55 Wheeler St., Cambridge, MA 02138, (617) 492-0246

An artificial intelligence program that organizes expert knowledge; learns from how an individual makes decisions; links graphics, text, and database information; and automatically diagrams a knowledge base for clarification. The program is one of the first in the "desktop knowledge publishing" category.

A knowledge base is created either by using an intuitive logic worksheet to specify questions, answers, and advice, thereby creating rules for a program to follow in offering advice, or by filling in examples on a standard spreadsheet form. MacSMARTS automatically constructs the underlying rules and puts questions to the user in the sequence that minimizes the number of required questions and produces the advice most quickly.

MacSMARTS can process up to 4,000 rules per knowledge base and 1,000 examples per rule.

MeasureUP

Logic eXtension Resources, 9651 Business Center Dr., Rancho Cucamonga, CA 91730, (714) 980-0046

A test-creation program that automates the creation and publication of free-form, multiple choice, and true/false tests. The program consists of two modules. The Questions module combines word processing, graphics, and database capabilities to simplify the generation of test items. Graphics can be integrated freely with text. All types of questions can be stored and related to specific instructional objectives. Questions can be of variable length and can be composed of various fonts, styles, sizes, and graphic images. The Design module assembles questions, either automatically or manually, to form a test. Statistical and prescriptive information can be tracked for each question.

MORE

Living Videotext, Inc., 2432 Charleston Rd., Mountain View, CA 94043, (800) 822-3700

A sophisticated idea processor that can convert an outline into a bullet or tree chart automatically. The chart then can be graphically modified with easy-to-use tools. Overhead transparencies for meetings and other presentations can be output on a LaserWriter with a minimum of user intervention.

More is the first program to convert ideas into typo/graphic forms automatically, which can improve their understanding and communication value. Charts can be transferred to page-layout programs for inclusion in other documents.

PAGE ONE

McCutcheon Graphics Inc., 130 Bridgeland Ave., Toronto, ON M6A 1Z4, (416) 789-2993

A program created with FTL's MacTEX's software that converts files composed with Microsoft Word into camera-ready book pages. Simple tags are embedded within the Word document to identify parts of the page, such as chapter headings.

The publisher selects from over 50 templates (representing standard book designs) and completes a simple form on the Macintosh screen. The publication then is sent to the LaserWriter or other PostScript-compatible printer. Some of the output options include right- and left-hand running heads, page density (leading control), and magnification (producing larger type for photographic reduction, thereby increasing resolution).

PS COMPOSE

PS Publish, 290 Green St. #1, San Francisco, CA 94133, (415) 433-4698

A desktop publishing program combining code input (based on the Compugraphic MCS code set) with an editable WYSIWYG display. Text can be input with tags using a word processor. The tags can be linked to style sheets in the program so the text can be cast into pages automatically. The program has complete hyphenation and justification control, as well as batch pagination capability.

The program is available in two versions: one for professional typesetters, outputting to the Compugraphic 8400, 8600, and all PostScript printers and typesetters, including the Linotype Linotronic 100 and 300; and one for business users, outputting to the Apple LaserWriter and other PostScript printers.

RAGTIME

Orange Micro, Inc., 1400 N. Lakeview Ave., Anaheim, CA 92807, (714) 779-2772

An integrated page processor incorporating forms generation and graphics, desktop publishing, word processing, and spreadsheet capabilities. The WYSIWYG program features split-screen capability with up to nine windows open at once; documents of up to 350 pages; screen grid; frame and contents protection; frame nesting; multiple rulers; sophisticated spreadsheet capabilities; compatibility with MacDraw, MacPaint, and MacDraft; and more.

SCOOP

Target Software, 14206 S.W. 136th St., Miami, FL 33186, (800) 622-5483

A desktop publishing program that is distinguished by its flexible, irregularly shaped text flow capabilities.

TECHSCRIBER

Mansfield Systems Inc., 550 Hamilton Ave., Suite 200, Palo Alto, CA 94301, (415) 326-0603

A desktop publishing program for technical applications, incorporating page layout, document formatting, text editing, diagram construction, table construction, and mathematical expression construction. Features include automatic creation of index, tables of contents, footnotes, figures, references, appendices, and tables; mouseless keyboard editing; discontinuous selection of elements; search and replace for style; and built-in diagram and table tools.

WRITENOW

T/Maker, 1973 Landings Dr., Mountain View, CA 94043, (415) 962-0195

An advanced word processing program incorporating a 50,000-word spell checker and desktop publishing capabilities. The 100 percent assembly language program rapidly reformats and repaginates long documents. Up to four columns appear in WYSIWYG form with embedded graphics appearing anywhere on a page, as part of a sentence or part of a paragraph. Graphics can be resized and reproportioned. An unlimited number of documents can be opened simultaneously. Additional features include auto-numbered footnotes; an unlimited number of odd and even headers and footers; date, time, and page number insertions anywhere on a page; find and replace forward, backward, wrapping, and wild card; and font-specific changes.

XPRESS

Quark Inc., 2525 W. Evans, Suite 220, Denver, CO 80219, (303) 934-2211

A high-end desktop publishing program oriented toward long documents. The pipelining feature maintains the instant reflow of text across all pages in the publication. Text can be made to flow around irregularly shaped objects. Other capabilities include automatic hyphenation; kerning; tracking; spot color; a spell checker; type sizes from 2 to 500 point; characters overlapping a screen of greater than 50% automatically change to inverse; text screening in any of six levels or seven colors; document size limited only by storage system; graphic displays in square, rectangular, rounded corner, round, and oval boxes; arrows and lines in any width, screen pattern, or color; color separation with optional register marks; rough proof printout; and direct insertion of PostScript commands. A powerful integrated word processor is at the heart of the program.

Atari ST

PUBLISHING PARTNER

Softlogick Corp., 4129 Old Baumgartner, St. Louis, MO 63129, (314) 894-8608

A page-layout program for the Atari ST 520 running under GEM.

CP/M, MS-DOS

SPELLBINDER

Lexisoft, Inc., P.O. Box 1950, Davis, CA 95617, (916) 758-3630

A word processing program with integrated office management capabilities. Features include on-screen help, database management, printer character assignment, flexible search and replace functions, hyphenation, spell-checking, grammar and usage checking, forms creation for automatic fill-in, data merge, real-time calculations, electronic address book, mail merge, conditional merge, and mathematical functions.

IBM XT/AT, Altos, Tandy, NCR Tower, Unisoft

SOFTEST DESKTOP PUB. SYSTEM

SoftTest Inc., 555 Goffle Rd., Ridgewood, NJ 07450, (201) 447-3901

A program available for a variety of computers, a variety of word processors (LEX, Uniplex, MultiMate, WordStar, IBM Displaywrite, etc.), a variety of laser printers

(HP LaserJet, Xerox 4045, Xerox 2700, etc.) and a variety of phototypesetters (Compugraphic 8400 and 8600, Varityper Comp/Edit, Autologic APS-5, Linotype 202, etc.) that adds about 15 English-like commands to the word processor in order to access typesetting capabilities. Among the features that are added are line and box drawing, font and type size selection, vertical spacing, character translation, multiple-column page formatting, hyphenation and justification, and automatic leadering.

IBM PC

ALEXANDER
Design Enterprises of S.F., P.O. Box 14695, San Francisco, CA 94114, (415) 282-8813

A word processing program that is capable of setting complex input, such as multiple languages, math, scientific, and music composition. Advanced word processing features include editing using the keyboard, light pen, and/or mouse; file transfer by telecommunication; text entry either left to right or right to left; and creation of multiple-character symbols with a single keystroke. In addition to supporting a number of printers, Alexander can automatically convert its word processing input into typesetting codes for AM Varityper, Compugraphic, and Linotype phototypesetters.

CALENDAR CREATOR
Power Up, 2929 Campus Dr., San Mateo, CA 94403, (800) 851-2917

A custom calendar-design program capable of producing yearly, monthly, and weekly annotated calendars. An unlimited number of events can be scheduled for any day, with any overflow continuing on an additional page. Periods as short as one week, or as long as one decade, can be shown.

CLICKART PERSONAL PUBLISHER
Software Publishing Corp., 1901 Landings Dr., Mountain View, CA 94039, (415) 962-8910

A personal page-layout program using a graphical interface that emulates an Apple Macintosh. Text is created using any word processor that can produce a plain AS-CII text file. Graphics can be created on the screen, using paint programs, or read in from one of a number of optional ClickArt collections. Features include automatic word wrap and picture wrap (text flows around images); vertical and horizontal rulers; one-to four-column layouts; variable column widths; point sizes from 10 to 48; unlimited font changing and mixing; freehand penciling; and image reversal, flipping, inversion, and duplication. Output is to any of a number of dot matrix and laser printers.

DESKSET
G.O. Graphics, 18 Ray Ave., Burlington, MA 01803-4721, (800) 237-5588

A desktop publishing package supporting output to any PostScript-compatible printer. The program's fully functional text editor has user-defined keys and macro keys, and is not dependent upon a stand-alone word processing program, although it can import files formatted on a word processor. Graphics from paint/draw programs and scanned graphics can be integrated with text. A WYSIWYG preview capability is included. Among the features are unlimited file size (limited by disk space), automatic character compensation and three-level variable-character compensation (tracking), user-modifiable automatic kerning (256 pairs per font), automatic and manual line-ending decisions, user-selectable justification parameters, automatic or discretionary hyphenation, up to 20 columns and 20 tabs, 248 point sizes ranging from 4 to 127.5 point, variable slant in quarter degrees up to 31.75 left or right, reverse video (white on black) characters, electronic character expansion and contraction, automatic cut runarounds, context-sensitive help, automatic ruling and boxes, and more.

FIRST IMPRESSION

Megahaus, 5703 Oberlin Dr., San Diego, CA 92121, (619) 450-1230

A WYSIWYG desktop publishing program incorporating style sheets for the production of newsletters, brochures, price lists, and long documents, such as technical documents. Features include text flow through whole document, global formatting, automatic headers and footers, vertical column justification, hyphenation, widow/orphan control, and text flow around pictures.

FONTASY

Prosoft, 7248 Bellaire Ave., N. Hollywood, CA 91605, (818) 765-4444

An on-screen type composition and drawing program for IBM PCs and compatibles, outputting to a dot matrix printer. The package supports full-page composition, with instant, automatic scrolling, and true-to-scale images of page elements. Page size is limited by computer memory, not by screen size. A two-keystroke sequence can be used to print a minipicture of the entire page.

The program supports multiple font selection, proportional spacing, right justification, kerning, centering, and magnification. A library of 28 fonts are included with the package.

FONTASY, VERSION 2

ProSoft, 7248 Bellaire Ave., P.O. Box 560, N. Hollywood, CA 91603-0560, (818) 765-4444

An enhanced version of Fontasy featuring 60 pieces of small clip art, clip art scan/select/resize/ reposition, improved dot matrix print resolution, selection of print-time margins, automatic multiple-page copies, semiautomatic hyphenation (the program recognizes embedded discretionary hyphens), user-designed clip art libraries, and an improved information status screen.

FRONTPAGE

Studio Software, 3001 Red Hill, Bldg. 210, Costa Mesa, CA 92626, (714) 957-0458

A page-composition program for the IBM PC/XT/AT that provides a graphic icon desktop environment for the assembly of text and graphic images. Output is to both laser printers and phototypesetters.

HARVARD PROFESSIONAL PUBLISHER

Software Publishing Corp., P.O. Box 7210, Mt. View, CA 94036-7210, (303) 799-4900

A WYSIWYG program with automatic kerning and tracking, hyphenation and best-fit justification, irregular runarounds, automatic page style formatting, automatic continuation messages, scanned image support, file importation from Lotus 1-2-3, automatic page numbering, hanging indents, and more.

LASERMAKER

LaserMaker Inc., P.O. Box 802140, Chicago, IL 60680-2140

A command-oriented program with on-line hyphenation and justification. The editor displays the current line measure, type size, type style, copy depth, indents, tabs, etc. Text-handling capabilities include search and replace, block operations, programmable format keys, and a spell-checker. Jobs can be previewed on the screen in sizes ranging from a 25% reduction to a 400% enlargement. Output is to a dot matrix printer, a laser printer, or a variety of phototypesetters.

LaserScript

Command Technology Corp., 1900 Mountain Blvd., Oakland, CA 94611, (415) 339-3530

A comprehensive batch composition desktop publishing program utilizing generic markup to produce lengthy documents on an IBM 3812 Pageprinter or HP LaserJet+. Graphics may be integrated from a number of programs, and fonts from third-party suppliers such as SoftCraft and VS Software are supported.

Components that comprise a document are called *text elements*. Their appearance on the page is controlled by a Global Style Definition. The definition details such items as headers and footers, text element numbering, page numbering, number of columns, page placement, indentions, first-line paragraph offset, odd/even page alignment, leading, change to uppercase, figure list entry, etc. Text elements themselves are identified as page headers and footers, footnotes, section headings (chapter, section, subsection), lists (numbered, bulleted, definition, simple), paragraphs, notes, warnings, figures (with raster or vector images), appendices, glossary entries, table of contents entries, figure list entries, index entries, and cross references.

A text editor or word processor is used to embed Laser Script commands within text. Commands are enclosed within markup delimiters. For example, a paragraph would be indicated as <p>, a chapter title as <h1>, and bold begin and bold end as <bb> and <be>, respectively.

Additional functions include extended character sets in the code range of decimal 32 to 255; support for a user-specified ASCII format hyphenation dictionary; tabs at arbitrary horizontal positions; flexible page imposition with trim marks; automatic column balancing and vertical justification; widow and orphan suppression; alternating odd/even margins for duplex page printing; combining of multiple input files to produce a single formatted document; mail merge of fixed text with a simple database file; automatic generation of table of contents, figure list, and index; parameter-driven macro definitions; and conditional processing based on IF, AND, OR, ELSE, ENDIF.

LaserType

Softlab, P.O. Box 879, St. George, UT 84770, (801) 628-4969

A software package for the composition of forms, manuals, reports, and business correspondence output on the Hewlett-Packard Laserjet.

LaserType 2d Plus

Softlab, P.O. Box 879, St. George, UT 84770, (801) 628-4969

A command-oriented program for the IBM PC and HP LaserJet Plus that supports the creation of business forms, letters, graphic illustrations, and mail merge. Pop-down menus and on-line help screens assist the user in creating and modifying input. Other capabilities include automated creation of table of contents, index generation, section enumeration, numeric and alphabetic lists, style profiles, and macros.

Lotus Manuscript

Lotus Development Corp., 55 Cambridge Pky., Cambridge, MA 02142, (800) 345-1043

A word processing program optimized for technical documentation. Graphics from Lotus 1-2-3, Symphony, and Freelance Plus can be imported, as can spreadsheets, charts, diagrams, and scanned images. Style sheets are used to globally format a document composed of multiple sections. An integrated outline function can be used to organize thoughts and ideas, as well as to collapse a document in order to get a general view of its contents.

MicroTeX Version 1.5A1
Addison-Wesley Publishing Co., Educational and Professional Tech. Div., Reading, MA 01867, (617) 944-3700

An improved version of MicroTeX that will run on a two-floppy system. System performance has been increased 24 to 35 percent.

NewsMaster
Unison World, 2150 Shattuck Ave., Suite 902, Berkeley, CA 94704, (415) 848-6666

A page-composition program outputting to a wide variety of dot matrix and laser printers. The WYSIWYG interface is controlled by function keys and consists of two basic sets of icons: one for editing text and one for editing graphics. Over 250 pieces of artwork are supplied in categories such as sports, business, foods, and design. Over 30 decorative and text fonts are included.

The program is easy to use and is consistent with the publisher's claim that the user can "go from purchase to print in less than an hour." Text elements can be typed in directly or flowed in from existing ASCII text files. Graphics can be stamped in place, moved, copied, enlarged, reduced, stretched, cropped, or flipped. Lines, boxes, and patterns can be placed anywhere on a page.

The screen is divided roughly into thirds, with the page view occupying the top 2/3 and the Icon menu the remainder. The page can be viewed in a number of ways, from full page to an eight-times enlargement. All editing functions remain active in any view. The initial page layout prompts the user to add or delete columns from the default two-column design, and to leave or remove the default headline area.

Text is added to a layout by selecting a typeface, positioning the text cursor, and keyboarding. The line orientation of the text is determined by selecting the justification icon, with options for centered, left, right, or justified text.

Artwork can be stamped over a column of text and can be made to change the reflow of text beneath it. A one-level Undo key can cancel or reinstate the last action.

PageBuilder
White Sciences Inc., P.O. Box 24756, Tempe, AZ 85282, (602) 967-8257

A WYSIWYG desktop publishing program supporting output through any Canon print engine and a variety of plotters and dot matrix printers. Over 300 fully proportional fonts, in sizes ranging from 3 to 72 point, are included. The program supports the integration of text, line drawings, and scanner clip art using the Enhanced Graphics Adapter with 16 on-screen colors.

PagePerfect
Beyond Words Inc., 180 Meernaa Ave., Fairfax, CA 94930, (415) 456-8909

A WYSIWYG program combining word processing, image processing, and file management. Among the text-creation features are multiple windows, color display of style commands, spell-checking, a thesaurus, and hyphenation.

PageWriter
The 'Puter Group, 1717 W. Beltline Hwy., Madison, WI 53713, (800) 545-3522

A program for the preparation of brochures, newsletters, forms, ads, bar graphs, and flow charts. Basic features include placement of text, screens, and rules; kerning; justified columns; hyphenation; scaling from 5% to 300%; border creation; and typeface modification (reverse, gray, condensed, or expanded). Output is to a laser printer or phototypesetter.

POWERTEXT FORMATTER
Beaman Porter Inc., 417 Halstead Ave., Harrison, NY 10528, (914) 835-3516

A text-formatting program that accepts input from most word processors and text editors and outputs to most laser printers. It can handle documents of almost any length, providing automatic type style selection, page layout, sorted bibliography, table of contents, sorted two-level index, outlining, footnote numbering and layout, hyphenation and justification and multiple-column capability.

The program uses the slash as its command character, preceding each of its format files, keywords, and sometimes, parameters. Parameters are numeric values that are enclosed within square brackets. The first entry in a file that is to be processed by the program must be the name of the format file. If the format is for producing a report, the first entry would be **/report**. To indent text 20 spaces from the left margin, for example, the correct command would be **/left [20]**. Graphics, tables, and other illustrative material are added manually to the text after printing. Space is reserved for them by using the **/block [x]** command, where x is the number of blank lines that are to be reserved.

SCENICWRITER
Scenic Computer Systems Corp., 14852 NE 31st Cir., Redmond, WA 98052, (206) 885-5500

A word processor with text-composition and page-layout capabilities. Embedded codes are required, and no screen preview is available. Output is to a variety of laser printers, including the LaserJet and LaserWriter.

SUPERPAGE
Bestinfo, 130 S. State Rd., Springfield, PA 19064, (215) 328-2900

SuperPage is a sophisticated pagination system (IBM XT or AT-based), supported by a Datacopy 700 image scanner, and output on a variety of laser printers and phototypesetters.

TYPE PROCESSOR ONE
Bestinfo, 130 S. State Rd., Springfield, PA 19064, (215) 328-2900

Type Processor One is a WYSIWYG program providing interactive page make-up on the IBM PC.

THE NEWSROOM PRO
Springboard Software, Inc., 7808 Creekridge Cir., Minneapolis, MN 55435, (612) 944-3915

An advanced version of The Newsroom, with the following improvements. Text can be deleted, moved, and copied within and between columns; five vertical line spacing settings are available; ASCII files can be imported from other programs, and files can be imported from The Newsroom; multiple copies can be printed at one time. The Newsroom Pro is completely hard-disk compatible (not copy protected); is mouse or keyboard controllable; includes over 2,000 clip art images; flips art left and right, top and bottom; and resizes art. Entire columns can be created on screen. Text and graphics can be positioned anywhere in a column. Text automatically scrolls between columns.

THE OFFICE PUBLISHER
Laser Friendly, 930 Benecia Ave., Sunnyvale, CA 94086, (408) 730-1921

A desktop publishing program that operates in the GEM operating environment; is compatible with all popular word processors, spreadsheets, and databases; supports all recognized laser printers, digital scanners, and computer accessories; provides an interactive WYSIWYG editor; supports kerning, leading, tracking, hyphenation, justification, gutter control, vertical tabs, automatic pagination, and more.

IBM PC/AT

PAGEWORK

West End Film Inc., 1825 Q St. N.W., Washington, DC 20009, (202) 232-7733

A WYSIWYG page-composition program that supports PostScript output devices, such as the Apple LaserWriter. Companion programs include ArtWork, for producing three-dimensional drawings; BrushWork, for scanning and painting captured images; and ChartWork, for adding business graphs and charts. Features include an unlimited number of fonts, unlimited size of fonts, large first-letter indent, wrap-around graphics, freehand run-arounds, and direct support for a number of popular word processors.

SUPERPAGE II

Bestinfo, 130 South State Rd., Springfield, PA 19064, (215) 328-2900

A menu-driven, format-oriented, interactive pagination program with a WYSIWYG display.

IBM PC/XT/AT

LASERWARE

SWFTE International, Ltd., P.O. Box 219, Rockland, DE 19732, (302) 658-1123

A memory-resident publishing program for HP LaserJet and LaserJet Plus laser printers. The program occupies just 45K of RAM and is compatible with virtually any MS-DOS program, supporting the real-time input of any of over 100 functions. Laser-Ware commands are input within the application program and exist transparently. When a document is printed, the commands for changing fonts, centering, aligning decimals, drawing boxes, and other functions are trapped by LaserWare, interpreted, and deleted from the output.

Graphics from other programs can be captured and merged with a text document. Graphics are captured by redirecting their output to a DOS file rather than to a printer, using the LaserWare Graphics Capture utility. Graphic screens also can be dumped directly to the LaserJet by using the Screen Graphics Dump function.

A series of LaserWare commands supports the integration of data into predefined locations on a form. Data can be processed in a delimited list or in tabular, fixed-length output. Most databases and spreadsheets conform to these two data formats.

A pop-up menu system includes an on-line help manual, a listing of font assignments, a font management system, and more.

MAGNATYPE

Magna Computer Systems, 14724 Ventura Blvd., Sherman Oaks, CA 91403, (818) 986-9233

One of the most powerful and full-featured typesetting front-end packages available on a personal computer. MagnaType was developed by Fred Rose and Burt Wigdor, who were instrumental in the development of minicomputer-based commercial typographic systems sold by Computer Composition International. The system uses a mnemonic coding structure composed of over 100 identities. Prior to output, the embedded codes are translated into the instructions necessary to operate a laser printer or phototypesetter. Additional software offerings include MagnaWord, the MagnaType program without the typesetter output module (appropriate for multiple workstations), and MagnaLink, a networking program that uses an IBM AT as a file server to XT or AT workstations.

Wang PC

PCS BOOKMAKER

Amtech Computer Systems Inc., 2389 Main St., Glastonbury, CT 06033,
(203) 659-2635

A program supporting all of the basic features of the Wang Word Processing program, with output to the Epson MX/FX, Diablo 630, and HP LaserJet. Features include printer sharing with printer buffer and queuing, mixed type styles, screen dumps, proportional printing, full-page formatting, and headers and footers.

Signs

Apple II

PROFESSIONAL SIGN MAKER

Sunburst Communications, 39 Washington Ave., Pleasantville, NY 10570,
(800) 431-1934

A sign-making program for the Apple II using dot matrix printer output. Signs may be up to 8 lines long, with individual letters up to 8 inches high.

CP/M, MS-DOS

MAGIC KEYBOARD

Woodsmith Software, Route 3, P.O. Box 550A, Nashville, IN 47448, (818) 988-2137

A program designed for the production of posters, signs, labels, overheads, banners, and headlines. Character sizes range from standard text to 10 feet, and output on a dot matrix printer. Features include a one-line text editor, a font library of 16 typefaces, automatic centering, underlining, proportional spacing, and adjustable margins. Fonts are editable and new fonts can be designed from within the program.

IBM PC

BANNER MAKER

Software Express, P.O. Box 2288, Merrifield, VA 22116, (800) 331-8192

A program that produces banners and signs in letters up to 7 inches high. Output, in a choice of decorative typefaces, is on the Epson or IBM dot matrix printer.

SIGN DESIGNER

Power Up, 2929 Campus Dr., San Mateo, CA 94403, (800) 851-2917

A program that prints sideways on standard-width printer paper. Three type styles, in sizes ranging from 1/4 to 8 inches, can be composed.

IBM PC, Apple II

DGI SIGNMAKER

Decision Graphics, Inc., P.O. Box 2776, Littleton, CO 80161, (303) 796-0341

A program that allows the user to create, edit, save, and plot text signs using a wide variety of plotters.

IBM PC, CP/M-80

SIGN-PLOT

Centerpoint Computer Applic., 500 N. Michigan Ave., Chicago, IL 60611,
(312) 467-0333

A program that creates signs using a pen plotter. A variety of fonts are available.

IBM PC, MS-DOS, PC-DOS

TYP-SET

Enter Computer Inc., 6867 Nancy Ridge Dr., San Diego, CA 92121, (619) 450-0601

A program for generating extremely small (.05-inch) 6 to exceptionally large (72-inch) typographic characters on a plotter or dot matrix printer. Features include a menu-driven interface, a wide selection of fonts, automatic design variations (condensed, extended, italicized, rotated, mirrored, reversed, shaded, overlapped, etc.), icon images and shape library, manual kerning, multiple-line justification (centered, right, or left), and on-screen preview.

MS-DOS, CP/M
BANNER

Custom Program House, P.O. Box 4710, Berkeley, CA 94704, (415) 652-8222

An inexpensive lettering program for the production of banners and signs.

Specialty Output

Apple IIGS
PAPER MODELS: THE CHRISTMAS KIT

Activision, Inc., P.O. Box 7287, Mountain View, CA 94039, (800) 227-9759

A companion program for Activision's Paintworks Plus, containing graphic images for creating Christmas decorations, tree ornaments, package designs and gift boxes, and three-dimensional displays. The kit includes a clip art disk, decorator's guide, reference card, heavy card stock, glue stick, red and green felt-tip markers, 6-inch ruler, and five jingle bells. This program is also available in a MacPaint version for the Macintosh.

Apple Macintosh
CALENDARMAKER

CE Software, 801-73rd St., Des Moines, IA 50312, (515) 224-1995

A program that produces calendars for wall display or inclusion in page-layout programs. Each day can have up to 255 characters and an icon. There are three calendar styles: Pictorial (with a large graphic image occupying the top half); Full Page; and Two Months. A collection of icons is provided, along with tools to create new ones and capture existing ones. Printing can be done in color on the ImageWriter II or at 300 dpi resolution on the LaserWriter. The MacBILLBOARD program can be used to enlarge the calendar to any size.

LASER FX

Tesseract Software, P.O. Box 937, St. Catherines, ON L2R 6Z4, (416) 685-4854

A special-effects typography program that processes standard PICT files using degrees of shading, tone, depth, angle, offset, and screening. Text also can be rotated or skewed. The program is compatible with all PostScript fonts, producing thousands of unique effects usually obtainable only through direct PostScript coding.

LP TEXT

London Pride Inc., 1 Birch St., Norwalk, CT 06851, (203) 866-4806

A program for producing special-effects typography in the form of shadow or circular set type. The program produces PostScript code for printing on PostScript output devices, or to disk for inclusion in programs such as JustText.

The Shadow Text option supports shadowing in the range of 0 to 100 percent, letters of any depth, or multiple outline letters. The Circular Text option supports the setting of a text string around the circumference of a circle in either a concave or convex fashion. The program allows control of letter spacing; type size; circumference size; and gray scaling of text, text background, and circle lines.

MacBILLBOARD & MacBANNER
CE Software, 801-73rd St., Des Moines, IA 50312, (515) 224-1995

MacBILLBOARD is a program for creating or modifying Macintosh artwork (pictures, text, graphs, digitized images, etc.) to be output to a maximum size of over 19 feet × 26 feet. Tools resemble those used in MacPaint, but multilevel magnification and split-window editing have been added. Posters are assembled by taping individual sheets together. Printer options also include a command to produce an Iron-On (laterally reversed image) and a Greeting Card (flipping images for a French fold).

MacBanner is a sign marker for producing single-line banners composed of text and graphics. Graphics can be copied from MacBILLBOARD, MacPaint, or prepared clip art. The program supports the use of color using an appropriate ribbon on an ImageWriter II.

MyDiskLabeler
Williams & Macias, P.O. Box 19206, Spokane, WA 99219, (509) 458-6312

A sophisticated label-making program for ImageWriter and LaserWriter output. Features include flexible file selection; inclusion of icons; icon editing; text borders; choice of fonts, styles, and sizes; automatic date stamping; automatic serialization; multiple printing; and a color option for the ImageWriter II.

POSTERMAKER
Strider Software, Beecher Lake Rd., Pembine, WI 54156, (715) 324-5487

A Macintosh printer utility program for the ImageWriter or LaserWriter that supports the enlargement or reduction of MacPaint-format documents from 1% to 3200% of original size. Posters larger than 8 × 10 inches are printed in sheets and are assembled manually.

STORYBOARDER
American Intelliware, 350 S. Crenshaw Blvd., Torrance, CA 90504, (213) 533-4040

A desktop publishing tool that facilitates the creation of storyboards for film, advertising, television, and audio-visual communications. The user can create graphics, split-screen montages, animatics, and real-time video animation with zooms, wipes, and dissolves. Dialogue and script notes can be included with numbered, formatted, and masked frames.

Images can be created using MacPaint or print and video digitizers. The images can be maintained in an image library. Images can be viewed and printed in various aspect ratios and TV masks. Each frame can have accompanying dialog, or script or production notes.

Animation options include moving images across, around, or off the screen; shrinking or enlarging them; zooming in or out; panning across, up, or down; flipping horizontally or vertically; and adjusting the timing of animation events.

IBM PC, Apple II

CERTIFICATE MAKER
Springboard Software, Inc., 7808 Creekridge Cir., Minneapolis, MN 55435, (612) 944-3915

An easy-to-use, screen-prompted program for automating the design and dot matrix printing of certificates, awards, diplomas, and licenses. The user selects one of over 200 prepared designs, chooses one of the 24 borders, adds a text message and signature and date, and prints the certificate. A selection of stickers and gold seals are included with the package.

Kaypro CP/M

3DD

Hawaii Mountain Works, P.O. Box 1573, Kamuela, HI 96743, (808) 885-4607

A program based on the principle of the stereoscope. It supports the printing of graphics on Epson printers. The graphics can be viewed through 3-D glasses as three-dimensional objects. The package includes two pair of glasses, one screen filter overlay, and the software disk.

Typefaces

Apple II

FONTS I

Tangent 270, P.O. Box 38587, Denver, CO 80238, (303) 322-1262

A large collection of fonts to be used with dot matrix printers.

Apple Macintosh

ADOBE TYPEFACE COLLECTION

Adobe Systems Incorporated, 1870 Embarcadero Rd., Palo Alto, CA 94303, (415) 852-0271

A series of downloadable PostScript typefaces licensed from the Mergenthaler and International Typeface Corporation libraries. The typeface packages include both the screen fonts for viewing on the Macintosh and the character outlines, which are processed by any PostScript printer. Each package includes the software for manually downloading a typeface (although the LaserWriter software can download requested fonts automatically) and for installing the screen fonts. The packages are available in single- and multiple-printer versions.

DECOWRITER LETTERS & FONTS

SEA-ESS Graphics, P.O. Box 451, Olathe, KS 66061

DecoWriter Letters are a set of decorative initials in MacPaint format. DecoWriter Fonts are more than a dozen decorative designs for output to the ImageWriter.

DESIGNER SERIES

Century Software, Inc., 2483 Hearst Ave., #175, Berkeley, CA 94709, (415) 549-1901

A series of downloadable PostScript typefaces including ITC Avant Garde, Terra, HelHeavy, Option, ITC Kabel, Gothica, ITC Eras, Micron, and Missive.

DOWNLOADABLE POSTSCRIPT FONTS

Allotype Typographics, 1600 Packard Rd., #5, Ann Arbor, MI 48104, (313) 663-1989

A collection of specialty fonts for typesetting Greek, chemical and molecular structures, Polish, and more.

FANCY FONTS

Genny Software R&D, P.O. Box 5909, Beaumont, TX 77706, (409) 892-5752

A single disk of exceptionally well-designed bitmap fonts ranging in size from 9 to 84 points. The contents includes borders, international symbols, calendars, forms, graphs, rulers, keycaps, flow chart symbols, and more.

FLUENT FONTS

Casady Company, P.O. Box 223779, Carmel, CA 93922, (408) 646-4660

A two-disk set of alternate bitmapped fonts.

FLUENT LASER FONTS
Casady Co., P.O. Box 223779, Carmel, CA 93922, (800) 331-4321

A collection of reasonably priced PostScript-compatible screen and printer fonts that are compatible with all Macintosh applications. The fonts have been created using the Altsys FONTographer program and are user-editable. The fonts have been optimized in size (compressed) so that more of them can fit into the limited RAM available on the LaserWriter. A full character complement, including accented characters, is included with each design. Available typefaces include Bodoni (italic, bold, bold italic), Sans Serif (italic, book, book italic, demi bold, demi italic), Ritz (italic, condensed), Right Bank, Monterey (italic, medium, bold, bold italic), Calligraphy, Regency Script, Prelude Script, and more. All designs also can be set in the standard Macintosh variations of outline and shadow.

FLUENT LASER FONTS DESIGNER COLLECTION
CasadyWare, P.O. Box 223779, Carmel, CA 93922, (408) 646-4660

A collection of downloadable PostScript fonts including Gregorian, Coventry Script, Zephyr Script, Dorovar, Bodoni Ultra, Sans Serif Bold, Sans Serif Extra Bold, Russian and Ukrainian, Gatsby Light, Micro Laser, and Micro Extended.

FONT COLLECTIONS
Altsys Corp., 720 Ave. F, Suite 108, Plano, TX 75074, (214) 424-4888

This collection of fonts was created by users of Altsys FONTastic and FONTographer. FONTastic Fonts include Doug Miles fonts (Gothic, Uncial, script, etc.), Foreign Language fonts (Cyrillic, Slavic, Greek, Coptic, and Armenian), and Math fonts, including a set of fractions. FONTOGRAPHER Fonts include Goudy Newstyle, Cooper, Cooper Extra, Cooper Oldstyle, Cooper Oldstyle Extra, Venezia, Venezia Extra, and Borders I-III.

FONT PAK
Power Tools Software, 5059 San Aquaric Dr., San Diego, CA 92109, (619) 483-3436

A collection of 30 ImageWriter fonts that self-install on the Apple Macintosh.

GAZETTE LIBRARY, FONTS
International Datawares Inc., 2278 Trade Zone Blvd., San Jose, CA 95131, (408) 262-6660

A collection of public-domain, shareware, and copyrighted fonts distributed with permission and organized into useful sets. The fonts are available at no cost, other than a charge for duplication, media, postage, and handling.

HEADLINE GRAPHICS
American Softwerkz, P.O. Box, Brandon, FL 34299, (813) 626-0755

A collection of decorative display type and images in MacPaint format.

LASERFONTS COLLECTION
Century Software, 2306 Cotner Ave., Los Angeles, CA 90064, (213) 829-4436

A series of Apple LaserWriter fonts that work with all standard Apple LaserWriter and LaserPrep files. These fonts work with almost every popular Macintosh program that can access the LaserWriter, including PageMaker, ReadySetGo, and MacPublisher. Font complements include a special set of printer's bullets, boxes, and arrows; fixed spaces (em, en, and thin); and accents necessary for printing in over 30 languages. Available styles include fat, thin, and micro variations of Times, Helvetica, and Courier; Williamette, a modern sans serif; Congo, a decorative stencil display; Thames, a traditional upright Carolingian script; Styx, a modern stencil display; Devoll, a decorative script; Cumberland, a general-purpose serif; Manistee, a modern sans serif; Trent, blackletter; and many more.

A special-effects package called Shadow Effects produces shadows, stacked, light gray, dark gray, drop shadow, filled, and other effects for Helvetica and Times. Symbols+ is a collection of over 200 popular symbols and graphic images, including people and icons.

LaserPerfect Fonts
NeoScribe International, P.O. Box, 6533-P, Hamden, CT 06517, (203) 782-2200

A collection of LaserWriter downloadable fonts, including Hebrew, OCR-A, and Devanagari, that include many typographic refinements such as tailored fit, kerned characters, old-style numerals, and printer's fixed spaces.

LaserType
Image Club Graphics, 2828 19th St. N.E., Calgary, Alberta T2E 6Y9, (403) 250-1969

A large collection of custom type designs featuring built-in kerning pairs.

MacMath
Linguist's Software, P.O. Box 231, Mount Hermon, CA 95041, (408) 335-2577

A set of fonts for scientific calculations related to the fields of engineering, mathematics, economics, chemistry, physics, and astronomy.

Professional Type Fonts
Kensington Microwave Ltd., 251 Park Ave., S., New York, NY 10010, (212) 475-5200

A two-disk set of fonts for outputting to the ImageWriter, with one disk composed of text fonts and the other display fonts. Designs are based upon famous Mergenthaler and ITC typefaces such as Times Roman, Helvetica, and Optima.

Soft Palette Font (Volume 1)
Decision Science Software, Inc., P.O. Box 7876, Austin, TX 78713, (512) 926-4527

A collection of 18 decorator fonts for the Apple Macintosh. It also includes borders and interior design symbols.

Soft Palette Font
Decision Science Software, Inc., P.O. Box 7876, Austin, TX 78713, (512) 926-4527

A collection of general-purpose ImageWriter fonts appropriate for business presentations, displays, and artwork.

Superfonts
Software Apple-cations, 11510 Alejandro, Boise, ID 83709, (208) 322-8910

A collection of 16 bitmapped typefaces for use in MacPaint, MacWrite, and other applications.

TechFonts
Paragon Courseware, 4954 Sun Valley Rd., Del Mar, CA 92014, (619) 481-1477

A two-font set—SciFonts for typing equations and ElectroFonts for typing electronic analog circuits.

Treacyfaces
Treacyfaces, Inc., 303 Conway Ave., Narberth, PA 19072

A collection of custom-designed PostScript typefaces.

ULTRAFONTS
Century Software, 2306 Cotner Ave., Los Angeles, CA 90064, (213) 829-4436

A two-disk set of fonts including technical and business designs, with special characters for engineers, scientists, lawyers, and doctors. Also included are a borders font, symbols font, international symbols font, and more.

WORKFONTS 3.0
Font Workshop, P.O. Box 3306, Oak Brook, IL 60522

A collection of 30 styles for the Apple ImageWriter I and II, ranging in size from 5 to 48 points.

WORLD CLASS FONTS
Dubl-Click Software, Inc., 18201 Gresham St., Northridge, CA 91325, (818) 349-2758

A two-volume set of word processing and graphics fonts named after cities around the world. Each volume is composed of three disks. Fonts range in size from 9 to 36 points and include theme fonts appropriate for religious, foreign language, chess, architectural, and decorative purposes. Also included are four accessory programs for determining character positions (BigCaps), changing the default application font (DefaultFont), displaying and printing font layouts (The Font Charter), and taking a break (TicTacToe).

CONOFONTS
Conographic Corp., available from LaserJet+ dealers only, Irvine, CA

A large collection of downloadable fonts, borders, and symbols for an HP LaserJet+ driven by one of the following word processors: MS Word (version 2.0 or later), WordPerfect (version 4.1 or later) WordStar 2000 (version 2.0 or later).

IBM PC, MS-DOS, PC-DOS

LASER FONTS
SoftCraft, Inc., 222 State St., Madison, WI 53703, (800) 351-0500

A program that automates the downloading of fonts to the HP LaserJet+, Canon Laser Beam, and other compatible laser printers. The downloaded fonts are compatible with Microsoft Word, Fancy Word, Fancy Font, and other word processors. New fonts and special characters can be created, and existing fonts (supplied with the software) can be edited using two additional programs supplied with the package.

Typesetting

Apple II

APPLE-BASED FRONT-END SOFTWARE
Imagemakers, 1030 G E. Duane Ave., Sunnyvale, CA 94086, (408) 245-2660

A typesetting program that provides real-time hyphenation and justification. Output is to a variety of different phototypesetters.

Apple Macintosh

MACTEX
FTL Systems Inc., 234 Eglinton Ave. E., Toronto, CN M4P 1K5, (416) 487-2142

A desktop typesetting product that is a complete implementation of the TeX typesetting system. The program offers a full set of professional typesetting features, including hyphenation and justification, kerning, ligatures, automatic pagination, headers, footnotes, automatic generation of index, table of contents, and bibliography. MacTeX supports over 1,100 built-in commands and macros, and provides page previewer. The program provides a number of standard templates for producing letters, reports, articles, and other types of common documents. MacTeX supports the importation of MacPaint images and also 248 PostScript commands. (PostScript cannot be previewed.)

MICROSETTER FOR THE MACINTOSH

Teletypesetting Co., 210 Nickels Arcade, Ann Arbor, MI 48104, (313) 761-7664

A software package that converts PostScript commands into typesetter driver codes for certain VariTyper, Compugraphic, and Linotype phototypesetters. Programs such as Microsoft Word, ReadySetGo, and MacDraw can be used.

IBM PC

/usr/tools

ETP Systems, Inc., 9730 SW Cascade Blvd., Portland, OR 97223, (503) 639-4024

UNIX-based software offering menu-oriented processing, publishing with standard fonts, laser printer interfacing, and support for text, tables, equations, and graphics.

BYSO PRINT

Levien Instrument Co., Sitlington Hill, P.O., Box 31, McDowell, VA 24458, (703) 396-3345

A typesetting formatter for certain dot matrix and laser printers that works in combination with any word processor. The BYSO PRINT formatter is loaded into memory prior to using the word processor. Typesetting-like codes, such as <PS14> (Point Size 14) are embedded in the text. When the word processor's printing command is invoked, BYSO PRINT intercepts the text and formats it according to the embedded typographic commands. A screen-capture utility provides for the inclusion of graphics within typeset documents.

Levien Instrument Company has digitized its own library of over 100 typefaces, which are available at a moderate cost.

MAXX AND MAXXPLUS

Varityper, 11 Mt. Pleasant Ave., East Hanover, NJ 07936, (201) 887-8000

A composition software package running on IBM PCs and outputting on certain models of the VariTyper Comp/Edit phototypesetter line. The program features hierarchical file management, scratch pad memory, a 10,000-word spelling checker, 36 user-definable keys, automated composition routines, and a command-suppress capability for easy proofreading. The Plus version features WYSIWYG capability.

PROFESSIONAL TYPOGRAPHY PROGRAMS

Edco Services, Inc., 3008 Sabal Rd., Tampa, FL 33618, (813) 933-8513

A group of specialized programs, most of which support the use of Alphatype phototypesetting equipment.

QROFF

QCAD Systems, Inc., 1164 Hyde Ave., San Jose, CA 95129, (800) 538-9787

Text-formatting software for the IBM PC and HP LaserJet combination. By adding simple commands to a standard text file, QROFF controls all of the following (and more): the mixing of fonts, the specification of page limits (margins, page number locations, automatic headers and footers, page length, and line spacing), the manipulation of lines (left, right, center, underline, indents), and the automatic creation of subject indices, superscript and subscript spacing adjustments, table formatting, etc.

TYPE-SET-IT

Good Ideas, 175 Lowell St., Andover, MA 10810, (617) 475-7238

A typesetting program outputting to a dot matrix printer, producing over 1,200 fonts at ''near-typeset'' quality. The system uses pop-up menus, and WYSIWYG processing.

XyWrite III

XyQuest, P.O. Box 372, Bedford, MA 01730, (617) 275-4439

An updated version of the XyWrite word processing program that features real-time automatic hyphenation and justification with syllable wrapping; within-column editing; up to nine overlapping windows of varying size and shape; automatic counting in alpha, roman, or arabic; up to six newspaper-style columns; multiple-file searching; full proportional spacing (definable printer file definitions); and on-line help.

IBM PC, Apple II

DGI Type Shop

Decision Graphics, Inc., P.O. Box 2776-B, Littleton, CO 80161, (303) 796-0341

A program that supports typesetting on a Hewlett-Packard plotter. Additional "plotsetting" typefaces are available.

IBM PC, MS-DOS

FinalWord II

Mark of the Unicorn, Inc., 222 Third St., Cambridge, MA 02142, (617) 576-2760

An exceptionally powerful text-formatting program with automatic generation of indices and tables of contents. The program is among the most flexible, proof of which is the following statement from the manual: "FinalWord II can support every printer in the world [with the exception of Fortran Carriage Control line printers], even ones we have never seen before!" Features include: multiple font variations, discretionary hyphenation, automatic line fill, indenting/outdenting, grouping of paragraphs and passages, formatting of verse, making lists, alternating of left and right page formats, vertical justification, equation writing, and creating one of multicolumn text.

IBM PC, MS-DOS, PC-DOS

RIMSystems

Telesis Systems, Inc., P.O. Box 5462, Lincoln, NE 68505, (404) 467-5652

A combination front-end composition and typesetting system outputting to the HP LaserJet Plus. The package consists of a full-featured text editor and utilities for moving files into the system from word processors or wire-capture sources. Files are created with embedded commands controlling typographic parameters, line orientation, tabbing, page formatting, and graphics (lines, boxes, etc.). Features include four levels of hyphenation, BitStream fonts, traditional typesetter commands (space only, flash only, floating tabs, run-arounds, hanging indents, multicolumn, etc.), menu-controlled system, ASCII text file input, extensive kerning pair tables, ligatures, and 158 characters per font.

MS-DOS

Micro Print-X

Composition Technology Int., 10646 Zelzah Ave., Granada Hills, CA 91344, (818) 368-8258

A program providing composition capability for output to either an Autologic APS-5 or Cordata laser printer.

Utility

Apple II

PS Lover's Utility Set

Big Red Apple Club, 1105 S. 13th St., Suite 103, Norfolk, NE 68701, (402) 379-4680

A collection of ten Print Shop utility programs for accomplishing such tasks as printing out Print Shop pictures and their names, creating labels from Print Shop pictures and text, and converting Print Shop pictures into Newsroom graphics.

Apple III

TYPEFACES

Quark Inc., 2525 W. Evans, Suite 220, Denver, CO 80219, (303) 934-2211

An accessory program for the Quark Word Juggler word processing program that translates Word Juggler formatting commands into a form understood by phototypesetting machines.

Apple *IIe/IIc*

LASERWRITER/APPLEWRITER UTILITIES

Synergetics, 746 First St., Thatcher, AZ 85552, (602) 428-4073

A program for driving the Apple LaserWriter by inputting commands in Applewriter files. The four-disk package includes utilities to produce letterheads and logos, isometric drawing, encoders, patches and insignias, grids and rulers, sequential numbering, electronic schematics, sunken initials, badges, signatures, graphs, and more.

Apple Macintosh

ATM

Boojum Computer Systems, Inc., 1327 High Rd., Suite J3, Tallahassee, FL 332304, (904) 576-9415

This program converts any Apple II screen to a standard Macintosh MacPaint document. Text screens can be converted to standard Macintosh text files. Apple II fonts for the Macintosh are included, providing the means to display text in exactly the way that it appears on the Apple II screen.

This program is particularly useful for publishers of Apple II software who have a need to produce their program documentation on the Macintosh. It is also useful for computer users who want to move graphic images from Apple II to the Macintosh.

The package consists of two programs, one for the Apple II and one for the Macintosh. The Apple II program converts a screen display into hexadecimal data that is sent through a serial connection to the Macintosh. The Macintosh must be set up with a communications program that is capable of accepting a standard ASCII text transmission. After a file is received, it is converted into MacPaint or text format using the AtM Macintosh programs.

DISKTOP

CE Software, 801-73rd St., Des Moines, IA 50312, (515) 224-1995

A collection of useful utilities provided as desk accessories. These utilities include the following capabilities:

- List, find, copy, rename, delete, move, and set attributes of files.
- Create folders, eject disks, and change the default drive or folder.
- Monitor the status of the LaserWriter.
- Set the date and time, adjust paper sizes for the ImageWriter, create a new startup screen, convert PICT files to paint files, print miniature catalogs of paint files on the LaserWriter, reset a LaserWriter, enable or disable the LaserWriter test page, and send PostScript files directly to the LaserWriter.

GAZETTE LIBRARY, UTILITIES

International Datawares, Inc., 2278 Trade Zone Blvd., San Jose, CA 95131, (408) 262-6660

A collection of public-domain, shareware, and copyrighted software distributed with permission and organized into useful categories. The programs are available at no cost, other than a charge for duplication, media, postage, and handling.

GRAPHIDEX
Brainpower, 24009 Ventura Blvd., Calabasas, CA 91302, (818) 884-6911

A graphics management system for retrieving, previewing, editing, and pasting bitmapped or object-oriented images into Macintosh applications. An on-line editing capability provides the tools to resize, rotate, invert, and more. Fonts can be defined to include graphics, small symbols, small pictures, diacritical marks, etc.

IMPORT/EXPORT
Telos Software Products, 3420 Ocean Park Blvd., Santa Monica, CA 90405

A data-exchange utility for the Business Filevision visual database program that supports the movement of data into and out of Business Filevision. It is especially useful for exporting data for reformation into word processed and typeset reports.

MAC+II
Meacom, P.O. Box 272591, Houston, TX 77277, (713) 526-5706

A program that is capable of converting Apple II Applesoft BASIC programs for use on the Macintosh.

MAC-HY-PHEN
Boston Software Publishers Inc., 1260 Boylston St., Boston, MA 02215, (617) 267-4747

This program, which installs as a desk accessory, overcomes the hyphenation limitation of many desktop publishing products. The use of hyphenation can appreciably improve the typographic fit, and therefore the readability of type. The program uses a 40,000-word dictionary to hyphenate by actual word division, rather than by computer algorithm. As a file is processed, invisible discretionary hyphens are inserted in all words found in its dictionary. Words not appearing in the dictionary are left for manual intervention. It works with any program that can recognize a discretionary hyphen, such as Microsoft Word, MacPublisher I or II, and PageMaker.

MACINUSE
SoftView, Inc., 4820 Adohr Lane, Suite F, Camarillo, CA 93010, (800) MACNTAX

A program for tracking the use of Macintosh applications, including name, date, start time, duration, and inclusion of an optional comment. The log is maintained as a text file that can be included in reports, correspondence, bills, and publications.

MACQWERTY
Paragon Courseware, 4954 Sun Valley Rd., Del Mar, CA 92014, (619) 481-1477

A keyboard utility providing options for reconfiguring the key identities of the keyboard, installing a Dvorak keyboard layout, and restoring the standard keyboard layout.

MACRO RECORDER
Genesis Micro Software, 106 147th Ave. SE #2, Bellevue, WA 98007, (206) 747-8512

A program that records a series of mouse movements and/or keystrokes for recall within applications programs. Option keys can be used as command keys for entering boilerplate text, starting or stopping a program, converting a series of program commands into a single macro, and more.

MACSAFE
Kent March Limited, Inc., 1200 Post Oak Blvd., Suite 210, Houston, TX 77056, (800) 325-3587

A utility program to apply password protection to documents and applications. Features include password protection for groups of documents and applications, encryption using DES or QuickCrypt, visual cloaking of keyboard input, and on-line help.

MICRO-SET

Mumford Micro Systems, P.O. Box 400, Summerland, CA 93067, (805) 969-4557

A software program, coupled with a special 5 1/4-inch disk drive, that supports a number of functions helpful in a Compugraphic MCS typesetting environment. Some of these functions are formatting MCS disks, displaying MCS directories, copying Macintosh files to/from MCS disks, listing MCS files on the Macintosh screen, and copying files from IBM disks to Macintosh disks.

MOCKPACKAGE PLUS

CE Software, 801-73rd St., Des Moines, IA 50312, (515) 224-1995

A set of four exceptionally useful desk accessories consisting of MockWrite, for word processing; Mockchart, for creating line, column, overlapped column, hi/lo/close, and pie charts; Mock Terminal, for telecommunicating; and MockPrinter, for printing files to the ImageWriter or LaserWriter in background mode.

NOTES . . . FOR PAGEMAKER

Layered, 85 Merrimac St., Boston, MA 02114, (617) 423-9041

A two-disk accessory program providing fast on-line reference to all PageMaker commands and functions; a tutorial program; a graphic design mini-course with expert design guidelines, tips, terminology, and guides; and 12 professionally designed, ready-to-use PageMaker templates for creating newsletters, mailers, manuals, catalogs, and more.

POSTCODE™

Mumford Micro Systems, P.O. Box 400, Summerland, CA 93067, (805) 969-4557

A program that converts Macintosh on-screen formatting to correct MCS coding, essentially letting the Macintosh serve as a WYSIWYG terminal for a Compugraphic MCS phototypesetter. PostCode works with most Macintosh programs, including Mac-Write, Microsoft Word, MacDraw, Excel, and ReadySetGo.

SET & SEND

Bree Communications Inc., 661D Market Hill Rd., Vancouver, BC V5Z 4B5, (604) 875-1622

A program that converts Microsoft Word files into coded files for a Compugraphic MCS phototypesetting machine. Converting Word files into typeset output requires three steps:

- Creating the document using Microsoft Word and Set & Send fonts.
- Creating a coded file with typesetting codes in place using Set & Send.
- Sending the Set & Send coded file to a Processing Center for typesetting. The file can be sent on disk or telecommunicated.

Set & Send conversion controls hyphenation (on or off), word spacing (standard, medium, or tight), letter spacing (standard, medium, tight, or none), headline kerning (standard, medium, tight, or none), text kerning (standard, medium, tight, or none), point size increase (none, 1/2 point), and leading increase (none, 1/4 pt., 1/2 pt., or 3/4 pt.).

A shipping instruction form is presented for billing, shipping, and special instructions. After the file has been processed, a statistics window is displayed showing the number of headline and text characters, MCS codes, and the total elapsed processing time.

SONAR

Virginia Systems Software Services, 5509 W. Bay Ct., Midlothian, VA 23113, (804) 739-3200

A free-text search and analysis program for the Macintosh Plus. The program can process an arbitrary text, such as a manuscript, book, or other document, searching for words or phrases and determining how or if text elements are related.

Although the functions of the program are limited, its performance is outstanding. It can search through a 400,000-character document for all occurences of a phrase in less than one second.

Sonar can be used to show if a relationship exists between two or more words or phrases within multiple paragraphs. For example, the phrases *desktop publishing* and *laser printer* could be entered. Sonar would find all paragraphs where both phrases are present. Using the automatic mode, Sonar also would select words that also exist in those paragraphs with either or both of the search phrases. It would eliminate words such as *the* and *and* that occur too frequently. Such an analysis might find words such as *near-typeset quality* and *Macintosh*.

This type of analysis is very helpful for locating specific information for research, such as scholarly inquiry or the review of court transcripts.

The use of Sonar requires that a text file first be processed by the SonarSetUp program. This program creates three working files that Sonar uses for its processing, leaving the original file intact. Files can be processed from disk or from communication through the Macintosh modem port.

A unique feature of the program is *sidetracking*, which temporarily halts the current search in favor of a new one, but maintains a place marker so that the user can return to the original easily.

TEMPO

Affinity Microsystems, Ltd., 1050 Walnut St., Boulder, CO 80302, (303) 442-4840

An intelligent macro production tool for optimizing the use of Macintosh software. Commands and/or keystrokes can be recorded and played back, with their results varying on the basis of conditions encountered during playback.

TOPDESK

Cortland Computer, P.O. Box 9916, Berkeley, CA 94709, (415) 845-1142

A set of seven desk accessories including Shorthand, a high-performance macro utility; MenuKey, for assigning command key sequences to menu selections; Encrypt, for encrypting and password-protecting files; BackPrint, a print spooler for printing files in the background; View, for giving any application multiple-view capability; and others.

IBM PC

BLUEBERRY SERIES 1, 2, BESTINFO

Blueberry Software, 7203 Bodega Ave., Sebastopol, CA 95472, (707) 823-2499

A utility program for automating the efficient translation of word processing files into an ASCII form (or word processor form) usable by most desktop publishing programs. Word processor font calls for italic, bold, and bold italic are converted into a pseudocode which can be replaced by using the program's TOGGLE command, into a form recognizable by the destination program. The program's MAKESWAP feature allows for the specification of up to 300 search/replace strings of up to 40 characters each. These strings can be used to convert information and formatting codes into more useful forms during the translation process. The DUMP facility is used to display the ASCII values of translated characters in order to identify "odd" characters. The MAKE-

TOG command handles the need to toggle certain characters or commands. The first encounter of the bold font command, for example, should be interpreted as a "start bold," while the second encounter should be interpreted as "stop bold, return to normal." The MAKETOG command provides the means to specify the two toggle states. The WIDOWS command automatically inserts a "forbid hyphen" in front of the last word of a paragraph to ensure that the printer or typesetter will not hyphenate it.

CALC-TO-TYPE

Calc-to-Type Co, 2004 Curtis Ave., #A, Redondo Beach, CA 90278, (213) 376-5724

A translation program that converts information input to a spreadsheet program (tables, charts, matrices, etc.), such as VisiCalc or Lotus 1-2-3, into tabular information which can be read by a Compugraphic MCS typesetting system.

ENCRYPTION/SECURITY UE 1.0

Public Brand Software, P.O. Box 51478, Indianapolis, IN 46251, (800) IBM-DISK

A collection of programs for protecting the contents of programs, diskettes, and hard disks.

EXACT

Technical Support Software Inc., 72 Kent St., Brookline, MA 02146, (617) 734-4130

A support program for Microsoft Word, MultiMate, WordStar 2000, Displaywrite 2 & 3, WordPerfect, Easy Writer, Perfect, Final Word, PC-Write, and other that allows for the printing of complex mathematical and scientific expressions within a document.

The program loads into RAM before the word processor and can be summoned at any time. A pop-up split-screen editor appears, supporting the input of EXACT (EXpression And Character Typography) commands at the bottom of the screen and the display of the mathematical expression at the top. After the expression is created, the user exits the pop-up editor and is returned to the word processing program. The user positions the cursor where the expression should be inserted and injects the command lines from the edit session directly into the text.

When the word processor is instructed to print, EXACT intercepts the print stream, scans the steam for EXACT commands, and sends a graphic image to the printer to construct the mathematical expressions.

Mathematical features include complete Greek character sets in uppercase and lowercase, unlimited levels of superscripts and subscripts, automatic equation centering, automatic positioning of equation numbers, automatic creation of boxes and borders, script and italic characters, and automatic selection of smaller characters when used in superscripts or subscripts.

The package includes 20 fonts with over 1000 symbols and characters. Any character can be rescaled up to 81 times its size. Also included in the package is a font editor, which allows users to create their own characters and use them as easily as standard fonts. The program also can be used to remap the keyboard for inputing in foreign languages.

Printer drivers are available for most dot matrix and laser printers.

FANCY PRINTING 1 & 2 UP 3.0/4.0

Public Brand Software, P.O. Box 51478, Indianapolis, IN 46251, (800) IBM-DISK

Two disks that provide a number of dot matrix printer enhancements. Functions include making large banners; printing "3 of 9" barcodes; producing letter quality on an Epson printer; printing sideways on a sheet; and producing a number of high-definition fonts (Helvetica, Palatino, and Sans Serif) on an Epson, ImageWriter, Proprinter, C. Itoh, or Star printer.

GEM
Digital Research Inc., P.O. Box DRI, Monterey, CA 93942, (800) 443-4200

The GEM desktop software provides the convenience of windows, icons, drop-down menus, and color. GEM works with many IBM programs, as well as a number of speciality written GEM applications for painting, writing, charting, and drawing.

GRAFPLUS
Jewell Technologies, Inc., 4302 S.W. Alaska St., Suite 207, Seattle, WA 98116, (800) 628-2828

A utility program that makes it possible to print any screen image to a dot matrix, ink jet, or laser printer at the touch of a key. The image can be printed white on black, black on white, or in any color that the printer supports. The image also can be scaled to any size that the printer can image.

HY-PHEN-ATOR PLUS
PlusWare Inc., 675 Fairview Dr., Carson City, NV 89701, (702) 355-6735

An automatic hyphenation and keyboard enhancement program for the IBM PC. It can work from within a word processing program, inserting soft hyphens as keyboarding proceeds, or can batch process text files, inserting soft hyphens in every word. Additional program features include a keyboard utility to store up to 1,000 keystrokes per key, a resident macro editor, a real-time clock display, and multiple timers to time tasks, telephone calls, etc.

INSET 2
American Programmers Guild, Ltd., 12 Mill Plain Rd., Danbury, CT 06811, (203) 794-0396

A memory-resident program that provides the capability to capture a text or graphics screen, edit it, and save it to disk. The saved image can be placed within a word processing document and merged in the printed output.

Screen images are captured (cut) by invoking INSET with the key sequence Shift-PrtSc (the default setting, which can be changed during setup). A two-line menu appears at the bottom of the screen with options to View, Save, Modify, Edit, Print, Output, Help, and Next. In the simplest scenario, the image is saved to disk. To place the image in a text document (paste), the image is specified within brackets at the specified location within the document, such as **[b:graphic]**. This identifier is called a [PIX] tag. The word processing document must allow sufficient room for the graphic, although INSET can resize a graphic to fit a specified space. Invoking INSET will produce a size box outlining the area that the graphic will require. INSET also can preview a representation of the image in its indicated position.

A simple paint program is part of INSET, supporting the creation and modification of graphics. Graphic images can be created while in a word processing program, and then added as part of a document.

Among the uses for INSET are enhancing images captured from other line-editing programs, merging a signature into letters and documents (password protection for images is supported), telecommunicating a file with text and graphics, transferring images between two different graphics programs, creating a quick screen hardcopy, and integrating graphics with word-oriented programs in a variety of ways.

KEYBOARD UTILITIES UH 3.0
Public Brand Software, P.O. Box 51478, Indianapolis, IN 46251, (800) IBM-DISK

A collection of programs for making customized function key templates, increasing the keyboard buffer size, storing macros, adding a keyboard click, and more.

LOGGER

System Automation Software Inc., 8555 Sixteenth St., Silver Spring, MD 20910, (800) 321-3267

A program that allows the user to keep accurate track of PC usage, i.e., what files and what programs are used, who is using them, and when. The program offers potential for editorial and typesetting services that need to account for the time spent on specific customer jobs.

MCS UTILITIES

Syscom, 320 W. Oak St., El Segundo, CA 90245, (213) 322-3378

A program for the IBM PC that supports the translation of text files into Compugraphic MSC-compatible form.

TEX PREVIEW

ArborText Inc., 416 Fourth St., Ann Arbor, MI 48107, (313) 996-3566

A TeX screen-display preview program for use with Addison-Wesley's MicroTeX.

WORD PROCESSING SUPPORT WP 3.0

Public Brand Software, P.O. Box 51478, Indianapolis, IN 46251, (800) IBM-DISK

A set of utility programs providing the following capabilities: converting WordStar or DisplayWrite documents to ASCII; determining the fog level of documents; counting characters, words, lines, and pages; counting the frequency of usage of each word; creating an index from a list of words; and more.

Kaypro, Radio Shack, IBM

MICRO-SET

Mumford Micro Systems, P.O. Box 400, Summerland, CA 93067, (805) 969-4557

A program that provides a software interface to the Compugraphic MCS typesetting system. Micro-Set permits a word processor to be used to prepare fully coded files for typesetting. It then will format an MCS disk in the computer and copy the prepared files onto it. The disk then can be taken directly to the MCS system for processing.

UNIX

DEVPS

Pipeline Associates, Inc., 39 E. 12th St., New York, NY 10003, (212) 598-4650

A collection of programs that support device-independent troff (ditroff) in the PostScript environment.

VAX/VMS, VAX/UNIX, Sun/UNIX, Apollo/Aegis

TEX DVI

Arbor Text Inc., 416 Fourth St., Ann Arbor, MI 48107 (313) 996-3566

A variety of device-independent (DVI) files for converting text files into a TeX-compatible form for output to a variety of devices. Among the devices supported are INPUT: VAX/VMS, VAX/UNIX, Sun/UNIX, Apollo/Aegis, VM/CMS, MVS, and IBM PC/XT/AT; and OUTPUT: Apple LaserWriter, QMS Lasergrafix, Imagen, Xerox 9700, Sun LaserWriter, Autologic APS-5, and Allied L300.

PERIPHERALS

Communications

ACI, ICI
Compugraphic Corporation, 200 Ballardvale St., Wilmington, MA 01887,
(617) 944-6555

ICI is the communications board option for the EditWriter series of phototypesetters. The ACI is the communication interface option for the MCS typesetting system and Quadex front-end system.

INTERCOM 100
Intergraphics, 106 S. Columbus St., Alexandria, VA 22314

A telecommunications device for accepting a wide variety of word and data processing coding formats destined for typeset output.

MULTICOM WP INTERFACE
G.O. Graphics, 179 Bedford St., Lexington, MA 02173, (617) 229-8900

Device accepts telecommunicated data from word processors, data processors, or personal computers to AM Comp/Set or Comp/Edit. Translation tables are user-modifiable. Some models have plug-in cartridges for holding conversion table information.

PC MACBRIDGE
Tangent Technologies Ltd., 5720 Peachtree Pky., Norcross, GA 30092, (404) 662-0366

A hardware/software solution for connecting IBM PCs to the Appletalk Personal Network. The LaserScript software converts PC files into PostScript form so that they can be printed on the LaserWriter. The MailBox software sends E-mail and other files to any other PC or Macintosh on the network. (The Macintosh requires Videx Mail-Center, which is available from Tangent.)

SHAREDATA
Extended Systems Inc., P.O. Box 4937, Boise, ID 83711, (208) 322-7163

A 20M hard disk with supporting hardware and software, which can be shared by up to four MS-DOS or PC-DOS 3.1 users. Each PC utilizes an RS-422 interface (which is 35 times faster than the RS-232 port), making it possible for users to conveniently share data and system resources (printers and plotters).

TELECOMMUNICATION OPTION
Allied Linotype, 201 Country Rd., Melville, NY 11747

Telecommunications option for the CRTronic phototypesetter. Communicates using asynchronous ASCII and synchronous EDCDIC.

TOPS
Centram Systems West, 2372 Ellsworth Ave., Berkeley, CA 94704, (800) 227-3900

A Macintosh network system running under AppleTalk, which supports the addition of the IBM PC. TOPS lets dissimilar computers share files and peripherals.

Displays

MEGASCREEN
micrographic Images, 20954 Osborne St., Canoga Park, CA 91304 (818) 407-0571

A 19-inch external monitor for the Macintosh Plus.

RADIUS FULL PAGE DISPLAY
Radius Inc., 1050 E. Duane Ave., Suite F, Sunnyvale, CA 94086, (408) 732-1010
An accessory large screen for the Macintosh.

THE BIG PICTURE
E-Machines, 7945 S.W. Mohawk St., Tualatin, OR 97062, (503) 692-6656
A large-screen display for the Macintosh.

THE GENIUS
Micro Display Systems, Inc., 1310 Vermillion St., Hastings, MI 55033, (800) 328-9524
A high-resolution monitor for the IBM PC large enough to display an 8 1/2-×-11-inch page.

VIKING ONE
Moniterm Corp., 5740 Green Circle Dr., Minnetonka, MN 55343, (612) 935-4151
A 19-inch display for the IBM PC featuring a resolution of 1280 × 960.

Ergonomics

SONEX
Illbruck/USA, 3800 Washington Ave. N., Minneapolis, MN 55412, (612) 521-3555
An acoustical foam material that greatly absorbs sound to create a quieter environment for computer input operations.

Graphic Input

DATA COPY MODEL 210
Datacopy, 1215 Terra Bella Ave., Mountain View, CA 94043, (415) 965-7900
A flat-bed image scanner with optional optical character recognition capability.

DESKTOP PAGE COMPOSITION SYSTEM
Vision Research, 1590 Old Oakland Rd., San Jose, CA 95131, (408) 298-8700
A desktop scanner for the IBM PC/XT/AT that is capable of scanning images at 300 dpi and of optically reading text.

DIPLOMAT VIDEO DIGITIZER
Computech Systems, 168 Finchley Rd., London, England NW3 6HP, 01-794-0202
A graphics-capturing system for the Apple IIe or II+.

JETREADER SCANNER
Datacopy, 1215 Terra Bella Ave., Mountain View, CA 94043, (415) 965-7900
A combination image scanner and optical character recognition device for the IBM PC/XT/AT. The image scanner works at a resolution of 300 dpi (optionally at 200 dpi), scanning at the rate of 43 seconds per page. The OCR software can read 12 different typefaces, and an optional package provides the user with the capability to train the system to recognize other typefaces.

LASERFAX
LaserFAX, Inc., 2000 Palm St. S., Naples, FL 33962, (813) 775-2737
An IBM PC-based digital scanner with black-and-white or color capabilities at resolutions of up to 200 dpi. Optional plug-in boards support optical character recognition and facsimile transmission.

LoDOWN

LoDOWN, 10 Victor Square, Suite 600, Scotts Valley, CA 95066, (408) 438-7400

An image scanner for the Apple Macintosh that connects to the SCSI port. Images can be scanned at resolutions ranging from 75 to 300 dpi, with up to 32 shades of gray.

MacScan

New Image Technology, Inc., 10300 Greenbelt Rd., Seabrook, MD 20706, (301) 464-3100

An interface for the Princeton Graphic's LS-300 tabletop optical scanner to the Apple Macintosh SCSI port. Resolution is variable, from 75 to 300 dpi. Images can be saved in formats compatible with MacPaint, MacWrite, PageMaker 1.2 and 2.0, and PostScript.

LS-300

Princeton Graphic Systems, 601 Ewing St., Bldg. A, Princeton, NJ 08540, (800) 221-1490

A desktop image scanner with 300 dpi resolution. An OCR option is available.

MacGrid

Diablo Valley Design, 4103 Hidden Valley Rd., Lafayette, CA 94549, (415) 283-4268

A set of plastic overlays useful for manually transferring sketches, photographs, or artwork to a MacPaint document for graphic enhancement.

MouseEase

Tacklind Design, Inc., 250 Cowper St., Palo Alto, CA 94301, (415) 322-2257

A set of Teflon paws for all Apple mouse devices. The paws improve the mouse's slideability over any surface.

P.A.G.E. Scanner

Printing And Graphic Enhancement, 150 Mt. Bethel Rd., Warren, NJ 07060, (201) 647-3678

A flat-bed scanner for the IBM PC/XT/AT that is capable of outputting line art or halftones at 300, 240, 180, or 100 dpi. The accompanying software is icon-driven and provides 20 fonts with text manipulation; undo; grids; filled and unfilled circles, ellipses and boxes; pencil and airbrush; scissors; and capabilities to draw, paint, cut and paste, and rubberstamp.

The Digital Paintbrush

The Computer Colorworks, 3030 Bridgeway, Suite 201, Sausalito, CA 94965, (415) 331-3022

A penlike freehand drawing device for the IBM PC and Apple II computers.

ThunderScan

Thunderware, Inc., 21 Orinda Way, Orinda, CA 94563, (415) 254-6581

A scanning head that is used in place of the ribbon cartridge on the Apple ImageWriter printer. Scanned images are received at the Macintosh, where they undergo modification using ThunderScan image-enhancement software.

Graphic Output

PrintMate Printer

Micro Peripherals, Inc., 4426 S. Century Dr., Salt Lake City, UT 84107, (800) 821-8848

A dot matrix printer with over 60 different type styles, characters up to 5/8 inch high, and a facility for user-created logos and fonts.

STYLEWRITER

Carolina Engineering Laboratories, 818 Tyvola Rd., Charlotte, NC 28210, (800) 222-9073

    A hardware device that can convert any all-points-addressable dot matrix printer into a multiple-typestyle, letter-quality printer. The basic unit comes with an 8K buffer and three typestyles. Both the buffer and typestyle selections are expandable.

TYP-SET

Enter Computer, 6867 Nancy Ridge Dr., San Diego, CA 92121, (619) 450-0601

    A software package to drive the Sweet-P line of single and multiple pen plotters. Characters can be created in the range of .05 inch to 72 inches.

Keyboard Enhancement

DVORAK STANDARD KEYBOARD

Drias Enterprises, P.O. Box CMU-145, Pittsburgh, PA 15213

    A modification kit to convert an H19 or Z19 terminal into a Dvorak keyboard.

KEYPORT 60

Polytel Computer Products Corp., 1250 Oakmead Pky., Sunnyvale, CA 94086, (800) 245-6655

    A flat-membrane keypad that adheres to the top ledge of the IBM PC and compatibles keyboard. The user can create and label each key with up to 10,000 characters of text and/or commands. The keypad works with any applications software.

LOC-DOTS

Prodigy Products Co., 14152 Superior, Cleveland, OH 44118, (216) 932-1413

    Adhesive-backed raised dots used to provide a tactile means of locating keys on a keyboard in order to increase typing efficiency.

MULTIFONT

Hash Tech. Co., 2065 Martin Ave., #103, Santa Clara, CA 95050, (408) 988-2646

    An add-on card for the IBM PC that enables the IBM monochrome adapter to support 256 user-definable symbols. The card includes a character/symbol editor, a printing utility, and ten fonts. Multifont works with any word processing software.

OMNI-READER

Oberon International, 5525 McArthur Blvd., Irving, TX 75062, (214) 257-0097

    A hand-held optical character reader attaching to the RS-232 port of a variety of microcomputers.

PENPAD 320

Pencept, 39 Green St., Waltham, MA 02154, (617) 893-6390

    A graphics tablet for the IBM PC that is capable of reading handwriting.

SAFESKIN KEYBOARD PROTECTOR

Merritt Computer Products, Inc., 2925 LBJ, #180, Dallas, TX 75234, (214) 942-1142

    A thin plastic skin that fits over an IBM PC or Apple IIe keyboard to prevent damage from liquid spills, dust, etc.

SMART KEY II

Software Research Technologies, Inc., 3757 Wilshire Blvd., Los Angeles, CA 90010, (213) 384-5430

    A program for the IBM PC, Kaypro, and other MS-DOS and CP/M computers that permits the user definition of new identities to keyboard keys.

XTRAKEY
Xpert Software, 8865 Polland Ave., San Diego, CA 92123, (619) 268-0112
A key-redefinition program for the Kaypro that allows the user to change the identity of any key on the keyboard into a string of characters.

Keyboards

ACCUFEEL KEYBOARD
Multitech Industrial Corp., 315, Fu Hsing N. Rd., Taipei, 104, Taiwan R.O.C., 02-713-4022
An alternate keyboard for the Apple II featuring function keys, numeric keypad, dedicated Applesoft BASIC command keys, and user-definable keys.

DATA SPEC EXTENSION KEYBOARD
Ora Electronics, 18215 Parthenia St., Northridge, CA 91325
A detached keyboard for the Apple II series of computers.

DATA SPEC KEYBOARD
Alliance Research Corp., 18215 Parthenia St., Northridge, CA 91325, (818) 701-5848
A detached-extension 87-key replacement keyboard for the Apple II. It features 90 preprogrammed functions and commands, as well as a 10-key numeric keypad.

DIGITEXT HIGH-SPEED ENTRY SYSTEM
Digitext, 325 E. Hillcrest Dr., Suite 250, Thousand Oaks, CA 91360, (805) 495-3456
A high-speed keyboard system that enables users to enter text into computer and word processing systems at speeds from three to five times faster than existing keyboards. The system consists of a 23-key computerized stenographic keyboard and a microprocessor-based digital translator.

ENIGMA RESEARCH MODEL 9000
Enigma Research, Inc., 4534 Vista del Monte, Suite 104, Sherman Oaks, CA 91403, (818) 784-0343
A replacement keyboard for the IBM PC/AT featuring 40 user-programmable function keys, IBM Selectric key placement, separate numeric and cursor keybads, built-in Smartkey II+ keyboard macro program, and removable plastic templates and labels for clear indication of each key definition.

KB 200
keytronic, P.O. Box 14687, Spokane, WA 99214
A detached keyboard for the Apple II series. Models for other computers, as well as keyboard devices for the handicapped, are also available.

KB 500
keytronic, P.O. Box 14687, Spokane, WA 99214
A replacement keyboard for the Radio Shack TRS-80 Color Computer.

KB5151 (jr.), KB5150 (jr.)
keytronic, P.O. Box 14687, Spokane, WA 99214
Replacement keyboards for the IBM PC, XT, and PC*jr*.

KEYTEC
Key Tec, P.O. Box 722, Marblehead, MA 01945
   Converts the existing Apple II keyboard into a detachable.

MAXI-SWITCH
Century Research & Marketing Inc., 10800 Normandale Blvd., Bloomington, MN 55437
   A keyboard device for the IBM PC.

OMEGABOARD II
Zicor Inc., 2296 Cascade Plaza N., Woodbury, MN 55125
   A detached, intelligent keyboard for the Apple II series.

PC-84 KEYBOARD
NMB/Hi-Tek Corp., 7274 Lampson Ave., Garden Grove, CA 92641, (714) 898-9511
   A replacement keyboard for the IBM PC meeting all DIN ergonomic standards and featuring the IBM international keyboard configuration, a 30-character buffer, and a keyswitch life of 100 million cycles.

PREH COMMANDER
Preh Electronic Industries, Inc., 8101 Milwaukee Ave., Niles, IL 60648
   A detached keyboard for the Apple II series.

PRO-100 KEYBOARD
Amkey, 220 Ballardvale St., Wilmington, MA 01887
   A replacement keyboard for the Apple II.

RAPIDWRITER
Quixote Corp., One E. Wacker Dr., Chicago, IL 60601, (800) 523-8356
   A combination keyboard and software program that optimizes the text-entry process by programming frequently used words, phrases, and paragraphs into a single key.

SPEEDKEY & KT2010 TOUCH PAD
Koala Technologies, 3100 Patrick Henry Dr., Santa Clara, CA 95052 (408) 986-8866
   A touchpad-based custom keyboard for the IBM PC.

Media Conversion

ALTERTEXT
Altertext Inc., 211 Congress St., Boston, MA 02110, (617) 426-0009
   A sophisticated hardware/software device for conversion of word processed or data processed media for typesetting.

ANTARES WP DATA CONVERSION SYSTEM
Antares, P.O. Box 159, Lake Elmo, MN 55042
   Code conversion hardware/software from word processing formats to user-defined code sets and/or media.

CONTEXT IV MEDIA CONVERTER
Computer & Communications Services, 8115 Fenton St., Silver Spring, MD 20910, (301) 588-8706
   A CP/M-based system providing telecommunications, disk sector and file analysis, directory and file comparison utilities, read/write/format CP/M and MS-DOS, and file-conversion utilities.

DCI, MDR
Itek Corp., 335 Middlesex Ave., Wilmington, MA 01887
DCI is the telecommunications board option for the Quadritek phototypesetter. The MDR is a media converter that attaches to the Quadritek. It accepts either 8-inch or 5 1/4-inch media from various word processor devices. The device is made by Baber of Australia, and is sold OEM to various vendors.

MACBYTE I AND II
Altertext, 211 Congress St., Boston, MA 02110, (617) 426-0009
A system that includes five (MacByte I) or six (MacByte II) disk drives, communications capabilities, and software for disk reading and writing. The system accepts jobs from virtually any source and can output to laser printers, typesetters, microcomputers, OCR scanners, and modems.

MEDIACOMM
Shaffstall Corp., 7901 E. 88th St., Indianapolis, IN 46256, (317) 842-2077
Media converters and telecommunications devices.

PC I AND II
Altertext, 211 Congress St., Boston, MA 02110, (617) 426-0009
A media-conversion system based on the IBM PC. Available with either three disk drives (PC I) or four disk drives (PC II), the systems support the reading and writing of a vast number of disk formats and the direct output to a range of devices, including laser printers, typesetters, mag tape drives, and computers.

SHAFFSTALL XT
Shaffstall, 7901 E. 88th St., Indianapolis, IN 46256, (317) 842-2077
The Shaffstall XT combines the Shaffstall 5000 disk-conversion unit with the IBM PC/XT. The system supports disk-to-disk conversion, as well as business application computing.

TRANSMEDIA 500
Applied Data Communication, 14272 Chambers Rd., Tustin, CA 92680
Media conversion hardware/software with many media options.

OCR

ALPHA WORD
Compuscan, 900 Huyler St., Teterboro, NJ 07608
An Optical Character Recognition device that reads typewritten pages composed in OCR-A, OCR-B, Perry, or Prestige Elite.

COMPUSCAN PCS
CompuScan, Inc., 81 Two Bridges Rd., Fairfield, NJ 07006, (201) 575-0500
A desktop OCR that is compatible with most word processors and IBM-compatible computers. It reads monospaced and proportional typefaces (optionally OCR-A, OCR-B) at the rate of 30 seconds per page.

CONTEXT 210, 310, AND 1205
Burroughs, Context Div., 9 Ray Ave., Burlington, MA 01803
An Optical Character Recognition device that reads typewritten pages composed in OCR-B or Courier. The unit can be connected directly to a typesetter.

DEST OCR
Dest Data Corp., 1285 Forgewood Ave., Sunnyvale, CA 94086
Scanners for OCR and graphic image capture.

ECRM 4000/5300, CONCEPT SERIES
ECRM, 205 Burlington Rd., Bedford, MA 01730
An OCR device capable of reading typewritten pages composed in Courier 72, OCR-A, OCR-B, Perry, Courier 12, or Prestige Elite. Can be configured on-line to a typesetter.

KDEM
Kurzweil, 185 Albany St., Cambridge, MA 02139
An omnifont OCR reader that can be user-programmed to read virtually any typewritten or typeset font. It can be connected on-line to a typesetter or to on-line magnetic or paper tape output.

TOTEC 5000B
Totec Co. Ltd., 19151 Parthenia Ave. ''A'', Northridge, CA 91324, (818) 993-9413
An OCR system for the IBM PC. It requires an RS-232 port and DOS 2.0 or higher.

WORD SCANNER
Dest Corp., 1285 Forgewood Ave., Sunnyvale, CA 94086
A tabletop OCR device programmable to accept up to four different typewriter faces. The unit can be cable-connected directly to a typesetter.

Output

HAMPSTEAD LASER SYSTEM
Hampstead Computer Graphics, P.O. Box 469, East Hampstead, NH 03826, (603) 329-5076
A Cordata laser printer with 64 on-line fonts from Compugraphic Corporation, in sizes ranging from 5 to 96 points. The printer works as part of the Hampstead Personal Computer Typesetting Software program (PC-TS) and can be used for proofing or final output.

LABEL EXPRESS
Composite Technologies, Inc., 3684 Forest Park Blvd., St. Louis, MO 63108, (314) 533-1216
A desktop unit that converts bond paper (as from a laser printer) into laminated, die-cut, pressure-sensitive labels.

MACBUFFER LW
Ergotron Inc., P.O. Box 17013, Minneapolis, MN 55417, (800) 328-9839
A large-capacity buffer connecting via Appletalk and available in 1 and 2 megabyte versions.

PRODUCTIVITY ENHANCEMENT PACK
Locker Typesetting Equipment, One Maple St., East Rutherford, NJ 07073, (800) 526-0192
An optional circuit board for the Compugraphic EditWriter that provides telecommunication capabilities. An optional feature allows the typesetter to drive laser printers that interpret PostScript.

Paste-up Aids

WAXTEC
Waxtec Inc., 9016 Owensmouth Ave., Canoga Park, CA 91303, (818) 700-0473
Adhesive waxers.

TYPESETTER VENDORS

Allied Linotype, 201 Old Country Rd., Melville, NY 11747, (516) 673-4031
CRTronic and Linotron typesetters
Manufacturers of a complete line of third- and fourth-generation phototypesetters, including PostScript-compatible models.

Alphatype, 7711 N. Merrimac Ave., Niles, IL 60648, (312) 965-8800
Berthold and Alphatype line of typesetters

AM Varityper, 11 Mt. Pleasant Ave., East Hanover, NJ 07936, (201) 887-8000
Comp/Edit, GTO, EPICS

Amgraf, 1501 Oak St., Kansas City, MO 64108, (816) 474-4797
MECCA III
A stand-alone desktop workstation based on the IBM PC/AT that provides real-time interactive page composition with integrated text and graphics. Output options include the Apple LaserWriter, Xerox 8700/9700, and the Autologic APS-5 and Micro-5 phototypesetters.

Autologic, 1050 Rancho Conejo Blvd., Newbury Park, CA 91320, (805) 498-9611
APS Microcomposer II
A plain-paper typesetting system with a full pagination option. Output can be to a laser printer or any Autologic imaging device.

Berthold of North America, 610 Winters Ave., Paramus, NJ 07652, (201) 262-8700
Berthold Phototypesetters

Compu-Page Systems, 1307 W. Sixth St., #127, Corona, CA 91720, (800) 553-9530
Compu-Page Laser Typesetting System
A typesetting system based upon the Apple Macintosh/LaserWriter with enhancements specifically for the needs of small publishers.

Compugraphic Corporation, 80 Industrial Way, Wilmington, MA 01887, (617) 944-6555
MCS typesetting systems, Quadex, Interleaf WS

Concept Technologies, P.O. Box 5277, Portland, OR 94043, (503) 684-3314
Concept 100
An IBM XT or AT based system that provides the interactive creation of high-resolution text and graphics, and page layouts. Output is to the Concept Writer laser printer.

Datacopy Corporation, 1215 Terra Bella Ave., Mountain View, CA 94043, (415) 965-7900
WIPS
Word Image Processing Systems (WIPS) personal publishing software runs on an IBM PC XT or AT, and handles page layout, image editing, and image capturing. Output is to a laser printer or phototypesetter.

Digital Composition Systems, 2501 West Dunlap, Phoenix, AZ 85021, (602) 944-0199
Signature

An electronic publishing system comprised of a text editor, spelling checker, thesaurus, controlled typographic aesthetics program, automatic table generator, widow/orphan control, automatic imposition, automatic index generation, art and photo scanner, image manipulation (cropping, scaling, and rotation), drawing capabilities, WYSIWYG copyfitting and forms design, input from word processors, IBM PC compatible operating system, and a large typeface library.

ETP Systems, Inc., 10150 SW Nimbus Ave., Portland, OR 97223, (800) 792-7600
The ETP Laser Publishing Package

A system consisting of an Imagen laser printer, a laser device driver, a version of AT&T's device-independent troff with simplified macros to ease text formatting, a selection of software fonts from International Typeface Corporation, a font-sizing program, and a tutorial.

Imagen Corporation, 2650 San Tomas Expressway, Santa Clara, CA 95052-8101, (408) 986-9400
Personal Publishing Systems

Information International Inc., 5933 Slauson Ave., Culver City, CA 90230, (213) 390-8611
High-Speed Digital Phototypesetters

Itek Composition Systems, 400 Amherst St., Nashua, NH 03063, (603) 881-8448
Quadritek and Digitek Phototypesetters

Kentek Information Systems, Inc., P.O. Box 78, Six Pearl Ct., Allendale, NJ 07401, (201) 825-8500
K-2 Non-Impact Printer

A 240-×-240 dpi laser printer with built-in diskette font and downloadable font capabilities.

Monotype Graphic Systems Inc., 509 W. Golf Rd., Arlington Heights, IL 60005
Laser Phototypesetters

The Electronic Publisher, 208 S. Marietta, Excelsior Springs, MO 64024, (816) 637-7233
The Electronic Publisher

An enhanced Apple Macintosh/LaserWriter system with additional RAM, a hard disk, and a graphics library of particular interest for newspapers and small publishers.

Titus Communications, 1001 Ross Ave., Dallas, TX 75202, (214) 954-0630
LaserSetter Models I and II

A personal computer, text editor, and laser printer combination created to meet the needs of the newspaper industry. The computer is based on the Bondwell 12A, and the printer uses a Canon CX engine. The typesetting coding system conforms to Compugraphic conventions. The typesetter is also directly compatible with the Harris front-end system.

Unidot, 602 Park Point Dr., Golden, CO 80401, (303) 526-9263
Laserset

A laser phototypesetter manufactured by Siemens. The device has a resolution of 720 dpi and can be driven by a computer, scanner, or OCR device.

USLynx, 853 Broadway, New York, NY 10003, (212) 673-3210
Lynx Laser

A laser printer OEMed from Ricoh with over 750 on-line fonts, including many ITC-licensed designs. The printer can be used as a desktop publishing typesetter or as a plain-paper proofer for phototypesetting output, emulating the output of Linotron 202, 202N, and 202W, among other devices.

PROFESSIONAL PUBLICATIONS

American Printer
Maclean-Hunter Publishing Co., 300 W. Adams St., Chicago, IL 60606

The oldest magazine to continuously serve the graphic arts industry. Articles about all aspects of the printing trade are offered monthly.

Clip Artwork for Groups
Norman H. Ludlow, 516 Arnett Blvd., Rochester, NY 14619, (716) 235-0951

A series of clip-art books devoted to the needs of group work organizations. Titles include Action People Artwork, Active Recreation Artwork, Disabled People at Work and Play, Faces to Tell Your Story, and Line Drawings of Everyday People.

Datamation
Thompson Division-Tech. Pub., 35 Mason St., Greenwich, CT 06830

A magazine concerned with the generation, gathering, reproduction, and distribution of information.

DeskTop Graphics
Dynamic Graphics, 6000 N. Forest Park Dr., Peoria, IL 61656-1901, (800) 255-8800

A monthly newsletter covering developments in desktop publishing and methods and procedures in design techniques.

DP: Bove & Rhodes' Report
PCW Communications, Inc., 501 Second St., San Francisco, CA 94107 (800) 351-1700

A monthly newsletter covering the desktop publishing industry, including product evaluations, market analysis, and trend reports.

Editor and Publisher
Editor and Publisher Co., 575 Lexington Ave., New York, NY 10022

A publication concerned with the editorial and technological aspects of publishing.

G. A. Literature Abstracts
Rochester Institute of Technology, One Lomb Memorial Dr., Rochester, NY 14623, (716) 475-2400

A monthly publication abstracting articles from over 300 magazines, journals, and research reports covering all phases of the graphic arts.

Graphic Communications World
Technical Information Inc., P.O. Box 12000, Lake Park, FL 33403

A newsletter with inside information concerning news in the graphic arts industry.

Graphic International
Graphic International, P.O. Box 4639, Margate, FL 33063

News of new and used printing and typesetting equipment.

Interface Age
16704 Marquardt Ave., Cerritos, CA 90701
  A magazine with many articles concerning innovative applications of personal computers.

LaserJet Unlimited
Peachpit Press, 2127 Woolsey St., Berkeley, CA 94705, (415) 843-6614
  A user's guide for the Hewlett-Packard LaserJet and LaserJet+.

LaserSampler II
MacTography, 702 Twinbrook Pky., Rockville, MD 20851, (301) 424-3942
  A looseleaf specimen book showing in a diverse sampling of fonts available for the Apple LaserWriter and other PostScript output devices. Sections include: Adobe Systems, Inc.; Casady Co.; Century Software; Zap Printing, Inc.; The Image Club; The Font Manager (a listing of screen and printer font storage requirements); The Keyboard Map (to locate character and symbol positions); and Area & Line Patterns (as produced by MacDraft, MacDraw, and PageMaker).

Ligature
World Typeface Center, 145 E. 32nd St., New York, NY 10016
  The typographic communication journal.

MacGraphics
GoldMind Publishing, P.O. Box 70295, Riverside, CA, 92513, (714) 785-8685
  A catalog of Macintosh clip art.

Macintosh Desktop Design
The Baxter Group, P.O. Box 61672, Sunnyvale, CA 94086
  The second in a series on Macintosh Desktop Publishing. Contents include the elements, tools, principles, and process of design; basic page composition; the grid system; and design examples.

Macintosh Desktop Typography
The Baxter Group, P.O. Box 61672, Sunnyvale, CA 94086
  The first in a series of books on Macintosh desktop publishing covering the basics of typography, elementary design concepts, and a listing of sources of information. Other books in the series include *Macintosh Desktop Design* and *Macintosh Desktop Production*.

Macintosh Typefaces
Houlberg Development, P.O. Box 271075, Escondido, CA 92027
  A reference guide to shapes, sizes, and styles of typefaces issued by Apple Computer Inc. The book contains specimens in all available variations.

Magazine Design & Production
Globecom Publishing Ltd., 4551 W. 107th St., Overland Park, KS 66207
  A magazine concerned with the technical, business, and creative aspects of magazine production.

New England Printer & Publisher
35 Pelham Rd., Salem, NH 03079
  A regional magazine with editorial emphasis on innovation in graphic arts technology.

PC Publishing

PC Publishing, 1800 Market St., Suite 154, San Francisco, CA 94114, (415) 864-0560

   A magazine devoted to IBM PC desktop publishers.

Personal Composition Report

Graphic Dimensions, 8 Frederick Rd., Dept. GE, Pittsford, NY 14534, (716) 381-3428

   A newsletter covering the use of personal computers in desktop publishing, typesetting, and imagesetting. Edited by Professor Michael Kleper.

Personal Publishing

The Renegade Co., 549 Hawthorn, Barlett, IL 60103, (312) 837-8088

   One of the first magazines devoted to the use of the personal computer as a publishing tool for the individual.

Picture This

The Write Words, Inc., P.O. Box 6446, Arlington, VA 22206-0446, (703) 820-5019

   A book of artwork composed of over 100 illustrations of computer terminals, mainframes, modems, printers, keyboards, icons, etc. They are useful for the preparation of computer documentation, instruction and training manuals, technical publications, newsletters, presentations, advertisements, brochures, and more.

PostScript Language Journal

Pipeline Associates, Inc., 39 E. 12th St., New York, NY 10003, (212) 598-4650

   A quarterly publication dedicated to the needs of PostScript language users.

Printing Impressions

North American Publishing Co., 401 N. Broad St., Philadelphia, PA 19208

   One of the oldest and most respected magazines in the graphic arts.

Publish!

PCW Communications, Inc., 501 Second St., #600, San Francisco, CA 94107, (800) 222-2990

   A bimonthly magazine providing how-to information on desktop publishing.

Publisher's Auxiliary

National Newspaper Assoc., 1627 K St., Washington, DC 10016

   A newspaper for people in the newspaper trade. Many articles deal with the use of personal computers and laser printers for traditional publishing.

Step-By-Step Graphics

The How-To Reference Magazine, 6000 N. Forest Park Dr., Peoria, IL 61656-1901

   A monthly magazine with detailed illustrated articles on a complete range of graphic arts methods and techniques.

The Book of Macintosh Hints

Philip C. Russell, 430 S.W. Crest Cir., Waldport, OR 97394, (503) 563-2501

   A collection of generally undocumented shortcuts and useful tips concerning the Macintosh and popular application programs, including PageMaker.

The Desktop

342 E. 3rd St., Loveland, CO 80537, (303) 663-1724

   A newsletter for desktop publishers.

The Katz Report
Desktop Publishers Intl., 105 Hudson St., Suite 310, New York, NY 10013
  A desktop publishing newsletter.

The Office
Office Publications, Inc., 1200 Summer St., Stamford, CT 06904
  A monthly magazine highlighting news and information about office automation and information technology.

The Seybold Report
Seybold Publications, P.O. Box 644, Media, PA 19063, (215) 565-2480
  One of the most authoritative sources of information on automated publishing systems.

The Seybold Report on D. P.
Seybold Publications, P.O. Box 644, Media, PA 19063, (215) 565-2480
  An excellent source of information on new products and software in the desktop publishing field.

The TypeIdentifier
Centennial Graphics, Inc., 1858 Charter Lane, Lancaster, PA 17604-9990, (800) 233-8973
  A guide for the identification of hundreds of different typefaces.

The Typographer
Typographers International Assoc., 2262 Hall Place N.W., Washington, DC 20007
  The official publication of the Typographers International Association. Articles include news concerning the association, its members, and the field of typesetting in general.

Typesetting On Your Computer
Accent Graphics, 226 S. 16th St., Lincoln, NE 68508, (402) 475-5533
  A no-cost, 48-page guide to using a personal computer to output text on Accent Graphic's phototypesetting system. Included are submission requirements, coding schemes, typographic measurement systems, information on a dedicated typesetting input program, costs and turnaround time, available typefaces, and numerous examples.

TypeWorld
TypeWorld Publications, 18 Oakridge Cir., Wilmington, MA 01887, (617) 658-6876
  The leading bimonthly publication for users of trade and office typesetting and page-composition systems.

U&lc
International Typeface Corp., 866 Second Ave., New York, NY
  A highly graphic and well-designed publication that highlights the typefaces licensed by ITC. Articles typically cover type design and typesetting technology.

VERBUM
Donovan Gosney, Inc., P.O. Box 15439, San Diego, CA (619) 463-9977
  The journal of personal computer art and aesthetics.

USER GROUPS AND TRADE ORGANIZATIONS

Apple Fontrix Club, P.O. Box 29857, Thornton, CO 80229-0857, (303) 451-7577
   A club for Data Transform's Fontrix enthusiasts.

Assoc. of G. A. Consultants, 1730 N. Lynn St., Arlington, VA 22209
   An organization of professional consultants serving the graphic arts industry.

Club 100, P.O. Box 23438, Pleasant Hill, CA 94523, (415) 939-1246
   A club for users of the Tandy Models 100, 102, 200, and 600 laptop computers.
The club maintains a BBS and a library of low-cost programs.

Desktop Publishers Intl., 215 W. 98th St., Suite 8B, New York, NY 10025,
(212) 865-6555
   A computer bulletin board dedicated to the needs of desktop publishers. Services
include technical support, product information, on-line graphic design assistance, and
a template library for MacDraw, ReadySetGo, MacPublisher, and MacPaint.

Desktop Publishing Association, 1795 Pearl St., Boulder, CO 80302, (303) 442-1100

Dvorak Intl. Federation, 11 Pearl St., Brandon, VT 05733, (802) 247-6020
   An information source for the Dvorak alternate keyboard arrangement.

Graphic Arts Tech. Foundation, 4615 Forbes Ave., Pittsburgh, PA 15213,
(412) 621-6941
   Technical information, seminars, books, and courses.

Graphic Comm. Computer Assoc., 1730 N. Lynn St., Arlington, VA 22209

In-Plant Printing Mgt. Assoc., 666 N. Lake Shore Dr., Chicago, IL 60611
   An association composed of members serving in various capacities in captive printing plants within large organizations.

Institute for Graphic Commun., 375 Commonwealth Ave., Boston, MA 02115
   An organization sponsoring educational programs and specialized publications concerning graphic communication.

Intl. Word Processing Assoc., Maryland Rd., Willow Grove, PA 19090

National Assoc. of Desktop Publishers, P.O. Box 508, Kenmore Station, Boston, MA
02215-9998, (617) 437-6472
   An independent, not-for-profit trade association designed to bring user feedback
to manufacturers, developers, suppliers, and vendors in the desktop publishing industry. The NADP also publishes the National Association of Desktop Publishers Journal
and the National Association of Desktop Publishers Buyer's Guide.

National Composition Assoc., 1730 N. Lynn St., Arlington, VA 22209, (703) 841-8165
   Educational programs, research, publications.

Print Shop Users Club, P.O. Box 216, Mercer Island, WA 98040
   An organization supporting the use of The Print Shop program on the Apple II
series of computers.

Printing House Craftsmen, 7599 Kenwood Rd., Cincinnati, OH 45236
An organization of printing professionals.

Technical & Education Center, 1 Lomb Memorial Dr., Rochester, NY 14623, (716) 475-2758
Seminar programs, technical information service, publications.

Typographer's Intl. Assoc., 2262 Hall Place N.W., Washington, DC 20007
An organization of professional typographers.

USED EQUIPMENT DEALERS

Atlantic Graphic Systems, Inc., 11164 Downs Rd., Pineville, NC 28134, (704) 588-6840

Baseline, 3800 Monroe Ave., Pittsford, NY 14534, (716) 385-6149
Phototypesetter repair, rebuilding, and computer interfacing.

Bob Weber, 23850 Commerce Park, Cleveland, OH 44122, (216) 831-0480

Capco, P.O. Box 1993A, Des Plaines, IL 60017, (312) 829-6220
Phototypesetting equipment buyers, sellers, brokers, and rebuilders.

Compugraphic, 80 Industrial Way, Wilmington, MA 01887, (617) 944-6555
Reconditioned and warranteed EditWriter equipment.

Craftsmen Machinery Co., 1073 Main St., Millis, MA 02054, (617) 376-2001

David John Co., 10178 Regatta Trail, Aurora, OH 44202, (216) 562-3750

Graphx, 1106 Hanover Ave., Allentown, PA 18103, (215) 439-1942

Hollenback Typesetting Systems, 823 Central Ave., Dubuque, IA 52001, (319) 556-2425

Inland Printing Equipment, P.O. Box 15999, Lenexa, KS 66215, (800) 255-6746

International PTS Exchange, P.O. Box 185, Sharon, Ontario L0G 1V0, (416) 473-3626
One of the largest phototypesetter rebuilders in Canada.

LFC Lessors, Inc., 4A Henshaw St., Woburn, MA 01801, (800) 225-6295

Locker Typesetting Equipment, One Maple St., East Rutherford, NJ 07073, (800) 526-0192

MBL Technical Services, Inc., R.D. 1, P.O. Box 264, Rte. 6, Mansfield, PA 16933, (717) 662-7488

Ober/Graphics, 7 Donald Cir., Andover, MA 01810, (617) 682-1139

Type Graphics America, 6280 150th Ave., Clearwater, FL 33520, (813) 530-4747

Type-Word Link, 601 13th St. N.W., Washington, DC 20005, (202) 745-1911
Specialists in phototypesetter repair and rebuilding.

MICRO FRONT-END SYSTEMS

AUTO-TYPE
Auto-Type/All-Tech Systems, 1501 Grandview Ave., Thorofare, NJ 08086, (609) 845-7300
A text input and editing system that can be used as either an off-line system (interfaced to a front-end system), or as a direct input system (interfaced to most phototypesetters).

COMPUWRITER PRODUCTIVITY PAK
Compugraphic, 200 Ballardvale St., Wilmington, MA 01887, (617) 658-5600
An MCS 5 input system, operating software, and an interface for the CompuWriter. This system provides disk storage and editing for B series CompuWriter model IV, 48, and 88 models.

CONCEPT 100 SYSTEM
Concept Technologies, Inc., P.O. Box 5277, Portland, OR 97208, (800) 631-2692
A personal publishing system based on the IBM PC/XT or AT supporting the integration of word processing and graphic pictures produced from applications developed with GSS VDI on the IBM PC Graphics Development Toolkit. Supported output devices include dot matrix and laser printers, as well as plotters.

CTI GRAPHIC SUBSYSTEM
Composition Technology Intl., 209 E. Alameda, Burbank, CA 91502, (818) 848-1010
A micro-based graphic system consisting of a personal computer, PC PreView screen, external hard disk, graphic scanner, LaserView 300 laser printer, and communications hardware for transmission to the Host Composition System.

DESKSET
G. O. Graphics, 18 Ray St., Burlington, MA 01803, (800) 237-5588
An IBM PC-based system outputting in PostScript to the Apple LaserWriter. The DeskSet software is available unbundled, and is code-compatible with the Compugraphic MCS. Features include a two-line status display, automatic white space reduction, automatic hyphenation (including an exception dictionary), up to 20 tabs or columns, batch or interactive hyphenation and justification, and kerning pairs.

FOCUS
Computist, 34 Chelmsford St., Chelmsford, MA 01824
A micro front-end system for the Compugraphic EditWriter.

HORIZON
G.O. Graphics, 18 Ray Ave., Burlington, MA 01803-4721, (800) 237-5588
An IBM PC or PC compatible software/hardware system that supports the preparation of hyphenated and justified text for direct output on a variety of different phototypesetters. The user prepares files by embedding mnemonic typesetting codes within the text. The system converts the mnemonics to the codes required by the typesetter.

MACINTOSH AD MAKE-UP TERMINAL
Concept Publishing Systems, 126 Monore St., Beaver Dam, WI 53916, (414) 887-3731
An enhanced Apple Macintosh system using a hard disk and graphics tablet. Features include a WYSIWYG display, the standard Macintosh visual user interface, an output to any PostScript-compatible device.

MAGNATYPE

Magna Computer Systems, Inc., 14724 Ventura Blvd., Sherman Oaks, CA 91403, (818) 986-9233

A total composition system incorporating every feature found on a large-scale type-setting front-end system. Features include up to 1500 automatic kerning pairs; four levels of white space adjustment (tracking); complete H&J control; multitasking capability; hyphenation by exception-word dictionary, 99 user-defined secondard dictionaries, temporary dictionary (for present job only), discretionary hyphenation, and rules of logic; and hyphenation in six foreign languages. Accessory packages include MagnaWord, a full editing H&J word processor, and MagNet, a private network linking Magna workstations.

MCS 8000 SERIES FRONT END

Cybertext Corp., 10th & Q Sts., Arcata, CA 95521, (707) 822-7079

A front-end system for the Compugraphic 8000, 8200, and 8400 running on an IBM PC. The system is available in two modes: a batch text processor mode, and an enhanced version with interactive counting editor.

MCS CONVERSION SYSTEM

G.O. Graphics, 18 Ray Ave., Burlington, MA 01803, (617) 229-8900

A program for the IBM PC that effectively converts it into an MCS workstation with Advanced Communication Interface (ACI) capabilities. Features include the creation of MCS-compatible disks, reception of copy from remote computers, file proofing on plain paper, user-defined translation tables, disk conversion from PC-DOS and MS-DOS, and conversion of MCS disks into word processing format.

METEOR/STAR

Bedford Computer Corp., Tirrell Hill Rd., Bedford, NH 03102, (603) 668-3400

An integrated Bedford Meteor keyboard and monitor with IBM PC to form a mark-up station for use in the Bedford Vision Network System.

MICROCOMPOSER FRONT END

Cybertext Corp., 10th & Q Sts., Arcata, CA 95521, (707) 822-7079

A front-end system for the Varityper Comp/Set 500 and 510 composed of three parts: microComposer, the driver software with hyphenation control; microMenu, the system control module that includes telecommunications software; and microWord, an intelligent text editor. Versions are available for a variety of CP/M and MS-DOS computers.

MORRIS PUBLISHING SYSTEM

Southeastern Newspapers Corp., P.O. Box 936, Augusta, GA 30913-0936, (800) 233-1339

A networked newspaper front-end system based on the IBM PC/AT.

NBI INTEGRATED WORKSTATION

NBI Inc., 3450 Mitchell Ln., Boulder, CO 80301, (303) 444-5710

A WYSIWYG document composition system outputting to the Apple LaserWriter. Features include typographic fonts in a variety of sizes and families; on-screen display of text and graphics; automatic real-time pagination; multiple-column text flow; automatic H & J; automatic numbering of footnotes, headers, and trailers; widow-orphan control; automatic box and line drawing; and more.

PUBLISH*ER7

Interlink, P.O. Box 134, Berrien Springs, MI 49103, (616) 473-3103

    A front-end system based on Commodore Business Machines for small newspapers and publishers.

RIMWRITER

Genesys Systems, Inc., P.O. Box 277, Ellinwood, KS 67526, (316) 564-3636

    An editorial system based on the TRS-80 Model II or 12 that drives a Compugraphic CompuWriter.

TURBO X

Xitron Inc., 1428 E. Ellsworth Rd., Ann Arbor, MI 48104, (313) 971-8530

    A software package for small daily or large weekly newspapers running on the Televideo 806H. The programs support the automation of the editorial, classified, and circulation functions in a multiterminal configuration.

TYXSET

Tyx Corporation, 11250 Rodger Bacon Dr., Suite 16'R', Reston, VA 22090, (703) 471-0233

    A software package running on a variety of computers including the IBM PC/XT/AT, Victor 9000, HP 9000, DEC PCP/11, DEC VAX, and others, and outputting on a variety of devices including Epson and Florida Data dot matrix printers, Canon T/10 laser printers, Allied Linotype 101, 202, TEGRA, Compugraphic 8400, 8600, and others. Special software features include strong mathematic capabilities, automatic indexing, footnoting, tabular composition, H&J, and multiple screen windows.

Notices

MS is a registered trademark of Microsoft Corporation.
Epson is a registered trademark of Epson America, Inc.
CP/M is a registered trademark of Digital Research Corporation.
Fontrix is a trademark of Data Transforms.
TPS-2000 is a trademark of Interleaf.
Lotus 1-2-3 and Symphony are registered trademarks and Jazz is a trademark of Lotus Development
  Corp.
Xerox is a registered trademark and Interpress is a trademark of Xerox Corporation.
IBM and PC are registered trademarks and PC/XT and PC/AT are trademarks of International
  Business Machines, Inc.
PostScript is a trademark of Adobe Systems Inc.
DDL is a trademark of Imagen Corporation.
WordStar is a registered trademark of MicroPro International, Inc.
MultiMate is a registered trademark of Multimate Corporation.
ProportionalStar is a trademark of Microlytics.
TTS is a registered trademark of the VariType Division of AM International.
Scriptsit is a trademark of Radio Shack, a division of Tandy Corporation.
FileMaker and FileMaker Plus are trademarks of Forethought, Inc.
Comic Strip Factory is a trademark of MacNifty Central.
Cauzin Softstrips is a registered trademark of Cauzin Systems, Inc.
InLine is a trademark of Hammerlab Corporation.
Ragtime is a trademark of Orange Micro, Inc.
WriteNow is a trademark of T/Maker.
The Newsroom Pro is a trademark of Springboard Software, Inc.
Conofonts is a trademark of Conographic Corporation.
MacTeX is a trademark of FTL Systems Inc.
Micro-Set and PostCode are trademarks of Mumford Micro Systems.
Notes is a trademark of Layered.
NamePro is a trademark of Computer Management Corp.
Rolodex is a trademark of Rolodex Corp.
DIF is a trademark of Software Arts.
Writer's Choice Elite is a trademark of Activision.
Mac3DF is a trademark of Challenger Software.
LaserBits is a trademark of Silicone Beach Software.
Z-3D is a trademark of Computer Graphics Center, Inc.
MathWriter is a trademark of Cooke Publications.
ArborText is a trademark of ArborText Inc.
Teflon is a registered trademark of DuPont.
UNIX is a registered trademark of AT&T Bell Laboratories.
pfs is a registered trademark of Software Publishing Corporation.
keytronic is a registered trademark of keytronic.
Apple is a registered trademark and Macintosh is a trademark licensed to Apple Computer, Inc.
MacScan is a trademark of New Image Technology, Inc.
Graph-in-The-Box is a trademark of New England Software.
DrawArt is a trademark of Desktop Graphics.
MacMemories is a trademark of ImageWorld, Inc.
InBox and LaserSpeed are trademarks of THINK Technologies, Inc.
Illustrator is a trademark of Adobe Systems Inc.
LaserPaint is a trademark of LaserWare Inc.
Scriptwriter and Storyboarder are trademarks of American Intelliware.
Spellswell is a trademark of Green, Johnson Inc.
FONTastic is a trademark of Altsys Corporation.
Scoop is a trademark of Target Software.
The Office Publisher is a trademark of Laser Friendly.
CalendarMaker and DiskTop are trademarks of CE Software.
LP Text is a trademark of London Pride Inc.
WorkFonts is a trademark of Font Workshop.
Graphidex is a trademark of Brainpower.
MacInUse is a trademark of SoftView, Inc.
TopDesk is a trademark of Cortland Computer.
MGMStation is a trademark of Upgrade Technologies.

Bibliography

Goodstein, David Henry. *Basic Computer Concepts for Typographers.*
    Washington: Typographers Int. Assoc., Inc., 1982.

Holscher, Dirck. *Phototypesetting and Its Word Processing Interfaces.*
    Washington: Electronic Publishers Technology Group, 1983.

Huss, Richard E.: *The Development of Printers' Mechanical
    Typesetting Methods 1822-1925.*
    Charlottesville: University of Virginia, 1973.

Kleper, Michael L. *The Illustrated Dictionary of Typographic Communication.*
    Rochester, NY: RIT/Graphic Dimensions, 1984.

_____. *Elementary Phototypesetting Systems Concepts.*
    Rochester, NY: Graphic Dimensions, 1979.

_____. *Practical Control of Phototypographic Quality.*
    Rochester, NY: Graphic Dimensions, 1978.

_____. *How to Make Type Easier to Read.*
    Rochester, NY: RIT, 1973.

_____. *How to Build a Basic Typesetting System.*
    Rochester, NY: RIT/Graphic Dimension, 1979.

_____. *Direct Entry Phototypesetting.*
    Rochester, NY: Graphic Dimensions, 1978.

_____. *Understanding Phototypesetting.*
    Philadelphia: North American Publishing, 1976.

Myers, Patti. *Telecommunicating for Typesetting.*
    Arlington, VA: National Composition Association, 1983.

Romano, Frank. *Handbook of Composition Input.*
    Arlington, VA: National Composition Association, 1973.

Roth, Stephen F. *The Computer Edge: Micro Trends/Uses in Publishing.*
    New York: R. R. Bowker, 1985.

Illustration Index

General Index